BY WATER BENEATH THE WALLS

BY WATER BENEATH THE WALLS

The Rise of the Navy SEALs

BENJAMIN
H. MILLIGAN

BANTAM BOOKS
NEW YORK

2024 Bantam Books Trade Paperback Edition

Published in the United States by Bantam Books,
an imprint of Random House, a division of
Penguin Random House LLC, New York.

BANTAM & B colophon is a registered trademark of
Penguin Random House LLC.

Originally published in hardcover in the United States
by Bantam Books, an imprint of Random House, a division of
Penguin Random House LLC, in 2021.

Illustrations credits are located on page 595.

ISBN 978-0-553-39221-0
Ebook ISBN 978-0-553-39220-3

Printed in the United States of America on acid-free paper

randomhousebooks.com

1st Printing

Book design by Edwin A. Vazquez

For all past and future frogmen,
but especially my grandfather, whose love of history,
and of me, more than any other factor, led to this.

In 705 CE, after having his kingdom taken away, his nose cut off, and his tongue split, Justinian II sailed across the Black Sea and led a small group of fighters under the impregnable walls of Constantinople by way of an unguarded aqueduct and captured the city. It was a victory that never should have been, by water beneath the walls.

Contents

Foreword

Jocko Willink

"KNOW YOUR HISTORY!"

As a young "new guy" at SEAL Team ONE in the early 1990s, this was barked at me many times by the older, more experienced SEALs. I had just graduated from Basic Underwater Demolition/SEAL training, or BUD/S, often called the most difficult military training in the world. It had lived up to its reputation, leaving a carnage of broken dreams as strong, confident men quit in droves.

But some of us didn't quit. I was one of those few. For my first assignment upon graduation, I was sent to SEAL Team ONE, just down the street from the BUD/S training, in Coronado, California. I was proud to have made it, and proud for the chance to serve at SEAL Team ONE.

So when the older guys told me to know my history, I could not have agreed more.

Hanging in the halls of SEAL Team One were pictures of SEAL Medal of Honor recipients Mike Thornton, Tommy Norris, and Bob Kerrey. I was told, "You better know their names!" That was not a difficult task—I already knew their names, and the actions that had resulted in their awards. Similarly, all of us new guys had learned that January 1, 1962, was the "birthday" of SEAL Team ONE—the day it was commissioned, or founded, at the direction of President John F. Kennedy. But most of us knew little about the history of the SEAL Teams, or about Naval Special Warfare prior to that date.

I did know some things about the SEALs in Vietnam. They had operated primarily at night, conducting ambushes and direct action raids from boats and helicopters. I knew they sometimes wore blue jeans and painted their faces green and carried Stoner machine guns, and I had heard that they killed the enemy with such ferocity and in such high numbers that SEALs were the most feared warriors in the jungles of Vietnam. Some of those warriors were still in the Navy at the time, in the early 1990s—and a few were actually at SEAL Team ONE when I reported there. They were our heroes, and while we young SEALs were eager to listen, they didn't talk much.

I recalled hearing of a group called the Scouts and Raiders, but I knew little more than the name and did not understand their connection to the SEAL Teams. I knew vaguely that the SEAL teams had originally been formed using "frogmen" from the Underwater Demolition Teams, whose roots were in a group known as the Naval Combat Demolition Units, or NCDUs. These were classic frogmen, and we still proudly called ourselves by that name, which they—not us—had earned.

I learned that these frogmen suffered severe casualties in World War II while clearing beaches for D-Day, and on islands in the Pacific Theater. And I knew the UDTs did some raids in the Korean War, but that was about it.

I knew only a few historical names beyond our Medal of Honor recipients. I had heard of Draper Kauffman and had been told he created our training. I knew about Phil H. Bucklew because my BUD/S training had taken place at the Phil H. Bucklew Center for Naval Special Warfare. I had been told that Bucklew was the father of Naval Special Warfare—but beyond that I knew nothing.

Sadly, that was about the extent of my historical knowledge of the SEAL Teams—and the extent of knowledge for just about all the SEALs from my era. In the SEAL Teams, there was virtually no written doctrine or history. Everything we learned, we were taught by our elders—and they chose to teach us the strategies and tactics of war, not its sagas and tales. When we asked older SEALS about our history, they always focused on teaching us how to fight: "Make sure you have cover fire when you move." "Keep your plans simple." "Try not to split your forces." "Make sure everyone understands the plan." "If no one is leading—you need to lead." These were important lessons—and since combat is the purpose and number one priority for SEALs, it makes sense that the number one priority for older SEALs in educating us younger ones was to pass on the knowledge of actually conducting warfare. Unfortunately, this meant knowledge of our history was deemed less important. Because of this, our proud history dimmed.

There were some more general phrases and mantras that were passed to us verbally, which guided our attitude and our standards: "Never quit." "Never leave your swim buddy." "The only easy day was yesterday." "It pays to be a winner." "If you ain't cheatin', you ain't tryin'." And while these slogans may have given us young SEALs some parameters on how to behave and formed some foundational level of culture, they also left a lot to interpretation—interpretation that was not always correct.

As time went on, our history faded further, as previous generations retired, aged, and died. Without a history to anchor us, we drifted. Our heritage dimmed, our roots withered, and our culture began to seem uncertain—we were not completely lost, but we did not have the clear soundings and bearings we needed to sail boldly, on a solid course, into the future.

Ben Milligan's book, *By Water Beneath the Walls,* has changed all that. In my opinion, it is the most important historical book about Naval Special Warfare and the SEAL Teams that has been written. For any reader of military history and anyone curious about the origins of the SEAL Teams, it's an essential and captivating read, a fact confirmed by the enthusiastic responses from the listeners of my podcast after Ben and I recorded over ten hours of discussion around the book. This book is an absolute must-read for anyone interested in history, war, leadership, or special operations.

But for me, as a fellow SEAL, it has an even deeper meaning.

Ben's perspective as combat veteran SEAL himself has allowed him to rediscover and solidify our history and our culture in a profound way. His book is now and forever will be a foundational source of the history and the culture of the SEAL Teams. It also answers the existentialist question that was always an enigma inside the SEAL Teams: *Why are we even here? Why wouldn't the Army or Marine Corps do the job of SEALs?*

Knowing the reason an organization exists is critical to its culture. History is also a key component in a culture—if not the most important component. Knowing where we come from guides where we will go and how we will get there. Understanding the past allows us to better maneuver into the future.

Ben's book explains why we exist, traces our origins, allows us to understand our heritage, and strengthens our DNA. He explains where Hell Week came from and why it is so important. He weaves our connection—and our debt—to the Army, the Marine Corps, and the Navy itself. He recounts operations in Europe, the Pacific, Korea, and Vietnam with more detail and precision than any post-operation report I ever filed, as a SEAL officer who had personally executed the missions I was writing about. He not only names our forefathers but explains their personalities, idiosyncrasies, strengths, weaknesses, and how they impacted our community. We learn about iconic leaders and innovators such as Gene Tunney, Phil H. Bucklew, Draper Kauffman, Milton Miles, and Robert Halperin; but we also learn about the heroes on the front lines—men like Ozie Mingledorf, Robert Christiansen, Roger Moscone, and Roy Matthews—who actually got the job done. Knowing the names, deeds, and reputations of those who came before us sets forth a venerated example to follow.

Of course, this book shares not only the success of the Naval Special Warfare and special operations but our failures as well. Operational disasters and personal meltdowns are plain to see. This book forces us to see and face the consequences of our mistakes, our politics, and our egos. These too are examples—of what not to do and of whom not to emulate.

In this book, Ben Milligan has captured no less than the roots of the SEALs' culture and the soul of our history. The result is, yes, a gripping read that I'd unreservedly recommend to anyone with an interest in our history. But for us SEALs, it's also a guiding light. This chronicling of history is what any purposeful organization needs. Without the past, there is no future. This book explains who we were and what we have done, which allows us to know who we are and what we will do.

Finally, this book also explains the price that was paid for our history and honors the men who paid that ultimate price. *By Water Beneath the Walls* is a tribute to generations of fallen frogmen, from World War II to the present day: their solemn duty, their suffering, their sacrifice. Each one a hero. They each gave their lives for the country, for the Navy, for the Teams, for their brothers—their fellow frogmen. And they will each live on, forever, as they continue to inspire and influence the young frogmen who now hold the line and carry on the proud traditions and feared reputation of the Teams. Thank you, Ben for writing this book. For capturing our history. And for memorializing the service and sacrifice of our brothers and our forefathers.

Thanks to you, we will never forget them—or the debt we owe them.

Thanks to you, we will *know our history.*

TEAMS!

Jocko Willink
BUD/S Class 177
March 2024

BY WATER BENEATH THE WALLS

Introduction

A Unit That Should Not Exist

First, a disclaimer. This is not an accounting of the modern US Navy SEAL teams. If that's what you're interested in, may I suggest you reach for one of the dozen or so recently published memoirs now crowding bookstore shelves everywhere. Instead, it is an attempt to explain a puzzle that no one ever has: the convulsive history of how and why the least likely branch of service in the US military came to foster the sort of unit it should never have needed; and more, the sort it should never have had the chance to create.

Let me explain.

The fifty-three-week process that creates a Navy SEAL—an acronym comprising Sea, Air, and Land—is essentially broken down into two parts. The first half is called BUD/S, or buds, which stands for Basic Underwater Demolition/SEAL training. It is a title that acts as a salute to the curriculum's origins but one so sterile that it also conceals both the course's range and its reputation as the US military's most notorious meat grinder. Included in this course are all the iconic scenes of arm-linked students awash in frigid surf, of sand-coated faces wrenched beneath the buckling weight of rubber boats or telephone-pole-sized logs, of air-sucking mouths bobbing for breath above wrists and ankles hog-tied with straps. Against a backdrop of surf and sand berms, swimming pools and fire hoses, BUD/S initially unfolds into a series of evolutions intended to test and build a volunteer's amphibious capacity—underwater knot-tying, the fifty-meter underwater swim, surf passage, ocean swimming, drownproofing, lifesaving, hydrographic surveying, contour diving, night diving, combat diving, underwater explosives. The crest of this training comes in the form of Hell Week, an almost completely sleepless five-day nightmare of uninterrupted backbreaking, skin-shredding wet and cold so intense that by the end, every candidate is contracted into a shouldered hunch from tendons swollen by shivering. By the end of these crucibles, each trainee has proven themselves as one of the US Navy's toughest, most torturously trained special operators—one of its naked warriors, its combat divers, its frogmen—and an expert in all the missions peripheral to the Navy's blue-ocean responsibilities: the demolition of underwater obstacles, the reconnaissance of enemy-held beaches, even midnight harbor infiltrations requiring ascent without bubbles beneath the shadow of an enemy ship to plant mines on its hull.

If BUD/S training stopped there, the Navy's premier special operations force would be undeniably remarkable but in operational scope not at all so. In other words, the SEALs would simply be a Navy unit capable of operations that extended just beyond the top edge of the surf zone but no farther; an area of responsibility so neatly tucked inside the boundaries of naval warfare that there never would've been a need for this book.

Instead, what follows in the final phase of BUD/S and carries on into SQT, or SEAL Qualification Training, is a curriculum more akin to what one would expect for Marines and Army Rangers—marksmanship and weapons training; land navigation, long-distance patrolling; then the tactics of ambushing, counterambushing, close-quarters battle, land warfare, even urban warfare. When married to courses in static-line and free-fall parachuting, it is a litany that enables graduates to perform a range of dry-boot missions entirely divorced from their blue-ocean origins. These missions range from the training of foreign soldiers—yes, soldiers—to the reconnaissance of enemy-held areas as far inland as mountaintops.

Most important, this training prepares its pupils for a mission that has emerged as the SEALs' specialty and carried them into the top rank of the world's best commandos. That mission—as everyone saw with the killing of Usama bin Laden in Abbottabad, Pakistan, a town some 800 miles from the nearest US Navy vessel—is the direct-action raid, the capture/kill. It is a mission so far removed from those performed by the Navy's original special operators in World War II that a comparable progression might be found only by imagining that the Army's tankers had developed into the US military's best submariners.

So, how did this happen? How did the US Navy create a unit whose operational center of gravity is not only directed at a mission performed on the 29 percent of the earth's surface that its ships cannot touch, but one so fraught with difficulties that most units of the Army and Marine Corps—the US military's traditional tenants of its land operations—are not able to perform it with anywhere near the same proficiency?

Most everyone who has ever tried to casually account for the Navy's inland creep in special operations has explained it away as simple evolution—essentially, a nearly thoughtless process of natural selection in which the Navy responded to a changing environment by inevitably adapting to new operational opportunities. As I saw firsthand, the problem with that theory is that the US military's various branches—and no less the US Navy—are legendarily hierarchical, thus legendarily stagnant, and thus require more than just a changing environment to turn the steam pistons of inevitability. In other words, these turns are not inevitable; at least not without the backs to crank-start their own evolution in the direction their own brains decide. Which brings us to the next explanation.

Probably to fill the holes in the aforementioned theory, there has—over the years—developed something of an agreed-upon origin story for the SEALs; a sort of creation myth that attempts to account for the contradiction of the Navy's inland adventurism. That story goes something like this: *After World War II, the Navy's Underwater Demolition Teams, or UDTs, transformed themselves into coastal raiders, prompting an internal grassroots campaign to formally expand the UDTs' charter to inland operations, a campaign that was beaten back by a hostile Navy—that is, until President Kennedy intervened and ordered the Navy to create commandos capable of operating from the sea, air, and land.* Framed like a fistfight between by-the-book bureaucrats and bootstrap-pulling rogues, this is a story that places the responsibility for the SEALs' creation and orientation with the SEALs themselves and at the expense of the Navy's leadership. How convenient. Never mind the theory's self-congratulatory ring, it's also one that collapses the moment you realize that President Kennedy's death so soon after the SEALs' creation afforded the Navy's planners a chance to renege on their infant creation. They didn't. This can mean only two things: first, that the SEALs hadn't simply authored themselves; and second, that the Navy's creation and sustaining of them as a land-focused commando unit was—against all obvious logic—deliberate.

But why? Why on earth did the Navy need commandos who could raid anywhere on it?

This was a question that I had first asked myself as a twenty-two-year-old BUD/S student but didn't really return to until some six years later, after a deployment to central Iraq during which my teammates and I had done little more than set rooftop ambushes and raid house after house in search of Al Qaeda insurgents. When I got home, my grandmother asked me why I, as a sailor, had been sent to the deserts of Iraq—"What in the hell were you doing there in the first place?"

"I'm not a sailor, Grandma," I answered, without a trace of self-consciousness or doubt. "I'm a Navy SEAL."

My response neither impressed nor illuminated her. And when I thought about it more, it didn't do anything for me either. The truth was, I didn't know the answer.

Several years later, not long after I left the Navy, I tried to find some answer to this question in the handful of history books about the SEAL teams; sort of a personal hunt to explore my own origins, something we all come to eventually. To my surprise, what I found was not much. Not only could I not find a book that didn't zip over the SEALs' creation or answer any of the questions I posed above, but maybe worse, I couldn't even find a history that was anything more than a meandering series of episodes selected for no purpose greater than each author's particular interest or one that explained the significance of those episodes or the men that made them so. As a person whose curiosity about the past had been sharpened since grade school by a grandfather who routinely dog-eared for me the most exciting battle scenes of whatever history book he was reading, and who thus grew up believing that it was one of the great endeavors to write something similar, I knew that I had found a topic. What I didn't know was anything else.

Begun at a small countertop desk in my kitchen with just enough width for a laptop and my two elbows, then finished in a spare bedroom cluttered with three-ring binders and so many notecards that they no longer fit inside the shoebox I originally believed they could never fill, the researching and writing of this book took no less than seven years (by the end, the same age of my youngest son, who had never known me not to be working on it). The prolonged development was partly due to the fact that in order to solve this riddle, I first had to find the scene of the crime—that specific moment in time when the Navy SEALs became what they are today: land-focused, capture/kill commando raiders. Once I established that this crime had occurred in the spring of 1968, during the Vietnam War, like a detective I had to collect the evidence that showed how and why it had happened—from archives and libraries, battlefields and personal collections; from tens of thousands of letters and diaries, reports and interviews; from the brains of the men still living whose memories could make sense of all the rest.

In the beginning of this backward search, the reasons—or motives—for the Navy's actions seemed to be always just out of reach, escaping every time I rounded a corner. That is, until the mists that clouded the timeline I had been painfully compiling shifted, revealing that each of the Navy's landgrabs seemed to follow a failure by one of the Navy's sister services to seize an obvious opportunity to permanently establish its own commando units—failures by the Army or the Marine Corps, even the OSS or its heir, the CIA, which were the logical entities to fill such an obvious and recurring need. The farther into the mists I plunged, the more I realized that many of these failures—for instance, the premature disbandment of the Marine Corps Raiders or the Army Rangers in World War II—had occurred at moments that unexpectedly stripped the Navy of its commando partners. It was a realization that snapped into focus every clue I had collected, and yet one that simultaneously told me that I would miss half the story unless I expanded mine to include the false starts by all those units of all those other service branches.

Anyway, here we are—writer and reader together. The first of us has finished the story, the other is just beginning. Since I have the benefit of knowing what twists and turns await you, please allow me one final word before you start.

Much noise has been made of late regarding the public's disproportionate interest in the SEALs and the costs that have come with it. That interest has led to too many ghost-authored books, too many movies, too many big heads, and in turn created among some SEALs—current and former—a sense of entitlement that likewise has led to a series of scandals. While this cycle among elite troops—as you will soon discover—is not a new phenomenon, it is one with the potential to cloud the reasons for the public interest in the first place. Having set out in part to understand that interest, an interest that captured me as a young man and obviously persists to this day, I found more than I ever anticipated: not simply a history of the early SEAL teams, but instead a prequel of that history that has never been told.

What follows is a story of raids and raiders; of leadership and bravery; of interservice rivalry and unintended consequences. More specifically, it's a tale of well-meaning American soldiers and Marines forced to make decisions amid magnificent tragedies, some of which created gaps for admirals and sailors with the foresight to tack into the wind of a rival's prerogatives, even when their ships ran out of water on which to sail. Best as I have found so far, it is the unlikeliest underdog story in American military history.

It is also one whose beginning is decided—as is entirely appropriate—by the water.

PART 1

NEGLECT

Chapter 1

The Reluctant Creation and Violent Demise of the Navy's First Commandos, the Marine Corps Raiders

Except for some magnificent excursions into the deserts of Libya and up the slopes of Chapultepec, the US Marine Corps—from the American Revolution to the American Civil War—was mostly an indentured adjunct of the blue-water American Navy. In peace, a ramrod insurance against mutiny; in battle, mast-clinging marksmen intended to replicate Admiral Nelson's fate upon the enemy—Nelson had been killed by a French sniper in a crow's nest. Later, after the Navy's conversion to steam stacks and the elimination of mast-top rifle nests, the Marines had adapted too, matching themselves to meet the national demand for foreign expedition. What followed was a Marine Corps of broad-brimmed campaign hats and leg-wrapped puttees, of guerrilla hunters like Smedley Butler and Chesty Puller, of brushfire victories in China, Haiti, the Dominican Republic, Nicaragua. It was a Marine Corps that had not only stretched the Navy's reach beyond the beaches that blocked its ships but along the way had also stretched the Navy's expectations for its own go-anywhere utility force.

Because of this history, the Marines of this period seemed poised to evolve into the Navy's very own corps of guerrilla hunters and amphibious raiders, but this was a logic that was upended during the First World War, when the Marines' battles at Belleau Wood, Soissons, and Blanc Mont proved as far removed from their small-war past as was a man from a monkey. More important, these meat grinders proved the Marines were every bit the battlefield equals of their soldier-cousins in the US Army, an upstaging that the Army sought to avenge by harnessing Congress's belt-tightening calls for consolidation in the early 1920s to turn the Corps' 13,000 Leathernecks into soldiers.

Threatened by consolidation with the US Army, by disbandment, by the elimination of their entire branch of service, the planners of the US Marine Corps scrambled for a solution. Their options: 1) decrease in size and thereby stature to return to filling the Navy's need for a shipborne utility force—essentially to return to their past as the Navy's guerrilla hunters and not-quite amphibious raiders; or 2) identify a future enemy and a future mission that would catapult the Marine Corps to an equal rank with the Navy and Army and thereby preserve it for half a century. Actually, this wasn't much of a choice at all; only one future appealed to the Marine Corps' planners: the option that would do nothing to satisfy the Navy's inland ambitions. More important for our purposes, it was a choice that would unintentionally produce a unit of raiders the Marine Corps didn't want, and a raid so near to disaster that its Navy planners wouldn't want any more of them, at least not from the Marine Corps.

2

A COMPOSITE OF ISLANDS and rapaciousness, the Empire of Japan was an enemy defended by water and fueled by a lust for resources. After the First World War, the only power that had stood between this lust and the vulnerable islands practically sinking beneath the weight of oil, tin, and rubber was the United States. If war ever came, it would come on these islands; if the US was going to win, it would need an army capable not simply of landing on them, but of stripping them clean of Japanese defenders. Of all the crusaders drawn to this cross and to the salvation it promised his service, none was as fervent as the man appointed to the office of the Commandant of the Marine Corps in 1936.

With a squat frame, round glasses, and retreating, tight-cropped hair, Major General Thomas Holcomb looked more like a frontier shopkeeper than a battle-hardened Marine. In fact, he was one of the Marine Corps' greatest heroes. At Belleau Wood, in response to an Army superior's question whether his battalion was "Holding or retreating," Holcomb had huffed in reply, "When this outfit runs it will be in the other direction." For an institution built upon smart appearance and fighting, the answer had made him a Marine Corps legend—a reputation he had springboarded to become his service's savviest partisan.

In a series of postwar assignments, Holcomb never lost sight of his ultimate objective: to build from the bones of his fellow First World War comrades the frame of the future Fleet Marine Force—an amphibious version of the US Army composed of all the same components, everything from artillery to aircraft. It was an objective that led him to seek out staff positions in operations and training, even to cultivate relationships with just about every Roosevelt who had ever served in the Department of the Navy—the closest thing the Roosevelts had to a family business. The most powerful example of this cultivation had been to achieve open access to the White House pool to rebuild the sickly body of his only son, an arrangement made possible by James Roosevelt, the president's second child and administrative assistant. Justifiably discredited now for his prewar testimony to a Navy panel in which he voiced his opposition to integration—"If it were a question of having a Marine Corps of 5,000 whites or 250,000 Negroes, I would rather have the whites"—Commandant Holcomb was nevertheless the man most responsible for the Corps' modernization of old equipment, the testing of new operations, the increase of amphibious exercises, and the improvement of coordination. Surrounded by office walls hung with the watchful portraits of his sixteen predecessors and a framed letter written 140 years earlier by the Corps' second commandant that exhorted a young Leatherneck to seek vengeance on a Navy lieutenant who had punched him, he was also the Marine most preoccupied with shedding the historic inferiority of the Corps and propelling it to an equal ranking in the US military's order of battle.

On December 7, 1941, the day the Red Sun wings blackened the skies over Honolulu, all Marines awoke to the world for which Holcomb had prepared; amphibious war was upon them. The next day, sitting beside General George Marshall in the House Chamber packed with legislators, secretaries, and black-robed justices, Holcomb listened to his old friend President Franklin D. Roosevelt articulate the terms of Japan's future. "No matter how long it may take us," the president promised, right hand gripping the lectern, his son James seated behind in a shadow to catch him should he stumble, "the American people in their righteous might will win through to absolute victory." Few could understand what this meant in terms of lives and logistics, method and strategy. For Holcomb, it meant a Marine Corps of 500,000 men capable of teaching the Japanese a definition of absolute victory not seen since the Mongols. It definitely didn't mean a Marine Corps of behind-the-lines commando raiders; especially not commandos whose service was indentured to the Navy.

3

IN JANUARY 1942, two memoranda arrived on Holcomb's desk within a week of each other suggesting the creation of Marine Corps commandos. The first was from his superior, Admiral Ernest J. King, the recently appointed Chief of Naval Operations. As enamored with defense as he was with temperance—"When they get in trouble they send for the sons-of-bitches," he was rumored to say upon appointment—King declared in his letter that the president was "much interested" in the "use of 'commandos'" for raiding expeditions in the Pacific. The second letter was from James Roosevelt, a recently activated Marine Corps captain—a subordinate by five whole ranks who had no business in sending his commandant a memorandum, except that his father was the president and the man to whom Holcomb owed the health of his only son. If these proposals were not imposition enough, attached to King's missive was a wholly unexpected backdoor suggestion as to the candidate who should lead this new capability. Unfortunately for Holcomb, the candidate was not a Marine but a former Army colonel clamoring for a Marine Corps commission. This unacceptable's name was William J. Donovan.

"Donovan served with distinction . . . during World War I," Holcomb began in a letter to Holland M. Smith and his senior subordinates, presenting the situation that he now faced. "He has since then observed practically all wars that have taken place; and in particular has specialized in Commando Operations (amphibious raids)." While this last was an overstatement and probably a rumor that Donovan himself had spread, it was not far from the mark. Twenty-two years earlier, when presented the Medal of Honor for actions on the Western Front at an award ceremony in the New York City Armory, Donovan had melodramatically unclasped the strap, then re-presented it to the four thousand veterans crowding the hall, saying magnanimously: "It doesn't belong to me. It belongs to the boys who are not here, the boys resting under the white crosses in France." When finished, he had left the medal behind with the armory. Sort of. Like so many men who receive such honors, he never really left it behind, nor had he ever failed to make use of it, especially when its blue ribbon and gilded bronze could double as a crowbar to pry open the doors that blocked his way. Since then, he had made a career as a New York lawyer, jet-setting whenever possible, ostensibly to provide counsel to overseas clients but in reality using his work as an excuse to witness the foreign wars in which he could not participate.

Despite being a Republican, intensely anti-union, a savage critic of the New Deal, which he called a "racketeering attempt," Donovan had tunneled into Roosevelt's inner sanctum, then outmaneuvered and out-imagined all the president's other suitors for the first-ever national intelligence job. Now, once again, with action and glory in his aperture, his crowbar was at Holcomb's door.

"All Amphibious Force Marines are considered as commandos and may be trained . . . under their own officers in this form of raiding," replied the commanding officer of the 1st Marine Division, Major General Smith, hardly containing his annoyance. "It is the unanimous opinion . . . of this headquarters that commando raids by the British have been of little strategical [*sic*] value." Concerning Donovan, who had "never been a Marine," Smith went from spark to flame: "His appointment would be accepted with resentment throughout the Corps" since it would seem that "the Marines had to go outside their own service for leaders."

A few days later, Holcomb poured out his heart on his Donovan problem. "I am terrified that I may be forced to take this man," he wrote in a letter to a friend. "I feel that it will be the worst slap in the face the Marine Corps ever was given . . . It will be bitterly resented . . . and I am afraid that it may serve to materially reduce my usefulness in this office."

While Holcomb sat under the portraits of the sixteen commandants who had gone before him and bemoaned his insufficiency to the task at hand, Admiral King, unburdened by such history or by the Marine Corps' ambition for a future on par with the Army's, throttled ahead, charting a course to the president's Pacific targets, even sending a small number of Marine officers and enlisted men to receive commando training from the British. On January 23, in accordance with King's expectations for aggressive activity, Admiral Chester Nimitz, commander of the Pacific Fleet, ordered his Marine subordinate to establish "units of 'commando' type." These units would be embarked upon submarines, rowed ashore in rubber boats, and trained to destroy enemy outposts on enemy islands, up to and including the destruction of a steel mill on Hokkaido or the detonation of a railroad tunnel on mainland Japan. Whether of "strategical" value or not, raids and commandos were about to be a reality. If Holcomb was not careful, so was an Army colonel in Marine Corps blue. He knew which threat was worse.

"As a means of forestalling the Donovan case, we must act and act quickly," Holcomb told his immediate subordinates. "We must prepare ourselves for . . . the execution of amphibious raids." In other words, to shield themselves from the former they had to arm themselves for the latter; they would have to create a unit of elite Marines specially trained to land on an enemy's beach, sneak through his lines, raid his facilities, then escape to do it all over again. At that moment, the closest entity the Corps had for accomplishing such a mission was the 1st Separate Battalion, a new unit commanded by Lieutenant Colonel Merritt "Red Mike" Edson, a veteran of the US occupation of Nicaragua, the author of the Corps' first-ever *Small Wars Manual,* and as perfect a Marine as has ever existed. He was the obvious choice to create and lead the Marine Corps' first commandos, except for one problem: Edson was a perfect Marine, and no perfect Marine has ever used his imagination unless ordered to do so. For evidence of this, Edson to date had focused his battalion's training not on behind-the-lines raiding, but mainly on the use of rubber boats to quietly paddle ashore ahead of a general invasion to knock out those beachside guns that threatened the landing fleet. After accomplishing this mission, Edson saw no reason his men should be held in reserve for future special assignments; rather, he wanted to refold them into the main advance. For Edson, his men weren't commandos, they were simply Marines.

As the first Marine in history to possess the right mixture of combat record and political skill to don the four stars of a general, it did not take long for Holcomb to see where his solution lay. The answer was to elevate Edson's 1st Separate Battalion to the 1st Raiders, then create the 2nd Raiders, a sister unit on the West Coast buttressed by a core contingent of Edson's troops and led by two men who possessed an interlocking perimeter of imagination and personal connections through which Admiral King would not penetrate and Donovan could not interlope.

For the first of the 2nd Raiders' leaders, Holcomb looked no further than the letter that had landed on his desk in January—or rather to its author, Captain James "Jimmy" Roosevelt. Better looking than both his famous father and his famous cousin Theodore, Jimmy was not as bright as either, or as diligent. Six feet four inches tall, bespectacled, and, in the words of one of his men, bald as a "polished grapefruit," he suffered from bleeding ulcers, persistent gas, and flat feet so bad that he should have been exempted from military service altogether. In 1937, he had become his father's administrative assistant, an appointment that earned him a cover story in *Time* magazine, howls of nepotism, and an ulcer so bad it had landed him at the Mayo Clinic for a barbarous cure in which 40 percent of his stomach had been removed. At the time of Pearl Harbor, Jimmy had already abandoned his various business ventures and had returned to government service, this time working for Colonel Donovan as a military liaison in the not-quite-yet-designated Office of Strategic Services, the OSS. Impatient at the pace of American retribution and hungry to achieve relevance in the coming war—like all fighting men at the time—Jimmy, because of who he was, was actually able to do something about it. Thus, his memorandum for a unit that, in his words, was specially trained to land "swiftly moving blows," not unlike "the jab in boxing"; but similar in character to the "British Commandos and the Chinese Guerrillas."

These last two words had no doubt revealed to Holcomb the hidden hand behind the proposal: the recently reactivated Marine officer Evans Carlson. It was a hand Holcomb had not been eager to accept, but the reasons for his reluctance were the same ones that now made this selection the perfect choice. Unlike the orthodox Edson, Carlson shared President Roosevelt's and Admiral King's belief that Marine Raiders could accomplish more with less than could regular Marines, but it was an idea as out of sync with Holcomb's future plan for the Corps as the others that came with it.

4

Though an accomplished Marine officer who could boast a guerrilla combat tour in Nicaragua, by 1942 Evans Fordyce Carlson was better known to his peers as an apostate author who had abandoned the Corps and his pension to travel the globe on a speaking tour, rallying support for the land that had long cleaved to his susceptible conscience: China. Before that, between 1935 and 1937, while assigned to the president's security detail in Warm Springs, Georgia, Carlson had not only developed a friendship with the commander in chief, but had also become something of a mentor to his son, an aspiring Marine and a future co-conspirator. Between 1937 and 1938, the same year the Japanese had used sword, bullet, and bayonet to kill the equivalent of 2,500 railroad cars' worth of men, women, and children in Nanking, Carlson had volunteered as a military observer to accompany Chinese Communist guerrillas along a thousand-mile march. Often under fire from Japanese dive bombers and artillery, he walked beside the guerrillas every step, admiring their flattened organizational structure, their everywhere-and-nowhere tactics, their willingness to strip down in freezing temperatures to cross rivers, and above all the ethical indoctrination that propelled the Chinese soldier's legs beyond all measures of human endurance.

Colonel Evans Carlson on board the USS *Nautilus.*

Forty-six years old, tall, almost gaunt, with sad eyes and a tucked-in smile intended to hide his crooked teeth, Carlson, like Red Mike Edson, was from Vermont. The similarities stopped there. The son of a minister in the Congregationalist church, a sect known for its individualism, Carlson was the very picture of nonconformity, a trait that extended everywhere his life did. Though reporters and rehabilitating biographers have forever since attempted comparisons with Lawrence of Arabia, Carlson instead reminded contemporaries of another New England–produced raider, one not so successful: the unfortunate zealot John Brown.

Not very well educated and thus overawed by the few books he had read, especially what he called the "lonely genius" of Mao Tse-tung's guerrilla warfare philosophy, when assigned to command the 2nd Raider Battalion on the West Coast in mid-February 1942 along with Jimmy Roosevelt as his executive officer, Carlson set to distilling all his previous combat knowledge into a moonshine that few in the corps wanted to drink.

Offered the chance to accompany the group of Marines headed to England for training with the British Commandos, Carlson dismissed the opportunity out of hand. After all, what could he possibly learn from the British that he hadn't already learned from the Chinese? When a young Marine officer named Oscar Peatross asked him for a recommended reading list, presumably to improve his understanding of the military art, much to his surprise the young man received a list of ten books—every one about China, including the ponderous two that Carlson had written. Forgivably, the young officer lost interest. Neither of those instances, however, could compare with Carlson's most presumptuous act—the dismissal of more than half the 197 men sent from Edson's 1st Raider Battalion meant to form the nucleus of Carlson's new outfit. His explanation for their dismissal: for failing to live up to his expectations of what a Raider should be. Having spent more than a year training these men, Edson fumed when he heard the news. "Whatever Carlson's so-called standards," Edson wrote to General Smith, "his refusal to accept . . . these men only confirmed my opinion that the Marine Corps had lost nothing by his resignation a few years ago and has gained nothing by his return." It was an opinion that only highlighted the fact that Carlson had been selected for his connections and not at all for his concepts or capabilities; moreover, it was an opinion that many Marines would soon come to share. Unfortunately for the Raiders, whose survival as a suborganization would depend in part on Carlson's ability to achieve a positive reputation, it was not a great start.

Of the four types of missions proposed in Roosevelt's (and Carlson's) memorandum, three required landing on a foreign shore. Among the qualifications listed to perform these landings was an individual's ability to march thirty to fifty miles in twenty-four hours; to exhibit initiative; to adapt to unexpected situations; to subsist on local food; to "subordinate self to harmonious team-work"; and lastly, to demonstrate "a deep conviction" in the "value of the democratic way of life." Not only did Carlson intend for his Raiders to fight like the Chinese Communists, he intended that they act like them too. To help instill this, Carlson adopted "Gung Ho" as the battalion motto, a Chinese expression vaguely meaning "work together." To reinforce it, he subdivided his nine-man squads into three-man fire teams, increasing his Raiders' tactical mobility and their opportunities for individual initiative. He also abolished nearly all perquisites of rank—enlisted men could see him without going through their chain of command and officers had to wait for chow like everyone else.

Considering that three of the four missions proposed for the Raiders were inextricably linked to the water, it should be noted that Carlson did not list as a mandatory qualification a volunteer's ability to swim, nor was it identified as a skill worth teaching. When the 2nd Raiders finally graduated to train with boats in the surf off San Clemente Island, then again off Barber's Point in Oahu, they no doubt linked their survival not to their own arms and legs, as they should have, but instead to the island of inflated rubber that they sat on. Whatever Gung Ho was, it was not a life preserver—as the Raiders' first mission would soon tragically show.

5

NEXT TO HOLDING HAWAII at all costs, Admiral King's main strategic objective for the Pacific Theater in 1942 was to preserve the supply line to Australia. If King had a third objective, it was this: to torpedo the US presidential policy of Germany First and stop thinking defense. "We must strike the enemy when and where we can and keep on striking him," King declared in a press release in the spring of 1942. The instrument to accomplish this striking was the blue-eyed, white-haired, square-jawed commander of the US Pacific Fleet, Admiral Chester W. Nimitz. A pioneer his entire career—first of submarines, then underway replenishments, fast carriers, and now naval commandos—Nimitz responded to King's directive and his limited resources with, said a *Time* magazine reporter, a series of "hell-for-leather, slam-bang affairs planned with the stealthy calculation of Indian raids, and executed with the bludgeon force of gang assassinations." In April, he had authorized an air raid on Tokyo by sixteen carrier-launched B-25s from an impossible distance of 800 miles. In June, Nimitz's dive bombers had buried four Japanese carriers in the waters off Midway at the cost of only one of his own. To make up for their fleet losses, the Japanese had responded the only way they could: by building a series of airfields around the island of Guadalcanal to threaten the US line of communications with Australia. And with this—ready or not—Nimitz ordered the Marines to war.

To initiate this operation, and to secure the 1st Marine Division's vulnerable flank, Red Mike Edson's 1st Raider Battalion was ordered to seize Tulagi, an island twenty miles to the north of Guadalcanal. Boasting the Solomon Islands' best anchorage, Tulagi was an obvious threat to the fleet and to those Marines splashing ashore to the south. Knowing the risks that his small force would face on a daylight assault against an entrenched enemy, Edson brought every man in his battalion, five companies' worth—as many as 800 Raiders—plus another battalion from the 5th Marines. Then, to further stack the odds, he brought mortars, abandoned his stealthy rubber rafts for the faster, more reliable Higgins Boats, landed his men at a single point, and once ashore, advanced on-line across the island until nearly every one of the 350 Japanese defenders was dead. Though this prevented the enemy from gaining an anchorage, the overwhelming use of force and firepower did nothing to distinguish or justify the remarkable nature of Edson's Raiders. They were just good Fleet Marines. Worse still, Japanese attacks on Guadalcanal continued unabated. Because this was the only theater where Americans were on the offensive, Guadalcanal suddenly became a concentrated target for the Japanese, for them a hair-of-the-dog curative that might suppress the nausea brought on by their recent defeats and return them to the good old drunk days of Tora! Tora! Tora!

To reduce this pressure on the Marines at Guadalcanal, Nimitz conceived of a second mission: a diversion in the form of a submarine-launched raid on the Makin Atoll in the lightly defended and faraway Gilbert Island chain. Though no one could have known at the time, it was an atoll upon which hung the fate of the entire Raider experiment.

For Carlson's men, preparations for this raid included more boat training, out and back through the surf, with motors, then without, with paddles, and finally with nothing more than rifle butts. Raiders studied unmarked maps of Butaritari, the southernmost island of the Makin Atoll and their first target, along with the likely locations of its Japanese defenders, whose numbers, character, and disposition Naval Intelligence had so far only guessed at.

On August 4, four days before their departure for the Gilberts, Carlson and his men boarded the submarines USS *Nautilus* and USS *Argonaut* for the first time. The short ride was incredibly cramped and hot. At sunrise, Carlson and his men executed their only dress rehearsal off Barbers Point on Oahu. On the beach, observing approvingly with his staff, stood Admiral Nimitz—waiting to see if a small force could unhinge a larger one, could extend the threat of the Navy's reach onto every patch of dry ground in the Pacific. If they could do all this, no doubt Nimitz would order more submarines with more Raiders inside, and the Navy would once again have the kind of inland reach that it had long since lost.

6

On August 8, at 0900, both submarines departed Sub Base Pearl Harbor and made for the open ocean. In the lead was the *Nautilus* with Carlson and 87 Raiders of B Company. Following almost a day behind was the larger and slower *Argonaut* with Roosevelt and the remaining 134 men, the majority belonging to A Company. For eight sweltering days, the Raiders lived crammed alongside one another, anywhere they could stretch, each man a prisoner to the heat, sweat, and stink of the one next to him. After 2,000 miles of the Pacific's omnipotence, slightly farther than from New York City to San Diego, the *Nautilus* finally arrived at its target on August 16.

At first, no one knew for sure if they were in the right place. The only confirmation came that night at 2100, when the *Argonaut* appeared for a moment only a few hundred yards away, then disappeared in a rain cloud. Except, perhaps, for the providentially minded, this was no confirmation at all, only the fact that both submarines were in the same vicinity of the same unknown island. Nor did it miraculously solve the problem of locating the Japanese defenses. Carlson could have resolved both unknowns by sending a scouting party ashore. Ever the fatalist, he did not. If they were in the wrong place, they were at least in the wrong place together.

Two Raiders prepare to depart the USS *Nautilus* for the raid on Makin Atoll.

On August 17, at 0300, in the pitch dark, the overhead hatches of the two submarines opened, releasing onto the helmeted heads of the Raiders crowded below a sharp wind and a cold rain, along with the first sign that their mission would not go as they had imagined. As they scrambled rung over rung, squeezing themselves through the hatch, their faces smeared with burnt cork, wearing black-dyed utilities and weighted down with as many bullets and grenades as each man could carry, they found themselves in another world. Now, topside, in the wind and rain and the battering waves, their hands at last overtook their thoughts. The months of preparation behind them, the Raiders were about to make their name a reality.

All across the wave-swept deck, men began heaving up, flattening, and inflating their rubber boats. Coxswains did their best to shield their gas funnels and outboard engines from the rain and seawater. It was all in vain. As soon as a boat was inflated and gassed, the men pitched it overboard into the black. Two boats floated away before anyone could board. One took with it the extra ammunition; the other, a heap of medical supplies. The boats "bounced around like toys," one Raider wrote later, and "blended so well with the ocean that you wondered if you were going to hit anything at all when you jumped for one." Without life vests, loaded down with as much as sixty pounds of equipment and some unable to swim a stroke, the men waited for a wave to bob their boats as high as possible, then jumped. In each boat, coxswains balanced themselves against the runnels and wrenched their Evinrude pull cords. Deaf to prayers and curses alike, only a few engines started. Most crews had to paddle, and paddle fast. Dawn was not far off.

Momentarily forgotten aboard the *Nautilus,* Carlson was the last Raider to board a rubber boat. When he leapt aboard, his right cheek bounced off a rifle butt so hard that it swelled up instantly. With his head ringing and his nerves taut from nearly missing his ride, Carlson told the surrounding boat crews to disregard the plan for separate landings of Companies A and B, and instead just to follow him directly to the beach. Over the crashing surf and howling wind, few crews could hear him. Only those around him got the message.

"It was organized grabass," Private Dean Voight would say years later, remembering the haphazard landing. Boats buckled under the breakers, slammed men together, then tipped them over the sides. On one boat, the dead engine acted like a paralyzed rudder, spinning them in circles in the surf zone before the men finally detached it and pitched it into the waves. Voight's own morning would consist of burning his crotch on spilt gasoline, then falling overboard—surviving only by grabbing an errant strap, since he could not swim, then ditching every piece of equipment on his body, including his gun.

Sensing his momentum eroding like the ground beneath him, Carlson sloughed through the soft sand, hastening to gather his men before the sun rose. If he could find and untangle his two reduced companies and point them in the direction of their targets, he might still have a chance. Because there had been no reconnaissance, however, no one knew for sure where they were or where to go. With four miles of beach to the left and another six miles to the right, their targets could be anywhere, if their targets were there at all. Worse still, one whole boat crew was missing.

Without target locations or knowledge of enemy strength, with thirteen men unaccounted for and possibly drowned, Carlson was blind and groping for answers in an ever brightening world, his men becoming ridiculously conspicuous along the white beaches in their uniforms of dyed black.

As Carlson considered his options, one squad happened upon a Japanese soldier riding a bicycle. Quietly they stopped him, then motioned for him to dismount. As this was happening, another Marine was loading a twenty-round magazine into his Browning Automatic Rifle. As he did, the bolt slammed shut, striking the primer and cracking open the silence with a burst of fire—and momentarily distracting every Marine within earshot. Seeing his chance, the Japanese soldier dashed for his bike and began pedaling for his life. The Marines gunned him down, killing any residual surprise they had left. Whether Carlson knew it or not, a raid was no longer an option.

7

In the absence of new orders, many of the Raiders began executing old ones. Primed for initiative, intermingled handfuls of Marines had already left the beach and advanced across the island's half-mile width to reach the far-side lagoon and assault their pre-assigned objectives. As they discovered huts and native buildings, they searched them. When a group of Raiders emerged from one, another group opened fire, missing them completely, condemning all at once their judgment, their unbridled jumpiness, their coordination, and worst of all, their aim. Two men, preoccupied with scavenging proof of their bravery, found time to fight over a liberated Japanese storm flag. They tore it in half. With his men ranging free, at 0543 Carlson transmitted a message back to the *Nautilus:* "Everything lousy."

But as handfuls dribbled back to his command post and rearranged themselves into squads, squads into platoons, and platoons into companies, they brought good news: The target buildings were abandoned and the wharf was unusable. Not only that, but the natives—mixing pidgin with broken English—had been all too eager to give them valuable information.

Where were the Japanese?

To the southwest, the natives had pointed.

How many were there?

Eighty, said some; *one hundred and fifty,* said others.

Absent from these initial descriptions was one article of information that would have helped: For some reason, the Japanese were on the alert. For three days snipers had been waiting, lashed to the tops of palm trees, supplied with native food, many with coconuts tied to their clothes to help them blend in. For unknown reasons, the natives forgot to mention this.

Just four minutes after his previous pronouncement of despair, Carlson began to see a brighter world. First, he knew where the enemy was. Second, by working mostly on initiative and unopposed, his Raiders had cut the island in half. If he could assert control over his distributed men, he could cork the Japanese into an inescapable bottle. Realizing this, or something close to it, he pulled back most of B Company to the vicinity of the command post. They would block to the left and shuttle reserves as needed. A Company, already on the far side of the island, would act as the cork. Once his orders had been issued, at 0547, he transmitted his last positive message to the *Nautilus:* "Situation expected to be well in hand shortly."

As A Company began ranging south along the dirt road, a lone truck about 300 yards away from them barreled into view. It stopped. Fifteen to twenty men jumped out and disappeared into the bushes. Behind them, another group arrived, raising the total to as many as thirty. If there was any doubt about who they were, it vanished the instant they planted a flag in the middle of their position. It was the Red Sun. The Marines scrambled for cover. As far as they could tell, they had not yet been seen. If they could not effect a raid, they could at least execute an ambush.

Stretched out on a hundred-yard-long skirmish line, the Japanese came on. While they did, the Marines ducked down, then—drawn instinctively to high ground—seized the low rise before them, spreading out in hidden bunches along a perimeter shaped like a cul-de-sac and now buttressed by the god of battle's most powerful natural phenomenon. With the rising sun at their backs—blinding the enemy, plus illuminating their shapes and green uniforms—the Marines reeled in the Japanese so close that their individual faces became clear, so close that the squad on the far left tip of the cul-de-sac became completely surrounded.

"Let 'em have it!" boomed Sergeant Clyde Thomason from Atlanta, Georgia, simultaneously firing a blast from his 12-gauge shotgun and unleashing the muzzles of his fellow ambushers. With that, the Makin raid became the Makin battle.

For four minutes or so, Thomason and the 2nd Raiders triumphed, unopposed and unrelenting. "Anything out in the open was riddled," the 1st Platoon commander would write later with satisfaction. Then came the counterattack.

For the next thirty minutes, A Company fought a suicidal enemy armed with four machine guns, two grenade throwers, automatic rifles, and a flamethrower. Each time the Raiders managed to silence a machine gun nest, another Japanese gunner would step over the piled bodies surrounding it and bring it to life. Worst of all, unseen and inescapable, were the snipers lashed to the tops of the palms. Not blinded by the sun and rewarded for their patience, each sniper sought out movement and took aim.

"[We] pleaded with [Thomason] to stay down," one man remembered years later. "There were snipers within 50 yards of us." He did not, compelled instead to shuttle between his men, pointing out targets as he went. His Medal of Honor was awarded posthumously.

"We had Japs in front of us, above us, alongside of us to our left, and behind us," remembered Corporal Young, exposed at the tip of the cul-de-sac. Even when they managed to fight free of the Japanese around them, their good sense kept them nailed to the ground. "I lay as flat as I could and tried to shrink myself as narrow as possible," said Private Glen Lincoln, playing possum under the palm trees and the scrutiny of two separate machine gun positions. In thirty minutes, nine Raiders from 2nd Platoon were dead; so was Thomason; so was Captain Gerald Holtom, the battalion intelligence officer, a child of missionaries and the one Raider who could speak Japanese. Also killed were four radio telephone operators, each one singled out by the antenna waggling above his shoulder, which was connected to a waterlogged radio that either lacked the power to reach Carlson's command post or did not work at all.

Using the one radio that did work, Carlson transmitted a request to the *Nautilus* at 0656 to fire on the enemy's rear. Seven minutes later, the *Nautilus* started its bombardment.

Ballasted by fatalism, the Japanese soldier in World War II was fearless. But the instant a prospect of defeat and shame breasted his gunwales, that ballast became an anchor. With Marines to their front and naval gunfire crashing around them, without prepared defenses besides the snipers in the trees, the Japanese defenders knew they were fighting a superior force. If there had been a voice of reason among them, it sank beneath the shouts of "Banzai" now clamoring from every throat. At the sound of two sharp bugle blasts, the coiled defenders raised their rifles above their heads and sprang into a charge.

Not sure what to make of the spectacle, the Marines at the cul-de-sac held their breath and watched. When the Japanese wave reached its crest and looked as though they would crash down on top of them, the Marines opened fire, killing every one. Afterward, surveying the corpses from the skirmish and the charge, they counted eighty-two Japanese bodies—though no one knew it, the bulk of the Japanese garrison. Despite the loss of twelve men, this was the closest moment that Carlson would come to a victory, and the closest the Navy would come to proving to the Marine Corps' planners the strategic value of Marine Corps Raiders.

8

For the rest of the day, Carlson picked his way through the battlefield, smoking his pipe and visiting with his men. Except for ordering B Company into the skirmish line, he issued no orders to advance, or retreat. For the moment, his mission objectives (to destroy installations, capture prisoners, and gather intelligence) hung suspended, waiting for what, no one knew. Supplied with one canteen and one candy bar each, the exhausted Raiders hunkered down, strained their eyes for sniper nests, and did their best to ignore their gathering hunger and thirst.

At 1130, two biplanes appeared. For fifteen minutes they scanned, then dropped their bombs and departed. No Marines were hurt. Two hours later, at 1320, twelve planes appeared. For one hour they bombed and strafed. Then two Japanese seaplanes attempted to land reinforcements in the lagoon. With machine guns and antitank rifles, the Marines shredded these to pieces, and took no additional casualties in the effort.

At that moment, despite the ineffectiveness of Japanese air sorties, Carlson's casualties totaled somewhere around 18 percent—a disastrous figure. But, when an out-of-breath Raider appeared at Carlson's command post with news that his missing boat crew had landed safely far to the south (and, in fact, had been harassing the Japanese rear all day), Carlson was elated. Not only was he saved from the psychological burden of thirteen drowned men, but now, whether he recognized it or not, he had an anvil behind the lines to hammer his companies against. Inexplicably, Carlson did nothing. With his mission half completed, he ordered his men to abandon their fighting positions, pull back, and prepare the boats. The raid was over.

At 1915, the moment darkness colluded with high tide to shield his force from planes above and the coral below, Carlson ordered his boats to peel off the beach from the flanks into the surf. "It did not look tough," said the official after-action report a few days later. "Not nearly as tough as other surfs we had worked in." With the tallest men pulling them seaward, others began paddling. All aboard, they struck a rhythm. As they neared the reef, the breakers tightened, throwing them back, collapsing their momentum and their gunwales, throttling them, souvenirs and all, into the surf. One of the wounded—lashed to a pole litter and balanced across the center of a boat—bobbed away in the blackness. To get through the waves, the men returned to the beach to lighten their loads. The Evinrude engines were the first to go, pitched into the sea. Plundered souvenirs came next, followed by clothes and shoes, concluding with every Marine's most precious article of faith, his weapon. Last to go were the wounded, valiantly volunteering to stay behind so their comrades might escape the same fate.

Thus unencumbered, propelled by the prospect of capture by Japanese reinforcements, the Raiders replaced their lost oars with palm fronds and paddled for their lives. After several hours, approximately ninety-three men arrived at the submarines. To those on board, the survivors possessed an appearance of "pale shadows," some of them stark naked, many "nothing less than zombies." More than one hundred men, including Carlson, had not made it off.

One of those who had not escaped was the man most responsible for getting them there in the first place. Though annoyed at having lost his glasses in the surf, up until that moment Jimmy Roosevelt, the silver-spooned son of the president, had demonstrated a clear head, an indifference to bullets, and best of all, a genuine concern for his men. Now, though, with the surf's remnants washed ashore all along the beach, many without weapons and clothes, all without food and exhausted, Roosevelt's presence hung like an anchor around Carlson's increasingly anxious mind. With tomorrow's promise of renewed air attacks and the likelihood of enemy reinforcements, the fear of Jimmy's death or capture unhinged him.

Then, when a Japanese patrol bumped into one of his beach sentries, sparking a short firefight and wounding another Marine, Carlson convinced himself that the enemy still existed in force and could attack at any minute. Buckling under this weight, he decided to do the unthinkable: at 0330 he dispatched two men, unarmed except for a note, to find the Japanese commander and surrender, and thus ending in humiliation the US military's first commando raid. Or so it would have happened except for one problem: the two messengers could not find a single Japanese soldier to whom they could surrender. When they eventually did—quite by accident, while bumming cigarettes at a native hut—the lone Japanese soldier reluctantly accepted the note (not exactly sure what it was), tucked it away, then marched off down the road, where some other Marines, unaware of Carlson's decision, shot the courier dead. Even Carlson's surrender was a failure.

The next morning, after one boat crew of desperate Raiders demonstrated that the surf could be crossed, Carlson ordered Roosevelt to make another attempt. With a full boat plus four men clutching boat straps, alternately dragging and swimming alongside, Roosevelt's crew emerged past the reef. When they made it to the *Argonaut,* they raced aboard just moments before a radar contact forced the submarine to submerge. If nothing else, Roosevelt was safe.

Freed of this burden and emboldened by native reports that only a few scattered defenders remained, Carlson steadied himself and resolved to keep fighting until all the wounded could be safely evacuated. But how? When a boat crew of five stouthearted Raider volunteers left the safety of the *Nautilus* on a mission to rescue their comrades and were strafed by Japanese aircraft, the rescuers were not only presumed dead, but daytime rescue attempts were abandoned. Worse still, the stranded Raiders now possessed only two rubber boats that had not been punctured by Japanese bullets, meaning that Carlson and his seventy survivors, many of them barely ambulatory, were now entirely responsible for solving their own problems—a tall order for most, though not for Marines.

Arming themselves with the weapons of more than eighty-three dead and decomposing Japanese soldiers, the Raiders ransacked the island's stores of canned fish, biscuits, and American corned beef, then refreshed their morale with Japanese beer. Lacking clothes, some men dressed in the only garments they could find, pink and blue silk underwear, becoming, as one Raider wrote afterward, "a child's-picture-book version of a gang of pirates." So armed and adorned, they burned gasoline stores, collected papers, wrecked anything of value for the Japanese sure to return, then set to patching their punctured rubber boats while a few men worked like "galley slaves" to dry out and prepare two motors. After lumbering four patched boats across the island to the lagoon, they lashed them side by side to a native outrigger and created by all accounts the "damndest contraption ever floated." When night fell, the Raiders blinked a flashlight message to the submarines, loaded their wounded, gave the Evinrudes a spin, then shoved off.

While the ride to the submarines was slow and uncomfortable for the wounded owing to their ungainly vessel and another sputtering motor, the placid lagoon entrance presented no surf. It was just the break the desperate Raiders needed. As soon as they arrived at the submarines, Carlson straggled aboard, staggering from exhaustion and relief, then reported his satisfaction that all survivors had been evacuated. With that the Makin Raid was over, and the fate of the Raiders was sealed.

9

Below a bright blue sky, tumbling white clouds, and the green mountains of Oahu, the USS *Nautilus,* after another week at sea, finally slipped into the channel that separated Pearl Harbor from the Pacific Ocean. Here she slid past Battleship Row, past the visible tips of the *Oklahoma* and the *Arizona,* the dead still diminishing inside their bellies, and finally turned the bend toward Sub Base Pearl Harbor. Crowding her forward deck—without helmets or covers of any kind, unshaven, disheveled, many still wearing the remnants of their black-dyed fatigues—stood the residue of the 2nd Marine Raider Battalion, now sons of Mars, awaiting their triumph.

"More brass than in a foundry," the submarine's commander said as a distant Navy band picked up the next verse to the Marines' Hymn ("From the Halls of Montezuma . . ."). On moored ships nearby, crews manned the rails, cheering as they passed.

Publicity photo of Carlson and Captain Jimmy Roosevelt leading the 2nd Raiders.

Waiting on the pier before them, in front of two rows of crisp Marines, stood the Caesar of the moment, Admiral Nimitz, still waiting to hear the details of the raid. As soon as the gangplank was secured, he was bounding down it, returning salutes, shaking hands, smiling broadly, congratulating the Task Force's commodore, who returned the praise with a captured Japanese sword. "Admiral Nimitz, here's a trophy from Makin on behalf of Colonel Carlson and his Raiders."

"First souvenir of the war," Nimitz said with a grin. "Damned good. Going to send it to the Academy museum."

"I hope the admiral is pleased by the results of our efforts," one Raider lieutenant awkwardly managed, his shot-up arm tucked into a sling.

"Very pleased," Nimitz responded. "Very pleased—a very successful raid."

It was a sentiment all too ready for an audience.

Though Nimitz had only intended the Makin Raid as a diversion, within weeks of its conclusion its story was taking center stage. "White House Hails Raid," declared one article; "We Mopped Up Makin Island," boasted another. On the heels of these, a Hollywood producer began securing the rights for a film titled *Gung Ho!: The Story of Carlson's Makin Island Raiders*—an against-all-odds picture made "for folks with strong stomachs and a taste for the machine gun." Though this was standard fare for military superlatives, in November *The New York Times* ran an article that described the actual benefits of "a raider group within an organization of raiders"; a unit designed to "strike quick, devastating blows . . . kill or capture . . . then swiftly withdraw"; a unit that was already "translating guerrilla warfare as practiced by . . . Lawrence in Arabia into Amphibious terms."

Though none of the articles actually said it, all were describing exactly the kind of unit that the Navy's planners had long since had a need for. As they would soon realize, however, it was also a unit whose actual performance had not nearly lived up to its accolades.

10

In the wake of the *Argonaut*'s return to Pearl Harbor, Carlson was finally able to tabulate his casualties at eighteen dead plus twelve missing—presumably drowned—and many more wounded. Already hardened to the lengthening lists of casualties in his theater, even Nimitz had to sheepishly admit to Admiral King that the "losses were somewhat larger than they should have been." It would take another year to learn that at least nine of the missing Raiders were not drowned off Makin, but rather abandoned. Among those was Corporal James Gifford, an Apache who had been left to die under a mesquite tree as a baby but had been rescued and raised by a local shopkeeper. Having grown up with the knowledge of his own salvation from certain death, Gifford had naturally volunteered to row back to Makin to rescue others—essentially to repay the kindness done to him—but it was a mission that had ultimately, for him and the other volunteers, ended in capture, imprisonment on Kwajalein, then death by beheading.

Worse than this—worse for the Raider organization, not for the men who had lost their lives—was Carlson's attempted surrender. Even Nimitz's belief in the surprise value of submarines and his desire to broadcast morale-boosting raids in his theater could not override his alarm: "Pfeiffer, have you read this?" Nimitz said while reading Carlson's after-action report. "I've never heard of anything like this in all my life. There is not as much iron in that man as I thought. You take this report back and get a hold of that young man and tell him that no report from my command will have any words or even idea of surrender in it!"

The assault on the Makin Atoll was bold, well equipped, and strategic. No other raid in the Pacific Theater would be conducted over such a distance or with as much audacity. But of its kind, it was the last. Though submarines would be used to great effect to launch other surprise landings throughout the war, including of Marine reconnaissance troops, Nimitz would never again give the Raiders a chance—eliminating not only one of the primary reasons for their creation, but also their primary advocate. At a request by Rear Admiral Richmond Kelly Turner for more behind-the-lines Raider operations on Guadalcanal, Nimitz didn't merely deny the request, he responded by declaring that "the basic training of all Marine Corps infantry units is essentially the same as that of the Raider Battalions"; and worse, that "all Marine Corps infantry battalions are potentially raider units." Commandant Holcomb could not have said it better himself.

Two weeks after Carlson and the 2nd Raiders arrived back in Pearl Harbor, Red Mike Edson and his 1st Raiders valiantly plugged a gap in the perimeter defenses around Henderson Field on Guadalcanal. Once again, they earned justifiable notoriety for their steadfastness by repelling wave upon wave of Japanese attack. From that point on, Raider missions—except for a few instances—edged toward those of Edson's battalion and those of the regular Marine Corps Infantry. The reasons for this were simple. Not only was the Corps leaning hard upon its amphibious Marines, but by 1943, rubber boats had become almost standard issue, even playing a decisive role when infantry officer Major William K. Jones (the "Admiral of the Condom Fleet" of rubber boats) landed almost 900 Marines on the second day of Tarawa. This seasoning of Marine Corps Infantry, plus the towering inventory of new aircraft carriers, planes, and amphibious vehicles capable of pulverizing Japanese defenses on the tiny islands of the Central Pacific, diminished not only the Raiders' marginal—even questionable—individual superiority, but, more important, the utility of their behind-the-lines guerrilla operations. What good is a jab if you can pile on the haymakers?

In spite of Nimitz's rejection, two months after the Makin Raid, Turner gave Carlson and the 2nd Raiders another chance. This time Carlson, desperate for redemption after the Makin debacle and still eager to prove his Gung Ho system—especially in light of all the praise erroneously heaped upon him in the press—led his men for thirty days behind the lines on Guadalcanal, launching just the kind of guerrilla attacks he had witnessed when marching with Mao's army. After this Long Patrol, the name by which it was later known, Carlson and Gung Ho were again the celebrated subjects of newsreels and magazine articles. In a jungle ceremony presided over by Nimitz and with Edson looking on (and barely hiding his annoyance), Carlson was awarded a Navy Cross, second only to the Medal of Honor. Not long after, he was promoted out of the battalion—replaced by as conventional a Marine as could be found—then sent home, ostensibly for medical issues and to organize more Raiders. It was not to be. "My opinion," said Nimitz staffer Marine Colonel Omar Pfeiffer, whose personal reaction to the Gung Ho motto verged on nausea, "is that [Carlson] missed his calling; he should have been a chaplain." Believing this, believing that all "orthodox Marines" looked upon the Raiders as "plain fools," Pfeiffer made the recommendation to Commandant Holcomb "that Carlson be detached from Raider activity, and never be given another command." Eventually able to wangle a set of orders as an observer to join in the assault on Tarawa—after which battlefield commander David M. Shoup said of his performance, "he may be red, but he's not yellow"—Carlson's fate was nevertheless already sealed: he would never again command his own Marines, Raider or otherwise. In 1947, at fifty-one, following well-publicized reports that he was associating with Communists intent on stripping US funds away from China's nationalist government, Carlson succumbed to a weak heart and died penniless, his wife dependent on Jimmy Roosevelt's charity to transport his body to Arlington for burial.

"Carlson's raid on Makin . . . was a spectacular performance . . . but it was also a piece of folly," wrote Holland M. Smith after the war, perfectly combining pride for his Marines with a contempt for commando operations. "The raid had no useful military purpose and served only to alert the Japanese to our intentions in the Gilberts," which was a roundabout way of laying the dead at Tarawa at the feet of the Raiders' failure. When affable Jimmy Roosevelt, who would love nothing in his past so much as his Raiders, returned to Makin for its re-invasion in November 1943 and learned the fate of those men left behind, he never talked about the Makin Raid again. Even for him, it was a failure.

In December 1943, two notable events in the history of the Marine Corps' Raiders occurred. The first was the release of *Gung Ho!,* the film that memorialized the Makin Raid for an entire generation of Americans. The second was Holcomb's victory in finally convincing Admiral King to dismantle the Raider experiment once and for all, in order to, in

Holcomb's words, "make all infantry organizations uniform." It is worth noting that King's concurrence was given only after Holcomb agreed that the Raider Battalions would form the nucleus of the 4th Marine Regiment (Raiders), the parenthetical clause acting as both a reminder of Raider victories and a charge—by Admiral King and the Navy—to not abrogate this capability. To this condition, probably suspecting what would happen, Holcomb wholeheartedly agreed. On February 1, 1944, the 4th Marine's new commander declared that "this is going to be a Marine regiment," then dropped for good the parenthetical "Raider" from the regimental letterhead. And with that, the Raiders were no more.

Though no one could have realized it at the time, it was a decision that initiated a process of repetition in which the need for direct-action raids—often launched from the sea—was identified by someone; then a unit for this purpose was created and committed to action—often with disastrous results; then that unit was neglected, refocused, or disbanded altogether.

With the Raiders consigned to an abandoned parenthetical remainder in the history of the Marine Corps' rise to greatness, so began the Navy's unlikely voyage to filling a need that its Marines had not.

Chapter 2

The Sidelining of the Army's Amphibious Soldier-Scouts and the Call-up of the Navy's Second-String Sailors

In the First World War, the US Army's expeditionary planners—as knowledgeable as Napoleon about the ocean's exclusive ability to swallow an army whole—were able to avoid the nightmare of amphibious warfare because of the timely availability of four French ports that made possible the invasion of two million dry-shod American doughboys by marching them down ten thousand different gangplanks. Rightly focused on a future of fighting land battles and wrongly assured of the Marines' willingness to lease their backs as gangplanks for soldiers, the postwar generation of US Army planners also avoided this elephant-sized burden by carrying its tail; Marine planners carried the rest. In 1924, the Marine Corps alone staged the first amphibious assault exercise near Puerto Rico. The next year, in Hawaii, the Army joined in—not in the landing, but as the opposing beach defenders, a role as important to the development of amphibious doctrine as Noah's neighbors were to the building of the ark. For ten more years, the Army pushed around the issue of amphibious warfare like a child pushes peas around his plate. In 1937, by special invitation, the Army finally participated in the FLEX-3 amphibious exercise but sent only a single under-strength infantry regiment. At FLEX-4, in 1938—in a sign of sudden attention—the Army sent three infantry regiments, but then apparently lost interest and over the next three years sent none.

In 1941—a year that found the headquarters for the US Army's Atlantic Amphibious Corps confidently placed at Fort Picket in central Virginia, a spot more than 100 airline miles away from the nearest surf—the US Army's planners suddenly awakened to the realization that all the world's villains were now barricaded behind moats as wide as oceans, and that despite their disinterest, their reluctance, even their fears, they would finally need to field an amphibious plan more ambitious than a gangplank.

After the problem of building the landing craft to transport the Army's troops from ship to shore, the next most important challenge facing the Army's invasion planners was how to get them there—essentially, how to find the beaches best suited for landing an entire army, then how to direct the landing craft to them. To solve that problem, in December 1941 the Army accepted the help of the Marine Corps, and together they created a joint unit called the Observer Group, a name so obvious that it accidentally achieved obscurity. Together, the group's soldiers and Marines cross-trained in every available technique for identifying a coastline in the dead of night and experimented with any idea that might help them land unnoticed on an enemy beach. From the Marines' surplus of various landing craft, they launched rubber boats of all sizes—ten-man, seven-man, two-man—then brought them to Groton, Connecticut, to launch them from the backs of submarines. They plotted coastlines, discovered gaps in sand berms through which tracked vehicles could escape a beachhead, and got a feel for the dangers lurking just offshore. In one test prompted by the imagination of an officer who happened to be a former employee of Firestone tires, they placed an entire jeep in a giant rubber bag, dumped it off the back of a destroyer, then towed it ashore with the idea that once on land, they might conduct a vehicle reconnaissance. "That did not work at all," one group member said.

Never mind. The Observer Group, just like the jeep condom, was not to be.

In June 1942, Marine Corps Commandant Thomas Holcomb finally slipped the noose of Army dominion and got what he had always wanted: an independent theater of operations in the Pacific. When he did, the Corps' contributions to the Observer Group came to an end—severing the Army's access to the US military's best experience in beach reconnaissance, along with the Marine Corps' surplus of landing craft. Worse still, the Army's first amphibious invasion was now set for only five months away, and not for a single, well-charted European beachhead, but for five unknown beaches in North Africa—all of which would have to be located first, and the farthest two separated by more than 800 miles of nearly indistinguishable coastline.

Abandoned by the Marines and only five months from an operation they had spent the past five generations avoiding, frantic Army planners turned at last to the only branch of service that might help: the Navy.

Though no one of that time could have predicted, it was an arrangement that would soon connect the Army's first full-scale invasion to a new kind of sailor, one whose instincts were not limited by the oceans' edges.

2

In May 1942, in anticipation of the Army's need, the Navy issued a narrow call for volunteers to join something called the "amphibious commandos." What made the call narrow was that it seemed to be directed at a single group. That group was, in the words of one reporter, the 600 or so "educated musclemen" who had signed on as assistant instructors to the Navy's Physical Fitness Program. These were led by the most educated muscleman of his day, Lieutenant Commander James Joseph "Gene" Tunney.

Six feet tall, equipped with a heavy, fist-shaped chin and a handsome smile that every man, woman, and child in the country recognized, Tunney was known to all as the Great War Marine turned heavyweight boxing champ who had not once but twice defeated Jack Dempsey. Unlike many boxers of his day—whose training consisted of, in the words of one competitor, "a haircut and a shave"—Tunney had managed this feat by relentlessly conditioning his body during the day and reading Shakespeare every night. After winning his second fight, Tunney had fought only once more, then quit the ring forever to follow that irresistible pull, as one contemporary reporter noted, to "do something big in other fields." This had included lecturing on *Richard III* at Yale and inventing "The Gene Tunney Exerciser"—a long board equipped with ropes and pulleys that would raise the feet and condition the abdominals. It sold for three dollars.

Biggest of all, he had swapped his old globe and anchor for the bronze oak leaves of a naval officer in order to rid his new service of what he considered its gravest threat: the potbelly. "I dare say that 50% of the officers and enlisted men . . . cannot properly stand at attention," said the newly commissioned Tunney in 1941. Partly blaming their ill-fitting dungarees, which stretched too much and induced the "wearer to stick out his belly to hold them up," Tunney reasoned that the problem was actually a threat to national security and would eventually lead, in his words, to "moral collapse." Like all Marines, Tunney believed that a strong physique undergirded a strong character. His efforts in the Navy, however, had so far met with only moderate success, most likely because sailors were not Marines, and as such had never cared for either fitness or character. To help make his case, he had gone on to recruit as many notable names from the sporting world as he could find, namely college athletes, then several from the up-and-coming National Football League. Having set out to create sailors like himself—both tough and intelligent—Tunney found that this last recruiting effort had brought him something else altogether.

When twenty-eight-year-old Phil Bucklew—a football star from Columbus, Ohio—had presented himself at an Army recruitment office immediately after Pearl Harbor to volunteer for the paratroopers, the recruiter had taken one look at his six-foot-two, 235-pound frame and said, "I could take two instead of you." Considering that the smallest soldier the Army could accept was a shadow heavier than 105 pounds, the recruiter was absolutely right. Disappointed to be passed up for the paratroopers and thus lose his chance to be dropped into a foreign land, Bucklew had settled for the Navy, then settled again for the Tunney program, ostensibly the best place in the military for someone with his background—but only ostensibly. After playing for Xavier University in Cincinnati and then for the Rams in Cleveland, Bucklew had since gone on to raise the money and recruit the players for his own professional football team—accomplishments that demonstrated not only the intelligence and toughness Tunney sought, but also leadership and the risk-taking of an entrepreneur. He was not the only footballer with hidden potential. "Big John" Tripson, a six-foot-five, bushy-haired all-American from Mississippi State, had already seen more of the country than most Americans ever would, having traded his life on the South Texas plains to play all-pro tackle for the Detroit Lions. And Robert Herrick, a mountain of muscle from the mountains of Colorado who stacked every bit as high as his Texas colleague, had enlisted in the Navy not only as a graduate of Colorado State but as its head football coach. Essentially, it was a roster with more potential than Tunney's program could tame.

When Bucklew and the other football players realized that their assignment would consist merely of leading others in unglamorous calisthenics, it didn't take long for them to begin looking for other assignments, assignments that would give them a chance at the big game, the biggest game, the whole reason the ancient Greeks had invented sport in the first place—war.

So, at the call for "amphibious commandos," Bucklew and nine other titan-athletes raised their hands. When they reported to their next assignment, a chief petty officer with a knowledge of angling and the Tunney regime took one look at the oversized new arrivals and dubbed them the Tuna Fish. The name stuck.

3

THE FIRST STEP in turning the Tuna Fish into amphibious commandos was supposed to be accomplished at the Navy's Amphibious Training Base at Solomons Island, a Maryland backwater of oystermen and crabbers located where the top teeth of the Patuxent River's narrow mouth met the Chesapeake Bay; ironically, the same area from which the US Navy had launched gunboat raids against British ships during the War of 1812. Now—for the moment anyway—Solomons Island was the East Coast hub for the Navy's scant supply of around fifty landing craft, the most common of these being the LCVP, or Landing Craft Vehicle Personnel—known to everyone as a Higgins Boat. Thirty-six feet long and shaped like a hollowed-out gray brick, the LCVP was mostly made of plywood and boasted a retractable drop-ramp on the front, and it was capable of carrying one infantryman for every foot of its length, plus a crew of four. As the Tuna Fish quickly learned, the only way to advance to the second phase of their training was to learn to command these first, a prospect that was more dangerous than it sounded. Right about the same time of the athletes' arrival, one of these vessels while on a routine night training mission was sideswiped by a careless mail tender, throwing overboard its skipper, whose body was not found until two days later, not quite yet consumed by the Chesapeake's crabs.

Over several weeks, the Tuna Fish were made to learn everything there was to know about maintaining and piloting an LCVP. "Everything" included painting boats, pumping bilges, checking equipment, navigating at night, embedding nautical procedures in their block-and-tackle minds, and learning how to sustain their craft's temperamental engines. "Well, Chief, it's not working so well," remarked a frustrated Bucklew on the state of a dead engine. "After chow I'll be back down."

"No," the Coast Guard instructor replied, "you'll have chow after you fix it."

It was a standard that the Tuna Fish took to.

"They learned everything we did and in a quicker time," said one landing craft sailor of the athletes. The one Tuna Fish who needed the least time to learn the intricacies of small-boat handling was also the least noticeable—at least at first glance. At a mere six feet and 225 pounds, Robert "Buck" Halperin was easily the smallest of the group, but stood out from his fellow footballers for a string of peculiarities, not least of which was a face not unlike that of Hollywood's Robert Taylor. Besides this, he was half a decade older than the rest and had a personality that was not only as dry as cabernet but also incomparably unflappable. Most peculiar of all, he had been raised and educated in the exclusive Chicago suburb of Oak Park, the second son of prominent Jewish immigrants—at the time, not exactly features that encouraged friendships with working-class White footballers. But try telling that to Halperin.

Unlike many sons of Jewish immigrants, Halperin had been raised to speak no Yiddish, to practice no faith; a boy so adrift from any spiritual anchor that he had adopted two regional substitutes as his sanctuaries. The first had been Lake Michigan, in which he swam so often and so well that he had once caught the admiration of a wading Al Capone and upon which he had learned to sail, eventually reading the Windy City's winds so instinctively that he had taken up competitive racing. The other sanctuary—a high holy place if there ever was one—had been the Notre Dame football stadium.

Robert "Buck" Halperin.

Asked why a Jew would submit himself to such a Christian university, Halperin had flatly replied, "Because it was the best." Indeed, it was. Between 1929 and 1930, while Halperin studied electrical engineering for his father and played first-string fullback for Knute Rockne, the team had gone nineteen games undefeated. No doubt Notre Dame would have sustained this trend had an ice-covered wing not been ripped off the plane that Rockne was flying in, killing him, seven others, and the hopes of Catholic football fans everywhere. After college, Halperin had joined the Brooklyn Dodgers football team, playing a range of positions on offense and defense until finally returning to his father's Commercial Light Company in Chicago to learn the family business—an apprenticeship not unlike those reserved for the second sons of all immigrants. Then the world had exploded.

For Halperin, the attack on Pearl Harbor was more than just an attack on the United States. In the days that had followed, while the rest of the nation was girding itself for war, he had braced himself for news of his oldest brother, a Harvard-trained radiologist turned Navy doctor who, Halperin was eventually relieved to learn, had not only survived the attack but had jumped into the action. Never mind his age, how could the younger Halperin do anything less? After accepting the help of a local union boss who convinced the Navy recruiters in Chicago to enlist the thirty-four-year-old, Buck Halperin had been snared into Tunney's program, then just as quickly had jumped at the chance to escape into the amphibious commandos. Or had he really? Best as Halperin could tell, he and the other Tuna Fish had simply been hoodwinked again, this time into a program for turning former football players into landing craft coxswains for Army troops.

In retrospect it seems unrealistically optimistic to think that men with such backgrounds could ever have been confined to a field of play as cramped as a landing craft. Especially considering the stakes, stakes on full display during their last week of training on Solomons when the Allies—on the other side of the world—attempted their first large-scale amphibious assault against a German-held beach at the French port city of Dieppe. There, as the Tuna Fish were soon able to read in newspapers, some 3,000 Canadians—of an original 5,000—were either killed, wounded, or captured because they were landed on shores with no inland exits, or on sand too spongy for tank treads, or on sections so far removed from those intended that their last living efforts had been to correct the mistake of landing on the wrong beach. There was nothing to guarantee that such a fate did not await the Tuna Fish.

4

In the last week of August 1942, Buck Halperin and the rest of the Tuna Fish—plus thirty-six enlisted sailors—left Solomons Island and were trucked more than 100 miles south to a point where the lower lip of the Chesapeake Bay met the Atlantic Ocean. Here the Virginia coast gave way to an isolated tidewater inlet called Little Creek and a dirt-road base with dirt-floor housing that made Solomons look like San Francisco. Upon arrival they were greeted by an Army officer: Lieutenant Lloyd Peddicord, Jr., the twenty-nine-year-old former commander of the Observer Group, who now wore the knee-high leather boots of a horse soldier and, in spite of his small stature, when standing at attention looked like a nail waiting to be driven into a rail tie. His personality wasn't far off. As one of few soldiers who had participated in the Marine Corps' FLEX exercises, he knew all too well the challenges awaiting the men he now welcomed to the intensely difficult course he had just created, a course of soft-sand runs, rubber boat races, and endless team calisthenics known as the Joint Army-Navy Amphibious Scouts and Raiders School. At last, the Navy's volunteers for the "amphibious commandos" were about to become them. Or not so fast.

Carrying the responsibility for landing the entire Allied invasion force on the correct North African beaches (a challenge that was only eleven weeks away), Peddicord, plus his staff of three Army officers and one Navy ensign, had created a curriculum that maximized the course's efficiency by dividing it in two, each half meant to train men only in what they needed to know to accomplish their specific part of the invasion. On one side of the Scouts and Raiders School was the Raider course. There, Peddicord and his three Army instructors would groom their soldier-students into over-the-beach scout-raiders of vulnerable shore defenses. On the other side of the campus lay the unfortunately acronymed Amphibious Scout School, where Ensign John Bell—the school's second-in-command—would turn the Navy's volunteers into Scout Boat Officers and Crews: experts in rubber boat handling, night navigation, silhouette identification, and signaling—all the skills needed to taxi the real commandos from ship to surf. Even more disappointing for the Tuna Fish was the realization that as soon as they completed their course, they would become its instructors, a future not much different from the past they had just abandoned.

By mid-September, both schools were full and frantically training soldiers and sailors for the invasion that was now less than eight weeks away. Special groups with special needs arrived, including two officers and eighty enlisted men from the US Army's 9th Infantry Division—2nd Battalion, 60th Infantry—to specifically learn how to land on a beach with rubber boats, deflate them, carry them to an inland body of water, re-inflate them, then paddle by stealth to assault a fortification from the rear. Having been in the Army long enough to recognize the difference between his raider-scouts and actual raiders being groomed for a genuine commando raid, Peddicord paid close attention.

Rubber boat training for Army Scouts at Fort Pierce.

The Navy too made peculiar requests. From Pearl Harbor came two naval officers and fifteen sailors, each one a volunteer for vengeance after nine months of nonstop salvage work raising the skeletons of ships and men put there by the Japanese. These sailors would receive one week's worth of training, not in beach identification or signaling, as all Tuna Fish had been subjected to, but for a bouillon cube's worth of instruction on surf passage, demolition, and the cutting of wire as thick as a child's arm—or in this case, as thick as a submarine net.

Toward the end of September, Major General George Patton appeared at Little Creek. As the commander of the invasion forces about to land in North Africa, he was eager to inspect his troops and just as eager to find fault with their readiness. As darkness descended along the Virginia coast, the old cavalryman stalked down the beach, the heels of his impeccable boots collapsing into the soft sand, his mind awash with worry. Beyond the surf and the range of Patton's clear blue eyes, narrowed now to catch any trace of shadow lurking beyond the breakers, Navy Scouts marked time with their oars in black rubber boats, their swimmers long since delivered. With his hands on his hips, the pulse of the autumn surf to his front, and the beaches of all his hopes and fears 3,600 miles across the Atlantic, Patton's attention was now suddenly interrupted by a black dummy grenade that landed at his feet. Then another. Then another. In one month, Peddicord had created raiders capable of sneaking through the surf to bushwhack the most aggressive American general since Stonewall Jackson. Even more important, as Patton lifted his eyes from the grenades and into the blackened dunes, he watched them light up with what looked like a dozen signal flashes.

Unable to contain his delight at his own notional demise, and now surrounded by the smiling black shapes of the men who had demised him, Patton launched into a warm, by-God speech. "I'm not going to make the world safe for Democracy," he said in his gravelly falsetto. "I'm going to make it unsafe for Dictators." With men like Peddicord's Army Raider-Scouts and the Navy's Scout Boat Crews, he now knew that at least the first step of this journey would take place on the right beaches.

5

On October 10, the Amphibious Scouts and Raiders School at Little Creek closed its doors. All students returned to their units; all instructors reported to various ships along the East Coast, consigned now to the fates of vessels and beaches they had never heard of. The Tuna Fish, who had been with one another for the most important period of their lives, would never again be all together. On board their individual ships, their fleet steamed north, back up the Chesapeake Bay to Solomons Island for final rehearsals to hammer in the final rivets of coordination between Army and Navy. Green sailors who had never been to sea struggled to make sense of new winches and davits that had, like their operators, never once lowered a landing craft. Once they figured these out and attached their climbing nets, raw soldiers wrapped nervous legs overboard, then clambered into their bobbing LCVPs for a single test landing on a single safe beach. Because Navy supply officers had failed to anticipate damages incurred during training, landing craft propellers consisted only of those already attached to the boats, a fact that convinced the commanding admiral to halt any further rehearsals, especially the all-important night run. When a flustered Brigadier General Lucian K. Truscott, Jr., heard that the Navy "considered landing-craft propellers more important than soldiers' lives," as he put it, he hitched a ride to shore, found a telephone inside an unoccupied shack, and called everyone from General Patton to Admiral Hewitt until he got permission to conduct the night rehearsal.

With that, with two rehearsals on flat water—one in daylight, another in darkness—the Army and Navy went to war, as comfortable with each other as virgins standing at the edge of an arranged-marriage bed.

6

ALIGNED AND ABEAM in a uniform pattern of straight gray followed by an endless crisscrossing of white wakes, the great convoy of Task Force 34, the mightiest to ever sail, was at last on the deep rolling blue of the Atlantic magnificence, bound for the African coast. "Like a file of Indian squaws trailing an Indian warrior" (or in this case a battleship), wrote Truscott, columned transports now stretched as far as the eye could see. On board eight different ships bound for eight different beach sectors were Peddicord and the rest of the Scout Boat Officers.

Halperin, plus his crew of four, plus their equipment, had not been expected on the USS *Henry T. Allen,* and had been welcomed aboard with all the hospitality reserved for stowaways. Without berthing or storage or a place to land, Halperin and his Scouts did what they did best, scurrying up ladder wells and through passageways, finally exercising the right of squatters in the sail loft under the bow.

On the USS *Leedstown,* bound for the Mediterranean and the Algerian coast, Phil Bucklew too—despite his size and chief's anchors—was an afterthought. When he and an officer were ordered to attend a conference on the coming invasion, for which he alone would lead the first waves ashore, an orderly ushered in the officer but stopped Bucklew at the door. No enlisted were allowed inside, no matter their skills or indispensability.

For thirteen days, while the convoy sailed east, the Scouts prepared themselves and their landing craft for action. With German submarines lurking in a solid line "from Dakar clear to Iceland," as one man put it, every minute not spent test-firing a machine gun or sharpening a knife meant an extra free moment to imagine an Atlantic grave. So motivated, Scout crews painted their boats a deep blue-gray, stood watch alongside the ship's crew, loaded drums for Thompson submachine guns, welded seven-foot-tall light stands to the center of their boats, trained themselves in the use of rocket launchers, and experimented with various strips of colored cellophane to cover their flashlights. At night, the men stared east, memorizing the stars. Each day, they studied maps, hydrographic charts, postcard photographs, and anything else they could lay hands on that might help them learn the silhouettes of beaches they had never seen.

On the *Allen,* without a single Army Scout assigned to him but still tasked to reconnoiter the Moroccan beaches of Mehdia south of the Sebou River, Halperin worried and chain-smoked, then received permission from Truscott's staff to handpick eleven soldiers for shipboard Scout training in rubber boat handling and everything else—an impossible task if ever there was one.

On November 4, less than four days until D-Day, the weather turned. Destroyers nosed under waves and shallow-bottomed transports rolled, launching out of racks anyone fool enough to sleep on their side. For Halperin and crew, lodged underneath the very bow of the ship, this meant feeling the maximum pitch of every peak and trough, and worse, the prospect of even poorer visibility of the beaches than anticipated. What this meant for the Scouts and Raiders was the likelihood of less accurate landings; for the invasion, a prospect as disastrous as the one at Dieppe.

7

On the night of November 7, 1942, Peddicord and Tripson—the pocket-sized soldier and the linebacker-sized sailor—ordered their crew to mount their machine guns and infrared lights, check radios, test their steering gear, then grab a bite to eat. Swells by now had mercifully fallen to less than four feet, along with the temperature, which was now in the low sixties but sharper over the water. Clouds blocked the sky above, but to the east, the only direction that mattered tonight, stars could be seen. After a last look at their maps and pictures, as if nervously cramming for a test, the men fingered their watch crowns until synchronized, crushed out their last cigarette butts, then loaded all hands. At 0030 on November 8, on a night so black that the winch operators couldn't see the cables directly in front of them, they lowered into the water. When released from their umbilical, the coxswain turned until his compass read 120 degrees, and with little else besides the thrum of the engine for distraction, motored toward Mehdia and war.

Nearby, Halperin and his boat crew, plus the eleven impromptu Army Scouts, were themselves being winched down into the unknown. Because the *Allen* had not been able to determine her position along the Moroccan coast, either in distance or in relation to Mehdia itself, the Scouts were left to determine their individual bearings. Relieved to finally be in command of his own vessel and confident in his seamanship (if not in what lay ahead), Halperin cast off into the black, found Jupiter, Prycon, and Servius in the eastern sky, and, no different from a Phoenician pirate bound for ancient Carthage, set a course for the unseen beach. After he'd motored for thirty minutes or so, a black smudge appeared before him. It was indeed Morocco. After another thirty minutes, finding no recognizable silhouettes, Halperin turned back north to skirt the outer edge of the surf zone. Just as he did, he heard the sound they had all hoped to avoid: the thrum of another motor.

Spreading his legs for balance, Halperin tucked his elbows against his chest and with palms sweating against black metal, brought the binoculars to his eyes. To the north, between him and what he thought might be his beach, was a patrol boat. Worse still, its crew had also obviously heard a motor.

"Battle stations," he said quietly. Conditioned to notice the tension in their skipper's voice, the men slid to their guns but held their fire. Halperin ordered his coxswain to take the boat into the surf and cut the engine. The patrol boat followed the noise, stopped, then circled around, trying to catch a glimpse of the intruder. With surf battering his gunwales but covering his escape, Halperin turned his boat south and eased into an idling speed, desperate to break contact before the ocean did the patrol boat's job and swamped him. After a few minutes that seemed like hours, the patrol boat sped off, unable to hear or see the Scouts. With the skill of a Lake Michigan whisky smuggler, Halperin had led his men through their first contact with the enemy.

Just then, with the luck that attends all great commanders, the northern rock jetty to the beach-dividing Sebou River appeared, along with the boat of Peddicord and Tripson, not seen since the exercises off Solomons. With these aids, Halperin had his exact position, and so set his speed and his clock. Beyond the river mouth to the east, a veiled loom could now be seen from the upriver lights of Port Lyautey.

For seventeen minutes, Halperin sped south until his watch told him he had arrived off Green Beach. Once there, at about 0300, he edged toward the spray of the first line of breakers, stopped, then unloaded the first six-man rubber boat team of Army Scouts. Two hundred yards south, he unloaded the second crew. With the first part of his mission complete, there was nothing left for Halperin and his Navy crewmen to do but wait.

At 0330, Peddicord and Tripson moved their boat to the center of the Sebou's massive rock jetties, faced seaward, and illuminated their ten infrared beach beacons. Because their lights were fixed to a seven-foot-tall platform and facing toward the bow, and because the river's current continued to push them out to sea, they were now repeatedly forced to throttle backward against the chop. After waiting for twenty minutes with no sign of any landing craft, Peddicord and Tripson conferred, then agreed to illuminate their underpowered, hooded white flashlights.

For another hour and twenty-five minutes the men waited, not sure if the invasion had been canceled or the fleet had been attacked by submarines. Finally, at 0515, the first wave of boats—if it could be called that—trickled over the horizon and into Peddicord's light net. The boat wave commander, the only one in the first wave with an infrared scope capable of seeing Peddicord's primary signaling lights, had long since been left behind with motor trouble. Now, without a commander or sense of direction, bemused landing craft skippers with barely any training throttled directly past Peddicord into the river's mouth, ignorant of the danger lurking before them.

8

Situated on a hill on the Sebou's southern bank—just over a mile from the river's mouth and looming high above the ocean's flatness—was a sprawling sixteenth-century Portuguese castle built of sand-colored stone and brick known to all invaders as the Kasbah. Recognized for its obvious place in an Arabian folktale, the misnamed fortress was complete with archers' battlements and spacious loopholes for French artillery. High as it was, the Kasbah commanded views of the jetties, any traffic that dared venture into the 500-yard-wide river below, and the river's only obstacle—and unlike the fort that overlooked it, it was anything but ancient.

Anchored to opposite banks of the Sebou and supported by four evenly spaced barges lay a stretch of one-inch cable, fashioned into an impenetrable net, blocking access to Port Lyautey and its airfield, the only such facility within bomber range of the Strait of Gibraltar. If the Allies could not take the inland airfield, they could not command the strait. If they could not command the strait, German submarines would be free to slip from the Atlantic into the Mediterranean to attack the Allied invasion in Algeria that Phil Bucklew was now leading to shore. The fastest way to secure the airfield was up the river; the only way to use the river was to cut the cable.

Planners had anticipated this problem early on, and so had plumbed the ranks of both Army and Navy for personnel with a knowledge of metal cutting. In the Army they found a veteran combat engineer, Lieutenant Colonel Frederick Henney. "Can the obstacle be removed?" they had asked. "Yes," he replied, with more bravery than brains—the best combination for a combat engineer—to which he then added "and I would like to try it." As most Army Combat Engineers had from the earliest days of planning been committed to the invasion force, once again the Navy had volunteered to fill the gap. With this mission in mind from the outset, the seventeen Navy salvage personnel had left Pearl Harbor for an abbreviated course of Scout and Raider training at Little Creek, then boarded the USS *Cherokee* for transit across the Atlantic. Now, as Peddicord and Tripson and every member of the Scout Boat Crew strained their eyes and voices to catch and correct wayward landing craft, a lone boat laden with men and explosives sped toward them with a singular purpose.

Bristling with tommy guns, pistols, knives, and grenades, at 0530 Henney and his Navy salvage workers breathed a sigh of relief when they encountered Peddicord and Tripson. Once their course was confirmed, Peddicord dispatched them upriver with a godspeed to the first Navy commando mission of the war—albeit one led by a soldier. To assist them in severing the obstacle, the salvage sailors brought equipment with which they were familiar, including an underwater torch, shallow-water diving gear, a one-inch cable speed cutter, plus an altogether foreign collection of custom-made shape charges that Henney had made during the Atlantic transit. Not sure if the cable net was also anchored to the riverbed and would require multiple cuts to unhinge it, they had brought two inflated rubber boats, now stacked on their landing craft's engine housing, that they could drop off at separate points and thereby minimize their time on target.

When the special river party left Peddicord and passed between the jetties, a white-capped groundswell of channelized surf lifted the boat and, as one sailor recalled, "shot us forward like an express train." Just as they passed, a signal rocket streaked overhead. If up until this moment their approach had been a secret, it was no longer.

9

ON BOARD THE UNGAINLY VESSEL, with nerves cinched tight with tension, was a second-class gunner's mate from Chicago named Bill Freeman. Possessing good looks but an incurably directionless disposition, Freeman—upon turning eighteen—had been loaded into a car by his frustrated father, driven to Arizona, then kicked out with no more advice than "make it back on your own." For a while, Bill made it nowhere. In short order, he had joined a gang of local toughs named Los Aventureros, then hitched a ride north to the Rocky Mountains. Once there, Freeman had enrolled himself in the Colorado School of Mines to learn, among other things, demolition. Now, at twenty-seven, he was launched on the adventure of his life; in his arms, a handmade underwater explosive, and in his head, a hope to make good on his father's advice.

As Henney, Freeman, and the rest of the salvage pirates trolled along the north bank of the river, edging past the ancient fort, a searchlight from the Kasbah's southwest tower blinked on, sweeping the opposite coast for movement. In a moment it found some. Trapped in this panic of light, Henney did the only thing he could and ordered the coxswain to hit the throttle. After a moment's rush, comically zigzagging to ditch the spotlight, an artillery piece from the Kasbah boomed, firing away on the landing beaches. A moment later, machine gun bullets ripped into one of the rubber boats stacked atop the engine housing, deflating it with a hiss along with any bravado the men had unconsciously brought. By the time they shook free of the light and evaded the machine gun, the notched outline of the Kasbah could be seen against the lightening sky. Upriver and barely visible in the shadow of dawn lay the barges and the net. Beyond: Port Lyautey's airfield.

Just then, the Kasbah's 75-millimeter guns opened up, plunging white geysers into the river all around.

"Let's get the hell out of here!" Henney yelled over the splash of artillery rounds and roar of the prop wash. The airfield, and the Strait of Gibraltar, would have to wait.

10

The first one to feel the Special River Party's failure was Halperin. Almost as soon as Henney and Freeman were fleeing back to the Atlantic, the waves of landing craft bound for Green Beach began passing Halperin's position on the edge of the surf zone. Just then, five or six French aircraft from Port Lyautey's unreachable airfield appeared overhead, ravenously circling for targets, eager to prove their fighting worth after two years of dishonor. The only craft on the coast with lights shining out to sea and not moving toward the beach, Halperin and crew were the proverbial sitting ducks—an exaggerated expression in nearly every case, but not in this one. For nearly two hours, the French pilots strafed the Scout Boat. For two hours, Halperin maintained his boat's position like a linebacker, his broad shoulders acting as the keystone for the entire landing. When the aircraft finally relented and returned to the still-unscathed airfield for fuel and ammunition, Halperin and crew were remarkably untouched, proving to all the favor the Almighty still held for his chosen people, especially for those who had played for the Irish.

Almost as soon as the aircraft departed, the Army Scouts that Halperin and crew had dropped off during the night now signaled the Scout Boat for assistance. On the beach, chaos reigned. Though the Army's landings on Green Beach had been completely unopposed, scores of capsized landing craft now bobbed in the surf and leaderless infantrymen milled haplessly on the shore. Landing amid this confusion, Halperin directed his men to do what they could to salvage the swamped vessels. Alone and without the combat loadout of even a buck private, Halperin drew his .45-caliber pistol and set off to scout a gap through which the Army's vehicles could fit, thereby becoming the first member in the history of Naval Special Warfare to advance himself beyond the beach.

After a short, plodding hike through scrub and sand as soft as powder, Halperin came upon a road running parallel to the beach. Here was the answer to the Army's problem. Before he could turn back to report what he had found, however, a foreign truck billowing black smoke rumbled into view. With no time to retreat but with the instincts of a fullback, Halperin raised his pistol. "Halt!" he yelled as the charcoal-gas truck bucked, then skidded to a stop. With empty hands and foreign tongues, two French officers stumbled out, dressed like dandies, aghast to find themselves in the custody of a hulking American. In his after-action report submitted later that month, Halperin summed up the entire episode with as much embellishment as his nature would allow: "I had no trouble taking them prisoner."

11

AT 1100, WITH SWOLLEN JOINTS, red eyes, and numb expressions, after more than an entire night's worth of no sleep and near-constant exposure to spotlights, then strafing, then artillery, Peddicord and Tripson returned to the USS *Clymer* to make their report. While they did, the suddenly jobless Scout Boat Crew dismissed their fatigue and volunteered to escort a boatload's worth of five-gallon gasoline cans to shore. Just as they hit the beach, a shell from the Kasbah slammed into their stern, killing their boat, but miraculously, nothing else.

Late in the afternoon, still with no sleep, Peddicord nevertheless climbed aboard a landing craft bound for Green Beach. When he arrived, the once gentle two-to-four-foot surf that had given the force's landing craft so much trouble had now metastasized into mountains of curling green breakers. And though he and his Scouts had helped the Army find their beaches—for the most part—by the time he reported to General Truscott's command post as an observer, it was apparent that beach marking alone had not compensated for the Army's lack of critical amphibious invasion skills.

When night fell, conditions only got worse. "As far as I could see along the beach," wrote Truscott years later, "there was chaos." Over the next two days, Peddicord would count seventy-seven abandoned landing craft, lost not to enemy machine guns or beach obstacles, of which there were none, but to insufficient training and overwhelming surf. Even General Truscott's jeep had been lost, only a few yards from the water's edge, stuck in a powdery sand that no one had thought to investigate before D-Day. For vehicles that remained mobile, drivers had no idea where to go. Those troops that did find the enemy had very little idea how to fight them. "You brave crazy," ran the response of a typical French soldier to American tactics. "You go by the front—why you no go by the flank?" But frontal assaults were not the only tactical area in which Peddicord saw room for improvement. Wherever he went, his soldier's brain spied missed opportunities for unconventional operations. So did others, not all of them soldiers.

12

The next morning, November 9, "all spirits rose," remembered Lieutenant Colonel Henney. The problem was, "so did the breakers." After the failed attempt to cut the Sebou River's cable, he had dropped off the Navy salvage workers on the *Cherokee,* then returned to the coast to form an infantry reserve of 150 lost souls who were wandering on the beach. In that time, the surf had gone from four feet to fifteen, making landing craft operations impossible. To the east and inland, still untouched by Allied assault, lay Port Lyautey and its invaluable airfield.

Patrolling just off the Sebou's jetties, like a hungry wolf pacing in a cage, was a 314-foot-long masterpiece of nautical minimalism. Built in 1920, the USS *Dallas* possessed a draft of nine feet three inches, as shallow as could be found in the US fleet and made even shallower after her stacks and superstructure had been cut away to further lighten her load. Now, the only thing that weighed her down were the seventy-five men of the Army's 9th Infantry Division—2nd Battalion, 60th Infantry—who had graduated from Peddicord's Raider curriculum less than two months before. If the cable net could be cut, then the *Dallas* and these Army Raiders could ply the Sebou's shallow waters in their rubber boats right up to the airfield's doorstep and, like all special operations, take it from the direction least expected. For two days the Raiders had waited for the go-ahead. For two days the call had not come. As the sun and temperature went down on November 9, Henney flashed a message out to sea. He would try again, just as soon as the Navy demolition team relaunched their boat and picked him up.

That night, the river pirates piled their Higgins Boat with the same explosives and cutting tools as before, but now, wiser from their first taste of combat, mounted two additional machine guns to their complement, proving that the lessons of war rarely require a second teacher. As they worked to improve their chances, the clear skies of the previous night began to choke with black clouds, which soon unleashed a bone-chilling rain and a sea state so high that landing craft operations remained out of the question. The river raiders were not planning on landing anywhere.

As the salvage sailors approached the jetties, the men spread their legs and released their pistol grips to stubbornly grab hold of anything they could that would anchor them to the floating plywood coffin that now ferried their lives to the Sebou River. The ride was even more perilous than last time, as the channelized surf met with the river's outflow to create waves nearly as high as the Higgins Boat was long. When they did finally emerge into the flat stillness of the river, their relief was overshadowed by the dangers ahead and behind. Even if they did accomplish their mission, the river's mouth would surely swamp them when they tried to make their escape.

Now, as their Higgins Boat inched forward, the men's eyes squinted through darkness and sheets of rain to locate their Army commander's flashlight along the bank. Ashore, Henney and a squad of infantrymen were still slogging through juniper and wet sand, trying to make their way to the rendezvous at the river's edge, when a machine gun opened up on the patrol. Skittish about the sounds of gunfire since they had just been its target, the river party eased away from the sound and the shore. The river raiders would have to go on alone, now led by Navy Lieutenants Mark W. Starkweather and James W. Darroch—neither of them soldiers. Ahead lay the cable and destiny. Overlooking all, the Kasbah.

With necks craning to spy the slightest movement along the steep battlements above, the demolition sailors laid the muzzles of their tommy guns atop the gunwales like men defending a foxhole. To their great relief, no movement could be seen. In fact, because of the reduced visibility, and no doubt also because the French believed that such an operation under such conditions was unlikely if not impossible, no one on the Kasbah seemed to have the slightest idea that the Higgins Boat had slid past.

When the cable finally came into view, the coxswain instinctively edged the craft toward the support barge third in line from the south bank and as far away from the Kasbah's guns as possible while staying in the center of the channel. As they eased alongside the wire net, the men stretched forth their cold fingers to at last grip the steel cable they had now twice risked their lives to destroy. On top of the net was a thin strand of wire supporting nothing but itself, with a purpose that no one could guess.

In a rush, the sailors affixed a handful of the cable-cutting explosives and drew off. With a flash of light and a sharp boom that raced over the river and echoed against the steep bank, the cable splashed into the water. The support barges that had supported it instantly sagged against the ebbing current.

Suddenly, the Kasbah was alive. Machine guns fired into the river and bullets stitched into the Higgins Boat's plywood hull.

In the space of a single breath the coxswain dropped his throttle, and the corresponding surge of power flung all hands into a scramble to drop their tools and reach for weapons and handholds. In an instant, their mounted machine guns were returning fire, blazing away at the Kasbah's cliffs while the coxswain twisted his craft downriver to escape the arching braids of bullets.

After no more than thirty seconds of terror, Starkweather ordered his men to cease fire, hoping that rain and darkness and distance would hide them from the Kasbah's guns. It worked. The Kasbah faded into the night, while the men held their breath for the ranks of white surf still to come.

When they arrived at the river's mouth, the men caught a glimpse of what lay ahead: mountainous thirty-foot breakers. With the focus that attends all men on the edge of peril, they threw overboard anything not living or bolted down. Then the coxswain waited for a break in the surf. When he saw it, he dropped the throttle to the floor. Shivering wet from the rain and surf, with knuckles as white as bones, the Pearl Harbor salvagers faced the waves, then mixed silent prayers with sailors' curses and held on for their lives. "I don't know how the hell we did it," Freeman said afterward, shaking his head in disbelief, the only casualty being the salvage crew's lieutenant, who broke his ankle when the boat's hull slammed into a breaker. But make it they did, and without a soldier holding their hand.

13

AT 0130, THE SKIPPER of the *Dallas* received the two words he and his Army Raiders had been waiting for. "*Steve Brodie, Steve Brodie,*" squelched the ship-to-ship radio, an indecipherable code to anyone listening in, but to those who knew, the signal that the Sebou River's obstacle had been cut. The path to the airfield was clear.

At 0600, the *Dallas* edged her bow over the first line of breakers cresting past the Sebou's jetties. As she slipped farther and farther into the channel, the surf pounded her stern and the ship tilted violently. Several times it appeared that she might strike the south jetty or, worse, grind to a halt in the shallows to be capsized by the indomitable surf. Piloted by René Malvergne, a French patriot smuggled out of Morocco by the OSS for this exact purpose, the *Dallas* edged parallel to the south jetty and squeezed into the channel.

When she arrived at the wire obstacle, Malvergne's eyes widened, alarmed to find that the demolition team had severed the cable above what he knew was an impassable shoal. Not only that, but the barges supporting the rest of the cable, though slackened, still appeared to be anchored to the riverbed, so the rest of the cable was apparently intact. Whatever had existed below the waterline most likely still existed.

Unable to turn back to sea, with no time to consider other options and with fire from the Kasbah raking the *Dallas*'s decks from above, Malvergne plunged the throttle to eighteen knots. At 0629, the *Dallas* struck the obstacle between the first and second barge. From the after-action report that followed: the *Dallas* "parted it without a tremor and headed on up the river." Though Freeman and the rest of the demolition team had twice braved a gauntlet of fire and mountains of surf, they had apparently done their work for naught.

The USS *Dallas* aground in the Wadi Sebou off Port Lyautey's airfield, Morocco, November 11, 1942.

Just over an hour and nine miles later, the *Dallas* ground to a stop on a sandbar just opposite Port Lyautey's airport. Dead in the water, the *Dallas* had nevertheless arrived. With 75-millimeter shells plummeting great geysers of water all around, eighty-two soldiers of the 2nd Battalion, 60th Infantry—all graduates of the Army's Raider Course—clambered into their rubber boats and cast off, paddling for Africa and their first solid ground in over two weeks. Hurrying from the south, threading through enemy strong points like a nervous father threads through a crowd to watch his son step up to the plate, Peddicord arrived just in time to watch his Raiders School students crush the last of the French resistance.

And with that, the challenge of North Africa's beaches was over; the challenge for the soldiers and sailors of the Scouts and Raiders School just beginning.

14

For everything that had gone wrong for the Allies in the invasion of North Africa—capsized landing craft, drowned soldiers, beach mix-ups—the Navy's Scout Boat Crews and the Army's Raiders were one of the few things that had actually gone right. The only problem: There had not been enough of them. "I think it very important that you set up certain Joint Schools," wrote Admiral Kent Hewitt after Torch to the new amphibious commander of North African Waters. Among the four listed, third was the Amphibious Scouts and Raiders School.

When Peddicord and the Scout Boat Officers returned to Little Creek at the end of November 1942, they were welcomed back into their positions at the Amphibious Training Command with a single mandate: more. The most immediate obstacle to their expansion efforts was Little Creek itself. When they had departed for Africa, autumn rains had already begun to turn their training area into a mudhole. Now, as December days fell away, so too did the temperatures. Unable to train men how to swim and handle rubber boats without having them slip into hypothermia, Peddicord made his way to Florida, borrowed an Army jeep, and drove along the coast. Frantic to find a stretch of Atlantic beach on which to train his men, he "bundled" himself in an Aquascutum trench coat and sloughed south from Saint Augustine until he found what he was looking for.

On January 25, 1943, with perfect boots that rose nearly all the way to his perfectly parted hair, Peddicord addressed the first class of 300 soldiers to attend the Scouts and Raiders School's new training site at Fort Pierce, Florida. Only "when our Army [has] been established ashore in sufficient strength to completely overwhelm the enemy forces, on their own ground," he began, the words of his clumpy Ohio baritone thudding like bricks among the crowd, "then and then only will the end of the war be in sight." This they all knew; even their mothers knew it. To land on this ground, Peddicord went on, required men with shoulders broad enough on which to "rest the responsibility of the entire operation." Shoulders like those of the small-boat sailors he had just commanded.

Navy Cross presentation for (left to right) Ensigns John Bell, Jack Byrom, Robert Herrick, Robert Halperin, John Tripson, and Kenneth Howe, the last of whom was killed at Anzio while transporting General Mark Clark to shore.

On May 1, 1943, five of the original ten Tuna Fish, including Halperin, donned their immaculate service dress whites, each boasting the newly commissioned rank of an ensign, then marched out to the grassy parade ground and came to attention. When the ceremony was over, each was wearing a Navy Cross—an award only one rank lower than the Medal of Honor, and one higher than the Silver Star the Army had seen fit to award Peddicord for the same effort. Perhaps an oversight, perhaps a sign of the Army's and Navy's disparate priorities, the awarding of this lesser medal was not to be the last time that Peddicord's efforts would be undercut.

In the year that followed Operation Torch, the Army and Navy demand for Scout Boat Crews and Raiders would continue, but not exactly at the same pace. In addition to Peddicord's joint school at Fort Pierce, Navy planners would dispatch Halperin back to Little Creek to prepare and command fourteen boat crews for the upcoming invasion of Sicily and would order Phil Bucklew to establish what almost amounted to a parallel school in Bizerte, Tunisia. Exactly the sorts of doors that opened onto hidden opportunities.

Having landed his scouts on an undefended beach in Algeria during

Operation Torch and so missed the avalanche of Navy Crosses that had hit the other Scout Boat Officers, Bucklew had instead had to survive two torpedo attacks and the sinking of two different vessels—the last one trapping him beneath the rack that had collapsed on top of him while he slept—before getting his chance to prove himself. When he emerged from the rack and the North African invasion, he had—in spite of thirty days due for "survivor's leave"—immediately volunteered for more duty. In Tunisia, that duty not only placed him in charge of his own Scouts and Raiders School, but introduced him to the British Commandos, who in turn introduced him to the use of cockleshells, or two-man kayaks, for closing within a whisper of an enemy beach and signaling the fleet from there.* No longer under the Army's supervision, Bucklew was already incorporating into his curriculum more than just cockleshells, but also ocean swims, rubber boat drills, running his men over the sand dunes for fifteen miles at a stretch—essentially, transforming them from Scout Boat Crewmen into simply Scouts. "Have sixteen navy volunteer swimmers," Bucklew wrote Peddicord from Bizerte on stationery swiped from New York City's Hotel Plymouth. "Have set-up gunnery, signaling, supplies, etc. . . . have our boats (the best, as usual). If we aren't blown to hell on the next play—well life isn't bad." In the coming months, no Scout or Raider during the entire war would come as close to getting "blown to hell" as Bucklew himself.

In the year since the formal establishment of the Joint Army-Navy Scouts and Raiders School, Peddicord had overseen the training of almost 3,000 Scout Boat Crewmen and Amphibious Raiders, a number that did not include those trained in other parts of the world—in other words, more than the Army would ever need. Sensing this glut and a growing irrelevance, and anxious to follow men like Bucklew and Halperin to active theaters of operation, Peddicord at the end of 1943 accepted orders to William Donovan's OSS, taking with him the Army's most enthusiastic expert on small-unit amphibious operations and the best advocate for the Army's continued participation in the joint training effort. When he left, the Army's departure was only a matter of time.

On February 2, 1944—just two months after Peddicord's departure—

* Two-man kayak use learned from the British: Undated book review by Jim O'Dell of John B. Dwyer's *Scouts and Raiders: The Navy's First Special Warfare Commandos* (Westport: Praeger, 1993).

the last Army officer assigned to the Scouts and Raiders School turned over to his Navy counterpart the last of the remaining Army documents that might be useful to future trainees; oddly enough, this included an analysis of Carlson's Makin Raid. With that turnover, the Army-Navy Scouts and Raiders School became the exclusive property of the US Navy.

Though no one could have anticipated how far such a decision would reverberate, in the near term the Army's abandonment meant an end to the previous restrictions on the type of training a sailor could receive. It also left the program's future in the hands of sailors who had spent their entire careers learning to run through any gap the opposing team had left unguarded.

Chapter 3

The US Army's First Commandos and the Raid That Wasn't

As the Navy was pressuring the Marine Corps' planners to create island raiders and the Army was begrudgingly partnering with the Navy to create Scouts and Raiders for marking beaches but not really raiding anything beyond the high-water mark, another unit had already started performing the actual mission of the commando raid. Because that unit wasn't American, however, the reasons for its creation had had nothing to do with American needs—but that didn't mean that Americans hadn't been paying attention. Considering the stories that had trickled into American newspapers and magazines, it would've been impossible not to.

Requiring "specially trained troops of the hunter class," the British Commandos—a name taken from the skulking, bushwhacking Afrikaners in the Boer War—had ostensibly been intended from their post-Dunkirk creation to, in Churchill's words, "develop a reign of terror . . . a ceaseless offensive against the whole German-occupied coastline, leaving a trail of German corpses behind." In other words, they had been intended to raid, to hit and run; the only offensive tactic left to a military that had just been chased off the continent. In keeping with the Dunkirk embarrassment, the initial results of the commandos' reign of terror had not been much. On their first cross-channel night raid—with faces blackened by makeup borrowed from a London theater—the commandos had stumbled ashore, startled two German sentries, killed them, then forgot to search their corpses or even pause to discover what the two guards had been guarding. Another group had botched their ambush when one of its members had accidentally ejected his magazine onto the rocky beach, prompting a counterambush and forcing the commandos to sprint for their boats, where the group's commander had

had to have his ear stitched back into place by a petty officer. When the British Coast Guard intercepted the commandos on the return trip to England, they found many of them drunk, which made their only successful raid the one that had been executed on their boat's liquor supply. For the British high command—desperate for soldiers to rebuild its army after Dunkirk—it was a mission whose potential rewards had not justified its risks; for Churchill—desperate for anything that might kindle hope in the British people—it was a start.

Initially created as a place-holder for Britain's offensive ambitions, in two years the British Commandos had not treaded water, but had gone on to so improve their own training and mission planning that they had come to amass a sensational record of "butcher and bolt" across coastal France, Norway, the Netherlands, even Africa. In so doing, they had proved that raiding could have a strategic impact that went far beyond just kindling hopes. Following their example, in November 1941 a group of Canadian commandos attempted a cross-channel raid meant to kidnap Hitler's famously overweight deputy, Reichsmarschall Hermann Goering, and carry him—"if they could"—back to their boat, then—and so long as he did not sink them—back to England. Successful in killing all the Germans at Goering's purported location, the mission's only failure concerned Goering's actual capture; as *Time* magazine explained, "the fat man wasn't there."

The high command's response to such near coups had been to formally establish the Combined Operations Headquarters, or COHQ, with the sole purpose of sponsoring more raids and raiders—"a steel hand from the sea," as Churchill called them. The status of COHQ was further elevated by the appointment of its six-foot-four, forty-one-year-old commander, Lord Louis Mountbatten, a handsome naval officer who had already commanded two ships in this war, both of them hit, the second one sinking with his silver cigarette lighter, a gift from his cousin the Duke of Windsor, brother of the king.

To anyone watching from the outside, such upgrades could mean only one thing: the British Commandos were no longer a sideshow; in fact, under the circumstances, they were now headlining the only show in town. More important for our purposes, their performance had already earned the attention of the top soldier in the US military, but a soldier who had no interest in the strategic potential of commando missions. For reasons peculiar to the man, it would prove a lapse that would ultimately commit the US military's first commandos to a raid that wasn't, leaving empty the stage for an altogether different kind of actor.

2

In early April 1942, the chief of staff of the US Army, General George Marshall, arrived in Britain prepared to oblige the requirements of English protocol. He dined at No. 10 Downing Street; he weekended in the country with Churchill; he lunched with the king and queen. To ease the monotony of rationing—Churchill's most sensitive pressure point—Marshall brought along a crate of cabbages and another of Brussels sprouts. On April 9, he met with the British war leaders and pushed for a cross-channel invasion. At this, the British winced. It would take more than Brussels sprouts to convince them to avenge the nightmare of Dunkirk. There was, however, one of Marshall's proposals to which the British commanders were almost too eager to agree: the inclusion of Americans on commando raids. Though Marshall didn't give his reasons for wanting to participate, he had them nonetheless. And his were not the same as Churchill's.

Six feet tall and silver-haired, "rangy" in the words of one contemporary, George Catlett Marshall—the Army's boss since A.D. 1940—had already been on active service for forty-one years, almost 25 percent of the US Army's entire history. Emerging from the First World War with a reputation as Pershing's best soldier in an army of two million volunteers, Marshall had stayed on to watch that same army deflate to its prewar levels, descending all the way to nineteenth among the world's armies, just behind Bulgaria's, a decline that had precipitated a corresponding shrink in budget and training, and worst of all, skill. Observing exercises in China in the 1920s, Marshall had watched one of the Army Infantry School's top-ranked graduates freeze when unable to draft an order to envelop an enemy flank since he lacked detailed information on the terrain over which his seventy soldiers would travel. Marshall had shuddered at the sight, and resolved to correct the problem. As assistant commandant at Fort Benning from 1927 to 1932, he had overhauled the Infantry School's dusty curriculum, and by default the entire infantry. When Marshall was made chief of staff and his service's most senior officer, his overhauls had taken on the entire Army. His earliest changes had included eliminating the complicated, close-order marches of Frederick the Great; tossing out the bolt-action Springfield rifles in favor of the semiautomatic Garands; replacing the khaki breeches and wrap puttees of the doughboy era with more comfortable everything. Disgusted by the resignation of many officers to a future of warfare that matched the trench-to-trench plod of the First World War, Marshall had pushed for the development of airborne troops and promoted magnificent cranks like Joseph Stilwell and George Patton, who better than anyone recognized the value of crashing troops behind an enemy's front.

Each one of Marshall's changes had been made to better prepare the Army for war; none to date had so far addressed his most complicated dilemma. Since his appointment, the US Army had swelled from 200,000 men into a legion of more than a million. Of the officers commanding this legion, barely 14,000 had been professional regulars; many of the best of these had never seen combat. Eisenhower himself, whom Marshall would soon select to command armies across North Africa and Europe, had spent the Great War in Maryland. Needing more than anything to supplement this lack of experience, Marshall now turned to the only English speakers who had it.

When Marshall and Mountbatten met, each impressed the other. By the end of their planning conference, they were decided on two actions related to joint unconventional missions. First, Marshall agreed to explore one of Mountbatten's long-range penetration schemes, one that required the development of a snow machine—a tractor of sorts—capable of speeding through snowdrifts and transporting a specially trained force of American and Canadian troops into Norway to blow up bridges and hydroelectric dams, and sow chaos generally. Second, Mountbatten agreed to Marshall's request to accept a group of Americans into British Commando training, then include them on a series of raids—Marshall's reasons: first, so they could serve as a nucleus for a similar American unit; and second, so that a group of his soldiers might gain "battle experience as soon as possible," which would then be passed on to the rest of the Army. Of the two, Marshall's more important reason was the latter.

On April 18, after departing London to review American troops in Northern Ireland, Marshall was confronted by reporters who asked a question on everyone's mind: Will Americans take part in commando raids in France?

"Inevitably," Marshall replied, his dry, "monotonal" voice brimming with suspense, "there will be American troops in Commando raids."

Few had reason to doubt his honesty, his confidence, his bright blue eyes, what swooning reporters were already calling his "short pugnacious nose," and "his stubborn upper lip." Already, his comments, no matter how soft, were rolling like thunder across the headlines. This one was no different.

"We have Commando training in our Army," Marshall continued, "but we call it by a different name. We have an Army corps trained now for amphibious operations." The very next day, *The New York Times* truncated the general's response into the headline Americans craved: "Marshall Pledges Action in Europe . . . Reveals Commando Corps." In fact, he hadn't—in fact, he had only revealed that some American troops had received amphibious training—whatever that meant; and some would participate in future raids—even vaguer. For the reporters, it was hair-splitting easily rebraided to boost newspaper sales. For the "Commando Corps," it was a hint that Marshall's heart wasn't fully in it.

To Marshall, both a product and a student of American history, Mountbatten's commandos were not at all unique. Within months of the Plymouth Rock landing, even the Pilgrims had adopted the skulking raids of their native allies and enemies. Some fifty-five years later, in King Philip's War, men like Ben Church had sharpened these into a campaign in which the central method had been the raid itself. In the French and Indian War, the numerically inferior French and Indians had launched terrorizing guerrilla attacks almost exclusively—that is, until men like the Marquis de Montcalm convinced the French crown to counter the British conventionals with a conventional army of his own. In fact, the French had been doing just fine without one. The British, on the other hand, evolved in the completely opposite direction, and more and more had come to rely on Indian tactics like those of Robert Rogers and his Rangers, who showed the British how to swap their red coats for green, march in single file, and save their hatchets until the last possible moment. In the Revolutionary War, the British forgot these lessons; their American cousins did not, and leaned on raiders throughout the conflict to tie down the British wherever they could. Four score and seven years later, both Northern and Southern cavalry units—from Abel Straight to Ulric Dahlgren in the Union Army; from John Mosby to Bedford Forrest in the Confederate—mimicked this history by scouting, raiding, penetrating, then returning to take their place in the firing line as highly mobile infantry. Because every professional American Army officer had a vague recollection of this history, raiding tactics were viewed with as much awe as any other technique on the continuum of military operations. Learning of the plan to create special soldiers for special missions, General Lesley McNair, head of the US Army Ground Forces, responded with the following: "Hell, we rehearsed trench raids in the last war and we didn't call them commandos." For Marshall, McNair had a point.

Indispensable to the country for his steadfastness, his energy, his foresight, most of all his unswerving commitment to raising the standards of the entire Army, Marshall lacked two attributes the American commando project required: imagination and the impulse to achieve more with less. He never imagined an elite unit focused on a single aspect of infantry tactics or that a unit explicitly purposed for such could be so effective. Once his "battle experience" was achieved and no longer a goal, the function of these commandos would fall to whatever theater commanders required at the moment. Like the apple in the garden, the downfall of the Army's first commando unit was present from the beginning. And its fall would soon reverberate past the life of the organization itself.

3

To OVERSEE THE DEVELOPMENT of the US Army's first commando unit, Marshall reluctantly assigned Colonel Lucian K. Truscott, Jr., a gravel-voiced, goggle-eyed, rock-jawed horse soldier from Texas who offset his saturnine appearance by routinely wearing the high-leather boots of the cavalry, a polished helmet, a striking red jacket, and a yellow scarf not unlike the one worn by Custer. "You are an older man than I wanted for this assignment," Marshall unflinchingly told the Texan at their first meeting. (In fact, he was only five years older than Mountbatten.) "But some of your friends assure me that you are younger than your years, and that your experience especially fits you for this assignment." It did not. Truscott, by his own admission, knew nothing of amphibious operations, had rarely dealt with the Navy, and had only twice been on a small boat on salt water. His only unique qualification for service on Combined Operations Headquarters and for creating the US Army's first commando force was that he, like Mountbatten, played polo. In the end, Marshall ignored Truscott's protests. Apparently, being a horse soldier from Texas was more than enough.

"You will keep in mind at all times that the principal objective of this program must be that of providing actual battle experience for as many as practicable of our personnel," stated Truscott's official orders. Focused on what should have been an ulterior benefit of a commando force and not the objective, Marshall failed to provide any guidance as to the type of unit he wanted created. Such nuances were not even mentioned.

Within two weeks of receiving his assignment, Truscott submitted a plan to Marshall for the creation of a battalion of something called "rangers." It was a name that echoed with the drums of Indian raids, and, in his words, "every war in which the nation [had] been engaged." Whether he recognized the influence or not, Rogers' Rangers had been the subject of *Northwest Passage*, a Spencer Tracy movie barely two years old. A day after the proposal hit his desk, Marshall telegrammed his approval for the name, and for the allocation of 35 officers and 450 enlisted men. Anticipating dropouts, planners approved a total of 575 volunteers. Soon published guidance would require the following standards for recruits: a height of at least five feet six inches; a weight described as "normal"; and an age ceiling of "not over 35." Requirements for race were, regrettably, predictable. In need of troops who already possessed a knowledge of "basic" infantry tactics, planners would nevertheless hold back from making this a requirement, as the need for basic competence was even higher. "Each applicant [must] be a true volunteer," the guidance would conclude, a warning to commanders who saw the Ranger program as an opportunity to jettison their worst troops. The result of the Ranger recruitment drive manifested some experience, but mostly a typical spread of citizen-soldiers: former shopkeepers, delivery boys, farmers, clerks, railroad workers, dockworkers, steelworkers, union laborers, mortician assistants; then a handful of misfits—one lion tamer, a bullfighter, "the treasurer of a burlesque theater," and, worst of all, a stockbroker.

In June, the recruits for the 1st Ranger Battalion traveled to Scotland. Wearing the tin-pot doughboy helmets of the previous war, they disembarked from their train cars, donned their packs, and fell in for what they believed would be a short walk to their accommodations. Accompanied by a wail of bagpipes and led by a Colonel Vaughan of His Majesty's Royal Army, they marched for miles. They had no idea where they were heading, and their pack straps cut like knives into their shoulders while their feet blistered at the pace. When they finally stopped, they found themselves at Achnacarry Castle, a gray cube on the banks of a rushing stream, surrounded by the rolling crests of the Scottish Highlands.

"Everything here," bellowed a British Commando instructor, "is done on the double." "You will even march to sick call on the double; and let me warn you that only the half-dead will be accepted."

Within a week, 104 men were returned to their units. In a river crossing, one man drowned. To desensitize the men to combat, the instructors fired live rounds just over their heads. If a man was hit, the Rangers would raise little white flags to tell the instructors to stop firing. In the "me-and-my-pal" course, the Rangers moved as pairs, jumping stone fences, sucking under barbed wire, crossing streams, the whole while shooting at pop-up targets over one another's heads. Using soap bullets at a distance of 200 yards, the Rangers even fired on one another; any closer, the soap would sting. Confronted by the "death slide," a forty-foot zip line strung across a "roaring river" and erupting with explosions, each man was forced to decide whether to jump or quit. "Better to find out now instead of in battle the guys who've got no guts," said the men who made the leap. Throughout all of this, the Rangers bathed in the icy stream and sustained themselves on the horror of British food—often getting nothing more than a "slab of fish for breakfast." To foster creativity and competition, the commando cadre split the men into groups, pitting teams like the Meade Rangers against the Martin Sharpshooters. "Martin, a lady killer," stated one of the operations orders, "makes love to the hotel proprietress at Spean Bridge, and is determined to keep Meade out." After the raid was over, after the troops had peppered the hotel with soap bullets and smashed its windows with live grenades, two lovely, middle-aged Scottish ladies crunch-stepped their way over broken glass to cheerfully serve them all tea. Within a month, the formerly blistered and wheezing volunteers had been transformed into troops capable of marching ten miles in eighty-seven minutes.

Throughout the manufactured haste and bluster of training, the men gained a sense of the interdependence of raiding elements. To raid an enemy's unguarded vulnerabilities, the men had to move at night; to move effectively at night—both quietly and together—their unit size had to be small; because their units were small, the units' targets had to be vulnerable. Any imbalance in this formula meant a weight shift in the opposite direction. For example, if a larger unit attacked a larger target at night, that unit became correspondingly harder to control, therefore less effective and therefore more vulnerable. This education in the interlocking elements of raiding was intended to guarantee the Rangers' future success. This was also an education that should have been imparted to the Rangers' superiors.

It wasn't.

4

THE MAN FOR WHOM this education was most important was the officer selected to command the Rangers: thirty-one-year-old Major William Orlando Darby. Born in Fort Smith, Arkansas, in 1911, the same guerrilla-studded year as Lord Lovat and Russell Volckmann,

Darby grew up believing that he was destined for greatness. Of average size and looks, his greatness lay below the surface. As it so often is with tragic men, a war would be required to uncover it. Black-haired, blue-eyed, wide-mouthed as a duck, Darby had a ruddy face divided into equal parts, forehead and chin. His left cheek bore a mysterious "brilliant red scar." Not particularly muscular, he nevertheless affected a chest-out, shoulders-back posture in which his arms seemed always cocked to the rear, as if never more than a moment away from snapping to attention. Son of a printer and musician, the second child between two sisters, he grew up scouting the Arkansas woods, and playing the saxophone. While he was in high school, his older sister died. In Texas, he married, then divorced. In spite of disappointment and tragedy, his attitude remained as it ever had been: good humored and irrepressible. In personality, just like his posture, he was direct, forceful, and never vacillating. Had the military gene not dominated and driven him to a life of soldiering, he would have made a born salesman. "He is the ideal Commando Leader," wrote Colonel Vaughan at the end of the course. "He possesses the energy, keenness and personality which produces the best out of those under his command."

Graduated from West Point in 1933, at the apex of the bell curve

Official Army photo of Colonel William Darby.

(ranked 177 out of 346), he was originally assigned as a field artillery officer. Like all soldiers who graduated then and with that assignment, he embarked on an eight-year career punctuated by the peacetime artillery's core elements, boredom and horse manure. In 1941, he was one of the few soldiers who attended the Joint Army/Marine Corps amphibious exercises in Puerto Rico. Disappointed at not snagging a combat command in the wake of the Pearl Harbor attacks, in mid-January 1942 he was made an assistant to Major General Russell P. Hartle, commander of the 34th Infantry, and assigned to Northern Ireland, the staging area for a theater of operations still two years in the future. Anxious to get into the war, when assigned to escort General Truscott on his base tour and Ranger recruitment drive, Darby made the most of it. Truscott duly rewarded Darby's professionalism and interest with an offer to command the 1st Ranger Battalion. Few offers have been accepted so enthusiastically.

At first glance, Darby's Rangers viewed him as a "pencil-pushing aide-de-camp." And why not? He was, after all, little more than a peacetime artillery officer, not even an infantryman. This perception died a quick death. Throughout their training at Achnacarry, Darby slung a standard-issue M1 over his shoulder and rotated between companies, marching, climbing, shooting, doing whatever the men were doing, and doing it better. After an intelligence officer from headquarters briefed the Rangers on the Allied procedures for surrendering to the enemy, Darby bristled and took the floor. "This information you have just heard is all very well for those troops who are going to be captured, but that is not for the Rangers . . . If there is any capturing to be done," he continued, "it is the Rangers who will do it." Within two months of training together, the men were reverently calling him "El Darbo." By the end, he would defy comparison. An Army staff officer wading ashore at Sorrento in 1943 would find a man wearing a Ranger patch and ask where he might find Darby. Smirking, the Ranger would reply, "You'll never find him this far back."

If the ideal Army officer was equal parts confidence, bravery, energy, and obedience, Darby was all these things but perhaps too much the last. Because of his unlikely origins, his humility, and most of all his courage, writers of Ranger history have always been generous with Darby's legacy. But a Robert Rogers or a Benjamin Church he was not. More than anything, he believed his men could (and should) perform any mission assigned to them—from the most audacious lightning raids, to the most ignominious rear-echelon duties, to the most spectacular seize-and-hold operations. Because of this, no one would be more responsible for proving the value of the Rangers—or for their downfall.

5

The Rangers' first combat experience was at Dieppe—the chaotic Big Bang from which all Allied amphibious operations evolved. Under the command of Lord Lovat and COHQ's No. 4 Commando Battalion, fifty Army Rangers splashed ashore and up the bluffs. They sprinted through farmhouses, dodged Luftwaffe sorties, and rained bullets and mortars onto their target, a German artillery battery. When a lucky mortar round exploded the battery's magazine, as lucky rounds tend to do when fired by men with skill, Lovat sent forward his butchers to finish off the Germans with bayonets. "My God, those Commandos can fight!" remembered one Ranger after the battle. "They'd kneel down or lie down and fire, then stand up, grab an apple off a tree, and start firing again." For Truscott, whose ship had been badly shelled during the raid and who spent the sad transit back to England rolling cigarettes for the wounded, the operation accomplished what he and Marshall had hoped. It provided much-needed battle scars to a handful of Americans. For a Ranger who returned from the raid, he summarized his experience with a shrug and an assessment of commando capabilities that was as close to perfect as any American soldier ever came: "You've got to fight like Indians in this war, I guess."

The next opportunity for the Rangers to don war paint came in Operation Torch, in Arzew, Algeria. "My God, Colonel, I've drawn a blank," said a chalk-faced young officer to Darby on board the *Ulster Monarch* before boarding his landing craft. "I can't seem to remember a thing. Please go over my job with me once more." The man had good reason to be nervous. Though already copying the handlebar mustaches and Vandyke beards of Mountbatten's British Commandos, this was the first time Darby's green American Rangers had operated without their mentors; the first time on their own. The mission: two nearly simultaneous night raids on two coastal forts whose cannons—if not taken by daybreak—would point directly into the ribs of the landing force.

In the first of these, the Rangers—two companies' worth—boarded landing craft that became so jammed with men that their crew members could hardly move. They rode these into the harbor's mouth, past its boom, past two docks that were "noisily" rammed in the darkness, and finally past two disembodied sentry calls of "*Qui va là?*" When the vessels reached the grand quay, the Rangers scrambled, slipped, and cursed their way to the top of the slime-coated seawall. Assembled there near barrels ripe with the stench of brining sardines, the Rangers silently patrolled through the darkness to the medieval ramparts and moat of Fort de la Pointe, where one group crept over barbed wire while another tucked in behind a French soldier balancing laundry on his head, following him right through the front gate. Within seconds of this, a quick clatter of machine gun fire and the writhing body of a French soldier produced a wail of sirens and voices, prompting one Ranger—T-5 Murray Katzen—to rush a barracks and capture forty-two Frenchmen by himself, marching them out with his hands tight-fisting a tommy gun and a grenade, the pin already pulled.

The second raid was even more dramatic. Victim of a winch that broke while lowering his landing craft—dumping him, his radios, and his equipment into the ocean—Darby nevertheless scrambled back aboard his boat, then led four companies plus one chaplain ashore. There, despite squelching wet boots, he and his Rangers marched uphill for three miles, every man carrying a full loadout of ammunition, plus fighting knives, bayonets, climbing ropes, one stick of dynamite, and two mortar rounds. The two unluckiest also pushed a mule cart bulging with still more mortar rounds. When the Rangers arrived at Fort du Nord, they found it was surrounded by concentric circles of barbed wire as high as eight feet and as deep as fourteen. With every snip, each man's nerves cinched tighter. Just as they were about to breach the last ring, a French machine gun barked and drove them to the ground. Darby, ever the artilleryman, wasted no time: "Roy, pull your company back a few yards, then hit 'em when the barrage stops." Lieutenant Murray had hardly gotten his men untangled from the wire when the first rounds thumped into the battlements. Thus persuaded, the French defenders abandoned their machine guns and retreated, chased by Murray and his Rangers shouting, "Hiho, Silver! Away!" Inside the ancient walls, the Americans stuffed Bangalore torpedoes down the barrels of the naval guns and dropped grenades down the ventilation shafts of a powder magazine in which the Legionnaires had taken refuge. In minutes, sixty shaken Frenchmen surrendered, including the fort's open-mouthed commander, who marched out wearing a peacoat, pajamas, and slippers. Had Darby not lost his radio and flares in the open ocean and been able to transmit his victory back to the fleet, the operation would have been nearly flawless. It was as compelling a case for raiders as the night in

1775 when Ethan Allen's handful of Green Mountain Boys had captured Fort Ticonderoga by banging on the front door.

6

WITHIN A WEEK, the Rangers were in the papers. Within a month, the best new children's game was Parker Brothers' Ranger Commandos, a Parcheesi knock-off in which little colored boats dropped little yellow pegs onto little foreign beaches. The objective of the game: destroy a tank factory, a railroad yard, or a munitions plant: "First one back with the most points of destruction wins." Had Parker Brothers directed the rest of the North African campaign, Rangers would have kept raiding and raided some more. Instead, Army commanders hesitated, not exactly sure how to employ the Rangers now that the beachheads were secure. Atop such slippery operational guidance, Darby tried to keep some balance. Within days, his men were stripped from him and cast into the battle. Speeding through Arzew on a motorcycle, pausing only long enough to yell at loitering GIs for not hurrying off the beaches, Darby corralled and directed his men in practically every possible infantry function. Charlie Company threw in with the 1st Division, launching daytime assaults on the fortified positions at Saint-Cloud; Easy Company attacked at La Macta, riding into battle on half-tracks like tankers. Those spared the glory of charging into machine guns in broad daylight were assigned the ignominious duty of guarding the forts they had captured. (Charging machine guns in broad daylight is an honor best reserved for the enemy.)

In January 1943, impressed by Darby's raids in Arzew, European Theater commanders requested the establishment of additional Ranger units for the invasion of Europe. General Lesley McNair, head of Army Ground Forces and a perennial crank on the issue of commandos, denied the request. He was not the only one to remain suspicious of the distinction between regular infantrymen and Rangers; the Rangers themselves were having doubts. After their head-spinning service in North Africa, Darby mandated that every man begin rotating through the most repellent of all military assignments: military police duty. "That does it," declared one Ranger, disgusted by the "fun-hating" assignment of rounding up drunk GIs. "I'm getting out of this no-good chicken outfit in a hurry."

To overpower the bitter taste left by such indignities and to demonstrate to his superiors just how effective a unit trained exclusively for amphibious raids might become, Darby thrust his Rangers into a training curriculum that would have made the British Commandos blush with pride. While the war raged beyond their reach, Darby and his Rangers began training for the mission they wanted most. To prepare them, Darby ordered two-mile swims in the harbor, cliff climbs along the coast, and mountain marches that stretched as far as twenty miles—often limiting the amount of food and water each man was allowed to consume along the way. To smooth out the stumbling choreography of nighttime raids, Darby developed ingenious systems of coordination: advancing company commanders would shine colored-pinhole flashlights backward to mark their positions—red for A Company, blue for B, and so on. Darby would then use a radio to move the flashlights (and the men they represented) like chess pieces into attack squares. To keep companies from intermingling in the dark, he had his men tape giant white letters to their backpacks—H, V, X, Y, Z. It wasn't long before Army commanders took notice.

In short order, rumors of a mysterious and important island raid began circulating among the men. When the Rangers set sail aboard a sleek new British assault ship, the rumors hardened into fact. "From here on in we'll be global terrorizers," one beaming Ranger said, relieved to finally be claiming his share of battlefield honors. The relief, however, was short-lived. "I'm sorry, damned sorry," squelched Darby's voice over the ship's loudspeaker after receiving word that the mission had been canceled. "I know you would have put on a good show."

Writing ten years later, Ranger James Altieri described the disappointment. "The terrible letdown of the raid that wasn't, the impatience for action, the uncertainty of our status as a fighting force—all combined to pervade the outfit with a futile sense of melancholia." That put it mildly. "I knew it!" barked one Ranger in disgust. "I knew it was all going too good. This damned unit is jinxed." Tired of training and disillusioned, many Ranger volunteers began unvolunteering. "If this keeps up," said one man of the exodus, "there won't be anyone left but Darby."

7

In January 1943, at the Casablanca Conference, Marshall and Mountbatten met again. No longer was Marshall fretful about gathering combat experience; no longer was Mountbatten the only way to get it. Since the disaster at Dieppe, Mountbatten's raiding schemes had, one by one, been plucked off the planning table. In spite of this, Marshall was still willing to test the limits of Rangers and raids. Despite knowing what Lesley McNair and other subordinates would say, Marshall promised Mountbatten more of both.

In February, Darby and his Rangers finally got what they wanted. At the head of three companies—A, E, and F—Darby led his men on a twelve-mile patrol across the desert to raid an Italian outpost of highly trained Bersaglieri mountain troops camped near Sened Station, Tunisia. Wearing woolen skullcaps instead of helmets, their dog tags taped together to prevent jingling, their boots saddle-soaped to keep from creaking, the Rangers marched all night, then hid out in the mountain clefts the next day. Darby and his executive officer, H. W. Dammer, snuck on ahead to spy out the enemy camp. "How close did he get?" asked a man after they returned. "Close enough to read their mail," came the reply.

That night, when darkness again collapsed around them, the Rangers picked their way for three miles over scrub and rock until within 200 yards of the Italian outpost, then dropped to their bellies and fixed bayonets. Using the flashlight-and-radio method developed during their Arzew maneuvers, Darby orchestrated his companies across a half-mile front. Sensing that something strange was afoot, the skittish Italians began shooting haphazardly into the night. Not a single Ranger returned fire. Instead, they crawled hand over hand, the "stygian blackness" covering them like a blanket. When the Rangers finally reached the sloping earthen barricades, they found themselves practically underneath the defenders' blazing muzzles. When the Rangers stood up, the Italians never knew what had hit them. In the assault that followed, more than 100 defenders were cut down without ever seeing their enemies. Ranger Sergeant Altieri stabbed a man, felt the blood spray his arm, then vomited where he stood. When Darby requested radio reports from his company commanders to determine the exact number of prisoners to be transported, Captain Max Schneider, an "excellent leader" with a healthy reputation for lax discipline, radioed back, "I think I have two, sir." A moment later, two shots rang out. "Well, sir, I had two." In total, Darby lost one man, his head plucked from his shoulders by a 47-millimeter round, plus twenty wounded. In exchange for those losses, the Rangers destroyed one 50-millimeter antitank rifle and five machine guns, and inflicted an estimated seventy-five killed or wounded, and marched off eleven captives. In short, it was—to that date—the greatest small-unit American raid of the war, and the best reason for more of the same.

8

After the raid on Sened Station, the assignments for Darby's Rangers continued to alternate between those fit for commando raiders and those for—in Darby's words—a "regular infantry battalion." Desperate for reinforcements, as battlefield armies always are, American commanders saw in the Rangers a well of untapped infantry potential. "There is a hell of a mess on our front," wrote General Terry de la Mesa Allen to Darby at the end of February during the Battle of Kasserine Pass. "Can you send me one reinforced company with a hairy-chested commander with big nuts?" Darby cheerfully sent Company D. It would not be the last time a superior would smile him out of his good sense.

On March 12, 1943, Army commanders in the European Theater again requested the expansion of the Ranger project. This time, Marshall overrode all objections and approved. A week later, Darby energized Marshall's endorsement by leading 500 Rangers on a ten-mile-long night march up the impregnable bluffs near the Tunisian town of El Guettar. Their mission: sneak in behind the Italian artillery positions guarding the pass. Dragging one another by the wrists and crawling hand over hand up sheer cliffs without once being silhouetted by the full moon, Darby's Rangers arrived exhausted, their pants ripped to shreds, their hands sore and bloodied. None of that mattered; like Lawrence at Aqaba, they were looking down on the breach side of the enemy's guns. At 6:00 A.M., rising like a GI version of Gideon, Darby initiated the attack with a bugle. Let loose, his men fell upon the sleeping Italians, shouting like wild Indians. By noon, 700 Italian defenders had been captured and the rest were dead; only one Ranger had been wounded. By 4:00 P.M., Darby's men were bivouacked on the heights, comfortably eating hot stew out of their helmets. As if to emphasize just how difficult those heights would have been to take in a frontal attack—planners had estimated it would have needed a conventional assault force of 10,000 men, or 9,500 more than Darby had used—the Rangers' dinner was cut short by an Italian counterattack that lasted not one night but six days—six days of reasons to justify the Rangers' unconventional commando tactics.

At the conclusion of the Rangers' mountaintop siege, Darby was summoned to Gafsa to meet with General Patton, the new commander of Second Corps. For his actions at El Guettar, Patton pinned a Distinguished Service Cross to his uniform, an award second only to the Medal of Honor, then offered him a prize that hardly any West Point graduate could refuse: a promotion to full-bird colonel and a regular infantry regiment. Darby turned down both offers.

In April, Darby was summoned to meet with General Dwight D. Eisenhower, Supreme Commander of the Allied Expeditionary Force, to discuss the invasion of Sicily. Asked how many Ranger battalions it would take to eliminate the coastal defenses at Palermo, Darby confidently replied fifteen. Eisenhower gave him three. To get three from one, Eisenhower used the 1st Ranger Battalion's companies like Adam's ribs, cutting out companies A and B to make the 3rd Battalion, and E and F to make the 4th. Veterans not assigned to the 1st, 3rd, or 4th battalions in Algeria went home to begin training two more battalions for the invasion of Europe—that is, the soon-to-be-established 2nd and 5th Ranger Battalions. To fill the staggering need for volunteers for these new units, Darby did the only thing he could and sent forth recruiters to raid the talent pools of every forward-deployed unit in Africa. "No bonus, no special privileges, nothing special," stated the Rangers' pitch. The only benefit: "swift action." Using the lessons learned in Scotland and sharpened in Arzew, Darby's veterans trained the volunteers in six weeks. Without approval to form a headquarters company, Darby kept direct tactical command of the 1st Battalion, plus overburdened his shoulders with command of the other two. There were oversights besides overburdening Darby's soldiers. Mostly, no one ever stepped back to assess the type of unit the Rangers were becoming.

At Gela, in Sicily, Darby led the 1st and 4th Battalions ashore like Richard the Lionheart at Jaffa—in the lead and unstoppable. After taking fire from a beachside hotel, he grabbed a squad and cleared it room by room with tommy guns and grenades. The next day, when 4th Battalion's F Company put up an Alamo-style defense at the Gela Cathedral, Darby appeared out of nowhere, his helmet gone, his shirtsleeves rolled up, standing in the back of a jeep and firing its 37-millimeter antitank gun into the turret of a death's-head Italian Panzer. After ducking the tank's rounds without flinching, Darby's shots exploded the monster into flames. If any of the men still bore a grudge for Darby's earlier misuses of the Rangers, those complaints were extinguished at Gela. "Take the regiment," General Patton told Darby after presenting him with another DSC, "and I'll make you a full colonel in the morning." Again, Darby—now the Hero of Gela—refused. How could he ever leave his Rangers?

Though historians enthralled by Darby's legend have always interpreted his refusals of advancement as proof of his commitment to com-

General George Patton congratulates Darby after Gela.

mando operations in general and more so to his Rangers in particular, in actual terms Patton's offer of promotion would hardly have been one. Within three days of the Sicily landings, promotion or not, Darby was commanding a small regiment: his three Ranger battalions—each with almost as many raiders as had attacked at Sened Station—plus an armored artillery battery of eighteen self-propelled howitzers. The 1st Battalion alone possessed some 200 pack mules to haul their equipment through the mountains. After the Sicilian campaign, Darby won approval to create a permanent Ranger Cannon Company of six self-propelled 105-millimeter howitzers. Just as the Vikings had swapped shallow boats and berserker fury for thundering horses and Norman armor, so too was Darby swapping speed and surprise for firepower and numbers. At Salerno, General Mark Clark ordered Darby's Ranger Force X to seize and hold the Chiunzi Pass until conventional forces could relieve them. Cut off from the Allied beachhead, Darby's force held out for twenty-two days—twenty longer than anyone had planned, and nine longer than the Texans lasted at the Alamo. Afterward the Rangers were folded into the troops doing the punishing uphill fighting along the Winter Line—patrolling to contact German units doing the same thing; attacking mule trains, mortar positions, even mountaintops, then turning right around and defending them from wave after wave of coordinated counterattack. After a month, by mid-December, the 1st Battalion had lost 350 men, 200 of them from exposure. Forget about raiders; by the end of the Salerno campaign the Rangers were barely distinguishable as elite infantry.

On January 29, 1944, after some forty-five days of uninterrupted combat, Darby's Rangers were called off the Winter Line to perform a raid. Unlike previous raids on coastal batteries, on beachside obstacles, even on mountain passes, however, this target was an entire town. No other raid in the history of American special operations would cost as much. No other raid in that history would be less like one.

9

After months of fighting on the impenetrable Gustav Line, a line just above the ankle of the Italian boot, the Allies tried to go around it. The solution was an amphibious landing at Anzio code-named Operation Shingle. Aimed smack in the middle of the Italian shin, the landing was intended to knock the legs out of the Gustav defenses from the rear. Led by General John Lucas, a plodding, bespectacled West Pointer known for service on the Mexican Punitive Expedition of 1916 and for looking at least twenty years older than his age of fifty-four, the invasion triumphed in all areas but one: speed. Within days, the Germans had matched numbers with the Allies, and left the US Fifth Army Commander, General Mark Clark, in effect the anxious owner of two mortgaged properties far beyond his means. What he and Lucas needed now was to cut the major supply line running between Rome and the Gustav Line, but where?

Cisterna di Littoria was a quiet Italian village whose houses of stone and rough cement could just be seen by the naked eye from the Anzio beachhead. Situated in an area described as "flat as a table top" and surrounded by nothing more than sparse orchards, vineyards, and the ditches that irrigated them both, Cisterna was important to the Allies for the simple fact that it sat at an intersection of roads. Nearly all battlefields do. The first of these was the Conca Road, running north and south from the beachhead to the town; the second was Route 7, a highway from Rome to Cassino, the back door to the Gustav Line. To cut this line, Clark and Lucas turned to the 3rd Infantry Division commanded by General Lucian Truscott. Afflicted with laryngitis and a limp from a shell blast to his left foot a few days before, Truscott proposed a night infiltration to seize Cisterna, followed by a conventional attack to cut the road. Truscott knew where to turn for the first part.

In the 598 days since Truscott had approved the concept for the 1st Ranger Battalion, Major Darby was now Colonel Darby, commanding the 6615th Ranger Force (Provisional). The force consisted not of a single Ranger battalion, but of three—plus a cannon company, the 83rd Chemical Mortar Battalion, the 509th Parachute Infantry Battalion, and finally, after much petitioning, a headquarters company complete with intelligence officers and clerks, radio operators and drivers. Just like a dreaming Solomon, Darby had been rewarded for his humility. His noble answer to Patton's temptations for regimental command had earned him so much more. Here was finally the infrastructure around which an entire regiment of Army raiders could form. The hitch, as always, was in the top-down, direct-from-Marshall prohibition on the Ranger Force as a permanent fighting unit. The Army's parenthetical "proviso" might as well have read like the living spouse's name already chiseled on the tombstone; the lifespan of the force was temporary at best.

There were other omens too. When Truscott asked Darby what he thought about the Cisterna mission, Darby said he thought the plan was fine, but in the days that followed, several men overheard him second-guess his answer. Courage is always strongest when not allowed too much time for thought. The men are too tired for another raid, he muttered to one man; it's not my plan, he said to another. Even the name of the town translated into a kind of foreshadowing. *Cisterna* in English means "cistern"; another word for a cistern is "tank."

10

THE MISSION WAS SIMPLE, but contingent on certain successes. The 1st and 3rd Battalions would play the part of the harpoon, cast north through a maze of ditches until they struck the outskirts of Cisterna. Once there, they would get on line and assault through the town. If the 1st Battalion was attacked on patrol, it was to slip by and let the 3rd clean up. Instead of waiting on the infantry as they had done in every other engagement, Truscott and Darby had agreed that this time the Rangers would largely support themselves. This self-support would allow the 4th Battalion, reinforced by the cannon company, the mortar battalion, and the 504th parachutists, to play the part of Ahab's whaler, pulling up the Conca Road until they reached the tip of the harpoon, where they would hack the thrashing German remnants to death.

Commanding the 1st Battalion was Major Jack Dobson, a thirty-year-old Virginian with a face so angular that even his mouth seemed to square at the corners. A graduate of Culver Military Academy, a boarding school in northern Indiana, then the West Point class of 1939, Dobson had a personality that allowed him to endure eight consecutive years of regimented military education. Though he had applied to the Rangers in 1942 and collected some thirty-nine endorsements, he had instead been assigned to a tank destroyer battalion in North Africa. His acceptance had arrived a year later, while he was serving in Tunisia. With the Rangers for barely a few weeks and with no time for commando training, or anything else for that matter, he would—improbably—lead the assault. In command of the 3rd Battalion was Major Alvah H. Miller. Described succinctly in British Commando reports as "very small," Miller was also an original Ranger, an amateur poet, and one of the fastest thinkers Darby possessed. In command of the 4th Battalion, and leading the whalers, was Major Roy A. Murray, Jr. Square-chinned, clear-eyed, with a profile more befitting a hero in a war movie rather than in a real war, Murray had trained in Achnacarry alongside Darby, then fought at Arzew, Sened Station, Gela, Salerno, and the Winter Line. Circumspect about the Rangers' decline as raiders and its rise as spearheaders, in November he had typed out a letter of concerns to the chief of Army Ground Forces, General Lesley McNair. Among his concerns were the growing numbers of untrained replacements in the Ranger ranks (especially among the officers) and the lack of a headquarters company able to decide whether or not a mission was a "proper" Ranger operation. (If McNair ever replied, or forwarded the concern on to Marshall, no such record has been discovered.) Why Darby chose the lock-kneed Dobson to lead the assault instead of Miller or Murray—his Ranger veterans—is a mystery.

Throughout the day of January 29, a cold, light rain fell, and the men of Darby's Ranger Force lounged in a wooded camp on a carpet of damp pine needles. Many were brand-new to the Rangers, green replacements for the scores already lost on the Gustav Line. Scratching six weeks' worth of growth, the veterans of the Salerno campaign now clipped their beards and waited in line for the barbers. Most men busied themselves by cleaning their M1s and Browning Automatic Rifles (BARs), muffling anything on their gear that might jingle, blacking out anything that might shine. Mostly they simply tried not to think about what lay ahead. Since reconnaissance flights had not been fired upon, German resistance in the area was presumed light. During the day, a Polish conscript of the German Army stumbled into American lines and chattered away to anyone who would listen. Unable to understand the man, the Rangers shuttled him on to Fifth Army Headquarters, where, according to the official report, he "tried to tell the troops not to enter the town." Whether or not the report was passed back to Truscott or Darby is not known. Suffice it to say, its advice was not followed.

At 6:35 P.M., as the last light of day faded into a moonless night, a message from HQ arrived: "The city may have considerable opposition." Worried about the lack of ground reconnaissance, the lack of aerial photographs, even the lack of clear maps, Dobson the amateur Ranger gathered his courage and confronted Darby. Darby treated his protests like temptations in the desert. "We've been ordered," he replied. An oak to his military roots, Dobson accepted the logic.

As the minutes ticked away, each man smeared burnt cork on his face and dumped his pack and bedroll onto a canvas tarp in front of the company mess cooks. Each rifleman slung two extra bandoliers of ammunition and stuffed his pockets with grenades. Mortarmen loaded their packs with three rounds apiece; the rest slung bazookas or found room for a ration of sticky grenades. At 7:30 P.M., minutes before the Rangers were set to depart, a Red Cross truck clattered into camp and dropped off several much-anticipated mailbags with news from home, the only news that mattered. With no time left, the men were forced to leave the bags unopened, to be distributed in Cisterna after the battle. At the command to move out, the Rangers split into two columns and set out for the staging area singing Bing Crosby's "Pistol Packin' Mama."

At midnight, Darby met with his company commanders just outside his command post, set up in a roadside farmhouse. The 1st Battalion will stop for nothing, he reminded them, his breath billowing warm clouds into the cold night. Radio silence will be strictly adhered to until one mile from Cisterna. With that, he bid them good luck, then walked off in the dark. Darby would not see two of the commanders ever again.

11

AT AROUND 1:30 A.M., under "cloud-choked skies" and surrounded by a light mist, 767 men of the 1st and 3rd Ranger Battalions began slipping into the drainage ditch to the right side of the Conca Road. An "ominous silence" gripped everyone. Standing at the head of the ditch to wish each man luck and remind them not to worry was Great War hero Brigadier General John "Iron Mike" O'Daniel. Wet and slick, the ditch—the first of many they would come to that night—varied from three to ten feet deep, with a rivulet of ice-cold water snaking through the center. Along the banks, a row of low bushes concealed the men up to their helmets. Here they split their single-file patrol into two lines, on each side of the water. In the lead, with knives not far from the ready, were Lieutenant James Fowler and 1st Battalion, F Company.

Thirty minutes after the 1st and 3rd Battalions departed, Darby ordered Major Murray and the rest of the Ranger Force to begin fanning up both sides of the Conca Road. At 2:48 A.M., four lost and bewildered radio operators, their antennas wagging lazily above their heads, wandered into Darby's farmhouse looking for the 3rd Battalion, which had long since departed up the ditch. Apoplectic at the sight, Darby snapped at the men to find the ditch and catch up with the 3rd. "That's the god-damndest thing I ever heard of," Darby fumed. In fact, the "god-damndest thing" was still to come.

At 3:00 A.M., as the 4th Battalion inched up the exposed sides of the road, a single machine gun erupted from the north. A moment later, an avalanche of fire cascaded down their entire front. With nothing to hide behind, the 4th Battalion Rangers flattened their bellies into the dirt. Barely a half mile from their line of departure, they now lay paralyzed three and a half miles from their target, completely unable to support the Rangers of the 1st and 3rd Battalions currently snaking up the ditch. There was trouble with them too.

Already, the foot-soaked harpooners of the 1st and 3rd Battalions had passed signs of a German buildup. Moments after the battle had ignited in their rear, a steady rhythm of pop flares had begun hissing into the sky. When they burst, veteran Rangers instinctively closed an eye to preserve their night vision, then slowly sank to their knees, avoiding any sharp movement in the hovering light that might draw attention to their positions in the swale. They were close to the enemy now. *"Alles geht gut"*—all is well—announced the various German positions around them. At one point, a German sentry clomped up to the edge of the ditch and asked Dobson for his identification. No one spoke a word. Gliding his knife from its sheath, a quick-thinking Ranger pounced on the curious guard and killed him before he could utter another sound. Several other German soldiers actually blundered into the ditch and folded into the patrol, completely unaware of their peril. They were killed too. "We passed two batteries of screaming meemies," remembered Corporal Ben Mosier—that is, they passed officers giving fire coordinates in German and soldiers in flared steel pots ramming shells into their breech ports. All of these were perfect targets for a commando raid. All of these were bypassed for one that wasn't.

At some point in the night—no one remembers exactly when—the rear element of the 1st Battalion lost sight of the lead element of the 3rd. The halting and starting of almost a thousand men had stretched the patrol until darkness had snapped the units in two. Despite unequivocal orders to keep moving, Major Dobson split his men—the head to push on to the edge of the town, the tail to wait for the 3rd Battalion. What had started as a harpoon was now cracking into kindling.

Eventually, Dobson and his men intersected with the Conca Road, a known point some two miles from Cisterna. There, while they hid in the ditch, Dobson's caution turned to dread as scores of Volkswagen jeeps and troop trucks barreled past him to join the battle against the 4th Battalion to the south. This was a division. At each break in traffic, Dobson shuttled his Rangers across the thoroughfare in pairs. When they had safely crossed to the left side, Dobson disobeyed another order and set up his radio. The mission to take Cisterna was clearly folly, but only Darby could approve a change in orders. Kneeling in a wet ditch less than 200 yards from the steady thump of a pair of German artillery batteries, Dobson pressed the handset to his mouth and requested Darby himself. Not only was there no Darby, there was no answer. After ten minutes of listening to the crackling static of a dead line—ten precious minutes of darkness—Dobson packed up his radio and gave the signal to move out. New to the Rangers and with his courage on the line, what other decision could he have made? Radio waves were not the only environmental failure. A mile and a half from Cisterna, the ditch ended. Exposed as cattle in a field, Dobson's 1st Battalion pressed on.

At 5:45 A.M., while still cloaked in darkness, Dobson's point men came across a stone structure—hereafter known as the Calacaprini House—and a battery of Nebelwurfer smoke mortars. Already that night, Fowler—the officer in charge of Dobson's point element—had stained his knife with the blood of two German guards. Now, another unfortunate sentry lingered under an olive tree, oblivious to the two crouching Rangers inching toward him. When finally close enough, the first of these struck the sentry with the butt of his M1, knocking him to the ground, while the second Ranger lunged in for the kill. Reflexively, the injured guard curled into a ball, and the Ranger missed the man's throat, slashing his knee open instead. The doomed sentry screamed. After a torrent of grips and thrusts, the man was silenced but the damage was done. Two other German guards panicked at the noise and fled. "Kill them!" Dobson yelled. Fowler's men opened fire.

As sure as the accidental discharge at Makin Island had sucked the surprise out of Carlson's raid, so did Fowler's botched knife kill now end the Rangers' chance for a silent assault on the town. Realizing instantly the danger to his mission—experienced Ranger or not—Dobson looked at Fowler and gave the only order he could: "Go for Cisterna!" If only.

Several minutes later, Fowler and his men were gliding through the night's last shadows of darkness and through an open field whose far end touched the edges of Cisterna's outlying buildings. Best as they could tell, nothing remained to block their path—that is, until they found themselves tripping over a series of foot-high mounds. Briefly pausing to examine the impediments, Fowler and his Rangers froze: beneath their feet—spread out in every direction—were hundreds of now-rustling bedrolls, an entire German bivouac.

What followed this discovery could be seen by Dobson, who was still gathering his forces near the Calacaprini House. In the dark distance he could see that something had startled Fowler, then halted his progress. Half a breath later, he watched Fowler's well-ordered skirmish line break apart as every man in it scattered in a different direction, followed by the flashes of downward-pointed muzzles, each one illuminating another snapshot of sprinting boots or thrusting bayonets—the massacre of what seemed like a hundred Germans.

On the far side of the field, Fowler and several of his cutthroats were sprinting for the safety of Cisterna's stone buildings. Leading the way—as was his wont—Fowler reached one of these and edged around its stone corner, where a burst of machine gun fire stitched across his body, killing him instantly. It was as close as any Ranger would come to capturing the town.

12

To THE SOUTH and still strung out in the ditch, about to be pinned down under the Italian sunrise, Major Miller, the diminutive commander of the 3rd Battalion, knew he was in trouble. Cisterna was far; the Germans were many and everywhere. After directing his men to seize several positions in their immediate reach, Miller clambered hand over hand out of the hip-deep water to high ground, then set up his radio. "Hit the dirt!" yelled a Ranger when he saw a tank clatter over a small bridge ahead. Instantly, the men scattered for cover. One officer even dove headfirst under the freezing water. Miller ignored them all. Fixed to the handset that could connect him with Darby and support, he never flinched. A moment later, the tank's first round blew his head off his shoulders. After that, two more tanks appeared.

Spared the effects of the blast but not the scare, Ranger Carl Lehman sprang to his feet and scampered west out of the ditch and away from the tanks. When he looked up, he found himself in a field dotted with blankets, each one lumpy with a German soldier stirring underneath. *"Kamarad!"* (friend), they yelled, throwing up their hands at the sight of the intruder. Bracing his M1 against his hip, Lehman chased the startled Germans like a flock of geese, firing until the clip pinged free from his rifle. When he reached a low hedgerow, he discovered he was not alone; several other Rangers had followed. As if on a training range, Lehman and his renegades fired anywhere they saw a German. By the time they ran out of targets, the wooden stocks on their rifles were smoking.

To the north—around the Calacaprini House—the 1st Battalion was already being encircled, their impromptu lines being probed. Hiding in a shed littered with broken bottles, Ranger Arthur Schrader spotted a German setting up a machine gun. Squinting hard at his weapon's front sight post, Schrader fired and heard a satisfying ping strike the flared helmet, forcing another German to take over the gun. At this, Schrader fired again, then eleven times more, counting each time another German took the gun. Ultimately it was for naught: Schrader would run out of bullets before the Germans ran out of heads. And still, there were worse things.

As the Rangers of the 1st Battalion traded rifle and machine gun fire with their German opponents, Dobson could already count in the lightening haze some seventeen separate German tanks and self-propelled artillery pieces, all closing in for the kill. At the sight of these, his inadequately armed men fanned out into kill squads to attack the monsters with what they had. Lacking anything else, First Sergeant Frank Mattivi clambered aboard one tank with nothing more than a sticky bomb, an explosive charge meant to cling to a tank's armor before detonating. As he did, a bazooka round blasted the turret on the other side and somersaulted him through the air. When Mattivi hit the ground—

miraculously, said one witness—he "landed running." Two other squads jumped onto separate tanks with tommy guns, then muscled open their hatches and machine-gunned the occupants. After dragging the Germans' bodies out, the Rangers commandeered the tanks and turned them toward Cisterna. Unaware of the identity of the new occupants—and in a tragedy typical of war—several other Rangers destroyed both captured tanks with bazookas.

As Dobson had already learned, there were limits to such bravery. Without the support of the 3rd Battalion, his indomitables were as good as dead. He needed more men and more ammunition, and both quickly. With his sister company spinning like a boat without a driver, Dobson prepared to dash south to shepherd the 3rd Battalion out of the ditch and into the fight. As he and his runner stepped outside the stone safety of the Calacaprini House, he counted fifteen armored vehicles on fire. He would have done better to sprint for Darby—to plead for a general retreat.

13

To THE SOUTH, Darby had his hands full too. After the 4th Battalion broke through the first machine-gun-raked field they hit another, then another. Fully conscious of the stakes, the 4th Battalion Rangers threw themselves across the fields like doughboys from the war before. At every cluster of buildings, they darted from house to house, blasting out Germans with grenades and tommy guns. At Darby's command post, mortars kicked up metal and dirt so thick that casualties in the rear tallied those near the front. Major Murray was already missing; Force Intelligence Officer Major Bill Martin, Darby's friend since their training in Scotland, was killed at the command post; so was Darby's runner.

At 6:20 A.M., Darby anxiously radioed his supporting artillery unit to ask if any fire support transmissions had been received from either the 1st or 3rd Battalion. None had. Because his own fighting line was now so intermingled with Germans, Darby's mortar teams had also been forced to cease firing. With their tubes so neutralized, Darby then ordered one young mortar captain to lead an assault with half-tracks. Three times the mortarman tried; three times he returned for more ammunition, each time with at least one fewer half-track and several fewer men. After returning from the fourth attempt, the dauntless mortarman threw open the farmhouse door, marched past the command-post radiomen, presented himself to Darby, then broke down sobbing. He couldn't do any more, he said. Despondent, the man turned, stepped out of the farmhouse, and fell dead—"hit through the head by an enemy sniper."

By civil twilight—the time before dawn when newsprint could be made out—the lead elements of the 1st Battalion around the Calacaprini House were established in a firing line some 800 yards south of Cisterna. Having reached the ditch and designated a new 3rd Battalion commander to replace the decapitated Miller, Dobson and his runner were now dodging Germans, racing back the way they had come to catch up with the 1st Battalion. Finding a German tank in their path with its engine turned off and its commander bobbing out of the turret, Dobson drew his pistol and shot the tanker dead. A tank destroyer by trade, Dobson then clambered aboard and dropped a phosphorus grenade into the turret, igniting something inside that almost instantly exploded in white smoke, blasting a chunk of armor plate into his left hip, spinning him to the ground. Dazed, he was dragged into a ditch by his Ranger companion, who shook sulfa powder into his wound to clot the bleeding, then left him—another battalion commander out of the fight.

At sunrise, through the dawn's haze, a tank finally appeared south of the Calacaprini House and the 1st Battalion's firing line. The men cried hoarse cheers at the sight; Darby's relief force had apparently broken through. As they reveled in another outlandish Ranger victory, a few relieved eyes followed the tank's turn, which suddenly revealed an Iron Cross emblem. "Then," a Ranger corporal recalled, "it opened up on us."

"What happened next," said a witness, "happened fast." Springing into action, the 1st Battalion Rangers shook off their mistake and unleashed their remaining bazookas. When that didn't stop it, they finished it off with a sticky bomb. As the stunned crew stumbled out of the smoking wreck, the Rangers shot them. It was a victory that, for half a moment, returned their sense of relief, a feeling that was again sucked out the moment ten more Iron Cross–marked tanks appeared to the south. The 1st Battalion Rangers were surrounded.

At 7:00 A.M., Darby finally received his first of several broken radio transmissions from the front and learned that Miller had been killed, Dobson wounded, and both battalions enveloped. At 8:35 A.M., in the usual roundabout way of radio traffic in war, a transmission was passed to the 3rd Division HQ that was then retransmitted to Darby. From this he learned that most of his Rangers were now "holed up" in sheds and ditches, or in a couple of outlying buildings. As if to say that nothing more could be done, the 3rd Division transmission closed its report by adding, "Can't adjust fire; enemy in buildings; town strongly held."

"Is 1st Battalion lost?" squelched a desperate voice from Darby's command post before cutting out. No one could have answered the question anyway.

At the front, desperate Rangers were shouldering the last bazooka tubes, running up to the tanks, and firing point-blank. If the armor was too thick, they aimed for the treads. When the tanks lurched, stalking Rangers pounced on the paralyzed monsters with grenades. Before long, the men ran out of these too. With four of the six company commanders in 1st Battalion severely wounded and Fowler killed, few knew who was in charge. Ducking constant sniper fire, two captains in Company D argued over which of them outranked the other. Throughout the argument, neither man took a moment to stop firing. Absurdity claimed other casualties too. Bleeding from his face, low on ammunition, and terrified of capture, one Ranger turned to his friend and asked him to shoot him. As the friend remembered afterward, "he wasn't so crazy."

14

SINCE HE'D BEEN blown off the top of a smoking tank, Dobson had somehow made it back to his men near the Calacaprini House. There, while organizing another defensive perimeter, he had taken more shrapnel in his right thigh. Now, lying in a ditch next to a burning self-propelled gun whose artillery rounds continued to cook off around him, he passed his command to Captain Charles Shunstrom, a Ranger since the Achnacarry days and Darby's tank-killing companion at Gela. Upon taking command, Shunstrom—as aggressive a soldier as the US Army ever produced—shored up his position with several companies of the 3rd Battalion and even attempted a flanking movement to either break free of encirclement, or—believe it or not—take the town. None of it worked.

At 10:45, solid communications were finally established between Darby and Shunstrom's radio, the care of which was now in the hands of Captain Edward Kitchens—"Kitch" to everyone who knew him—who was set up in the 1st Battalion's makeshift aid station and whose feet were gradually becoming more and more encumbered by wounded Rangers. At 11:15, Darby told Kitch to "hold on" and that the 4th Battalion was making slow but steady progress. Thirty minutes later, Darby reiterated his encouragements and even asked Kitch to put together a rescue party for a 3rd Division reconnaissance company that reportedly had been captured in his vicinity. "Maybe you can break up the thing and rescue them," Darby said, his suggestion as tone-deaf as his original expectations. Operationally employed like infantry, Darby's Rangers were now dying like them too. At the Calacaprini House alone lay some sixteen dead Rangers, another twenty-two wounded, and only five men still fighting—barely three loaded weapons among them. At 12:15, Kitch became so "overwrought and weeping" that he could no longer make himself understood. Darby asked for another voice, and Kitch quit the house altogether, preferring to die outside in battle rather than trapped inside manning the radio.

Grasping the receiver now was a hulking Ranger, Master Sergeant Robert Ehalt from Brooklyn, New York, one of Darby's originals. "Some of the fellows are giving up, Colonel," said Ehalt, his voice scratching out of the speaker box. "We are awfully sorry . . . They can't help it, because we're running out of ammunition . . . But I ain't surrendering."

In his farmhouse command post, Darby became frantic. "Don't let the boys give up," he pleaded. "Get the old men together and lam for it . . . How many men are still with you?"

"They are coming into the building now," Ehalt replied, gunfire snapping in the background. "We're out of ammo—but they won't get us cheap!" Moments later, Darby heard Ehalt's voice for the last time. "So long, Colonel. Maybe when it's all over I'll see you again."

With a violent *wham! wham!* Ehalt's transmission cut out.

Darby squeezed the handset and steadied himself. "Use your head and do what is best. You're there and I'm here, unfortunately, and I can't help you." It stung to say the words into the dead line, his 4th Battalion still a mile from Cisterna. "But whatever happens, God bless you . . . God bless all of you."

With the mention of God, Darby's voice choked, his eyes watered. "Ehalt, I leave everything in your hands. Tell the men I am with them to the end." After a moment he set down the handset. Bracing himself, he wrapped his hands around a telephone receiver and called General Truscott. "It apparently was too much for them," he said, muffling his emotions. Replacing the receiver in its cradle, Darby asked his staff to leave the room. "As enemy shells beat a steady tattoo around the house," he crumpled into a chair, dropped his head into his arms, and sobbed.

Several minutes later, Darby appeared outside, his shoulders "straight and his chin thrust forward defiantly." He was still in command. But in command of what, no one quite knew.

15

AT 1:30 P.M., the survivors of the 1st Battalion destroyed their radio, their last chance of rescue. At 2:30, the 3rd Battalion Rangers did the same. With his carbine gone, shot out of his hands earlier in the battle, the 3rd's Lieutenant William Newnan—a "little fellow with big thick glasses" who always "loved a fight"—leapt into a "machine gun nest with only his pistol," breaking his glasses in the jump. Unable to see well enough to shoot or escape, he was captured by the Germans immediately. For the men of the 3rd Battalion who were still shivering in wet ditches, the tanks rumbled right up to them, lowered their guns, and demanded surrender. Cut off from support, bereft of ammunition, what other option did they have? With hands raised above their heads and guns at their backs, the bedraggled prisoners were marched north in columns of four, the Germans bayonetting in the back anyone who resisted. Panzers equipped with loudspeakers blared out in broken English the consequences of continued fighting: *For every Churman killed, two prisoners would be shot!*

As the line of prisoners came on, one 3rd Battalion lieutenant and several of his Rangers attempted an ambush to free their comrades, but they had only enough ammunition to kill two guards, and in the end their effort simply prompted more executions. With the line of eighty-some captives continuing to march toward the Calacaprini House, Shunstrom ordered his men to hold their fire, then hastily tried to prepare his own ambush for when the column got closer. As the word was being passed from group to group, one nervous Ranger fired a shot that killed a captive, startling other Rangers into killing even more captives and forcing the Germans to take cover and "spray" the entire column.

Overwhelmed by the threat of the Germans' terrible logic, many Rangers, said the official report, immediately "got hysterical" and gave themselves up—unwilling to shoot their own to save themselves. Even Shunstrom's attempts to shoot those men failed. Ranger Larry Kushner, with an ID card marked "H" for Hebrew, stripped the trigger housing from his tommy gun and buried it along with his tags. Staff Sergeant Wayne Ruona did the same, then turned to face the muzzle of a machine-gun-cradling, gray-clad jackboot. "Shoot!" Ruona barked, disgustedly. The German shot the two men next to him, their arms held high, but left Ruona alone.

Outside Calacaprini House, Master Sergeant Ehalt, now a prisoner, looked up at the perfectly accented English-speaking German tank commander with bewilderment. The German smiled, then told his new prisoner that he was, in fact, a graduate of New York University, one train and a bridge away from Ehalt's native Brooklyn. Expecting compassion, Ehalt asked the NYU graduate for help with the wounded still inside the stone house. Instead, the commander dispatched his Germans with guns. At the horrified look on Ehalt's face, the tanker responded simply, "It's war, sergeant."

Shot through the lung and shoulder, a helmetless Ranger named Clarence Meltesen tied his white Red Cross handkerchief to the end of a broken cane reed, raised his working arm above his head, and limped toward three German soldiers, each wearing a captured American Airborne helmet. In broken German, Meltesen told his captors he was a Ranger. Hearing this and unable to contain his excitement at the score, one of the German soldiers broke out into a "little jig."

16

THAT NIGHT, WITH EYES red from tears and exhaustion, with a face stubbled rough from two days' worth of growth, Darby stood silently above the piled packs and bedrolls of the men who would not return. Already the bodies of Rangers killed in Cisterna's fields and ditches were freezing stiff in the Italian winter. Beyond the reach of the Army, local farmers would dig holes and pitch them in, where they would wait for GI bulldozers to push them into the ditches in which they'd fought. Those not dead—well, it would be some time before anyone knew. Of the 4th Battalion, at least 50 percent was gone, sent to hospitals or as frozen on the ground as their comrades to the north. Of the more than 500 men who had started at Achnacarry, only 87 remained. In a few days the remnants of the 4th Battalion, along with a handful of cooks and drivers, would be snatched away, attached to the 504th Parachute Regiment, then thrust back into combat. Darby's Ranger Force—the product of all his energies; the unit for which he had risked his life again and again, and turned down two promotions to senior command—would be gone, either in captivity or reassigned. As Darby stared at the stenciled names on the packs that would never be claimed, another Ranger kept his eyes fixed on this broken legend. After a while, the witness remembered, Darby just went away.

For the disaster, General Mark Clark laid some of the blame on General John Lucas, but mostly on Truscott. "[Clark] says they were used foolishly as infantry which they were not equipped to do," General

Lucas confided to his diary. "I told Clark the fault was mine as I had seen the plan of attack and OK'd it." Clark was not appeased; men with egos so large rarely are. So self-assured was he in his understanding of Ranger capabilities and limitations that he bypassed his immediate subordinate Lucas altogether, and first thing the next morning appeared at Truscott's headquarters looking for answers to explain the catastrophe. In the meeting, Clark bemoaned the inevitable publicity and the embarrassment, and threatened an investigation. There was no need, Truscott said; he accepted the full responsibility himself, but reminded Clark that as the author of the Ranger concept, no one in the Army better understood the Rangers' capabilities than he. Clark said no more, Truscott remembered, and the threat of investigation was dropped. Had Clark pursued the investigation, had he tried to understand why the town—unlike an artillery battery—was too big for a raid, the Army might have understood the difference between raiders and infantry decades earlier. Clark was right about another thing: Few episodes in the Second World War would make the US Army collectively wince as hard.

On February 1, after two days of short truck rides and long marches, sustained on snatches of food and shivering sleep, the captured Ranger survivors trudged into Rome. Wearing mismatched coats and hats, some with their pants still bloused, the men shuffled five abreast, crammed together like stock. On their flanks, spaced every ten feet, gun-cradling guards herded them along by the elbow. Lining the streets and only slightly less captive than the guarded masses before them, Italian men and women watched the triumph in hushed despair. Some cried; a handful threw rotten food. Salivating at the prospect of manipulating the triumph, German propagandists positioned "black uniformed Fascisti" next to "bemedaled Nazi officials," then marched the procession behind an open truck armed with a bank of motion picture cameras poised to capture the Rangers' historic humiliation in front of the Colosseum. To assuage the sting of defeat, Ranger captives stretched their fingers into secret Churchill Vs and muttered obscenities. Some groups sang "God Bless America." Remembering the hopeless moment years later, Ranger Charlie Eineichner said, "Not until I was marching through Rome did I realize that help may be a long way off." Taken prisoner, Dobson was spared by his debilitating wounds from the humiliation of the march, but nothing else. German doctors removed the "hunk" of tank turret in his hip with no anesthetic, then handed him the souvenir. When he came to, interrogators gushed over their victory.

Six weeks after the battle, the German propaganda machine released what Clark had known they would. "The Rangers have at last entered Rome," crackled the lightly accented radio voice of Axis Sally. "They have come not as conquerors but as our prisoners." Leaflets followed: "Over one thousand American soldiers were made prisoner at one blow." Exactly what ends the derisive messages were supposed to achieve remains a mystery. Months later, after the 1st Special Service Force had broken the Anzio wall and the rest of the Fifth Army had driven through the gap, Colonel Robert Frederick took the recently escaped Ranger William Newnan for a drive. When they stopped at the remnants of a rubble-strewn, brown smudge of a town, Frederick asked his nearsighted passenger if he knew where they were. Newnan looked around, and shook his head. Frederick answered his own question. "This is Cisterna."

When General Mark Clark and his superior, Lieutenant General Jacob Devers, contacted Marshall in the aftermath of the battle, they recommended disbandment of the 1st, 3rd, and 4th Ranger Battalions. According to Lesley McNair's office at Army Ground Forces, reconstituting them would take six months, an outrageous statement considering that recruitment and training of Darby's original battalion had taken only a third of that time.

In fact, Clark's and Devers's real reasons were more straightforward. Constituting just 11 percent of the Army, the infantry—after two years of combat—had nevertheless absorbed some 60 percent of the service's total casualties, most of these accrued in the European Theater of Operations. This meant two things: first, that the infantry in Europe needed replacements, and second, that the infantrymen who had fought there had already learned a lot about combat, which meant they had already blurred the distinction between themselves and the Army's elite commandos. Never mind for a moment that the Rangers were no longer being used as elite commandos. For Clark and Devers, nowhere was this blurring of capabilities more obvious than in the Rangers' humiliation at Cisterna. They were not alone in this thinking.

For Marshall—less worried now about the infantry's combat experience than about the availability of more infantrymen—the recommendation not to rebuild Darby's 1st, 3rd, and 4th Battalions presented him with an opportunity to ease the apprehension he faced in robbing the infantry to pay the Rangers. Having created the Rangers himself, however, he hesitated. Was there really no longer any special mission in the Italian theater for which a Ranger battalion could be used? Again, Clark and Devers said no. Marshall accepted their judgment and split Darby's remaining survivors into two groups. The veterans were ordered home to pass on their experience in training—Marshall's original goal for them; the newer replacements, many of them with as little as three days' worth of Ranger training, were ordered to join Robert Frederick's 1st Special Service Force. When the Rangers reported to their new unit, Frederick ordered them to remove their Ranger patches. Darby's Rangers were no more.

17

VARIOUS HISTORIANS AT various times have blamed the Rangers' failure at Cisterna on a variety of factors: the lack of night combat skills among the new replacements; the unnoticed German buildup around Cisterna; the lack of pre-mission reconnaissance; faulty intelligence; the twenty-four-hour schedule bump; the screaming German sentry; the sun—a phenomenon as predictable as gravity. Enough. The Battle of Cisterna did not destroy the raiding capacity of Darby's Rangers. The Army did that before the Battle of Cisterna took place. After the Rangers' early successes against small targets at Arzew and Sened Station, planners had assumed they could increase their winnings by increasing their bets. This had worked when Darby's Rangers were fresh from training at Achnacarry, but as they fought instead of trained, exchanging veteran Rangers with replacements along the way, the odds on audacity grew longer. Too "clumsy" to hide in the shadows, said one observer, too light for the hardened targets they attacked, the Rangers were crushed under the weight of contradicting raiding elements. No one seemed to recognize the peculiarity of raids as a distinct type of infantry operation, requiring men able to function on their own, at night, and nearly always surrounded. Darby himself had assigned Dobson—an untested Ranger officer—as his lead battalion commander. If Darby hadn't understood the difference between elite commandos and conventional infantry, who could have?

Following the defeat at Cisterna, Darby was relieved as commanding officer of the Ranger Force. After shuffling between a few different units, he was finally assigned to lead the 179th Infantry Regiment. Though any normal man would have felt deflated at the loss of three battalions, the hurricane of Darby's personality had hit land and gained speed. "He actually seemed to enjoy fighting," one man remembered. When his troops met resistance, he crushed it not with shock troops anymore, but with, as one writer described, a "promiscuous use of artillery." When Darby met his new officers, one recently defeated major approached him and said, "I guess you will relieve me for the loss of my battalion."

"Cheer up, son," Darby replied, putting a friendly hand on the man's back. "I just lost three of them, but the war must go on."

Anxious that the theater's greatest combat leaders would be killed in the Italian fighting, General Mark Clark requested that "certain exemplary soldiers" be sent home for "inspirational purposes." Few were as "inspirational" as Darby, and so he went, ostensibly assigned to Marshall's plans division at the War Department, but in reality assuming a vague position in which he could tour the country, inspecting training installations and delivering speeches. Probably his most important inspection visit was paid to the Infantry School at Fort Benning, Georgia. There, just four months after the Cisterna debacle, he passed along the nighttime flashlight tactics developed by his Rangers and produced a seven-page assessment of the overall course, which he dubbed "excellent." It was just one more example of the infantry's rise to the Rangers' example—George Marshall's number one reason for creating them; Mark Clark's number one reason for their disbandment; and after Cisterna, the best legacy for which Bill Darby could have hoped. For proof of Darby's commando misgivings, one needed only attend his lecture at the Army and Navy Staff College in Washington, D.C., where, with a split finger—"[his] most blood lost since the war began," he joked—he joined with the rest of the Army's orthodoxy and abrogated his earlier belief in elite troops because, as he said, "they become egotistical and feel themselves apart from the ordinary soldier"; they shirk the "normal requirements of discipline, dress, and sanitation"; and most impractically, they steal from the Army's replacement system. Given the chance to do it all over again, Darby said, he would not recruit volunteers who wanted to be raiders, "but would select a unit for a particular job, and give it the special training and equipment for that particular job." General Lesley McNair could not have said it any better. In the end, even the Army's greatest raider turned his back on the concept.

In March 1945, swinging at a last-ditch attempt for a combat command in Europe, Darby attached himself to a battlefield tour of the Italian theater. Once there, all he had to do was wait. Within days, the assistant division commander of the 10th Mountain Division was wounded, and Darby was installed in his place. On April 30, 1945, the same day Hitler committed suicide, Darby drove out to inspect his battle line. While he was stopped at a quiet town on the edge of Lake Garda, a single round from an 88mm antiaircraft gun struck the hotel right behind him, wounding two officers in the legs and hips, and all but decapitating the master sergeant next to him. Knocked unconscious but apparently uninjured, Darby was carried away by his men. Two minutes later, after they discovered a hole in his chest "half the size of a dime," Darby died. He was barely thirty-four years old. The Army recognized his incomparable impact by posthumously promoting him to brigadier general—the only officer to receive that honor. Lost along with him was the impact he might have had in maintaining the Rangers in the postwar Army, or advising the Army high command on the relevance of raiders in general. Considering his previous comments, it was probably lost anyway.

Within four months of the end of World War II, every one of the Army's six Ranger battalions was disbanded. This was due partly to the US Army's predictable downsizing, but mostly for the same reasons that had killed the 1st, 3rd, and 4th Ranger Battalions after Cisterna. Cut from the ribs of Darby's Rangers in 1943 while still in North Africa in order to pass on their combat experience in Stateside training camps, the men of the 2nd and 5th Ranger Battalions had gone on to the front rank of the D-Day invasion: the 5th Battalion leading the 1st Infantry Division off the killing fields of Omaha Beach; the 2nd Battalion performing one of the most daring operations of the war: the cliff-scaling raid on the heights of Pointe du Hoc that eliminated the guns threatening both the 1st and 4th Infantry Divisions' landing sites. Then, having proved their chops as raiders, both had spent the remainder of the war—not surprisingly—used simply as spearheaders, often at great cost and often operationally indistinguishable from the infantry for whom they spearheaded. Only in General Douglas MacArthur's South Pacific Theater had the story taken a different turn. There, the 6th Battalion Rangers—recruited in-theater from a pack-mule artillery unit and so far from the European Theater that they had not even heard of other Rangers or their misuse—had been held in reserve for specific raiding missions. The most significant of these had been the raid on the prisoner-of-war camp at Cabanatuan that rescued more than 500 captives and—better than any other operation of the war—justified the Army's investment in dedicated raiders. Or would have, if anyone had still been paying attention. In fact, according to an exhaustive search by Ranger historian David Hogan, the lessons of the Cabanatuan raid are barely mentioned in the Army's "postwar doctrinal documents."

Superficially modeled on Churchill's "butcher-and-bolt" commandos, the US Army Rangers—by the time of their disbandment—looked nothing like them. This was, in the end, the predictable result of different parents. Preoccupied with the readiness of his front-line soldiers, George Marshall had created the Rangers not to perfect the art of Churchill's coastal raids, but to serve his infantry: first, by gaining battlefield experience that could be transferred to the rest of his troops; second, by handing them off to infantry commanders who committed the Rangers to missions with impossible odds and then either blamed them for their failures or diminished their uniqueness by using them no differently than the regular infantry.

Though no one could have guessed the consequences, it was a prioritization that produced a lasting gap in the US military's order of battle for a unit that specialized in raiding, one that could best be filled by a branch of service less preoccupied with its infantry.

And there was only one branch that didn't have infantry.

PART 2

OPPORTUNITY

Chapter 4

Draper Kauffman and the Course That Cracked the Atlantic Wall, Then Laid the First Bricks of the Legend of Naval Special Warfare

In February 1943, Admiral Kent Hewitt—fresh from amphibious invasions in North Africa and equipped with the sailor's gift to see a red sky at morning and predict the storm to follow—sent a message to the US Army's commander of ground forces requesting a curriculum addition to the Scout and Raider program to begin training men on the destruction of beach and underwater obstacles. At this suggestion, the Army planners balked. As far as they were concerned, there already existed a solution for such a problem: the Army's combat engineers. This was an opinion bound to collide with that of Admiral King, the chief of naval operations, who—more and more—was considering the scope of his authority to be whatever he could get away with. In the spring of 1943, when reconnaissance flights began discovering a variety of coastal defenses popping up along the beaches in France, Admiral King consulted no one—especially not the Army—and on May 6, 1943, ordered his amphibious force commanders to "communicate what they required in regard to the proposed demolition units." To transform these requirements into a workable program, King assigned his chief of the Readiness Division, Captain Jeffrey Metzel, who in turn summoned to his office one of the US military's top experts in explosive ordnance—not a grizzled combat engineer but a bookish lieutenant who had been in the Navy for just over six months.

"Have you seen the pictures of the obstacles the Germans are building on their beaches in France?" blared Captain Metzel to the junior lieutenant, comporting himself in the manner of all senior commanders as he hustled down the corridor to his next meeting with Admiral King.

"No, sir," said the lieutenant, now striding to keep up.

"Well, they're putting obstacles up in six feet of water that will stop the landing craft," Metzel said—his hands gesturing wildly, his famously unruly eyebrows as wild as his "thought-a-minute" mind. "Do you know how much an infantryman's pack weighs?"

"No, sir."

"Well, neither do I, but they'll all drown. I want you to put a stop to that!"

As the lieutenant struggled to absorb Metzel's orders, his mouth began to form the front end of a question.

"Now, look here," Metzel cut him off, "you know perfectly well that you're not supposed to ask the 'what, how, when, why' questions of the Commander in Chief's staff. That's your job. Speed, speed, speed, that is the key."

With that, Metzel and his eyebrows disappeared into the conference room. Around the corner, a female yeoman handed the lieutenant his official orders stamped with his name. That name was Draper Kauffman. And though the man who bore it didn't look like much, in actuality he was a boulder of stored energy balanced on the lip of a cliff—a man whose personality and past experience would combine to forge a training course so intense that its graduates would go on to play a leading role in breaching the worst section of Hitler's Atlantic Wall and would keep rolling until they formed the nucleus of the most combat-conditioned unit in the history of the US military.

2

Tall and thin, lanky even, with dark hair, a narrow face, and a chin that stretched down like a teardrop, Draper Laurence Kauffman also possessed poor teeth and spectacles as thick as submarine glass. Given to bouts of indolence, he was absentminded, a failure in any subject that did not capture his interest, and alarmingly progressive on the issue of race—at least so thought his mother, a shrew on the topic. As a young man, Kauffman had wanted nothing more than to attend the Naval Academy and command a destroyer as his father had. When poor eyesight threatened to torpedo this dream, he submitted himself to doctor's orders, however medieval, and for one hour a day held a palm over each open eye. When his appointing congressman suddenly died, leaving his academy application in limbo, he told no one his plans, escaped from his Connecticut boarding school, got a bunk at the Washington, D.C., YMCA, then walked the halls of Congress, slipping past secretaries and performing a rehearsed sob story until someone—anyone—gave him an appointment. Once finally accepted, he rowed crew, acted in school dramas, and, in cruel foreshadowing, spent thirty days on a prison ship for sneaking off campus. When he graduated in 1933, a year when Navy pinchers stalked the ranks looking for any excess ballast to pitch over the side, he was given his diploma and a physical disqualification from the Navy—a steep four-year price to pay to achieve the rank of civilian. Thus betrayed by his childhood dream, Kauffman packed in his pride, shelved any ideas of glory, and settled for an onshore operations job in the shipping industry, his life suddenly devoted to endless manifests for the onloading and offloading of cargo. In January 1939, after six years' employment, Kauffman was made an assistant operations manager and sent on a six-month assignment to Europe.

In Germany, he experienced something few Westerners would: He attended two speeches by Adolf Hitler. Though he did not speak German, he did not need to. The mania of the speaker, the tempo of his voice, and worst of all, the rabid howls of the crowd were enough. Kauffman shuddered at the spectacle. In Hamburg, Hitler and his striding entourage passed so close that Kauffman could have palmed a pistol into the Führer's face. A year later, he confessed to his mother that he wished he had.

When he returned to the United States, Kauffman was like Moses come down from the mountain. Though he had not been in the presence of God, he had caught a glimpse of the Devil, and now he suspected what was coming. Worst of all, because of his abysmal eyesight, he knew that he would be left out when it did. Ignoring the taunts of his friends, as all true believers are wont to do, he began speaking four nights a week on a free lecture circuit, inspiring his audiences to a mixture of boredom and outrage. "You limey lover! Why don't you go over and join them yourself?" an irate woman had heckled. "Don't send my son to war." After months of such treatment—and to the hand-wringing astonishment of his friends and family—Kauffman took the woman's challenge.

To be accepted in the American Volunteer Ambulance Corps, an adjunct unit of the French Army, one was first required to submit a down payment of $3,500 to cover living expenses and the cost of one ambulance. In 1940, this was almost the price of a house. Even more alarming, volunteers were bound to follow the orders of the French military. To a man with purpose in his boots and adventure in his guts—just the sort of Hemingways the French cause had attracted in the last war—no price was too high. Actually, it was. With no friend fool enough to loan him the money, Kauffman scraped together a thousand dollars, practically bankrupting himself, then relied on a sympathetic benefactor to raise the rest. Having been born six hundred years too late to take up a Crusader's vow, the day before he departed he did the next best thing and renounced the dry Episcopal faith of his youth to kneel like a knight before the darkened, candlelit mystery of the Catholic Church. When he left, he weighed 165 pounds.

On May 10, 1940, Kauffman arrived at his post six miles beyond the protection of the Maginot forts in the Saar River valley, in the northeast shoulder of France, where the borders come to a point and jut like a salient into the ravenous mouth of Germany. The same day, Hitler launched one hundred divisions through the Ardennes Forest. As he had known it would, the Second World War had begun. By nightfall, French troops were giving ground, leaving wounded men behind. With three stretcher bearers in the back and a small bell in front to announce the approach of noncombatants, Draper jumped into the ambulance driver's seat and dropped the clutch. Using the momentary loom of shell explosions as a guide, he inched toward the battlefield. When artillery fire erupted around him, he abandoned caution and hit the gas, bouncing his men into the roof over the rutted fields. In a moment, they were surrounded by the dead and dying. With the haste of men caught in a pelting downpour, Draper and his stretcher bearers jumped from the ambulance and began collecting anyone they could. Amid shrieks of pain, he turned the vehicle back toward friendly lines. Arriving at the field hospital, Draper ran for cover—not from shellfire, but from the view of others. When he finished retching his guts out, a French officer found him and ordered him to return to the front for another load. "I can't tell you how close I came to running," he said afterward. But return he did.

Again and again for two unrelenting weeks, Draper drove to the front, picked up survivors, and returned, the inside of his ambulance slippery with blood. The whole while he sustained himself on bits of food and the horror of French cigarettes. The only sleep to be had was taken in snatches, never in a bed and never with his boots off. Responding to the deliberate fire of German gunners—Boche barbarians, he called them—he and his fellow ambulance drivers began draping dark blankets over the sides of their vehicles to cover the giant Red Cross emblems. By the end of his third week in combat, two ambulances had been shot out from under him and he had lost ten pounds.

As expected, the French had been totally unprepared to withstand the German juggernaut. The only French unit (at least in Kauffman's area) that seemed to carry on in spite of this rout was the outfit known as the Corps Franc. Made up entirely of volunteers, and all proven fighters, the men of the Corps brooked every regulation except the one that mattered: in the face of the enemy, no group fought harder. "They were foolhardy in a lot of ways," said Kauffman, but if they accepted you, "they were absolutely wonderful." If a member of a six-man patrol was cut off from his group, the remaining five would fight to the death to free him.

On June 16, 1940, eight French soldiers desperately needed to get to a hospital. The only one close enough to save their lives was four miles inside the rapidly advancing German lines. Adopting the Corps Franc philosophy, Kauffman and his thirty-five-year-old lieutenant—a former manager for Coca-Cola in Germany—volunteered for what they knew was a one-way mission. It ended as expected. Though they got the men to the hospital and saved the unfortunates from certain death, Kauffman and his lieutenant were taken prisoner and sent to a prisoner-of-war camp.

Eight weeks later, Kauffman surrendered his passport and perfunctorily signed a statement vowing to never again take up arms against the Third Reich. When freed, he weighed 125 pounds, 40 less than when he had enlisted. For his service in the Ambulance Corps he was awarded two of France's highest military honors—a Croix de Guerre with Star and another with Palm—small consolation for the psychological and financial trauma he had sustained. At home, his frantic mother was on the edge of a nervous breakdown. The rest of the family was, in his father's words, "one step ahead of a fit." With a passport stamped by the Germans "Not Valid for Travel to England," he was eligible to travel only to those countries not yet at war with Germany, namely the United States. In short, Kauffman had every reason in the world to return home. He refused.

On August 8, 1940, on board a Portuguese freighter bound for Scotland—he had illegally smuggled aboard as a second pantryman with responsibilities mainly in potato peeling—he wrote his parents. "I am going to England to do everything in my power (admittedly very very little) to help them fight our battles for us"; not only to defeat Germany, but—in Kauffman's words—to level her towns and smash her people. If the American Navy would not accept him, perhaps His Majesty's would. "God knows [I am] not doing it for adventure—it's too horrible to be adventure . . . It's simply because as long as I believe all Americans should be in the war I can't very well be anyplace else myself."

On the afternoon of September 7, 1940, a thousand German planes attacked London and the surrounding areas, killing 400 men, women, and children, and wounding 1,200 more. The next day, 412 were killed, wounding nearly double that number. For fifty-seven consecutive days, London was hit. Had he arrived any earlier, who knows what the Royal Navy's reaction would have been to his request. As it happened—as it always happens when opportunity meets courage—Draper arrived at exactly the right moment.

The day Draper Kauffman volunteered for the Royal Navy, he presented himself to the Admiralty at nine o'clock in the morning. When asked to present verification of his peculiar résumé, he excused himself, marched over to the office of the US naval attaché, Captain Alan Kirk, his father's friend (and the future commander of naval operations on D-Day), and asked him for a letter of introduction. Kirk begrudgingly obliged. "As far as I know everything in his dossier is correct," Kirk wrote, somewhat annoyed to be losing such an obviously aggressive volunteer to the British. "I have known him all his life." After lunch, Kauffman returned to the Admiralty for a short physical examination. Considering the darkening skies above, the British needed every man they could get—bad eyes or not, British citizenship or not. By five that afternoon, young Kauffman was a sublieutenant in His Majesty's Navy. The only hitch: Once again, he was barred from duty at sea.

Several weeks into his new career, a German bomb landed just outside the hotel in which Kauffman was billeted. Had it detonated upon impact, Kauffman's story would have been buried along with the hotel, another footnoted condottiere of military history, nothing more. As it happened, the bomb hit but did not detonate, its only damage being a thirty-foot tunnel gouged into the earth. Before long an Army bomb disposal team arrived, cordoned off the area, and set to work. With hand tools alone, the squad painstakingly dug a path to the bomb—enlarged the hole, and shored up the sides in case of collapse. The objective: reach the bomb without disturbing it, gently unscrew the fuse, winch the inert remains from the earth, and, accompanied by police car sirens and loudspeakers—"Unexploded bomb coming through!"—transport the carcass to a nearby cemetery. Usually this method worked. In this case it did not. The entire bomb disposal team was killed. The next day, Kauffman volunteered for bomb disposal.

For eight months, from September 1940 to May 1941, Hitler waged war on the British people. More than 40,000 civilians were killed; more than a hundred thousand were injured. The instrument of all this de-

Lieutenant Draper Kauffman, Royal Navy.

struction was the bomb. Many of these weapons were defective or deranged—as in, they failed to detonate upon impact or were timed to detonate after a bomb disposal team had arrived. After British papers praised the heroism of the bomb disposal groups, the German bomb makers began tinkering with even greater malevolence. On the fuses, they placed devices to detect disturbance and prevent withdrawal. On mines, they added acoustic sensors.

Often working for days at a time with no rest, in water up to his armpits and some thirty feet below the surface in absolute darkness, Kauffman spent the next year gliding his fingertips over mud-caked metal to feel for the tiny screws covering each bomb's fuse housing. In that year, he learned more on the subject of bomb disposal than any other American alive. He also learned what it meant to possess both skill and courage, and when to use them. "You have not the right to take an unnecessary chance in war," a French doctor had told him during his ambulance days. "Your duty is to save yourself for the necessary ones." For bomb disposal, nothing could have been more relevant.

"I'm about to unscrew nut number three a quarter of a turn to the left," Draper would whisper into his telephone headset before making the slightest movement on the bomb. Most of the time, this worked. On occasion it did not. If a screw turn initiated a low buzzing sound, a man knew he had between one and seventeen seconds to either run like mad or die in a hole. On one snowing, windswept day in early January, in a seaside Welsh village, Draper and a British sailor eyed an unexploded 300-pound parachute mine that had landed in a field some 125 yards away from a railway line. Sending the sailor to wait across the tracks, Kauffman finished his cigarette and knelt down over the bomb. With numb hands, he brushed the snow away, gripped his wrench, and inserted it into one of the turn holes. Just as he began his methodical quarter turn he slipped, his hand faintly slapping the side of the bomb. Immediately he heard the sound—a hushed, mechanical buzzing.

"Down! Martin, down!" he yelled, jumping to his feet, running like mad to make the tracks. He didn't even make it halfway. The explosion ripped up a small tree by the roots and threw Kauffman into the air. When he came to, his first thought was to ask about his tools.

During his year performing bomb disposal, Kauffman risked his life again and again. For his bravery and his circumstances, he was a unique attraction. When Churchill reviewed the mine disposal group, he made a special point to find the American.

"How did you happen to join our Navy?" the prime minister asked, his heavy face relaxed into evident delight at meeting as strange a human specimen as himself.

"Well, Sir, after I got out of the prison camp I left the French Army . . ." The answer caught Churchill off guard, who pleasantly interrupted to ask for more details. He was hooked. So was anyone else who heard Kauffman's story. If he went to a pub in uniform, the only thing he had to do was open his mouth and "The place was mine," he said afterward. In April, in what Kauffman described as a "little ceremony" at the Admiralty, he and Martin were honored for "bravery and devotion to duty" by King George VI. On July 4, 1941—still five months away from the Pearl Harbor attack—he was asked to broadcast a propaganda message on BBC radio, to which he wholeheartedly agreed. "Believe it or not the British are celebrating the fourth of July this year . . . Their appreciation is amazing in a way . . . It seems to me that it is we who should be grateful to them . . . for keeping a barrier between the Huns and ourselves." In spite of his many near misses, Kauffman was undiminished, eager for more. "What do you do now?" an American reporter asked him in November over a pint. "Nursing these goddam land mines," Kauffman replied bitterly. "They won't let me go to sea."

Then, gesturing to an RAF pilot stumbling toward the door, he shook his head and muttered, "Get ashamed of myself every time I see those guys."

Eighteen months after he had left the United States, Kauffman finally accepted a breather and sailed home. When he arrived in Washington, D.C., he was asked to visit with Rear Admiral William Blandy, the US Navy's chief ordnance officer and his father's former groomsman. Receiving the young hero in civilian clothes, Blandy made a pitch for the Navy as if he were offering a friend's son a job selling Oldsmobiles: "I want you to come with the United States Navy and set up a navy bomb disposal organization." Politely rebuffing the offer, Draper reasserted his commitment to the war against Nazi Germany—a war the United States had not yet formally entered. Three days later, Draper was ordered back to Blandy's office, this time in his dress uniform. While he stood at attention, Blandy let him have it. "If you think the United States Navy is not at war, I suggest you consult your father," the admiral said, his avuncular attitude gone. "Our ship the *Reuben James* was torpedoed yesterday by a German submarine, and your views do not make sense." With that, the admiral dropped a message on his desk from the Royal Navy announcing that Kauffman had been discharged—transferred back to the service that had rejected him eight years before. Having no objections left, or the power to voice them even if he did, Kauffman characteristically poured himself into his new assignment.

In December, while he was preparing to receive his first batch of bomb disposal recruits from Northwestern University's ROTC program, the Japanese attacked. After two years of waiting, the United States was finally at war. In a few days, a message found Kauffman, ordering him to "Get out to Pearl Harbor. Right now." Imagining that Japanese trickery extended beyond strategy and into engineering, Draper prepared for the worst. When led to an unexploded 500-pound bomb that had landed near Schofield Barracks, he sent everyone else to cover, then examined it, sketched it, and telephoned each nail-biting step back to his controller. It had been dropped too low, he determined, landing on its side instead of its nose. What he had visualized as an "old-fashioned oriental puzzle" turned out to be the easiest job he had ever had. "I couldn't have set that bomb off if I'd had a sledgehammer," he said later. To those who had witnessed the bespectacled master push past the line of gawkers to single-handedly disarm the bomb, there were few actions as deserving of praise. "D.C. Man Takes Live Jap Bomb Apart, Gets Navy Cross" ran the headline in *The Washington Post;* "All

Florida will rejoice with Rear Admiral James L. Kauffman . . . on being the father of so worthy a son," broadcast WQAM radio in Miami. In early 1942, at thirty years old, Kauffman was the country's youngest and most feted naval officer since Decatur or Cushing. As such, who better to start the Navy's underwater demolition course in the Second World War than the man who had seen the most of it? A sailor for whom no barrier had ever held, and who was about to squeeze his biography into a syllabus like none that had ever existed.

3

To CREATE THE TYPE of amphibious engineer that he envisioned, Kauffman needed elbow room. Like Peddicord before him, he found his elbows had ample space in Fort Pierce, Florida. Situated along the Atlantic coast in an area once called Mosquito County, the town had grown up around an Indian fort built by President Franklin Pierce's brother during the Second Seminole War of 1838. The area was remote, but according to a Navy study not too remote, and possessed the essential features of docks, piers, ramps, water lines, and a "sewerage" system. Despite a blazing Florida sun in the summer months, temperatures in the winter were comparably mild, rarely dipping below 56.9 degrees, a temperature that allowed year-round water training without immediately inducing hypothermia. Most attractive, attached to Fort Pierce was the offshore Causeway Island—seemingly endless in length—built of dredged coral and sand, on which men could experiment with all manner of tactics and explosives, disturbing no one but the resident herons.

Shaped like a sausage in one man's estimate, the island was less than a mile at its widest point and less than a half mile everywhere else. A channel break guarded by rock jetties split the island, naturally separating the halves into north and south sections: the south for habitation; the north for training. Both sides shared an environment of pinewoods, elephant grass, and swampland. On the western coast, between the island and the mainland, lay a mile-wide expanse of brackish intercoastal water called Indian River. To the east, the irresistible Atlantic produced a clawing surf that looked like every breaker would drag the beach beneath the waves. Up and down the island lay miles and miles of sandy beaches covered not with tourists, but with an invisible, buzzing tyranny of flies, sand fleas, and gnats, desperate to bite onto any living thing before the onshore winds swept them out to sea. In the water, especially in the summer months, lounged a stinging tangle of jellyfish and Portuguese man o' wars.

Since the Scouts and Raiders had arrived there in January of 1943, the base had undergone a transformation. Latrines had been built, space for nine hundred wood-floored tents had been budgeted, and many of those now lined South Island in ranks as sun bleached and straight as tombstones. Even more transformed was Fort Pierce, which was turning into the sort of place where anything was possible. Instead of settling for the Army's usual training mock-ups of plywood vessels staked in the dirt, Fort Pierce planners had already begun the process of fielding scores of actual Higgins Boats and building a forty-foot-tall, net-draped tower in the middle of Indian River to simulate a ship's side that recruits would descend into a bobbing landing craft. Besides these physical attractions, Fort Pierce was also now drawing a variety of skill sets: those of the Scouts and Raiders, the Army Rangers, the Army Amphibian Engineers, even Fighting Frenchmen from across the ocean. At any time of day on North Island, a man could stroll up the beach to see black shapes crawling out of the surf. No stroll was necessary to hear the crack of gunfire and the jarring boom of TNT. Both were as constant as the flies. So too were classes on kicking, choking, escaping, tying up a prisoner, fighting with clubs, killing sentries with hatchets, killing sentries with piano wire, and plunging a knife into a man's back to avoid bending the blade on a bone.

When Kauffman arrived at Fort Pierce in June 1943, he encountered a seemingly untended garden of opportunity, an isolated world where imagination could grow. Stimulated by his combat experience, Kauffman aimed to develop an organization similar in character, if not in function, to the unit that had so impressed him in 1940: the Corps Franc. Surrounded by sand, commandos, and surf, and armed with orders from Admiral King's office, he got to work.

To create such a unit, he would require students with, in his words, both "temperamental stability" and "individual initiative." To that end, Kauffman insisted that candidates be subjected to "very heavy" physical training—"very heavy," he emphasized again. As he knew from his own career—first in France, then in the blitz—this type of experience would show students that they could push beyond their physical limits, doing without sleep and food and warmth, and still function without their arms falling off. More important, training of such intensity would create in its students a sense of purpose and unity like nothing except actual war.

With the energy of someone racing against the clock—indeed, racing against Rommel—Kauffman turned his attention to manpower. He'd need not only instructors, but students too. At that moment he had neither.

"I was standing at a bench in the machine shop shaping a device . . . to remove Italian bomb fuses [when] Draper came storming in," remembered Jimmy Warnock, a good-natured Georgian turned bomb disposal officer and one of the first to whom Kauffman offered a position. "Give me an answer in an hour or two, or at the very latest, first thing tomorrow morning," Kauffman said. The next day, after much thought and discussion with his new bride, Warnock approached Kauffman with not a little drama and gave him his answer. "Draper, I'm with you," he began, his voice solemn, on the edge of a monologue. "I can't think of anything I can do to make a greater contribution . . ."

"Fine," Kauffman cut him off. "Here are your orders."

4

FLUSH WITH AN OBVIOUS officer candidate pool from the mine and bomb disposal schools, Kauffman took the pick of the litter and sent them south. Needing enlisted men also, and believing they probably knew something about explosives, he asked for volunteers from the Seabees based at Camp Peary, Virginia. He got these too—a steady stream of them. Before going south, demolition volunteers were subjected to an intense evaluation by Camp Peary's Marine Corps instructors that consisted mainly of calisthenics and forced marches. By all accounts it was an evaluation second only to the one they'd face where they were bound.

Every day at Fort Pierce equipment arrived. In July, so did the students: nineteen officers and eighty-three enlisted sailors reporting for a course they and their instructors knew virtually nothing about. Immediately they were divided into competitive boat crews of six men: one officer, five enlisted—the same as the Corps Franc squads Kauffman had seen in 1940 and the number that could fit into a six-man rubber boat. To build a sense of unity, crews were instructed to adopt names—Heideman's Hurricanes, Simmons's 6 Saintly Sinners, Locke's TNTeetotalers, Baird's Battling Blasters, and so forth.

Short on time, eager to "screen out the obvious people that would not make it physically," and long on his desire to simulate an experience that was as close to war as possible, Kauffman decided that all three problems could be solved by the same solution: one week of misery. Never reluctant to ask for help, he walked south along tent row until he came to the section reserved for the Scouts and Raiders. There, still six months away from being transferred, Peddicord listened to Kauffman's proposal. He had never been asked to compress the Scouts and Raiders eight-week physical conditioning course into one block of uninterrupted training. Certainly men could be pushed, indeed nearly broken, but what Kauffman asked was another matter. In the end, Peddicord agreed. What else could he do? This was Kauffman; seas parted at his arrival. What Peddicord did not know—no one did—was that he was about to help create the sacramental cup from which nearly all future naval commandos would drink.

"You were wet, chafed with sand—just completely miserable," remembered Frank Kaine years later. In the daytime, men melted under the sun. At night, they shook so hard from the wet and the cold that their hip flexors swelled and cramped. Their teeth chattered like jackhammers. Shouldering boats sloshing with water, they marched for miles in sand and dunes that collapsed beneath every step. Sodden fatigues adhered to the sand and grit, turning armpits, thighs, and scrotums into raw meat. If an instructor detected a student on the Stealth and Concealment Problem as he wormed his chafed and dripping body to the plantation house, the man was punished by being sent to sit inside, where swarms of mosquitos feasted on his misery. In addition to simple surf drills, rubber boat training included hours of paddling while harassed by the nearby air station's squadron of F4 pilots, who would try to nail the floating rafts with sacks of flour bombs. Jetty landings and night portages were attended by base ambulances and performed over boulders as broad as dinner tables, the crashing surf smashing the paddles and men against the rocks. Intended to simulate the long drain of a campaign march before a battle, this seemingly endless harassment ultimately culminated in a daylong mock skirmish known as the Extended Order Problem—or to the students "So Solly Day." Beginning before dawn, students raced off the ramps of their landing craft just as "the beach erupted in a thundering sheet of flame." For a whole day, instructors armed with charges unleashed a torrent of exploding "columns of water" and "showers of mud and debris." The students belly-crawled on throbbing knees and elbows into hip-deep mud, swamps, and surf as the explosions chased them from cover and foxholes.

Until Kauffman's regime, no Navy unit had been subjected to a training course whose essence so closely resembled that of a real war—the frantic harassment, the inescapable cold, the relentless exhaustion. Not only did it prepare the men for what was to come, it set them apart from everyone else in the Navy. Even in the early classes, as many as half the men who started did not complete the week. That was entirely the point. Modeling his project on the culture of the Corps Franc, Kauffman had set out to forge both an esprit de corps and the reputation that always accompanies it, exclusivity. "If you haven't been through [it]," he would say later, "you're not a demolitioneer."

In August 1943, Kauffman volunteered for his own program. At thirty-two years old, with eyesight not good enough to qualify for his own demolition standard of 20/15, he was hardly an ideal candidate. "I think I have never seen a man struggle so desperately," Warnock said after witnessing Kauffman's performance. The moment he finished his ten-mile beach run, he passed out. During the ocean swim, Warnock thought he would drown. "We all knew he wasn't a great athlete," said Frank Kaine, "and we thought, 'Hell, if he can take it, we can too.'" Throughout the training, Kauffman listed but never sank, alternately encouraging and bullying his boat crew from start to finish, as one remembered, with his "bloody battle cry of 'Corps Franc!'" When men showed signs of cracking during another bone-chilling dip in the ocean, Kauffman turned it into a joke, annoyingly repeating the same mocking phrase: "The water," he boomed in his strong mid-Atlantic accent, "is never cold!"

The Monday after Kauffman completed this week, he was ordered to report to Captain Clarence Gulbranson, the base commander of Fort Pierce. Swollen from head to foot, with fingers like sausages ready to burst, he crawled out of bed and staggered into the commander's office.

"What is this I hear about forty percent of your class either being in the sick bay or quitting?" the captain barked. "I don't think you have any idea what you're putting these men through, Draper."

"I do," Kauffman responded. "It was hell."

When Kauffman's trainees completed Hell Week—the name his week of misery inevitably took on—their demolition training progressed to its next phase: two weeks of explosives, two weeks of reconnaissance, and three weeks of practical exercises. In the summer and fall of 1943, this too was an experiment. Kauffman certainly had an understanding of bomb disposal, but he did not know the first thing about applied explosives. To help, scientists, physicists, and engineers from the Naval Demolition Research Unit arrived and began teaching the demolitioneers how to demolish. Adding to the delay in this education was a lack of recent intelligence. Aerial photos showed a hodgepodge of various obstacles at various distances from the high-water mark on the French beaches of Hitler's Atlantic Wall. No matter. Even if Kauffman had possessed perfect replicas of these obstacles, he still would have lacked the backs to build them. To solve this, Kauffman turned to the Seabees—two full companies' worth, along with a full stock of equipment. "It became a contest," Warnock would remember. The Seabees welded rail ties together and poured [tank teeth]; the demolition trainees blew them up. "If you had waited till the concrete set," went an oft-repeated Seabee objection, "you never could have taken it out."

NCDU night demolition of stake obstacles at Fort Pierce.

"A ticket to sure fire danger and excitement in the most explosive form is furnished every man who volunteers for the Seabee demolition units," said a military publication in October 1943. When it is over "he is an expert in destruction, qualified to blow up everything from a milk bottle to a man." So qualified, each graduate was assigned to a six-man Naval Combat Demolition Unit, or NCDU, a name too small for the wake that trailed it. Upon receiving his first batch of Fort Pierce–trained NCDUs for duty in the South Pacific, one officer bristled at their attitude. "It seems the men who have gone through training there get the impression that they are a commando outfit." A visitor to Fort Pierce said as much to Warnock. "This outfit doesn't know much about saluting, but you sure as hell know how to fight." Whether that was true remained to be seen, and would depend on a variety of factors, the most important being leadership—an attribute the NCDUs had never lacked, but were about to.

In November 1943, the first batch of Kauffman's NCDU graduates departed Fort Pierce for the southwest coast of England to await the impending invasion of the Continent. Missing from their contingent, however, was the NCDU's most important asset: Kauffman himself, kept behind for his indispensability in running the course he had created. It was a decision that would deprive his men of an advocate who could protect them from misuse, which meant they would be left with only one advantage they could fall back on: their training. This was the same thing that would now permit them to be pushed into the front rank of the D-Day invasion.

5

In November 1943, Rear Admiral John Hall took command of the 11th Amphibious Force and assumed the responsibility for depositing the Army's Fifth Corps on the landing site designated as Omaha Beach—nothing less than the most important operation in American history. Remembered by his peers as a "big, blonde, good natured Virginian," a handsome, three-sport athlete who had left the College of William and Mary in his third year to start all over again at the US Naval Academy, Jimmy Hall was now fifty-three years old, with hair already gone white and the kind of linebacker frame that was soon to stoop beneath its own weight. Because of an easy laugh and an ability to get along with nearly anyone he worked with, Hall—at first meeting—gave an impression of someone almost too genial to be entrusted with an operation of this magnitude. In fact, it was an affability as real as Eisenhower's—and just as illusory. Already, in the invasions of Sicily and the Italian mainland, Hall had been bombed by airplanes, torpedoed by submarines, and shelled by shore guns, thus becoming one of the most battle-scarred American sailors above the rank of captain.

Hall now took command and applied that history to the imagination he would need for planning, a demand that would require for the next six months that he lash himself to a desk except for meals, sleep, and the very occasional game of golf. Among the signs of his suitability for the task before him, none resounded more than this: Shown the underground command and control bunker that the British Navy had built for him and wired with hundreds of communication lines to direct the D-Day landings, Hall chuckled, then demurred: "I'll be with my men off Omaha Beach." To Eisenhower's staff, who hesitated to lavish praise upon anyone in naval service, Hall was already known—both for his experience and looks—as the Viking of Assault.

Because Hall was the Viking most responsible for the successful transfer of troops to Omaha Beach, his authority extended over everything that would touch or support them. Increasing the number of landing craft. Evaluating the untested, inflatable skirts that would float the first wave of tanks to shore. Assembling the naval guns that would be able to fire into the loopholes of the enemy's defenses. "Any tiny island invasion in the Pacific can get plenty of gunfire support ships. Why am I not able to get enough destroyers?" the normally affable Hall thundered while pounding his footballer's fist on a conference room table in mid-February.

"You have no right to talk like that," his superior blustered in response.

"Who has a better right?" demanded Hall, his deep bass filling the room. "I'm landing the Fifth Corps and the Rangers. I don't want them all killed because we didn't have enough Naval guns." No one else said a word; he got his destroyers.

After the conference, Hall's concerns grew and shifted. Now his greatest challenge was not the Germans, or even the number of landing craft and naval guns, but rather untangling his prerogatives. "It is always necessary," Hall wrote to his superior, "to convince the Army commands that the landing and support of the troops is the Naval Commander's responsibility. I hope someday that this will be very clearly stated from the highest commands and will not just remain a unilateral Naval declaration." On February 23, an agreement to that effect was reached, cementing in doctrine that which had always been a vague understanding: the "Naval task force commander had full control of both services after embarkation until the commanding general was established ashore." Few other documents would be as consequential to the Omaha Beach landing.

Among the more important opportunities this new arrangement presented to Hall was the command and control of the pre-invasion demolition of beach and underwater obstacles. Prior to this moment, the Navy's preparations in this area had gone no further than the creation of the NCDU course. In the meantime, more than a dozen six-man NCDUs had shivered their way down icy gangplanks in Falmouth Harbor, where "until such time as they could figure out who they were, what they were sent for and what their job might be," said the official record, they were placed under the improbable direction of the US Navy's European command for Landing Crafts and Bases. Having arrived just two days before Christmas, a group of fifty-four Fort Pierce–trained demolitioneers had checked in, dropped their sea bags, and the next morning assumed seven days of ignominious guard duty. Lacking a commanding officer to deflect their involvement in such menial tasks, the NCDUs had stood their posts and done what all men do under the tyranny of petty assignments. They had complained. In between watch standing and complaining, they had set up what training they could, but mostly had just enjoyed the scenery: in other words, the local brew and the Cornish women.

Among the first demolitioneers to enjoy these temptations had been twenty-eight-year-old Chief Petty Officer Bill Freeman. Slightly above average in height and thinly built, with handsome features and a glare in his blue eyes that could have stopped a Panzer, Freeman had, since his arrival, submitted himself to the care of a hotel proprietress and her daughter, who had welcomed the American with a room, then "drowned" him in good Scotch. And why not? For two full years now, Freeman's life had been dominated by the war—first as a salvage diver in the corpse-floating aftermath of the attack on Pearl Harbor, then as one of the intrepids who had cut the cable blocking the Sebou River in Morocco, and last, as one of the first sailors to complete the nightmare of Kauffman's NCDU course. Naturally, Freeman had wanted a break; instinctively, he had known he couldn't take one. Already a recipient of a Navy Cross for his role in cutting the Sebou cable, plus near-perfect fitness evaluations for mechanical skills and leadership, it had not taken long for Freeman to employ these latter attributes in scrounging up for his teammates what training he could, an effort that had coincided with Admiral Hall's assumption of responsibilities for beach demolition. And not a moment too soon.

6

By February, Hall's increased authority had shifted the NCDUs out from under the tyranny of Landing Crafts and Bases and placed them with the Navy's Beach Battalions. The change was felt almost instantly. In a few days, heretofore listless NCDU officers were shaking off their hangovers and attending the British Army's Assault Demolition Course. The changes went beyond training too. When NCDU officer Lieutenant Junior Grade Carl Hagensen, a pocket-sized Pennsylvanian and graduate of the University of Maine, invented a self-securing canvas pack to hold two pounds of C-2 in the shape of a bratwurst that could be wrapped around an obstacle in a matter of seconds, the Navy—under Hall's command—contracted with "'sailmakers' in lofts throughout England" to temporarily abandon their trade and begin sewing "ten thousand canvas sausages of explosive." An evangelist for live rehearsals that mimicked realistic conditions, Hall demanded that his demolitioneers train on obstacles as close as possible to those they would see in France. Even after the debacle at Slapton Sands in April, in which hundreds of American troops were killed in training by lurking German torpedo boats while rehearsing to land on Utah Beach, Hall still insisted that his landing craft and demolitioneers get the same realistic training. Most important, Hall sent a dispatch requesting that his NCDUs get a commander, one with sufficient rank to guard their interests and shepherd them through the final weeks of their preparations. With Kauffman just assigned to the Pacific Theater, the men could only wait and hope for the best.

For planners, the beach demolition problem was still predominantly the Army Combat Engineers' to solve—a reasonable assumption as it was mostly Army lives that would be lost should they fail. By spring 1944, however, the Army was still not prepared to wreck its way onto Hitler's beaches. In a 1944 training film titled "Hand Placed Charges Against Beach and Underwater Obstacles"—a film set to the brassy pomp of a John Philip Sousa march—a narrator described the Army's procedures for eliminating a row of barbed wire on an enemy shore: First, the landing craft would drop its ramp, a single engineer would rush out—barely wetting the cuffs of his pants—and thrust "fifteen feet of Bangalore torpedo" under the wire, then race back aboard, where two sailors waited to hand-crank the ramp until it shielded the huddled assaulters. Had the US Army's planners asked for advice from Hitler himself, they could not have developed a method more suited for preserving his Atlantic Wall. A wall that was growing more sinister by the day.

Sensing the immaturity of the invasion's clearance plan, some soldiers began to balk. On March 29, Fifth Corps' chief of engineers, Colonel R. K. McDonough, noted several Army objections. Among those were the amount of time allotted in the invasion schedule, the numbers of men earmarked for clearing the obstacles, the insufficient ordnance dedicated for air and naval bombardment, and most worrisome, "the effectiveness of demolition parties, both Army and Navy, working in water under heavy fire."

"I am rather disturbed about the progress being made on training . . . with the removal of underwater obstacles," wrote Major General Leonard Gerow, the Fifth Corps commander, on April 10. Of the two Army combat engineering battalions designated for the dry portion of Omaha Beach, only one, the 146th, had arrived. The 299th, made up of volunteers recruited almost exclusively from western New York and trained at Fort Pierce, presumably in tactics not unlike those taught in the demonstration film, would not arrive in the United Kingdom until April 26, less than six weeks before D-Day. (In fact, the 299th had received three days of training at the Scouts and Raiders School in mid-January—a month after Peddicord and the rest of the Army cadre had left.)

"We are as disturbed as you are," wrote Brigadier General William Kean in response to Gerow's letter. "I realize that this whole subject has been worked out far too late. I will push it to the limit."

On April 15, Admiral Hall and General Gerow—another Virginia gentleman—called a meeting with the Navy's demolition officers, none of them possessing a rank higher than lieutenant, and asked their "advice on obstacle clearance under certain hypothetical conditions." Exactly what was said is not known. Whatever it was, however, must have awakened both commanders to the disaster that would befall the invasion if Army and Navy efforts did not combine forces. Within days, the Navy's NCDUs and the Army's combat engineers bound for Omaha Beach were reorganized into a single unit designated as the SETF, or Special Engineering Task Force. So organized, all NCDUs were subsequently transferred to the Assault Training Center in Woolacombe, on the west coast of southern England, to join the 146th and 299th Combat Engineer Battalions. Once there, the Army augmented each six-man NCDU with an additional five soldiers.

Within days of this restructuring, soldiers and sailors were learning from each other. From the soldiers, the sailors learned the "defensive tactics of the rifle squad"—whatever good that would do them. From the sailors, the soldiers learned the Navy's two top specialties: working in the water and using condoms—in this instance as thread-tied, waterproof casings for explosive pull fuses; for some of the younger men present, the only use for a condom they would ever have. The reason for that approaching tragedy was now filling every section of the beach on which they would soon meet their fates.

7

By the spring of 1944, the soldiers and sailors who made up the SETF bound for Omaha Beach knew from aerial surveillance photos what awaited them: a wall built by Field Marshal Erwin Rommel—probably Hitler's most devious genius of war—and so a wall like none that had ever existed, a wall built from bricks whose layers now stretched out in four parallel belts as far as the eye could see.

In the first belt—that is, the one closest to the water—the line consisted of an obstacle with as many names as a German prince. Variously called a De Cointet after the Frenchman who originally designed it and Element C by the Germans who stole it, the Belgian Gate was best known for the people who had manufactured and employed it four years earlier. Seven feet high and ten feet wide, the Belgian Gate was shaped like a prison door and buttressed in the rear by a pointed tangle of crossbeams intended to sink its anchor the harder it was pushed—hardly a necessity considering its weight of 3,000 pounds. In the tragedy of 1940, the Belgians had confidently connected more than 70,000 of these in a zigzagging barrier across their frontier. Alas, the German commanders had simply gone around them, a tactic the Allies would be denied the moment the tide concealed every randomly placed one of them until they buckled the front ends of the landing craft.

Farther up the beach the Atlantic Wall consisted of a line of wooden stakes, each twice as wide as a man and almost twice as tall. Though it had originally required as long as forty-five minutes for a piledriver to drill deep enough into the sand to insert a single stake, the innovative German defenders had cut that time to three minutes by drilling the holes with fire hoses. The second belt of defense was a veritable forest whose trees were topped with iron spikes called "thorns" designed to eviscerate the guts of a landing craft.

Beyond these, the third belt of defense employed an obstacle made from two beams joined together—one set straight down into the sand, the other set diagonally toward the ocean. Shaped like an upside-down checkmark, this innocuous-looking contraption had a purpose that was as sinister as those that preceded it: in this case to act as a ramp that could flip a landing craft and disgorge its passengers at the critical moment of vulnerability.

If by some miracle a landing craft did manage to thread its way up to the last belt of defenses—that is, the one farthest from the water—there still remained one final set of obstacles with which the invaders would be forced to contend, an obstacle meant not for men or boats but for the one weapon that the Germans both loved and feared more than any other: the tank. To stop these, they had assembled a legion of what were known as Czechoslovakian hedgehogs—four-and-a-half-foot-high knucklebones that looked like toy jacks for the gods, each welded from three separate lengths of L-angle iron, then planted in concrete. Often weighing more than 500 pounds, it would take no fewer than four men to lift them, and if run over, they could strand a tank.

Taken individually, no single obstacle on Hitler's Atlantic Wall was insurmountable—not the Belgian Gates, the stakes, the ramps, or the hedgehogs. In order to make them truly impassable, the German defenders had relied on three final deterrents.

First, they had topped every type of the aforementioned obstacles with antitank Teller mines, millions of them, and then added millions more improvised versions made from artillery shells whose explosives had been recased and protected from the corrosion of salt water by ingeniously corking each mine's fuse canal with a wooden plug and rubbing each one's cavity with a tarry oil. Whatever space remained inside each cavity had been filled with asphalt—asphalt that now waited to be exploded into the bodies of the invaders.

Second, the Germans had taken advantage of the beach's rising backdrop—in some sections, an escarpment that rose to the height of a fifteen-story building. Here they had staggered trenches, pillboxes, and bunkers as big as barns, then armed them with an interlocking chessboard of weaponry: mortar tubes, artillery pieces, and a Western Front's worth of the smokeless, tracer-less, 1,200-round-a-minute MG-42 machine gun whose roughly 400-yard distance to the low-water line was barely an underhand toss. In short, for an invader it was a backdrop no less intimidating than a battlement ranked with archers and vats of boiling oil.

And still there was more—a peril less obvious than all the rest but as inevitable as gravity. The third and final enhancement to the obstacles at Omaha Beach was also in many ways its most effective. That was the beach's staggeringly quick tide—either rising or falling a foot every eight minutes. At its lowest point, this tide revealed a watery no-man's-land where not even a seagull could hide and where parallel runnels of trapped seawater waited to suck at the boots of men sprinting for their lives. At its highest point, this tide shrouded every mine-topped obstacle that waited to drown the Allied troops even before their ramps dropped. Counting on this blanket to protect their defenses from air and sea bombardment—the Allies' two greatest advantages—the Germans knew there was only one alternative method for their destruction: Each would have to be removed by hand.

One at a time.

8

ON APRIL 23, as if suddenly awakening to find the Army taking control of all beach demolitions, the Navy finally appointed a temporary commander for its NCDU forces. A graduate of the Naval Academy class of 1921, Captain Timothy F. Wellings was a member of a family defined by the service. In a short time, he would be a rear admiral, along with three other men in his family. Forty-five years old, old enough to know what he did not, Wellings possessed no demolitions experience at all. Despite this, his first missives to superiors rang with confidence. "Training," he wrote on May 6, two weeks after taking command, "has progressed most satisfactorily . . . Cooperation and the facilities extended by the Army have been excellent." A week later, after receiving an additional fifteen NCDUs to his task force, his confidence had evaporated. "These units were flown to this theatre and arrived without equipment or operational gear," he began, before reporting that this lack of preparation had only been solved through "strenuous effort," and worse, by the Army. Most alarming of all was the method of training. "Attention is invited to the fact," Wellings concluded, "that all Naval Combat Demolition Units are being employed for this operation in a manner which has prevented deep water training to date . . . [and has been] subordinated to the task of breaching obstacles in the dry." Wielding only the authority of a temporary commander, and with no demolitions experience, Wellings was hardly equipped to improve the NCDUs' training situation, let alone their operational employment: "It is my opinion that the beach obstacles will prove most troublesome." The demolitioneers were headed for rough waters and he knew it, but what could be done? Years on ships had taught him this: Inertia was as true as gravity. Only so much could be reversed.

At a joint Army-Navy conference in early May, Admiral Hall listened to the Army's proposed invasion plan. At H-Hour—0630—on the low edge of a flooding tide, the Army's tanks would trundle out of the surf, bulldozing their way through the obstacles. The first wave of infantry assault troops would tuck in right behind them. Third to land would be the NCDUs and combat engineers, each to be folded into a single joint unit called a Gap Assault Team that would clear one of sixteen paths fifty yards wide, all the way up to the shingle, a raised ledge of large stones at the far edge of the high-water mark. Dreading what would happen to "his demos," not to mention the infantrymen, when the surf began lapping at their heels, "Hall pleaded to land his forces on the half-falling tide." Not only would this land the soldiers farther up the beach, he argued, but it would give his NCDUs more time to accomplish their mission. No one else agreed. In the end, Hall shrugged his athlete's shoulders and H-Hour was set.

On May 3, Hall's request for a permanent commander of his NCDUs was answered in the person of Lieutenant Commander Joseph Gibbons, a Kentuckian of moderate height but moderate in nothing else. Described as "powerfully built" by one contemporary, and a "pug-nosed fighting bantam" by another, Gibbons was also "stern, direct, and outspoken"—the enlisted man's least favorite attributes. Though he had graduated from the Naval Academy in 1924, he had decided against a career at sea and instead opted for the Coast Artillery. After service there, he had transferred all his vaunted education and military training to employment with the New York Telephone Company, and there he had remained until the attack on Pearl Harbor had made him—like everyone else with a diploma from a military academy—frantic as Doctor Frankenstein to resurrect a dead career. Now, with no knowledge of underwater demolition or even what his men had gone through to earn the right to be there, Gibbons assumed command of a unit whose training and lack of oversight had conditioned them to operate with no commander at all.

Two days after Gibbons took command, the NCDUs received another surprise: 100 volunteers, all second-class seamen just graduated from boot camp and shipped across the ocean to join the invasion. "A number of these men do not appear qualified for the task, and in the process of screening, will be rejected," Captain Wellings wrote to Hall on May 6. Oddly enough, it was the unqualified Gibbons who would decide which men to keep and which to cut. Whether or not he noticed the irony inherent in this task is lost to history.

On May 15, orders arrived to begin preparing demolition charges. Each man would carry 40 pounds of explosives on his person—hung on his sides in haversacks as big as saddlebags on a mule or draped front-to-back like a poncho in specially made mortar vests. Around the outside of each man's helmet were attached five to six fuse assemblies, each one inside what looked like a limp balloon, readied for the greatest task for which a prophylactic had ever been used. Some men carried what looked like reels of yellow telephone wire. This was, in fact, primer cord, an explosive rope that could connect an entire field of obstacles with a single fuse. Some men carried carbines; some did not. In addition to what each man planned to carry on his person—and though they had never practiced this method in training—each team decided to hand-carry another 400 pounds of supplies and explosives in a rubber boat, piled up like Christmas presents. In fact, each supply boat would weigh more than one of the hedgehogs they were lugged ashore to destroy.

In the last days of May, Gibbons was finally handed the assignment that all had hoped would never come. With lumps in their throats, the demolitioneers of Force "O" packed up their bombs and boats and, on May 31, transferred them to the docks at Portland Harbor on the southern coast of England. There, each Gap Assault Team would board its own LCT (Landing Craft Tank), a roughly 115-foot-long, open-aired, flat-bottomed gray bathtub. Crowding the inside of each bathtub were no fewer than three Sherman tanks, sometimes four, plus an additional jeep or two, leaving only the wet steel between tank treads and tires on which to lay a bedroll. For food, the men had K-rations. For toilets, they shared a bucket. To replenish their canteens, they drew from the LCT's 3,000-gallon supply of brackish water made potable with chloride pills.

On June 3, all NCDU officers of Force "O," including Bill Freeman—the only enlisted man in charge of his own team—reported to the USS *Ancon* to attend the demolition briefing given by Lieutenant Commander Gibbons. Included in this briefing was a description of Omaha Beach—five miles wide, "as flat as a tabletop," and backdropped by a roughly 150-foot-tall green escarpment with only five possible exits through which a mechanized Army could drive. Oriented west to east, the beach had long since been divided by planners into three main sections—code-named Dog, Easy, and Fox—and then subdivided into colors—Green in the west, White in the middle, and Red in the east. Matching themselves to their missions, Freeman and the others jotted notes on their assigned sections, each of which—except for Easy Red, the largest at 2,000 yards—was allocated just two Gap Assault Teams, each of which consisted of roughly twenty-six combat engineers, plus a fourteen-man NCDU made up of six Fort Pierce–trained demolitioneers, five soldier augmentees, and two or three volunteer support sailors. According to plan, once on the beach the Army engineers would focus on the obstacles closest to land, the hedgehogs mostly; the NCDUs would handle the stakes and ramps and Belgian Gates.

NCDU 11, with Bill Freeman standing (second from right).

At some point during the briefing, a ship door clanked open and someone called "Attention on deck." The men snapped to their feet and in from the passageway ducked a man with white hair and a sportsman's frame. It was Admiral Hall, come to talk with the men he was now about to send to their destinies. "I knew that they had a very tough job," Hall would say years later, remembering the moment. "I wanted to be with them." Over the next few minutes, Hall did his best to assure his demolitioneers, if not himself, that the preliminary air and naval bombardment would clear out most of the defenders before they arrived. "Not a living soul will be left alive on that beach," one man recalled Hall saying. If there was, "if enemy artillery started banging" around on them, Hall promised that he would, in his words, "close it off."

"I'd like to go ashore with you," the former athlete told them, the moment thick with tension, "but I can't." For the next several minutes, he told the men a story about Justice Oliver Wendell Holmes and his pride at having participated in the Battle of Fredericksburg, another great engineering victory over water. Hall finished his story portentously. "If you courageously carry out your duties," he said, not dreaming what this unit would ultimately become, "your descendants will be proud of your bravery." When the men responded that they were ready,

Hall's eyes dropped to the floor and, "deeply moved," he murmured just above a whisper: "How do we get such truly brave and fearless men?"

As he prepared to leave, once again someone called "Attention on deck!" Once again, the men snapped to their feet.

"God bless you," Hall told them, looking into their young faces. "And good luck!"

9

On June 4, every man not already on a vessel was ordered aboard and issued seven sticks of chewing gum, twelve seasickness pills, three blankets, and two vomit bags. Thus equipped, the Gap Assault Team's LCTs slipped their moorings and made for the English Channel. The invasion was on. Nothing could stop the tide of ships, planes, tanks, and men now bound for the Normandy coast—nothing except the weather. In no time, men were soaked to the bone and seasick, adding their regurgitated effluents and vomit bags to the slosh now drowning their boots. By midnight, the invasion had been postponed; their misery had not. Finding a tiny enclosure toward the bow of his ship, one scared demolitioneer knelt to pray. "I saw an opening in the dark clouds, like a window into heaven," he wrote after. "Standing in the opening . . . was Jesus."

By the morning of June 5, the battered ships and men, nearly all more religious than they'd been twelve hours before, had returned to the safety of Portland Harbor to assess their boats, if not their souls. There were plenty of damages in each. When darkness descended that evening—barely enough time to dry their clothes, let alone finish all their repairs—the invasion force departed again. Immediately, there were problems. Still a hundred or so miles from France, LCT 2075 "foundered" in the Channel, forcing Gap Assault Team 6, bound for the center section of Omaha, to cross-deck themselves and their supplies into their towed landing craft, a boat originally designed for a river. Left behind were the precious tanks and any hope for the protection they might have offered. Next to fail was LCT 2227, carrying Gap Assault Team 2. A few miles away from the coast, NCDU chief Jerry Markham, a former paper maker from Jacksonville, Florida, discovered that Gap Assault Team 11's LCT was sucking in water, then "impounding it." After reporting the vessel's condition to his team leader, Ensign John Bussell ordered his men to abandon ship. Shortly after 0200, the LCT sank.

Despite the problems, most transports arrived at the rendezvous point as scheduled at 0330, some eleven miles from the Normandy coast. The Gap Assault Team members straightened up, donned their forty-pound haversacks bulging with charges, slung their carbines wrapped in clear pliofilm, shook hands with the Army tankers and wished them luck, and in pitch-black darkness clambered down the cargo nets into their bobbing landing crafts. For two more hours they waited, crammed on top of one another while the LCTs turned endless circles, like so many diesel-churning sharks. Before long, the smell of exhaust joined with the four-to-six-foot chop to kindle a "seven-bag case" of vomiting so bad that many men lost their fear of landing. In Boat 15, one combat engineer drew a lucky two-dollar bill from a pocket and passed it around for his friends to sign. Thirty-nine men scribbled their names or the name of a sweetheart; nine of them would never sign anything again.

When the boats stopped circling, it was time. The date was June 6, 1944.

10

As THE FIRST WAVE of landing craft turned south to close the final leg to Omaha Beach, the men who rode them could see nothing of what lay ahead except for the wave crests that the crosswind was whipping into white curls. Suspended in darkness and diesel thrum, this lull was finally interrupted at 0530 with the opening scream of a rocket salvo to their rear that sent a flinch through every close-shouldered rank, snapping heads from hypnosis and eyes skyward to watch the suddenly visible cloud-gray ripple with glowing red strips. A moment later, explosions like heat lightning could be seen against the mist-draped hills before them. Seconds after this, the unseen thunder-roar of ten thousand airplane engines shrank every helmet beneath them into its corresponding collarbone and lifted every eye to the still-distant shore and the promised light-splash of bombs. At the wall of assembled battleships now lined up parallel to the beaches, the armada of landing craft slid through the gaps. Among these was Boat Team 8, which passed just under the prow of the USS *Texas* as its first broadside of ten fourteen-inch guns erupted in satanic tongues of red flame and smoke so black that it turned the night into a mine explosion—a blast so powerful to the passersby that it jolted away any remnants of nausea and, in the words of Lieutenant Wes Ross, "would have blown the helmet off my head if the chinstrap had not been fastened." As they motored toward the beach, Boat Team 12 approached a floating tank, its entire crew huddled on the turret, "waving and yelling frantically," as their improbable vessel sank beneath them. His boat crammed with men and explosives, the team's coxswain shrugged and motored on toward the black shore. There was nothing else to be done.

When the bluffs behind Omaha finally became visible, the men in their landing craft could see little more than clouds of black smoke drifting across an escarpment dotted with grass fires. On the hills disjointed muzzle flashes appeared—too far away to be synced with the sounds of their explosions, and around them, plumes of white water from the distant shore guns erupted. Before troops had reached the beach, they could see facedown bodies ahead, buoyed by their life belts. In a moment, they had been passed—left like driftwood to wash between ten thousand boat wakes. Without orders, landing craft crews went to work. Skippers scanned the shore for any familiar landmark. Sailors in their turrets double racked their twin .50-caliber machine guns, some letting loose a deafening response, others holding their fire. Coxswains—much better trained now than two years earlier—palmed throttle knobs waiting for the first touch of ground, ready to cut their engines if needed to dip the bow and backwash the stern over any sandbars that might stop them too far from shore.

Forced left—east—by the current and away from their assigned beaches, boat officers struggled to decide what to do. As soon as the first bullets drummed against the walls of their landing craft, nearly everyone in the fleet arrived at the same decision. "Take us on in—there's fight there anyway." For many Gap Assault Teams, not a single tank or infantryman had yet landed. Alone and unsure of their locations, the demolitioneers did their best to steady their nerves, gripping their charges in one hand and boat handles in the other, and waited for the ramps to drop.

11

AT 0633—PRECISELY THREE MINUTES after H-Hour and right on schedule—Boat 1's ramp splashed down. In a scramble of clomping boots, Gap Assault Team 1 plunged up to their chests into a fifty-four-degree surf, too filled with fear and adrenaline to notice the cold. Remarkably, no one was shooting. Looking to the right as he waded to shore, Chief Petty Officer Bill Freeman—now in command of NCDU

11, the only enlisted man so entrusted—could see the cliffs of Pointe du Hoc, where the 2nd Rangers were already supposed to be ascending. Though Freeman did not know exactly where he was, he did know that he was east of Dog Green—several hundred yards at least. No matter. To his front, where tanks and infantrymen and Rangers were already supposed to be barreling ahead, there was no one. Neither was there a single crater, a single wrecked obstacle, or any sign of Hall's promised bombardment. Before him lay Rommel's perfect forest of deterrence—Belgian Gates, stakes, ramps, hedgehogs—all untouched. Born and raised in Chicago, already tested and hardened in Morocco, and now as skeptical of assurances from superiors as he was of those by Bible-thumping chaplains, Freeman waited for no officer and led his men forward—his thighs lunging out of the water, the bone-chilling waves shoving him shoreward. For reasons unknown to all in the first wave, the enemy was holding his fire.

As Freeman made the most of this lull to hustle to shore, so too did everyone else, including his Army superior—Lieutenant Bill Kehaly—who wasted no time and pointed his engineers toward the first belt of obstacles—a line of Belgian Gates not yet covered by the waves. After sprinting upright through the damp sand to reach them, Kehaly and his soldiers used frantic fingers to strap each one with sixteen strategically placed charges. Running past these, Freeman and his demolitioneers were equally exposed and did not stop until surrounded by the second belt—a mine-barnacled thicket of wooden stakes and log ramps, all of

Painting by Navy combat artist Mitchell Jamieson of an explosives-laden rubber boat being dragged to shore by NCDUs at Omaha Beach.

which they immediately started to wrap with haversacks. Left behind in this rush were Seamen Farrell and Conti, two of the boot camp graduates who were straining against bow lines to drag their rubber boat through the surf, the only cover around them a 400-pound pile of explosives. Through all this the only sound to muffle their voices were the guns out to sea and the gentle rhythm of waves crashing behind them. It was—for those few tense moments—not at all the kind of battlefield for which Kauffman's Hell Week had prepared them. Then it was.

First, an MG42 machine gun started barking in the hills, then another, their bullets stitching across the sand, splintering the wooden stakes. Mortars followed, slamming into the earth and surf, and splashing hot shards of metal in every direction. Next came the dreaded 88s, antiaircraft guns used by Rommel as beach artillery, the shells exploding plumes of sand and water in terrible groups of three.

First of Gap Assault Team 1 to be hit was the boat—through the rubber skin—buckling it into the waves with all the extra charges. Beneath the whip and snap of machine gun fire, Seamen Farrell and Conti frantically grabbed what they could—the beach markers—then turned and ran toward the shingle. As they did, Farrell was shot through the knee, Conti through the back. Immediately an Army medic rushed to their aid, dragged them from the surf, tucked them behind stakes, and then dropped dead from a sniper's bullet. Gunner's Mate 2nd Class Ozie Mingledorf, a Fort Pierce graduate from Douglas, Georgia, who had valiantly left a sickbed just two days before so as not to miss the invasion, strapped his charges to the wood pilings just as he had in all those months of training. As he did, a bullet slammed into his leg.

As his demolitioneers crawled and sprinted between posts, Freeman dashed around them all—paying out his telephone reel of yellow primer cord and connecting the charges into a single trunk line. Then, better late than never, the first Sherman tank trundled out of the surf, the sea draining off the beast in waterfalls. As it shook free of its flotation skirt, it turned parallel to the shingle, firing toward the enemy. With every round, it drew attention away from Freeman and his men. When it turned back, threatening to overrun and cut his trunk line, Freeman sprinted from cover, waved his arms like mad, and cursed the tankers until they went around it.

Less than twenty minutes after landing, the Team 1 engineers were ready to blow the gates. Gripping the condom-protected fuse lighter, Lieutenant Kehaly sucked the smoke-filled air into his lungs and yelled *"Fire in the hole!"* In the same breath he pulled the fuse, dropped it, and ran, tossing a purple smoke grenade as he went. Freeman and his sailors saw the signal and pressed their bellies into the sand.

As soon as the gates exploded and flattened beneath the waves, the landing craft flooded past. Rushing down their ramps, infantrymen fell back at the sight of mortars and artillery bursts and instinctively crouched forward against the machine gun bullets now drumming into the wooden posts and human flesh. As if caught in a hurricane, soldiers huddled next to the only cover available, falling in behind log ramps and stake posts. Around them, the demolitioneers inspired open-mouthed expressions of amazement as they "shinnied up the stakes and stood on each others' shoulders" to crown each mine with a charge to ensure that it blew apart at the same moment the pole did.

With terrified soldiers frozen in place, neither advancing nor retreating, Freeman and Kehaly sprinted between posts, yelling obscenities and kicking the infantrymen away. Once clear, Freeman gave the signal, tossed a purple smoke grenade, and Petty Officer Bass pulled the fuse. *"Fire in the hole!"*

At 0655, only twenty-two minutes after landing, the whole area exploded in a roar that "drowned out the battle's din," shooting skyward a hell's mixture of "water, smoke, wood, sand and steel high into the air."

The defenders' response was vicious. As soon as the smoke and debris settled, the fire from the hills became unbearable. As Mingledorf, the Georgian with a hole in his leg, crawled hand over hand to the seawall and safety, a round slammed through his helmet into his forehead, killing him instantly.

With the obstacles blown and all beach cover gone, Petty Officer Bass, a former Seabee from Durham, North Carolina, resisted the urge to run and instead found Seaman Farrell alone, still writhing from the hole in his knee and with a fresh wound to his right eye. Bass bent down to cradle the boy to cover him, and as he did, a bullet tore through his back, entering just to the right of his spine and blowing a hole out of his right shoulder. Sergeant Murphy, one of the Army's naval augmentees, found them both and dragged them to the seawall.

Wounded himself, and with nearly everyone in his crew either shot or dead, Freeman was unstoppable—blasting obstacles, clearing out infantrymen before his charges blew, helping his wounded to cover. Though they had been cut to shreds, Gap Assault Team 1 had completed its mission; their fifty-yard gap was clear.

But now the tide was coming in.

12

Along the five miles to the left of Dog Green Beach, Gap Assault Teams struggled to achieve a similar feat, but because of the tide and a thousand other factors, their results were mixed. Team 2, having been forced to abandon their sinking LCT nearly 100 miles from France, was still motoring south, somewhere in the middle of the Channel, and would not arrive for another hour. When the soldiers and sailors of Team 3 hit the beach at Dog White, they gritted their teeth and leaned forward like everyone else, then took an artillery round in the center of their boat, lighting off their stored charges and blowing men across the sand and surf, either dead or incapacitated. The same thing happened to Team 14. Landing on the eastern half of Omaha, they managed to get ashore unscathed, only to be cut down as they worked, nearly every man wounded. Like Freeman's crew, Team 5 landed alone and unsupported, placed all their obstacles in a record-setting fifteen minutes without a single casualty, then watched in horror as infantrymen rushed ashore to take cover behind their explosives.

Paralyzed by the same problem, and in spite of the bullets whizzing past his head, Lieutenant Junior Grade William Jenkins of Team 6 squinted through his glasses at the chaos at Dog Red and arrived at a solution. Tall and thin, with a high forehead, dark wavy hair, and the warm smile of a Sunday school teacher, Bill Jenkins looked like any-

Sketch of NCDUs laying charges on a Belgian Gate at Omaha Beach, by Mitchell Jamieson, 1944.

thing but a man in charge of an explosives team. In normal settings, he was as mild as the Pacific Northwest climate in which he'd been raised. Now, he was unleashed, his soft face transformed into hammered steel. Grabbing Chief John Jacobsen, his friend since Hell Week, he quickly laid out his plan: They would abandon the trunk line and instead blow each charge individually. Sprinting from obstacle to obstacle, the pair ripped two-minute fuses from their helmets, attached them to each obstacle's charge, pulled them, then ran on, screaming at the soldiers left behind to clear out or die. In the madcap race to load them all, Jacobsen and another sailor were killed. Jenkins, out of breath but alive, was untouched. He and his friend had cleared a gap almost a hundred yards wide. Then, on the beach where so many sacrifices gave birth to tragedies, this victory was smothered almost the moment it was finished when two separate landing craft drifted outside the cleared gap, hit mines, and breached, almost completely blocking what Jacobsen had given his life to clear.

The men of Gap Assault Team 10, who had been assigned a portion of the 2,000-yard monster section known as Easy Red, had crossed the Channel in relative comfort. In command was a tall, handsome, coolheaded twenty-five-year-old Army lieutenant from Elko, Nevada, named Joe Gregory. Leading the Navy contingent was Lieutenant Junior Grade Lawrence Karnowski of Tampa, Kansas, a twenty-eight-year-old reservist with oh-gosh looks who'd been in the service for barely more than a year and married for less than that. While most had simply endured the Channel transit, Karnowski had tucked himself under a tank on a pile of warm bodies and slept. When it came time to cross-deck from the LCT to the landing craft, he rubbed the sleep out of his eyes, and then, like everyone else, gripped the cargo net, kicked his legs overboard, and in the process lost his helmet, which sank to the bottom.

Landing at 0625, one of the earliest crews to arrive, Gregory and the Army engineers had dragged their rubber boat into the surf, lashed it to a wooden stake, and run for the farthest belt of hedgehogs. "It looked impossible to be there without being hit," one of Karnowski's men remembered afterward. It looked even worse without a helmet. Despite the chaos, Karnowski and the demolitioneers laid their charges, ran out their primer cord, tied in, and blew their charge. "The first shot was magnificent," remembered one man. After it, nothing else was. As soon as the charge blew, machine guns opened up from everywhere, and men pushed their bellies into the sand. Conrad Millis, a quiet California carpenter—made chief petty officer for the example he had set during training—grabbed the primer cord reel and sprinted for the next row of obstacles. He was identified later by the "pack of explosives" around his neck, with a "big hole in his chest."

As the waves of infantry landed, the demolition job grew even more complicated. Terrified soldiers either did not notice the purple-smoke warnings swirling around them or did not care. "I thought I'd never get one of the infantrymen out from behind a piling," a demolitioneer confessed later. "He moved out just in time and our second shot went off." As obstacles blew apart, the Army and Navy sections began working together, mingling as a single team, regardless of the advancing tide. Lieutenant Gregory, having destroyed the tank-crippling hedgehogs at the far edge of the beach, turned away from the enemy and splashed back into the surf. Like a man possessed, he waded or swam to each remaining stake, where he waited until someone threw him a charge, then—using the lessons taught to him by the NCDUs—stretched his arms as far as they could reach and placed his bomb next to Rommel's, then blew them both to nothing.

Carrying the Army and Navy demolition commanders, Command Boat 1 dropped its ramp in waist-deep water at 0645, twelve minutes behind the first wave. Moments earlier, the high-value passengers had held their breath as the coxswain tried to wrench his craft away from a mine-topped stake and failed. The only reason Lieutenant Commander Gibbons was still alive was thanks to the Germans' inability to waterproof their weapons. Now it was the water that threatened him more than anything else. Stepping into a runnel, he sank. Inflating his life belt, his bounce to the surface stripped him of every article of usable equipment and "popped" him above the surface, where he found himself gasping for air and besieged by what one man called "a sleet of bullets." Scrambling for cover, Gibbons did the only thing he could and jettisoned the life belt, then dove, moving to shore with as little of his body above the surface as possible. With his men stretched out along a five-mile front and lacking the demolitions knowledge to be able to help, Gibbons—when he finally did make it to shore—had little that he could do except survive. When he dove into a ditch with one of his sailors, the man shouted back, "Get the hell out of my foxhole!" He did.

Except for Karnowski and Gregory's Gap Assault Team 10, nearly every one of the demolition units that fought on the left flank of Omaha Beach suffered staggering losses. Scheduled to land dead center on Easy Red, Boat 11 instead came ashore on Fox Green, as far as 1,000 yards east of their intended target. When their ramp dropped, the six-man

Army crew wrenched their rubber boat free and machine gun fire cut them down. When the survivors finally did set their charges, a fuse described as "faulty" stymied their detonation. The Navy crew had better luck, but only for a moment. Once again, a mortar round hit the reserve explosives and blew one demolitioneer's head "completely off his body." Ensign Bussell, who only hours before had ordered his men to abandon their sinking LCT, now "lay facedown in the water," dead from "where chunks of shrapnel had taken his life in a second." With only half the gap clear but more than half their number either dead or badly wounded, Chief Markham—the former Florida paper maker—gathered his survivors at the shingle. Three men dug a trench in which to shelter, then hunkered down to wait it out. When a nearby mortar collapsed the whole thing on top of them, burying them alive, Markham rushed to the hole and dug with his fingers until he uncovered their panicked heads.

At 0830, two hours after touching ground, the beachmaster at Omaha halted further landings. Although five of the sixteen planned gaps had been cleared, as the tide had come in, many had clogged up with the debris of landing craft and vehicles. Now, just past the surf zone, landing craft zigzagged back and forth through a forest of mine-topped stakes and ramps looking for a hole where they could drop their troops. Nary a spot could be found.

As low on explosives as they were high on casualties, several demolitioneers ran along the beach collecting charges from the surf or slipping them off the shoulders of dead friends. Three NCDU men commandeered three beach battalion bulldozers and drove them right into the surf zone, nothing protecting them from being shot from their seats.

In short, the prospect of landing more troops on Omaha was narrowing, and the beach was only getting smaller by the minute. What the NCDUs needed was a miracle. What they got was the Viking of Assault.

13

OUT TO SEA, huddled with his staff around a transmitter in the bowels of the USS *Ancon,* General Clarence Huebner, commander of the 1st Infantry Division, dispatched an aide to the bridge with a message saying that he was considering the unthinkable: evacuation of Omaha Beach. When the aide arrived, said one witness, every flag officer on deck was wearing an expression of worry, all except for Admiral Hall, who—in a garrison cap and a fur-lined weather jacket—received Huebner's message at the rail of the bridge wing by barely dropping the binoculars from his eyes and reminding the aide that the Army could not order a withdrawal as long as the Navy was still in command. Then, in the next breath, Hall gave a five-word order that fulfilled the promise he had made to his NCDUs: "Get those destroyers in there," he said, unleashing eleven ships—eight American, three British—to levy a broadside attack not seen since Farragut ran the gauntlet at Mobile Bay.

Within minutes of this order, remembered James Knight, a combat engineer on Fox Red, "a destroyer loomed out of the sea . . . headed straight toward me. Even though she wasn't listing or smoking, my first thought was that she had either struck a mine or taken a torpedo and was damaged badly enough that she was being beached." All down Omaha, men saw the same thing: destroyers charging the beach at flank speed. At approximately 800 yards from the beach, well within range of the German MG42s, they turned sharply to the right, sailing westward, their guns rotating to face the shore, then erupting in bolts of flame and cylinders of gray smoke. With hulls just scraping the Channel bottom, gunnery officers strained through binoculars, watching to see where troops and tanks were firing, then aimed their guns at those locations, blowing the defenders into eternity. When one observer spotted an artillery observation post in Vierville's church steeple, the commander of the USS *Harding* hesitated, then radioed Hall for permission to fire. Hall hesitated not an instant: "Destroy it." When one of the vessels went dead in the water, the men on the beach fully expected to see her stern as she banked back out to sea. Instead, the destroyer shuddered, then reversed, chopping the water as it went, all the way to where it started, its guns never ceasing.

"There was one element of the attack [the Germans] could not parry," a 1st Division Colonel wrote to Admiral Hall two days later. "Without that gunfire we positively could not have crossed the beaches." After the battle, despite being overshadowed by just about every other commander at Omaha, Hall was made an honorary member of the 1st Division.

To him, however, there was only one Navy unit that deserved such recognition.

14

By morning's end, and with the help of Hall's destroyers, the Gap Assault Teams had partially cleared five of their sixteen target sections along Omaha Beach; by nightfall, the total was ten—for the NCDUs, an accomplishment that came at a cost prematurely estimated at two dozen dead, at least that many wounded, and fifteen more missing. These last had either been blown clear of their landing vessels and drowned or, in the words of one writer, had "run off to fight" with the Army. In fact, some had done just that, or at least had abandoned their section of beach.

After loading his wounded at 1900, Freeman—having lost nearly every man in his crew, and now more than ever convinced that the "Old Man" would only allow "the bastards and screwballs [to] live through this stuff"—capped off his almost twelve hours of direct combat by following the 2nd and 5th Rangers off the beach and up the Vierville Gap, digging in at the foot of the ridge. Lester Meyers, a machinist from Freeport, Illinois, assigned to Team 10, also reportedly ran off, not out of fear but to try his hand at hedgerow combat. Karnowski and his Army comrade Lieutenant Gregory, the unstoppable stake-clearing swimmer, also advanced, trudging up the St. Laurent Gap together, escorting their wounded to a makeshift aid station. On the way a shell exploded in their midst, splashing hot fragments into Gregory's thighs and guts. Collecting his friend in his arms, Karnowski alternately attempted to stanch the soldier's wounds and reverse the hopeless words that spilled from his lips, then simply held him until he died, dug a foxhole for another wounded man, and finally collapsed from exhaustion. The next dawn, Karnowski returned to the beach to direct clean-up operations and find a helmet.

On June 10—D plus 4—the Gap Assault Teams on Omaha Beach finally cleared the last of their sixteen assigned objectives. Their mission completed, the soldiers of the 146th and 299th Combat Engineering Battalions would now be reassigned to the regular Army and the traditional engineering duties of bridge building and minesweeping; the NCDUs would go on to more training in the demolition of beach and underwater obstacles, and in two months another assault on Rommel's obstacles in Operation Dragoon, the invasion of southern France, an action that was nothing compared to what they had already accomplished.

At 10:30 a.m. on September 27, 1944, a Wednesday, Secretary of the Navy James Forrestal addressed a crowd of high-ranking naval officers and reporters in room 3601 of the Pentagon. The purpose: to award the NCDUs of Force "O" the Presidential Unit Citation—the highest award a military unit could receive and, despite the service of hundreds of Navy units at Omaha Beach, one of just three such honors that Admiral Hall had recommended.

"I am very glad to have the opportunity to draw particular attention to the kind of work this [unit] has done in this war," Forrestal began. "Some day when the story is told, I think you will all agree it's a conspicuously gallant undertaking." After reading the citation—much of which was the same catalogue of bravery described in Hall's initial recommendation—Forrestal made what he called a "rather unforgivable plug" to draw attention to the service of one NCDU sailor from his own hometown of Beacon, New York: "a gallant fellow," Forrestal added to the usual ribbing by the press pool ("Good old Beacon," one reporter replied). At this, Forrestal turned and pinned the unit citation on the left breast of Lieutenant Commander Gibbons, then handed him over to the gathered press.

"They say here casualties were 41 percent but we heard they're over fifty," said one reporter. They were. Of the 190 NCDU demolitioneers who had participated in the assault on Omaha, Gibbons explained, 32 had been killed, while the actual number wounded had not been known for some time, as so many had simply ignored the shrapnel in their bodies to carry on with their missions. Jerry Markham, whose furious digging had saved the lives of three men, had not even noticed his own blast injuries for four days, not until an alarming trip to the latrine had revealed "severe internal bleeding." Eventually, the total number of demolitioneers wounded at Omaha more than doubled from 32 to 65—earning a total casualty ratio of 51 percent—10 percent higher than the Light Brigade at Balaclava—everything from Markham's hemorrhaging to one man's fingers blown off his hand by a pull fuse.

After Gibbons's explanation, Forrestal turned the reporters' attention back to the training that the NCDUs had received at Fort Pierce, and—quickly ensuring that there was a security officer in the room—continued by detailing the difficulty in planting explosives underwater. His description was ultimately expunged from the record, but the task's importance was not. Though he didn't say so, Forrestal might also have added that now—with the pullout of the Army's combat engineers from beach and underwater demolitions—the Navy's NCDUs were the only unit in the US arsenal still trained to perform them.

As a handful of planners had expected, the most difficult aspect of

Rommel's Atlantic Wall had been the beach and underwater obstacles, a problem that had been overcome only because of the Navy's commitment—first in identifying the issue, next in commissioning Kauffman to solve it, then in sharing those lessons with the Army's combat engineers. Ultimately, however, the Navy's greatest contribution had come from the NCDUs themselves. In addition to the Presidential Unit Citation, Admiral Hall had gone on to recognize the demolitioneers by recommending for them a trunkful of individual awards, including six Navy Crosses, one of which went to Chief Petty Officer Bill Freeman. "I kicked myself ever since that I didn't recommend him for a Medal of Honor," Hall said later. "I never heard of anybody . . . who did a greater job than that fellow did."

Responsible for getting the Army past the underwater obstacles on Omaha Beach, the NCDUs' achievement was—in the end—made possible only by their training at Fort Pierce. There they had learned not only the technical skills of underwater demolition—the explosives, the pull fuses, the minimum safe distances—but also, as Kauffman had insisted, the ability to push past the limits of normal human endurance to withstand cold, hunger, raw skin, exhaustion, even the chaos of combat; the kind of fortitude that made winning wars possible. "Only our vigorous training held us together," one survivor said afterward. But what about after that?

With the collapse of the Atlantic Wall the mission of the NCDUs had been accomplished, and therefore no unit in the US military was in greater threat of disbandment. Or at least would have been if not for one final hang-up: The Navy's planners were loath to disband a unit that had just performed so effectively. After all, the war was far from over. And there was no shortage of needs for sailors so conditioned to the combat that lay ahead.

Chapter 5

The Evolving Contest That Created the Mermen of War—World War II's Only Indispensable Special Operations Unit

In the late summer of 1943, right about the same time that Draper Kauffman was putting himself through NCDU Hell Week, US commanders in the Pacific were about to initiate two campaigns with one ultimate objective, the invasion of Japan. Blocked by a swath of ocean five times the size of the Sahara and whose every atoll had been turned into a Japanese fortress, the strategy to accomplish this objective was one in which the Allies would leapfrog most islands—especially the most robustly defended (let them "wither on the vine," said Douglas MacArthur)—and seize a handful upon which they could build airfields substantial enough to support the long-range four-engine bombers needed to soften up the next handful on the way to mainland Japan. In the South Pacific, this path would progress from the mountainous jungles of Guadalcanal to a nearby group of similar islands—many well charted and populated, and all of them battlefields large enough for the US Army's and MacArthur's ambitions. In the Central Pacific, this path would start some 2,000 miles west of Hawaii in the Gilbert Island chain—the first lily pads large enough to support bomber-sized airfields, but so small, so remote, so daunting, that their volcanic spines of white sand and green palms could almost be mistaken for the ridged backs of a thousand sea monsters. And there was only one branch of service that could lead the hunt against those, the same branch that would soon go on to break Hitler's Atlantic Wall, but employing an altogether different kind of method—indeed, a method unlike any in military history.

Like every other amphibious campaign in the Second World War, the island-hopping advance through the Central Pacific was made possible only by the technological advancement in what planners had euphoniously called that "bridge to the beach," those landing craft that would transport soldiers and Marines from their ships to their shores. The first improvement to these vessels had been discovered in May of 1938 at a fifteen-boat trial in the Chesapeake Bay near Portsmouth, Virginia, in which one vessel had outshone all the rest. The winner had been a flat-bottomed river runner popular with loggers and called the Eureka by its designer, Andrew Jackson Higgins, a tireless, bourbon-swilling industrialist—the only man President Roosevelt ever met who had done all the talking. Higgins's principal innovation had been a hull whose stern concealed a "recessed tunnel" that shielded the propeller from running aground. The second advance in landing craft design had been discovered by 1st Lieutenant Victor Krulak, a Marine Corps observer at the Japanese invasion of Shanghai, in 1937, who had commandeered a tugboat, enlisted a Navy photographer, then sailed right into the middle of the Japanese landing fleet. There he had seen an odd-shaped vessel whose peculiarity was a bow ramp that dropped as soon as it hit the beach: "That's it! That's it!" he had shouted above the booming artillery. Now, both developments were about to make it possible for the Navy to land Marines directly on any beach in the Central Pacific, including the first ones awaiting them in the Gilbert Islands. All except for one problem: the wall of coral that surrounded nearly every island in the Central Pacific. It was an obstacle that would inadvertently write the opening chapter to the history of the Navy's first permanent special warfare unit, a chapter initiated by an argument over prerogatives, assets, and how best to adapt to the physical environment—the way evolution always begins.

2

Before the invasion of Tarawa—the central island of the Gilbert Island thrust—the Navy's hydrographic analysis showed that on the morning of assault the coral reef that surrounded the island would only be submerged to a depth of four feet six inches. A fully loaded Higgins Boat had a draft of four feet—just enough. When it was discovered, however, that the invasion force would have to contend with an annual peculiarity called a dodging tide, in which the difference between high and low water would hardly be noticeable, those six extra inches of water would disappear altogether. "You won't have three feet!" declared an Australian major familiar with the regional tides. Both Navy and Marine Corps planners recognized this as a problem but, being married, disagreed on how to deal with it.

Advocating for the Corps' position was General Holland McTyeire Smith, a former Alabama attorney who was now in command of all Marines in the Central Pacific and whose given name had long since been modified to Howlin' Mad in order to match his personality. Caustic and canny, with round spectacles, a mustache trimmed equidistant from nose and lip, and a jowly face that relaxed into a scowl (as every good Marine's does), Smith had long since learned to use his temper and lawyer's logic to turn a Navy bureaucracy built on anything but logic to argue for more training, better boats, more shells, and better ship-to-shore guns. Well informed by years of research into the mechanics of various landing craft, he viewed the coral as a technical problem with a technical solution. To him, that solution was variously known as an amphibious tractor, an alligator, an amtrac, or by its most common name, a Landing Vehicle Tracked, or LVT for short. Conceived by Donald Roebling—grandson of the builder of the Brooklyn Bridge—as a rescue vehicle for the aftermath of Florida hurricanes, the LVT had the looks and characteristics of a decapitated tank—not exactly a vehicle associated with speed or buoyancy. Because of their disadvantages to the Higgins Boats—lower troop capacity, lighter transport weight, significantly slower water speed—the LVTs had so far only been used in a noncombat capacity to haul supplies to inland troops on Guadalcanal. Unlike the Higgins Boats, however, the LVTs possessed one trait that made up for all the rest: an ability to crawl over coral and at least seven consecutive rows of barbed wire, an incomparable advantage on islands surrounded by both. Reacting to the Navy's preference to rely on the Higgins Boats at Tarawa, Smith's mustache curled into a snarl: "No LVTs, no operation!" he insisted—a demand the Navy accepted, though not enthusiastically, for reasons more important than the loss of an argument.

On the day of battle, the first three assault waves consisted entirely of LVTs: 125 in total, carrying some 1,464 Marines. As Navy planners had feared, their plod had forced H-Hour to be bumped from 0830 to 0900, a delay that complicated a number of things, but particularly the coordination of carrier bombers and naval gunfire—coordination that was especially needed now as the LVTs fell under the crosshairs of the Japanese guns erupting on the beach. Another repercussion of deploying such an ungainly fleet on the high seas was the sinking of some thirty-five of its vessels (almost 30 percent of the total), plus a rolling five-hour transit from ship to shore that created an exceedingly nauseated assault force made even more so by the residue of the Navy's standard pre-invasion breakfast of steak and eggs. To anyone riding in these waves of LVTs, they must have seemed like a distant last place to the more seaworthy Higgins Boats—that is, until the first rank reached the reef, where their tank treads grabbed the underwater coral and cranked across (except for twenty-six of them swamped in the effort). Those that made it rumbled forward into the blasts of antiboat shells and the criss-crossing belts of machine gun bullets that pinged like bells off the LVTs' overlapping armor plates or clattered through their skins like so many empty oil drums. Against this, the surviving LVTs crossed a nearly half-mile-long lagoon as open as the last stretch of Cemetery Ridge. When they finally breasted the surf, many LVT drivers—slightly braver than smart; the best ratio in combat—drove onto the beach, where they eyed the defenders' five-foot-high coconut-log seawall and plunged headfirst into a landscape of fractured palms that looked like "the broken teeth of a comb." LVT 4-9, nicknamed "My Deloris," stalled halfway up the wall as if cresting a wave, allowing Japanese machine gunners to puncture her hull with a planetarium of light holes and rip off her coxswain's head.

For all the horrors suffered that morning by those aboard the LVTs, they were not the worst ones encountered. Immediately after the last tank tread cleared the coral, two ranks of flat-bottomed Higgins Boats lined up to fall in behind, then scraped to a halt the moment their hulls hit the reef. Blocked from the lagoon and the beach beyond it, coxswains did the only thing they could and dropped their ramps. Marines who survived long enough to touch coral immediately found themselves exposed to the pre-sighted "soprano whine" of Japanese guns. One man, frantic to get off the reef, glanced behind just in time to see his friend's face shot off, leaving just the red-black shell of his skull. Those not shot, blown to mist, or immediately sunk, raised their rifles above their heads and began the two-hour wade to shore.

For the next three days of battle, not a single Higgins Boat was able to cross the reef. Except for the rubber boats, the only craft that could were the LVTs. But of the 125 that did, half were destroyed by the end of the first day—shot to pieces, broken down, or sunk. As a result, one Kingfisher pilot who flew above the blood-clouded lagoon remembered, "The water never seemed clear of tiny men. I wanted to cry." Of the 1,009 Marines killed during the battle—a four-day total that almost surpassed the number of Marines lost in six months' worth of losses at Guadalcanal—it is not known what percentage were attributable to the reef, but only about half were identifiable afterward, a fact in no small part to blame on the lagoon's salt water, which washed away men's hair and swelled their bodies beyond identification.

Because nothing else at Tarawa had made so terrible an impression as the reef, nothing else had so proved its value as the LVTs, a triumph dimmed only by their scant armor, slow speed, and the Navy's reluctance to bring extras. As a result, the solution for future reefs, according to the 2nd Marine Division's after-action report, was summed up in three words: tougher, faster, and more. Missing from the report was any mention of alternative means for dealing with the coral; one-track minds tend to prefer dual-tracked solutions. This was an answer that didn't really solve anything; it just drove over it, ignoring all the risks of relying on LVTs. As it had at Tarawa, the coral would remain to complicate everything from timetables to resupply runs to medical evacuations to fire support at every island.

As the Navy saw it, the Marine Corps' solution was more than just an oversight. It was unacceptable. The coral wasn't simply a technical problem, it was a tumor—one that needed to be found and cut out. The problem: At the time of the Tarawa operation, there had been only two units that might have been capable of such a venture, both of which had been allocated to other missions. The first of these was the 2nd Marine Division's regimental Scout-Sniper Platoons—units originally designed for inland reconnaissance of tactical targets, but which at Tarawa had been dispatched just ahead of their fellow Marines with grenades and flamethrowers to assault the island's 500-yard-long pier, whose machine gun emplacements had threatened to cut into the flank of the entire length of the landing fleet. The second of these was the Fifth Amphibious Corps Reconnaissance Company, or VAC Recon Company, a unit formed from the Marine Corps' half of the disbanded Observer Group and whose counterpart had gone on to create the Army-Navy Scouts and Raiders. On the day of the Tarawa invasion, this company had been transported aboard the USS *Nautilus*—the same submarine that had taken Carlson and his men to Makin—to conduct a reconnaissance-in-force of the satellite island of Apamama. Both units—the Scout Sniper Platoons and the VAC Recon Company—had performed exceptionally well. Both could probably have been reoriented to handle the Navy's preoccupation with finding and destroying the coral. Neither was, because neither unit belonged to the Navy.

For one admiral, that fact was even more unacceptable than the Marine Corps solution to the coral.

3

Rear Admiral Richmond Kelly Turner—the recently appointed commander of the Fifth Amphibious Force—was the closest the US Navy had ever come to creating an actual Captain Ahab: a man obsessed not only with vengeance and the Navy's preeminent role in exacting it, but also with dealing the death blow himself. It would prove a compulsion with many consequences, for our purposes none as important as the creation of the most closely held unit the Navy had ever devised.

With jib-sail ears, a "solemn owlish expression," and a nose wider at the end than at the nostrils, Turner at first glance looked less like a Melville character and more like a country parson, maybe a schoolmaster. "Courtly in courtesy [and] affable in an academic manner," said a contemporary, one was "tempted in the first five minutes of acquaintance to make the snap judgment that he [was] a quiet, softly philosophic man." Longer acquaintance, however, revealed that this calm was simply the center of a hurricane. "As abrasive as a file" and celebrated by his sailors for his legendary profanity, Turner's every trait seemed to indicate a manic personality—a gaunt frame that looked almost "loose-jointed"; an addiction to whatever bottle he was holding; and a faithful monogamy to every chain-smoked cigarette that touched his lips, right "down to [its] last soggy half-inch." Devotedly married but childless, since the day he had left his home in Portland, Oregon, for the US Naval Academy in Annapolis—an appointment that had required him to first name every body of water one would pass through on a voyage from Yokohama to the Suez Canal to St. Louis—Turner's entire life had been dominated by the Navy. He had dominated the Navy right back.

When given the assignment in 1942 to take command of the amphibious force bound for Guadalcanal, Turner immediately boarded a plane to New Zealand, where he set sail with his Task Force three days later. "Damn the torpedoes, damn the airplanes, damn anything Japanese," a reporter wrote of Turner's pace. In Japan, the coming of Turner was like the coming of the fourth horseman. He is a "devil man," said one broadcast. Like Patton of the Pacific Theater, the enemy feared and admired him. On one occasion, a Japanese reporter described Turner to his listeners: "He is known as the 'Alligator.' Once he bites into something he will not let go." These characterizations were actually tame compared to the reality. On any issue that touched his ships, his Navy, or his tactics, Turner's mind and pace towered above all, superiors often included. A subordinate of Admiral Ghormley in the South Pacific,

Rear Admiral Richmond Kelly Turner off Kwajalein supervising the invasion of the Marshall Islands, February 18, 1944.

Turner nevertheless dominated all conversations with him. When Admiral Jack Fletcher informed him at a planning session that he would remove his carriers from Guadalcanal, leaving the Marines without air cover, Turner took the news with as much equanimity as he could muster. "You son of a bitch," he told Fletcher without blinking, "if you do that you are yellow." Of the fight that followed, a witness remembered, "I had never heard anything like it."

Nor had Turner's dominion stopped at the waterline. Handed a plan by an [Army] general, Turner had examined it for several moments, then declared, "It stinks. Whose is it?"

"It's mine," replied the general.

"It still stinks."

To Robert Sherrod, a reporter as well acquainted with the military as any rifleman, Turner could not travel from shore to ship "without lecturing the coxswain on how to bring the boat alongside," an impulse that extended to the Marines—to Turner, members of a mere department of the Navy, as subordinate to his orders as any coxswain. Impressed with the performance of Edson's 1st Raider Battalion on Tulagi and Guadalcanal, Turner—without consultation—had decided that every Marine should be retrained as a Raider. "Without authority," said one of the affected, Turner had then bypassed the entire chain of command to break up "the uncommitted remains" of an entire Marine regiment. Generously described by one Marine as a "frustrated general," Turner prompted a wave of righteous protests that did not subside until Nimitz himself had become personally involved, telling Turner to "cease tampering." Easier said than done.

Though Turner's belief in the divine right of Navy admirals over Marine Corps generals was inherent, it had also been the result of a regulation, Fleet Tactical Publication 167, or FTP 167 for short. With an authority as dust-covered as Deuteronomy, this regulation codified the relationship of a Navy amphibious force commander to a Marine landing force commander as that of senior to subordinate. In practice, most Navy men had recognized the limit of their knowledge and delegated the authority for ground operations to their Marine Corps juniors. Turner, however, had not. Having landed and supplied his Corps, he thought it only natural to keep commanding them. "By and large naval officers . . . were wary of trying to run land operations," remembered Marine Corps colonel Omar Pfeiffer. But not Turner; "Turner knew everything!"

In November 1942, well into the Guadalcanal campaign, even Admiral Nimitz had recognized that FTP 167 was a dinosaur and sent along a revision to Admiral King. Both Nimitz and King knew Turner; both knew he would never be constrained by good manners; both agreed to the revision—henceforth establishing the Marine Corps' invasion commander as the equivalent of the Navy's amphibious commander. From this point on, the Navy's Marines would be—at long last—just Marines.

It was an order that not only officially cut Turner off from any operational authority over the Corps' special units—the Raiders, the Scout-Snipers, even the VAC Recon Company—but also one that cut him off from any solution to the coral that did not involve an LVT. Or rather it would have, if Turner had been the sort who had ever met a problem he didn't instantly try to overwhelm; in this case, by invigorating a rear-echelon unit of Seabees—the Navy's builders—that Nimitz's staff had already tasked to start developing methods for blasting channels through coral under combat conditions. It was a unit not nearly prepared for Turner's interpretation of the word "invigorate."

4

On November 24, the day the battle for Tarawa ended, Turner's staff forwarded a training syllabus to Lieutenant Thomas Crist, the commanding officer of the coral-blasting Seabee unit back in Hawaii, calling for the creation of two provisional units capable of dealing with underwater obstacles—something called the "underwater demolition teams," or UDTs for short. In just over three weeks, 30 officers and 150 enlisted men began training together on Oahu—a hodgepodge of Army and Marine Corps engineers, Navy Seabees, plus some recently arrived NCDUs from Fort Pierce.

To command these teams, two men were selected. For UDT 1, the mantle fell on Commander E. D. Brewster, a stout Seabee. For UDT 2, the challenge could not have fallen on a man more prepared to create something out of nothing. Thirty-nine years old, with a bald head, straight back, and frameless glasses, Commander John T. Koehler (pronounced "Kayler") looked less like a leader of combat engineers and more like a tax attorney, which in fact he had been. One of ten children of a part-time house painter in Pittsburgh, Jack Koehler had an early life that was a series of obstacles overcome: rust-belt poverty, parental pressure to enlist in the ministry, disownment when he had refused, and the full burden of putting himself through Princeton (where he had arrived with so few belongings that he placed a wooden board in his suitcase to keep the clothes from balling up at the bottom). There, he had worked every day to pay his tuition and survive, taking jobs in the dining hall, at a men's boardinghouse; anywhere. Ultimately graduating from Harvard Law with nothing but his degree and a conciliatory check his father had just palmed into his pocket, Koehler had immediately torn up the check and gone to serve in the Treasury Department before setting up a lucrative private practice in Baltimore. Cerebral and somewhat solitary, Koehler had spent these years as a bachelor, sustaining himself with his two passions: memorizing poetry—mostly Keats, but Byron and Yeats too, anything but Shakespeare—and raising orchids, a hobby that had required such care and attention that it had become an obsession. When the war came, Koehler—given his age, gift for precision, and sophistication—had seemed a perfect fit for an administrative billet or the legal branch; instead, he volunteered for the Beachmasters, a decision that brought him face-to-face with Hermann Goering's Panzer Division at Gela. Now, as the recently appointed commander of UDT 2, Koehler was about to face an enemy not human, but physical. He had five weeks to prepare his men.

"Our year of attack," said Admiral King to a reporter in January 1944, "has just begun." Indeed it had. Within the month, Turner and the Fifth Amphibious Force launched Operation Flintlock, the invasion of the Marshall Islands. Composed of more than thirty atolls, each one a miniature solar system of islands and islets, the Marshalls had been guarded as military secrets by the Japanese for the past twenty-five years. Now, they concealed a galaxy's worth of mysteries from their invaders. From Kwajalein, the heart of the Marshall Islands, only rumors had escaped. Called "Execution Island" by US airmen, this was the place where American POWs had reportedly gone to die. Carrying the scars of the Gilberts, and fearing the worst of the Marshalls, Turner now brought to bear 30,000 men and two million tons' worth of ships—more weight than had existed in the entire prewar Navy.

Fresh from the first successful ground reconnaissance in the Central Pacific Theater, General Smith sent forth his VAC Recon Company like the twelve spies into Canaan. At Majuro Atoll, one of the VAC Recon platoon commanders, Lieutenant Harvey Weeks—a former Yale wrestler, former attorney, and former enlisted man—captured the Japanese commander with a half nelson, then negotiated the support of the local Marshallese trader, who paid out his allegiance in chickens and a 220-pound boar. Assisted by the Divisional Scout-Sniper Platoons and the Army's Alamo Scouts, the VAC Recon Marines went on to franchise the Majuro coup and secure more than fifty more islets, which in turn secured the Fifth Amphibious Corps' flank and, presumably, their essential place in all future invasions. The same could not be said of Turner's experimental demolition unit.

At the outset, the provisional UDTs did not impress. At Enubuj, UDT 1 attempted to destroy the coral reef with remote-controlled boats packed with explosives. The first of these burned out its water pump; the other two shared the same radio frequency, so only one could be used. It buckled under the weight of its charges and sank on its way to the reef. In the end, the failures didn't matter. With four tanks in on the invasion, Enubuj was secured in twenty minutes, no thanks to the UDTs.

Fifty miles north at Roi-Namur—two islands separated by a causeway as long as a hyphen—Marine Scouts took control of Koehler's UDT 2 for a night reconnaissance of the lagoon reefs. Riding rubber boats through choppy water, they searched for mines and found none. The next day, UDT 2 attempted their own remote-controlled boat mission. This time the drone drifted so far off course that it began heading back toward the fleet, forcing a UDT crew to ram it with their LVT just in time for a man to leap on top of the explosives and cut the fuse. Had the UDTs continued on in this fashion, they no doubt would have found themselves on the same path to disbandment as the Marine Corps' Raiders.

When Turner saw the reconnaissance photos of Kwajalein's western beaches, he saw something that made him straighten up and take notice. Just as at Tarawa, and Dieppe before that, there was an unbroken seawall. Compiled of wooden posts slanted out toward the sea and buttressed from behind by concreted rocks, the wall was designed to stop the LVTs and tanks in their tracks. To crush the defenders and the wall that protected them, Turner ordered an unprecedented barrage of metal: 7,000 rounds from naval guns, plus 25,000 artillery shells fired from Enubuj, all topped off by 96 sorties from carrier aircraft, then six B-24s dropping 1,000- and 2,000-pound bombs. "The entire island looked as if it had been picked up to twenty thousand feet then dropped," said one veteran, remembering the dusty smudge that Kwajalein became. Under this tyranny of metal, Turner dispatched his UDTs, but not to demolish; he had already taken care of that. He needed them to look. And not just at the reefs, but at the wall.

Trained to operate like the Scouts and Raiders—to work at night, to scout from boats, to wear helmets and Army greens—the UDTs planned to conduct their reconnaissance accordingly. Or at least that was the plan, until their coxswain got within 500 yards of Execution Island and faltered; he had no interest in going farther. Unable to see the wall so far from shore, two UDT men—Ensign Lew Luehrs of the NCDUs, and Chief Bill Acheson of the Seabees—stripped down to their black swim trunks, strapped on goggles, and dove overboard. For forty-five minutes they swam, looking for mines or other man-made obstructions, pausing only to stand on the reef, measuring the depth of the water at high tide with their bodies. When they raised their eyes to the shoreline, they could see the locations of gun emplacements and the entire length of the log wall. It was untouched. Swimming unprotected and alone, more than once they expected the Japanese to fire at them. They never did. Pinned down by Turner's barrage, or simply confused by what was happening, the Japanese held their fire.

Within minutes of being plucked from the water, Luehrs and Acheson were whisked to the USS *Monrovia,* where—dripping water all over the deck—they described to Turner the coral heads and, most important, the wall—as yet still standing. Almost immediately, Turner saw that his investment in the UDTs had paid off, at least partially. Here was a reconnaissance method that had uncovered the hidden world beneath his boats and the beaches in front of them, two mysteries concealed from an airplane's camera and a submarine's periscope. That afternoon, at low tide, he moved his ship guns even closer to shore and sent his UDTs out again. "The Japanese seemed unaware of what was taking place," one of Turner's contemporaries said afterward. Even Turner himself wasn't yet entirely sure. "We have certain theories we go by," said a Navy strategist to a reporter in Pearl Harbor, describing the planning process for amphibious invasions. "After that there is the Jesus factor—the unpredictable." Though Luehrs and Acheson had not walked on water, they had been baptized in it, and returned as apostles for a new method.

For the rest of Operation Flintlock, the UDTs made themselves as useful as they could to the invasion force but never quite matched the strategic relevance Luehrs and Acheson had in that singular moment. In the days following their initial reconnaissance, UDT 1 blew gaps in the coral for the LSTs and lent a hand wherever one was needed, even donating their surplus explosives to Army engineers, then volunteering to help plant them. One UDT squad even worked their way up to the front, past the line of tanks with names like Killer and Baby Satan, crunching over ground strewn with empty ammo boxes, shredded palm fronds, and the bodies of naked Japanese. When they arrived, they joined an assault on a Japanese pillbox, sprinted to the wall side, stacked haversacks full of tetrytol against it, and ran. Writing with all the enthusiasm of a foster parent, Brewster summed up the squad's work as "blasting enemy strong points." On Roi-Namur, Koehler and UDT 2 also tucked in behind the ground troops, an experience so piercing it would cut through his dreams until the day he died.

After Flintlock, and despite wounds received at Eniwetok, Brewster made several recommendations for improvement. First, the UDTs should develop the "closest coordination" with the beachmaster, a recommendation that added ballast to the argument to keep the UDT confined to the water and not trailing behind Baby Satan to the center of hell. He also recommended that each UDT should be assigned to "one vessel to be used as an operating base." With these suggestions approved and implemented, more changes were still to come from on high. To relieve operational disorganization, Army and Marine Corps engineers were returned to their units, making the UDT an all-Navy outfit. This was likely not accidental.

Anticipating the sticky fingers of Marine Corps planners who would no doubt covet the UDT capability as an adjunct arm of the Fleet Marine Force, Admiral R. L. Conolly, Turner's "round-faced, round-bellied" subordinate commander of the Northern Attack Force at Roi-Namur, passed his own recommendation on to Turner. Demolition parties of underwater obstacles "should not be attached to the Assault Division." The UDTs "should be part of the Navy's effort to get the boats and vehicles into the beach." Had Conolly been preaching to a choir, his recommendations to Turner could not have been more welcome.

5

After Operation Flintlock and eighteen months of nearly continuous combat operations, Turner was a changed man, and not for the better. Behind him were the ghosts of the Gilberts and the Marshalls; ahead were the double horrors of the Marianas and the Japanese Home Islands. Having suffered a back injury, he now lived in almost uninterrupted pain, a pain he medicated with a back brace and a bottle. For the rest of the war, he held on to both. "When I came back from the Marshalls I was dead tired," he said years later. "I stayed dead tired for the rest of the war." On his map of former and future tragedies, islands ceased to be anything except citadels of death. The longer it took to attack them, the sturdier each one became. A partial answer to this problem, glimpsed at Kwajalein, was clear: find the path of least resistance and blow it into a highway. Like any convert struck on the road to Damascus, Turner went forth to proselytize. One man who required no conversion was the man most like him.

Admiral King "listened with utmost enthusiasm," wrote Captain James Doyle, Turner's operations officer, when describing the UDT efforts at Flintlock. "Excellent," King interrupted in the middle of Doyle's briefing, "that business of the hydrographic survey at the first possible moment is a pet hobby of mine." For Turner, however, a unit capable of doing for the Navy what the VAC Recon Company was doing for the Marines was not so much a hobby as, in the words of one witness, "his baby." It was, in Turner's own words, "something entirely new to naval warfare."

To create exactly the kind of "entirely new" unit that Turner wanted, he first had to implement a new structure. He broke apart the provisional UDTs and used the remnants as nuclei for a series of permanent ones—Teams 3, 4, 5, 6, and 7—then goosed their allotted size to ninety-six men per team; enough for four platoons of eighteen swimmers each, plus a headquarters element of signalmen, drone technicians, machinist mates, and coxswains. To fill these teams, Turner opened their doors to the NCDUs from Fort Pierce and local Seabees, the main requirements for joining being an ability to swim one mile through choppy water and dive to a depth of fifteen feet—skills so hard to find in the fleet that the ranks were soon opened to ratings of every sort; as one man described, "cooks who never cooked, shipfitters who never worked on a ship, and storekeepers who never kept a single store." To carry all these men and their equipment, Turner allocated to each team its own APD, a high-speed transport (AP) fashioned from an overhauled World War One–era destroyer (D). Last and most important, he flipped the UDTs' reconnaissance method from the Scouts' and Raiders' nighttime use of rubber boats to Luehrs's and Acheson's daytime use of nothing more than swimsuits and goggles. In order to implement all these changes—to grow the UDT recruits from seedlings to trunks—the prodigious Koehler was made the commanding officer of the recently established Naval Combat Demolition Training and Experimental Base on the boulder-ringed beaches of Kamaole, on the west coast of Maui. Now all Turner needed was a combat commander who shared his vision. That man was on his way, but he had never had good vision; he had never even liked swimming.

6

In March 1944, Draper Kauffman arrived on Maui. In the twenty months since his creation of the NCDU's Hell Week and training pipeline at Fort Pierce, the stories of his Navy Cross and his wont for holding conferences into the "wee hours of the morning on matters big and small" had already earned him, among his demolitioneers, nicknames that ranged from "the brain" to a "combination of Don Quixote and Richard the Lionhearted." Because of this reputation, he had recently been offered positions with the two most innovative and secretive groups in the US military, the first being Donovan's OSS and the second Admiral Milton Miles's Sino-American Cooperative Organization, or SACO, operating in China. Eager to return to action but even more so to serve at the front rank of the institution that had always held him at arm's length, he had rejected both offers and instead had pulled every string within reach for a job in the theater in which the Surface Navy still reigned. Unknown to Kauffman, he had not been the only one pulling strings.

Despite being the son of Rear Admiral James "Reggie" Kauffman—an officer whose sense of fairness had led him to ignore the Navy's prohibition against issuing condoms to sailors on port visits but had also prevented him from using his influence to prevent his son's expulsion from the Navy for bad eyesight—Draper thus far had had a naval career remarkably free of intentional nepotism. Having been classmate, friend, and groomsman to the elder Kauffman, however, Kelly Turner had known Draper all his life, was well aware of his unconventional biography, and ever since Tarawa had been angling for him to leave Fort Pierce for the Pacific in order to teach his men how to get "ashore against heavy opposition." Now, at their first meeting, Turner explained his idea for the next big invasion.

"The first and most important thing is reconnaissance for depth of water. I'm thinking of having you go in around eight."

"Well, Admiral," Draper replied, momentarily taking his eyes off the map laid out before him, "it depends on the phase of the moon."

"Moon?" Turner snapped, his calm vanished. "What in hell has that got to do with it?"

In May, a fresh batch of NCDU recruits arrived on Maui. Per the direction of Koehler and Kauffman, the men were told to abandon the bulk of their gear—their green fatigues, their boots, their Mae West life jackets, even their helmets and sidearms—and slip into a pair of black Maui swim trunks and dive masks, their rough rubber edges sanded down to prevent them from biting into the face. What followed were nine seemingly endless days of training on how to systematically map an underwater landscape and blow it up—"Rocks, coral, night swimming, blasting, no rest, no sleep, suicide stuff," one trainee remembered. For no fewer than six hours a day the recruits lived in the water, perfecting their strokes until they could swim a mile before breakfast. Their only day off was Monday—"when possible." Seeing that this was the first time many of them had handled explosive fuses or tied primer cord into a trunk line, accidents were routine: "fingers blown clear off or hanging by bloody shreds of skin." Asked how long he could swim underwater with 100 pounds of powder, recruit Knorek replied, "with 100 pounds of powder I could probably stay under forever."

To accustom the men to the flat-trajectory fire of surface vessels, Turner loaned Kauffman a brace of battleships, three cruisers, and a squadron of destroyers to blast the barren island of Kahoolawe while his swimmers plotted their advances, the rifled shots skimming mere feet above their heads. The average age on those heads hovered not above twenty-four. Though most had been through the torment of NCDU Hell Week, some recently enlisted Seabees had not. Recognizing their unpreparedness for the hell that lay ahead, Kauffman requested a Marine Corps liaison for the ostensible purpose of translating his team's findings into usable data for the LVTs, then responded to the arrival of 1st Lieutenant Alan Gordon Leslie—a Canadian-born combat engineer who had shouldered a flamethrower on the pre-invasion raid of Tarawa's pier—by offering the Marine command of one of UDT 5's platoons. The legendary Leslie agreed, making himself the Corps' only representative in the pre-invasion reconnaissance that should have been the responsibility of VAC Recon Marines, who would instead be relegated to the ignominy of command post guard duty in the upcoming battle for Saipan. For Turner—a man so jealous of his domain that in the days before deployment he responded to a six-ship harbor fire by commandeering a tugboat and throttling to the scene, shouting to a retreating Navy skipper, "Go back in there and stay or I will shoot you"—the reconnaissance of Saipan's beaches would be handled by his UDTs or no one.

At the end of May, ready or not, Kauffman and the men of UDTs 5 and 7 returned to Pearl Harbor and boarded two APDs, the *Gilmer* and the *Humphreys*. In their sweltering holds the men found racks that consisted of ninety-five rectangles of steel pipe stretched with canvas and stacked in towers five high. Each rack included a pillow described by one man as simply "miserable." Underneath the bunks, the men deposited a double layer of tetrytol and nearly two tons of extra gear and explosives. When stowed, the ships slipped their docks and made for the Pacific. Watching them depart was Draper's father, whose preceding weeks had been punctuated by briefings with Nimitz in which Turner had adamantly described his idea for scouting Saipan's beaches in broad daylight and during which he had never uttered a word of protest. When the ships were gone, he returned to his quarters and penned a letter to his only son that he knew might never be delivered. He closed it as helplessly as the millions of civilian fathers all over the world: "Lots of love, lots and lots of good luck, and God bless you."

7

Silhouetted at the first breath of dawn and smoking from bombardment, to Robert Sherrod, "Saipan looked like a low-lying prehistoric monster." Just fourteen miles long and half as wide, the island rose in the middle to a single point at Mount Tapotchau. Halfway up the west coast sat the town of Garapan, the administrative center for the Japanese in the Marianas. Complete with theaters, factories, wide avenues, palm-shaded plazas, white churches, and parks, Garapan, wrote a reporter, looked like "Honolulu seen through the small end of a telescope." Hidden beneath Saipan's jungle canopy waited some 32,000 defenders—30,000 more than had been at Tarawa—numbers that allowed the Japanese to mount a defense not only at the beaches, but also from Saipan's teeth to its tail. And they had the guns and the elevation to do it.

Around the island's edges, especially in the east and north, the narrow beaches sank under the weight of tall rock cliffs. On the western side, the beaches lifted gently out of the blue lagoon, the only visual blemish to that paradise being a series of sixty-foot-long, half-sunk barges, apparently abandoned. Guarding the lagoon—except in a few spots near harbor entrances—lay a crisscross of reefs, each one thicker than a battlement, some as wide as 200 yards, some as far as a mile from the shore.

On the bright, clear morning of June 14, 1944, Turner positioned his fleet 4,000 yards to the west of Saipan in the same way a Crusader might have positioned his siege engines. His biggest question: Where were the walls thinnest? To find out, he planned to send UDT 7 to scout the approaches to the southern flank and UDT 5 to scout the northern. In the latter section, the approaches had already been broken down into four beaches: Red 2, Red 3, Green 1, and Green 2, each 700 yards wide.

At a little after 0800—while being straddled by plumes of water from Japanese shells so close that they had already wounded two sailors near the fantail—Kauffman, Leslie, and the rest of the men of UDT 5 began assembling near the side decks of the APD *Gilmer*. There, they made final adjustments to gear, including the topping off of several water jugs filled with post-mission "café royale," the chief pharmacist's medicinal brandy. This completed, each man crowded onto one of four LCPRs (Landing Craft, Personnel, Ramped, a Higgins Boat variant), where they waited for winch operators to lower them into the blue and craned necks over gunwales to glimpse the island's smoke-beclouded beaches. It was a sight like none of them had ever seen before—but the same could be said of them.

From the Celts to the Plains Indians, human conflict has seen several groups who could be classified as "naked warriors," but these groups also had the protection of a warrior's weapons. Besides his black swim trunks, life belt, canvas gloves, and kneepads, each UDT swimmer was about to go into combat with no more protection than a blue helmet, a pair of blue-dyed low-cut tennis shoes, and a thin smear of blue paint "from toe to chin." To measure every inch of real estate by means of human depth gauges, Kauffman had ordered each man in UDT 5 to stripe his body with black ship paint—thick lines at every foot and dashed lines in between. To record depths and locations of obstacles, each man carried at least two lead pencils and hung around his neck (or strapped to his leg) at least one four-by-eight-inch sandblasted plexiglass slate. For weapons, the men carried nothing except knives to cut themselves free of entanglements.

At 0840, the last of the LCPRs was detached from its winch lines, whereupon the anxious coxswains transporting UDTs 5 and 7 all turned east and plunged their throttles to the floor. From that moment, the gunners on the battleship *California* and the cruiser *Indianapolis* knew that each round they fired would whistle over the heads of their own men. The dual wakes of the UDT boats quickly shrank to single white lines, ever tinier the farther they slipped under a bank of cloud cover and the morning shadow of Saipan, where dense smoke was already curling in black waves from the sugar factory at Charon Kanoa. At 500 yards from the reef, the Japanese guns began popping with tufts of gray and red flame, followed a breath later by the roar of their shells and the white plumes of their impacts now jetting up all around them. So intense was the barrage that it forced the flotilla's coxswains into a zigzagging approach that launched swimmers into gunwales and hands onto anything that could hold them upright. Only if the blue-painted swimmers had been naked could they have felt more exposed.

When the LCPRs reached the edge of the reef, each boat turned sharply right and trimmed its speed. With shells bursting in their wakes—one landing craft was trailed by twenty-six consecutive plumes—the men dropped their helmets onto their boat decks and with nervous fingers pulled their dive masks down over their faces. Every 100 yards a pair of swimmers jumped, practically skipping across the water before collapsing under the waves. As they jumped, each pair was tossed a weighted buoy by landing craft sailors. The swimmers connected to them an 1,800-yard reel of fishing line floated by two empty powdered milk cans welded shut on the ends and connected by a wooden flange. This done, the pairs faced east and swam. Ahead were the beaches, and history. Nothing like this had ever been done before.

As the first swimmer alternately towed and paid out his reel, taking soundings at every twenty-five-yard knot in the line, the second man dove to the bottom, searching for any sign of mines, barbed wire, or other obstacles. To direct the reconnaissance, Kauffman and the other helmeted team leaders each rode a two-man rubber raft thick as a mattress and shaped like a backward surfboard that was powered by a detachable motor not much bigger than an eggbeater and just as reliable. Unable to see the bobbing swimmers in the water, the Japanese gunners trained their fire on the rafts. As mortar rounds pelted black water all around them, one raft was upended before it got off the reef. Another was hit by machine gun fire and deflated; another's motor simply died. One raft pilot, Shipfitter 1st Class Robert Christiansen—"one of the finest and best-liked men on the team"—was shot through the head, killed instantly.

"I was the center of attention for a thousand slant eyes," said one officer, casually invoking one of the tamer racisms unleashed that morning.

Sharing his raft with Boatswain's Mate 2nd Class Alex Paige—"his seeing eye"—and gripping a pair of 630 binoculars in one hand, an SRC-536 brick-sized radio in his other, Kauffman (call sign Blowgun 5) now keyed his handset and revealed the true limit of his vision: "For God's sake, tell the support ships they're firing short!"

"Skipper, those aren't shorts," squelched the reply, "they're *overs*. They're not ours."

Seeing what was happening to every other raft pair, Kauffman and his pilot ditched their mattress, anchored it to the reef, and swam. So did the rest.

Out to sea, practically every sailor and Marine in the fleet was now manning the rail of his ship, watching the UDT boats in the distance and listening in on their radio frequency. When the control tower of the USS *California* was hit by a shore battery, the UDT swimmers' protection was left entirely to the guns of the USS *Indianapolis*—at exactly the time they needed the big guns most.

Surrounded by perfect blue and a chaos of drifting black smoke, the men reacted by diving deep, many ditching their life belts, then "dolphining" for breaths, pulling themselves under the cover of water where they marveled at the husks of spent lead tumbling to the seafloor like bubbles in reverse, catching them in their outstretched fingers and tucking them away as souvenirs. As they scouted the sandy bottom, about the only thing they found were large tree-limb-fashioned tripods anchoring the white flags that Japanese artillerymen were using as range markers. On the surface, the reel men kicked and pulled and dragged their cumbersome reels, pausing among the plunks of bullet splashes to jot down depths and obstacles, or to cut tangled lines and retie them, or simply to uncross theirs with that of another pair. While they were at this, at least six swimmers had mortars explode beneath them; one man—Gunner's Mate 3rd Class Harold Hall—was blown completely out of the water. Despite their internal injuries, each man kept swimming.

To ensure that at least a partial account of what had been learned about the approaches to the Saipan beaches was successfully transferred to Turner, at the halfway point one swimmer in each pair spun around and swam back, leaving the remaining swimmer to carry on alone, and under more fire than ever. At 1000, after almost an hour of swimming and cataloguing, just when the swimmers' lives were most in jeopardy, the guns of the *California* and the *Indianapolis*, as well as various other smaller ships, lifted their fire off the beach. A planned sortie of Navy aircraft was about to swoop down from above and drench the entire shoreline with bombs and machine gun fire, making it possible for the swimmers to discover the last of the lagoon's secrets. Inexplicably, the aircraft never came. In that moment of relief, with no bombardment and no fighter bombers, the entrenched Japanese gunners—some only 10 yards from the waterline—stood up in their trenches and unleashed "point-blank" fire at the bobbing face masks in front of them.

The closer his swimmers got to the beach, the more nervous Kauffman became. At 100 yards, he tried to turn them around, but most of them kept going. At 50 yards, some began to pivot back but some didn't, closing to within 30 yards of the shore and 40 yards of the guns—so close that they ceased swimming and dug the toes of their sneakers into the sand, pulling themselves along with their gloved hands. When that last line finally did run out of water, each man backed off slightly, turned left, then sidestroked along the beach for 25 yards—edging his mask out of the water with every breath, careful to remember the locations of any gun positions; under the circumstances, not an easy thing to forget.

On the swim back, each man ignored his exhaustion and ever worsening leg cramps and stayed as close to the bottom as possible. When they neared the reef, Kauffman reboarded his mattress and offered a nearby swimmer a tow.

"Get that damned thing out of here!" yelled the swimmer.

On the other side of the now surf-slammed reef, each swimmer waited for pickup. When the landing craft arrived, the coxswains took turns motoring to each man and either dropped him a Jacobs ladder or reversed engines until he could grab hold and pull himself up. Throughout this cumbersome boarding—a period packed with "vociferous" cursing, said one survivor—every man aboard fully expected a mortar round to drop square into the boat.

As soon as the last man was loaded, Kauffman tallied his numbers and realized that—in addition to the officer killed on the air mattress—two of his swimmers were missing. Pulled in separate directions by his instinct to rescue and his orders to rush back to the fleet, Kauffman looked around at his blue-tinged, black-striped men and chose the more painful option. With the fleet waiting for his information, Kauffman ordered his boats back to the APDs.

When the men of UDT 7 arrived back at the *Humphreys,* they discovered something remarkable. Though several men had been wounded—some with serious internal injuries from the mortar blasts—not a single one of their swimmers had been lost. In fact, the only men killed had been the ones who had remained on the LCPRs as they waited for the swimmers to return. Kauffman's UDT 5 swimmers had been slightly less fortunate, with one killed, several more wounded, and two still missing, but it was nothing compared to the bloodbath that had occurred just one week before at Normandy. Turner's method—rather, the method that Luehrs and Acheson had improvised at Kwajalein—had worked.

When a cruiser reported that one of its lookouts had seen two men bobbing in the lagoon, Kauffman, former ambulance driver that he was, dropped everything, grabbed three fresh swimmers, jumped in a landing craft, and sped back to the reef. Under a rain of mortar fire, Kauffman and his volunteers scrambled across the coral, then swam like mad to within fifty yards of the figures, only to realize they were not men at all; they were coral heads. Disgusted by their credulity and under fire, the men turned around, hoping now only to save themselves. However painful that discovery must have felt, it was forgotten the moment Kauffman and his braves arrived back at the landing craft to find the two lost men sitting on board. Left behind, they had seen the landing craft and saved themselves.

8

But what had the UDTs' recon accomplished? That afternoon and all through the night, the men of UDTs 5 and 7 deciphered the pencil scratches on the dripping pile of their plexiglass slates and consolidated them into several charts, then reproduced those into several hundred copies—a precise and exhausting chore that the men of UDT 5 accomplished while the crew of the *Gilmer* fought off five Japanese gunboats that left no fewer than eight holes in her skin. At dawn the next day, two red-eyed UDT officers delivered their charts to the *Rocky Mount,* Turner's flagship. In a few hours, D-Day on Saipan would commence.

Though both men expected to hand-deliver their reports and return to their teams to prepare for their demolition assignment later that day, both were instead instantly hustled before Turner to make their reports in person. Joining the admiral for this session was General Smith. For an hour, the admiral and the general peppered the men with questions. First, and as expected, the UDTs had covered the underwater landscape, confirming the absence of mines and obstacles for the LVTs. Not so expectedly, they had drawn into the open every Japanese gun emplacement on or near the beach—a series of five trenches, with machine guns stationed every forty to fifty yards. Most important, with Leslie's help, UDT 5 had discovered that the course originally planned for the tanks was a disaster waiting to swallow them whole. Kauffman's swimmers had discovered a far better route—a narrow diagonal path of high ground from the center of Green 2 that cut northeast over the reef toward the center of Green 1. Had Jones and the VAC recon men worked every night for a week, they could not have exposed as much information as the UDTs had in two hours, nor with as little loss. "Are you the man who's been ordering my tanks around?" barked Major General Thomas Watson when confronted by Kauffman's report. "Whose tanks do you think they are?" In the end, even Watson was convinced.

At 0545, Turner's guns started. An hour after that, flights of fighter-bombers lifted off from their decks to pound anything that the guns had missed. When the invasion force launched, thick waves of black smoke from the fires burning at the sugar mill towns of Charon Kanoa and Garapan obscured everything from the beaches to Mount Tapotchau. Guided by the information gained the day before, plus the highway of buoys laid out by the UDTs, 732 LVTs cut through the smoke to land some 8,000 Marines on the beaches in no more than twenty minutes. Close behind, Kauffman and Ensign Jack Adams of UDT 5—going into their third day with almost no sleep and still wearing nothing but swim trunks—boarded separate LVTs to lead in the tanks. As Adams probed for the path from his LVT, Kauffman tossed buoys from his to mark the way, taking fire all the while. Following close behind was Leslie in a tank transport, coaxing the reluctant coxswain to land on the surf-washed reef to drop his ramp and his tank. When the tanks were finally ashore, Kauffman and Leslie—dressed as conspicuously as tourists, remembered one man—hailed a passing LVT and rode it to the beachhead to receive their reef demolition instructions. It would be several days before anyone could pull Kauffman away from the beach. It would take even longer for Turner to decide if he needed to—if he needed Kauffman and his UDTs for an altogether different kind of mission.

9

IN THE WEEKS that followed the Saipan invasion, the 2nd Marine Division seized Garapan, halfway along the island's west coast. This provided ground forces with a logistics hub that could cut the time it took to get supplies from the ships to the front lines—or it would, just as soon as two small island redoubts in Garapan's harbor were wrested away from the Japanese. With the VAC Recon Marines still relegated to command post guard duty, Turner now looked to the only unconventional unit over which he still had authority—the UDTs. The man acting as Turner's voice was his workhorse chief of staff, Captain Paul Theiss.

When Draper frantically appeared on the *Rocky Mount* at two o'clock in the morning to attempt to reverse this assignment, Theiss, true to form, was still awake.

"I don't think there are three men in the UDTs who have ever fired a rifle," Draper protested. In fact, he continued, he had not fired one himself in over ten years.

"Now, look," Theiss pushed back, "your UDT people are a special unit for all kinds of operations"; so much so that even Captain Carl "Squeaky" Anderson—the indomitable beachmaster of Saipan—had already begun calling the UDTs "his own All-American football team."

Though Kauffman possessed more bravery than ten average men combined, he had none of Bucklew's, Halperin's, or Leslie's instincts for offensive combat, or, more important, their training. Nor did he have any long-range plans to extend the UDTs' mission past the surf zone. Indeed, when several of his men had gone missing on Saipan, having attached themselves to a Marine battalion (just as many UDT swimmers and NCDU demolitioneers had done at Kwajalein, Roi-Namur, and Normandy), Kauffman gave them a choice: leave UDTs for good or spend five days on burial duty. The men had chosen the five days, and Kauffman had only made them stay for three. Now, Theiss was giving Kauffman a choice, a military euphemism for an order. Just as Kauffman was about to accept the order, or the consequences for refusing, Captain Jack Taylor appeared at the door of Theiss's stateroom wearing a bathrobe. When Taylor heard the subject of the conversation, he took Kauffman's place in the argument and won. By the time Kauffman departed, Theiss had canceled the order.

Two nights later, Kauffman was again awakened to learn that the UDTs had been volunteered for another unusual mission: this time to clear six Japanese vessels, all half sunk in Garapan Harbor, all just as dangerous as the booby-trapped sniper nests that had attacked UDT 7 in the lagoon. Once again, Kauffman frantically sped back to the *Rocky Mount* to protest.

"Now, just calm down, Draper," said Captain Taylor when Kauffman arrived. "The message will be canceled . . . You can go back and relax." What Taylor didn't address was the possibility of future messages. After all, it had taken only a few weeks of operational employment before many Navy planners had begun to see the UDTs as more than just reconnaissance and demolition units, and instead as something comparable to Jones's VAC Recon Force—in Kauffman's words, *jacks of all trades, capable of anything.* They weren't. The question that Turner and Navy planners had to decide: Did they need to be? What happened next would give them their answer.

10

Two miles south of Saipan, cliff-shrouded Tinian rose out of the water as flat as an aircraft carrier, which was exactly the reason that Army and Navy planners wanted it. On July 1, ten F4F Wildcats escorted a single torpedo bomber on a special reconnaissance mission to study every yard of Tinian's coast, searching for a break in the cliffs through which the Marines might squeeze. On board the torpedo bomber was Kauffman, who, while "hedgehopping to as low as 25 feet" above the rocks, squinted through his Coke-bottle glasses and noted every cleft.

Short on beaches but long on defenders—as many as 9,000 Japanese soldiers, more than three times the number at Tarawa—Tinian possessed an obvious front-door path of entry made up of a mile-long beach on its southwest coast, just in front of Tinian Town, the island's most significant population center. With a beach that wide, Turner would be able to replicate his storm landing of 700 LVTs in twenty minutes. General Smith snorted at such logistical precision. Because the Tinian Town beaches were out of range of his artillery positions on Saipan, because they were so obvious a target, and because they possessed the fiercest defenses on the whole island, he had opposed them even before the fleet had left Hawaii. Instead, he preferred two "infinitesimal" beaches on the rocky northwest coast—White 1 at 65 yards and White 2 at 130.

"You can't possibly land two divisions on those beaches," said Turner. "You need ten times that amount of room . . . The Japs will move in on you before you get all your men ashore and then you will be in a jam!"

"If we go ashore at Tinian Town," said Smith in his Alabama drawl, "we'll have another Tarawa—sure as hell. The Japs will murder us."

"You are not going to land on the White beaches. I won't land you there."

"Oh yes you will," said Smith. "You'll land me any goddamned place I tell you to."

"I'm telling you it can't be done. It's absolutely impossible."

"How do you know it's impossible," said Smith. "You're so goddamned scared that your boats will be hurt."

Watching this encounter was Kauffman, whose presence did nothing to douse the "sparks."

"All right," said Turner. "We'll send Draper in with his teams into the White beaches, and see just how good they are."

"The hell we will," said Smith. "What you'll do is tell Draper he's to come back and say they're impossible to land on."

In the end, the admiral and the general agreed on a compromise: a reconnaissance of Tinian's beach approaches, plus the beaches themselves, by the Marine Corps' and Navy's respective reconnaissance units, the VAC Recon Battalion, and the UDTs; units that had never worked together, nor worked in the method that was about to be employed, at least not in any real operation. The method would reflect the concerns of both Turner and Smith, who needed to conceal their intended landing sites from the enemy. In order to do so, the reconnaissance would have to be conducted at night, by just a handful of swimmers and amid

Japanese patrols whose front-row seats to the ransacking of Saipan now guaranteed them to be the jumpiest soldiers in the entire Pacific, making these beaches the most dangerous in the world.

To prepare for this mission, on the night of July 9, the Recon Marines and UDT sailors met in Saipan's Magicienne Bay to conduct a rehearsal, during which they tried to iron out the wrinkles in their respective tactics. It didn't go well. Weather, waves, surf, darkness, personalities, and vastly different swimming levels all conspired to prevent the teams from finding the dummy mines that had been hidden and prolonged the rehearsal so that the last swimmers did not return to their rubber boats until dawn. What they needed was another week of exercises; what they got was a few hours of sleep.

On the afternoon of July 10, the reconnaissance teams boarded APDs *Stringham* and *Gilmer,* then began preparing their rubber boats and equipment: plexiglass slates, dive masks, Ka-Bar knives, life belts, condom-encased penlights, even some recently acquired dye packets reserved for aviators who had crash-landed in the water. Aboard the *Stringham* were twenty men from VAC Recon Company A and an eight-man squad from UDT 7; there was a similar disposition for the *Gilmer,* except drawn from Company B and Kauffman's UDT 5. Naturally, Kauffman included himself in the force list; because Jones admittedly swam badly, he did not.

In charge of the reconnaissance would be the overall commander of the Tinian Assault Force, Rear Admiral Harry Hill. Having already commanded a group for Turner at Tarawa and orchestrated the bombardment of Engebi—a bombardment that had even outdone Kwajalein's—Hill had since then become, after Turner, the Navy's most enthusiastic advocate of pre-invasion reconnaissance. As such, he planned to personally monitor the Tinian reconnaissance mission from his flagship. Silver-haired, black-eyebrowed, known to the press as "Handsome Harry" and to the fleet by his brevity code "Pin-up," Hill's involvement now inspired additional call signs: swimmers in the water would be identified as brunettes; those safely recovered as blondes.

At nightfall on July 10, under a moonless, cloudy sky, both sets of brunettes departed their APDs aboard a daisy chain of blacked-out rubber boats now towed by landing craft whose coughs had been silenced by repositioning their exhausts underwater. Instead of blue paint and black hash lines, each man now wore a thin smear of silver ship grease and a gray monk's hood to hopefully conceal his silhouette on the ash-colored rock-sand beaches. None of them carried any weapon heavier than a knife.

At around 2030, as the wind and the slap of rubber against the chop kicked up flecks of salt water into the men's faces, each boat crew cut their umbilicals, dipped their oars, and began the long pull toward the shadow of Tinian. At some 500 yards from the shore, still outside the gathering swells of surf break, the *Stringham*'s swimmers eased themselves into the waves and started stroking toward a stretch on Tinian's east coast that planners had designated as Yellow Beach. On the way in, UDT swimmers dove and slid along the sea floor like blind men over braille marks. At about the halfway point, the team discovered a heavily mined reef interrupted by gnarled volcanic boulders. As they scratched waterproof chalk and pencil marks onto their slates, several explosions detonated near the shore, prompting the UDT swimmers to turn back to the boats. The Marines—being Marines—kept going. Crawling ashore (one officer made it 30 yards inland), these intrepids discovered a beach guarded by sentries, pillboxes, and double belts of barbed wire, and bookended by 100-foot cliffs that Japanese work crews were noisily transforming into ramparts capable of cutting into the flanks of any invasion force. So much for Yellow Beach.

On the west coast, the *Gilmer*'s reconnaissance teams were having problems of their own. Having compensated for an anticipated southward current that had actually been going in the other direction, the northern team reached the coast and instead of finding their intended beach, White 1, found nothing but rock cliffs. Led by Navy lieutenant Jack Debold, both the Recon Marines and the UDT swimmers turned north, then half swam, half crawled over wave-lashed rocks for some 300 yards, found nothing, then repeated the effort in the other direction.

To the south, Kauffman and his team had also drifted north, and now, instead of landing on White 2—the 130-yard back door to Tinian that had prompted Smith's ultimatum—found themselves at White 1, the 60-yard plot of sand just wide enough to park sixteen LVTs so long as not an inch of space could be seen between them. On the way in, Kauffman and his swimmers had found a shelf of coral some twenty yards from the waterline but nothing more. Even a line of suspected mines that intelligence analysts had spotted in aerial photographs turned out to be nothing. Now, with no sign of defenses—no mines, no aprons of barbed wire, no pillboxes—both Marines and UDTs crawled out of the surf and into the trees, hunting for gaps in the bluffs large enough to squeeze the tanks through. Once the inland reconnaissance was complete, the men backed out to sea, sweeping away their tracks with palm fronds as they went. So confident had the Japanese been in the beach's unsuitability for a landing that the only excitement of the reconnaissance had come from one UDT swimmer goading a Marine into sneaking up behind Kauffman and wrapping a garrote around his neck.

Chased from the coast by a sudden cloud shift that had uncovered a nearly full moon, the swimmers on both sides of Tinian were now kicking for the boats. As they did, a light fog blew in and collided with a deepening chop, making it impossible for brunettes to see anything unless cresting the top of a swell. The consequences of this were separated swim pairs who succumbed to an irrational fear that they were being pursued, prompting many who encountered another swimmer in the blackness to silently circle until confirming he was not a Japanese tail. The loss of orientation and direction caused many to swim past the waiting rubber boats, then past the landing craft too, finding themselves adrift in the Pacific.

Despite the coming assault, a logistical nightmare that pushed the boundaries of any person's capacity for detail, Admiral Hill remained awake. Every half hour, landing craft coxswains heard the same voice crackle over the TBS radio: "How many blondes? How many brunettes? This is Pin-up himself." With no blondes yet, Hill directed his ships and planes to be ready to conduct a "full-scale air-sea rescue" at dawn.

At around 0430, eight hours since the swimmers had departed their landing craft, Hill finally got an initial report on their status. The first group to be found was Kauffman's, picked up by the *Gilmer* while they were treading water somewhere between Tinian and Saipan, all staggering with exhaustion, their tongues swollen from salt water. The *Gilmer*'s rescue was soon followed by many more, including one by a minesweeper whose crew spotted a swimmer by the moonlight he used to reflect off his dive mask.

Once all the Recon Marines and UDT swimmers had been recovered, their information was collected and passed on to the respective staffs of Turner and Smith. Missing from the reports was any mention of the beach at White 2, the reason Smith had insisted on a reconnaissance in the first place. This failure meant that the teams would have to repeat their work.

On the next night, planners took no chances and entrusted the mission to Kauffman, who led a team of twelve UDT swimmers and six Marines, a ratio reversed from that of the night before. To ensure the team hit the right beach, the rubber boats were outfitted with small "window" reflectors made of wire and SCR-200 radios so that the *Stringham*'s radarmen could track the rubber flotilla's progress and its radiomen could transmit course corrections. So aided, Kauffman and his men swam right to the center of White 2. Except for the rhythm of the surf, it was a stretch of beach as silent as a graveyard. As Kauffman readied himself to crawl ashore, he picked up the unmistakable sound of two of his men having an audible conversation. Furious at their lack of discipline, Kauffman prepared a rebuke before realizing just in time that the voices he was hearing were Japanese. Pressing his hands into the sand, Kauffman slowly lifted his body and pushed himself backward, then repeated the movement until safely submerged. Turning left, he swam north about half the length of a football field and stopped. Fearful that his black swim trunks would stand out against the light-colored earth, he stripped them off, edged to a dry patch of sand, rolled until every inch of his naked body was covered, then crawled inland to scout for beach exits. To the south, two other UDT swimmers also crawled ashore to locate a potential string of shore mines. As they did, a Japanese patrol appeared on the beach, suddenly casting shadows across the sand from their oil lanterns. Clutching their sheathed Ka-Bars, the pair froze, suddenly feeling "as big as houses," and held their breath as the patrol approached, then walked right past, blinded by the light of their own lamps.

The next morning, at a briefing for Admiral Turner and General Smith, Kauffman and Jones presented the respective reports of the UDTs and the VAC Recon. Regarding White 2, Kauffman and Jones reported only one drawback: an outlying reef too pitted with potholes for wheeled vehicles. Except for its size, the beach was perfect. Having never seen Turner "so mean and cantankerous" on an issue, which was saying something, "Handsome Harry" Hill listened to the reconnaissance report and held his breath. He needn't have; it was clear that Smith and the Marines had won the battle of the beaches.

It would take several more weeks to be clear that Turner too had won a victory, his for the future of pre-invasion reconnaissance.

11

On the morning of July 24, Jig Day, Admiral Hill positioned a portion of his fleet off the southwest coast of Tinian Town, then launched a single flotilla of landing craft. Each of these was packed to the gunwales not with rifles and Marines, but with explosives and the 100 or so swimmers of UDT 7. Their purpose: to make such a racket when blowing the southwestern reef that the Japanese would turn their attention away from every other potential landing site—the equivalent of clutching a man by the collar so he doesn't notice the bottle about to land on his head.

Supporting UDT 7's diversion were the sixteen-inch guns of the USS *Colorado,* now rifling engine-block-sized shells above the swimmers' heads and into the Japanese defenses. The response was a multi-shot volley from a Japanese shore battery that slammed a hail of six-inch shells into the *Colorado*'s ribs, killing forty-three American sailors and wounding more than four times that. Commander Seymour Owens, husband of Kauffman's cousin and skipper of the destroyer *Norman Scott,* aware of how critical the *Colorado*'s guns were to UDT 7's survival, maneuvered his comparably smaller ship in order to draw the Japanese fire. The ploy worked, and in seconds the *Norman Scott* was shuddering beneath the impact of six successive rounds, ultimately killing twenty-three of her crew, including Owens, who was posthumously awarded a Navy Cross, but whose name today is just another black-shoe legend to have faded from memory after his role in supporting Naval Special Warfare.

While Owens was giving his life defending UDT 7's diversion, Kauffman and UDT 5 were to the northwest under a wind-whipped sea struggling to drape the reef with explosives, an effort that Kauffman was ultimately forced to abort. No matter; Kauffman and his team had already performed a function more important than underwater demolition.

At 0717, after Kauffman and his men had cleared the coral, sixteen LVTs carrying the first wave of 200 Marines embarked on a twenty-six-minute, knuckle-clenching transit to White 2, during which every man aboard feared the assault would be another Tarawa. It wasn't. At the unexploded reef, the LVTs crawled right over; at the pocket-sized beaches, the major problem was parking space, quickly solved by the fleet's enterprising coxswains, who simply "nosed up against the rocky cliffs" and let their Marines climb up.

So fast and unexpected were the landings on Tinian's White Beaches that during the entirety of the mission, the whole of the 4th Marine Division suffered just five casualties—the first not incurred until they had penetrated 1,500 yards inland. It was, wrote Smith, a "singular success," a result of surprise—"fatal to the Jap mentality"—and "the most unorthodox plan of assault ever attempted in the Pacific." Such a plan had been made possible only because of a reconnaissance that had found a strip of sand as useful to an invasion force as had been the goat path that carried the Persians around the Spartans at Thermopylae. It was an achievement that helped clarify the future of the men who had made this goat path possible.

12

Before the summer of Saipan, the American strategy of island hopping in the Central Pacific had been something of a misnomer. Intending to limit the casualties of US troops by limiting the number of island targets they had to take, planners had nevertheless treated every atoll like it was a traditional battlefield, the flanks being every island that surrounded the main one, all with flanks needing to be scouted, seized, or held. It had been more like island smothering. Had the war been prosecuted this way on the enormous islands of the South Pacific, planners would have surely needed all sorts of special units for all sorts of special missions—blowing railways, arming natives, mining shipping, sowing chaos; missions that exceeded even the scouting and raiding capabilities of the VAC Recon Marines. In the immediate wake of Tinian, the only unit in the Central Pacific capable of such operational flexibility was UDT 10, a team whose ranks—including its commanding officer—were bolstered by twenty-nine recently inducted operatives from the OSS Maritime Unit, who had brought along eleven tons of special equipment, or 750 pounds per man, of everything from the bubbleless rebreather systems and motorized submersibles needed to cripple an enemy ship or land a partisan agent on an enemy coast. Yet none of this proved as valuable to the Pacific War effort as the OSS's simple demonstration of feet strapped with swim fins. After the achievement at Tinian—and except for a series of submarine-launched missions to determine the enemy's presence in Palau in August 1945 that ended in the capture and death of two OSS operatives and one UDT swimmer—Navy planners like Turner no longer felt compelled to treat every unsecured island on their path to Japan as a vulnerable back door; they just needed to find the easiest one to get on. And of all the special units in the Pacific Theater, only one had been created for that explicit purpose.

By the fall of 1944, the Navy's Underwater Demolition Teams were the most indispensable of all the US military's special operations units, a fact directly attributable to the Central Pacific planners who would no longer go anywhere without their reconnaissance reports. "[The UDTs] are an essential part of our amphibious organization for the remainder of the war," wrote Turner on the last day of combat on Tinian. "It is questionable if we could have made our landings except after great losses, if we had not had these teams to prepare the way." This assessment was immediately echoed by Admiral Conolly, who concluded his invasion at Guam by declaring that without the UDTs' discovery and demolition of some 640 obstacles along the 3,000 yards of beaches—including the nearly car-sized coconut log cribs filled with loose coral—the "landings could not have been made." There, in spite of orders forbidding them to do so, three demolition swimmers—including Gunner's Mate 1st Class Henry L. Green—had grown so convinced of the UDTs' worth that they had planted a white butcher-block-sized sign at the water's edge with the following message: "U.S. MARINES, WELCOME TO USO, GREETINGS FROM UDT-4." Hearing of this, Admiral Conolly had summoned the team's commander to his stateroom in order to hand him a starched counseling, but instead had neutralized his own admonishments by stopping the young officer at the door and declaring, "Wait till I tell Turner. He'll have those Marine Generals eating crow!"

To recognize their contribution in the taking of the Marianas, Turner showered the UDTs with awards: more than 60 Silver Stars and 300 Bronze Stars, reportedly "the largest mass recommendation" for sailors and Marines in the war up to that point. Given the "importance of the job," Conolly would have pinned Navy Crosses on the commanding officers of UDTs 3 and 4 but in the end settled for Silver Stars, each of them presented by none other than Admiral Kauffman, Draper's father. As for Draper himself, rumors circulated about his nomination for the Medal of Honor, an accolade his father, chairman of the awards board in the Pacific, lobbied against for fear of the medal's association with recklessness. In the end, Draper received a Navy Cross, his second, pinned on by his father with a comment that allowed the photographer to catch the serious young man in a laugh: "Thank the Lord you found a clean shirt!"

Along with the awards came upgrades: more comfortable dive masks,

Rear Admiral James L. Kauffman presents the Navy Cross to his son, Lieutenant Commander Draper Kauffman.

Owen Churchill–patented swim fins, wrist compasses, even better tennis shoes that—like those in style for teenage girls—laced above the ankle but whose soles were thick enough to allow them to walk on coral. Within two months of Tinian, Turner was swapping out each UDT's dilapidated APD for a newer one with topside bunks—forever endearing himself to the men who rode them—and overseeing the creation of a formal curriculum at the Experimental Training base in Maui through which all UDT swimmers would now pass. Most important, he established a heretofore nonexistent position to command all UDT operations and enlisted for the job Captain B. Hall "Red" Hanlon, a bulldog-faced battleship skipper of "flight-speed tempo" who looked like he "could lick any man in the house," and who, one subordinate would say, was "the only guy who didn't take Hell Week" who we ever "[bought] as a true UDT man." "Have patience with screwball ideas and people," Turner told Hanlon upon taking command. "Many of them have value." Aboard his flagship, the *Gilmer,* Hanlon not only tolerated the screwball ideas, he encouraged them, personally directing the fleet's guns during landings, improving safety standards during training, instituting rehearsals, staggering landing craft to avoid the attention of Japanese gunners, and drastically speeding up the process of transferring all the data scrawled onto each plexiglass slate into the heads of the fleet's landing craft coxswains. In short order, Turner's experiment was ready to move beyond the narrow lane of Nimitz's Central Pacific.

In December 1944, Turner sent two of his UDTs to support the mine-packed landings at Lingayen Gulf in MacArthur's South Pacific. They came with a note to Task Force Commander T. S. Wilkinson describing how the UDTs in the Central Pacific had already developed "into a big business," and would soon number around forty teams, or roughly 4,000 swimmers. The post-invasion reaction by amphibious force commander Admiral Daniel Barbey was effusive: "The results achieved by these UDTs," Barbey began, "are far above anything that anyone, not informed, might imagine. It seems incredible that men in small boats and men swimming should be able to close a heavily defended, hostile beach in broad daylight to almost the high-water mark without receiving such severe damage . . . That they are able to do so is due not only to the gunfire and plane barrage, but to the skill and intrepidity of these men themselves. When one watches them perform under the gunfire of the enemy, one cannot fail to be impressed by their boundless courage. The Nation's future is safe when it is defended by such men as these." It was remarkable praise for a unit that had not even existed twelve months earlier, and noteworthy because in the entire Pacific War no other special unit's acclaim would even come close. And the evidence was obvious.

With no pressing need for the types of operations they seemed to have been intended to perform, the swimmers of UDT 10—a third of whom were Donovan's specially trained Maritime Operatives—had been forced to abandon their eleven tons of OSS equipment in Maui before being loaded aboard the APD *Rathburne* for whatever Turner and the Fifth Amphibious Force needed. What was needed was a series of daytime beach reconnaissance missions like the other UDTs performed: swimming on line right up to the water's edge while assailed by mortars, machine guns, and in the Palaus, even by sharks, the biggest one some six to eight feet long. Personally recognized by Admirals Nimitz and Jesse B. Oldendorf for its superlative performances—including the white-knuckling of the *Rathburne*'s deck guns to shoot down two kamikazes, one within fifty feet of her fantail—UDT 10 would also make a name for itself as the UDTs' "Golden Horseshoe," a nickname earned for incurring no casualties. Besides this, however, and in spite of their training in everything from limpet attacks to land warfare, UDT 10's record was no more remarkable than that of any other team in the fleet, and the unit would never employ a single pound of its eleven tons of OSS equipment. Subordination to the UDTs' mission would not be a fate limited to the OSS Maritime Unit, but would extend to other units too.

13

NOWHERE WAS THE PREEMINENT RANKING of the UDTs in the Fifth Amphibious Force's list of special units more evident than upon the sulfuric wastes of Iwo Jima, a battle in which the US Marine Corps' contribution to victory outweighed the Navy's in every category—every category but one. There, on the cloud-banked morning of February 17, 1945, Red Hanlon dispatched a lone flotilla of twelve landing craft toward Mount Suribachi and into a curtain of metal fired from the guns hidden inside her rail-tracked caves. Aboard these vessels, open-throttled and cutting hard swerves to avoid the geysers of raining mortars, was a 120-man reconnaissance force, each man gleaming as white as a terra-cotta statue—the result of being smeared with silver paint to blend in with the sun-glinting swells, then coated with cocoa butter to retain body heat in the bone-chilling fifty-nine-degree water. Making up this army were 100 swimmers pulled from UDTs 12, 13, 14, and 15, then augmented by 20 more from Jones's VAC Recon Marines, conspicuously without their green fatigues and without their own mission.

Diving to the ocean floor and venturing upward only when the need for oxygen demanded an ascent through so many descending bullets that they looked like "falling leaves" in an underwater forest, each UDT swimmer at Iwo Jima did his best to improve his chances by timing his breaths to coincide with a wave trough and not a swell; even so, each breach filled his ears with so much chaos that it sounded like he was inches from a passing freight train. Tasked to fill small tobacco bags with black sand from the beaches in order to determine if they could support the weight of the tanks, the reconnaissance swimmers were now required to get so close that one UDT man carried a pack of cigarettes so he could later boast that he had smoked ashore before the Marines had even landed (they wouldn't light, he said afterward) and another who came face-to-face with a Japanese soldier who "disgustedly" threw his rifle on the ground to "shake his fist at the swimmers" he could not hit.

Knowing the unprecedented proximity that his men would have to get to the enemy, Hanlon had prepared by subordinating the fire support of an entire fleet: six battleships, five cruisers, sixteen destroyers, and twelve LCI(G)s (Landing Craft Infantry gunboats). These last—painted black, brown, green, and gray, and splashed with "zigzag orange"—looked like a staggered line of bizarrely elongated fishing trawlers, but because of the white wakes behind and the red flashes before, seemed as heroic as the front rank of a cavalry charge. Lacking spurs and outstretched sabers, these sailor-cavalrymen nevertheless rode to the UDTs' rescue with the nautical equivalent of the reins in their teeth—launching rockets, firing machine guns, hand-loading tray after tray of shells into their 40-millimeter cannons.

LCI(G) 633 en route to Iwo Jima.

Within moments after they crossed the threshold to the enemy's farthest range, Japanese shells began slamming into the LCI(G)s, ripping three-by-four-foot holes at their water lines and shredding the bulkheads through pilothouses, radio shacks, captain's cabins, crew's heads. All down the line, the gunboat sailors rushed to dog doors, plug holes, fight fires, and to pump water out of compartments to prevent sinking or to pump it in to douse flames about to spread to ammunition stocks. While the UDT and VAC Recon swimmers were able to shield themselves beneath a protective blanket of salt water, the LCI(G) gun crews were unable to shield themselves with anything more than their helmets, the flimsy rings of two-inch plastic armor that surrounded their open-aired gun tubs, and the smears of flash cream meant to keep gasoline flames from peeling the skin from their faces. The impact on the sailors ranged from one gunner's hands stitched with shrapnel to another's hands blown clean off. Others died crumpled in their seats, their feet almost buried beneath blood-flecked shells they fired defending the UDTs' reconnaissance.

At 1,500 yards from the black-sand beaches, the center LCI(G) carrying Draper Kauffman—now Hanlon's chief of staff and the overall commander of the UDT swimmers—was struck by an eight-inch shell, almost immediately slowing the vessel to a four-knot crawl and knocking it into a starboard list. As damage controlmen fought to stop the flow of seawater into the ship's hold by plugging the hole with a mattress, Kauffman's command post was hit with a fresh volley that killed his radioman and forced him to cross-deck to another gunboat. Stepping aboard the vessel—a vessel whose decks were so awash with blood that some sailors were on their hands and knees to keep from slipping—Kauffman ignored the chaos, "climbed to the conning tower"—the most exposed part of the ship—"and stood there peering through his binoculars, like nothing was going on." Within five minutes of transfer, this vessel too was on fire, forcing it to make for the open ocean. "[Like] a general who had his horse shot out from under him," Kauffman hailed a passing destroyer whose captain recognized the bespectacled face and shouted, "Get away from here, you Jonah!"

As it had been with Admiral Hall's destroyers in the assault of Omaha Beach, the success of the reconnaissance of Iwo Jima's eastern approaches was largely due to the audacity of Hanlon's LCI(G)s, whose crews had never stopped plugging the holes in their sides and whose skippers had never stopped requesting to "return to the firing line." By the end of the UDTs' mission—a mission that cost just two UDT swimmers (one missing and most likely drowned; one shot through the head)—the LCI(G)s' losses had totaled 47 sailors killed and another 153 wounded, including one UDT liaison, Ensign Frank Jirka, who had both feet blown off and whose first response had been to apologize for the loss of his borrowed shoes. Of the twelve vessels that had made the assault, eleven had been "put out of action" and the other had sunk with three men aboard. It was a staggering sacrifice but one that, by midnight, had helped produce three hundred copies of every chart the landing force would need for Iwo Jima's invasion. More than that, it was a sacrifice whose cost demonstrated—better than anything else to date—the importance that the Navy's planners now placed on the UDTs.

14

RESOUNDING PROOF OF THE UDTs' importance to the future of amphibious reconnaissance—if indeed it was still needed—came in April 1945 at Okinawa. An island with twice the square footage of Chicago and surrounded by a similar number of islet suburbs, the battlespace exhibited all the unguarded flanks that Central Pacific planners had long had the luxury to ignore.

Created explicitly for this purpose, the Jones-led VAC Recon Battalion once again found themselves tasked with their own force-level,

Ship Fitter 1st Class John Regan with brandy after Borneo, Balikpapan Operation.

inland reconnaissance missions. These included the clearing of several islets capable of reaching the main landing beaches with artillery and the sweeping of many more to separate the pockets of Japanese soldiers from Japanese children. Both missions were strategic, and required both nerve and talent to accomplish. However, except for the addition of some Army Scouts and Marine dog handlers, both missions were allocated no more resources than that of the VAC Recon Battalion's roughly 250 Marines—an allocation far below that already assigned to the UDTs, and an allocation for the UDTs that could only mean one thing: higher expectations.

The force assembled for the reconnaissance of Okinawa's beaches consisted of ten UDTs of 100 men each—almost a thousand swimmers—plus fourteen APDs and another flotilla of LCI(G) gunboats. It was more protection than they'd ever had before. Thus supported, the UDTs went on to discover and destroy some 400 plywood suicide boats hidden in caves and intended as nighttime kamikazes, then blew channels blocked with sunken vessels and cleared nearly 3,000 man-sized wooden posts wedged into the coral from more than 4,000 yards of beach approaches. On the morning of the invasion, UDT swimmers ensured that the troops would land on the right beaches by riding the first wave of landing craft themselves—one blond UDT petty officer named Samuel Conrad even jumped free of the safety of his craft to lead a line of tanks ashore by walking upright and ahead of them as a human depth gauge through a three-foot-deep lagoon besieged by sniper and mortar fire in nothing more than a swimsuit and a helmet. They did all this while "freezing by inches" in water so cold their legs doubled up in cramps and their hands grew too numb to mark their slates; one man mistook the sound of "the incessant machine gun fire in the background as the chattering of [his] own teeth." Hostages to the cold and beset by the threat of the kamikazes, the only relief a UDT swimmer experienced during this campaign came when—dripping black water mixed with oil—he collapsed into that "small heaven" that was the bottom of his landing craft to wrap himself in a wool blanket and suck down a post-mission two-ounce bottle of brandy.

As they had in every battle since Kwajalein, the UDTs at Okinawa predictably demonstrated to planners the indispensability of their investments in the water phase of an amphibious operation. It was also, unpredictably, the battle where they began to demonstrate an interest in wider operational responsibilities. This interest just happened to coincide with a recent addition to the UDTs' equipment—rifles for every enlisted man and shoulder-worn pistols for every chief petty officer and higher. At the islet of Kamiyama, not long after the VAC Recon Battalion cleared the island of Japanese, a boat crew from UDT 19 brazenly paddled ashore armed with nothing more than a carbine and a pistol. When Japanese snipers interrupted their reconnaissance and shot one officer through the wrist and leg, Ensign Robert Killough grabbed the wounded man's .45, ordered his men to swim the officer to safety, then charged the snipers, firing "clip after clip" as he ducked "behind rocks and trees." As short on ammunition and clothes as he was long on bravery, Killough held off the snipers and multiple grenade attacks until he saw his men clear the reef, then sprinted for the beach and swam for his life. Ensign Killough was not the only swimmer to push the envelope of his training and mandate. After scouting the approaches to the island of Tsugen Shima, one UDT chief petty officer "bawled" out a pair of his swimmers for extending their reconnaissance past the beach. "I was perfectly safe, chief," the accused responded indignantly. "My buddy was covering me with his knife."

For Operation Olympic, the invasion of Kyushu, the southernmost island of Japan, Turner planned to employ thirty UDTs—more than 3,000 swimmers. Anticipating even more beaches for Operation Coronet, the follow-up invasion of mainland Japan, planners decided to open the ranks of the UDTs to Army and Marine Corps volunteers. At Maui in June, Koehler began training Team George, what would be a UDT made up of soldiers drawn from MacArthur's Sixth and Eighth armies. In the same month, UDT trainers began hustling Marine Corps volunteers through a hasty three-week underwater demolition course on Okinawa's beaches. Whether it was the presence of these new infantry veterans at Maui or Okinawa, the UDTs' yearlong partnership with the VAC Recon Battalion, or the influence of Marine liaisons like Gordon Leslie (the flamethrower-wielding Scout-Sniper whose twelve months with UDT 5 had made him the team's executive officer), Koehler-the-orchid-grower now began splicing Maui's training with marksmanship, patrolling, even small-unit tactics. Had the war continued for another year, who knows how far he would have stretched the scope of UDT operations? But it was not to be. Not yet.

On August 15, 1945, while MacArthur and all the other titans of the Pacific War stood in ranked silence aboard the USS *Missouri,* Kauffman led his UDT swimmers into a harbor on mainland Japan that was said to be holding a cache of two-man suicide torpedoes. Reaching a pier that cut the beach in two, he climbed the ladder in fins and dive mask, and instead of finding any treachery at the top, was faced by a formation of some 400 white-uniformed Japanese troops, whose immaculate commander approached and in intelligible English asked to see Kauffman's commanding officer. "I am the commanding officer," he replied, ignoring the Japanese officer's outstretched hand and doing his best not to trip over his fins. "It was really about the most undignified surrender that was ever accepted," Kauffman said afterward. The next day, after his mission was complete, Kauffman and four of his UDT comrades disobeyed MacArthur's orders, donned Marine Corps fatigues, and enlisted a jeep for a road trip that took them through the devastation that stretched from Yokohama to a small store on the outskirts of Tokyo, where they gave the owner five dollars for five glass-encased dolls. Two weeks later, when Kauffman finally admitted his crime, Admiral Oldendorf exploded. "Dammit to hell!" he said. "I knew it was [you] damned UDTs. I knew nobody but you guys would do such a damn thing as that! Now you listen to me . . . Don't you ever, ever go into Tokyo ahead of General MacArthur again!" It was not the last time the Navy would beat the Army in a foot race.

Though intended simply to solve the problem of the Central Pacific's coral, what Turner had created instead was his own on-call reconnaissance and demolition unit—one that he had never had to argue with Howlin' Mad Smith to employ. Because the results of their missions had become so central to the Navy's amphibious operations, no other special unit in all of World War II had grown as fast or as large, or become as indispensable—not the Raiders, the Rangers, the Marauders, the VAC Recon Battalion, and certainly not the OSS Maritime Unit. The UDTs' indispensability was proven once again at the war's end when planners in every branch of the US military began to unceremoniously disband their special units; by the time the culling ended, the OSS Maritime Unit was gone, as was the VAC Recon Battalion, with the Marine Corps' reconnaissance missions left to division-level units. Only one special unit had survived: the UDTs. Downsized to two half-size teams on each coast, they were nevertheless a nucleus of stored knowledge for future amphibious landings. To the American public, it meant that the UDTs were the last standing heroes of the war.

Unlike Carlson's Raiders, Darby's Rangers, and Merrill's Marauders, the UDTs were never featured in stories by newspapermen during the war. For the Navy, they were a weapon too critical to future invasions to be exposed to press coverage. Even the irrepressible Ernie Pyle had been muzzled. Now, with the end of the war, articles with titles like "Warriors in Trunks" and "The Paddlefoot Commandos" were appearing in publications ranging from *All Hands* to North Carolina's *Washington Daily News,* each one an attempt to satisfy the public's growing curiosity. Even *Yank*—the US Army weekly—ran a two-page article. On October 25, 1945, just seventy-one days after the Japanese surrender, Wrigley's Spearmint Gum presented a radio program titled "The First Line!" in which the narrator introduced the show by saying, "Ships, planes and submarines . . . the world knows what they did . . . But there were other men about whom little has been spoken or written—men to whom thousands of soldiers and marines owe their lives—men who went to war in bathing trunks and webbed feet! Tonight, we bring you the amazing story of the Mermen of War." In the end, the nickname didn't stick, and reporters settled on one with a hundred different claims to its origin, a name the UDT swimmers had long since adopted for themselves: the frogmen.

15

After almost five and a half years of war and a career that had culminated with a ten-day stint as commander of all UDT forces, Draper Kauffman, the thirty-four-year-old veteran of three separate services and five separate campaigns, the author of the NCDUs and Hell Week, weighed a scant 126 pounds, 50 fewer than when he had been commissioned. If his appearance alone didn't signal a change, his personality did. Normally affable, polite, and sincere, he was now, said his father, "rather high strung and intense," on the verge of disrespectful, even to his seniors—the most hazardous of traits for a naval officer. By all indications, he was finished.

Partly to check his downfall, partly because he was the best man for the job, he was, as soon as the war ended, transferred back to San Diego as the underwater demolition training officer at the new UDT base in Coronado, where he was finally reunited with his wife and baby daughter in one of the most beautiful places in the country. On paper, his duties were to teach all the tactics that he and his fellow frogmen had spent the past three years perfecting; in reality, he spent much of his time untangling the three years' worth of administrative problems that the UDTs' hasty creation had accumulated. These included those of 1st Lieutenant Alan Gordon Leslie, the Canadian-born Scout-Sniper Marine whose transfer to the UDTs had caused a fourteen-month stop to his pay and who now wanted to transfer from the Marine Corps Reserves to the regular Navy as a UDT officer—an affront to the Corps that Holland Smith himself stopped. Leslie's response to Kauffman's attempted intercession and Smith's rejection was to slap his $4,000 worth of back pay on the front desk of the Hotel Del Coronado, a favorite of Navy admirals, to secure a "peninsula" of suites for a thirteen-day, twelve-night, brandy-fueled bash that Kauffman was forced to create a watch bill of sober UDT officers to chaperone. Not exactly the kind of assignment fit to stimulate a mind fresh from five and a half years of war.

Almost as soon as Kauffman took the job in Coronado he was "itching" to leave, itching to look beyond the downsizing of the UDTs, their end-of-war creep toward inland operations, and all the way to a future in which he was wearing the uniform of a regular line officer in the United States Navy—the service that, in his youth, had rejected him. "I would like very much to work with you on your Atom Bomb Project," Kauffman wrote to Admiral Blandy just two months after returning home. "On the off chance that you have an opening for me, I will keep my affairs in shape so I can easily leave here within four hours."

During the next decade and a half of his naval career, Kauffman's passions—like his father's—cleaved to the conventional Navy, and his involvement with the UDTs dwindled to proofreading manuscripts of UDT histories and turning down offers from publishers to ghost-write his memoirs. His reasons: lack of time, lack of writing ability, and his chief concern, "loss of stature" among his teammates.

As Kauffman concentrated on his naval career and raising a family, several of the UDT history books for which he had provided comments hit the shelves, including one with a three-page foreword by Admiral Turner himself. In it, Turner described the amphibious warfare efforts that had been made by the Navy and "its Marine Corps," then justified the provision of Navy Scouts as the proper response to the service's responsibilities from "the deep sea to the high-water mark." Probably not at all what the publisher wanted, Turner's foreword hardly dipped below a 30,000-foot view of the topic, except to conclude by saying, "To these Naked Warriors: Hail! You earned and have my sincere admiration and respect." For Turner—"sentimental as an old woman," said one of his subordinates—it was a statement brimming with emotion, the kind characteristic of a father, which of course he was.

In March 1960, in command of a cruiser and finally in the top echelon of the conventional Navy, Draper was now also on the cusp of turning fifty, an age when his thoughts seemed ready to turn back to his

World War II experiences, so much so that he typed out a letter to Turner, his old mentor. In the letter, he expressed his admiration for Turner's career—unequaled "or even approached by any officer of any service," and asked for an autographed picture. He closed by saying that the eighteen months he'd spent in the UDTs was "by all odds the most interesting and vital part of my life so far." Five days later, Turner—now seventy-five, and within a year of his death—scribbled a note back, saying that "the UDTs turned out to be exactly what we needed, and I've been very proud of what they, and you, were able to accomplish."

For the remaining two decades of his life, a period that included the honor of a three-year stint as superintendent of the US Naval Academy, Kauffman's interest in his underwater demolition service could be seen in his yearly attendance at UDT reunions, where he was always celebrated as the undisputed "Grandpappy Bullfrog" for his generous mentorship of any junior UDT officer who approached him and, before retirement, his request for authorization to wear the service insignia of the UDT—a request that the Navy's interminable bureaucracy approved "with pleasure" in just one month. Dying suddenly just two weeks after his sixty-eighth birthday from a heart attack while touring Budapest, his funeral at the Naval Academy Chapel included three decades' worth of shipmates and twenty-five pallbearers, two of whom were his World War II teammates. Having never gotten around to writing a memoir of his service, he left behind a 648-page transcript of an oral history interview meant to cover his entire thirty-three-year naval career but whose most significant bulk was spent on just one topic: the frogmen that he had helped create, then—in some of their most pivotal battles—had led to indispensability, thereby ensuring their postwar survival.

Though never interested in creating commandos, Kauffman's hand in helping his fellow frogmen to remain the only special troops in World War II to avoid disbandment had practically guaranteed that they soon saw themselves as the closest thing to commandos the US military had left.

Chapter 6

The Contest for the Guerrilla War in China and the Organization That Had "No Damn Business" Fighting in It: The US Navy's Army of Sailors

Literally Spanish for "small war," the word "guerrilla" originated to describe the wrench-faced, pitchfork-clutching partisans that Wellington had employed to bushwhack Napoleon's regulars in Spain. Because of the way it sounded to English-speaking ears like some form of "bestial" savagery, the term had ever after been co-opted by American military thinkers to describe every nonuniformed, American-led fighter from the Indians who had fought alongside the Pilgrims to the Filipino scouts who had thrown in with the US Army. Ultimately, this three-hundred-year stretch of bloody history had abruptly ended in the trenches of France, where churning tank treads and spinning propeller blades had hypnotized an entire generation of American soldiers into thinking that this was the future of warfare—that is, until the US military found itself locked in a total war on three continents. Now, that same generation of planners was glimpsing an opportunity to connect the richest country on earth to the world's nearly inexhaustible supply of disaffected manpower, the base element of all guerrilla armies before or since. But where to start?

Nowhere was the prospect for a guerrilla army greater than in China, a country buckling under the weight of Japanese occupation and overflowing with potential recruits. If such an army could be created there—or so believed William J. Donovan, the guerrilla-advocating director of the OSS—it would tie down at least 600,000 Japanese soldiers, but it was a strategic opportunity that General Joseph Stilwell, the uncompromising, vinegar-tongued commander of the China-Burma-India Theater, wanted to have nothing to do with—"No irregulars. That's not my kind of war," he had scoffed. This was a gag reflex triggered by the prospect of joint operations with China's impenetrable chain of command

and Donovan's increasingly intrusive OSS, whose eclectic and often well-educated operatives were viewed by most conventional Army officers as little more than thin-necked Ivy League dandies—"east coast faggots," as one not particularly nuanced soldier had described them. Eventually, both objections were overcome by a proposal for a guerrilla detachment led by one of General Stilwell's old friends—a 250-pound former boxer and gunslinging narcotics agent named Carl Eifler—and located in the strategically less consequential country of Burma. It was, however, a compromise that blocked Donovan from the one landscape he viewed the way an oilman eyes a desert—a country just waiting to be sunk beneath the weight of his very own OSS-led guerrillas. It was an ambition that Donovan and the OSS would have eventually achieved if only they hadn't been beaten to the punch, and beaten to it by the most unpredictable foil in American military history—the US Navy.

The account of the US Navy's sailors in China during World War II was, according to the naval supply officer turned amateur historian Roy Stratton, "A cloak and dagger story, a story of Cops and Robbers," a story of American-led guerrillas "under the cover of darkness" destroying "highways, railroads, bridges and supply facilities, kill[ing] a few Japs and puppet troops . . . and then run[ning] like Hell." Stratton couldn't have known it at the time of his writing, but it was also a story that would prove to be more than that. Though the sailors in China would suffer no Makins, no Cisternas, nor triumph in the headlines over any Pointe du Hocs or Saipans, the snap of their bullets would echo far beyond the mountain walls among which they fought and, most important, would set the example for the generation that came after them.

2

If General George C. Marshall was the country's cavalry bugle—crisp, resonant, proud—then Admiral Ernest J. King was its foghorn. At no point was this more resonant than in those early days of the war when King's shark-bald head had cocked in disgust at any mention of "Germany First." His reason: The Japanese had just destroyed his fleet and thus deserved a beating. A student of Napoleon, an apostle of the decisive battle, a man who had never met another who so impressed him as himself, King now wanted to destroy his enemy not like Wellington at Waterloo, but like Nelson at Trafalgar—his resurrected fleet leading the way. But how? Situated on the farthest western edge of the

Pacific, Japan's geography would not only force King's ships to contend with an ocean crisscrossed with Japanese wakes, but now—with the loss of every Allied outpost and weather station from the Philippines to the Gilberts—one without any ports of supply or meteorological stations warning of the winds that blew down from Siberia to whip white every swell in their path. Without that support, King knew his ships and planes would be forced to tiptoe into the Pacific, and he therefore hoped there might be a single solution—both a hub for his radar stations and a backdoor base from which to launch his final battle.

To explore this idea, King summoned to his office Commander Milton Miles, a forty-one-year-old destroyer sailor and China veteran who—despite being an advocate of US involvement in China—was currently girding himself for a war fought from inside a ship's hull. Standing at his desk, his eyes hardly lifting from the papers spread across it, King motioned for Miles to sit and then, without any pleasantries, launched into a hasty assessment of the obstacles bedeviling his plans in the Far East, concluding, "We are going to have tough sledding out there."

Bracing for the inevitable basis for King's monologue, Miles then heard what he had hoped he wouldn't—that his next stop would not be a destroyer; in fact would not be a ship at all. His mission, King told him, was to set up weather stations, then "to prepare the China coast in any way [he could] for US Navy landings in three or four years."

"In the meantime," King said, "do whatever you can to help the Navy and heckle the Japanese."

"But, Admiral," Miles protested, "I'd like to go to sea."

"You have your orders," King concluded, then—after reiterating the mission's top secret nature—ordered him out, neither defining the meaning of the word "heckle" nor the instrument through which Miles was to accomplish such a mysterious undertaking. Shortly, the instrument's existence would be the mystery.

Born Milton E. Robbins in 1900 in Jerome, Arizona, Miles had spent his first years in a mountainside mining hub called by the New York *Sun* in 1903 "the wickedest town in the West." The only child of a lumber cutter who had been nearly thirty years older than his mother at the time of their marriage, Miles—by the time he was eight—had lost his father, which was something of a blessing, as it had given his mother an opportunity to move and remarry, then settle in Seattle. From his stepfather, Miles had received the last name he would live with but not much else. At fourteen, Miles ran away from home. On his seventeenth birthday and before graduating from high school, he enlisted in the Navy. Despite his origins in a town choked with prospectors and prostitutes, despite little in the way of an education or stability, and after only one year as a boot seaman, Miles—though suffering from Spanish flu at the time—had been one of two competitors at an exam held in Ireland to win a spot at the US Naval Academy. If nothing else, life had taught Miles to make the most of opportunities.

Commander Milton E. Miles, circa 1942, before being sent on his mission to China.

Topped with curly brown hair, always cut close and high on the sides, Miles had a slightly upturned nose, cheerful eyes, and a smile as pleasant as a country pastor's. He was well liked at the academy, where his friends and peers had almost instantly dubbed him "Mary," after the rhyme and rhythm his name shared with the silent film starlet Mary Miles Minter. Even with a no-nonsense major in electrical engineering, Mary had ranked in the top 10 percent of his class and graduated forty-fourth of 539. No small accomplishment for a man from Jerome.

Within three months of graduating in 1922, Miles deployed to China to begin a five-year tour. Patrolling up and down the nearly orange waters of the Yangtze River during the Warlord period, Miles learned leadership, diplomacy, geography, small-boat handling, how to shoot his way "out of a hold up," and, unlike most Westerners, he picked up various coastal dialects. Most important, Miles learned to love China and the Chinese, and to hate the treaty-port supremacy of his American and European peers. Later, in 1936, the same year Mao and his Communists embarked on their Long March, Miles returned for another three-year stint. This time his sea bag included a wife named Wilma, whom everyone called Billy, and three sons, whom Miles cheerfully shouldered wherever he could. In March 1939, Mary and Billy packed five suitcases, a gas stove, a typewriter, and their three sons, ages ten, seven, and five, then spent the next four months on a US government–authorized return to the United States by way of the Burma Road—or what amounted to a Grand Tour of South Asia. Hitching, driving, sailing, and flying, Miles and family braved bandits, disease, weather, and Japanese soldiers, traveling from Kunming to Rangoon to Calcutta to Agra to Lahore to Kashmir to Kabul to Herat to Tehran to Baghdad to Damascus to Beirut to Alexandria to Greece to Naples to Rome to Florence to Genoa to Marseilles, and finally, to Boston. While riding an elevator in New York, Miles's five-year-old boy looked up at the Black attendant and remarked, "Daddy, there aren't very many natives in America, are there?"

Whether King knew it or not, he had selected the right man for an adventure.

3

Because half the world was now under Axis occupation, Miles's orders to China required as circuitous an itinerary as his Asian tour—from New York to India by way of Brazil, Nigeria, and Egypt—this time aboard an eastbound flying boat that suffered at least one midair engine failure along the way. During the flight to the mountaintop-refueling airfield at Myitkyina, the pilots learned that the Japanese had just seized it, which forced all future Allied traffic into a frigidly pressurized three-and-a-half-hour midnight dash over the Himalayas thereafter known as "the Hump." When he finally did land, it was on a cobblestone island airstrip between the confluence of the Yangtze and Jailing rivers. There, Miles stared up at a mountain accessed by 300 broad steps that rose to the base of the walled fortress-city of Chungking, now a magnet for refugees, rats, and daily Japanese bombings.

When Miles finally took his last leg-burning step, he was picked up by a mysterious car and driven to an even more mysterious location, for a secret reason about which he had already been warned. Miles knew that prior to his arrival, American attempts at forging a unified effort with the Chinese had been stymied by lots of issues: the personality of China's leader, Generalissimo Chiang Kai-shek; the divergence in opinion over China's greatest threat, the Japanese or the Communists; and the methods of the man that Miles was now on his way to meet. "Seldom photographed, never interviewed," General Tai Li, head of China's Military Bureau of Investigation and Statistics, or BIS, was known to American intelligence officers for being Chiang's closest confidant, but also the reason that every inductee to this theater could expect to have his suitcase ransacked the moment he set it down. Variously known as the "thought police," the "Himmler of China," and the man most responsible for the death or imprisonment of "scores of liberal college professors," Tai Li's worst crime was rumored to have been, like Nero's, the murder of his mother—a falsehood that persisted because the reality that he had simply moved her to a mountain village was less interesting. Together, the truths and lies had turned Tai into one of the most targeted men in China, so much so that he now insisted that a bodyguard sit next to him whenever he went to the bathroom. "He's a skunk of the first order," read the US War Department's military intelligence card. "No one should associate with the cut throat."

With a bald crown framed by lush black hair and an upper lip shut as tight as a portcullis to protect his mouthful of golden bridgework, Tai Li—at Miles's first meeting—looked less like the leader of China's gestapo and more like a vaudeville comedian. More important, Miles found Tai to be entirely amenable, an impression that only deepened when Miles presented him with a camera and a snub-nosed .38 revolver that matched his own. Not only was Tai delighted by the gesture, but he immediately found in Miles a man with whom he could work.

"Commander Miles has gotten off to a flying start and has been taken completely into the confidence of the Chinese Secret Service," wrote the US ambassador's naval attaché Lieutenant Colonel James McHugh to Secretary of the Navy Frank Knox. "He has seen and done things I never thought any foreigner would be able to do." Within two weeks, Miles and Tai were bouncing their way across hundreds of miles of China in a Dodge truck, wicker chairs bolted in the back, inspecting the coast and surveying potential weather stations. At stops, Tai Li alternately introduced Miles as a salt commissioner, a customs official, and a missionary. He looked most like the last.

One predawn morning in Hai Chang, while Miles's face was still half covered in shaving cream, the growl of a Japanese sortie thundered overhead. As bombs fell and machine gun bullets stitched the ground around them, Tai, Miles, and an interpreter sprinted for cover, found none, and, out of options, squatted in a rice paddy. As Miles scrambled like a war correspondent with his home movie camera to film the attack, Tai nonchalantly asked him to arm 50,000 guerrillas and to train them to fight the Japanese. Before Miles could blink, Tai asked a second question: "Would your country allow you to accept a commission as general in the Chinese Army, so that we could operate these men together?" Miles was speechless. He knew the political complications of subordinating himself to Chinese control, especially Tai's control; he knew how upside down it would be for a sailor to command soldiers; but mostly, he knew that Tai was offering an investment opportunity to "heckle" the Japanese that he would likely never come across again.

"OK," he said, then shook Tai Li's hand in the light of the burning buildings around them. At that moment, Donovan had only just recently won permission to establish his first guerrilla detachment, and that was in Burma.

4

Though he had set out on his tour to find the future real estate for his weather stations and landing beaches, what Miles had actually found in his two-month trip was so much more. Proving his mettle by braving bomb runs, burning houses, quarter-sized black scabs of cellulitis, malaria-spiked fevers, river pirates, and even a headfirst counterattack into a Japanese machine gun—"the most important gun battle" the Americans in China "ever fought," said Tai afterward—Miles had returned with a scribbled, unapproved outline for a US Navy–led guerrilla army in China. If both American and Chinese authorities approved, Tai Li would be in charge with Miles as his deputy, each of them sharing equal operational veto power. After the Navy doctor in Chungking skimmed over the chunk of metal shrapnel in his shinbone and told him "you should stick to the sea," Miles had gone on to formally propose the plan to Admiral King. His response, as usual, was full speed ahead, and he immediately authorized Miles to draft the agreement. What followed was several weeks' worth of negotiations in which Miles and Tai met every day to haggle for hours over each paragraph.

Upon its completion, planners in Admiral King's office viewed the agreement as propitious as Excalibur rising from the lake. When Miles flew to India to explain the plan to the Army, however, Stilwell objected to everything: objected to guerrilla warfare and sabotage, calling them both "illegal action," but more than anything to the Navy "running loose in his theater." As suspicious as Tai, Stilwell barely trusted his British allies, let alone the Chinese. To him, the offer was no Excalibur, but rather a wooden horse outside the walls. Pointing to an editorial in the *Washington Daily News,* Miles pleaded his case. After all, a defeat of China's government would release one million Japanese soldiers into the Pacific Theater. Why not allow the Navy to arm and operate the guerrillas, a low-cost investment with the potential to achieve "the most for the least"? As free of guile and vanity as Miles, a fellow hater of bureaucracy, Stilwell was already more annoyed by the meddlings of Donovan and the OSS than he was with this amateur sailor-soldier. Moreover, all the OSS plans he had seen so far had more potential to ruin Chinese-American relations than to hurt the Japanese. Also, Stilwell liked Miles; it was hard not to. In the end, Stilwell shrugged: What did he have to lose? "I'll tell the boys to include a few pounds for you in each plane that comes over the Hump." It was a start.

When Miles arrived back in Chungking, he ordered 2,000 tommy guns, 3,000 revolvers, and 10,000 grenades, then began hunting the surrounding countryside for real estate on which to use them. Eight miles

Happy Valley.

northwest of Chungking—far from the Japanese—he found 200 acres overlooking the Jialing River. Coincidentally, the land was Tai's personal property. Mostly rock-strewn, terraced farmland, from the sky Miles's new camp looked like a sea of green swells switchbacked with trails and surrounded by hazy spade-shaped mountains. Hot in the summer, cold in the winter, the fields were fertilized with human excrement that contaminated the air and water. Cold drinks would be forbidden, and woe to the man who disobeyed. Arrivals by boat would climb 100 laborious steps to reach the top or pay to be carried by sedan chair.

In September 1942, the first seven sailors arrived: all radiomen trained in radio intercept. A month later, seven more men came, three of them Marines. Before long, white-painted mud huts with thatched roofs dotted the grounds and hillsides. Eventually the camp's architecture would grow to ten permanent buildings plus tents. For beds, the men slept on cots of interlaced ropes. In no time, ship-trained sailors would harness the mountain spring—abundant enough to supply each man with two baths a day and the reason Miles had selected the spot in the first place—and would fit together a crisscrossing system of bamboo pipes, bamboo toilets, and gravel filters. To prevent dysentery, each man would carry around his own teapot, refreshing himself by "sucking" boiled water "through the spout." Maybe the worst feature of all would be the insects—twelve-inch-wide "belts" of black ants that would unpredictably snake through the camp, plus mosquitos so numerous that all would agree that they should be the unit's mascots. In due time, all who served there would know the camp to be hot, pestilential, completely free of women, mostly free of booze, and as miserable a place as could be found in all of Asia. They loved it. As if to anticipate the nostalgia that would one day attach to it, they even named it Happy Valley, and adopted as their flag one of Miles's own designs: a triangular white pennant with three red characters in triplicate—three question marks, three exclamation points, and three stars—???!!!★★★. To them, the flag would mean "What the hell?"—an appropriate question for a Navy base some 600 airline miles from the nearest salt water; the first of its kind.

Recognizing the uniqueness of this assignment and also that he had just been granted more autonomy than any naval officer since the age of sail, Miles now charted a course to build what he believed would be the only kind of organization with which he could succeed: a decentralized series of almost completely independent camps from Indochina to the Gobi Desert that would support a number of almost completely independent guerrilla armies. Raised in the only branch of service where estrangement from one's chain of command was routine, Miles nevertheless knew that such a plan would not only isolate its members with unheard-of distances but would also force them to fight the enemy in seas not of water but of people—a people that nearly every American viewed as backward but that Miles knew to be descendants of one of the most ancient civilizations on the planet.

SACO's "What the hell?" pennant.

To smooth those points of friction that would stunt the teamwork so needed in his plans, Miles dressed his sailors and Marines in rank-free Army khakis, then issue them a list of don'ts: Don't say "Chinaman"; Don't say "coolie"; Don't call American food "civilized"; Don't use pidgin English. "Treat the Chinese around the camps and station with the respect due to a soldier fighting for his country," he would insist. Boys grown tall on American meals and exceptionalism would quickly learn to eat Chinese food with chopsticks or go hungry. To further foster this teamwork, Miles would request from the Navy a particular kind of recruit: "No high hat, rank conscious, red tape clerks or Old China Hands," the latter "A title highly disapproved by all Chinese" and one that usually foretold a "foreigners' contempt" for "Oriental" shortcomings. "The less our recruits know about China the better," he would say.

What he really wanted, he would soon write, were the kind of men who could "fight the Nips in any job assigned" but also the kind who could do so "without fighting his shipmates." "[Volunteers] must be slightly crazy but not so much as the Skipper on account of the Old Navy custom of RHIP (rank has its privileges) and I won't stand for trespassing." In short, Miles wanted men like himself, personalities with the potential to fight a kind of war the Navy had never faced.

Unlike "Wild Bill" Donovan, the ostentatiously insatiable commander of the OSS, Miles would be unassuming, faithful, mildly introverted, almost forgettable. Mostly, he would be easy to underestimate. Nearly always in shorts and often without a shirt, to his troops Miles would never be "Captain" or later "Admiral," but always "Mary," and completely indistinguishable from them—a superficial abrogation of authority that Miles made up for by example. "You are expected to learn Chinese," Miles would say to a new arrival in what amounted to an interview while running along next to him through the mountains at a crippling pace he could keep for forty miles a day, even when racked by malaria. To officers returning from an operation he would nearly always insist that they take his room for a night so they could sleep on an actual mattress. To raise spirits even higher, Miles would eventually take to a makeshift pulpit where he would preach Sunday sermons to his men, who in turn would count the number of times he said "goddamn" during them. Equipped with all the dash of a tax attorney, Miles to this day has never been compared with the greatest of guerrilla leaders, but he did share their greatest strengths: enthusiasm, forbearance, and a nearly evangelical belief in the equality of his men with the guerrillas they led. "I didn't get the impression that he was a very efficient man," one officer would later say. "But he had the personality to deal with the Chinese. He was as pagan as they were. He could sit up and negotiate with them all night long with just cup after cup of tea." But that was far from all.

Having never planned to command an army of any sort, Miles nevertheless responded to this surprise assignment with an immersion so deep that no other Navy flag officer in the entire war—in any war—would so closely resemble an infantryman. What would follow were endless meetings of operational planning; innumerable escapes from Japanese offensives; more than forty assassination attempts, three of which almost succeeded, including one knife attack at a train station in which he walked away with his "shoes filled with blood"; and an untold number of nights spent shivering in the grass next to his guerrillas while they waited to waylay a Japanese patrol.

Though Miles was not yet quite able to glimpse all this through the fog that hid his future, to Donovan it was a fog so thick that he took it for gunsmoke, and naturally rode toward it.

5

In September, Donovan attempted to compensate for his delayed arrival in China by secretly negotiating with the Joint Chiefs to have Miles made the Far East Coordinator of the OSS. In October, three weeks after this agreement was officially signed, Miles was informed of his new status as an OSS officer. Tai had already heard. While Miles was still adjusting to this news, he was visited by Dr. Joseph Hayden, an old China hand turned OSS officer, who arrived so hot and soaked with sweat that his red tie "left a blur of color on his white shirt." More alarming than Hayden's appearance was his message: that Donovan—without consulting the Chinese—was preparing a plan to parachute into China a contingent of British and Norwegian commandos.

Annoyed by Donovan's messenger and his apparent obliviousness to China's well-earned distrust of the British, Miles offered Hayden a hot towel and a hot tea, and then told the OSS officer that he planned to kick him out of the country. In the end Miles refrained, and the proposed plan was canceled, but things were already off to a bad start. "Mary has a lot of nerve telling us to not send Old China Hands to China," exclaimed OSS Colonel David K. Bruce in early 1943. "He should realize that [his] whole project would crack up without Donovan." In no time, Miles's reputation with the OSS sank to that of "a renegade white man 'gone native!'" That wasn't Miles's only problem.

Because Miles now worked part-time for Donovan, and because all OSS operations required the approval of each individual theater commander—who in this case was Stilwell, a soldier—Army planners naturally saw the Navy's gathering arrangement as theirs to control. To this end, General Marshall informed Stilwell that he aimed to put Miles under his command—a reversal of Stilwell's and Miles's original unofficial arrangement.

At this proposed change, Captain Jeffrey Metzel, Admiral King's implementer of ideas and Miles's Stateside handler, immediately attempted to intercede. Metzel, the same typhoon of energy that tasked Draper Kauffman to create the NCDUs, was impatient, impertinent, and equipped with the uninhibited tongue typical to all post-command flag officers. Now, as both the Army and the OSS attempted to strangle Miles, he smoldered. "A big-hearted gent, that Marshall," Metzel said, "consenting to leave Tai Li under the generalissimo." Ultimately, it was neither Miles nor Metzel that blocked the Army, but a soldier, the crankiest in history. "After investigation," wrote Stilwell to Marshall on February 21, 1943, "I believe that the Chinese will not accept [an] agreement if any agency comes between them and Miles. Tai Li's organization is super-secret and super-suspicious. Miles's work would be hampered if they knew he was under my command. I have enough confidence in him to recommend that in view of the peculiar and unusual circumstances connected with this matter he be allowed to operate as heretofore, and I believe that any conflict that arises can be adjusted between us." Not explicitly an endorsement of Navy-led guerrillas, nor a tactical withdrawal from what was historically an Army specialty, Stilwell's statement was an honest, if unexpected, recognition of realities. When it came to guerrilla warfare in China, the Navy had not only gotten there first, but it also had none of the Army's institutional hang-ups to overcome.

When Miles and Metzel, plus an entourage of two admirals, one Chinese colonel, and one OSS man, arrived at General Marshall's Washington office in February 1943 to obtain his agreement to the arrangement—an arrangement that cut the Army out of guerrilla warfare in China except by way of its OSS levers—a staff officer kept them waiting in the anteroom like children sent to see the principal. With smoke practically rising from his head, Metzel announced that if they waited any longer he would interrupt the general himself. When they were finally ushered inside, Marshall greeted them "straight-mouthed," never standing from behind his desk and leaving the six men locked at attention in the middle of the room. All Marshall had to do, said one of the admirals, respectfully, was initial the agreement and it would be whisked to the president's desk. At this, Marshall paused. There were, he said, still "somc minor changes to make."

Instead of retreating before the guns of Marshall's four stars, instead of addressing him deferentially as was customary inside his office, Metzel broke rank and marched right up to Marshall's desk—an act so abrupt that, as Miles remembered afterward, it made the "very office" seem "to gasp."

"Do you mind if I smoke, General?" asked Metzel as he lit his cigarette with nary an ashtray in sight. Metzel then braced a hand on Marshall's desk—a desk once owned by Civil War legend Phil Sheridan—and leaned in, his free hand ready to deposit ash all over the wooden antique. "To attempt to make changes will delay things for months, even if we get the Agreement back without additional Chinese requirements. All you have to do, General, is put your initials here next to Admiral King's."

Barely a footnote today, Metzel—for a moment—was on history's stage, playing all the way to the last row. When he stopped speaking, the entire room was silent. If there was ever a moment when the Army might have disabused the Navy of its unconventional warfare ambitions, this was it.

Then, remarkably, Marshall's mouth cracked into an almost imperceptible smile. From one of his drawers he produced an ashtray and handed it to Metzel. Then he produced a pen and pulled the paper toward himself. "Carefully," Miles remembered, the grand general "wrote his initials." With that, the yoke of Army control slipped from Miles's neck. Only the OSS yoke remained, a burden much easier to ignore.

On his way back to China, Miles received a message from Donovan to stand fast in Karachi. According to the note, an unspecified issue with Stilwell had arisen, and Miles might have to reverse course to fly the 12,000 miles back to D.C. in order to resolve it. Miles compared Donovan's flimsy missive to the stone tablet he now held from Admiral King and chose the heavier. It was a snub that Donovan would not forget.

On April 1, 1943, President Roosevelt completed the pyramid of signatures and created the Sino-American Special Technical Cooperative Organization, later simplified to Sino-American Cooperative Organization, or SACO. The months-old common-law marriage was official. "We're no longer bastard," Metzel exclaimed in a letter. As if to reiterate the organization's intended guerrilla purpose, Navy planners agreed that SACO would be pronounced "socko," to sound like a "powerful or sudden attack." Tai could hardly have been more pleased. "Every time we meet he produces a toast to SOCKO!" exclaimed Miles in a letter back to Washington. It was, he said, the only English word he ever heard Tai speak.

To command the Chinese guerrillas, Tai commissioned Miles a lieutenant general in the Chinese Army. Months later, in a meeting with a river pirate, Tai introduced Miles as a "Brigadier General of the Sea," a fact that reportedly made the former secretary of the Navy then sitting in the White House "belly laugh" with delight.

Now officially charged with using China as a base from which to attack Japanese harbors, airfields, mines, factories, warehouses, depots, and anything else he could think of, Miles broke ground on the series of camps he had long been planning.

From Washington, Donovan listened for battle—any sound that suggested that SACO's founding had cleared the way for OSS guns in China. He heard nothing.

6

On February 1, 1943, the first batch of American advisors—three Marines and three sailors—piled as many weapons and supplies as they could aboard a half-dozen beat-up trucks and set out on an adventure like none of them had ever known. With engines variously configured to run on gasoline, alcohol, or charcoal-generated gas, the men clattered out of Happy Valley enthusiastically bellowing songs "about tigers." On April 1, 1943, after a two-month-long, 2,000-mile journey on barely visible roads, usually walking alongside their battered transports, the men stumbled into a mountaintop village in Anwhei Province. They had long since stopped singing. Three months later, after a monumental effort to build a camp from scratch, the first batch of 320 Chinese recruits reported for training. Gaunt, hungry, exhausted, and racked by diseases so numerous as to be considered by the Americans as "300 per cent" disabled, most of the recruits had also never used a tool more sophisticated than a shovel. "Besides being tiny," said Major John "Bud" Masters, the Marine camp commander, "these guys are too weak to hold a gun and some of them are too dumb or sick to learn." They were, another officer remembered years later, "the walking doomed."

In June, Camp Two was established along the Yangtze River in Hunan Province. Half the distance from Happy Valley as Camp One and therefore twice as close to supplies, Camp Two nevertheless took just as long to get organized. Intended from the start as a base for river raiders, command was given to a naval officer, an officer whose health did not improve until he was relieved. When his health did, so did the camp's. In September, an OSS officer led eighteen American advisors 600 miles north of Happy Valley and established Camp Three. Within three months, almost half the time it had taken Camp One, Camp Three graduated 421 guerrillas, but they might as well have taken their time. Due to a lack of supplies coming from Chungking made worse by lackluster leadership, Camp Three could not field its guerrilla graduates for four months.

China's sheer geographical size complicated everything. A typical mailbag to Camp Four in Mongolia, the farthest of SACO's camps, required a plane from Chungking to Sian, then a train to Pao Ki, a truck to Langchow, a skin boat for a 100-mile descent down the river, then an ox to Ningshia, and for the final stretch, a camel. Because anything heavier than a mailbag would sink the inflated goatskins, equipment to Camp Four had to wait for winter when the river would freeze.

In addition to third world realities, officer problems, distance, and lack of supplies, SACO was further hobbled by Tai's implacable policy that restricted Americans to an advisory role, which meant no combat. Critics insisted that Tai was keeping Americans out of direct combat so he could stockpile troops and supplies to fight the Communists, not the Japanese.

To minimize supply issues—just about the only problem that could be controlled—Miles secured four DC-4 airplanes and loaned them to the Army Air Forces in exchange for 150 tons of supplies flown over the Hump each month. It did not solve his problem of transferring supplies from Chungking to the various camps, but it was a start. On June 23, 1943, a plane carrying SACO's first regular shipment arrived in Chungking.

"With supplies rolling," Metzel wrote to Miles two months later, hardly enough time for SACO's camps to feel the impact, "we are hoping you will very soon begin reporting scalps. How we need such reports! . . . It is almost impossible to get either personnel or equipment except for scalps on the barrelhead. We are pleading against mounting competition for every item . . . We don't give anybody sixteen days to draw blood in any theater." Forced to negotiate with the Chinese leadership over every operational decision, Miles found that Metzel's appeals for such reports were far easier asked than achieved. In October, when they finally came, the reports were nothing glamorous. A few guards killed, a few buildings burned, a few locomotives damaged. In mid-November, a Japanese advance in the east prompted Camp One's Chinese commander to evacuate, leaving Bud Masters and his advisors on their own, responsible for rescuing themselves and every precious commodity in their inventory. When Miles and Tai met with Masters to adjudicate the situation, Masters promised to resign unless the Chinese started cooperating and letting the Americans share the burden of direct combat. "I shot the Chinese general responsible," Tai responded in defense. "Does that not show my cooperation?" Ultimately, Masters stayed, but only after Miles promised to unleash him against the Japanese. Masters was not the only one braying for a fight.

7

AT SIXTY YEARS OLD, thick-jowled and with white hair parted just off center, "Wild Bill" Donovan—a nickname he had earned as a volunteer leading soldiers through the mud, gas, and death of the Western Front—

looked in his uniform nothing like the head of an insatiable unconventional warfare organization but more like an overweight toddler playing dress-up. For signs of the former, one had to look elsewhere: first, to his left breast, where he had humbly affixed a single ribbon, his Medal of Honor, in effect saying to his peers that no other awards mattered; and second, to a career as a New York attorney and politician—occupations that had introduced him to everyone from movie stars to Mussolini, and taken him farther around the world than most presidents. He had been to Siberia to size up the Bolsheviks, the Far East to hunt down business, Ethiopia to tour the Italian front, the Balkans, Turkey, and Spain as the president's unofficial envoy. In past ages, a hero-millionaire like Donovan could have responded to a world crisis simply by raising his own regiment, equipping it, and leading it into battle. In the twentieth century, such impulses had been curbed by the increasing complexities of modern warfare and a corresponding bureaucracy that recognized the limited value of eccentric amateurs, Medal of Honor or not. Now, blocked from commanding regular troops, Donovan—courageous, entrepreneurial, imaginative, and most of all, unstoppable—had set his sights on the only field of action whose battle lines had not yet been drawn, and on the one man who stood in his way.

On December 2, 1943, the plane carrying Donovan touched down in Chungking. He was accompanied by an entourage that included Holly-

Camp Ten dinner with Miles (standing) and Tai Li (seated, right of Miles).

wood director John Ford and a movie crew. His visit had three objectives: first, to replace Miles as the head of the OSS in China; second, to elevate the OSS to an equal position with SACO; and third, to divvy up all strategic responsibilities in China and keep the best parts for himself. Under this new arrangement, Donovan planned to take the guerrillas and leave the Navy with little more than the weather stations. After all, said Donovan sympathetically to Miles at their first meeting, the burden of operations in China was "far too heavy for any one man to carry."

"Harangued on three sides" by Donovan and his senior staffers—all "expert professional lawyers"—Miles alternated between disputing the OSS accusations and pretending he did not understand all their "assessments, procurare, assizes, testaments, instruments, pax vobiscums," and ultimately demanded that they simply speak to him in "common American slang." This they did by telling Miles that it was impossible for him "to do both the Navy job and the OSS job," and it was "necessary to relieve [him]."

"I am afraid I enjoyed the situation too much to let it pass as simply as that," Miles wrote immediately afterward.

Several nights later, Tai Li held a reception in Donovan's honor at the Orphans' Primary School, a night of wine, food, and singing that culminated in several short operas, the last one a parable about three bickering brothers. During the banquet that followed, Tai Li offered Donovan both booze and women. Donovan, a teetotaler, normally indulged only in the latter, but not on this night; he still needed to divest SACO of its guerrillas and infuse the OSS with its stock. At around nine o'clock, the arguing commenced and a full-scale fight broke out. Donovan "yelled and became ungentlemanlike"; another OSS officer "butted in and made them all mad"; Tai's deputy and interpreter grew so angry that his "English fell off . . . and [he] became unintelligible." At one point, Donovan bluntly told Tai that he planned to jump-start China's guerrilla war and would send his OSS agents into China whether Tai liked it or not.

"If OSS tries to operate outside of SACO," Tai responded with customary tight-lipped gravity, "I will kill your agents."

"For every one of our agents you kill," replied Donovan, his fist rattling the dishes, "we will kill one of your generals."

At the table, Miles watched two years of diplomacy burn up like tissue paper, and attempted to douse the flames by countering every shout with a lowered voice, so much so that the entire table was forced to shut up to hear what amounted to a whisper.

When Donovan and his film crew left China a few days later, he flew out confident that he had buffaloed the Chinese into submission and shunted the Navy out of the guerrilla warfare business for good. Miles, dejected, was sure that he had too.

In January, Miles returned to Washington to meet with Admiral King's staff in an attempt to, in Miles's words, fix the "Humpty Dumpty [he] had broken." At a subsequent meeting at the Navy Department at noon on February 23, Miles again defended himself against Donovan and his OSS staffers, who reiterated all their problems with SACO and with the Navy's involvement in guerrilla operations in general, which—in spite of Donovan's demands—had continued to gather momentum. This increased involvement could even be seen in the Navy's appropriation of one of Donovan's many abandoned schemes to allocate $800,000 to send advisors by horseback into Thailand to recruit, arm, train, and lead ten battalions of guerrillas. After admitting that "the Navy was [now] performing functions in China which did not have much relation to conventional naval duties . . . but that were of the OSS character," Rear Admiral W. R. Purnell stood to hand Donovan a draft of the Navy's proposed plan for future operations and asked if it "would be satisfactory to him." Donovan said it wouldn't. At 1:07 P.M., the meeting ended, and with it SACO's OSS support. The Navy was now on its own.

Despite a temperament perfectly evolved for diplomacy, Miles found that his three months in the unrelenting current of interservice competition had left him disenchanted and wistful for the simplicity of a surface ship. "I should be relieved in China," he sheepishly told Admiral King at a face-to-face meeting. "I've made enemies among our own people and SACO will be saddled with them."

King brushed aside Miles's objection. "We know you want to go to sea," King replied, his "piercing" eyes repelling any objections, "but you're more useful to us in China."

On Miles's return trip, a cloud of doubt descended. What possible success could he now have without OSS funding and support? How could SACO survive with such a ravenous competitor for supplies over the Hump? How could he possibly repair his loss of face with Tai Li? At Nouméa, New Caledonia, Miles slipped into the blue waters for a swim. If he had hoped to emerge with clarity, he did so only with an ear abscess. Then, on a transport between the Polynesian islands and India, he was struck with dysentery. Exhausted and aching from his head to his guts, he stretched out his hand to silence the telephone ringing in his Bombay quarters and heard a familiar voice from Calcutta. "Happy

Birthday, Mary! Do you have your new shoulder marks?" With that, Miles learned that he had just been promoted to the Navy's recently established rank of commodore—"Commodore of the Yangtze Rapids," it was decided over celebratory drinks at the Gymkhana Club—in effect, a rank equal to Donovan's, and one that doubled as both a shield and a sword against interservice attacks.

"It may be that I soared on my own power over the Hump," said Miles of his flight from Calcutta to Chungking, "for I hardly remember the trip." A few days later, Miles received another gift. Along with his promotion, King elevated SACO to Naval Group China, an act that likewise elevated each camp to a formal naval unit and invested Miles with all the authority of a group commander, increasing his rolls to 600 officers and 2,400 enlisted men—about 300 more than that allotted to a World War II battleship—and a commitment by the Navy that was further augmented by various numbers of Marines, Coast Guardsmen, and radio operators. To supply all of these men, Miles received two planes—their engines rarely idle—with which to ferry loads from Chungking to the various camps. The gas alone for these planes gobbled up as much as half of Miles's monthly tonnage allotment over the Hump, but for the first time in the war, SACO's camps began receiving at least a portion of what they deserved.

8

In May 1944, Tai Li and Miles traveled to Camp Two in Central China—now Unit Two after King's promotion of Miles's command to Naval Group China—to attend the graduation of a new class. There, Tai met Lieutenant Joseph Champe, a small, blue-eyed thirty-one-year-old from coal country West Virginia who, like Draper Kauffman, had been mustered out of the Naval Academy in 1932 because of a failed eye exam. A possessor of practical talents, he had taken up his studies at Cooper Union college in New York City, majoring in electronics. When the Japanese attacked, he had immediately volunteered for the Navy Reserve, accepting orders to a minesweeper before the smoke over Pearl Harbor had barely dissipated. Dissatisfied with his selection, he had next volunteered for the OSS, and in the disentangling of the Navy from the spy service had been assigned to SACO. "I'm sending Joe Champe to you . . . best of the experimental group," Metzel had written to Miles in October 1942. "He don't look so tough, but he made the Navy wrestling team and rates top everywhere he's worked." It was not an understatement. Given no more than a perfunctory education in infantry and commando tactics, Champe had picked up what he could from the Marines around him, then taught himself. Before long he was teaching Camp Two's guerrillas "standing-room-only" classes on how to turn glass candy jars into roadside explosives, to seal the ends of bamboo shoots to make underwater pipe bombs, and most ingenious of all, to oh-so-carefully fish Japanese mines out of the water, then move them to other parts of a river, a process that Miles liked to call "jujitsu." In these operations, Champe led his guerrillas up to the moment of attack, at which point they shunted him to the rear for fear that he would be wounded or worse. Blue with frustration over these flirtations with combat, as most Americans were, Champe had resorted to working with an ever-shadier cast of Chinese guerrillas. When Camp Two's commander reported Champe to Miles for "consorting with the wrong type of people," Champe had demanded a court-martial to clear his name. What he got instead was an opportunity to tell Miles and Tai exactly what he wanted—his own river unit that he could lead right into the Japanese strongholds. Face-to-face with West Virginian sincerity, Tai began to crack.

A few days later, the Japanese launched an advance into Unit Two's area that halted Champe's raiding plans but freed him to now trade jabs

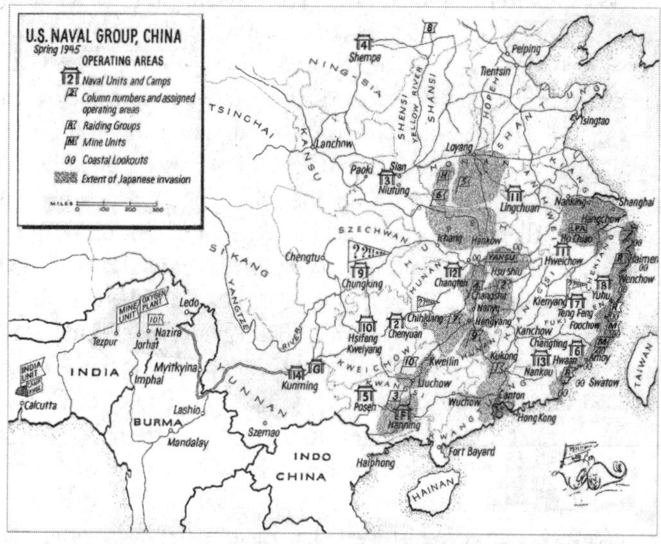

Map created by Admiral Milton Miles, edited by Charles Miles.

with the enemy. Gathering a handful of American advisors and some Chinese guerrillas, Champe led a rescue party into the eye of the Japanese hurricane to save nine stranded missionaries in Changsha. When they finished, Champe's crew struck out for the north, 900 miles by foot and by oar, where he and his Americans donned peasant clothes and big straw hats, built an army of 1,000 raiders and assassins, and proceeded to turn the lakes and rivers of central China into highways of terror for striking the remotest outposts of the Japanese Empire. When he finally relinquished command to a Marine captain, Champe's grateful Chinese raiders lined the path leading out of camp for a mile and a half, tossing firecrackers as he and another sailor and Marine walked the hero's gauntlet. Reddened by the sun and jaundiced by antimalaria medicine, the young sailor who had become the first American to lead Chinese guerrillas into combat was given the highest compliment Tai could conceive: "He looks like a Chinese."

Two months after allowing Champe to raise his Yangtze River Raiders, and after an "explosive argument with Miles," Tai finally relaxed his ban on allowing Americans in combat and expanded his permission across the board. "This is the green light you have been waiting for," Miles radioed his men. "Good hunting!" The only problem was that not all of SACO's sailors were hunters as instinctive as Champe.

Prior to the spring of 1944, the typical preparation of a SACO-bound sailor had consisted of a specially designed psychological evaluation that determined a candidate's ability to adapt to other cultures, followed by a three-week-long pressure cooker of training in Quantico, Virginia, that had included instruction in pistols, rifles, explosives, snowshoeing, kayaking, judo, and land navigation—hardly enough time for proficiency in one skill, let alone in seven. If SACO in 1944 was a body built of sailors—specialists in aerology, weather, ship engines, carpentry, and storekeeping—then it was a body held together by a spine of Marines—experts in gunnery, tactics, all the hard skills that guerrillas needed and sailors didn't have. For a time, that specialization meant that Marines would command some 70 percent of SACO's guerrillas, eventually even Champe's River Raiders, while making up just 4 percent of SACO's total, an imbalance that temporarily made the Navy's portion of SACO look like a gigantic tail behind a mouthful of Marine Corps teeth. Not only did this imbalance threaten to place the Navy's SACO legacy squarely on the shoulders of the Marine Corps' insufferable propaganda machine—also known as every Marine in history with a mouth—but it also often complicated Miles's efforts. "We have a clique out here which has embarrassed me several times," Miles had written in December 1943. "Probably it originated because they are all Marines, but at any rate it exists." Among this clique's offenses were an obvious anger at their assignment, a refusal to eat Chinese food, and the physical kicking of a Chinese servant, an act made even worse by telling the servant that his mother had been a turtle. The obvious solution to such problems was to engineer sailors who fought like Marines but didn't act like them. Good luck. Short of that, the only other option was to make Marines who were simply more susceptible to the Navy's authority. An even unlikelier prospect.

To solve this problem, Admiral King—in August 1944—ordered the commander of amphibious training in the Atlantic to create at Fort Pierce a special twelve-week-long course with a curriculum "divided equally between" that of the NCDUs and the Scouts and Raiders—not exactly a revolutionary proposition, since this was already happening with the UDTs in the Pacific. Moreover, the order did not foretell a Navy mission much beyond an arm's length of the high-water mark. Additional guidance from Admiral King was more explicit. After recommending that volunteers for this program possess prior combat experience and a good digestive system, King's memo went on to list among its training requirements several topics not usually associated with a naval assignment: map reading, booby traps, machine guns, and even Ranger principles: "Officers must combine fighting qualities with patience, and must have enough assurance to be ready for independent command of raiding expeditions." In a few months, the course would culminate with a week of survival and reconnaissance, finished off by a raid on the landlocked Florida town of Okeechobee, a running assault made more realistic by the flash of cherry bombs and all the terror the shouts from 100 or so human voice boxes could inflict. Ultimately, as another memo would state, it would be the kind of curriculum that would soon allow Miles to "substitute" a special kind of sailor for his Marines.

Because their mission had been usurped by the UDTs, the Scouts and Raiders were the Navy's best candidates for a new assignment; because of their long association with the Army, they were also the Navy's most primed unit for a ground war in China. So obvious was this fact that in short order Fort Pierce's commander would recommend that the Scouts and Raiders School be "dissolved" to make room for the one described above. Previously pigeonholed into the limited field of amphibious reconnaissance, volunteers to the Scouts and Raiders suddenly found themselves being upgraded into a new program with a new title—the Amphibious Rogers. The name was chosen to conceal their exact purpose beneath a cloak of ambiguity and to suggest they were the Navy's cutlass-clutching pirates beneath a whipping Jolly Roger. Though no one seems to have acknowledged it at the time, the course's graduates were the Navy's first attempt at creating commandos. Before the year was out, the first batch would depart Fort Pierce by train and in California board a thirty-day transport for Calcutta. There, the group would encounter Miles, who, after interviewing the officers and men, would pronounce them "the most outstanding that [he had] seen to date." It wasn't false flattery. "I have previously looked over the syllabus of training," he would write in a follow-on letter to Fort Pierce's commander, "and although half of the training periods do not appear to have any relation to what we originally had in mind when we requested these units, I have received a lot of ideas and may completely revamp our operating training program to fit the training. This, I know, is backwards. But we in China are often backwards anyway." He closed his letter by saying that he was looking forward to seeing these boys in action—action he now needed more than ever.

Scouts and Raiders School sign at Fort Pierce, alongside a sign for the Amphibious Rogers.

9

In October 1944, Marshall recalled General Joseph Stilwell from the China Theater for good. As his plane lifted off, Miles "swallowed a lump." A week later, General Albert Wedemeyer was officially given command of all US troops in the theater. In November, Wedemeyer flew to Chungking, where he and Miles discussed SACO at an Army party. "I just stumbled into this," Miles remembered telling him above the clink of glasses and the din of conversation. "Admiral King gave me a green light after I had Stilwell's permission, and now the guerrillas are really beginning to pay off." In this relaxed setting, Wedemeyer seemed easygoing, open-minded, and even "friendly to the Navy." Most recently assigned as the chief of staff to Admiral Mountbatten in Calcutta, Wedemeyer possessed smart looks, crisp gray hair parted down the center, ample height, and was known in the Army for having attended the pinnacle of Prussian military education, the Kreigsacademie. In the not too distant future, *Time* magazine would call him the Army's "Big Brain." In short, Wedemeyer was smart, pleased about it, and like all career staff officers, concerned chiefly with his career and secondarily with his staff. Moreover, he had thus far avoided a field command but also possessed a Prussian general's disinclination for peripheral operations. Now, he found himself in command of an operation as peripheral as ever existed. More than anything, Wedemeyer wanted a neatly aligned pyramid chart, one with clear, bold lines and one soldier at the top. Miles's worst fears had coalesced in a single person.

In January 1945, the Year of the Rooster in China, Wedemeyer crowed the coming of a new dawn. Almost as soon as Stilwell had gone, Donovan had returned, this time finding a willing buyer for his ideas on OSS-led commando teams—and unlike SACO's guerrillas, not shared with Chiang's Nationalist government. In every meeting about the OSS and SACO, Wedemeyer stressed the importance of "coordination," an innocent word that Miles quickly learned to interpret by its Army meaning: "subordination." As Wedemeyer prepared for a trip back to Washington for a meeting with the Joint Chiefs, he met with Miles in Chungking. With a voice so "raised" as to prompt a passing general to pop his head in "to see who was getting murdered," Wedemeyer told Miles that he planned to request that the Joint Chiefs "abrogate" the SACO agreement, because "it was the most awful thing that ever existed!" The argument tied the men in knots.

Wedemeyer: "Admiral Nimitz would not allow an Army unit to operate in the Pacific Ocean without his full control."

Miles: "Nimitz does not have a major ally with whom he must coordinate."

In fact, chain of command was only part of the problem; the other part was the Navy's presence in the first place. Months later, Miles met for lunch with Wedemeyer's planning officer, General George Olmstead. Friends since their days at rival service academies, even Olmstead bristled at the Navy's role in China's ground war. As Miles recorded afterward, the typical Army question ran: "What is the Navy doing in 'our' business anyway?" Even naval officers squirmed at the thought. When Admiral C. M. Cooke, a plans officer on Wedemeyer's staff, traveled to Happy Valley to tour Miles's operation, he told him that "a seagoing sailor has no damn business fighting guerrillas in the hills" and admitted that he had been sent "to see about closing [him] out." If fellow sailors could not understand what the Navy was doing out there, then what chance did Miles ever really have?

In the first week of March, Wedemeyer returned to Washington in order to brief the four Joint Chiefs—Marshall, King, General Henry "Hap" Arnold, and Admiral William Leahy. He put forth his various plans to capture a port on China's east coast, to solve the problems in transporting supplies over the Hump, to further the progress of Stilwell's road. Then, as Miles watched from the "slopes" of the room in "a kind of shocked horror," Wedemeyer outlined what he later described as "a rather embarrassing problem"—that of a US Navy group in his theater "undertaking operations of a clandestine nature" outside his chain of command. (In Wedemeyer's five-hundred-plus-page autobiography, this instance was the only time SACO and "Commodore Miles"—first name not given—were ever mentioned.) As Miles remembered the scene afterward, Wedemeyer repeated every sensational charge that had ever been made about Tai Li, and even "assured" the chiefs that the generalissimo had agreed to a modification of the SACO agreement that would place him in charge of all Americans.

Being one of the president's closest confidants, Admiral Leahy looked around at his peers like an impartial judge before sentencing.

"I am in favor," Marshall said. So was Arnold, the chief of the Army Air Forces. And with that, King was cornered. Without a word he "shrugged his shoulders a little and turned up both hands." It was done. The Army was now in control of the Navy's guerrillas; for SACO, this was a threat even greater than the Japanese: disbandment. As Metzel had warned, only one route remained to prevent such a fate: "scalps on the barrelhead"; an offering not as simple as it sounded, especially for those camps most removed from Happy Valley and most densely surrounded by the Japanese. The camps near the coast—the focus of SACO's original mandate—were now the best chance of forestalling its demise.

10

ESTABLISHED SOME SIX MONTHS earlier as a jumping-off point for capturing the Japanese-held harbor island of Amoy, Camp Six possessed a target area that most of its assigned sailors had so far never laid eyes on. The explanations for this were varied. Situated near Huaan in a "well hemmed" valley along the banks of the Nine Dragons River, the camp was surrounded by mountains that provided a natural protection from Japanese attack but simultaneously complicated every other aspect of its mission. Among those complications were the fifty airline miles that separated the camp's sailors from China's southeast coast—no small distance by foot—by way of routes that were notoriously treacherous—either a twisting stripe of road etched into a sheer-drop cliff or a rapids-choked mountain sluice crowded with bean curd sampans. Pilgrims to the site, said one witness, emerged from this experience with "a strange feeling of relief to be somewhere—in fact—anywhere"; but this was an anywhere made of rice paddies and water buffalo that had not noticeably changed since the days of Marco Polo. Lacking construction materials, the camp's first members had had to cram themselves, their hand-cranked radios, their weapons crates, and their alcohol-powered refrigerator stolen from an abandoned American mission into the candlelit second story of a traditional square building whose lower level housed several Chinese families who shared their space with the snorts, quacks, and clucks of their pigs, ducks, and chickens. After a month, the camp's sailors had upgraded their accommodations to an ancient tiled Chinese temple large enough for several desks, an armory, a sick bay, a mess hall, and a galley, but plagued by roof leaks, a propensity for flooding, and a perfect profile for a Japanese bomb target.

More disheartening than the camp's physical limitations had been those of staffing. Invested by Miles with the operational authority of a destroyer skipper, Camp Six's commander—one of the few Navy officers in charge of a guerrilla unit—had been forced to shoulder responsibilities that went far beyond any with which he was familiar: intelligence gathering, camp payroll, counterespionage, aerology, physical security, direction finding, even gasoline rationing. Most incongruous of all had been Miles's mandate to plan an operation capable of not only capturing the Japanese-held island of Amoy, but also seizing the Japanese code and radio rooms intact without suffering a "crippling" loss to themselves. "Since you are to be tangled up with that action," Miles's orders had specified, "it is your neck if you don't train [the task force] properly." Quite a mandate, considering that the camp's initial roster had included only two Marines.

The camp commander's response to this pressure had been to funnel it downward—formation every morning at 7:00 A.M., where, according to one sufferer, all had been "issued orders right and left." A forgivable annoyance considering the circumstances, but the commander's reputation had suffered a bigger blow when he challenged one of his enlisted storekeepers to a pistol shooting contest, lost twice, then resented the sailor until he was replaced just two months after his appointment. The next commander—a former FBI special agent—appeared to be more competent and was certainly much more formidable on the pistol range, but except for commissioning a full-scale sand, glue, and sawdust model of the Amoy target area, he spent most of his time preoccupied with rescuing the camp's properties from the threat of typhoon flooding and misery. Ultimately, this preoccupation resulted in moving the headquarters to a patch of high ground at the top of 500 stone steps, improving the lives of everyone with generator-powered lights and the discovery of an underground stream that—through an improvised series of pipes—fed a water heater of repurposed gasoline drums and a refrigerated slaughterhouse stacked with the "luxury" of steaks, chops, and roasts. The creation of a pistol and rifle range notwithstanding, these had been the kinds of improvements aimed inward, not outward, the only direction that really mattered.

In early September 1944, guerrilla training had begun with classes on ship and plane identification, and progressed to a single course in pistol shooting—a slow start caused by the fact that no other weapons shipments had yet arrived in Huaan, but also by the reality that most of Camp Six's sailors would not have known what to do with them if they had. Leaning on the Marine Corps skills of Captain Earle B. Dane, Jr., and Sergeant Harrison Rainey, however, instruction had quickly ramped up to include courses on M1 carbines and Thompson submachine guns, and then—for a handful of Chinese—had rolled right on into scouting, patrolling, grenade throwing, and first aid. In between volleys at the range and sometimes during them, Chinese children scurried about collecting the hot brass or huddled by the targets, waiting to dig the spent bullets out of the dirt.

On December 10, Camp Six's commander was abruptly removed and returned to the United States, leaving the unit without a boss at the same moment the skies unleashed forty-seven days of uninterrupted rain and cold. With the grounds resembling an "unpleasant bathtub," training slowed to a drip and the men responded as all do in the absence of leadership and the advent of bad weather: they "cultivated" elaborate beards, played cards with Chinese money, puffed on fairy-tale-length pipes, hurled insults at Roger the houseboy, and spent their nights belting forth a bawdy assortment of "off and on key" songs hammered out by Doc Coleman on an upright piano—another luxury that had been muscled up the camp's 500 steps by twenty-six peasants. During breaks from painting his model of Amoy, one sailor sketched the images of salacious women on a bulkhead. At night, Camp Six's advisors allowed their Chinese wards to play their favorite game: "Get the Americans Drunk." In short, the experience of Camp Six to date had led most of those assigned there to believe they were "backing a tortoise," and allowed them to join in with the rest of SACO's coastal units whose members had already started calling themselves the Dead End Kids.

On January 8, 1945, Captain Dane—Camp Six's lone Marine Corps officer—had returned from a monthlong reconnaissance of China's southeast coast. Aside from gathering information on Amoy, Dane had also returned with tales of an area rife with Japanese troops, several island garrisons, and innumerable isolated patrols of never-before-molested mainland foraging parties—"ideal" targets for raiding and providing Camp Six's advisors and guerrillas with "sorely needed combat experience." The only problem with such a plan: the lack of adequately trained men. Within two days of his return, Dane had made a formal request that Camp Six be assigned not just more men, but seven Marines, "as they are the only men qualified." "If these cannot be secured," his request had continued, "no others are needed." It was a blunt indictment of the lack of combat skills among SACO's naval personnel, but it was a request that went on to make an exception for sailors "with specialized training in demolition and/or field work." Men not unlike the one who was to be Camp Six's new commanding officer, but whose weeks of delayed arrival had—said the official record—turned him into something of a myth. Soon that man would be one of Naval Special Warfare's first legends.

11

In February 1945, the same month Miles found himself en route to the meeting meant to strip SACO of Navy control, the members of Camp Six welcomed into their midst a small caravan that brought the mail, three more American sailors, a little black dog named Hash, two bottles of Johnnie Walker, and, finally, the commanding officer long since promised; the kind of commanding officer SACO now needed more than anything.

Wearing a peaked cap and the fur-lined leather jacket of a naval aviator, Lieutenant Commander Robert "Buck" Halperin—as conspicuous in his features as the actor Robert Taylor, and still built like the NFL quarterback he had been—looked like neither a Marine nor an Amphibious Roger but more like Hollywood's version of both. It was an appearance made even more auspicious by the weight of its owner's notoriety. More than three years now since Halperin had enlisted, his talents as a Lake Michigan sailboat racer, Chicago business owner, and professional football player and coach had carried him far beyond his early days as a thirty-four-year-old seaman recruit and Gene Tunney conscript. The first Scout Boat Officer to go ashore in the North Africa invasion and the first sailor of the campaign to level a weapon at an enemy soldier and take him prisoner, he had since volunteered for repeat performances in Sicily and Normandy, invasions that had claimed five of the original ten Tuna Fish—two killed and three discharged for wounds. Although Halperin had initially been afraid of missing the war because of his age, his experiences had turned him into one of its heroes. In three years he had leapfrogged thirteen ranks and been awarded a battlefield commission. And in spite of service in a unit described as a "top secret within a top secret," he had been repeatedly lionized by the press: first with a two-page story in the Navy's *Amphibian* magazine that included a front-page sketch of him reconnoitering an enemy beach, followed by mentions in radio broadcasts, the *Chicago Sun*, and *The Daily Times* of Beaver and Rochester, Pennsylvania. "His job is to mark beaches for the assault . . . a daring, intricate job calling for as much brain as courage and barrels of both," said the *Canadian Jewish Chronicle* of him in 1944. "[A job] which not one man in a thousand would like to have."

For being that one man in a thousand, Halperin had, after the final Allied invasion in Europe, been reassigned to the Scouts and Raiders

School at Fort Pierce to pass on his knowledge of amphibious reconnaissance. It was an assignment that would have finally allowed him to relax, to take pride in his achievements, even to reconnect with his wife—a relationship that had long since been strained by the stress of war. Alas, if only Halperin hadn't been Halperin. This was an incomparably personal war for all Jews, especially those only one generation removed from the Old World, and Halperin was—despite a personality abounding in kindness, humility, camaraderie, and humor—still the same man whose drive to be the best had overridden his heritage and carried him to Notre Dame and, more important, one whose appetite to personally confront the enemy had not yet been slaked. It was an appetite that happened to coincide with the Scouts and Raiders School's transformation into the Amphibious Roger Program.

In late 1944, Halperin had been ordered to the Navy's Interior Control Board in Washington, D.C., where he had been escorted to a windowless room whose walls had been hung with drapes to conceal the maps beneath them. Inside, he had been greeted by the usual uniforms, plus a pair of uniforms he had never seen, both attached to the smiling faces of two Chinese officers. After introductions and a few pleasantries, said a later account, the assembled officers "gave him the business": a ground war being waged by Chinese guerrillas that were being trained and advised—for the most part—by US Navy sailors, but trainers and advisors with only slightly more experience than their students. Having demonstrated his knack for training sailors and soldiers alike and leading them in combat, having shown a willingness to personally pursue the enemy no matter if it pushed the normal boundaries of maritime operations, Halperin was—for the second time in one war—as ideal a naval officer as could be imagined for the assignment ahead; this time to lead Camp Six, one of SACO's last, best justifications to remain under Navy control. Though no one had the context to realize it at the time, he had just been named the first ground force commander in the history of Naval Special Warfare; a title that would be earned in no small part by his insistence that every Marine, sailor, and Roger under his command "participate directly in combat action." It was a policy that would not only crush the motto of the Dead End Kids, but replace it with another: Every Man a Tiger.

12

UPON ARRIVAL, HALPERIN was welcomed to Camp Six with a "Bam Bam Boo" party that had ended with him being carried back to his room by sedan chair. His first morning in command was met with a hangover followed by an introduction to all the problems that had awaited him. Not only were many of his guerrilla trainees racked with malaria, cellulitis, and various digestive maladies, they were also without shoes or even a single change of clothing—all of which had prevented them from training in the near-constant rains lest there be an increase in the number of those with pneumonia. Further detriments to combat preparedness were the result of an inexplicable habit among the Chinese commanders to rotate weapons among those who had not been trained with them, and a cadre of twenty-nine American instructors who largely could not correct these deficiencies for the same reason. Those who could have—like Dane, the camp's "restless" Marine officer—had already departed the camp to initiate Operation Whiskers, his plan to launch raids against the coastal mainland, and for which he had taken Camp Six's best guerrillas. The camp's most aggressive operational undertaking to date, even this was already stumbling; not only had Dane's Chinese radioman been unable to assemble the transmitter needed to communicate with Camp Six, but the Navy officer attached to the patrol had lost a musette bag containing Dane's entire plan of operations.

Realizing that many of Camp Six's problems originated from a lack of training, Halperin made it his first order of business to initiate an

Camp Six photo, with Halperin in the front row, center.

overhaul. To improve the weapons competence of his guerrillas, he first ensured that all Americans assigned to him received training in the camp's entire arsenal, a measure that cascaded into advanced instruction in demolition, the mysteries of Morse code, marksmanship and weapons maintenance, and for 100 students, a special class in the Lewis machine gun, a Western Front–era vintage weapon that despite its age could still magnify a small unit ambush from droplets of rifle fire into a downpour of lead. So that his students could absorb such training, he augmented the already Herculean medical efforts of Lieutenant Ernest "Doc" Coleman and his corpsmen—everything from treating ankle sprains to at least one "greatly elongated prepuce" that required circumcision—and started issuing to every guerrilla volunteer the gold equivalent of 530 Chinese notes per month, plus enough to buy each man one pair of sandals. To synthesize these improvements, Halperin organized a two-day mock battle between his 1st and 2nd guerrilla battalions that he umpired on horseback, including all of the following challenges: river crossings, dawn attacks, night raids, running retreats, and hasty hilltop defenses; not exactly the standard fare of most naval exercises.

Not willing to wait for the return on these investments, Halperin approved the creation of a subcamp at Changchow as a jumping-off point for the operations of Demo Detachment Number 1, an all-Navy sabotage unit conceived in part by Charles Robinson, one of Draper Kauffman's former protégés at the mine disposal school. After this, he doubled down on Camp Six's riskiest venture. Instead of recalling Dane and his guerrillas for the loss of the musette bag and their radio failures, Halperin generously reasoned that "the element of surprise would be lost after the first operation" anyway, so he not only decided to keep them in the field, but also sent them one of his own radiomen. Emboldened by such confidence, Dane went on to make the most of his independence and planned his group's first nighttime raid on a thirteen-man Japanese barracks in the town of Tayee. Setting aside the mission's faults—the inability of Dane's bazooka squad to keep up, forcing him to leave it behind; the failure of Dane's guide to locate the target in the blacked-out town, forcing him to knock on the doors of random locals to find it; and worst of all, the miscalculation of the barracks' size, forcing his three squads into a terrifying, interior shoot-out with fifty Japanese soldiers—it was nevertheless a start. Camp Six had struck a blow. Now all Halperin needed were the fists to strike more.

As it happened, March was the month the first men of Amphibious Roger Group 1 began arriving in Camp Six.

13

Just as planners seemed to have finally solved the manpower issue that had long stymied the Navy in China, Wedemeyer decided that SACO should receive no more American troops except replacements. Almost immediately this order caused a logjam at Camp Knox, the Navy's way station in Calcutta, and indefinite confinement for what would soon be 1,000 Amphibious Rogers in a holding pen built for 450 transients. Worse still, Wedemeyer followed up this order with another that instructed Miles to begin limiting SACO's guerrillas to "those directly essential to the protection" of groups acquiring "naval intelligence and other information as may be required by the Commander-in-Chief, U.S. Fleet." Essentially, Wedemeyer was telling Miles to keep tabs on the weather.

Alternating Benzedrine to stay awake with sleeping pills to go to sleep, Atabrine for his malaria, and as many as forty aspirins a day for everything else, Miles responded to the Army's "roadblocks" with an almost sleepless schedule—more hours than he had ever spent fighting the Japanese, he said—to create a compromise "acceptable" to Wedemeyer, the Chinese, and most of all, to him. More than a comprehensive operations plan, it was an effort that also taught him a lesson that no one at the beginning of this war could have expected to learn.

Incredulous at how far the Army had fallen from Mosby's freewheeling Civil War Rangers to Wedemeyer's bean counters trying to control every operational detail of China's irregular war from the safety of their "little Pentagon" in Chungking, Miles was now not only convinced that the Navy should have a seat at the table for future guerrilla wars, but that that seat should be at the table's head. Likely the first Navy man of the century to arrive at such a heretical idea, on March 20, Miles circulated a letter to the entire staff of Naval Group China with instructions to make available to the Army all the Navy's routine services, from its weather stations to its radio nets, but also added an unequivocal order to the skippers of his fleet's camps to "prosecute the war in every possible phase in which the US Navy is interested . . . making sure that our effort is all directed at the enemy." Conveying no self-consciousness about a Navy-run guerrilla army, and written in the usual Navy way to lend as much latitude as possible to its recipients, Miles's letter went on to order his units to "clean up all Japs" on China's coastal islands—specifically Amoy—and to reiterate his insistence that his men physically accompany each guerrilla column. Whether or not the Army's planners could recognize how their missteps in China had made this possible, SACO's sailors were nevertheless about to launch their very first ground campaign—something no living American sailor had ever done before, and something they had not chanced upon by accident.

At no point would the Navy's intentions to insinuate itself into the Army's prerogatives be more apparent than in Admiral King's insistence on fielding the men who had been created to do just that. Furious after watching five months' worth of training and investment being squandered in Calcutta because of Wedemeyer's bureaucratic petulance, King reminded Miles of the cost it had taken to create the Amphibious Roger School and warned him that if he did not hijack the Army's transports, then he wouldn't be able to demonstrate the Rogers' value, and the program would likely "go out of existence." If that happened, the Navy's chances of ever "[obtaining] comparable material [would] be very remote indeed." As it happened, Miles wouldn't have to do anything to demonstrate the Rogers' value; they were already doing that themselves.

14

By April of 1945, Halperin was on the cusp of initiating two programs that, along with the work being done by Dane's Operation Whiskers Raiders, would officially transform his training camp into a full-fledged operational weapon; that is, Naval Unit Six—one of eleven such outfits within SACO and one of just four not commanded by a Marine officer. The first of these programs was a training plan that would in short order produce some 2,500 Chinese guerrillas, enough to form a large American regiment or a small brigade, and a size that would invest Halperin with all the battlefield authority of a regular Army colonel, two ranks above his pay grade and fifteen higher than on the day of his enlistment. The second of these was the operational unleashing of Demo Detachment 1 and all the "malicious gadgets" they had been devising to demolish Japanese infrastructure around the island of Amoy, including what the official record described as "undesirable persons." Taken together with Dane's Whiskers Raiders—now planning an ambush on a 100-man Japanese convoy in Fuchang—Halperin's Unit Six was already shaping up to be as aggressive and can-do as any of the SACO units run by Marines, and with Halperin, would no doubt have remained so. With the arrival of the first batch of Rogers to the camp, however, Unit Six would soon become something else altogether; it was the outfit that came closest to fulfilling the original concept of the OSS Maritime Unit.

Within weeks of the first Rogers' arrival, the Chinese at Camp Six organized a sampan regatta on the Nine Dragons River that included a swim meet. In attendance was Ensign John "Matty" Mattmiller, a recently arrived former swimmer from the University of Idaho and former enlisted Marine who had second-guessed his commissioning as a naval officer by volunteering for the Amphibious Rogers, and who only days earlier had learned of his brother's death at Iwo Jima. With more reasons than anyone for vengeance, Mattmiller watched the race and arrived at an idea to get just that. After selecting the four best Chinese swimmers, he proposed his idea to Halperin, who in turn sent a message to Miles and Tai Li for permission, along with a request for fifty limpet mines—"RPT FIFTY," said the message. Once the concept for Operation Swordfish was approved, Mattmiller started his recruits on a month of calisthenics, swim practices, and rehearsals. On the day before they were meant to depart, one of his swimmers went missing in the river, initiating several days of bottom searches that resulted in nothing found.

Ten minutes after midnight on May 6, 1945, Mattmiller and his three remaining Chinese swimmers boarded a junk and, on the surge of a rising tide, motored toward the blackened silhouette that was the island of Amoy. Once they reached the outskirts of Amoy's harbor, they stripped down, strapped twenty-pound, OSS-made, magnetized limpet mines of composition C to their backs, then slipped into the water and began swimming. After 300 yards of furtively raising their faces to the surface and concealing their arms beneath the black water, they reached the cadaver-cold hull of a 1,000-ton Japanese oil freighter moored against a newly filled land dock. Treading water in the dark, each swimmer silently wriggled out of his pack, and cradling his charge, headed to its designated location. One was easily placed amidships above the waterline, the magnets softly clunking a hollow thud as they grabbed the hull. Two swimmers were forced to hold their breaths, descend, then use their hands to blindly feel their way past the sucking threat of the ship's various intake valves to place one mine on the rudder's strut and another on the blade of the screw. Once all mines were affixed, each swimmer quietly cracked the tube of a four-hour acid-eating time fuse, then pushed away from the ship. As they prepared to slip away into the darkness, one swimmer kicked against the water beneath him and heaved a final mine directly onto the ship's deck. With that, the swimmers disappeared.

When the junk finally arrived back on the mainland, Halperin welcomed the swimmers ashore, then quietly led the shore party to the top of a hill overlooking the harbor. As the clock approached the four-hour mark, Mattmiller told the anxious crowd that the explosions should begin in about fifteen minutes. As the deadline came and went, Mattmiller lost hope; "Damn pencils must not have worked," he said. Then, as the group began to murmur, a light flashed in the distance. Instantly, the men stopped talking. In a few seconds, they heard the report—"a great rumbling noise." At the first of these, the lights around Amoy blinked on and the ship's crew began rushing up from the hold to gather on the deck. Halperin and his men watched the Japanese sailors look skyward for the thrum of bomber engines, but there were none. Then, without warning, a "geyser of fire" erupted from the hold, followed by another explosion that splashed the decks with flame. Within thirty minutes, the entire ship was ablaze; by morning, it was settled on its side and filling with mud, blocking the much-needed pier to thwart future Japanese resupply and evacuation. Within days, Miles's chief of staff sent a telegram to Admiral King's office that recognized Halperin for a "no casualties" raid that had left the entire "Amoy area in a state of confusion." Halperin wasn't done.

15

LARGER IN SQUARE FOOTAGE than Manhattan, the island of Amoy had been under Japanese occupation since 1938 and was now guarded by some 4,000 Japanese troops, about twice the number that had been at Tarawa. Responsible for "cleaning up" these troops, but possessing less than two-thirds of their numbers or the boats or weapons needed to launch a frontal assault against them, Halperin really had only one course of action: to isolate their outlying garrisons and attack them one by one. It required him to initiate a campaign unlike any other in the history of the US Navy, and for which he had first had to receive full approval from Miles and Tai Li. As with Operation Swordfish, it was an approval that was eagerly granted.

To begin this operation—Operation Wild Horse, as it was named—Halperin assembled a specially trained company of 120 Chinese guerrillas and 18 American advisors. With his Marines—Captain Dane and

Sergeant Rainey—embittered by the failures of Operation Whiskers and now anxiously awaiting their orders to return to the United States, Halperin was forced to fill out the latter group exclusively with sailors, most of them Amphibious Rogers—except for the Chinese, the first all-Navy raiders since William Cushing's in the American Civil War. Thus organized, Halperin led this company to China's southeast coast and from there organized the kinds of reconnaissance missions he had been perfecting since his first days at the Scouts and Raiders School, the only difference being that now he was the raider.

On the night of June 24, 1945, Halperin led his men over "the steepest, rockiest, most slippery trail any American in the group had previously travelled" to reach their jumping-off point at the fishing village of Tau Be. From here, across some six miles of Japanese-patrolled waters, they could see the shadow of Amoy and, in between, a series of smaller islands strung out from south to north like stepping-stones. The closest was their target of Wu Su—from their reconnaissance, manned by fewer than a hundred defenders.

With the full moon shielded by a shifting veil of black clouds and the dawn of one of the longest days of the year fast approaching, Halperin wasted no time in assembling a flotilla of whatever vessels his men could find and setting up an aid station and a command post. From here—the first time since Morocco in 1942 that he would not personally be along for the invasion—he would oversee the entire operation, the tactical command of which now fell to Navy Lieutenant Richard Plank, commander of Demo Det. 1. Plank in turn would oversee three raiding groups, each led by a Fort Pierce–trained officer—Ensigns Matty Mattmiller, Robert Hoe, and James Treanor—and each supported by a handful of enlisted Rogers. Individual group assignments included the (ironic) elimination of all sentries atop the Goddess of Mercy Hill, plus the capture of several machine gun nests, two houses, three forts, and the disabling of an air alarm station; all targets more appropriate for Army Rangers than Navy anything. Or it would have been, had there been any Rangers within a thousand miles.

As soon as the various sailboats and junks were ready to push off, Halperin and Plank assembled the men for a hasty briefing. While they were detailing the mission's objectives, several signal lights flashed in the hills behind them—whether a warning to the defenders on Wu Su, no one knew. Not wanting to scrap the mission for what could be a completely unrelated occurrence, Halperin looked over the men, then ordered them to go ahead.

For a while, the transit—and therefore the entire mission—seemed to go smoothly: Plank and his machine gun crew managed to set up on their abandoned island without incident; the weather cooperated; all the men remained poised inside their vessels, clutching their carbines and tommy guns, some even clicking through the beads on their rosaries. Then the problems began to arise.

Straining against the rolling Pacific current, most of the Chinese oarsmen quickly began to tire; many became nauseous. As this was happening, the clouds began to shift, exposing a full moon that turned the flotilla into a creeping rank of black silhouettes on a shimmering sea. As if suddenly realizing their nakedness in a dream, each man tucked low or tightened his grip on a gunwale, anxious to feel the dull scrape of sand on the hull so they could leap out and splash ashore. They never did.

When Mattmiller's group was fifty yards from the beach, a rope of tracer fire disintegrated the night. Though initially ineffective—as night fire often is—it nevertheless shattered the men's nerves and broke the flotilla into a "clamor" of "sampans, junks, tracers, and gunfire," each vessel scrambling to escape in a different direction. Seconds after this initial burst, the shore fire tracked from right to left, stitching past Hoe's group and drumming into Plank's position on the abandoned island; it was enough of a shift to permit most boat crews—all of whom refused to paddle forward—to turn around.

As they did, the first of several Japanese gunboats slipped from the docks of Amoy's harbor in the distance and began heading straight for them. Their only hope was to scatter or make for the protection of Plank's island. When Hoe's group landed on the latter option, the Japanese gunboats turned off, making a chess-like move for Tau Be, to cut off the flotilla's retreat.

Just off the beach from the point where the Rogers had launched their raid, one of the gunboats lowered its antiaircraft guns to near water level, then blasted shells across the town. As fragments "splattered" about the temple walls where Halperin's men had established their aid station, Doc Coleman and Pharmacist Mate William Powers flattened onto the ground. Before long, the Japanese garrison on Wu Su also opened up and "literally plastered the mountain side with fire." When a frantic Chinese guerrilla officer appeared with word that a detachment of Japanese soldiers had just landed and were now advancing on the temple, Coleman and Powers ran for their lives.

Back on the abandoned island, Lieutenant Plank was cut off from advance or retreat. Experienced enough to know that no choice was still a choice, he picked the least bad option and ordered his boats back to the mainland while darkness could still conceal them. He and his command party would remain behind and cover the withdrawal. If the Japanese gunboats wanted to sink his men, they would have to do it under the pain of his Lewis gun.

If the boat ride out had been a struggle, it was nothing compared to the ride back. In Hoe's group, the Chinese guerrillas refused to relieve their collapsing peasant comrades because, as Hoe remembered, "this was below their position." When the men finally did reach the mainland, they were exhausted, scattered up and down the shoreline just as haphazardly as Carlson's Raiders had been on Makin. As one exhausted group struggled to negotiate a trail back to the rendezvous point, it ran into a tiger. Another group landed so angry at being outgunned by the Japanese that they went hunting for a bazooka, found one, and fired it at one of the roving gunboats. With the first aid station abandoned, the peasant oarsmen saw their chance and began sloughing off down the beach with Doc Coleman's medical supplies.

When all the crews were finally safe on the mainland, Plank and his command party loaded their boat and pushed off from their island. Somewhere between the island and the mainland, the boat sank. One of his sailors was unable to swim (obviously not a Roger), so Plank removed his pants, tied the legs off at the ends, then slapped them full of air and gave them away as a life preserver. By this means the desperate sailor managed to float like flotsam all the way to shore. Lieutenant Charles Robinson, Kauffman's former protégé, abandoned all hope of reaching the mainland under his own power and swam back to the island. He was picked up later. Separated in the dark from his men, Plank likewise found a rock, climbed on top of it, and waited there naked until rescued.

16

In the end, SACO's first all-Navy-led raid was no less a botched execution than had been the Marine Raiders' on Makin Island. Lack of intelligence, lack of weapons, lack of reliable boats—mostly the lack of experience to know that they had lacked those other things in the first place—had all demonstrated an operational immaturity that should have led to a lowering of operational ambitions. What made the failed raid on Wu Su so important was that it did no such thing. Supported by a chain of command whose only response was the same autonomy it had always given, Halperin responded the way he always had and immediately prepared to try again. As it happened, he wouldn't have to.

Within days of the raid's failure, Halperin received intelligence from SACO's spies that the Japanese sailors on Amoy were eating all of the Japanese soldiers' food and now were under the double threat of the American raiders and starvation. The Japanese Army commander's response was to place an order for three hundred black business suits to be worn by an advance party that would prepare the way for a mass evacuation of Japanese soldiers from Amoy to the mainland, where they would escape south along the coast. Naturally, Halperin eyed these impending convoys like a shark eyes a pod of seals and ordered Unit Six to scrap the raid, then fall in with the 75th Chinese Division for the chase. It was an experience that no American sailor who had enlisted in the US Navy during World War II could have anticipated.

For twenty days and nights, often with no sleep, often with little more than a single bowl of rice in their stomachs, Halperin and his men—many of them Rogers; many of the officers mounted on horses—redeemed their failure at Wu Su by leading their guerrillas over mountains and through valleys planting explosives, laying ambushes, escaping encirclement, directing naval air sorties, storming hilltop redoubts, even kicking their Chinese comrades into action. Though barely heard by most Americans, who were already deafened by four years of uninterrupted combat, SACO's guns—especially those wielded by outfits like Halperin's Unit Six; especially in the silence that followed the Battle of Okinawa—were some of the very last ones being fired by Americans in the Second World War, a fact that made them reverberate all the louder in the ears of the Navy's planners. No doubt these would have continued to build to a crescendo had they not been drowned out by the loudest explosion ever heard in any war.

In Changchow, Halperin received the news of the war's end with circumspection and dispatched his men to find out what they could—"with or without" their Chinese troops. After sending two bottles of Scotch and a case of beer ahead of himself, presumably to discourage the Japanese from any suicidal last stands, Halperin boarded a boat and crossed to the island of Amoy. There he was met by Amoy's commanders—Admiral Halata and his chief of staff, Captain Motsomoto—who, said a reporter, "turned their swords over to the American naval officer who had made their last year miserable." Even Halperin agreed: "we cut them up, no doubt about that," he said. At the conclusion of surrender formalities, the men of Unit Six hoisted above Amoy's Japanese garrison both American and Chinese flags, along with SACO's "What the hell?" pennant. Significant for its war-ending symbolism, the flag-raising on Amoy was also important for undercutting a CNO-directed raid on Amoy's heavily guarded airfield to capture a secret Japanese codebook. Designed to be supported by Unit Six and conducted by Phil Bucklew and a specially trained force of twenty-two former Scout and Raider veterans, it was the kind of raid whose success could not only have redeemed the Navy's failure at Wu Su but illuminated the increasing maturity of the Navy's past investments in the arts of scouting and raiding, and the returns that could be expected from further speculations. However, it was not to be. Not yet.

17

For Miles, the war ended much like it had begun. To disprove Army accusations that SACO guerrillas had attacked OSS-sponsored Communists, Tai had escorted Miles on an overland trek to Shanghai. There, once again, they had both been forced to jump from a window to escape an assassination attempt. Afterward, with Miles's teeth chattering from a malarial fever of 103 degrees, his guerrillas had packed him up and shuttled him from house to house, mountaintop to mountaintop, always moving at night, never too far ahead of the threat of Japanese encirclement. Days later, on August 7, from the crackling voice of an army radio operator, Miles heard "something about a 'big bomb.'" Like most people, he had no idea what that meant. Though he would not know it for a few more days, the war was over. On August 13, 1945, Miles was promoted to admiral.

"The end of the war should have been the happiest day of my life," wrote Miles afterward. Tasked with an impossible mission and yoked to impossible partners, he had nevertheless achieved something greater than had ever been asked of him: a Navy-run guerrilla army and intelligence infrastructure that had stretched from Indochina to the Gobi Desert. Assisted by Marines, his sailors had trained as many as 100,000 Chinese guerrillas, rescued airmen and missionaries, blasted open Japanese tanks, blown up some 158 bridges, derailed some 66 Japanese trains, sunk 35 Japanese ships, raided uncountable Japanese camps, and led at least one cavalry charge on camels. Best estimates of the time placed the number of SACO-inflicted Japanese casualties at around 26,717 killed, 8,702 wounded, and 346 captured. Of the roughly 2,500

Americans who served in SACO, 5 were killed. As is almost always the case with successful wartime generals, Miles's victories had come at the price of his sleep, his health, his family's happiness, and even his sanity. For his sacrifices he had been heaped not with praise and press releases, but with troubles, bureaucracy, and overweening scrutiny. In the end, SACO—along with the Navy's guerrilla warfare effort—received a reward as glamorous as an obituary. As Miles bitterly concluded, "the month that followed the surrender of Japan was the worst through which I have lived."

By the time Miles arrived back in Chungking for the official surrender of Japanese forces in China, the ceremony had already ended. So had many formal and material discussions about the postwar division of labor. Despite the fact that SACO Units 6, 7, and 8 were in "almost absolute control of the coast"—from Halperin in Amoy to Bucklew in Hangchow—Wedemeyer was preparing to have the Army replace them. Most important, Wedemeyer was already petitioning the Joint Chiefs to terminate the SACO agreement immediately. Considering the rattled state that Miles was in, there was no time to spare. After a long day of celebrations in Shanghai in September, Wedemeyer retired to his private chambers, only to have Miles barge in, "roiled as a ship's wake." Exhausted, angry, sick, and self-medicated, Miles moved about the room like a squall. Impassioned, perhaps shell-shocked, Miles lectured his superior on his and SACO's accomplishments, on the burden of Wedemeyer's bureaucracy, on discovering "a method of warfare that not only suited the Chinese" but one that had maximized the Army's "trifling quantities of supplies." Like a blinded ironclad, he fired every gun he had.

"Miles, I don't have to take that from you," Wedemeyer finally snapped.

Depleted of ammunition, Miles proclaimed to Wedemeyer that he actually liked him personally, but that he "never wanted to serve under him again."

In the second week of September, a brace of press releases declared SACO "the greatest joint operation of its kind in history," a superlative due to the work of its units, including that of Unit Six, which was mentioned explicitly, but whose efforts had been made possible only by the "never two stranger partners" of Miles and Tai Li—the "visionary" and the "black-cloaked mystery." Finally recognized for his monumental efforts, just days later Miles received his worst blow yet when Admiral Cooke issued a report to Admiral King saying that word on the street had it that Donovan was already crowing about how Wedemeyer was on his way to Washington "to get Miles thrown out of China." A week later, Miles spontaneously stood up in the press club dining room in Chungking and announced that the next day he would hold a conference, promising to tell them how he planned to "crack the whole theater wide open." Asked by a Chinese officer for his reaction at seeing the Navy's 7th Fleet coming up the Whangpo River, Miles's face lit up and he responded for all to hear, "Now General Wedemeyer can stuff his entire army."

"Arrest that man," responded Wedemeyer's furious chief of staff, an order that was avoided when a quick-thinking Phil Bucklew grabbed Miles and bundled him out of the dining room.

Two nights later, after hosting a dinner for many of his SACO officers, Miles began a rambling, seemingly endless lecture on what the atomic bomb would mean for the US Navy's future. As men awkwardly drifted out of the room, Miles continued, unaware when every man had left and when the lights had been turned off. After the camp doctor confined him to his stateroom, Miles jumped from the window and took off sprinting through a rice paddy. Chased by a group of American advisors and Chinese guerrillas, he escaped them all and stole a jeep. As he rattled past his pursuers, he was heard muttering over and over, "I must get to the drill field."

"Block the road, goddam it, that's an order!" shouted the camp's doctor to the driver of a 6x6 truck.

When the jeep reached the roadblock, Miles jumped out and ordered the truck driver to move. The doctor countermanded the order and told Miles to return to his quarters, whereupon Miles accused everyone of lying to him.

"You're on the sick list," the doctor finally managed.

"What are you saying, Doctor?" Miles spat. "I'm all right."

"I don't think you are, Admiral," the doctor replied nervously, "and have to officially inform you that you're on the sick list and have been relieved of your command."

As the words drilled into Miles's delusion, the doctor could feel himself "shaking like a leaf."

Finally, Miles relented. "Aye, aye, Doctor," he said, then hopped back into the jeep and returned to his quarters. The next morning, he was placed under house arrest and his razor was confiscated. In Washington, Metzel met Mrs. Billy Miles and informed her that her husband had

had a "complete mental breakdown" and they could only hope that "he had not suffered permanent brain damage."

Three days after Miles's incarceration, Admiral Cooke issued a four-point report to Admiral King entitled "Opposition to the Saco Effort." Among the Army's objections were Miles's "affiliation" with Tai Li, the "integration" of Chinese and American troops, and the "exchange of materials and services . . . on the basis of friendship." The final objection was the most obvious, and the only one that would be relevant after the war: "Guerrilla activities are not Navy business."

To protect Miles from embarrassment, neither Tai Li nor Chiang Kai-shek was permitted to see him. Rumors of straitjackets circulated. On September 28, two Chinese generals presented themselves at Miles's quarters with a citation for the Order of the White Cloud and Golden Banner, China's highest award. After the men finished draping the two "plate-sized medals" with red-and-white sash over his head, a Chinese photographer snapped a picture of Miles that captured his immaculate white uniform, his unfocused eyes, and an awkward, forced smile. The presentation of the honor to an American, said Captain Irwin F. Beyerly, Miles's chief of staff, "set a precedent in the history of China." The next day, Miles was unceremoniously bundled onto a canvas-seated Army transport plane and flown home, then hospitalized, and ultimately given a quiet sinecure in the Navy's Office for Historical Research—a good subject matter for all lunatics. On September 30, 1945, a day after his departure, Naval Group China—SACO—was dissolved and Miles's rank of admiral was reduced to captain. In muted consolation, President Truman had demobilized the OSS on September 20 and hustled Donovan out of uniform altogether. Miles's organization had lasted ten days longer.

18

At the time of Japan's surrender, Rudy Boesch—a seventeen-year-old volunteer with the Amphibious Rogers—looked up from the middle of a training exercise in the swamps near Lake Okeechobee to hear the class instructor announce, "Stop what you're doing. The war is over." Told to return to Fort Pierce, Boesch and his classmates were then given a single, final order: tear it down. What followed was the sacking of three years' worth of construction—mess halls, classrooms, offices, ranges, towers. Before a backdrop of flaming white tents—tents that had once proudly lined the macadam roads, sheltering nearly every special group in the US military from the Rangers to the UDTs—the Rogers who had not gotten a crack at China took out their frustrations by demolishing everything with their bare hands. By the end of the week, the only thing that suggested the past existence of a naval base was the pool.

Last to go were the men themselves.

As soon as they had completed the destruction of Fort Pierce some 500 of the Navy's Scouts and Raiders turned Amphibious Rogers were packed onto troop trains for transport to California. While in transit they learned of their disbandment. Combined with the news of the war's end, the result of this announcement on the men was some half-dozen scheduled cases of court-martial and the disappearance of about 250, who jumped from the train whenever it stopped and disappeared into the hills. Just a few weeks later, a front-page exposé in *The Washington Post* titled "The Unsung 200 Whose H-Hour Was Minus 4" would laud these sailors' wartime accomplishments as easy to confuse with those of the Army's Rangers.

For the Amphibious Rogers that Wedemeyer had kept shackled in Calcutta—as far from SACO's headquarters and SACO's war as was San Diego from St. Louis—there was no silver lining. On August 12, three days before Japan's official surrender, 17 officers and 168 enlisted men of Amphibious Roger 3 refused to wait for the Army's permission any longer. In one hundred 6x6 trucks they drove through Hell Gate, the entrance to the Patkai Range, and onto Stilwell's Road—as one man called it, "the goddamndest road ever built." With mud chains attached, the raider-sailors ground past sun-bleached shells of trucks and jeeps, around switchbacks as tight as stitches, down muddy sluices that a "destroyer might have navigated," next to cliffs shored up by sandbags, through blinding clouds of dust or towering above valleys carpeted in white clouds. The Rogers completed the 1,072-mile journey in seventeen days, losing four trucks along the way and one man when his vehicle tipped off a 200-foot cliff. Months later, on December 1, an Army-Navy football game was held in Shanghai. Coached by Bucklew and fellow Scout and Raider alum G. G. Andreasen, the forty-four-man Navy team included no fewer than eight former Rogers. Held down by the Army during the war, the Navy won 12 to 0.

Notably missing from the game was Buck Halperin, already departed from China on what would be an unsuccessful search for his brother, whose plane had crashed in the Philippines just six days earlier. Before Halperin had departed China, however, he had been, like Miles, awarded the Order of the White Cloud and Golden Banner, the only other member of SACO this author has been able to find that was so honored. In the end, he would return to Chicago to run his father's highly successful Commercial Light Company, then go on to travel the world, competing everywhere in two-man sailing competitions and even in the 1960 Olympics, where he won a bronze medal in Rome at the age of fifty-two. Of the indispensable role he had played in pushing the Navy beyond the surf, or the similarity of his wartime service to more modern special warfare experiences, he never spoke.

19

On March 17, 1946, seven months after the Japanese surrender, Tai Li's plane crashed into a mountain not far from the grave of his hero Sun Yat-sen. Charred beyond recognition, Tai's body was identified by his golden teeth and the serial number on the .38-caliber pistol Miles had given him at their first meeting, in 1942. Admiral Nimitz, the newly installed chief of naval operations, personally telephoned Miles with the news. Recovered now from his breakdown, Miles ignored the rapidly deteriorating situation in China and orders not to travel, and returned. Embarrassed by his reduced rank, Miles was nevertheless afforded by the Chinese the honor of a face-saving private train car from Shanghai to Nanking. In the auditorium at the headquarters for the Bureau of Intelligence and Statistics, Miles saw four large pictures displayed: Sun Yat-sen, Chiang Kai-shek, Tai Li, and himself.

Miles's remaining thirteen years in the Navy included command of the cruiser USS *Columbus,* the directorship of the Navy's Pan-American affairs, and command of the 15th Naval District in Panama. At his retirement ceremony in 1958, while watching his two-star flag lowered, he did his best to choke back his tears but failed. After his retirement, he paced around his house ruminating on SACO and its legacy, and dictated his remembrances to his wife, who dutifully typed them out. With scissors he carefully cut out passages, reordered them chronologically, then used uncountable rolls of Scotch tape to turn his slivers into Frankensteined sheets of paper.

There's "an awful lot of pages for a 'minor operation,'" Billy would often tease.

"We can always cut," he would invariably reply, undeterred, "but what we miss now we can never recover."

One of the things he most wanted to preserve for posterity was how accidental it had been for the Navy to "[stumble] upon the guerrillas," but also how ideally the Navy's principles of autonomy and trust—words that for many of the theater's Army officers might as well have been in Chinese—had made them so effective. "At least a dozen of my young officers," wrote Miles of his sailors in those final months of the war, "were handling operations which, except for their smaller scale, were of the type and complexity that are usually reserved for generals or field marshals—intricate military elements requiring the use of two or three languages, three or four different kinds of troops and, from beginning to end, unfamiliar fighting techniques that had been almost entirely forgotten by Americans since the days of the Indians in western New York, Pennsylvania, and Kentucky." He wrote these lines in a paragraph that preceded another on Unit Six's campaign to seize the area around Amoy—if nothing else, a nod to Halperin and the Amphibious Rogers who had made this campaign possible, and an example of what future Navy commandos might do under unconventional Navy direction.

In 1961, his third year of writing, Miles was diagnosed with prostate cancer and admitted to the naval hospital at Bethesda. His immigration to the United States having already been sponsored by Miles, Happy Valley's former Chinese cook learned of Miles's illness and came running, ready to prepare Miles's favorite meals right up until the end. On March 25, just twelve days before his sixty-first birthday, Miles died, nine months before the founding of the Navy's answer to guerrilla warfare. At his funeral at Arlington National Cemetery, his SACO men prepared a eulogy, quoting the final tragic words about Brutus from *Julius Caesar*. "His life was gentle, and the elements so mixed in him that Nature might stand up and say to all the world, 'This was a man.'"

In 1967, less than a year before the Tet Offensive in Vietnam, Miles's book, *A Different Kind of War*, was published by Doubleday. Called as colorful as anything published to that date on Lawrence of Arabia, it was not simply an account that described "a sideshow of a sideshow," as those books on Lawrence had already done, but also one that could—at that point—be considered a prequel to a prequel: a sign of the Navy's ambitions to tack into the wind and challenge a rival's prerogatives. It was also a book that described a venture destined to implode under the dual pressure imposed upon it by the OSS and the US Army, but an implosion also fated to pockmark every sailor in its orbit with the shards of memory, experience, and most of all, ideas for the future.

Part 3

RELEVANCE

CHAPTER 7

The US Navy's Postwar Plight, and the Sailor-Raiders Who Led Her Back to Significance in Korea

On October 5, 1949—one month and two days after the Soviets detonated their first atomic bomb, and with it the whole world's hopes for a lasting peace—the House Armed Services Committee convened a reporter-packed inquiry into President Harry Truman's postwar drawdown of the US military, an inquiry prompted by the outraged members of the branch most battered by the reductions and known forever after as the Revolt of the Admirals. Mostly this outrage was due to Secretary of Defense Louis A. Johnson, a bald and bulky West Virginia lawyer whose glad-handing past as Truman's campaign director concealed a mind that never saw an arm without considering how to twist it. In the seven months since his appointment, he had canceled construction of the Navy's first supercarrier (its keel already laid in Newport News), cut an additional $353 million from the Navy's already emaciated budget, and probably worst of all, installed former USO director Francis A. Matthews as secretary of the Navy, a man who explained his lack of naval experience at his Senate confirmation by joking, "Well, I do have a rowboat at my summer home."

Johnson's castrations were more than just penny-pinching. He had also adopted the Army/Air Force belief that the Navy's relevance was waning. "Admiral, the Navy is on its way out," he was rumored to have told—of all people—Admiral Richard L."Close-In" Conolly, hero of multiple Mediterranean battles and Lingayen Gulf. "There's no reason for having a Navy and a Marine Corps. General Bradley tells me that amphibious operations are a thing of the past. We'll never have any more amphibious operations. That does away with the Marine Corps. And the Air Force can do anything the Navy can do nowadays, so that does away with the Navy."

Meant to reverse Johnson's abuses by appealing to public opinion with eight days' worth of broadside testimonies from every blue-water hero save Kelly Turner and John Paul Jones, the resulting congressional hearings actually produced the reverse. When it came time to rebut the Navy's warnings, Johnson rolled out a lineup that matched the Navy's pound for pound. This murderer's row culminated with testimony by Chairman of the Joint Chiefs Omar Bradley, "the soldier's general," who—with head down and eyes lowered behind spectacles to read his handwritten, unedited statement—belittled the Navy's Jacobin "martyrs" as prima donnas, soreheads, fancy Dans (whatever those were), and worst of all reiterated Johnson's libel that "large-scale amphibious operations, such as those in Sicily and Normandy, [would] never occur again." When he finished, said one reporter, "there was stunned silence in the committee room." Not only had Bradley impugned the Navy's honor, like Johnson he had questioned its future as an instrument of offensive combat.

Comparable to a boxer accused of having a glass jaw, the admirals emerged from this humiliation spoiling to prove the Navy's offensive worth across any rock connected to the water. As it happened, events would soon provide them with their opportunity.

In the same month as the Revolt of the Admirals, Mao's Communists finally defeated Chiang Kai-shek's Nationalist forces. Under an umbrella of nuclear deterrence, world Communism was on the move. Though political and military leaders in the United States had not quite grasped what this meant, Stalin had ensured that, at least for the foreseeable future, wars would be limited, unbalanced, and would take place far from the USSR's center—in other words, on the fringes.

This was exactly the sort of battlefield the Navy was made for—the Navy and one other sort of entity: the US military's commando units, the Raiders, Rangers, VAC Recon Marines, Amphibious Rogers, and UDTs. Or at least it would have been if the parent services of those units had not already disbanded them. All except for the last. The unit least like the others.

2

On the morning of June 25, 1950, still dark and raining, some 90,000 troops of the In Min Gun, or North Korean Army, silently crossed the 38th parallel into the Republic of Korea. Their purpose:

erase forever the line that for the past five years had separated their north and south peninsula into East and West sides. Supported by Soviet-made T-34 tanks and supplied by trains running on secretly rebuilt rail lines snaking all the way back to Vladivostok, the In Min Gun—half of them veterans of the Chinese Civil War and masters in the footsore slog of guerrilla warfare—circled behind their American-advised capitalist foes and cut roads, laid ambushes, shot up command posts, waved truce flags ahead of attacks, drove peasants before them like shields, and ultimately rolled up their South Korean cousins like a carpet. They did all this with barely more arrows in their quiver than darkness, surprise, and good soldiering; an example that few troops in the US military could, at that moment, come close to matching.

Within twenty-four hours of the In Min Gun invasion, Truman committed US air and naval forces to do what they could in halting the advance and petitioned the UN Security Council for help. On the fifth night of the crisis, General Douglas MacArthur, supreme commander of the Allied powers in the Far East, informed Truman that none of these prophylactics would work. Returning from the front to Tokyo's Dai Ichi Insurance building—his colossal gray cube of a citadel, still looming over Japan's Imperial Palace—MacArthur told Truman that only an immediate commitment of US troops could douse the fires now leaping toward the south. Out of options, Truman agreed. Over the next nine days, the US Air Force landed two infantry divisions in Korea, both made up of regiments short an entire battalion, of troops grown dull in occupation duty and lacking even basic equipment. Though Johnson had promised to touch only fat, never muscle, it was now clear to everyone that his cuts had nicked the US military to the bone.

Between July 1 and 12, the US Army's 24th Division tumbled backward some sixty miles, from Osan to the southwest city of Taejon, where they tucked behind the wide moat of the Kum River. In a manner typical of guerrilla armies, the In Min Gun forded the river, then slid around the 24th's flanks in an attempt to cut the American retreat to the south. On July 18th, the US Army's just-landed 1st Cavalry Division galloped to the rescue as cavalier as cowboys, the commanding officer promising a bottle of champagne to any man who could bag a Communist tank. His men arrived just in time for Taejon to fall and to see the 24th's survivors fleeing the battle in overloaded jeeps or barefoot, and on as many trains as were capable of clattering through the gauntlet, their engineers frantically blowing their whistles to clear the tracks. The 24th's doomed commander, Major General William Dean, found himself reduced to leading squad-sized attacks, even personally destroying an enemy tank with a hand grenade. In the end, he too was captured.

In less than one month of fighting, US forces fell back to a siege-like perimeter around the southeast coastal city of Pusan, where only two options remained: stand and fight, or evacuate in Dunkirk-sized humiliation. As incapable of attack as were the British in 1940, several planners in the US military suddenly arrived at the same idea that had so beguiled Winston Churchill. In a few months, a reporter from the *Seattle Post-Intelligencer* would write that the American soldier in Korea was desperate for a military unit capable of doing "unto the enemy as the enemy was doing unto" him; units that could "range behind the enemy's lines [and make] a bloody nuisance of themselves." The first military branch to attempt this was also the least likely.

3

If the US Army suffered every possible disadvantage at the beginning of the war—in terrain, supplies, preparation, and notably commanders—the US Navy conversely could boast two distinct advantages: leadership and geography. The chief of naval forces in the Far East, Vice Admiral Charles Turner Joy, shared none of MacArthur's bearing, his fame, or his reputation for genius; instead, he had the look of a jowly farmer from Missouri, the place of his birth. He was, however, in possession of a farmer's good sense in forecasting the yield of his terrain. Though Army commanders would see in Korea only mountains, the insuperable cold, the inexhaustible supply of Communist soldiers, and the depth of the US military's fall from World War II–era greatness, Joy couldn't help but spot the opportunity staring back at him on every map. Awash on three sides by ocean and spined like a stegosaurus, Korea's geography pushed almost every highway and rail line to the edge of the peninsula's thumb, often to within 100 yards of the surf. Except for a handful of North Korean torpedo boats, no fleet guarded the peninsula's skin or the arteries that lay beneath it. In the east, where mountain cliffs dropped steeply into the Sea of Japan, giving way only rarely to harbors and landable beaches, the peninsula exposed to Joy's ships more than 1,000 miles of track, 956 bridges and causeways, and 231 tunnels—almost a bridge per mile, and a tunnel every five.

In World War II, Joy had commanded fire support groups in eleven separate battles from Bougainville to Okinawa, had commanded training for all US-based amphibious forces for the invasion of Japan, and had relieved Mary Miles as the senior naval officer in China. Few shared his wide-ranging exposure to naval gunfire, to UDT reconnaissance swimmers, and to the Navy's recent experiments in guerrilla warfare. As UN ground forces thrashed and kicked for a foothold from which to pivot retreat into advance, Joy's experienced eyes saw the peninsula for what it was: an endless flank from which to hack at the enemy. Two years after the Korean War ended, he would confess a perspective that no ground soldier of the war ever would: "The Navy could not have fought in a more favorable distant area."

Ignored by reporters until the end of the war, when General Matthew Ridgway assigned him as the UN's chief negotiator at the armistice talks, Joy nevertheless had all the traits of a great commander: patience, fortitude, a sarcastic sense of humor, compassion, creativity, tenacity, and, most important, the instinct to win and the imagination to figure out how to do so when the answer wasn't apparent. A father of three, with one son a sailor and another a soldier fighting on the mainland, Joy would day after day during the armistice negotiations suppress his impulse to end the war at all costs and instead met the Communists as defiant as Job, once sitting for four and a half hours deadlocked in silence, staring at his adversaries. "We are losing men at the front every day because I can't negotiate this damned truce," he would tell an interpreter, his head facedown on the table after the room had emptied. But every day he would return. By the end of the war, Peking radio would call him "Stonewall Joy." Except for the indomitable Ridgway, no fighting man in this conflict would stretch his mind so far to win the war without widening it.

On the day the war started, Joy's Far East Naval Forces consisted of one cruiser, the USS *Juneau,* and four destroyers—five ships in all to blockade a coastline six times the length of California's. With reinforcements a month away, most commanders would have husbanded their ships as Jack Fletcher had at Guadalcanal. Instead, Joy released them against the coast, as one historian described, "like hungry dogs in an unattended butcher shop." After the *Juneau*'s repulse of four North Korean torpedo boats, an unexpectedly sharp contest made sharper by the decrepit shooting skills of the *Juneau*'s crew, Joy's ships ranged freely, gunners listening into their crackling headphones for lookouts to call out the location of smoke puffs, truck lights, or any other giveaway target worth shooting at. When guns ran dry, ships nosed back across "the little slot," that stretch of water separating Korea from the US Navy's base in Sasebo, Japan, for a refill of shells and a night on the town.

Noble efforts aside, the effectiveness of these attacks was mixed. When southbound locomotive engineers expected a broadside on their left, they simply waited for darkness or, if time was of the essence, tucked into a tunnel or behind the slope of a hill. Against fixed targets like bridge stanchions, the Navy's gunners fared even worse. Later in the war, Admiral Arleigh Burke would bet ten cases of Scotch whisky that the skipper of the battleship *Los Angeles* would not be able to hit a railroad bridge in ten shots. For every shot past ten, the skipper would owe Burke a bottle. The skipper accepted the wager, but after thirty misses finally quit and wrote Burke an IOU for twenty. If hitting the side of a truck or a train from 4,000 yards out to sea was considered a bull's-eye, then hitting a railroad track was the equivalent of splitting an arrow.

On July 6, only eleven days after the North Korean attack, Joy sent a message from his headquarters in Tokyo to Admiral John Higgins, his eastern blockade commander, ordering the fleet to "disrupt the east coast rail line in the vicinity of Rashin," just south of the Russian border. Already aware of the challenges connected to this mission, Higgins summoned the *Juneau*'s top two officers to discuss the best location and method to accomplish the assignment. Armed with a sheaf of maps and charts, the *Juneau*'s executive officer, Commander W. B. Porter, convinced Higgins to let him try something new.

One of the few survivors of the Asiatic Fleet's corpse-cluttered dash from Corregidor to Australia in 1942, Porter had risen in that war to command a destroyer, on which he had taken the initiative to organize what he described as "a small commando outfit." The day after the meeting with Higgins, Porter selected the following from the *Juneau*'s manifest: one Marine officer, four Marines, and four dungaree-wearing "bluejacket" gunner's mates. "You are all volunteers," Porter said, a map of the target area laid out before them. "None of you have to go on this mission if you don't want to."

On the night of July 11, the men assembled on the deck of a destroyer, the USS *Mansfield*, bedecked with carbines, tommy guns, walkie-talkies, shovels, detonators, explosives, and primer cord, these last three items borrowed from the US Army. Several of the men wore sneakers. Porter estimated that his own backpack weighed as much as fifty pounds. As the whaleboat was lowered into the water, several men on deck shuffled their feet, unable to conceal the weight of loads and nerves. "Well, this is it," Porter finally managed. "Let's go over the side."

Attended by darkness and launched on a calm sea for their two-mile transit, the men sank onto the benches of their whaleboat and worried that the unmuffled rattle in their motor would betray their mission before it began. When they were sixty yards from the shore, a coastal spotlight momentarily flickered on and flattened each man to the bottom of the boat until the beam was extinguished. At thirty yards, the boat's coxswain paid out the stern anchor for 270 feet and, feeling no bottom, kept on paying it out until the line fouled the propeller. As the men quietly dipped their paddles and pulled through the surf, a train passed right in front of them. Unable to restrain himself any longer, Porter slipped out of the boat and immediately found himself underwater, bobbing for air against the weight of his pack and frantically splashing toward the shore.

After finally reaching solid ground, the men found themselves nowhere near their flat beach target; they were blocked by a sixty-degree gradient of rocks so loose that Porter feared an avalanche. Dripping wet, Porter posted two Marines, then using his compass and chart led the remaining nine up the rocky slope to a hilly plain of grass that reached his gun belt. For an hour and a half, the men scoured the ground for any sign of roads or rails but found nothing—until a train clattered behind them, exposing a slightly curved track that disappeared into a tunnel cut from blasted rock. (Apparently, Porter had led his men over the top of the tunnel.)

Posting his remaining Marines at the tunnel's ends, Porter and his sailors crept into the blackened center and quietly dug with their shovels and bare hands a four-foot-deep, five-foot-long trench beneath the track, then packed it with explosives. The only casualty in the whole affair was Porter, who slipped on a rail and slightly skinned himself in the fall. When the men arrived back on the *Mansfield,* they were met by warming shots of brandy and an eager *Time* magazine reporter named Wilson Fielder.

"It wasn't bad after we got ashore," said a slow-talking sailor to Fielder. "It was just the long pull. Standing by, waiting to go in is always the worst."

As Fielder and Porter's men watched the coast from the *Mansfield*'s fantail, a distant locomotive disappeared into the tunnel and never emerged. Having heard no explosion and seen no smoke, they wondered if the locomotive's engineer had simply stopped. Two days later, an Air Force plane captured some pictures showing the train's tail still "sticking out" the end.

Encouraged by the *Juneau*'s attempt and probably inspired by the partial redemption it promised for the Navy's offensive ambitions, Joy—over the next several months—would do as much as any man to propagate the Navy's employment of amphibious raiders.

4

SINCE NOT A SINGLE ONE of the US military's commando-type units from World War II had survived disbandment—not the Raiders, the Rangers, or even the Amphibious Rogers—Joy's first action was to create some.

On July 24, less than a month after the North Korean invasion, Joy tasked Rear Admiral James Doyle, the commander of Amphibious Group One, to order his Marine Corps cadre in Mobile Training Team Able (MTTA) to stop training US Army soldiers in vehicle waterproofing, landing craft embarkation, and all the skills necessary to execute another D-Day, and instead to begin rearranging themselves and their curriculum to train "Special Raiding Forces"—none of which were yet identified—"to conduct small scale harassing, destruction, and reconnaissance operations along North Korean lines of communication." Even for the Marine instructors, who were known for their "flexibility," this transformation would take several weeks. Impatient for results, as is every man not a gardener, Joy waited only four days before issuing Operation Order No. 11-50, directing Doyle—at "earliest possible"—to employ an APD (the same class of ship commissioned for the Raiders in 1942) to immediately carry forth with the 1st Marine Division's Reconnaissance Company. Unlike Joy's "Special Raiding Forces," which did not yet exist, the 1st Division's Reconnaissance Marines had been ready for just such a mission since 1947, when the Navy had allocated to its training several special-purpose submarines that could ascend and launch troops, a Higgins Boat, and a jeep, then descend and maintain radio contact with them all by way of a sonobuoy-floated antenna. In short, these were exactly the kind of troops Joy needed, but there was one problem. They weren't yet in-theater—and the closest alternatives weren't troops at all.

Because the Recon Marines had not yet arrived, the man who read Joy's order was technically at liberty to do nothing but wait. Yet because the reader was James Doyle—a man as thin as a cadaver and just as warm—he did no such thing. Raised in Queens, New York, the country's cradle of hostility, and the implementer of Kelly Turner's destruction in the Solomons and subsequently the top amphibious planner on Admiral King's results-oriented staff in World War II, Cadaver Doyle was in possession, said a fellow officer, of a well-earned "hairtriggered" mouth and mind, and was as enthusiastic as Joy to increase the Navy's collateral in the war. Since he had arrived in the Korean theater, his contributions had consisted mainly of shuttling supplies from Japan to Pusan and executing one "administrative" landing at Pohang. In this last feat, not a single Navy casualty had been incurred—a fact that had done nothing to plane down the chip still perched on the Navy's shoulder. So, upon receipt of Joy's directive, Doyle immediately summoned the Navy complement to his Mobile Training Team of Marines, a ten-man squad of UDT 3 swimmers. It's worth noting that Doyle did not ask if such a mission was within their purview.

Shrunk from thirty teams to four after World War II, the UDTs' narrow role of beach reconnaissance and demolition had devolved into a collage of extracurricular Navy assignments: collecting postblast radioactive water samples; exploding ship paths through Antarctic ice; even ignominiously standing duty as base lifeguards. Given this misuse—misuse that foreshadowed disbandment—and with the role of fleet raiders already filled by its traditional tenant, the UDTs' senior East Coast officer and engine of innovation—Lieutenant Commander Doug Fane—had attempted to secure his organization's future by emphasizing its underwater potential.

Born in Scotland, correspondingly "raw," redheaded, and hard-drinking, Francis Douglas Fane possessed an eye for publicity just shy of P. T. Barnum's. When he had taken command of the East Coast UDTs,

UDT swimmer Lieutenant John Booth showing the Lambertsen technique, 1947.

he had almost immediately boosted their profile by recruiting the OSS Maritime Unit operative Dr. Christian Lambertsen to teach a handful of UDT swimmers the use of the Lambertsen Lung, the predecessor of the modern scuba apparatus. So qualified, Fane then created a unit for Submersible Operations (thereafter known as the SubOps Platoon) and with them perfected the art of submerged exits and entrances from a submarine's escape trunk and from its twenty-one-inch-wide, coffin-like torpedo tubes. Drawing upon the World War II lessons of OSS, British, and Italian attack swimmers, Fane resurrected the cranky, canoe-sized, British-made submersible, the *Sleeping Beauty.* Concerning any UDT activity removed from the water, however, he had shown practically no interest. In half a decade, Fane would co-author the first comprehensive history of the UDTs in World War II and Korea, in which he confessed his own belief that the UDTs' "responsibility was strictly underwater," and that "raiding behind the beach was a task for better armed and specially trained men." Though other Navy planners and frogmen had already hinted at a future that stretched beyond the surf, Fane had only been able to imagine a future in the opposite direction. Thanks to Admirals Joy and Doyle, his imagination was about to get a nudge.

5

When the ten UDT swimmers arrived at Doyle's flagship, the USS *Mount McKinley,* the team's officer in charge—Lieutenant Junior Grade George Atcheson—found the atmosphere thick with "confusion and uncertainty." The "urge to get in" on the war was obvious, but as Atcheson listened to Doyle's staffers bandy ideas off the bulkheads, several of the proposals sounded more like "suicide missions." Whether they were or not, Atcheson was in no position to judge.

Though nearly every other serviceman who fought in Korea would blanch at the stench, to George C. Atcheson III, the smell was home. Born in Beijing in 1923 and raised in China, a boy witness to Japanese atrocities, he was the son and namesake of George C. Atcheson, Jr., the up-from-his-bootstraps diplomat who had risen from journalist to translator to *Panay* attack survivor to become the acting US ambassador who had, at the end of World War II, gone against Mary Miles by recommending the arming of Chinese Communists. Thought a Red by many, Atcheson the elder had, in the postwar era, shuffled off those suspicions to become one of MacArthur's most strident anti-Communist advisors and was well on his way to becoming US ambassador to Japan.

On August 17, 1947, at the height of his career, the plane carrying him from Kwajalein ran out of fuel some 100 miles west of Hawaii. "I'm sorry it had to end this way," a passenger said to Atcheson on their way down. "Well," the diplomat replied calmly, a tragic smile stretching across his face, "it can't be helped." Rescue planes from Barber's Point found the site awash with Mae West life jackets, "gaudy souvenir kimonos," five floating dead, and only three survivors. The future ambassador's body was never found. Now, as Atcheson the younger plied the Pacific waters that had swallowed his father, about to fight the Communists that his father had once supported, one can only guess what thoughts dwelt within him. One thing is known: It was a topic about which he never spoke, even to his closest friends.

A sailboat racer before World War II and fluent in Chinese, Atcheson shared his father's wandering impulse, his bravery, his easygoing style, and his intelligence, but none of his father's bookishness, or paunch. In 1943, he had abandoned his Berkeley studies after only one semester and joined the Navy, becoming an aerial navigator by the tail end of the war. In 1947, the same year his father died, he won a regular Navy commission, spent a year on a destroyer, then volunteered for the UDT for the same reasons everyone else had.

As one of Fane's first SubOps divers, Atcheson had performed the heart-pounding, leg-cramping art of entering a submerged and moving submarine, describing it afterward as the swimming equivalent of "catching a train." So dedicated had he become to his position as the UDTs' West Coast director of underwater and submarine operations that during a class on how to avoid contaminating the Lambertsen Lung's sensitive breathing bag with carbon dioxide, he had donned the system, demonstrated the commonest mistake, then passed out in front of his students. Already off the coast with Doyle's Amphibious Group during the invasion, Atcheson and two other officers (a Marine and a beachmaster) had been flown to Korea, where they had hitchhiked in trucks the six miles north to the city of Pohang, where they had weaved through a sea of "waving arms, hands and flags," past the nervous smiles of a people about to be overrun. At the harbor's gray stone quay, Atcheson had stripped off his uniform for a pair of swim trunks, stretched flippers over his feet and a mask over his face, then finned himself from one end of the harbor's canal to the other, noting the notches on the lead line as he went—and in so doing had performed what normally required 100 men to do.

Now twenty-seven years old, single, and accustomed to the UDTs' growing role as the Navy's utility force, Atcheson had not blinked at the prospect of going ashore to conduct a raid, but he should have. Despite his experience in every other medium of naval warfare—air, surface, and undersea—this was a type of operation about which he knew nothing. A fact about to be made obvious for anyone who cared to notice.

When the planning on board the *Mount McKinley* ended, Atcheson plus his nine men plus their "war bags" packed into a seaplane and flew to Sasebo, where upon landing they were immediately cross-decked to an LCPR and zipped across the harbor at flank speed to board the USS *Diachenko,* an APD whose crew was already hauling anchor to transport these enigmatic raiders, a title most discomfiting to the men who now bore it. Already enviously dubbed "the Big Ten" by the Marine Corps' base guards for their swagger and reputation as experts in explosives and everything, Atcheson and his men actually knew all too well, wrote one of the men afterward, that "their training had been only to the high water mark [and] that they had no training what-so-ever in commando tactics." Nothing made this more abundantly clear than when the Big Ten was mustered on deck and issued Thompson submachine guns, weapons that none of the swimmers had any familiarity with except from gangster movies and which they learned to use by firing "thousands of rounds from the fantail" at inflatables tossed from the bow by a shirtless boatswain's mate whose tattoos would have made "an old China Hand blush."

UDT 3 members before the Yosu raid. Left to right: Boatswain's Mate Warren Foley, Signalman Phillip E. Carrico, and Signalman B. Johnson.

On August 4—just before midnight and just eight hours after the crash course in submachine guns—the *Diachenko* reached the tangle of islands off the southern Korean coast. Ahead in the darkened distance was the coastal town of Yosu. Nearby, and visible only on ship's radar, was an isolated cliffside tunnel that opened onto a small bridge some ten feet off the ground. This was their target.

As Atcheson and his swimmers—their faces blackened and their bodies clothed in ill-fitting Marine Corps fatigues and caps—descended into a TNT-laden landing craft that would tow their ten-man rubber boat to shore, the lip of a nearly full moon rose, drawing perfect silhouettes around every blackened object on the water. Though Atcheson cursed it as a "bad omen," he might as well have cursed himself for being surprised by a phenomenon more regular than rain.

At 1,000 yards from the shore, Atcheson and his men unhitched their boat to start their paddle, but not before the same boatswain's mate who'd taught them how to shoot that afternoon blew them a kiss and whispered, "Break a leg." At 500 yards, Atcheson and frogman Warren "Peekskill" Foley slipped over the side and into the cool water carrying a brace of tommy guns and several pineapple grenades apiece. Having never considered until this moment the unbuoyed weight of a ten-pound machine gun with bullets, both Atcheson and Foley quickly decided to leave these weapons behind, swimming toward their first raid with nothing but grenades, knives, and Atcheson's .45-caliber pistol. After a thirty-minute swim against a stiff current, both men collapsed onto the pebble-strewn beach "panting" to catch their breath. When they had, they discovered a twenty-foot seawall that neither the ship's radar nor their undated charts had warned them about. In a few minutes they overcame this too. At the top of the wall they found the tunnel and bridge, whereupon Atcheson turned his penlight toward the sea and flashed the signal to bring the explosives to shore. Foley slid down the seawall to meet the reinforcements at the beach.

For the first time since leaving the *Diachenko,* perhaps since leaving Sasebo, Atcheson relaxed, the result of a sudden sense of confidence in himself and the mission he was about to complete. The feeling was premature.

As the Big Ten's rubber boat breached the surf zone, Atcheson cringed at the squeal of a handcart rattling out of the tunnel behind him. On it were roughly ten North Korean soldiers, who emerged onto the bridge and naturally looked out toward the moonlit sea. There, "laid out before them" was a "panorama" of ocean and blackened islands interrupted by five unknown vessels. Not sure what to do, Atcheson slipped under the tangle of trestles ten feet below the bridge and froze, his eyes fixed on the Communists bustling above and his mind on his men, all of them oblivious to the ambush awaiting. Only Atcheson could save them, but carrying only a pistol and a pouch full of grenades, he was hopelessly outmatched.

Below the seawall and out of Atcheson's view, Foley had likewise heard the handcart and was already splashing into the surf, his legs and arms straining against the slow motion of sucking water and the bad dream unfolding behind him. When he reached the rubber boat, he gave a hushed alarm to the crew, grabbed a tommy gun, and splashed back through the surf, swimmers Limey Austin and Dennis McCormick wading behind to keep up.

Under the bridge, Atcheson held his breath, waiting for an opportunity. Suddenly a shadowy figure breasted the seawall and charged the tunnel firing a machine gun from the hip. Instinctively, both the North Koreans and Atcheson opened fire at the same target—apparently just in time to hear the figure yelling, "Hang in there, LT, I'm coming!" It was Foley. Whether or not Atcheson realized his mistake, the flash of gunfire unfroze him. Grenade in hand, he pulled the pin and threw it toward the North Koreans. Then he threw another, and another. The sequence of explosions—all of unknown origin—chased the North Koreans back into the tunnel. Glimpsing his moment, Atcheson tore himself from cover and sprinted to the seawall.

As soon as he reached the top of the wall, one of the armed swimmers huddled at the bottom spotted a human head poking over the lip and made the same mistake Atcheson had and stitched the wall with fire. One of the rounds tore a hole in the bill of Atcheson's hat. Half a second later, Atcheson identified himself—"You idiots, hold your fire, it's me!"—and poked his head over again, then scraped down the wall and onto the rocks. At the bottom, he found the rest of his men. Having rolled himself away from danger and over the seawall, Foley was now alert but "gritting his teeth," shot through the hand and thigh, a kneecap smashed by his fall. Once they were together, McCormick scooped up Foley in his arms and everyone ran for the surf—the medium that, until this mission, the UDT had always considered the furthest limit of their operations.

Though the first ground raid in the history of the UDTs had produced next to nothing in actual operational value, it had—after doctors determined that no American bullets had struck Foley—at least spared Atcheson the guilt of shooting his own rescuer, and moreover had elevated Foley into becoming the Navy's first hero-casualty of the war. For his "John Wayne"–level bravery against an unknown number of North Koreans, he would soon be awarded a Silver Star and an invitation to the Little Creek premiere of the World War II–era UDT film *The Frogmen,* which his wounds would require him to attend in a wheelchair. Beyond these results, the Big Ten's audacity and Foley's sacrifice had also expanded Navy planners' expectations of what a squad of UDT frogmen could do—and, slightly, where they could go.

6

ATCHESON'S MISSION HAD BEEN, as all missions are, an audition for future ones, but the mistakes in planning, preparation, execution, and even marksmanship had shined a spotlight on the UDTs' five years of plateaued interest in the art of raiding. Though no one counts on failure before an undertaking, Admiral Joy had at the very least ensured that the Navy's raiding hopes rested on more than one squad of demolition swimmers.

On August 8, the USS *Perch,* one of the Navy's special-purpose submarines built specifically for launching raiders, arrived in Yokosuka "ready to"—in the words of Joy's war diary—"carry out her assigned mission as a submarine transport." The next day, at 0800, Doyle's Mobile Training Team instructors ushered into Camp McGill's base theater 130 fatigue-dressed volunteers for service in the Eighth Army's hastily assembled General Headquarters Raider Company—GHQ Raiders for short. After some opening remarks, the GHQ volunteers received a quick lesson on the history of amphibious reconnaissance—the prerequisite to amphibious raids—immediately followed by an ocean swim. In less than twenty-four hours, the volunteers would be learning how to "silence" an enemy sentry at night—as sanitized a euphemism as was ever printed in a training plan. Over the next three weeks the Marine instructors would cram into their soldiers every conceivable lesson needed for amphibious raiding: inflating, deflating, paddling, bridling, towing, capsizing, righting, and beaching rubber boats; motor cleaning; APD and submarine boarding; beach identifying; scaling; street fighting; ambushing; and all types of raiding. Just about every lesson implied a future long-term partnership with the training's author, the Navy—

the only service capable of launching, shadowing, and recovering a flotilla of rubber boat raiders. The kind of raiders just days away from hitting the Korean coast.

Right about the same time that the volunteers to the GHQ Raiders were first sorting out their surroundings, the USS *Horace A. Bass,* another APD, was departing Yokosuka for her first raiding target. Riding in its hold were twenty-five Marines from the 1st Marine Division's Reconnaissance Company and all fifty-six members of UDT 1. Upon reporting to Doyle's command, the two units had been formed into a single entity called the Special Operations Group, or SOG, explicitly purposed to cut the North Korean coastal supply line. Officially led by Navy Commander Selden C. Small, the entire group now bowed to the incontestable experience of the Commanding Officer, Raiding Forces—a thirty-one-year-old, cropped-haired, green-eyed, jib-eared Rhode Islander: Major Edward P. Dupras.

A volunteer for the Corps at the first whiff of gunpowder in 1941, Dupras had almost immediately volunteered again, this time for "Red Mike" Edson's 1st Raider Battalion. Then, after avoiding the cull and transfer from Edson's battalion to Carlson's, he had embarked on a career in elite units that spanned the chasm between these men. As a junior officer in the 1st Raiders, Dupras had raided Tulagi, an island sweep as much like a raid as was the Rangers' on Cisterna. After that, he had landed on Guadalcanal and survived Edson's Ridge, a two-night Little Round Top. By the end of the Solomons campaign, at age twenty-three he had proved a capacity for combat that earned him a promotion to captain and command of an entire company. Only malaria and a jeep accident had stunted his rise and forced him to return to the States to a training billet. By June 1944, Dupras was back in combat, this time in China, and this time under Mary Miles. After mentally adapting to the nonchalance of SACO and the footsore intensity of Chinese marching, Dupras took command of Camp Two, SACO's largest, and then did something that Edson had never imagined and Carlson could have only dreamed about: he led five American-advised Chinese guerrilla columns into combat. After the war, Dupras had taken the top position at the Marine Corps' Amphibious Reconnaissance School, a Coronado posting that practically shared a property line with the UDT and thereby benefited from all the various underwater and submarine experiments. Like Atcheson, he too had been in-theater during the invasion, assigned to Doyle's staff, and summoned to Joy's headquarters to advocate for Marine Reconnaissance raids—for which his entire career now seemed but a prelude.

7

As Dupras and Lieutenant Commander Kelly Welch, the UDT commander, pricked and spun their compasses over plotting maps, the men of SOG test-fired their machine guns, waterproofed their radios, prepared towlines, stacked paddles, inflated rubber boats, and secured those boats with radar reflectors that would enable the *Bass*'s navigators to correct the paddlers' course headings. Next to each rubber boat was a 400-pound pile of C-3 explosives broken down into 20-pound canvas-covered packs, not unlike the Hagensen packs used at Omaha Beach.

On August 12, at about ten minutes before sunset, the *Bass* abruptly turned west and dropped speed to seventeen knots. Across twenty-eight miles of ocean lay Target King—a railroad bridge and two tunnel mouths—carved into North Korea's east coast, now just a darkening silhouette of rock cliffs. As night fell, the Marines bedecked themselves with weapons and ammunition, and the UDT swimmers donned a hodgepodge of dungarees, surplus uniforms, and shoulder-worn .38-caliber revolvers (their only weapons), then wrapped their wrists and waists with primer cord—the explosive rope that would connect their C-3 packs for simultaneous detonation. Once dressed, they painted their faces green and black, appearing to Dupras like a "torture crew right out of Dante's Inferno." When finally ready and with nothing more to do but wait, the men crowded the *Bass*'s wake-churning fantail to acclimate their eyes to the dark, then drew on cigarettes whose embers accomplished the opposite.

At 2120, the *Bass* crew spotted some fishing trawlers and maneuvered to avoid them. At 2152, it arrived at a position 3,500 yards off the beach, whereupon the ship's crew slung out and lowered one landing craft with UDT commander Welch aboard, who started the engine as it hit the water. Next came seven rubber boats, Able through George, all daisy-chained together for the tow to shore, which quickly filled with men as they peeled off the cargo nets. At 2340, Dupras gave the order, and the landing craft pilot spun his bow westward, instantly snapping taut the dripping towline. After motoring to 500 yards from shore, Welch flashed the signal to detach, and the boat crews plunged their paddles into the black, each one swirling a miniature galaxy of phosphorescence. When the flotilla reached the far edge of the surf zone, a pair of swimmer scouts silently lowered into the water and finned themselves into the rolling white-cut blackness. As the raiding party scanned the beach, straining to see the familiar signals from the red flashlight, the swimmer scouts instead popped up alongside the boats to report the beach crawling with "considerable enemy activity." The mission untenable, Dupras directed his flotilla back to the ship. At sunrise, Commander Small steamed the *Bass* inshore, where his gunners unleashed fifty-six five-inch rounds at the enemy's railroad yard and bridge—small consolation for the aborted raid.

Aftermath of a UDT rail demolition.

Later, at sunset, the *Bass* and SOG reiterated every step of the previous night's choreography, now at Target Baker—a pair of railroad tunnels. The only difference: This time the scouts were accompanied by a boatload of Marines, who, upon landing, established a hasty perimeter, then flashed to seaward the signal for "all clear." When the remaining boats hit the shore, the Marines secured a beachhead, then scouted inland for the tunnel entrance. As they did, two trains appeared and did the job for them, revealing the locations of the two rail tunnels. At the southernmost, the scouts "put to flight" one sentry armed with nothing but a wooden rifle and bayonet. After securing the southern tunnel, the UDT swimmers sloughed some 2,000 pounds of explosives 300 yards past the beach, where they stacked pack after pack into the tunnel's mouth and under a bridge. At 0305, the UDT swimmers pulled their fuses, initiating a hasty six-minute retreat to the beach and the boats, followed by a concert of oars through the surf. At 0330, noted the task force diary, "charges exploded." Twenty minutes later, the men of SOG climbed back onto the *Bass* and into history as the Navy's first successful raiders of the modern era. For Joy and many of the Navy's planners, it was just a start.

8

On the very same day as SOG's first success, a representative of Her Majesty's West Coast blockade fleet—under US control since June—informed Joy that the British Admiralty had approved the US Navy's request for a small squad of Royal Marine Commandos. The offer was quickly accepted and returned with a request for the squad's estimated time of arrival at Camp McGill, where Doyle's Mobile Training Team waited to outfit them with American fatigues, M1 rifles, and three weeks of lessons in all the same skills the GHQ Raiders were currently learning. Named for their commander, Royal Marine Lieutenant Derek Pounds, and not for the weight of their punch, "Pounds Force" was hardly the kind of commando unit Joy had been expecting; it was a ten-man contingent, half of whom were ship volunteers, not commandos at all. When they arrived at Camp McGill, Doyle's men trained them anyway.

While Joy was supplementing his fleet with this third raider force, SOG was returning to Target King, the location of their first night's aborted mission. On the night of August 14, the scout Marines from Able Boat patrolled 150 yards inland, "wormed" their way up to a pair of tunnels connected by a rail bridge, and discovered two unmanned bunkers holding four sleeping peasants—two men, a woman, and a young boy quaking with fear. Upon landing the rest of the team, the frogmen tied the captives with primer cord and bundled them away from the site, then returned to the tunnels and set their charges. The next morning, the *Bass* steamed inshore to examine the wreckage and saw both tunnel entrances blocked and the railroad bridge demolished.

The next night, at Target Sugar, the SOG Marines again spearheaded the landing, and the frogmen pack-muled their explosives 200 yards inland. After twenty minutes ashore, however, the frogmen grew so cocky that, in Dupras's words, they began "chattering like a bunch of magpies." To silence them, Dupras climbed a railway trestle and at the top of his lungs shouted, *"Quiet!"* If Dupras had hoped to rein in their exuberance, he failed. At the first sight of an armored truck barreling toward the road bridge, the UDT swimmers unholstered their pistols and prepared to engage it. Only a direct order by Dupras forced them to lie down and let the truck pass.

The blue flames from the explosion rose 150 feet and rattled the *Bass* some 5,000 yards out to sea. The next morning, the *Bass* returned inshore, discovered the rail bridge "wiped out," and for good measure fired forty-two more five-inch rounds at the still-standing highway trestles. At 7:25 A.M., running short of explosives, the *Bass* turned toward the rising sun and Japan.

Almost as soon as the last flame of the last explosion died out, SOG received a warning order: Upon arrival in Japan, immediately prepare to return to Korea, not to cut the east coast rail lines as before but to scout a series of beaches on Korea's west coast.

On the night of August 24, Dupras led SOG on a beach reconnaissance near Kunsan, one so urgent that the mission had been launched despite the danger of a full moon. A half hour into the reconnaissance, a machine gun drove the men of SOG back to their boats and dropped one Marine with a bullet through his stomach, who used his fingers to stanch the holes and contain his guts while Dupras and a radioman dragged him to the surf. Back at the *Bass,* the head count revealed one rubber boat sunk, the wounded Marine paralyzed, and another UDT swimmer with a bullet wound that had skimmed his midsection but left no serious internal damage. The count also revealed nine Marines missing, perhaps killed, captured, drowned, or stranded. First to volunteer for the rescue mission was a UDT officer named Ted Fielding, followed by three enlisted Marines and four UDT swimmers, one of them Atcheson, ready to try his luck again, and Fred "Tiz" Morrison, the first Black sailor to join the UDT after desegregation. At 150 yards from the beach, the rubber boat rescue party received the first snaps of rifle and machine gun fire, but nevertheless paddled into the surf, where they found the Marines, two of them wounded and not one able to swim, all nine "standing patiently in water up to their necks." With hardly any room left in the boat, the survivors clutched the raft's sides and the paddlers stretched their backs against the surf. The subsequent entry in the mission log bluntly stated that "the beach is hydrographically unsuitable for amphibious landing."

Back in Yokosuka, the men of SOG received the congratulations of Admirals Joy and Doyle, a flood of Silver Stars for all the senior officers, and the same reward as every other previous raider force in American history, disbandment. Unlike the Rangers or the Raiders, however,

SOG's dismissal had been brought about not by any great disaster but because of an exigency that suddenly made its components more valuable than its sum. By the time SOG had returned, Doyle's amphibious group needed every Marine, UDT swimmer, and APD it could get—not to cut the enemy's supply lines, but to cut the enemy itself in half.

9

Located some 200 miles from the Pusan Perimeter on the opposite, northwest side of the Korean Peninsula, the port of Inchon presented to MacArthur as promising a path for a sneak attack as had been Hannibal's in Italy but at a beach as perilous to the Navy's ships as were the Alps to the elephants. Located at the end of a forty-mile-long gauntlet of sentinel islands, Inchon's tide rose and fell a staggering thirty-five feet each day, one of the most extreme ranges in the world, making its unmarked channel a six- to eight-knot sluice of mine-hiding, muddy water. That was just the pathway; the landing site was worse. Like Dieppe, and unlike every other invasion site in World War II, Inchon was a harbor and a city, protected by seawalls of unknown height and those protected at low tide by mudflats of unknown density, stretching in length from 1,000 to 4,500 yards—exactly the sort of terrain for which the machine gun had been invented. Smack in front of the beaches sat the heights of Wolmi-do, an island that stretched into the harbor's center like a tomahawk, ready with artillery to chop any landing force in half. Taken together, it was a series of obstacles unlike any that Marine Recon or the UDTs had ever faced, and as such would require something altogether different.

At 5:30 p.m. on August 23, a Wednesday, all senior theater commanders—including Admirals Arthur W. Radford, Arthur D. Struble, Joy, and Doyle—crowded into MacArthur's sixth-floor wood-paneled conference room in the Dai Ichi Insurance building. Joining the meeting were two superiors from Washington: the recently arrived Army chief of staff, Joe Collins, and his peer, Forrest Sherman, chief of naval operations. What was the purpose of such a mighty host? To moderate MacArthur's evangelic zeal for Inchon and to select another beach, one like Kunsan—less perilous, closer to the Pusan Perimeter.

After eighty minutes listening in lock-lipped silence to the ranks of naval objections, a feat for MacArthur, he stood and paused. As tense hands gripped chair rails, his gusty baritone took his audience on a tour of his shared history with the Navy—his PT-boat flight from Corregidor, his island-hopping campaign through the South Pacific—then launched a salvo describing his supreme belief in surprise and the amphibious landing, "the most powerful tool we have." With every word, he soothed the nerves still raw from the humiliation left by the Revolt of the Admirals. The anchor to his speech was a brief reminder of the last great battle of the French and Indian War, in which General James Wolfe surprise-landed his comparably smaller force of British regulars on the Quebec shore, then had them scale the unscalable cliffs to crush the French on the Plains of Abraham—a battle whose very name resounded with Old Testament assurance. "I might have more [faith] in the Navy than the Navy has in itself," MacArthur concluded before delivering his next line directly to Sherman, but "the Navy has never let me down in the past, and it will not let me down this time."

To ears that had only a year earlier listened to Omar Bradley predict an end to amphibious warfare and the Marine Corps, and an early twilight for the Navy's relevance, MacArthur's words were both a salute and a gauntlet. Having kept his mouth shut the entire meeting, CNO Sherman finally spoke: "General, the Navy will take you in."

10

THOUGH HE HAD NOT mentioned it in his speech, the French and Indian War battle that MacArthur had used to prove the genius of Inchon had actually hinged on a preliminary assault of twenty-four bayonet-wielding volunteers who had climbed Quebec's cliffs in darkness, then cut a hole through the French sentry line for the rest of the Army to walk through. Those volunteers had served under the command of Colonel William Howe, the brother of the man most responsible for integrating the tactics and green coats of Rogers' Rangers into the British Army's light infantry regiments. Not quite two hundred years later, planners of the Inchon invasion realized a need for a similar spearhead, but for that assignment chose not a Ranger (there were none), but a sailor as shipbound as Ulysses.

On August 26 at the Dai Ichi Insurance building, Navy staffer Lieutenant Gene Clark was told to report to his superior, Captain Edward Pearce, head of Far East Command's naval geographic intelligence section. Medium in build and slightly above average in height, with oak-brown hair and eyes that were never unattractive to the building's secretaries, Lieutenant Clark had, just one month earlier, turned thirty-nine years old—an age too old for his rank. Exiting the elevator, Clark threaded past a bustle of military orderlies to arrive at the office where Pearce and a fellow officer—two-war hero Major General Holmes Dager—greeted him with looks of anticipation. After some small talk, the two superiors took turns revealing MacArthur's secret plan to land at Inchon Harbor on September 15—just twenty-one days away. Having spent the last year of his life working for Pearce—cataloguing old Japanese nautical charts, fishing reports, anything that might inform him about regional harbors, tides, and terrain—Clark knew better than anyone else how little information the Navy had collected on Inchon, a lapse that MacArthur's Prussian-born chief of intelligence, Major General Charles Willoughby, had received with "grave dissatisfaction." Prussian generals are always gravely dissatisfied. The problem well stated, Pearce shifted in his chair and thrust his white-haired head forward.

"Gene," Pearce began, his face blank but his eyes "twinkling" portentously, "I believe we've cooked up a little rumble you're going to like."

What came next was a laundry list of everything the Navy needed to fill the gaps in Inchon's intelligence—the size and location of island garrisons, the position of antiship guns on Wolmi-do, the consistency of the mudflats, even the height of the seawall. Before Clark could comment or posit a question, General Dager cut in: "How would you like to get us that information?" It was not a question most staff officers ever expect to get.

Wary of the enemy-held islands that lined the path to Inchon, Clark immediately began to envision a "rumble" that spanned the entire spectrum of unconventional operations—operations of a sort for which SOG and the GHQ Raiders and even Pounds Force had been conceived, units which were either about to be broken up or earmarked for other missions. Clark considered the offer—even his unsuitability for it—and then let his excitement get the better of him.

"I'd certainly like to take a crack at it," he said.

Pleased with the answer, Pearce replied that for the duration of the mission Clark would fall under Far East Command's intelligence branch, to which he would radio his reports directly.

Within minutes Clark was back in his office, staring out the window, a pipe clenched in his teeth, trying to force his mind to focus on the thing for which he had just volunteered. When his world stopped spinning, he asked his secretary to pull every file they had amassed on Inchon, and for the next several hours he scratched notes on the various islands and inhabitants, then listed everything he guessed he might need, from guns to rice. One thing was for sure: With only twenty-one days to go before the operation, there was not a moment to lose.

Born in 1911 on the empty plains of South Dakota, Eugene Franklin Clark had endured an early childhood as bleak as his surroundings. Following the death of his mother when he was three, his father had dropped him and his two siblings at a California orphanage, where his sister was eventually adopted, his brother reclaimed, and young Clark was abandoned for good. An early life of bad breaks seems to have taught him to never miss an opportunity.

Before graduating from high school, even before turning eighteen, he had married and joined the Navy, accomplishing the latter feat by having his estranged father sign the waiver—apparently his only meaningful contact with him since abandonment. By nineteen he was a yeoman, the Navy's equivalent of a clerk, and stationed in Panama, where he seems to have picked up passable Spanish. Over the next ten years he sailed the world and steadily worked his way from seaman to chief petty officer. When assigned to a shore command in San Francisco, he rented a cheap flat in the city's red-light district so he could afford the double expense of night law school and two infant children—first a girl, then a boy. During World War II, he grew dismayed at his vocation aboard what he called an LMD—a large mahogany desk—and so, to get himself "into the warzone," accepted appointment to Officer Candidate School, learned Japanese, and volunteered for assignment to the Army's Military Government Group, becoming what is today known as a civil affairs officer, a cross-functional specialty intended to protect civilian populations from starvation, disease, reprisals, and infiltrations. In practice, these sorts of vague disciplines tend to expand beyond their original charter. In this capacity he served in the Philippines, then in the full three-month campaign at Okinawa and the surrounding islands, where he received what one official Navy historian described as a "forced-draft education in soldiering." He witnessed an amphibious landing, a final banzai charge, a flamethrower assault; he even survived an ambush in which the two backseat passengers of his jeep were "riddled" with bullets. After the war, Clark stayed in the Far East, where he was first assigned to a cargo ship, progressing from department head assignments in navigation, communications, and gunnery, then took command of a flat-bottomed LST in which he launched a series of clandestine missions up and down China's coast in dhows and sampans, all in support of Chiang's Nationalists in their ill-fated war against Mao's Communists. After a stint commanding an attack transport in the Pacific between Saipan and Palau, Clark was sent to Guam to serve as chief interpreter in the trials of Japanese war criminals, then to a permanent assignment on another mahogany desk at MacArthur's Dai Ichi in Tokyo, a position that permitted his family to join him but confined his chances for excitement to the occasional weeklong trip north to debrief a Japanese soldier released from Russian captivity.

In the words of a Navy historian, Clark was mature, deliberate, and calculating. In manner he was agreeable, somewhat quiet but not overly so, and like all sailors, was never shy of tobacco, Scotch, or a joke, which he told often, never once betraying a smile in the telling. Having spent almost eight uninterrupted years in Asia, he had grown fond of all the amenities: geisha houses, massage parlors, hot baths, cold showers. Unlike most servicemen, however, the luxuries did not seem to have dulled his inclinations or imbued him with any sense of superiority to Asian peoples, thus making him a veritable descendant of Mary Miles. Gifted in languages and in the written word, his ambitions could easily have drifted toward those of a scholar, had it not been for an equal pull toward action. It's a comparison too often made because no one can really compare, but it is worth noting that another raider phenom also possessed a gift for languages and specialized in geographic intelligence before he was plucked from a staff job. That raider was T. E. Lawrence.

II

When Clark finished his notes, he packed off for home, where he told his wife and children he had another prisoner assignment up north. The next morning, he kissed them goodbye, then caught a flight into the Pusan Perimeter in order to recruit a fellow pilgrim with whom he might shoulder the weight of his newfound burden. A natural partner for such a mission would have been one of the northern refugees or South Korean (ROK) soldiers already being trained as guerrillas by the CIA's director of Korean operations, Lieutenant Colonel Vincent "Dutch" Kramer, a polymath Marine and SACO's former Camp Three commander, who was, at that moment, enlisting seafaring partners to raid the northern coast. After what appears to have been at least a day of interviews, Clark selected two men, both of whom measured a full head shorter than him in height but supplemented his lack of ground combat. The first was a forty-two-year-old former ROK Army colonel named Ke In-Ju, fired from his counterintelligence post by none other than South Korea's president, Syngman Rhee, for failing to predict the invasion—he could have gotten in line for that; the second was a thirty-year-old ROK Navy lieutenant named Youn Joung, the handsome son of a Japanese-murdered industrialist who had survived the last war by joining a group of Manchurian guerrillas. Besides Korean and English, both men spoke Chinese and Japanese. With his team selected, Clark linked up with an old Army buddy who jeeped him to the Pusan Front, where a cluster of mortars chased them back.

When the three companions arrived back in Japan, Clark found an old friend and current Navy supply officer who transformed the team's wish list into a pile of M1 rifles and M3 grease guns, a pair of .50-caliber machine guns, several .30-caliber machine guns, crates of bullets and grenades, thirty cases of C-rations, several boxes of Halazone water purification tablets, a five-pound can of insect repellent, a tent, several cots, a high-frequency radio to transmit reports, one million won in South Korean currency, two hundred pounds of rice, seventy pounds of dried fish, cigars, and two cases of Canadian Club whisky. They also requisitioned flashlights, binoculars, compasses, canteens, and everything else a Marine had but Clark didn't.

While Ke and Youn sorted the supplies, Clark made his way to Sasebo Harbor, where he stalked the piers until he found HMS *Ladybird,* Her Majesty's flagship to Admiral Joy's west coast blockade force. Presenting his letter of introduction, Clark was ushered into a wardroom of royal portraits, rugs, and Scotch and soda, where his hosts arranged for him a predawn departure aboard HMS *Charity,* a destroyer.

On the morning of August 31, under a blanket of stars that seemed "etched in deep blue velvet," Clark, Youn, and Ke stood at the rails aboard the *Charity* while she slipped her moorings and broke rank with the rest of the bobbing warships. For Clark, who had spent the past five sleep-deprived days and nights in almost constant preparation and planning, the momentary peace of churning engines and intersecting ship wakes allowed his mind to drift. Beyond Sasebo's corridor of green hills lay uncertainties of every sort, not least of which concerned his suitability for the task ahead, a task more portentous than he could know. Never trained as a commando, Clark now embarked on a commando mission that, if successful, would clear the way for invasion and redeem the Navy's offensive purpose. The corollary: His example would also validate for the Navy the use of amphibious commandos for far more than scouting beaches and cutting the enemy's supply lines.

12

On September 1, exactly twenty-four hours after departing, the *Charity* arrived off the island of Tokchok-do, approximately thirty airline miles west of Inchon. Nearby was the twelve-gun cruiser HMS *Jamaica* and Clark's next ride, an ROK patrol craft, *PC 703*, a single-stack, 173-foot twin diesel submarine chaser, armed with .50-caliber guns and a three-inch cannon on the bow. Of the vessel's crew, only the skipper wore a uniform. Clark now wore a set of green Marine Corps fatigues (too short in the sleeves), his .45-caliber pistol in a leather shoulder holster, a hand grenade (in case he was captured), and his black-billed, tan Navy officer's hat whose gold trimming and silver-winged emblem inspired authority but drew attention like a spotlight. As Clark and his men cross-decked their supplies to the PC, the *Charity*'s crew further burdened them with two additional bottles of Scotch, and the *Jamaica*'s skipper eagerly brought his gig alongside to offer gunfire support in case of emergency. Anxious to find a base from which to stage his reconnaissance missions, preferably one closer than thirty miles from the target, Clark spoke with the patrol craft's skipper, Commander Lee Sung Ho, who described in perfect English what he knew of each island's inhabitants. Lee and his crew had already raided Tokchok-do, seized its sampans, and freed the island's fifty or so villagers from their Communist masters, whose status—living or dead—Clark was diplomatically reluctant to investigate. Like Mary Miles, Clark had the capacity to work cheerfully alongside the grayest of characters.

Ashore at Tokchok-do, Clark listened in as Ke and Youn spoke in Korean with the village chieftain and the son of a Christian schoolmaster from nearby Yonghung-do, a six-mile-long, three-mile-wide oval-shaped island that lay some fifteen miles from Inchon and, just as important, was guarded by a single squad of North Korean soldiers. The island, however, contained one significant drawback: a low-tide mud bridge in the southeast that twice a day connected it to its island neighbor, Taebu-do, which was guarded by a well-armed North Korean garrison, a garrison that might reinforce the lone squad at any minute.

With no time to lose, Clark and his men reboarded the patrol craft and informed Lee of their intent to seize Yonghung-do as a base. Lee in turn offered Clark a landing party of eleven sailors. Clark accepted, then outfitted them with six M1 rifles and five M3 submachine guns, and during the twenty-minute transit had Ke and Youn provide the volunteers a crash course in how to use them. Three miles from the target, Lee commandeered two fishing junks and towed them around Yonghung-do's rocky northeastern tip, where Clark and his raiders high-stepped over the lifelines, stacked the junks with piles of crates and supplies, then armed the wooden bows with .30-caliber machine guns. With no radio to connect him to the patrol craft or the British ships, Clark told Lee to "come in for breakfast" the next morning, an offer that probably did nothing to mask his nervousness but that guaranteed that someone would check up on him. As they heaved free of the safety of the PC, and raised the sails of their ancient vessels, Clark lifted his binoculars to the shore of Yonghung-do and scanned the island's rock cliffs and pebble beaches, its lone ferry landing, its 500-foot-tall scrub-covered hills, and the swamp-plain valley that cut the island in half.

The accounts differ on what happened next: One says the *Jamaica* dispatched a platoon of Royal Marines to join Clark's sailors, then initiated the assault with a single eight-inch round at the island's jetty, killing a lone Communist sentry and scattering the rest. Another account says that Clark's raiders were welcomed ashore by a crowd of villagers waving little white flags and that after a brief meeting with village leaders they chased a boatload of "frantic" Communists off the opposite side of the island, then adjusted their fire by the splashes of their bullets until the enemy corpses receded with the tide. However it happened, Yonghung-do was secured by 10:30 A.M., and by afternoon Clark, Ke, and Youn had set up a command post on the northern hill overlooking Inchon Harbor, complete with an eight-man pyramidal tent, a four-foot latrine, three cots, the radio, a map table, a single kerosene lamp, chairs from the village, and a hibachi. They also set up defensive positions, including one overlooking Taebu-do, and from the island's pool of 150 teenagers recruited seven boys for service in what Clark called the Young Men's Association, a grenade-armed guard with orders to "watch and run."

For Clark, Ke, and Youn, the next two days and nights would be a blur of interviews, guard duty, radio dispatches, black coffee, and a typhoon. Sleep and food would be extremely infrequent. Throughout, Clark would compare his tidal estimates to what he saw around him: like a drain being pulled from a sink, he thought, and enough water to uncover a three-story building. Though he and his men had already established a base of scouts near the enemy's back door, Clark knew it was not enough. To find the answers to Inchon's other secrets—the mud, the mines, the guns, and the seawall—he knew he would need to move beyond his island redoubt and beyond his relative comfort as a mere spy handler. Clark was not the only one who could sense the necessity for change.

13

Back in Japan, the raiders at the Navy's Mobile Training Team schoolhouse were being plucked like ripe apples. On September 5, the US Army–dominated United Nations Command combined the GHQ Raiders and Pounds Force into a single entity: the Special Activities Group, or SAG, a nominally joint unit but one in which the Navy seemed destined to devolve into a mere subcontractor for SAG's training and transportation, this latter activity subcontracted further to Her Majesty's fleet. A few days later, Admiral Joy tried to reassert the US Navy's custody of SAG's operational future by sending a dispatch to the skipper of HMS *Whitesand Bay* with orders to, at "earliest possible," conduct "amphibious raiding operations and beach reconnaissance" near Kunsan, an order that—by virtue of the players—had to receive concurrence from the rest of the stakeholders at UN Command. In fact, the Navy's unilateral raiding ambitions appeared likely to be at an end, finally relegated to its traditional train-and-deliver role. Joy was not about to let that happen.

At about the same moment on the other side of the world, a group of 200 or so men of the 41 Royal Marine Commando—pronounced "four-one," not "forty-first"—were climbing a set of jetway stairs and boarding a civilian airplane in England. They were dressed in a mishmash of ties, pinstripes, and vulcanized military boots, a thin secrecy made transparent by the crowd of journalists on the tarmac and the exploding flashbulbs. When they arrived in Japan, they dropped their ties and blazers and reported to Doyle's Mobile Training Team to receive their American uniforms, guns, radios, mortars, and bazookas, their pride of service preserved only by their lopsided green berets badged with the crown and lion of the British Empire. Uncomfortable with his unit's assignment to the Army-dominated Special Activities Group—he was a Marine, after all—Major Douglas Drysdale, the unit's commander, presented himself upon arrival to Rear Admiral Arleigh Burke, Joy's recently appointed chief of staff, with hopes of finding an advocate who was familiar with the types of amphibious missions his unit had been trained to perform.

Burke was confused. He had only just arrived in Korea a few days before, and so was apparently unaware of all the coastal raiding the Navy had thus far sponsored.

"I don't know how the hell to use commandos," Burke told Drysdale. "Have you got any ideas?"

By the end of the conversation, Burke and Drysdale had settled on a plan to attach the 41 Royal Marine Commando to the USS *Perch,* the Navy's long-since-prepared troop-carrying submarine, in order to reinitiate the Navy's raids on the North Korean coastal supply routes. In the next week, a third of Drysdale's men would do little else but train on the *Perch* as the US Navy's "Undersea Raiding Force." At the end of the week, Joy would send MacArthur a formal dispatch requesting the permanent transfer of this submarine-trained group to the US Navy's "operational control." The first service to raid in the Korean War, the Navy—under Joy—apparently refused to be the first service to stop.

14

After five days on Yonghung-do, Clark had achieved some notable successes. To capture local vessels sailing from Inchon, he had enlisted the junk fleet of the local fishermen's association—essentially part-time pirates. To separate infiltrators from Yonghung-do's islanders, he had issued crudely torn slips of paper that would only match the slips from which they had been torn. To confirm the functionality of the lighthouse on Palmi-do Island, he had led an armed night reconnaissance, then left a teenage machine gun crew to guard the only landing site.

Working on meager rations and even less sleep, he had created a courier network, captured an infiltrator from Taebu-do, and sent daily reports back to Far East Command. Still, it was not enough. Clark needed more, and faster.

Learning that a North Korean platoon in a village on Taemuui-do was protecting a Communist political commissar named Yeh, someone who probably knew everything there was to know about Inchon, Clark decided to capture him.

At 7:00 p.m. on the night of September 5, Clark, Youn, and nine fishermen scouts boarded an armed junk and set sail for Taemuui-do. On the voyage, Clark poked chopsticks around a bowl of rice and cold fish, then stripped off his fatigues, blackened his entire body with charcoal, slung his pistol rig over his shoulder, and hooked to his belt a knife,

Korean guerrillas on Yonghung-do before Inchon with Youn (standing, center) and Eugene Franklin Clark (standing, right).

a flashlight, and three hand grenades. Lying on the wooden deck and listening to the creak of bamboo and the slap of sails, Clark passed out and woke to the junk crew using poles to push the boat to the shore. Under a moonless sky, Clark and his men slogged through the sucking mud, then uphill, threading a path of deep grass and branches, the darkness so thick that the guides had to lead by instinct. After two and a half hours, the patrol stopped on a hillside overlooking a seaside village of kerosene-lit homes, a school, and a central rowhouse now occupied as a barracks. As the would-be raiders squatted in a semicircle, Clark whispered out an assault plan that Youn translated, one that split the untrained raiders into two groups, with orders to sneak into the town and position themselves in such a way that they could simultaneously grenade the barracks and capture the commissar.

Descending into a rice paddy, Clark, Youn, and the guide continued into the surf, paralleled the shore, then waded up to the village's center, where the sight of a guard flattened them momentarily onto the sand. Clinging to the shadows, the three darted from house to house until they found the commissar's, where they saw him inside, talking to three policemen. Hiding next to the house's paper door, Clark and his companions nervously clutched their knives and waited for the sound of the other group's grenades.

Then it happened. In an instant the sound of bullets and the flash of grenades tore open the night, prompting a rush of policemen through the door that Clark and Youn quickly blocked, prompting the commissar to scream and kick open a door leading in the opposite direction. Retrieving his knife from one of the policemen's ribs, Clark pulled out his pistol and clubbed the commissar into unconsciousness. When the commotion stopped, Clark noticed his guide slumped on the floor, lifeless and bleeding from his head. With no time to lose and the battle raging outside, Youn secured his own knife, and scooped up the commissar like a bundle of rags while Clark slung the guide over his shoulder. Outside, a wave of bullets forced them to their bellies, a position from which Clark fired his pistol to lock-back, killing two North Korean soldiers. With the village burning behind them, Clark and Youn hefted their human bundles back to the ocean, then retraced their path to the rice paddy and back up the hill, a climb that left Clark's lungs burning and his leg muscles twitching uncontrollably.

At the rally point, without any light except the distant flickering from the burning village, Clark and Youn placed their fingertips on the guide's and the commissar's throats, feeling for any sign of a pulse. There was none. Apparently, some of the bullets that had forced Clark and Youn to their bellies had been stopped by their human shields. The commissar's death would have made the mission a failure, except for what happened next: While being pursued by a four-man patrol of North Korean soldiers swinging a dim lantern, Clark staged a hasty ambush, eliminating half the pursuers and hog-tying the rest. It was the Navy's first successful capture mission of the war.

15

THE MORNING AFTER A DAYLONG sweep of Yonghung-do that flushed out seven North Korean soldiers, followed by a nightlong examination of a lighthouse that proved unusable, Clark received a breathless report that a flotilla of North Korean junks from Taebu-do was preparing to attack at any moment. Without hesitating, Clark took command of his pirate fleet and sailed out to meet the threat, a six-junk flotilla carrying eighty to ninety North Korean soldiers, their flagship a three-sailed monster called a Kwantung whose principal weapon was a forward-mounted recoilless rifle.

Perched like Ahab on the bow of his own junk, binoculars to his eyes, a sandbagged machine gun at his feet, Clark ordered his fleet to sail directly into the Kwantung's fire. After a few minutes spent closing the distance, one of the Kwantung's rounds "raked a gash" along the full length of Youn's boat, killing or wounding half of his eight-man crew, and struck another boat just below the waterline, forcing her pilot to the beach. Like the French maneuver at Trafalgar, Clark ordered his fleet to turn slightly, a move that opened his flank to the recoilless but set up his flotilla for a broadside right down the enemy ship's bows. After two shots tore through the hull of Clark's boat, a third crumpled the mainmast, splaying Clark on the wooden planks and splashing his pirate captain's thigh with a "miserable looking" pincushion of splinters. It was time. After untwisting the .30-caliber's belt and rebracing it in the sandbags, Clark stepped back to avoid the inevitable shower of brass and ordered his gunner to open fire on the Kwantung. In seconds the bullets "melted" the enemy vessel's entire bow, toppled its recoilless end over end, and exposed the whole top deck that was crammed with North Korean soldiers, who now dove overboard to be drowned or sniped in a red cloud of salt water. The other boats sank even faster in a clean sweep of Flying Fish Channel that now enabled Clark to push closer to his intended target.

That night, he and Youn popped their first Benzedrine tablets, washed them down with a pot of camp coffee, then set sail for Wolmido, the former island resort turned citadel that towered above the Inchon beaches and that Admiral Doyle considered the "whole key to success or failure." Coating themselves with thick tidal mud that smelled like rotting fish, Clark, Youn, and a third scout crawled over sharp rocks, rubbing their skin raw in the process, and avoided the sentries made visible by the glow of their cigarette tips. Clark's radio report that followed listed roads, barbed wire, beach exits, waterline foxholes, machine gun nests, an artillery observation post, and two antiaircraft guns, but on the bright side, no mines or underwater obstacles.

The next day, the skipper of the USS *Hanson,* a destroyer, sent a whaleboat of armed American sailors to Yonghung-do with a resupply of cigarettes, bandages, penicillin, sulfa powder, and a hundred pounds of sugar with which Clark could barter. For good measure, the skipper bombarded the North Korean garrison on Taebu-do, then arranged for a follow-on flight of Marine Corps fighter-bombers. In the afternoon, Clark's fishermen-pirates presented him with a captured one-cylinder, diesel-powered white junk called a pompom, complete with a small pilothouse, a smokestack that shot sparks ten feet in the air, and an old, toothy, grease-covered mechanic whose loyalty lay only to his engine. Clark called the monstrosity his flagship and, so armed, began plotting the missions that would finally give him the answers for which he had been sent.

16

THAT NIGHT, AFTER ATTENDING an island wedding in a kimono, Clark stripped down into his UDT attire but this time cross-taped a knife to his bare back so the hilt touched the base of his neck, then similarly secured a grenade behind his right hip. Thus prepared, he and Youn boarded a sampan for Inchon in moonless darkness so total that they "seemed to be suspended in blank space." When they reached Inchon, Clark and Youn tied a line of braided safety rope between them, then sank up to their thighs on a mudflat as firm as a can of grease. After a 500-yard, thirty-minute slog to shore, Clark and Youn took the parts played by Bucklew and Halperin in the previous war and used the starlight to sketch the silhouette of hills and smokestacks. At the seawall, with no lead line to measure depth, Youn stood on Clark's shoulders and stretched his hands to the lip while Clark prayed that his partner's fingers would not land on a sentry's boots.

The next day on Yonghung-do, Clark learned of three important developments: first, despite his best efforts infiltrators had crept ashore and practically beheaded one of his teenage guards; second, a band of guerrillas hiding in the hills south of Inchon had sent a message that they wanted to join Clark's forces; third, the Navy planned a preliminary bombardment of Inchon a full forty-eight hours before invasion. The last two developments suggested an opportunity. If he could join up with the Inchon guerrillas before the Navy's gunships arrived, he could seize a vantage point from which to plot and report the enemy's counterbatteries.

On the night of September 12, the same night the GHQ Raiders and Pounds Force Commandos launched an unremarkable raid on Kunsan's beach, Clark, Youn, and a guide boarded the pompom flagship, this time to raise an army on the mainland. At the shoreline, three men "materialized out of the scrub" to lead Clark and his companions up the slopes with only the fires from Inchon's saltworks to light the way. At the guerrilla campsite, Clark met the group's leaders—one with a top hat, one a woman, all malnourished—whose only request was weapons and ammunition. Clark agreed to supply them with all the surplus weapons he and his pirates had captured, then asked the guerrillas to help him seize and secure a hilltop from which he might see the bombardment now only a few hours away. The leaders immediately offered ten guerrillas who would lead Clark and his companions to an isolated hillside camp whose thirteen-man North Korean guard would rotate an hour before sunrise.

Retracing the path by which they'd come, the guerrillas led Clark and his raiders to an outpost with one campfire and a scattering of stilt-raised thatch shelters. Leaving his Navy cap behind, Clark crawled around the enemy camp, then ordered Youn and the guerrillas to cover the likeliest escape route and placed himself on an overlooking ridge, forming something like an "L" ambush. Lying on his belly just twenty feet from a pair of sentries, Clark quietly covered himself with grass, laid his pistol magazines in front of his face, then placed his head on his arms and promptly fell asleep. Waking abruptly, he popped a Benzedrine tablet just in time for the sunrise, the arrival of the new guards, and the sensation that his entire body was crawling with ants and spiders. There was nothing to do but endure it. At 9:00 A.M., unable to wait any longer, Clark stretched out his pistol, oriented its front sight post on the sentry, and gently squeezed the trigger. The shot shattered the morning's silence and dropped the convulsing guard on his companion. As Clark rose to fire again, Youn and his guerrillas charged into the camp firing at anything that moved. The whole ambush took less than a minute, and cost two guerrillas killed and two wounded. As soon as the firing stopped, Clark rose and stripped off his clothes and shook out the insects while Youn collected the bodies and covered them with thatch from the huts. It was Clark's second successful raid in less than a week and was rewarded with the distant sight of four gray ships emerging from Flying Fish Channel to turn their broadsides toward the shore.

The rest of the day, Clark, Youn, and the guerrillas sat on the hillside watching the bombardment and passing binoculars among them. By day's end, Clark had marked his map with the location of twenty of the enemy's counterbatteries.

17

Having transmitted to Far East Command the answer to every question he had been sent to resolve, Clark had planned to spend the final day before invasion preparing for his final mission to illuminate the lighthouse on Palmi-do, which would guide the entire fleet down the narrow corridor of Flying Fish Channel. Unfortunately for him, the enemy had other plans. At noon, a mud-covered teenage guard appeared at Clark's tent with news that North Korean soldiers had seized the ferry landing. Immediately, Clark and Youn led parallel patrols across the island where they fought off an attack, then returned to the tent to organize an evacuation and defense of Yonghung-do's inhabitants. By sunset they had loaded their equipment aboard the flagship and evacuated not quite a third of the island's men, women, and children. That night the enemy attacked in force.

Alternating between directing tracerless machine gun fire and throwing grenades at the waves of North Korean soldiers, Clark, Youn, and Ke fought as long as they could, until they too had to evacuate to the flagship, an evacuation that ultimately left some fifty of the island's inhabitants behind to be executed, a cruel price to complete the final leg of their mission.

When Clark, Youn, and Ke—emaciated and exhausted from two weeks of little food and less sleep—stepped onto the spit beach of Palmi-do island, the sand at their feet exploded with a burst of machine gun fire discharged by the teenage guards they had forgotten to warn of their arrival. After Youn silenced the attack with an explosive shout, he seized Clark's arm and dragged him to the top of the hill and up five steps to the base of the tower, where together they unbolted the double doors, hustled past the triple row of dry batteries and stripped wires, and climbed almost forty feet of iron-rung ladder to reach the light deck. There, they lifted a small glass chimney labeled "Made in France" and lit the wick to the light by which the invasion fleet would navigate.

Depleted of strength, his heart "beating like a trip-hammer," Clark stumbled through the hatch to the external catwalk and collapsed, the entire black channel spread out before him. Eventually someone handed him a blanket, which he wrapped around his shoulders. He awoke to Youn shaking his shoulder and pointing to the water. There, 200 feet below in moonless darkness, was the silent vanguard of the fleet—three of them APDs: the USS *Bass, Wantuck,* and *Diachenko*—stretched out in a line and pulsing toward Inchon.

18

IN THE PREDAWN OF SEPTEMBER 15, Doyle's ships glided into Inchon Harbor on the pull of a rising tide and turned their broadsides toward the island rump of Wolmi-do. It was "dark as the inside of a cow's belly," one witness said, so ship gunners calculated distances on the only lights available, those flecks of fire still burning from the previous two days' bombardment. At 5:45 A.M., Doyle ordered the fleet to open fire. The first round sounded like a "slammed door," wrote a reporter floating in a landing craft. Moments later, the slammed door gave way to the "kettle drum" pound of eight-inch guns, the rolling snare of the 40-millimeters, followed by a constant drone of fighter-bombers and the "thump" of bombs, shells, and rockets splashing onto the "quivering" crust of Wolmi-do. "I thought it would roll over and sink," said one Navy pilot after watching the drubbing. As the fleet's guns roared and smoked, the APDs each lowered four landing craft. With no Rangers left in the US arsenal, each was filled with something just as terrifying: Marines.

At 6:29 A.M., the firing stopped and the first seven landing craft hit the Wolmi-do beach. Right behind were ten more, then nine Pershing tanks: three slick, three equipped with flamethrowers, and three fronted by bulldozer blades ready to entomb any North Korean soldier not smart enough to flee the island's caves. By 6:55, some twenty-five minutes after landing, the Marines reached Wolmi-do's crest and to the top of a naked tree tied an American flag. The capture cost the Marine battalion no dead but seventeen wounded, the most serious case shot through the chest and another who lost a leg at the thigh. The obstacle that had threatened to cut the invasion force in half could now be transformed into an island of artillery.

Having strained through binoculars to watch the assault from the bridge of the *Mount McKinley*, MacArthur returned to his stateroom and scratched a note to be broadcast to the fleet: "The navy and marines have never shone more brightly than this morning."

Not long afterward, lookouts aboard the *McKinley* spotted a strange white junk motoring toward them, coughing sparks out of her smokestack. Atop the pilothouse was a bearded man in green fatigues waving a tan hat above his head. Placing a hand around the ship's megaphone, the *McKinley*'s skipper ordered the approaching hulk to "stand off!" The junk complied, but the man kept waving. The skipper ordered an LCVP to intercept.

A few minutes later, the LCVP was circling the junk, its redheaded officer leveling a tommy gun at the mysterious hat waver. When close enough, the officer called out, "Who the hell are you?"

"I am Lieutenant Eugene Clark of the U.S. Navy. Put that gun down before you hurt somebody."

When the LCVP officer relayed the response to the *McKinley*, an incredulous voice radioed a response, asking the officer how he could be so sure that man was an American sailor.

"He's got a naval officer's cap on his head," he responded.

With that, Clark was ushered aboard the LCVP and shuttled to the *McKinley*. His mission was over. Whether it was successful or not was about to be seen.

19

THAT AFTERNOON—AFTER THE HARBOR had drained and refilled, reflooding the uncrossable mudflats with water—the Navy's guns and rockets and fighter-bombers began again, this time focused on Inchon itself. In minutes the city was "choked with fumes and cinders" and buried, wrote a *Time* magazine reporter, under a "pall of purple smoke." Behind the shoulders of ship guns, the flotillas of landing craft—many piloted by UDT swimmers—were cutting "endless" white circles in the "dirty yellow water," waiting for their moment. Though anxious, perhaps on the cusp of eternity, many of the Marines inside these vessels had ignored their nerves and hung signs over the lips of their bow ramps that read "Truman Police Force"—a defiant protest of the president's famous dismissal of the Marines as no more than "the Navy's police force."

At 5:30 P.M., an hour before sunset, Doyle gave the order and the circling boats wheeled into ranks. At the bows of the landing craft, the Marines heaved and propped ladders, often pairs of them, making the vessels appear like giant, antennaed beetles. Only fifteen seconds before the first wave reached the shore, Doyle silenced the fleet's guns just long enough for each invader to brace for the rock-slab seawall that with every second was growing, remembered one witness, as tall as the RCA Building. Into this the coxswains slammed their bows and the Marines—one at a time—runged to the top. When ladders fell short, the men simply catapulted each other over the lip and into the snap and skip of machine gun fire, a hail of bullets that was often inescapable due to the warren of enemy-prepared, plate-covered trenches.

Behind the landing craft barreled the first of several wide-mouthed LSTs, their throttles opened to ram and crush the seawalls, then strand themselves on the low-tide mudflats as improvised supply dumps. Though casualties for the landing fell far below almost anything encountered in similar World War II operations, those first over-the-wall minutes cost the Marines eight dead and twenty-eight wounded—nothing to shrug about. At 6:45 P.M., the setting sun emerged beneath the overcast sky to illuminate a city of smoke and fire, and also a Navy and Marine Corps restored to their rightful place as instruments of offensive warfare.

On September 18, just three days after the invasion, for reasons both material and political, Secretary of Defense Louis Johnson—the US Navy's and Marine Corps' Haman—was fired.

20

ON THE SAME DAY that Johnson was fired, the 41 Royal Marine Commando graduated from Doyle's Mobile Training Team schoolhouse ready to join SAG and assume its role as a raiding force for MacArthur's Army-dominated Far East Command. Joy had other ideas. The day after their graduation, he sent a message to MacArthur asking that the Navy assume operational control of the entire unit—a far cry from his original request for one troop to serve as an Undersea Raiding Force. MacArthur's reply came the same day: "Why is the Navy so keen to use Brits, but not UDTs?" Joy had his reasons.

Now that the siege of the Pusan Perimeter was lifted and UN ground troops were preparing to steamroll north, the Navy was planning to support this drive with a series of amphibious landings, landings that would require every UDT swimmer in-theater. The other reason can be found in the Pacific Fleet's own assessment. "The urgent need for [the UDTs'] unusual employment as raiders," stated the Pacific Fleet evaluation report published that November, "was recognized as a special situation" brought on by the fact that the "peacetime Marine organization [did] not provide . . . trained raider units," thus making the "interim use" of UDT swimmers "a logical solution" but not a popular one. "UDT commanding officers are concerned," the report continued, that such "unorthodox employment" for "dangerous tasks for which they are not trained" will become "a possible future additional function" for the UDTs, which "could jeopardize their primary function" as "highly specialized swimmer-demolition experts." In short: Though the Navy's offensive instincts had pulled the UDTs from the water, the Navy's obligation to its most offensive mission—the amphibious landing—had put them back. In response to MacArthur's question, Joy said none of this, instead stating simply, "The 41 Royal Marine Commando was formed and trained especially to conduct commando raids," an oblique answer whose corollary was obvious: The Navy could make no such claim about the UDTs.

MacArthur approved Joy's request the same day, and the 41 Royal Marine Commando was released from US Army control and assigned to the US Navy as its coastal raiding force. Except for a four-month period during the Chinese Emergency when assigned to the 1st Marine Division in the fight for the Chosin Reservoir, the commandos would serve in this capacity until December 1951—wrecking railroads, collapsing tunnels—each time shuttled to shore by US Navy vessels, guarded by US Navy guns, and usually guided to the beaches by US Navy frogmen.

When after more than a year the commandos finally did depart the Korean theater, they left under a veritable ticker tape of congratulations from nearly every senior US naval officer. For his part, Admiral Joy promised that the commandos would "go down in history's brightest pages"; Vice Admiral Harold Martin declared that their departure concluded "one of the most glorious chapters yet written in the Korean War." So appreciative was the US Navy of its bootstrapped British raiders that naval planners embarked on a six-year bureaucratic slog of signatures and approvals culminating in a private ceremony at the US embassy in London, where Drysdale and five others received on behalf of their comrades the Presidential Unit Citation—the highest US award available to an entire unit.

21

As it had been with SOG, the departure of the British Commandos would not end the Navy's appetite for raiding. Into this vacuum, the Navy would again cast its APDs and a small portion of its UDTs to support the CIA's guerrillas (notably organized and directed by Major Vincent "Dutch" Kramer, US Marine Corps, a former SACO officer, not an OSS one), all in the hopes of replicating the bird-dogging raids of Eugene Clark, which had, better than any previous such actions, supplied the Navy's guns and carrier-launched bombers with targets. The most notable example of this symbiotic relationship between raiders and the fleet would occur in October 1951, when CIA guerrillas alerted the fleet to a meeting of Communist officials in the stone-and-plank buildings of the village of Kapsan, which the Navy's Skyraiders and Corsairs then drenched with so much explosive and napalm that nary a stone or plank was left standing. The "decapitating" strike reportedly killed more than 500 North Korean and Chinese leaders.

Marine 1st Lieutenant Thomas L. Curtis, UDT Lieutenant Junior Grade George C. Atcheson III, and Sergeant 1st Class James C. "Joe" Pagnella, Joint Advisory Commission, Korea, advisors to Special Mission Group on Yonghung-do.

Among those tapped to support Kramer's joint CIA and Navy raids would be none other than Lieutenant Junior Grade George Atcheson, the first UDT officer to conduct a raid in the Korean War, and who, upon return to this role in January 1952 (the month after 41's departure), would lead a demolition raid against a North Korean bridge in which he would also ambush an enemy patrol, killing fourteen and capturing one. In this capacity he and other UDT men would serve until November 1952, almost a year, at which point the CIA would dissolve the program, leaving the Navy in possession of an empty holster.

Though the Navy would achieve numerous successes in the Korean War, none would quite match the offensive contribution it had made at Inchon. And of all the contributions to that victory, none was as critical as Eugene Clark's. The effort had almost broken him—he recalled that he lost forty pounds in the process—but Clark had unlocked Inchon's secrets, and more than that had demonstrated better than anyone before him how small-scale direct action could achieve a strategic impact.

Looking to replicate that impact, the Navy's planners had, within a month of the invasion, dispatched Clark again, this time to lead a flotilla of six oceangoing sail junks and 150 guerrillas and spies (four women included) against North Korea's west coast islands. Wearing a khaki Navy uniform and a winter jacket, and standing at least a foot taller than every one of his fighters, Clark used quail hunting tactics and common sense to improvise nine separate island raids, including one on Paengnyong-do that killed some seventy-five North Korean troops at the cost of thirteen of his own guerrillas—a "mass of gore," he remembered—in which at least two men standing next to him were shot down by snipers. After hopscotching his way to the mouth of the Yalu River and reporting the massive Chinese buildup around it, Clark had had enough. "No more behind the lines for me," he told a Navy historian when he returned to Japan. "No more wind, waves, and rocks."

Not quite. In February 1951, Clark and Youn were again tapped for a behind-the-lines mission, this time to escort MacArthur's top medical officer to the mainland around Wonsan to investigate North Korean reports of bubonic plague—that scythe of the fourteenth century known as the Black Death. Staged from an island base, Clark and Youn again ran two weeks' worth of reconnaissance missions in which nine two-man CIA-trained guerrilla teams were sent ashore, eight of which were captured. Not to be denied, Clark and Youn paddled the doctor ashore themselves, then led him past the enemy's layers of barbed wire, mines, and patrols, all the way to a hinterland cave crowded with victims, all feared to be infected. As the doctor examined them and disproved the fear and the propaganda, Clark and Youn roamed the cave's outskirts and even staged the hasty ambush of an enemy patrol. For this final mission Clark was awarded the Navy Cross.

As a result of interviews by Navy historians, the broad strokes of Clark's Inchon story became public knowledge as early as 1952. Since then, they have been a footnote in every history of the Inchon invasion. The outline of his story informed not just the public's perceptions of the Navy's involvement in commando work, but also those of the Navy's planners, whose expectations for naval commandos increased with every telling.

The remainder of Clark's Navy career included command of various ships, and staff postings to Germany, Japan, and Washington. While living in Arlington, surrounded by his Japanese paintings and relics, he would return every day from the Pentagon and, accompanied by a cold beer and a bowl of nuts, would peck away at a typewriter, squeezing his memories of those fourteen days on Yonghung-do into a stack of white pages upon which the bulk of this account is based. When he finished, he made no attempts to publish it, merely handing it to his college-age daughter saying, "Here you go, Susie. Do with it what you want."

In his account, Clark clearly imagined commando-type companies landing by ship or plane or helicopter and operating behind enemy lines, their mission to raid the enemy's supplies, to force an enemy commander to "shunt off a large body of troops," and to "act as rallying points for both dissident and resistance groups." Unpublished, the account of Clark's actions would—like the Inchon invasion itself—eventually fade from the public's memory, a fact that did not diminish their importance in redeeming the Navy's reputation or in demonstrating the kinds of missions that could sustain it. Devoted to that goal to the end of his life and to the institution that had salvaged his youth and given him opportunity and purpose, Eugene Clark hoped in his final disposition to be cremated and committed to the deep from a US Navy vessel. At eighty-six years old, when such was his fate, the yeoman handling his remains made no special distinction, but rather read down the list of sailors containing Clark's name and rank, then cast his cloud of ashes into the blue. No matter. The monument to Clark's life is better represented by the institution that eventually copied his example.

Chapter 8

The Resurrection of the Army's Rangers, and the Guerrilla Raid That Failed to Forestall Their Second Death

In early July 1950, Colonel John McGee loaded his wife and nine-year-old daughter into the family car, then drove them north from their seaside posting at Monterey's Fort Ord, the Army's jewel, and up to San Francisco's Travis Air Force Base. Only five days earlier, McGee had received orders to drop everything and report to Eighth Army's Headquarters in Japan for reasons becoming more obvious by the day. Having missed out on a combat command in the last war—a career killer for the career Army officer—he found it a not altogether unwelcome order. Straight-jawed, gray-eyed, forty-two years old, nineteen of them spent in the Army, McGee remained as starched as the uniform he now wore. His only real sign of age was his unmistakable silver hair, all slicked into ranks and retreating across a forehead whose age was marked by lines as distinct as tree rings. At the tarmac, neither McGee nor his wife shed any tears. This was not the first time they had said goodbye for war.

In Yokohama, McGee was immediately informed of an initiative conceived by MacArthur's pontificating, Alabama-born chief of staff, General Ned Almond, to employ in Korea something like an amphibious version of Mosby's Raiders from the American Civil War. In the 1950s, southerners were as yet not at all self-conscious about drawing on the legacy of Confederate dash, but Almond's idea would take a lot more than dash. Since 1945, every attempt to resurrect the Army's raiders had left the tombstone right where it started. Now, McGee was being ordered to create such a unit from scratch and without drawing from any of the combat units preparing to depart for Korea. Those probably would not have helped anyway.

Though the US Navy and Marine Corps had taken the brunt of

Johnson's cuts, the Army had not been far behind. In 1945, the US Army (including the US Army Air Corps) had peaked at 8.25 million men. By 1950, it had sunk to 591,000, a number still too big for its budget. Without enough money to go around for equipment, repairs, and training, quality had diminished too. Lured into service by sugar-coating recruiters who promoted the ease of occupation duty over its boredom, most postwar soldiers, one reporter noted, had quickly discovered that the "sugar-coating" was actually "thicker than the pill." Once the jungle-slogging bushwhackers of the South Pacific, MacArthur's Japan-based Eighth Army was now fat, oversexed, undermanned, plus road-bound, day-bound, dismissive of "Orientals," and incapable of even elementary infantry functions, let alone the graduate work of raiding.

Undaunted by the challenge, McGee set to screening rear-echelon troops—clerks, typists, mechanics, essentially the only kinds of soldiers left in Japan—and within a week of his arrival had raised more than 130 volunteers for service in the Eighth Army's General Headquarters Raider Company—GHQ for short. He then turned them over to the US Marines of Admiral Doyle's Mobile Training Team for three weeks of instruction in rubber boat handling, beach identification, and all of the other skills necessary for amphibious raiding—skills that the US Army had apparently found superfluous. Instead of McGee, command of the GHQ Raiders was turned over to Colonel Louis B. Ely, an appropriate selection since Ely's service in the previous war had included a lengthy posting to Fort Pierce, where he had lent a hand in creating the Army-Navy Scouts and Raiders program. McGee could boast no such affiliation.

Having contributed to creating the Army's first raiders since World War II, McGee was once again ordered to board an airplane, this time bound for the K-9 airstrip in Taegu, close enough to the Korean front that the pilots had to radio ahead to make sure that the field had not been overrun. When McGee arrived, he picked his way through the hollowed-out campus of grid-squared Quonset huts that made up the Eighth Army's forward headquarters to report to the command operations officer. In their meeting, the operations officer placed McGee in charge of the Eighth Army's entire Miscellaneous Division, a division that at the moment consisted of not a single person, and whose supplies included not even a desk or chair. Before the afternoon ended, McGee was ordered to prepare a "staff study for [the] conduct of guerrilla warfare in North Korea."

To McGee, this was an assignment for which he had long been waiting, and, more important, one that would erect the structure of the US military's first go-anywhere commando unit—but a structure that the US Army's planners would eventually overwhelm, then blame its collapse on the builder.

2

BORN IN 1908 in Minot, North Dakota, fifty airline miles south of the Saskatchewan tundra, John Hugh McGee, the eldest of four, had rejected the wagon-rut destiny of his father's career as an attorney and judge, and instead selected for his life the adventure promised by an appointment to the US Military Academy at West Point. Following his commissioning in the infantry in 1931, McGee spent the next decade at peacetime posts in Wyoming, Colorado, Texas, Hawaii, Texas again, Georgia, New York, and finally Mindanao. In 1937, the same year his younger brother George graduated from West Point, McGee attended the Infantry School at Fort Benning, Marshall's brainchild. In December 1940, when the stomach growls of Japan's imperial hunger sounded an alarm throughout Asia, McGee packed his pregnant wife onto an evacuation transport and sent her into a typhoon so terrible that the

John H. McGee, circa 1953–1954.

ship's doctor had to strap her to a radiator for fear she might follow several crewmen over the side.

A year later, McGee was at the center of history, hopelessly commanding Moro troops in the Philippines against Japanese bombers in the snake-choked, malarial hills around Del Monte airfield; then at kilometer 117 of the Sayre Highway, becoming the only American of the eleven who fought there to survive the war.

After six months of resistance, on May 10, 1942 (his birthday), McGee swallowed his pride, obeyed his superior, and with a humiliating, blindfolded salute surrendered himself and his American and Filipino troops to an imperious Japanese officer wearing a kimono. Many of the Filipinos were tied to stakes, shot, and buried in pits, the Japanese soldiers never bothering to confirm they were dead. At thirty-three, McGee's dark brown hair had already faded to an iron gray.

For the next twenty-five months, McGee survived beatings, trench foot, dysentery, malaria, mosquitos, cages, and slavery. For nourishment, he and his fellow prisoners were fed a meager diet of rice and a few vegetables that occasionally included yams, dog meat, wafer-thin candy bars, and cigarettes—the last two purchased with a monthly allotment of forty pesos that the Japanese could turn into a lever to pry the prisoner's submission. So sensitive did the men become to their hunger that when fearful of transfer, they gorged themselves on every scrap they had hidden, one man even devouring a litter of puppies born the same day.

Along with his Catholic faith, to which he cleaved, McGee sustained his mind on a series of escape plans into the Philippine jungle, even making use of a urinary tract infection that kept him up at night to memorize the guideposts of the constellations. To each plan was attached an obvious corollary—obvious to him, anyway: Once escaped, he would raise and lead an army of Filipino guerrillas against the Japanese. For two years he plotted, mentally choosing men for work details not for their strength, but for their knowledge in gunnery and logistics—men around whom he could build the guerrilla army in his mind.

On the night of June 12—two years, one month, and two days after his capture—he finally got his chance: While anchored off the east coast of the Zamboanga Peninsula on a prison transfer ship, McGee palmed off his rosary beads to a friend, dropped every stitch of his ragged clothing to the deck, then tiptoed over his sleeping comrades, placed a naked foot on the top railing, and dove into the racing current. Through an initial volley of bullets and past two other prison ships, McGee drifted for miles until rescued by a native in an outrigger, who paddled him to land and gave him a T-shirt, which McGee turned into a loincloth. Ashore, two native boys eventually found, fed, and clothed him, tied undersized sneakers to the bottom of his feet like "heelless slippers," then pushed and pulled his emaciated frame over jungle trails lit by nothing more than a torch "as bright as a cigar tip." For the second phase of his journey, he held on to a native rider atop a water buffalo and with his free hand kept his balance by clinging to the stump of the animal's tail. At the end of the bruising ride, Colonel McGee was presented to a lieutenant of the US Army Air Corps, now a local leader in a two-year-old guerrilla army. The authority for this army—an army of thousands—could now be traced all the way back to General MacArthur.

Having spent the previous two years imagining how to recruit, train, and lead a guerrilla army, McGee was not at all prepared for insinuating himself into one that already existed. Men that he had outranked before the war, in both grade and experience, now stood close to equal in grade and far beyond in experience. While recuperating in northern Zamboanga, McGee impatiently skipped protocol and sent a message directly to Colonel Wendell Fertig, American commander of all Filipino guerrillas. In his message, McGee enthusiastically described his plan for using guerrillas in the coming campaign of Philippine reconquest and his anxious desire to prepare the guerrillas in southern Zamboanga for it. The message was a mistake. (In the Army, officers are more readily forgiven the loss of a battle than a breach of protocol.)

The recipient of McGee's message was not a graduate of West Point, not even an infantryman. Before the war, Fertig had been a civilian engineer working in the Philippines and an Army reservist, a mere logistics captain. When American forces had collapsed, however, Fertig had benefited from his more nonchalant affiliation, unburdened as he was by the "duty, honor, and country" of a West Point education. As his active-duty peers had followed orders and laid down their arms, a panicky fellow officer had asked Fertig what he planned to do. "Any damn thing but surrender," Fertig had replied. Afterward, Fertig had escaped into the Filipino jungle, raised a guerrilla army, puckishly promoted himself to brigadier general (an act that MacArthur later begrudgingly confirmed at the rank of colonel), and for two years, with hardly any help, grew his force into a cancer that the Japanese could not cut out. Thus unimpressed by his professional peers, especially the ones that had marched off to slaughter, Fertig not only denied McGee's request for a leadership position but also disparaged his ideas and, worse, his comparably "easy time" as a POW.

Embittered toward Fertig and forgivably homesick (he still had not met his daughter, born four years before), McGee retreated inward, glued himself to the radio, solitarily sketched Japanese positions from memory, and sulked through a six-week wait for promised evacuation by a US Navy submarine. His only operational service in Fertig's guerrilla army came when he was asked to trek over to Sindangan City to take command of eighty-one survivors of a torpedoed prison ship. Knowing he might miss his chance at evacuation, McGee went anyway, and within a week of arriving had created a camp to feed, clothe, and stabilize the wounded. He later claimed that he had scratched out a plan to turn his rabble of convalescents—ten with bone fractures, eight with bullet wounds, twenty-eight with punctured eardrums, and nearly all with intestinal parasites—into a band of unarmed guerrillas. It was not to be. In late September, the submarine arrived and rescued the entire group. On November 7, 1944, McGee passed under the sanctuary of the Golden Gate Bridge.

Almost as soon as McGee was reunited with his wife and daughter, he began angling to leave them again. In July 1945, he packed off to Manila with a dream of commanding troops in the coming invasion of Japan. On August 7, he got his wish and took charge of the 169th Infantry Regiment, just in time for the atomic bomb and the total surrender of the Japanese Empire.

As a professional soldier, McGee possessed ample quantities of all the professional's traits—courage, obedience, confidence, patriotism. As an indigenous leader, his main attribute was a conscientiousness for his troops that few of his American peers could match. Though circumstances had cheated him out of a meaningful contribution to the war while elevating his brother George to Army fame (George had become one of Frank Merrill's most competent and celebrated Marauder battalion commanders in Burma), McGee exhibited no outward insecurity. He remained, said one man who would serve under him in Korea, "invariably courteous and kind to everyone with whom he came into contact"; one of the "most charming and unaffected men I have ever met." His account of his World War II experiences—commendably published without the crutch of a ghost writer—purposely concealed many instances of his own bravery. (When still unsure of the rescue submarine's capacity, he had composed a manifest of eighty-one evacuees by placing his wounded at the top, then cast lots for the remainder, ensuring that his own number was eighty-two, dead last.) In short, McGee was a comprehensively good man, plus a capable soldier, organizational entrepreneur, and administrator. To the tasks given him in Korea, he would apply energy, passion, creativity, foresight, all the things he had wanted to apply in World War II but had been denied.

If there was any ingredient that McGee lacked for the tasks ahead, it was unquestionably this: experience, and the ability to recognize that his other traits did not compensate for it. Not a Ranger in World War II, or an OSS operative, or even a Marauder like his brother, his interest in unconventional warfare had grown mostly out of necessity. Conservative in preferences, conventional in outlook, he was first and last an infantryman, and one accustomed to alternately likening war to a crusade or a football game—an inexorable advance to Jerusalem or an end zone (it is usually neither). Being a conventional soldier, he viewed sabotage and raiding and assassination as mere prerequisites to what he called "a final liberating advance," a typical Army framing that denigrated the value and complexity of unconventional operations. For all his conventional shortcomings, however, no one else would so closely resemble a father to all the various unconventional US Army units born of the Korean War. When McGee was ordered to prepare a study for promoting guerrilla warfare, the ideas that had sustained him as a prisoner spread out from him like spokes in a wheel. In part because he lacked the experience to know any better, and in part because the organization from whence he sprang didn't either, he pointed those wheels toward ground too rough to turn, and upon which their thin spokes would predictably splinter and break. But this didn't mean that others wouldn't be paying attention.

3

To McGee, Korea's western islands—innumerable, defensible, close to shore—promised the greatest offensive platform. Staged from them, guerrillas could rescue downed pilots, gather intelligence, raid coastlines, erode enemy resolve, eventually spearhead the reconquest of South Korea. But how? Rice, boats, weapons—they all cost money, and Eighth Army planners had none to give, at least none to give to Asians. Practical solutions were even scarcer: McGee's initial plan—Plan Able, as it would soon be called—proposed that guerrilla recruits act like the Moro tribesmen in the Philippines and sharpen their plowshares into bolo knives—presumably to hack the guns out of their enemy's hands. The predication for Plan Able rested on this assumption: The refugees wanted to stop running and fight. When McGee left his barbed-wire campus to investigate (campuses often make their inhabitants deaf to realities), he discovered the Naktong riverbed "choked" with souls full of despair. In their arms and on their backs the refugees carried children and old people, not revenge and certainly not bolo knives. They were, he said, an "apparent cowed people."

Confronted by this reality, McGee took a logical next step. Instead of arming guerrillas, he proposed to plant the west coast islands with US-led South Korean soldiers and marines. This too was untenable, as no South Korean soldier or marine could be spared from the Naktong Line. With that, Plan Able was shelved.

McGee was then "directed to organize a unit capable of penetrating [and reconnoitering] the rear of the [Pohang] Pocket." So ordered, he scoured the file cabinets at Eighth Army and Far East Command for a table of organization and equipment (TO&E) for the Sixth Army Alamo Scouts, the same reconnaissance unit that had hacked open the path for the 6th Rangers on the Cabanatuan prison camp raid in World War II. Such a TO&E, if found, would have acted like an architect's schematic, an organizational shortcut to creating a unit from scratch. No such TO&E was found, but another one was: for a World War II Ranger Company. On the path to guerrillas, McGee had tripped through the door to an adjacent address.

As had been the case with the GHQ Raiders, McGee's manpower pool for this new unit was again limited to cooks, clerks, typists, and mechanics—most of these drawn from the replacement depot or from the excess quota already found in the GHQ recruitment drive. In the course of his interviews, McGee spoke to a 1st lieutenant named Ralph Puckett—West Point class of 1949, a boxer like himself, a recent Airborne graduate—and asked him if he would like to command a Ranger Company. "I'll do anything to be a Ranger," Puckett replied. "You can make me a squad leader or a rifleman if you want." McGee immediately liked the young man's pluck and made him the company commander on the spot. In turn, Lieutenant Puckett signed up a pair of his West Point classmates as his two platoon commanders. Together, the trio of lieutenants cautioned each batch of applicants with the following: "If you are not willing to volunteer for anything dangerous, you are free to leave the room right now." Typically one-third of the applicants walked right out. In total, McGee and his three officers found seventy-three enlisted men, ten of whom were Korean.

The training for this new unit would be located inside the Pusan Perimeter on a hill just north of the city of Kijang. Curriculum would be cobbled together from notes on McGee's experiences with his Moro tribesmen, from his time at the Infantry School at Fort Benning, and from his younger brother George's notes on Merrill's Marauders. After seven weeks, Puckett's men would be capable of patrolling, ambushing, reconnaissance, and raiding.

On August 24, before this training even began, Eighth Army Headquarters officially designated the new unit as the Eighth Army Ranger Company. This seemed to mean that the unit would answer directly to the Eighth Army commander and be reserved for strategic-level missions. This arrangement would have wrapped the Rangers in a layer of protection against the kinds of tactical misuse that they had experienced in World War II. It would also have meant that Eighth Army Headquarters would have been responsible for the Rangers' food, supplies, billeting, and transportation, which a headquarters unit was not typically equipped for. Ultimately, it was decided to redesignate the unit as the 8213th Ranger Company (though everyone would still call it by its original name) and place it under the 25th Infantry Division. The 25th Infantry Division begrudgingly assumed all those functions that Eighth Army had avoided.

On August 29, 1950—still six days before the Eighth Army Rangers started their training—Army Chief of Staff General J. Lawton Collins issued a directive to Army Field Forces to begin forming units of "Marauder Companies" for service in the Korean theater. Initially, Collins imagined these not as a reincarnation of Merrill's foot-slogging Marauders in Burma, but as a copy of the Nazi Brandenburgers: jeep-driving SS troops who had disguised themselves in American uniforms to cut behind the Allied lines during the Battle of the Bulge. The misnomer was confusing. To untangle this confusion, a conference between Collins's staff and Army Field Forces was held a week later at the Pentagon. Representatives for the CIA attended. At the conclusion of the conference, the assembled planners agreed to strike the Marauder name and recognize the new unit as the officially resurrected entity that everyone already knew it to be, the Army Rangers. And yet a unit whose past foretold its future.

Made up exclusively of volunteers from the Airborne, the best troops in the US Army, the new Rangers' potential advantages were—even from the very beginning—limited by one fateful provision: First, instead of forming them into a full-scale battalion (as they had been in World War II), they were to be disaggregated into companies and assigned to separate infantry divisions—exactly the same sort of parasitic arrangement that had befallen the Eighth Army Rangers in Korea. It is worth noting that throughout these decisions the commander of Army Field Forces was General Mark Clark, one of the men most responsible for the raid on Cisterna and for dissolving Darby's Ranger Battalions in its aftermath. His involvement in the Ranger restart practically ensured that the birth announcement was written on a tombstone.

4

On September 15, the same day of the Inchon invasion, Colonel John Van Houten reported to Army Field Forces in Washington, D.C., for assignment as commanding officer of the Ranger Training Center. He was not a former Ranger, Marauder, or Devil's Brigader, not even a parachutist, but one of Lightning Joe Collins's most grounded regimental commanders at the Battle of the Hurtgen Forest. In several months, a generous reporter from *The Detroit News* would describe Van Houten as tall, quiet, and handsome. Of the adjectives, only the first two were accurate.

Thin, dark, and droopy-eyed, Van Houten was forty-six years old but looked not a day younger than sixty. The only prop for his deflated face was a pair of arching eyebrows that when cocked left his eyes as droopy as always. A graduate of the University of Georgia, his home state, and not West Point, Van Houten had had a prewar career much the same as McGee's—dusty and monotonous. Unlike McGee, however, Van Houten had fought from the Falaise Gap to the Rhine, as impressive a warpath as any in history, rising by talent from chief of staff of the 9th Infantry Division to command the 60th Infantry Regiment. Though Collins's selection of Van Houten had notably demonstrated a casual disregard for the uniqueness of Ranger operations, and even for those of the Airborne, it nevertheless succeeded in finding a man incapable of commanding troops whose burdens he himself had not shouldered. It was almost enough—almost. In a few months, while perched in the doorway of a C-47 on the edge of his first jump, Van Houten would holler above the propwash to the jumpmaster, "Come on, son, tap me out." When they found him on the drop zone later, bleeding from his oversized mouth and ears, Van Houten would be heard to mutter, "Let this be a lesson to you. Never leave me alone again in the back of an airplane."

To fill the holes in Van Houten's résumé, planners ransacked personnel files looking for men with unconventional warfare experience of any kind. For executive officer, Van Houten got Edwin Walker, last commander of the 1st Special Service Force, the Devil's Brigade. The rest of the officers' mess was filled with men like Bull Simons, Cabanatuan raider and 6th Ranger veteran. He also got two of Darby's men: Jack Street, a Panzer killer at Gela and Admiral Hall's liaison for the 2nd and 5th Rangers at Omaha Beach; and Bill Bond, an up-from-the-ranks law school dropout who fought from North Africa to Cisterna, where he had been captured. Least like the others was Jack Singlaub, a high-and-tight OSS Jedburgh in France who had stuck with the gumshoes all the way to China. The list was impressive and diverse, maybe too much of the latter: If Collins's initial idea for Marauders had been confusing, then tying together the loose strands of nearly every unconventional Army unit from World War II was like braiding hair that had never been combed.

Not having been issued a formal mission statement, the newly minted, quasi-Ranger officers groped for one of their own making. In due course, Major Bond—the Cisterna POW and man most sensitive to operational misuse—authored a statement of doctrine that attempted to confine the Rangers' future missions to raiding "command posts, artillery [positions], motor pools, communications centers, and other rear area targets." In other words, no towns, and no "sustained combat," just the "short, hard jab," the "limited objective," the hit-and-run raid. The statement was sent to Mark Clark's Army Field Forces for approval. It was never approved. In the end, this attempt at cohesion probably would not have mattered anyway. Since when has any American military officer paid any attention to doctrine?

To compensate for the lack of a written constitution, Van Houten and his officers instead tried to anchor their future to history. Not a bad idea. Speaking from the stage at Fort Benning's Theater Number 11, Van Houten would greet new recruits with a drawly, meandering journey through time and past dead ancestors: Robert Rogers, the French and Indian War Ranger; Francis Marion, the Swamp Fox who had bedeviled Cornwallis in the Carolinas; Confederate raiders John Hunt Morgan, J. E. B. Stuart, and Nathan Bedford Forrest—every famous pioneer, scout, and mountain man, including the fictional Hawkeye of

The Last of the Mohicans. "You see, sir," a thoroughly indoctrinated sergeant would tell a lingering reporter who had come to see the show, "they were all Rangers, just like us." They weren't, but never mind. At every breather in training, instructors would "pound away" at what Rangers were supposed to be. Seen with history's backward lens, it is easy to find the purpose in such sermons: If the high command would not define them, then the Rangers would define themselves.

5

ON OCTOBER 1, 1950—one day before Van Houten began training his first batch of Rangers in Georgia—McGee completed a two-page report on the training of his Eighth Army Rangers in Korea. Though they had started as cooks, typists, and mechanics in an oversexed occupation army, four weeks of runs, hikes, push-ups, and patrolling had transformed them into soldiers—good ones. They were, concluded McGee, capable of all the things intended: trail blocks, motorized detachment, combat patrolling, reconnaissance, and, most important, raids. As if to double down on his claim, McGee recommended cancellation of the last ten days of the seven-week curriculum in favor of combat duty. Such a move, he said, would afford decision makers the opportunity to study the "combat value of this company immediately . . . with the view of either expanding it into a Ranger Battalion" or deactivating it altogether. McGee probably saw the collapsing North Korean Army and feared another lost chance at contributing to an enemy's defeat. A soldier can only take so many missed battles.

The report came with just two warnings. First, McGee repeated his critique that without trucks, kitchens, drivers, and cooks, the Eighth Army Rangers would unduly burden the regular infantry battalion to which they would soon be attached. Not a recipe for popularity. Second, he warned that his Rangers' comparably faster foot speed and round count would be easily squandered if they were not given enough time for "detailed" mission planning and reconnaissance—the bedrock of successful raiding. He was speaking into the wind.

From October 10 to November 21, the Eighth Army Rangers folded into the 25th Infantry Division for the northward advance to the Yalu—that portentous 2,500-yard-wide river of melted snow that cut the boundary with China. At first, Puckett and his men were kept to the rear to sweep up pockets of enemy stragglers that the main assault had missed. It was not exactly raiding. In that time, there had been just one

Ranger casualty: a corporal on patrol accidentally shot in the arm by a South Korean police unit. He was back with the company in no time. Though the past had been mild, the future loomed like a storm cloud.

Every day, the increasingly plummeting temperatures froze more engines and shallowed more foxholes. In mid-November a snowstorm blanketed the deck of the USS *Philippine Sea* so thoroughly that flight operations had to be suspended. Rations and canteens not tucked under a soldier's armpit often froze solid. Worse still was the terrain. Every step past the imaginary line that stretched between Pyongyang in the west and Wonson in the east sucked the UN forces into a widening map that pulled UN units farther apart and closer to China. Faced with this widening front, the commander of the 25th Infantry Division did what anyone else would have done, and dipped into his Ranger reserve.

On November 21, Puckett's Rangers were loaned to Task Force Dolvin, two battalions of mostly tanks and reconnaissance troops intended to range ahead of the rest of the division. For a unit whose motto in the last war was "Rangers Lead the Way," the promotion from rear guard to skirmishers was an improvement, but still not what had been intended.

On November 24, at 2:00 P.M., machine gun fire forced the Rangers off their tanks and into the scrub. From the valley floor, Puckett led a daytime attack to seize and hold Hill 224 during which one Ranger was mortally wounded. In the chaos, TF Dolvin's tanks fired on Puckett's men, killing two and wounding six. The next day, during TF Dolvin's phased movement north, enemy fire again opened up on the column, this time from behind. Realizing they were suddenly surrounded, the Rangers bundled off the tanks into the middle of a frozen rice paddy and sprinted up Hill 205. Enemy fire wounded three more Rangers and convinced one of Puckett's two platoon commanders to desert the company and hide in the valley command post. As darkness fell, the Rangers clawed out frozen foxholes amid the hill's emaciated pine trees, and Puckett scratched down an artillery support plan. His roster numbered fifty-eight souls.

At around 10:00 P.M., the sounds of drums, whistles, and bugles rattled the night's silence. A moment later, a cascade of sparks crackled forth from the slope below, followed by the hard thud of mortars and grenades, then a wave of attackers in tan, winter-padded uniforms.

The fight that followed was not the one the Rangers had been promised. Under the ghostly loom of waning red flares, the men fought from the lips of foxholes like trench soldiers, relying on artillery to splash their slope clean. As with all rising tides, every wave inched closer and eroded a little bit more: bullets, grenades, courage, men. After five hours and five waves, no Ranger had more than a few rounds left. Any man who had not already done so fixed his bayonet.

Then came the sixth wave. Shot through the chest with shrapnel in his shoulder, Puckett ducked into the bottom of his foxhole, wrapped white knuckles around his radio's handset, cupped the receiver close to his mouth, and begged for another salvo of artillery. The response: Get in line. A half second after Puckett's last transmission, two mortar shells exploded next to him, killing his remaining West Point classmate and peppering holes from his feet to his shoulders. When he woke up, he laughed. There was nothing else to do.

All around, Puckett's men either snaked down the hill or fought to the death. "Holy Mary of . . . Goddamn this rifle," one Catholic Ranger was heard to curse as he wrenched open his frozen bolt. The last report of Wilbert Clanton, one of the US Army's first Black Rangers, was the unmistakable sound of him "roaring in rage" as he charged a cluster of enemy troops with an empty rifle. He was never seen again. Three privates first class nearly made it to the valley floor when they were stopped not by the enemy but by that wind that fills the sails of bravery—their duty. Past looters and battlefield executioners, the three stalwarts crept over scrub and bodies until they found Puckett—alive, but reeling on his hands and knees. As they dragged him away, he was heard "muttering" the same thing over and over, "I'm a Ranger, I'm a Ranger." Months later, McGee would pen a letter to Puckett in the hospital commending him and the Eighth Army Rangers for carrying forth the "fullest" interpretation of "Duty, Honor, and Country." "This personal satisfaction of doing the job," concluded McGee, "is the highest and often the only reward of a soldier." In the entire letter, McGee betrayed not a trace of bitterness at the Rangers' misuse.

Of Puckett's fifty-seven men who started the battle on Hill 205, seventeen were wounded and eleven killed, their bodies destined for the same fate as those at Cisterna. The enemy was estimated to have numbered around 600—and they were not North Koreans. With some 300,000 troops, China had entered the war.

6

To RESCUE HIS ARMY (and what was left of his reputation), MacArthur abandoned his Home-by-Christmas offensive in favor of a new plan: a series of Navy-led, Dunkirk-style evacuations—from Chinnampo and Inchon on the west coast; Hungnam and Wonsan on the east. But first his soldiers and Marines had to get there. To this new mission every back and brain now strained, including those attached to the Army's Rangers.

On November 30, Major Jack Singlaub—the high-and-tight Jedburgh turned Fort Benning Ranger instructor—landed at Tenth Corps' east coast headquarters at Hamhung. Just four days since Puckett's mauling, Singlaub's ironic mission was to educate Far East commanders on the proper use of Rangers—presumably with the same quick-hit raiding doctrine that Mark Clark's Army Field Forces had not approved. Had he arrived but a week earlier, his Ranger briefing might have met with open minds. Now concern on the faces at headquarters lay as thick as the snow that topped their tents. "I felt a little useless," Singlaub wrote afterward, "trying to brief officers . . . [who] were naturally preoccupied with extricating their forces." A few days later, Van Houten himself arrived not far ahead of three of his brand-new Ranger companies (the 1st, 2nd, and 4th)—some of the best-trained soldiers in US Army history—but still, it was no use.

December 1950 was a month of misfortune so dark that the silver in its lining looked like glints from a guillotine, but silver they undoubtedly were. The highlights from this period included an intentional crash landing by a White wingman to rescue from flames or enemy capture the Navy's first Black aviator—a failure in all but example; then, a jeep accident that killed the Eighth Army's commander—a tragedy that led to the appointment of the unparalleled Matthew Ridgway; and most often remembered, the trapping of Tenth Corps at the Chosin Reservoir—a frozen fistfight that led to the greatest escape in Marine Corps history. Culminating at the Port of Hungnam, it was a flight and evacuation only made possible by Admiral Joy sewing to their retreating heels the shadow of seven different aircraft carriers—enough to maintain a constant wheel of forty to sixty fighters overhead—and by dispatching his UDTs with 400 tons of frozen dynamite, 500 thousand-pound bombs, and some 200 drums of liquid gasoline on a seventeen-hour, jaw-rattling mission that produced the largest nonatomic, nonvolcanic explosion in history to that point and left the Chinese little more than a G.I.-scribbled sign that read: "WE DON'T WANT THE DAMN PLACE ANYWAY." Dubbed by reporters the Miracle at Christmas, the evacuation rescued some 350,000 tons of supplies, 17,500 vehicles, and 105,000 soldiers and Marines. It also rescued some 91,000 shock-faced refugees all clamoring for sanctuary against certain Communist retaliation, a kind of rescue that elevated the campaign's conclusion from a simple miracle to a Christmas ending crafted by Dickens himself. In other parts of the country, other such endings were not necessarily so happy.

USS *Begor* (APD-127) stands offshore during the evacuation and demolition of Hungnam, Korea, December 24, 1950.

On January 8, 1951, the commander of ROK Naval Task Group 95.7 radioed Eighth Army headquarters and estimated that the refugees in Hwanghae Province numbered around 10,000 souls, with just about one rifle for every tenth person. On January 13, around 500 refugees crammed onto seven sail junks—all that was available—and fled the night of Communist return by sailing west from a shoreline collapsing like a disintegrated elbow into a tangle of reefs, shoals, and rock-channeled sluices to a crust of coastal islands that—to every man, woman, and child aboard—glowed like the dawn. Some 150 volunteers remained behind to guard their escape. The next day, the Chinese advanced on this Dunkirk behind a wall of artillery and a shield of captured peasants. The result was predictable, and not at all isolated.

Forget the promise of Airborne Rangers for behind-the-lines raids: To anyone who heard the stories of similar last stands, it was obvious that there was a powder keg already positioned at the enemy's back door. All it needed was a match; one soldier just so happened to have it.

7

For his miracle in resurrecting the first Ranger unit since World War II, McGee had been ordered not to combat, but to take command of the UN Reception Center in the southeast city of Taegu. There, his responsibilities had been to receive, prepare, and dispatch to the front all the various UN troops from Australia to Turkey. Since the only combat that far in the rear came from North Korean infiltrators, he might as well have been back in California. About to be pushed to the fringe of another war, McGee reversed his opinion on refugees—how could he not, with reports of such stunted bravery?—and on January 13 resubmitted his Attrition Warfare study.

In this second version, McGee reiterated his idea for island-based guerrillas—they were already there anyway—and his belief that such a force could mature into a conventional partner for the reconquest of North Korea. He also proposed something new: an attached force of Airborne Rangers capable of raiding strategic objectives behind enemy lines, even including in his memo a subplan (the memo's only subplan) titled "Employment of a Ranger Company in a Penetration Operation." Like the war's earliest Navy raids, the subplan targeted a railway tunnel. Unlike the Navy's raids, however, this one would require the following: a parachute drop behind Pyongyang; Korean cargadores to lug enough explosives for 530 meters of tunnel; and troops hardy enough for a mountainous eight-mile hike to the coast for pickup by a Navy destroyer. Logistics for such a unit would require "landings, pick ups, air drops, air support," legs too complex for Eighth Army alone, but not for the ostensibly multiservice Far East Command. Only a theater-level command could unlock the Rangers' "maximum utilization"—Armyspeak for "full potential." [So necessary was the Navy to the entire plan that McGee proposed a command structure that included a Navy executive officer, two Navy department heads (he wanted four in total), and a Navy commander to head the guerrilla operations section. Mary Miles could not have asked for more.]

The plan was creative, comprehensive, enthusiastic, forward thinking, and like all great plans, well-timed. On January 15—just two days after submission—it was approved, but stripped of every idea that made it forward thinking. No Navy involvement, no assignment to Far East Command, no Rangers. Never mind. Ten years and two wars since he had first dreamed of leading guerrillas into combat, McGee finally had in his hands a version of the castle he had long been building in his mind, but a version that fell far short of its potential. A version he was not yet ready to surrender.

8

When Ellery Anderson, a former British Special Air Service (SAS) officer seeking employment, presented himself to the snow-capped Quonset hut containing the Eighth Army's Partisan Command headquarters, he found the anteroom occupied by a paperless typewriter, a folderless file cabinet, and a single attendant, a private. McGee's office contained little more than a desk, a "thin haze of cigar smoke," and one entire windowless wall draped by a mysterious black cloth. During the meeting, McGee was "charming," "invariably courteous," one of the most "unaffected men" the Brit had ever met. That was on the outside. Inside, McGee was a cyclone of activity, mentally conjuring up plans to select and build island bases; to find, buy, and steal boats to supply them; to recruit instructors; to recruit North Korean refugees; to pay all these people without money and without any promise of South Korean citizenship in return; to arm their hands with surplus guns and ammunition; to clothe their bodies with surplus uniforms and boots; and to fill their bellies with every extra grain of rice that could be grown. The US Army bureaucracy's reaction to such requests was less than enthusiastic. At a sit-down meeting with the Eighth Army's top supply chief, McGee's superior officer and nominal advocate chose a seat across from McGee rather than next to him, and joined with the supply chief in a cross-examination that made McGee feel like a "school boy." Anyone else would have been deflated. McGee was not.

When Anderson presented himself for a second visit, he found McGee's Quonset hut cluttered with unpacked crates, ringing telephones, and alive with a "constant flow" of hustling attendants—like "a large disorganized family in the process of moving house." Beneath the mysterious black cloth—now drawn back—hung a giant map of Korea pockmarked with circles and crosses, each representing a different agent or sympathetic area, plus the two islands upon which McGee would build his empire. The first of these, Leopard Base, was located seven miles from North Korea's west coast and Hwanghae Province on a windswept, hilly rock called Paengnyong-do; its twin, Task Force Kirkland, was located ten miles from North Korea's east coast and Wonsan Harbor on a smaller island called Nam-do—both well situated for hitting the Communists in the ribs. To the south of these, in Pusan, McGee staked out Baker Section, a miniature partisan airborne school on the same ground on which he had trained his Eighth Army Rangers.

Across these three bases—Leopard, Kirkland, and Baker—McGee spread his full force of seventeen Army officers and ten enlisted men with orders to build, recruit, train, and supply. To find volunteers, Leopard's first commander boarded a leaky, lice-infested fishing boat and sailed for one month across the western satellite islands, a voyage that landed him in the hospital but succeeded in recruiting some 2,000 volunteers.

As his men recruited refugees, erected Quonset huts, and issued supplies, McGee hustled from coast to coast, shore to ship, meeting officials, deconflicting his plans with the parallel efforts of the CIA, enlisting support from everyone, and pleading for supplies and bodies, each day blending into the last. Landing aboard a truck-crammed LST on Paengnyong-do's southeast beach—a beach so endlessly flat and hard at low tide that a C-47's wheels hardly left a track—McGee strode ashore like MacArthur to address his first batch of recruits.

Ranging from young boys to old men—their dress ranging from peasant rags to the red-piped greens of Communist officers—the forty or so North Korean recruits stood on average no taller than five feet five and were mostly illiterate. In McGee's remarks, translated by an interpreter, he promised training, weapons, and food, and in return asked them not to venture too hastily back to the mainland for vengeance, where they would no doubt be destroyed and thus unable to support "the coming advance." Their behavior, McGee cautioned, "must be like the wise mule when entangled in wire . . . not like the foolish horse. The horse kicks until it destroys itself. The wise mule carefully waits out its entanglement." From this group would grow more than sixteen partisan units, called Donkeys (possibly named from McGee's speech), alternately purposed for either coastal or hinterland service, their operational capacity mainly limited to the small-unit raid. Though he did not notice, McGee was inadvertently establishing a competitor for all the missions toward which Van Houten and his Rangers had long been striving. At the moment, it was the last thing they needed.

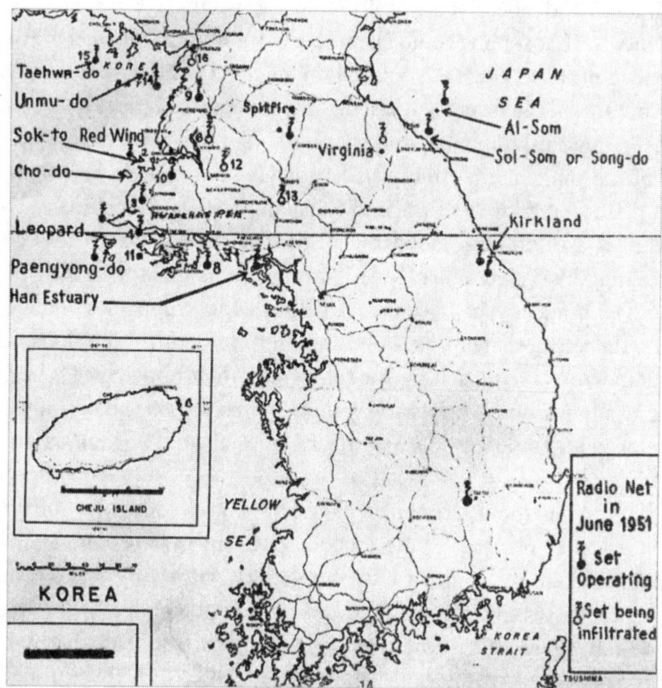

Map of McGee's plans (annotated by McGee).

9

When the 4th Rangers debarked in Yokohama en route to their assignment with the 1st Cavalry Division, the receiving officer took one look at them and told the commander, "this Ranger Company is the first unit through here that has looked and acted like a military force." He wasn't kidding. With their morning runs, their Mohawks, their gear bedecked with grenades and switchblades, the 4th Ranger Company looked like a unit with something to prove. "I cannot remember being so impressed with the sheer doggedness and cold, anxious anticipation for battle from a group of men," wrote a public information officer to Van Houten; they're "something out of a Warner Brothers movie." But apparently it was a movie that the Army's division commanders had no interest in watching.

In the first week of February, Eighth Army asked its relevant division commanders for status reports on each Ranger Company's employment. Almost none could claim to have used their Rangers for their intended purpose, and each pointed the finger at a different reason. The lack of targets, the distance to them, the mountains in the way, even the Rangers' physical unpreparedness for both. Not one commander placed the blame on himself—not even Major General Claude Ferenbaugh, who had taken custody of the 2nd Rangers, an all-Black company, then used it as a dumping ground for all the "negroid" replacements contaminating his White units. To "Lightning Joe" Collins, the Army chief of staff whose idea it had been to create Marauder companies in the first place, then scatter them like seeds among the infantry divisions, Van Houten wrote a letter stating the following: "their impatience is beginning to show around the jaws." By the required response date, only one division commander could claim to have promulgated a genuine Ranger raid.

Starting on the afternoon of February 6 and continuing into the night, all three platoons of the 1st Ranger Company hiked nine airline miles north into a country of dog yelps, boot-freezing streams, and mountain passes so steep the men had to slide downhill as if they were riding toboggans. When they reached Changmal—a headquarters hub for a North Korean division—the Rangers crept into town, found a building bulging with enemy soldiers, then opened fire. "Like bees out of a hive," remembered one man, the panicked Communists poured out of doors and windows into a world of white snow, orange explosions, and red tracer fire. In the fight, the Rangers amassed an uncounted heap of Communist dead at a cost of only three Americans wounded. On the return trip, when still six miles away from friendly lines and racing against a looming sunrise, the company commander decided to stash his wounded in an abandoned hut with a seven-man guard and promised to send a rescue helicopter—at that point, still an unreliable technology. After several failed attempts, the rescue was effected by a single, knife-faced Ranger from Maine, 1st Sergeant Romeo Castonguay, who hiked alone over mountainous enemy territory to find the men, then fashioned a litter and led them back.

From this raid, Van Houten's command squeezed every drop of publicity, probably in a vain attempt to steer the Army by the tail toward a future of similar scrapes. "Rangers Answer to Prayers," ran the headline on an article that described the raid; "New US Rangers Make Life Tough for Reds" said another. The latter article conjured an image of soldier-Indians who struck and ran "like hell for home," and in this case forced the retreat of two whole Chinese regiments and made the "Red" commander feel no better than a "pincushion." Other articles were less specific on facts but very specific on what constituted a proper Ranger target: enemy artillery positions, command posts, railroad centers, road hubs, truck parks, observation posts, and rear headquarters. The articles said nothing about using Rangers as infantrymen to seize and hold a hilltop trench; quite the contrary. "Because they depend primarily on surprise, speed, and the shock effect of their weapons," wrote a *Chicago Tribune* reporter in mid-February, "the Rangers do not engage in prolonged fighting. They hit and run. They withdraw on foot or . . . [are] picked up by airplanes, boats or submarines." If only reporters instead of generals had commanded the Army's Rangers, the history that followed would no doubt have been different.

Within five days of the raid, the commander of the 2nd Infantry Division allowed the breakup of the heroes of Changmal, then attached one Ranger platoon to an infantry task force and ordered the whole to retake a hilltop to the south of Chipyong-ni—Ridgway's Gettysburg—to turn the Chinese tide. Naturally, the Ranger commander protested: He knew his company's edge should not be dulled on such attacks; the infantry officer knew the opposite. "Christ, John, but I'm glad to see you here," said the exasperated task force commander to a newly arrived infantry officer. "I can't do anything with these Rangers." Ultimately, the Rangers' daylight assault succeeded in briefly seizing the hilltop, but at a cost of thirty-one wounded and eleven killed, including the valiant Castonguay, shot in the face.

Within a week of the battle, the 1st Rangers—now reduced by half—were back to patrolling like infantrymen. Unless their operational trajectory changed, and quickly, the new Rangers appeared destined for the same fate as the old: misuse, decimation, disbandment. What the Rangers really needed was a mission that would demonstrate their ability to outperform a straight-stick infantry company, not in fighting but in operational complexity. In other words, they needed a raid—and not just any raid, but one in the enemy's backyard. It was the kind of opportunity that rarely presented itself when confined to an infantry division's area of operations, but as it happened, just such an opportunity arose.

10

Frustrated by the Communists' growing knack for restoring cratered rail lines near the coast, in early February Navy planners approached McGee with a question: Could partisans airdrop behind enemy lines, blow a hard-to-reach-thus-hard-to-repair rail tunnel, then scratch their way to the coast for a Navy pickup? Barely three weeks old, Baker Section still had not yet received a single partisan recruit; moreover, its campus was still just a skeleton of airborne jump towers and platforms for practicing parachute landing falls. Because of this, no partisan had yet acquired the experience needed to lead such a complex operation. Equipped with an entrepreneur's sense, McGee knew he could not turn away such an opportunity, especially one from a customer as important as the US Navy. But how to win approval? Already, Eighth Army planners had rejected McGee's original proposal for a Ranger penetration operation for fear that the Rangers might get trapped and annihilated. The ideas advanced to mitigate this risk—helicopters or overland escape by foot—were ridiculous: helicopters in their current state of development lacked the range and capacity for such rescues, and White faces and American tongues could slip south only at the gravest peril. The solution was obvious: hastily train a body of Korean volunteers to parachute, patrol, and handle explosives, then attach them to an experienced Ranger head. After all, if Rangers were going to be attached to a division, then why not McGee's?

Having narrowed the risk to American lives by widening it to Koreans', Eighth Army approved the mission, now code-named Virginia I—a name that presumed a sequel—and set the launch date for March 15. This date allotted just five short weeks to recruit, train, plan, and rehearse. The target—a tunnel near the mountain river town of Hyon-ni—lay thirty airline miles inland from North Korea's knife-edged east coast, twenty-two miles farther than the tunnel in McGee's original proposal. To lead the mission McGee chose Captain Eugene Perry, his current Baker Section commander.

To the Rangers, the prospect of such a raid seemed to be precisely the sort of thing they'd been waiting for. Success would prove them worthy of all the newspaper claims, of Van Houten's propaganda, perhaps even rescue them—at least a portion of them—from the woodchipping routine of patrols and hilltop assaults. When the chance to perform "an OSS type mission in North Korea" was posted to the 120

Mohawked scalps of the 4th Ranger Company—the most underused Ranger company in the whole Eighth Army—all but five men volunteered. McGee's subsequent interviews yielded four men—not one above the rank of corporal, but three of them veterans. The selectees were as follows: Edward Pucel, a thick-browed, thick-nosed OSS veteran with combat experience in Yugoslavia, Italy, and China; Raymond Baker, a Pacific-tested parachute Marine in World War II, recently demoted from sergeant to private for knocking out a regular Army lieutenant; and least forgettable, the bear-framed Corporal Martin Watson, a twenty-seven-year-old veteran of Darby's Rangers who had fought through Italy only to be captured at Cisterna. Last of the group was William Miles, a fresh-faced twenty-one-year-old radio-telephone operator from Philadelphia.

To recruit the Koreans for his raid, McGee strode onto the assembly hall stage at the ROK's officer candidate school in Tongnae and spoke to 400 or so wide-eyed officer candidates, promising adventure and, even better, an immediate end to officer training should they volunteer. When the time came, 400 hands were raised; no one likes training. After interviews, McGee and his officers picked 40 men and split the group, trucking one half to the old Eighth Army Ranger campus for demolition training and the other to the US Air Force's K-3 airfield at Pohang for a hasty airborne school, intending to rotate the groups after two weeks. Unfortunately, the airborne instructors dropped their green recruits on a frozen rice paddy, resulting in eleven broken bones, nine other injuries, and the purging of half the partisans from the Virginia mission. Instead of improving training and safety protocols, Anderson, the augmenting SAS officer, recommended to McGee the cancellation of further partisan parachuting until the actual jump that would drop them into North Korea. You read that right. Not a Ranger, not even airborne qualified, McGee lacked the eye to tell tin from silver, in either the idea or its author. After all, the solution to a military deficiency—to any deficiency—is very rarely less training. If ever a decision showed McGee's inexperience for his own assignment, this was it.

11

ON MARCH 5, the four Ranger volunteers reported to mission commander Perry at K-3 airbase, fully expecting a period of intense training, rehearsals, and integration with their Korean counterparts. There would be none of that. Instead, Captain Perry briefed them on the mission concept and, not being a Ranger himself, asked for their suggestions. Neither officers nor planners, the enlisted Rangers nevertheless recognized that the mission's timeline, the mission's support, the mission's everything, all rested on a bull's-eye airdrop. Why not insert a pathfinder team to mark the landing zone? Perry championed the idea up the chain of command, where the suggestion received little more than a shrug. A pathfinder team would risk early discovery, and discovery was the same as mission failure. Not only was the idea rejected, but planners resolved to further limit the chance of compromise by disguising the team as a North Korean patrol escorting a group of captured American prisoners. To sell the ruse, the Rangers would not take their rifles and their usual load of every-bullet-they-could-carry, but instead would bring only their .45-caliber pistols—fine weapons on the streets of Chicago, not in the mountains of North Korea.

Late in the day on March 13, nineteen of the forty original Korean officer candidates arrived at K-3 airbase for their first introduction to the Rangers. As the historian Edward Evanhoe noted in his account, only fifty-eight hours remained until mission launch—hardly enough time for a dress rehearsal, never mind that the cast did not speak the same language. In the final two days before the launch, Miles checked his radio, a forty-pound, cinderblock-sized SCR 300 with a frequency range optimized for ground-to-air communications, then packed extra batteries and colored ground panels should all the rest fail. Every man packed seventy-two hours' worth of food, water, and cigarettes, plus gold rings to be used for bartering in case of emergency. Divided among the nineteen Korean packs was 300 pounds of explosives, primer cord, and fuses. To supplement his meager allotment of six pistol magazines, Watson loaded a sack full of white phosphorus grenades—an explosive for immolating the contents of an enemy tank. (Cisterna was an experience hard to shake.)

The next day, McGee—from his Quonset hut in Pusan—sent a blithe report to the Eighth Army's assistant operations officer stating that the Virginia I team would launch at 2300 hours, adding that he had already "secured" a new group of Korean volunteers for a second iteration, presumably Virginia II, a batch of unhatched eggs already counted. Now, he just needed more Rangers.

Back at the airfield, Captain Perry, the four Rangers, and the nineteen Korean volunteers loaded weapons, sharpened knives, and packed parachutes. When the C-47 arrived, they removed the lateral waist door, then taped down the threshold's sharpest edges so none would cut a static line when a man stepped through it. As before every other long-shot mission in history, the men scratched out letters to loved ones, picked nervously over last meals, and tried to shield their mind's eye from those potential disasters that could befall them. Now just hours away from takeoff, the oversights and corrections that had plagued the mission's preparations seemed to dim as quickly as the sky. This close to launch, no more surprises could interfere. At least so they thought.

As they waited for the hours to tick away, McGee received one final order from Eighth Army's intelligence chief. For fear that his capture, interrogation, and torture could uncloak every one of Miscellaneous Division's covert programs, mission commander Perry was ordered scratched from the operation. Of all the carpets that had been snatched from beneath the Virginia team's feet, this was the worst. In response, McGee protested and Perry threatened to escort the jumpers to the drop zone in order to accidentally fall from the airplane. Both were noble gestures, but alas, though Perry's mind could encompass both defiance and bravery, McGee's—as he had already shown in the Philippines—could not. Orders were orders. To prevent any attempts at insubordination, McGee assigned an additional officer to the C-47 with one responsibility: Keep Perry on the plane.

With Perry out but the mission not canceled, Virginia I needed a new ground force commander, and fast. Of the four Americans remaining—Miles, Pucel, Watson, and Baker, the first three all corporals—McGee had really only one choice: the only one of them who had been a Ranger in the last war, and a man who'd almost been born fighting.

12

Raised in Hartford, Connecticut's Frog Hollow district by the competing lash stripes of an Irish Catholic diocese, a German grandmother, and the local French bullies, Martin R. Watson—red-haired, fair-skinned, and small—had survived by learning the languages of each group, by building his body until his back was the size of a dinner table and his legs could not fit into store-bought swim trunks, and by joining up with a gang of local Irish toughs who were destined for the usual options of East Coast Irish destiny, law enforcement or crime. With seventy-five arrests by the time he was nineteen—the last one requiring seven police officers to detain him—Watson's future would have undoubtedly been the latter if the Japanese had only stayed on their island.

Martin Watson prior to the Virginia I raid, undated.

A member of Darby's 1st Ranger Battalion since North Africa, and thus a veteran of blazing heat, bitter cold, three amphibious landings, and more than a few mountaintop Alamos, Watson and his Echo Company platoon had been among the few groups to reach Cisterna's outskirts. There, with all hope lost, Watson—at just twenty-one—had volunteered to stay behind to cover his squad's retreat, a sacrifice that resulted in humiliation in the streets of Rome followed by fifteen months at Stalag 2B, situated on the northeastern fringe of the Reich and known above all for its cruelties. Watson had responded to captivity by murdering the camp commandant's German shepherd and by attempting so many escapes that the guards had nicknamed him the *hase,* German for "rabbit." Upon liberation, Watson had vowed that he would never be a prisoner again. It was a promise his personality was able to keep for just five months, whereupon he was jailed for thirty days in East Hartford for "inciting a riot" and resisting arrest, crimes that preceded six more similar episodes—breach of peace, assault, intoxicated assault, and assault and battery of a police officer. For the last charge, Watson would have faced as much as nine months in jail had he not reenlisted in the Army, then revolunteered for the Rangers.

At that interview for the Virginia I mission, McGee had seen in Watson a man physically distinct from the others: six feet four, 240 pounds, a chin shaped like a fist, hands the size of country hams, a reddish-brown Cadillac mustache with ends as sharp as tomahawks. The real difference in Watson, however, had lain just below his eyebrows, a gaze so comfortable and confident that he looked fifteen years older than his twenty-seven years suggested. There was only one issue. Imposing, experienced, eager, a preternatural fighter, Watson had ended World War II with a rank of T/5—technician fifth grade, essentially a corporal. In the five years since, he had advanced not a single rank, a fact that belied his leadership potential—which was ample—but spoke volumes about his exposure to a military leader's responsibilities—from mission planning to command and control. For an institution whose central commandment was the officer's supremacy in operations, no action so fully framed the Army's dismal valuation of raiding than the promotion of a corporal to lead its first penetration raid, now just moments away.

As the wait for zero hour flattened to minutes and the moonless dark shrank the world to inches of visibility, the Rangers donned their long johns, their winter green fatigues, their Army-issued ushanka hats, and the partisans pulled on their quilted puffball tans. Once everyone had been cinched into their parachutes, with backpacks buckled between their knees, jumpmasters checked straps for twists and tears, and concluded every inspection with a satisfying hand-slap to the shoulder. For the Koreans, this would be their first jump.

When McGee arrived at the airfield, he gathered the Rangers together, noting their warm clothing, then "wished them Godspeed" and told them that their mission would be "closely followed," and the "utmost effort" would be expended to ensure their safe return. As the C-47's twin props coughed into an angry hum, the men shuffled, lumbered, gripped their way into the dimly lit fuselage, and collapsed into fold-down canvas seats, their backs against a hollowed-out rib cage of curved metal trusses. If anyone in the dark noticed that Miles—the Philadelphian—had brought his M1 rifle plus two bandoliers of ammunition, no one protested.

At 8:00 P.M., the plane lifted off and banked north. Immediately the fuselage was awash with air from the hole left by the extracted waist door. For three hours, in deafening silence, each man sat with his shoulder touching his neighbor's but was, in effect, completely alone, a captive of his thoughts and the penetrating cold. Unaccustomed to flying, almost all the Korean soldiers became nauseous, proving once again that no one goes into combat comfortably.

Just before 11:00 the team stood, faced the rear of the aircraft, and hooked their static lines to the wire cable running the length of the cabin. Had anyone's eyes been able to focus beyond the red light above the doorframe, they would have noticed—not too far below, probably no more than 800 feet—a racing landscape of undulating tree shadows relieved by a neverland of white snow. At 11:04, the red light blinked off and a green one replaced it, initiating a hasty rearward shuffle to the door and eternity. Because this was each Korean's first jump, there was an understandable stutter, a hardly noticeable hesitation in the aircraft that would have consequences for distance on the ground.

Stepping from the fuselage and into the prop blast, each man attempted to glue his feet together as best he could, counting aloud—one thousand, two thousand, three thousand—hoping with every syllable to feel a jolt and a sudden cradle of leg straps. After the relief of having survived, each man had but a moment of silent drifting—probably less than thirty seconds—before his feet, knees, buttocks, and back collapsed into a heap on the frozen ground.

To a chorus of dog yelps, Watson crashed into the roof of a peasant's hut, after which he collected himself, then rolled up and slung his parachute as calmly as if it had been a backyard hose and trotted out of the village holding his knife in one hand, his pistol in the other. Outside of town, Watson encountered none of his teammates nor any of the terrain features he had expected to find. Equally dangerous, the temperature on the ground was easily forty-five degrees colder than it had been in Pusan, well below zero. Disoriented and alone, cold and practically unarmed, Watson faced the steepest slope and started climbing.

Remarkably, scattered from the valley floor to the other side of the mountain, the rest of the team had landed unharmed, then mostly arrived at Watson's conclusion and crunched their way over packed snow to the summit of the tallest peak. There the Virginia team reassembled and in the early daylight compared their maps to the landmarks around them. Instead of landing within a four to five hours' walk from the Hyon-ni tunnel, a detailed map study showed that the Air Force crew had, as the Rangers feared they would, inserted them some eight miles short of their intended drop zone. You're welcome. In the best of conditions, the time to target was now at least one cycle of darkness away, maybe two. If they destroyed the tunnel in two days, this would leave them with just one day's ration for a thirty-mile sprint through the mountains to the coast.

As the Rangers deliberated, white flakes dusted the ground around them. By day's end, a Siberian storm piled one to two feet of powder in the team's path, a path made exceedingly more difficult by their failure to bring snowshoes. On top of everything else, the intense cold had already sapped all strength from the radio's batteries.

13

AT PRECISELY 11:15 A.M. on the other side of the world, commander of Army Field Forces General Mark W. Clark strode for the first time into Fort Benning's Ranger Training Command. His be-starred entourage included General Church, General Hartness, General Kennan, General Uncles, Colonel Hill, and at least eight other high-ranking officers, a saluting, murmuring pyramid of authority deferential to Clark and imperious to everyone else. When they arrived, they promptly met with Van Houten and his second-in-command, the former Devil's Brigader Colonel Edwin Walker. For thirty minutes, Van Houten and Walker answered the general's questions, described training, and respectfully parried suggestions for a Ranger organization and Ranger mission that departed from the vision they had been imparting to their students. It was no use. Having commanded at Anzio and by default at Cisterna, Clark—surrounded by his entourage—already knew everything he needed to know about Rangers and their missions. They could fight—better than just about anyone else—but their missions could go horribly awry, and worse, they "siphoned off" the best infantrymen in the Army, making the infantry worse all the way around. At the meeting's conclusion, Van Houten and Walker received an assignment as attractive to them as Nineveh was to Jonah: "prepare and submit ideas on the use of Ranger Training Command as a means to raise the standards of the entire infantry." George Marshall's idea from the start.

Whether Van Houten or Walker knew it or not, their best argument for rescuing the Rangers and elevating them from divisional misuse to a strategic-level raiding force was already up to its knees in snow.

14

WHILE MARK CLARK was in Georgia examining ways to stanch the flow of Ranger talent, McGee was back in Pusan trying to open another vein. To the executive officer at Miscellaneous Group, he clacked out an optimistic memo advising that once his Virginia Rangers completed their mission he wanted to reward them with rest and recovery in Japan, and nothing less than officer commissions. On this last point, he said, "I look for no trouble." (As if any West Pointer would ever object to vaulting three corporals and one private into their ranks.) On the overall concept of American-led, deep penetration missions, he could hardly contain his enthusiasm for more: "When do you desire additional Rangers?" he asked.

In the afternoon, McGee and Perry boarded a C-47, then flew north toward the zone where Perry—only a few hours before—had watched the Virginia team jump out of sight. According to plan, they knew that Miles would soon unfold his radio's antenna and cast his first transmission into the sky. When they neared the appointed time, they leaned into the radio's crackling static to catch the vaguest squelch of Miles's voice in the airwaves. After several minutes of straining, they had heard nothing.

What McGee felt in that moment, he did not commit to any lasting record. Perry's actions in the coming days suggest he wished he had followed his first instincts, disobeyed orders, and jumped with his men. In his defense, it would not have changed anything.

In the coming days, McGee would attempt two more reconnaissance flights and Perry's feet would hardly touch the ground, flying every day over enemy territory, listening for any break in the radio's crackle and straining his eyes against the snow for any sign of Miles's colored ground panels. After a few days, McGee issued an alert to Eighth Army requesting that a priority message be sent to all UN units cautioning them to be on the alert for a joint American-Korean Intelligence Team—code-named Virginia I—that might attempt to cross over to friendly lines.

15

ON THE GROUND, the Virginia team had heard the drone of the C-47, but with near-frozen batteries—in their radio and their flashlights too—there had been nothing to do but listen. Separated from support by distance, mountains, cold, and Communists, Watson had nevertheless pointed them toward their objective. After two full nights of a leg-burning plod through snowdrifts, the Virginia team finally dropped their explosives-laden packs at a mountaintop lay-up point just within striking distance of the Hyon-ni tunnel. With rations short, with everyone exhausted, Watson wasted no time and sent forward a handful of his disguised Koreans to scout the target and to trade barter rings for food and cigarettes. When they returned, they reported that the tunnel was now a sandbagged fortress, the headquarters for a North Korean railroad repair battalion. On top of that, it seemed that the enemy knew that a team had parachuted into their backyard and was now organizing patrols to track them down. The area was, remembered one operator, crawling with search patrols and as busy as an anthill. That night, the hum of Perry's C-47 was no longer heard, replaced by a silence that told a most unwelcome message: McGee had already given them up for dead or captured.

With his men unable to accomplish their mission, unable to coordinate their rescue, unable even to communicate their existence, Watson studied his map, counted his options, and ultimately decided to abandon the original tunnel in favor of one nearer the coast and the obvious proximity to rescue that it promised. Two nights later, they arrived exhausted at the secondary tunnel only to find in the morning light that it too had been fortified with bunkers on each end and was now a daytime air raid shelter. Eight days since their night jump, the Virginia team was out of food and cigarettes, and now survived by burning small chunks of explosives to melt snow into water, into which they dropped their meager bouillon cubes. Out of options, Watson ordered his men to dump and bury their excess weight—explosives included—then booby-trapped the entire cache with a forty-eight-hour time delay. The objective was now the coast and survival.

On the tenth day, while nearing the last ridge that separated them from the coast, another snowstorm forced the entire team to cram inside an abandoned hut. For two days they waited. When the storm did slacken, the temperatures spiked, a welcome change but one that turned every mountain cleft, every oxcart trail, every frozen stream into a cascade of icy water.

On March 29, a day as bright as it was warm, Miles unbundled the dead weight of his cinder-block-sized radio, removed its batteries, and laid them out in the sun. After a while he picked them up, his cold fingers clutching their warmth, and reinserted them into the radio. As he twisted knobs, the handset receiver suddenly crackled. After some adjustments, the radio's wobbly antenna caught a conversation between a forward air controller and an artillery battery some sixty miles to the south. Holding the handset to his mouth, just inches above where his heart was now pounding in his throat, Miles pressed the push-to-talk key and spoke. Exactly what Miles said is not known, except that he signed off the transmission with his call sign. That was enough.

"Virginia One, Virginia One," crackled back the voice of the air controller, unable to conceal the urgency in his voice. "Hold on while I turn this shoot over and I'll be right back to you."

Within four hours of Miles's transmission, Captain Perry was buzzing loops overhead in his C-47, promising a night drop of provisions and a morning helicopter rescue. To the men of Virginia I—cold, practically starving, and long since given up for dead—it was an incomparable moment of relief. For fifteen days they had marched untold miles over unimaginable terrain, had endured bitter cold and two snowstorms, and despite a country crawling with Chinese and North Koreans had managed to snake through a briar patch of checkpoints and patrols, all without suffering a single casualty. Even though they had failed to execute their mission, their survival alone had been an achievement. And one worth copying.

Whether it was Perry's circling plane, or Miles's radio signal, or just Virginia's overextended luck that finally brought the enemy to their doorstep we will likely never know. In any event, as the Virginia operators endured what they believed would be their last night on a North Korean mountain ridge, the sharks began to circle their life raft.

16

THE NEXT MORNING in the navigational plotting room of the USS *St. Paul,* a two-stack Navy cruiser, Admiral Roscoe Hillenkoetter—just fired from his directorship at CIA—welcomed all the meeting's attendees, then introduced an overworked, underrested operations officer to brief three helicopter pilots on Virginia I's rescue mission. For several minutes, the officer "rubbernecked" the pilots' attention from wall to wall on a tour of clip-hung charts and topographic maps—their contour lines so crammed together as to suggest a landing zone of cliffs and thermal updrafts. At this prospect, remembered one pilot, a "stony silence" gripped the room. With their attention captured, the briefer then abandoned the maps, ransacked his notes, and in a state of hasty distraction confessed his fear that a "fully complemented" North Korean division had probably already discovered the Virginia team's snowy footprints and surrounded them on a mountaintop. There was, he concluded, no time to lose.

Ninety minutes after the sun rose on that crisp Pacific dawn, three

Navy helicopters—each one painted a deep blue, and as lean as a dragonfly except for its pig-snout plexiglass cockpit—lifted free of the *St. Paul*'s rolling flight deck, thwopped aft over her green wake, then dipped their noses west above the white-tipped blue waters of the Sea of Japan and on toward the cold, mile-high mountains in the distance. Before long, a squinting eye could pick out little more than three flecks as small as flies.

Flying in the lead was Lieutenant Junior Grade John Thornton, the Department of the Navy's 298th qualified helicopter pilot. Barely five feet four, Thornton now resembled an arctic explorer, his body zipped into a flight suit wrapped in a fur-lined leather jacket, his combat boots in a winter overlayer. Near his feet, in reach of his hands, lay the only weapons his craft could boast: an M1 carbine and a satchel full of grenades—as Thornton had learned after four months in Korea, a loadout hardly sufficient for the mission with which he and his fellow pilots had been tasked, something that could also be said for the platform that now carried them into combat. Barely wider than a man's shoulders, each Sikorsky-made HO3S-1 could carry one pilot (no copilot) and three passengers, all practically stacked on each other's laps. Rescuing the twenty-three-man Virginia team would require three round trips, each taking at least two hours, six in total—an exceedingly optimistic timetable that the fleet was now crowding the coast to accommodate.

After thirty or so minutes of flying, Thornton and his men traded the backdrop of flat blue for an inclined slope of snow-covered mountains. A glance skyward through their pig-snout canopies revealed the incomparable V-shaped echelon of twelve single-engine Navy Corsairs from the USS *Philippine Sea,* their wings pitchforked with a devil's arsenal of rockets, bombs, and napalm. After another thirty minutes, Thornton spotted Perry's twin-engine C-47 looping lazy circuits around what he assumed was the target zone. With no time to lose, Thornton claimed the lead and pulled away. Though it was still morning, Thornton sensed "a long night . . . approaching."

17

Alternating his hands on the cyclic stick between his knees, Thornton did what he always did before descending on a hot landing zone and slid open both cockpit doors. The move unleashed upon his small body a frigid gust of gale-force wind and upon his ears the unmistakable pops of rifle fire in the distance. Below and around him lay either a hill or a trough, and a nearly colorless texture of dirty white mixed with deep shadow. In another moment, Thornton caught a tiny glimpse of brilliant color stretched out like a blanket in the middle of a lumpy mountaintop clearing. Suspicious that the enemy had staked a stolen marking panel to the ground—a known tactic, and one often accompanied by a staked pilot—Thornton flew a low racetrack pass and locked eyes on the Virginia team, now defending a Korean burial ground about half the size of a football field. Beyond the clearing, the hill's frozen slopes fell away at what Thornton estimated to be a thirty-five-degree drop into a rocky tangle of pines, brush, and leafless trees. From this black veil surrounding the slopes all the way to the valley floor erupted sudden puffs of gray smoke, each chased by a crack or boom that ricocheted off the neighboring mountains into a symphony of chaos.

Though Thornton wanted to drop right down in the center of Virginia's perimeter and get out as quickly as possible, his left hand could feel from his collective—the lever that determined the helicopter's altitude—the unnavigable updrafts emanating from the valley floor. The only way to land was to circle back into the valley, charge up a slope with the fewest smoke puffs, and try to ride a thermal to the top.

As Thornton turned away from the summit to gain enough room to make a runway, he radioed the plan to his flight team. To better the rescue's chances, the first flight of Corsairs banked free of their altitude fortress, dropped to treetop height, then fired cannons, rockets, and napalm into the mountain slope. Hoping that the attack had "carved a trench" through the enemy's ranks, Thornton pointed his nose at the mountain's base and twisted his throttle. The first moments of his "escalator ride" seemed to work. The collective responded, and Thornton began straining his eyes for a patch of ground on the summit's crest where he might rest a single wheeled strut—just enough platform for three passengers to scramble aboard. But as his helicopter lifted, his eyes caught a subtle movement beneath the trees, one he instantly recognized, a sight that made the eyes practically "bug out of his head." As he tried to pull up, a seeming "hailstorm" of what sounded like "ballpeen hammers [on a drum]" struck the underside of his fuselage. The enemy's bullets shredded his cabin and tore "away entire chunks of sheet metal." Momentum alone carried him past the tree line, where twenty-five feet above the ground he hovered for a pregnant second, then "dropped like a stone."

As the helicopter crashed sideways, its top weight carried its spinning rotor into a downward, chopping roll. Not Thornton's first crash, he dove into the roll and into the frozen ground, scrunching as small as a prayer, or at least as small as his diminutive frame could get. When the helicopter had passed by, he paused. He was alive, his only injury a broken rib. After checking for Communists, he crawled down the hill after his helicopter, already settled upside down in a clump of brush and trees, a severed fuel line still pumping gas. From the wreckage he grabbed his horsecollar rescue harness, whereupon the snap of enemy bullets chased him back up the hill to the only safe place within sixty-five miles.

18

When Thornton reached the summit, he was quickly ushered into the Virginia perimeter. There, he saw bedraggled faces all stubbled with beards, and a hodgepodge of guns and uniforms. Every human shape was now hunkered behind a boulder or a grave mound. If Thornton took a moment to discern who was in command, it did not take long. In the perimeter's center and tethered to the radio, Watson was now alternating between encouraging his men (often in Korean), shifting their fire, and directing the Corsairs overhead. This was not his first time in a desperate battle, and it showed. Embarrassed by his crash, Thornton edged into the center, where Watson, betraying no sympathy, simply asked the pilot how badly he was hurt.

Not badly, Thornton replied, cradling his rib. He then told Watson that the only way off that mountain was by hoist and the horsecollar sling in his hand.

Wasting no time, Watson waved over Pucel, the former OSS operative, and Thornton draped him with the sling. At a lull in wind gusts, the first helicopter trembled into a seventy-five-foot hover, its rotor wash kicking up a blizzard of grit and loose snow, and inspiring a fresh clatter of bullets. From his tenuous perch, the pilot lowered his hoist. As soon as Thornton could reach it, he swapped the empty horsecollar with the one wrapped around Pucel, then stretched out an arm and an eager thumb. As soon as Pucel's feet jerked free of the ground, Thornton looked for a second victim.

Watson's next pick was Miles, the M1-armed Philadelphian, who threaded into the sling and turned over his rifle to the men who needed it more than he did. When the helicopter's empty hoist returned, Thornton repeated his horsecollar exchange. As he did, a bullet sliced into Miles's face, snapping his head back. Dazed but still conscious, Miles clung to the sling through a snapping shower of metal so thick that when he finally reached the helicopter, Pucel pulled him in and the pilot pulled out of the rescue altogether although the cabin contained enough room to carry another man.

The next helicopter pilot fared even worse. As Thornton connected the hoist to Baker—the recalcitrant parachute Marine—all eyes turned upward, expecting to see the slackened cable snap into a hard stripe. Instead, everyone cringed as a sheet of fire stitched "white blotches" across the helicopter's blue-painted belly. If Baker considered squirming out of the horsecollar and taking his chances on the ground, it was an idea that arrived too late. Without warning, the helicopter jerked up and "wrenched" Baker through the air "like the tail of a kite." The men watched the helicopter pull away over the valley as "quickly" as a "leaf in an autumn storm."

"What the hell do you call that!" Watson barked at Thornton, the only target to turn on. "Your goddamn pilot got his ass out okay, but the hell with my guy. Bullshit!"

The words stung, but not nearly as deeply as the numbers in Thornton's mind. That morning, three helicopters carrying three men each could have neatly rescued the Virginia team in three round trips. Instead, one helicopter had crashed—adding a man to Virginia's roster—and the other two had evacuated with a grand total of three men. As Thornton calculated the time and trips it would now take for two helicopters to rescue twenty-one men, he failed to account for the darkest variable of all: By the time the helicopters returned, there would not be twenty-one men to rescue. It was the kind of realization guaranteed to collapse a normal man's courage, but the commander of the Virginia team was not a normal man.

19

WHEN THE LAST HELICOPTER DEPARTED, Watson, as worried about tomorrow as a barroom brawler, instantly swung back into all the tasks that had thus far preserved his tiny perimeter: He scurried about under a canopy of withering fire; he checked his wounded; he directed his partisans' muzzles; and mainly, he radioed fire missions to Perry in the C-47, who unwound each wheeling Corsair into an ever-closer hillside bomb run. Before long, Perry radioed Watson that the C-47 was "bingo" for fuel and must depart, a move that would sever Virginia's umbilical to the Corsairs and, more important, to their wall of splashing rockets and jellied flame.

Edward Pucel (second from left) and William Miles (second from right with visible gunshot wound to the face) on the USS *St. Paul* after rescue from the Virginia I mission.

Without Watson's directions to guide them, the Corsair's attacks, though punishing, quickly fell behind the forward edge of the advancing line of enemy soldiers—bad timing, as Virginia's ammunition supply was beginning to dwindle. To retrieve his helicopter's extra carbine and sack of grenades, Thornton and Watson belly-crawled beneath a curtain of rifle snaps and raining tree branches until they reached the wreckage—still unexploded. As they rummaged through the twisted frame, a torrent of machine gun bullets pinholed through a sidewall, "cartwheeling" Watson and Thornton out of the fuselage and back up the hill to the perimeter. As they sprinted, the enemy's machine guns tracked just behind, chasing their feet with "evil little geysers of dirt."

Just about the same time that Watson and Thornton slid back into the perimeter, a large group of Communist soldiers rose, rushed forward a few paces, then dropped into firing positions. Under this cover, a separate group stood and leapfrogged forward. "This is gonna be it!" Watson roared, the desperation in his voice not concealable. All around, Watson's Korean soldiers pulled triggers until their weapons stopped firing. At the implacable wave of tan-clad soldiers, many Koreans stood and ran, only to be shot, their bodies collapsing down the hill, tangled and contorted in the underbrush. When the enemy closed to within throwing range, Watson unleashed his pitcher's arm and his bucket worth of white phosphorus grenades, each exploding into "showers of glowing white streamers" that caught hold of the enemy's cotton-quilted garments and transfigured each wearer into a running, screaming banshee of flame. On one follow-through, Watson's "ham-like paw" slammed so hard into Thornton's head that the pilot thought he heard the sound of glass breaking.

"Keep your head down!" Watson bellowed, flexing his hand into a fist. "You nearly broke my goddamn knuckles."

As Watson nursed his hand, he could see that at least half of his partisans lay dead or dying, ashen-faced lumps on the frozen ground. Sensing a sudden halt in the enemy's tightening advance—probably a collective flinch at the prospect of sparking into a human torch—Watson decided that the time had come to make a run for it. If he considered covering his team's escape as he had in Italy, he quickly abandoned it; there were not enough grenades or ammunition left to cover anyone. Rushing from man to man, Watson quickly gathered his survivors—Thornton and just six Koreans—then, taking a deep breath, led them on their hands, knees, and bellies through the scrub toward a shred of tree line, the only sector where he had not seen muzzle flashes. Reaching the sanctuary of the trees, Watson's relief instantly cramped into a seizure of panic: He had forgotten the radio. "Take this," he told Thornton, passing him his rifle, preparing to rerun the gauntlet.

"No, wait!" Thornton protested. He knew that Watson was the only man who could operate the radio, not to mention the only man capable of leading the team out of those mountains. After a moment of intense argument, Watson ordered back one of the Koreans, who not surprisingly refused until Watson threatened to beat the man himself. Scrambling to the clearing, the Korean soldier seized the radio by the backstrap, then dragged it behind him, "bouncing, rolling, smashing over rocks" and "leaving a trail of broken knobs, handles and antenna."

"Bastard's got his brains in his ass!" seethed Watson as he watched.

When the runner reached the trees and presented the radio, everyone could see that it was destroyed. With their only hope for survival buoyed upon the ability to communicate their position to the Navy's fighters and helicopters, the radio's destruction meant Virginia's was not far behind. Had Watson wanted to repay this cruelty in kind, his rage was instantly short-circuited by the shredding sound of machine gun fire and the terror of Communist soldiers lunging across the body-strewn clearing. Without a word, as Thornton recalled, the Virginia survivors plunged into the trees and "careened down the hill in a wild melee," . . . "stumbling, rising, running and falling again," hoping with every bruise to break through to the valley floor before the enemy cinched the "noose" around their necks. After running for what seemed like half a mile, the men collapsed into the relative protection and shadow of a ravine.

As their lungs pumped miniature fogbanks into the cold air, their ears caught the growing but unmistakable hum and chop of two helicopters echoing through the valley. When the first helicopter made it back to the clearing, its pilot edged into a hover, kicked out a bundle of supplies, then leaned out his window, coming face-to-face with a staccato volley of muzzle flashes. Banking hard, the pilot escaped the ambush only barely. With the clearing obviously overrun, both pilots rolled their helicopters into an anxious racetrack search around the mountain, flying so low that Thornton could easily make out each pilot's face. Without a radio, without even marking panels, the Virginia survivors waved frantic arms but betrayed not a sound, since any noise would only alert their hunters, not the engine-deafened pilots. For thirty or so minutes the pilots searched, then ascended and retraced their path to the ocean. Virginia was alone. "Except for the blowing wind and the rustle of the leafless trees," remembered Thornton, "there was silence—lonely, empty silence."

20

Separated from UN lines by some sixty-five miles of 3,000-foot snowcapped mountains, Watson had wasted no time on despair, but gathered his men and supplies—two rifles, a few pouches of ammunition, a pistol per man, a map, some knives, and Thornton's wallet—then pointed them all south on a trek that would no doubt take at least two weeks to survive. During the days, the men hid in the terraced hillsides, their sleep always threatened by the presence of white-clad peasant farmers. When awake, they nursed injuries—mostly their blackening, frostbitten feet—and gnawed on acorns and chewed spindly grass shoots. Most days, Watson sat alone, a fraying map in hand, comparing it to the hills around him and talking to himself, guessing at which valleys and towns concealed the busiest enemy concentrations. Often the concentrations were unavoidable; often they contained a rear-echelon supply dump or railroad hub, just the sort of lumpy target perfect for a Ranger raid. When Watson spoke to Thornton—whose condition and resolve decreased by the day—he nearly always returned to his time as a POW and this refrain: "They'll never get me."

At night, Watson led the survivors—their hands often glued to the shoulder in front—through a dark world of clattering trains, whistles, blinking truck lights, and the echoing voices of people singing. In the pitch-black hills, the men weaved their way through the switchbacking, slithering lines of hand-carried supply chains—"procession of the dead," Thornton called them—intermittently lit by the orange licks of stick-bundle torches. Believing that an enemy search party was pursuing them, on one occasion Watson hid his team, then "like a demon popping out of the ground" managed to snatch and silently bayonet the enemy patrol's rear security man in the guts.

At the edge of each ice-crusted stream, the men stripped and piled their clothes atop their heads to prevent them from freezing to their bodies on the other side. On one of these crossings, Thornton tripped and lost his boots, a miniature calamity that forced him to hike wearing only his slip-on winter overlayers. When challenged by enemy sentries, which happened three times, Watson eased his height into a hunch and the partisans launched into a torrent of Korean or Chinese, each time miraculously managing to talk the group past without a close inspection. At each heart-stopping, mouth-drying confrontation, Thornton "died a little" more.

After six days and nights of this routine, the men were physically wrecked. With one rib broken, his toes frostbitten, and the flesh peeling off the balls of his feet, Thornton could no longer maintain Watson's unforgiving pace. Too far from sanctuary to bully the man any further, Watson relented and ordered two Koreans to stay with the pilot while the rest of the group continued south. Eventually the Koreans also abandoned the pilot, and Thornton was captured. Steadfastly adhering to his vow to avoid reimprisonment, Watson continued, but not for long. On April 10—ten hallucinatory days since the mountaintop battle and just two to three miles from UN lines—the last remaining members of the Virginia I mission were cornered in a cave, captured and ransacked, then beaten and bound with wire so tightly that Watson's arms soon swelled to twice their normal size. For the second time in his life, this veteran of Darby's Rangers was a prisoner of war; as fate would have it, captured while escaping from a disaster as consequential for the Rangers as Cisterna had been.

21

Exactly one day after Watson was captured, his 4th Rangers were given a second opportunity to prove their worth: a mission to capture or destroy an enemy-held dam at Hwachon Reservoir. The Rangers' first amphibious raid of the war and exactly the sort for which Van Houten had prepared them, it was—similar to the Virginia I mission—a chance to demonstrate their supremacy in raiding and perhaps convince the Army's planners to assign them more of the same. Alas, that is not what happened.

On the predawn morning of April 11, without life preservers, motors, or time to prepare, the 4th Ranger Company paddled eight 400-pound plywood boats across Hwachon Reservoir, landed silently—probably too far from the dam—and seized an outlying hilltop redoubt. It was a seizure that squandered their surprise, the only element that would have permitted a small force to best a larger one. Within an hour of landing, they were surrounded on a hilltop and the dam as far from their grasp as Cisterna's had been. By noon, they needed ammunition or reinforcements even to retreat. A subsequent investigation of the raid by an Army historian produced seventy-four typed pages of interviews with participants—none with any of the Rangers—criticizing every element of the mission's planning and preparation. One operations officer summarized these critiques in a single, cumbersome sentence: "there was an inadequacy of knowledge of such operations among the people who handled this operation." As complex as the Virginia mission, the Hwachon Dam raid had been allotted the same amount of forethought: not much at all.

On May 18, the 1st Ranger Company fought a rearguard battle on Hill 710 known afterward as the May Massacre. The battle cost fourteen Rangers killed, including the commander—shot through the head—plus numerous wounded and eight captured, all dragged off to various North Korean prison camps, where a promise of torture awaited them and for several, a miserable death. The very next day, General Matthew Ridgway, the Far East commander of all UN forces, issued a dispatch to the Army chief of staff's office asking for an immediate inactivation of all Ranger companies in Korea. Just six months since the first company of Airborne Rangers' arrival in-country, Ridgway did not blame this reflex on their bloodbaths—there were bloodbaths everywhere, especially among the infantry. Instead, he blamed his decision on the enemy's dismal treatment of POWs and the inability of Caucasians to blend into the population, conditions that had made it "impractical" to employ the Rangers in their intended role. Those reasons had made raiding "impractical" for almost every American raider since King Philip's War, and would have been ignored had the Virginia mission succeeded. When the Army's senior planners received the dispatch from Ridgway—a man whose reputation in the Army had already leapfrogged MacArthur's—they immediately began contemplating not only a disbandment of the seven Ranger companies in Korea, but of the fifteen companies stationed around the world, including those in Europe, where the Rangers' White faces matched the enemy's—a sign that the real reasons for disbandment had not yet been named.

In the aftermath of Virginia I, McGee blamed the failure on a variety of actors and circumstances: the carrying capacity of the Korean partisans, the Baker section commander, the weather, even the Navy planners who had suggested the raid in the first place. He never blamed the Rangers themselves, who—McGee believed—would have succeeded had only Eighth Army allowed him to use an entire Ranger company—a direct contradiction of Ridgway's reasons for disbanding them. After the mission, McGee doubled down on his investment by trying to recruit convalescing Rangers to be partisan instructors and by attempting the permanent annexation of the three Virginia survivors. Of the three, only the face-shot twenty-one-year-old Miles volunteered to stay with McGee. He shouldn't have. Several weeks later, McGee launched a second penetration mission—this one code-named Operation Spitfire—wherein he replaced Baker and Pucel with two British soldiers of questionable credentials. On June 18, the team parachuted some eighty miles behind enemy lines to recruit, arm, and lead a hinterland force of guerrillas. The mission proved as badly executed as Virginia, resulting in no one recruited, a botched extraction, and a similar hike to the south. After three weeks of evading the enemy, young Miles went missing and was never again seen by American eyes. Instead of raising a standard for Ranger penetration raids (something McGee had hoped to do), his failures had actually helped reinforce Ridgway's indictments against them.

22

On July 10, just nine months after the re-inception of the Ranger companies, the Department of the Army accepted Ridgway's request and ordered their inactivation in the Korean theater. While that order was being carried out, a Pentagon conference convened to determine the fate of the rest of the Ranger companies and to consider an alternative idea, but one with a charter far more comprehensive than simply raiding. Stalemated by a Communist horde in Korea, the Army's planners had discovered the limits of American technology and now wanted a horde of their own. To achieve this, they entertained a briefing by Colonel Aaron Bank and Colonel Russell Volckmann—the first a former OSS operative, the second a former Filipino resistance leader—who briefed them on a conceptual unit that would be capable of employing indigenous guerrillas across the entire spectrum of warfare, not unlike what McGee had already envisioned in Korea. The force would require special soldiers and a special organization, similar to the operations branch of the OSS and quite removed from division-level abuses. In the course of the meeting, one officer asked if these "special forces" would be capable of conducting "Ranger activities." Bank responded that they would, but added that the use of such "highly trained and specialized personnel" for "raids in force" or as "front line" assault troops "would be a terrible waste." Bank said more than he probably knew: of the roughly 748 Rangers who had fought in Korea, 130 had been killed, or 17 percent—a staggering casualty figure that did not include the wounded.

On August 1, all Ranger companies were disbanded, freeing up enough troop spaces in the Army's order of battle to create the Special Forces. All that remained of the Rangers was Van Houten's Training Center, repurposed as a sort-of graduate school to spread Ranger tactics throughout the infantry—George Marshall's dream, just nine years late. It was a decision that instantly cut off US military planners—including those of the US Navy—from access to the US military's only explicitly named commando raiders, and one that also placed the future of American raids in the hands of troops that weren't even American.

In the wake of the US military's flinch away from behind-lines commando raiding, the planners at Eighth Army, and later at Far East Command, restricted the Partisan Command's American advisors to actually advising; in other words, no more front-line operations. This policy helped attract to the partisans a type of Army officer focused on island girls, drinking, ample liberty, just about anything other than combat. The policy's most aggressive violator, but not the only one, was Roy Meeks, a veteran of the 1st Ranger Company—Changmal, Chipyong-ni, the May Massacre—who trained his partisans every day, fought beside them even when surrounded, and once carried a dead Korean guerrilla over his shoulder for about 7,000 yards while chased by some 400 angry Chinese soldiers. There were not enough Meekses to go around. Without Americans to plan and lead, and dismally supplied, the partisans' raids quickly devolved into coastal harassments and "spur of the moment" attacks, usually unverifiable except for the booty they captured—oxen, film projectors, sewing machines, or simply sacks of enemy ID cards and shoulder boards.* Of the 19 total Virginia-style penetration missions (the last 17 of which included no Americans, and thus received only casual planning and preparation), all 19 failed; and of the 389 Korean partisan raiders who parachuted behind enemy lines, it seems only 2 were ever seen by Americans again, both of whom were found to have earned their freedom by promising to spy for North Korea. They were executed.

By the end of the war, Far East Command's principal objective for its partisans was simply to keep them from escaping their island cages and overwhelming South Korean society with a sudden influx of 20,000 North Koreans, all of them now practiced in the arts of black-market trading, thieving, and bushwhacking. If there was a second objective, it was to continue bird-dogging targets for Air Force planes and Navy bombs and guns—the exact sort of mission that Virginia I had become and that had decided the fates of the men most responsible for it. At least, decided them in part.

23

On July 27, 1953, the armistice that effectively ended the Korean War was signed, and within days the Chinese and North Koreans began publishing daily lists of UN prisoners of war earmarked for release. For a printing press operator at *The New York Times* who received each list directly from the front, this initiated a nightly series of breath-holding, paper-clutching searches through line after line of names, not one of them belonging to his son, of whom he had had no information for two years, five months, and twenty-six days. After thirty-two nights of this routine, and having recently been informed that only one more list of 110 names remained to be published, this father left his co-workers and his post behind and made for the Connecticut shore to be alone. There, hours later, he was found by the local police and informed that the North Koreans had—at the last minute—added a 111th name to their final list. A name the local police knew all too well.

In the twenty-nine months since his capture, Corporal Martin R. Watson—a soldier no guard or prisoner had ever believed was actually

* The Korean partisan volunteers were paid just nine handfuls of rice per day to eat and barter, and allotted the same annual dollar amount for indigenous cigarettes as they were for boat maintenance, their only conveyance to the coast.

a corporal—had set an example for captivity that to this day has never been exceeded. Thirty days after he was captured (eighteen of which he had been starved in a cave to make his 240-pound size somewhat easier to handle), Watson and a South Korean comrade had knocked out a guard with a rock and made for the surrounding mountains, where they had survived for five days until their pursuers had disabled them by rolling a grenade into their hideout. Never medically treated except with some shreds of brown paper to cover his wounds, Watson had nevertheless escaped again, this time by wriggling out of his rope restraints and jumping free of a moving truck as it slowed around a bend. This time he survived a week before inadvertently walking right past a wide-eyed North Korean patrol. For these attempts and one other (plus an attempted suicide with a piece of broken glass), he had been relentlessly beaten with rifle butts and boot heels, and periodically starved and almost always isolated, once in an unsheltered hole for seventy-two days with rations described by the record as "sparse." Rightly suspected as an OSS spy and saboteur, Watson had also been subjected to almost daily interrogation by the North Koreans, the Chinese, even the Russians, who had drilled him on his exposure to the Gestapo in World War II, but especially on the organization, methods, and tactics of the "paratroop" unit to which they knew he had belonged. Watson's response to these and other questions had been a mixture of stony silence or intentional contradiction, responses that had invariably earned him a switch across the eyes, a pistol barrel across the face, or hours of kneeling with his nose pressed against a wall and a stone on his head. Throughout these deprivations, Watson had never lost his bearing or conviction, once standing during a packed camp lecture by a British speaker from the London *Daily Worker* to say that he "didn't know what Communism was and didn't care to find out," nor did he and his fellow POWs want "to listen to this traitor, commie SOB." For this affront, and as an example to other prisoners, he was eventually frog-marched before a military tribunal, informed of the armistice, then sentenced to death by firing squad. He still didn't talk. In the end, after he had been starved from 240 pounds to 120, his was an example that earned him the final distinction as the second-to-last UN POW to be released across the Freedom Bridge. On the other side, he learned that the Rangers that he had so steadfastly protected from exposure no longer existed, as far removed now from the Army's interest as was the man who had resurrected them from the grave. A man whose accomplishments had disappointingly matched those of his past.

About the same time that Operation Spitfire had been unraveling, Colonel John Hugh McGee—the Korean War author of the Army's Rangers and Korean partisans—had presented himself for the third time to the Quonset hut maze of Eighth Army's headquarters in Pusan intent on securing a date for a partisan advance into North Korea, a date for which he had long been waiting. The reply from his superior had been simple: never. After a yearlong tour, McGee left Korea as dejected as he had left the Philippines, never again to have a chance to lead a partisan Army on a campaign of liberation. On top of everything else, he was "branded" the "scapegoat" for the failure of Virginia and Spitfire, failures with consequences beyond a battered reputation.

When McGee returned home from Korea, he accepted a student appointment to the US Army War College, hoping upon graduation to be selected to teach guerrilla warfare at the Command and General Staff School. His missteps in commanding the Miscellaneous Division, however, meant that his application was denied. Though he went on to other successes in the Army, eventually earning the rank of brigadier general, he was never quite able to shake the scorn of his failure. For the remainder of his life, he maintained detailed accounts of his partisan achievements (like most people, precious few on his failures) and wrote two books (only one of them published) defending his belief in the growing importance of guerrilla warfare. Nearing the end of his life, he typed a letter to a former partisan associate in which he remarked that every "new war is marked by surprise adaptions [*sic*] . . . in the closing period of the last." Not exactly Clausewitz, it was still as true a military maxim as any ever written. Not a great commander, McGee was nevertheless sincere and conscientious, and well respected by his peers. Until the end of his life he kept in contact with Ralph Puckett, talked daily with his brother George, the Marauder, and attended Ranger reunions. In 1995, the US Army Ranger Association voted him into the Ranger Hall of Fame. It was an honor earned—in part—for his greatest contribution to the Army: a vision of strategic, go-anywhere raiders that leveraged all the mobility and power of the entire US military. Alas, McGee's proposed organization had simply been ahead of its time to all except the branch of service that had requested the Virginia I raid in the first place.

The US Navy.

Chapter 9

Arleigh Burke, the Bay of Pigs, and the Launching of the Navy's Limited-War SEALs

On March 17, 1960, President Dwight D. Eisenhower—the former commander of Allied Armies in Europe, whose "New Look" defense strategy relied less on armies than on spies and a mounting stockpile of nuclear projectiles—approved a CIA program to recruit and train a paramilitary force of Cuban exiles to overthrow the upstart regime of Fidel Castro. The United States had already accomplished similar feats in Iran and Guatemala, yet this plan was different in one major way: instead of a coup d'état from within, this would be an invasion. In the summer, the CIA commenced beach assault training for some 1,500 volunteers on the Pacific coast of Guatemala and busily gathered a force of M41 tanks, cargo ships, twin-engine B-26 bombers, even two LCIs—160-foot-long Landing Craft relics from World War II. Because the mission's success required American deniability, its planning was largely concealed from the heads of the US military; because Cuba was an island and support might be needed in case of emergency, some exception was given to the one branch that could provide it: the US Navy, a branch of service not normally associated with covert action, but one that—for reasons to be explained—was already priming its sailors to lead the way.

Among the Navy's first assistance to the CIA's Cuba invasion plan occurred on the white beaches of Vieques. There, twelve Cuban volunteers—all either competitive swimmers or sons of Cuba's formerly well connected—were secluded on a remote beach in two tents staked just twenty-five feet from the ocean on cots whose mosquito netting was so insufficient against the gnats that sleeping required pants, long sleeves, and hats. Here, the volunteers fell under the guidance of a tough but standoffish UDT instructor known only as Bob, whose initial lessons included all the traditional UDT sacraments of endless calisthenics, soft-sand runs, breath holds till each man could go for at least two minutes, and ocean swims till each man's ankles could endure the tyranny of duck fins. Later, after imparting a practical education in beach reconnaissance and marking, then underwater explosives and navigation using a rebreather and a compass, a second UDT instructor known only as Steve—a more accessible "old-timer" with a wealth of experience—expanded their curriculum to not-so-traditional topics, meaning, remembered one participant, topics with "more emphasis on the land." This new emphasis included improvised "kitchen explosives"—mainly just concoctions of charcoal and urine; marksmanship with submachine guns and World War II–era BARs; and escape and evasion from the CIA-contracted support staff of merchant marines who resembled a gang of pirates and upon capturing a student were supposed to "beat the shit out of him." Toward the end of their time on Vieques, Steve assigned his students demolition raids on inland installations similar to those of the Korean War–era UDTs, and even challenged them to sneak aboard the merchant marines' anchored vessel in the middle of the night to wrap their sleeping wrists with tags to signify a simulated kill. Before they left Vieques, these UDT-trained Cuban frogmen—whose training had included a daily interruption for Mass—were so assured of their newfound faith that they were already referring to themselves as the 12 Apostles, and, whether they knew it or not, were about to go forth into the world as one more set of disciples of a gospel whose converts would extend far beyond the narrow halls of the CIA.

During the period of the CIA's preparations for the covert invasion of Cuba, the US Navy was led by Admiral Arleigh Burke, the fifty-eight-year-old CNO whose most conspicuous features were a tight shock of curly bleached hair, a fist of a chin that fell into a loose and swollen neck, and a sizable bulk that had long since settled into his hips, a trait that gave, said one witness, a "sea roll to his stride" and to his shape the impression of an upright bass or a freighter. Besides making him easy work for the fleet's cartoonists, it was—along with a wide smile—a combination of features that suggested a "sunny" personality, "like a cheerful skipper of a . . . fishing boat." Outwardly conventional, plus never a veteran of any of the Navy's elite branches—aviation, submarines, or UDTs—the principal detail that suggested Burke's exceptional abilities was the five years that he had spent as CNO, more than twice the normal stint in a post that was known as notoriously grueling, and for which he had been vaulted over ninety-one higher-ranking admirals. The other obvious distinction was a chestful of combat awards—the only awards the secretary of the Navy could convince him to wear, and an indicator of Burke's bias that such was the only kind of naval service that mattered. More important for our purposes, it was evidence of Burke's willingness to propel his ships into any conflict they could reach, a past that now hinted at his eagerness to propel his sailors into conflicts his ships could not—conflicts that would soon require a unit unlike any the US Navy, or any navy, had ever possessed.

2

FEARING THAT A morning blizzard would block the road to the Naval Academy entrance examinations, young Arleigh Albert Burke had left his 170-acre farm in the foothills of Boulder, Colorado, ridden into town the night before, and "slept in a stable with his horse." On test morning, every smarter candidate had been a no-show. Accepted on a "fluke," Burke's subsequent Naval Academy career had revealed no indication of his future standing. Never a natural student or athlete, his most standout achievement had been that he never stood out. Like a

Admiral Arleigh A. Burke, USN (center), takes the oath of office as chief of naval operations during ceremonies in Dahlgren Hall, US Naval Academy, Annapolis, Maryland, on August 17, 1955.

shooting star in daylight, Burke had not really been noticed until the skies began to darken, and then only because of his two great farmboy virtues: an unequaled capacity for hard work and the foresight to see the storm clouds in the distance and position himself where most others had not thought to.

Summing up Burke's first five years aboard the battleship *Arizona,* where he demonstrated an almost unparalleled skill in gunnery, a shipmate obliged the future CNO with the first superlative that indicated any promise: "Arleigh Burke will be dead before he's fifty, or he'll be chief of naval operations." Looking to increase his knowledge of explosives, Burke ignored his academic handicaps and for his postgraduate requirement attended the University of Michigan to earn a master's of science in chemical engineering, a course so intense that he had to study until midnight six days a week. His breaks—if you can call them that—were usually spent with colored pencil in hand, jotting notes across one of several wall-pinned *National Geographic* maps of the Far East, explaining to a peer, "one day, my friend, our country will be at war with Japan . . . When that time comes I intend to know that area of the world as intimately as possible."

In 1943, when Burke finally arrived in the South Pacific to take command of Destroyer Squadron 23—DesRon23; the Little Beavers—he pinned himself to a drop-leaf desk in the sweltering belly of his command ship and crammed into his head a year's worth of combat reports, every battle from Coral Sea to Savo Island. Appalled at the micromanagement of destroyers at the Battle of Tassafaronga—"The Night of the Long Lances"—in which permission to launch torpedoes against an already discovered enemy fleet was denied for four interminable minutes, Burke crafted an entirely new doctrine of employment: Instead of spreading his destroyers around the fleet's larger ships as nighttime submarine pickets, all dependent on permission from above to break guard duty to engage the enemy, Burke proposed to concentrate his ships at the head of the fleet and to govern his skippers under what has since been called "the Doctrine of Faith," an unprecedented delegation of authority in which an enemy sighting would be immediately followed by a "coordinated torpedo attack WITHOUT ORDERS." The use of all-caps was Burke's. To convey this attitude to his sailors, Burke issued them a twelve-page mimeographed memo whose very first lines read: "If it will help kill Japs—it's important. If it will not help kill Japs—it's not important. Keep your ship trained for battle!" Burke's list of non-battle-related orders was succinct: There were none.

"CORRECTIONS TO THIS SECTION WILL NOT BE PERMITTED!" It took less than a month to make his point.

A little after midnight on Thanksgiving 1943, while patrolling the black waters off Cape St. George, near New Guinea, Burke's five-ship wolfpack spotted a Japanese radar contact. Immediately and without permission, Burke radioed his squadron, "Hold your hats, boys; here we go." Into the dark and into the enemy's guns, Burke's destroyers dropped throttles to flank speed and launched torpedoes, exploding two Japanese ships outright, then wheeled to starboard like Parthian horse archers into the face of three more enemy ships that immediately tucked tail and fled. In the nightlong pursuit, Burke's deck sailors discharged and loaded their guns so fast and so long that many passed out in their turrets from the fumes and from "sheer exhaustion." When Burke's squadron finally returned to port, said a *Time* magazine reporter, "every ship in the roadstead turned up its searchlights" and every bluejacket in the fleet "manned the rails" in tribute. It was, said Halsey afterward, "the classic sea action of this war."

For thirteen months, Burke commanded his destroyers like Patton did his tanks. To every order he invariably responded, "proceeding at 31 knots," a "boiler-bursting" pace, said one historian, that caught Admiral William "Bull" Halsey's attention, who addressed his future dispatches to "31-Knot Burke." The name stuck.

In the last two years of the war, Burke was forced to give up command of his own squadron in order to become chief of staff to Marc Mitscher, a famous aircraft carrier admiral. Neither a pilot, nor possessing any experience in aircraft carriers, Burke was at first out of place in this new staff role, an "onlooker" to the aviators and a jolt to his morale that almost immediately expanded his waistline. Essentially confined to the flag plot—the ship's tactical command center—Burke was forced not only to learn everything he could about aircraft carriers and their tactics, but also to elevate his operational understanding beyond the amateur's urge for the battle at hand in order to plan for the next one: beyond the Marianas to the Philippine Sea, beyond that to Leyte Gulf, then on to Iwo Jima. When submarine intelligence told him the battleship *Yamato* was spotted en route to an unknown location, he spent all night hunched over his charts, a caliper in hand, then launched 400 planes "against the spot" where he would be if the roles were reversed, and sank the ship with more than 3,000 men aboard. Before his planes returned, Burke had already switched his attention to the next battle.

By the time they reached Okinawa, the final terrible fight of World

War II, Burke had settled into a punishing routine: Always up at 0330; the sleep he did manage was usually interrupted by some twenty calls a night. In his waking hours, Burke watched nightmares unfold, his only sanctuary the flashes of courage that "for years to come," said a biographer, would seem to whisper to him "something about the meaning of the U.S. Navy." The worst of these, and the greatest, was the final transmission of a newly commissioned ensign who had taken command of his crippled destroyer after everyone else in the chain of command had been killed. Before the ship sank and the transmission was cut off, Burke heard the young man say: "I will fight this ship to the best of my ability and forgive me the mistakes I am about to make." The voice would haunt and steel him for the rest of his life.

The next five years of Burke's career coincided with the push by Truman's consolidationists to break the Navy's warhorses into supply-line wagon teams. Assigned to the Navy's General Board, an advisory body of Marine Corps and naval officers, Burke pushed the group to develop a forecast of where the Navy needed to be in ten years, and for him, any answer besides the front rank was not a future he could stomach. "Combat," he would say, "is the profoundest experience of the male, corresponding to childbirth in women." Unable to fully shake its impact, and not wanting to, Burke was ever after committed to producing a Navy offspring that reflected the inclinations of its most battle-hungry ancestors—an attitude that manifested itself when the CNO personally called to ask how quickly he could leave for Korea to take over as Turner Joy's chief of staff for the Inchon invasion and he replied, "Two hours."

Publicly critical of the Army's failure to adapt to "another type of war [that] not only scared us to death" but also "kicked the hell out of us," Burke—as commander of Cruiser Division 5 on Korea's east coast—never missed an opportunity to enlarge his slice of combat involvement. "He was his own Chief of Staff, his own intelligence officer, his own operations officer. He was even his own [radioman] on the bridge," said one of Burke's shipmates in Korea. "You endangered your life if you got between him and the phone." Never content to sit off the coast to wait for action, Burke routinely rode a helicopter or plane to tour American fighting positions, casually surviving one fuel-soaked crash landing in the process. In part to ease the burdens of soldiers and Marines, in part to bird-dog targets for his own guns, he outfitted members of his staff with radios and rotated them to the front as naval gunfire liaisons. During a meeting with UN commanders, one Korean general went so far as to awkwardly introduce Burke as his "artillery commander." Burke took it as a compliment. On another occasion, Burke personally accompanied ROK troops on a nighttime ambush during which his watch alarm sounded, initiating a ground-sucking firefight. An eager advocate of Douglas Drysdale and the US-sponsored raids by British Commandos, he was forever pleased that the Navy had not lost them to the Army. During breaks in the armistice talks, in which he served as Turner Joy's deputy, he so often wore Army fatigues and organized rifle-range time for the soldiers under his charge that they routinely called him "general." On whether he ever corrected them, the record is silent. Not since Mary Miles had there been a naval flag officer as eager to engage in ground combat, or as eager to bend every gun in the fleet to support the troops engaged in it—but a disposition not determinative for the Navy until Burke was placed in charge of it.

If Burke's first priority as CNO had been the nuclear modernization of the fleet, then his second had been to articulate a future vision of the Navy's core functions. To gather ideas for this, one of his first actions had been to establish an Office of Strategic Studies with a mandate to conceptualize the Navy's future—"five years ahead, ten years ahead."

"Think," he had told them. "Just think. And don't stop thinking."

To do this himself, he had traveled to South Vietnam, Thailand, even Laos—a landlocked country—to meet with leaders and to learn about the insurgencies there; he had made a special effort to cultivate a close relationship with Britain's First Sea Lord, Admiral Louis Mountbatten, the former World War II commander of the British Commandos; he had even created an "open-mailbox policy" to accept letters from sailors of any rank, and required his staff to respond to every one of them, working weekends if needed.

Puffing clouds from his MacArthur-style corncob pipe like a "battleship smokestack," said one writer, Burke invariably worked every day for twelve to fourteen hours straight—a "man-killing personal example"—and held as many as twenty conferences a day. With no hobbies and no children, weekends for Burke did not exist. "The only man who ever had his work done by Friday," Burke had been known to say, "was Robinson Crusoe." "You could hear the sighs of relief all over the Pentagon when he finally went home for the day," remembered one officer who served there during those years. At home, Burke usually retired to one of two offices—one upstairs, one in the basement, and each complete with a globe and world maps. The second office was created because he had grown so tired of the first.

By the time of the CIA's proposed invasion of Cuba, Burke had already sensed that the peace promised by Eisenhower's threat of mutually assured destruction was not peace at all, but a fraud. From Hungary to Cuba, from Iran to Guatemala, Burke had seen the flames of brushfire wars igniting all around him. As neither Americans nor Soviets had been keen to risk nuclear holocaust over such a tributary interest, Burke had joined a rising chorus of strategic voices clamoring for the US military to resurrect its capacity for nonnuclear limited war, and fast. For the Navy's ability to land Marines, to bombard from afar, to sit off the coast in international waters and thus avoid a "direct foreign commitment," it was not long before naval planners had started promoting their service as the natural leader for such conflicts—one naval historian had already called the Navy the "champion of limited war and of preparedness for it." It was a promotion that quickly coincided with the presidential election of John F. Kennedy, who in his inaugural address stated his belief that the horror of nuclear war could deter none of the causes of revolution—tyranny, poverty, disease, and war itself—nor could they defeat the revolutionaries themselves.

"I have never heard a better speech," said Burke afterward. "It's the best statement of policies in which I believe that I have ever heard."

Three months later, Kennedy ordered the CIA to launch its invasion of Cuba.

3

Just before midnight on April 16, 1961, three squads of Cuban frogmen cut the towlines to their twin-engined catamarans and began paddling three black rubber Zodiacs toward three separate beaches near the Bahía de Cochinos, the Bay of Pigs. Just days earlier they had been slogging through the final phase of their training in a grimy pool at a deactivated naval depot on the banks of the Mississippi River, and upon completion had been granted two days' leave in New Orleans, where they had hit the French Quarter's bars and restaurants, and taken in the epic tragedy *The Alamo,* in which the characters of Davy Crockett and Jim Bowie had been played, respectively, by John Wayne and Richard Widmark—an actor better known to all of them as the enigmatic commanding officer in the World War II UDT film *The Frogmen*. Now, like the title characters in that movie, two of the squads were being led by two equally enigmatic CIA commanders—commanders who were supposed to have remained in the catamarans, but, more important, commanders who had not been content to command only frogmen. The first of these was William "Rip" Robertson, a high-and-tight Pacific War Marine and leather-skinned Texan who smiled so infrequently that his men called him "the Alligator"; and the second was Grayston Lynch, a veteran of Omaha Beach and the Army's Special Forces whose own Texas roots had crossed with an easy laugh to take his personality in the opposite direction. Under these two final trainers—the Marine and the commando—the frogmen had evolved into something else.

Members of the 12 Apostles training at a deactivated naval depot pool along the banks of the Mississippi River near New Orleans.

No longer naked warriors armed with just a lead line and a plexiglass slate, Lynch's frogmen instead now looked more like Marine raiders from World War II—each one in green fatigues bulging with magazines and grenades, his face smeared with kitchen soot, his hands clutching a Thompson submachine gun. Scraping their hull against a line of coral that CIA planners had assured them was simply a line of seaweed or a shadow in preliminary aerial photographs, the frogmen responded to its danger not by slipping into the water to chart its depth and location, but rather by simply lifting their Zodiac over it—their eyes fixed on the shoreline, their hands leveling their Thompsons. Instead of a darkened beach, the Playa Girón section that planners had selected as the primary landing zone was now awash in the loom of several overhead arc lights that illuminated a beachside bar alive with chattering locals. Still aboard the Zodiac with a BAR trained on the bodega, Lynch responded by ordering his men to edge their course toward a section of the beach that remained shrouded in darkness. Once reoriented, the squad resumed their so-far-undetected scull through the surf—undetected, that is, until one of the red lights that was meant to mark their landing site started flashing uncontrollably, illuminating the inside of their boat. They scrambled to extinguish it; when they succeeded, they looked up to discover a jeep turning its high beams out to sea, so close they could hear its brakes squeal over the surf. Intending like nearly all UDT swimmers who came before them to land in secret and prepare the way for armed invaders, Lynch's frogmen now responded to their high-beam exposure the way their enhanced training had taught them.

Erupting with a deafening clatter of automatic fire, the squad shredded the jeep with their Thompsons, while the tracers from Lynch's BAR skipped off the vehicle's skin into the trees beyond. With the jeep lights extinguished and the nearby locals alerted, the frogmen now hustled their boat to shore to complete their mission. First, they positioned their red lights to guide the landing flotilla; second, they scattered the local drunks, seized the bar, and extinguished its lights; third, they took cover behind a rock jetty to ambush any of Castro's counterattackers and shined a directional white light out to sea to mark their position. Within minutes of commencing their raid, Lynch's radioman—Eduardo Zayas-Bazán, just twenty-five years old and a new father of a five-month-old boy—was frantically yelling into his handheld radio to lift the invasion flotilla's guns from the frogmen's white directional light and to strike an incoming truck full of Castro's militiamen. Already dissimilar to the vast majority of the UDTs' past operations, the mission of Lynch's frogmen finally differed in one fundamental way: After eliminating the enemy's beach defenders, the frogmen completely forgot to alert the landing fleet of the coral. Never mind for a moment their abrupt evolution from reconnaissance swimmers to amphibious raiders, it was an oversight that would be compounded by a series of other failures, all of which would soon gather to unravel the invasion's future prospects and turn these frogmen—like the rest of the brigaders—into defenders as doomed as those in the movie they had just watched. As doomed as the Texans at the Alamo.

4

When Burke's alarm clock woke him at 6:00 on the morning of April 17, his first thought was to wonder why no call had interrupted his night's sleep. Eighteen minutes later, he was standing in his Pentagon office, dressed in full uniform, listening to an aide rattle off some of the night's misadventures. Coral, capsized landing craft, waterlogged radios, friendly fire—the headaches typical to every amphibious landing since Dieppe. Untypical, and most consequential, was the president's cancellation of an airstrike on Castro's airfields, a decision that made reprisal by Castro's airplanes a sinister inevitability. About the same time that Burke was learning this, six of Castro's airplanes attacked the invasion force's five support ships, sinking two almost immediately and chasing the three survivors so far from the beaches that they ceased to support anything. An hour later, six brigade airplanes dropped 177 paratroopers at critical road intersections to block Castro's reinforcements from the beachhead. Much of their equipment splashed down in nearby swamps and sank.

Suspicious from the start of the CIA's planning, its logistics, its command and control, and most of all its promises, Burke would—over the next three days—press harder than any other for the immediate intervention of regular US forces. To save the invaders, he proposed a series of increasingly overt solutions: the insertion of a radio-armed US Marine or naval officer onto the beach to give real-time updates, maybe even to direct a pair of destroyers in "wiping out" Castro's tanks by replicating the Navy's run on Omaha Beach. At a White House meeting, Burke watched in "stricken" horror as the president picked up a tiny magnetic destroyer from the map that represented the Navy's proximity to the besieged beaches, then moved it beyond the line representing the horizon. "Let me take two jets and shoot down these enemy aircraft," Burke pleaded to no avail, even offering to whitewash the US Navy tail identifications before launching them. At the suggestion of a treetop overflight by Navy planes to intimidate Castro's forces, Kennedy responded, "Burke, I don't want the United States involved in this."

"Hell, Mr. President," Burke snapped back, "but we *are* involved!"

5

In the three days since they had seized the beachhead at Playa Girón, Lynch's squad and the rest of the frogmen had folded into an almost continuous battle, but in a way that few frogmen ever had. Dressed in black-dyed swimsuits and sweatshirts, thus more closely resembling their UDT forebears than Lynch's men, the squad led by Rip Robertson—the Pacific War Marine and real-life John Wayne—had nevertheless also been transformed into far more than just reconnaissance swimmers. This fact was evidenced by the beards they had cultivated in case defeat forced them into an inland guerrilla war—the only beards in the brigade, remembered one frogman—and by their pre-mission adoption of the heavy-barreled BARs instead of the more lightweight and swimmer-friendly Thompson submachine guns; "Throw those fucking things away," Robertson had told them before embarking to their landing site at Playa Larga. There, two trucks full of Castro's militiamen had interrupted their beach-marking mission with fire so close that frogman Andrés Pruna had been forced to flatten under a "goddamn fireworks show" of tracers snapping just inches from his head—an ambush that Pruna and the others were able to escape only by unleashing their BARs, machine guns that Robertson had taught them to fire as accurately as rifles. Since that firefight, half of the 12 Apostles had been (along with Robertson and Lynch) pulled back to the support fleet—ostensibly to serve as supply couriers between the ships and the invasion force; in reality, held back to limit the number of brigade members about to be betrayed by Kennedy's second thoughts.

As for the frogmen left behind—namely those who had originally landed with Lynch—the battle that remained for them was exactly that, a battle packed with all the horrors of infantry combat: mortars, rockets, machine guns, and grenades; positions being overrun and retaken; desperate radio calls for ammunition, water, the evacuation of wounded, all unanswered. Throughout, the frogmen—just like the brigade's infantrymen—manned a section of the brigade's perimeter, a section dug from sandy foxholes near the bar they had initially seized. The only real interruption in this defense was a last-ditch attempt by Brigade Commander Pepe San Román to enlist the squad's radioman and the squad's Zodiac for an all-night, over-the-horizon dash to transmit a rescue plea to the American fleet. It was a failed attempt made worse the following day when the same radioman left the safety of his foxhole during a break in strafing only to be shot below the knee by a group of jumpy brigaders whom the radioman had been trying to clear from the beachside bar that had become a favorite target of Castro's planes. In the end, when San Román ordered the brigade to escape into the nearby island swamps, about the only feature that distinguished the frogmen as such was their refusal to leave their wounded behind.

For the overwhelming majority of invaders who were ordered to flee—a majority that included all the frogmen in Lynch's boat crew—the fates had other plans. Instead of escaping into the mountains to wage a guerrilla war, each of these unfortunates was captured by Castro's forces and packed off on an eight-hour drive to internment in Havana, many of them inside sealed trucks so asphyxiating that the men had to scratch out air holes in the aluminum bulkheads with their belt buckles, a solution that still didn't prevent the suffocation of nine brigaders. Spared this torture because of the bullet hole below his knee, Eduardo Zayas-Bazán—the twenty-five-year-old frogman and radio operator with the five-month-old son in Miami—was instead seated in the back of a Buick, taken to a local police station, and dumped in a cellblock to be taunted by its inmates. "Take your shoes off," he was told. "You won't need them when we execute you later tonight."

Hoping to forestall the capture and firing-squad executions of as many brigade members as possible by the notoriously vindictive Castro regime, Burke now stretched his leash to the very limit of its length and authorized a handful of his ships to lend a hand to the rescue of survivors. More than eager to accept the help, Lynch and Robertson told their six remaining frogmen to get their gear, then cross-decked them from their unmarked and ramshackle CIA-owned LCIs to the irrefutable supremacy of an American destroyer. From this platform of deterrence—often crowded to within 200 yards of the coast—the ad hoc rescuers spent the next four sleepless days and nights motoring whaleboats and rubber Zodiacs around Cuba's skin, beckoning survivors with whistles and bullhorns, and, as they already had, trailblazing ashore. In this case, trailblazing meant armed patrols through an often shadeless terrain of scrub, undrinkable swamp water, and bush thorns so thick that Lynch had two sets of khakis ripped from his body in two days. Predictably, it was also terrain being flattened even further by overflights of Castro's hovering helicopters and ground-pounding patrols of militiamen. Not exactly a mission that American-led frogmen had ever performed, it would soon prove—especially for the men they rescued, but not only for them—among their most consequential.

Of the 1,500 men in the invasion force, 26 were rescued, all emaciated and barely ambulatory, their bodies clinging to remnants of shredded clothing or completely naked. Many of them were mute or hallucinatory from drinking seawater. One escapee had hidden for days with only his face above water, a state that left him so disoriented that when he saw Lynch's European features, he took them for a Russian's and desperately tried to sink into the swamp. Several more were so delirious that when rescued they invariably asked, "Did we win?" For the dead brigaders they found, the frogmen clawed out graves with bayonets and bare hands—a courtesy these Catholics even extended to a crash-landed Communist pilot.

Throughout these days, the Navy's attentiveness to the frogmen's mission was felt in numerous ways: in the eagerness of American sailors to detail the frogmen's guns after returning from the swamps—"I'd never seen them so clean," remembered Andrés Pruna; in their being welcomed into the officers' wardroom for white-tablecloth meals while still dripping with mud; and, ultimately, in the Navy's provision of a submarine to continue the frogmen's mission when the presence of an American destroyer became too overt. For some of the frogmen—now benefiting from the gift of nearly sixty years of hindsight—this attentiveness was equally on display in a personal cable by Burke himself commending their "incredible" efforts. Efforts that he had always tried to support. Efforts that would now serve to inform his vision for a future Navy connected to the future of combat.

6

BEGINNING ON APRIL 22—just three days after the brigade's surrender and two days before Lynch, Robertson, and the frogmen would conclude their rescue efforts—the president convened an inquiry into the invasion's planning and execution. Besides the commission's chairman, Maxwell Taylor—a former Army chief of staff and current limited-war advocate—the rest of the commission's principal jurists were also its principal defendants: CIA Director Allen Dulles, Admiral Burke, even a representative from the administration: the "slouching," flop-haired, sleeve-rolled attorney general, Robert Kennedy, the president's younger brother and his top torch-wielding witch hunter. Over the course of three weeks at the Pentagon, with no recording equipment or even stenographer, the group would interview some fifty witnesses; enough to weld a bracelet of animosities connecting every institution involved. The president's brother blamed the Joint Chiefs; the Joint Chiefs blamed the CIA; the CIA blamed the president. No witnesses were more compelling on this last charge than CIA officers Lynch and Robertson themselves, their skin sunburned black, their luggage a cardboard Hershey bar box, Lynch's paratrooper boots crusted white with salt water. Not since the disaster at Dieppe in 1942 had a postmortem revealed so many cracks in a country's readiness for its battles to come.

Sensing these battles, on May 3, 1961—still in regular attendance at Bay of Pigs interviews—Burke issued a memo to his senior staff suggesting a canvass of Navy records for personnel, particularly officers, experienced in guerrilla and psychological warfare, underwater demolition, "and what the Army [called] 'Special Forces Training.'" As the search would soon show, the Navy possessed just ninety-three officer-graduates of UDT training, and only six remaining from its World War II–era Scouts and Raiders. The projected numbers for those slated for training were even worse: just one naval officer for the Army's six-week-long Special Forces Officer course in 1961, and none planned for the Army's Ranger School or its Jungle Operations Course. Probably already anticipating such a paltry answer, Burke "recommended"—CNOs don't really recommend—that the Navy create training pamphlets on such subjects, plus equipment lists (both based on Army examples, if necessary), and also suggested sending Navy personnel, particularly men under the age of thirty-five, through the Army's and Marine Corps' unconventional warfare schools, adding that the Navy should "probably set up [its own] courses."

"I know this is going to be difficult," Burke added, before naming South Vietnam as a probable future theater of Navy operations, "but our people will have to know thoroughly how to fight and live under guerrilla conditions."

Exactly one week later, the CNO's director of strategic plans, William Gentner, answered Burke's memo with a six-page response that began with a single question: "How can the Navy improve its contribution to the U.S. guerrilla/counterguerrilla warfare capability?" Gentner provided a laundry list of eight recommendations—A through H—including new shallow-water boats, new mines, a comprehensive study of naval assistance to indigenous fighters, an increased emphasis on guerrilla training, a manual for operations in restricted waters, and, last, the "establishment of a unit" that was specialized to perform "naval guerrilla/counterguerrilla operations." For this last recommendation, Gentner attached a two-page concept of employment intended to shortcut the Navy's "historically" haphazard tendency to "hurriedly improvise" such forces—a "consuming, expensive, wasteful" process, he wrote—and burden their success on the "ingenuity and adaptability" of individual soldiers, sailors, and Marines. That list could have included Peddicord, Kauffman, Turner, Miles, Halperin, Bucklew, Atcheson, Dupras, Eugene Clark, the 12 Apostles. Enough.

Imagining a unit that could coordinate and "cross-pollinate" with the CIA and the Navy's sister services, Gentner suggested that training for this unit could include elements from the Army's Special Forces and the

Navy's UDTs. Employment could range from Mobile Training Teams to "deployed trouble shooters." Ultimately, the unit would serve as a "focal point" to "channel" the Navy's guerrilla and counterguerrilla warfare efforts; a unit able to flex from limited war to the actual thing. "An appropriate name for such units," stated the last sentence of the attachment, "could be 'SEAL' units, SEAL being a contraction of SEA, AIR, LAND, and thereby, indicating an all-around, universal capability." It was the first time in official correspondence that that name was used.

7

THE DAY AFTER this memo was issued, the Taylor Commission met for the fourteenth time and discussions turned to the future of US-sponsored guerrilla warfare. Just as the failures at Makin Island and Cisterna had cooled Marine and Army leaders on their services' respective raiders, so the Bay of Pigs was about to have a similar effect on the CIA.

"I'm first to recognize that I don't think the CIA should run paramilitary operations," confessed agency director Allen Dulles. "I believe there should be a new set-up."

"It's a tough, dirty business," agreed Robert Lovett, the former secretary of defense and not exactly a proponent of unconventional military employment. "But in today's world, I don't see how we can avoid going in to guerrilla type operations . . . [and] we literally can't survive on a dual standard where we are the good boys. We can't fight these fellows successfully until we are prepared to go to the same lengths they are."

"Since we must have an effective paramilitary capability," asked the meeting's moderator, "where should this capability be established?"

Opinions differed. But no one missed the question's implicit consensus: The military was the only logical instrument for such work.

"In the Army," responded one attendee, "they have the Special Forces, which are organized with the concept that they would be the cadre put into a hostile country in time of war for the purpose of utilizing and organizing assets there."

To this, Burke responded skeptically, his deep voice stretching out each word like he always did before clipping it off at a trot: "Technically, the Americans can train people of other nations. What you cannot control is what they do with their training." For the Navy, it seems that guerrilla warfare was—even from the beginning—believed to be an art too important to be left to its clients.

Two days after this meeting, another memo landed on Burke's desk echoing the previous memo's call for SEAL units. Referencing Admiral Turner Joy's Korean War employment of "small amphibious raiding parties, made up mostly of UDT personnel, for the conduct of demolition raids," the memo envisioned the Navy's future conduct in such warfare as serving two roles: "The first," read the memo, was "a logical extension of naval warfare to restricted water areas," meaning the rivers, canals, streams, sluices where the Navy's deep-hulled ocean cutters could not venture. "The second role in which Naval forces might become involved," said the memo, and this was, by comparison, not at all logical, was in operations where "water-borne forces" would act "in support of land warfare, which," the author admitted, was "the primary responsibility of the Army." Even at its conception, the SEAL team's authors could conceive a future for it stretched beyond its birthplace.

As Burke and his crew rigged the sails of their limited-war solution, a fair and following wind began to blow.

8

Even before reading the Taylor Commission's report, the president had begun to implement the recommendations of its chairman, a man whose unconventional credentials had few equals. Polished, cerebral, aloof, and handsome, Maxwell Taylor had graduated fourth in his class at West Point, was fluent in six languages, and had not only been the first general officer to jump on D-Day, but on a separate occasion had also infiltrated some seventy-five miles behind enemy lines to gauge the offer of a disaffected Italian marshal who promised to support an Allied airborne drop in Rome. "The risks he ran," said Eisenhower afterward of Taylor's efforts—hitching rides aboard blockade-running PT boats, hiding in dusty truck beds, and escaping the continent in an Italian airplane—"were greater than I asked any other agent or emissary to undertake during the war."

Though he had seemed the perfect fit to serve as President Eisenhower's Army chief of staff, Taylor had instead become the military's most vocal captain for conventional strength, a ship that had soon crashed upon the rocks of the doctrine of massive retaliation. Thus forestalled, Taylor had adopted a caretaker's schedule—out of the office by four o'clock, tennis, a relaxing shower, an early dinner—and after four years had resigned a failure. "I think Napoleon himself could have been Chief of Staff in that period and looked like a bum," said one colonel of Taylor's performance. In response, Taylor had published *The Uncertain Trumpet*—known in Air Force circles as *The Unclean Strumpet*—a 197-page rebuttal to massive retaliation that proposed, in its place, a "strategy of Flexible Response"—essentially, a case for rebuilding the military's capacity for limited wars. As a senator, Kennedy had been so impressed with Taylor's argument that he had provided the publisher a short blurb praising the book's "unmistakable honesty," its "clarity of judgment," its "genuine sense of urgency"—attributes as president that he needed as much as he did absolution for the disaster he'd just authored.

On May 25, 1961, President Kennedy appeared before a joint session of Congress to deliver what was billed as a "Special Message on Urgent National Needs." What was so urgent? As he explained, the "entire southern half of the globe"—the "land of rising peoples," he called it—was beset by an unseen and villainous list of guerrillas, subversives, saboteurs, insurrectionists, and assassins—"assassins who [had] taken the lives of four thousand civil officers in the last twelve months in Vietnam alone." Besides his lofty commitments to reduce unemployment, to close tax loopholes, and to land a man on the moon, the rest of the speech might as well have been a blast from Taylor's *Trumpet:* For the subversive threats uncowed by nuclear deterrence, Kennedy announced a range of actions as broad as his New England accent—a modernization of the Army's divisions, new helicopters, new armored personnel carriers, new howitzers, a larger Marine Corps, a larger reserve force, additional Polaris submarines, nearly two billion dollars for military assistance programs to countries besieged by Communist insurgencies, and last (and most important for our purposes), the "rapid and substantial" expansion and "orientation of existing forces for the conduct of non-nuclear, paramilitary operations and sub-limited or unconventional wars." In addition to these "existing" components, Kennedy promised that "special forces and unconventional warfare units [would] be increased and reoriented." Not since Churchill had a head of state taken such a keen interest in the development of unconventional units.

9

ON JUNE 5, just eleven days later, Burke's office dispatched four secret pages detailing the SEAL concept to the commanders of the Atlantic and Pacific fleets, plus Naval Forces Europe. Unlike the Army's Special Forces, whose principal role was the training of indigenous fighters, Burke's message proposed for the SEAL teams a list of eleven possible tasks—A through K—the first three of which were different forms of direct action: A) "attacks on enemy shipping"; B) "demolition raids in harbors . . . and other enemy installations within reach"; and C) destruction of "lines of supply by demolition of bridges, railway lines, roads, canals, etc." The training of indigenous fighters did not appear until letter "I," an afterthought tucked between two others: the inevitable development of special operations equipment and the unlikely delivery of a backpack nuclear bomb.

Proposed as separate and distinct from the fleet's UDTs, the recruits for the two new SEAL teams (one on each coast) would, like Adam's rib, be drawn from them—ten officers and fifty enlisted men per team, all graduates of the training first conceived for the Scouts and Raiders, then modified by Kauffman for the NCDUs. The "specialized training" needed to create the SEALs, said the memo, would occur at "existing Army and Navy schools," or could "be added to the present UDT curriculum, as required."

Before long, rumors of a naval commando unit began to hover so thickly above the UDTs that many took the clouds for smoke of their own making. In the coming years, two UDT officers—Lieutenant Commander Bill Hamilton and Lieutenant Junior Grade Roy Boehm—would enlist the same ghost author to pen two self-congratulatory books insisting that it was Hamilton's idea, and then Hamilton's letter, that awoke Burke's office to the need for such a unit. To bring the SEALs to life, he and Boehm would claim to have waged a two-man war against a Navy bureaucracy hostile to anything new. Colorful and profane—mostly profane—Boehm's book, *First SEAL,* would describe a pile of dubious interactions with mostly foolish superiors in which every argument would end the way we all wish they did. In his telling, he would arrive at the idea of "Sea Warriors," and commandos "for all seasons," by conversing with a gray-bearded Chinese holy man at the end of World War II, then by reading Confucius, Mao Tse-tung, Che Guevara, and Mary Miles—impressive, since Miles's book would not be published until 1967.

Not to diminish the importance of Kennedy's commando interest, or the efforts of individual frogmen to escape their sandy confines, the establishment of the SEAL teams would require far more than either to lever the weight of the Navy's legendary bureaucracy into concurrence. It would require another six months of CNO-level conversations, meetings, and memoranda to allocate funding, to carve out basing, to hammer out organizational plans and chains of command; to purchase commercial watercraft and fund new research for silent motors; to resurrect six mothballed APDs from retirement; to study the country of South Vietnam, and there to embark on a type of riverine warfare, said one memo, that the Navy had not "seriously attacked . . . since the war between the states." At the end of that six months, the Navy would quietly, and without any ceremony, commission SEAL Team ONE on Coronado Island in San Diego, and SEAL Team TWO at Little Creek in Virginia Beach. Alas, the man most responsible for their creation would, in the end, not have the pleasure of commanding them.

10

On August 1, 1961, more than two months after Kennedy's speech and four months until SEAL Team ONE and TWO's commissioning, Arleigh Burke presented himself before a Naval Academy audience, this time to relinquish command for good. On the left breast of his white uniform he wore just one row of medals, almost every one of them earned in combat. After the usual speeches and the sharp reports of a nineteen-gun salute, Burke turned to the honor guard and gave his final order: "Will you please have my flag hauled down." As he said it, his thickening voice broke.

In the 2,176 days that he served as CNO—the longest term in history by almost two years, and to this day not matched—Burke stretched the Navy's combat reach from the floors of the ocean to the edges of the atmosphere. As Maxwell Taylor's failure had shown, this achievement was anything but inevitable. Confronted by Eisenhower's tightening military expenditures, Burke had defied expectations and tacked the Navy toward every breach left by a rival service: He had challenged the Air Force's hegemony on ballistic missiles by placing them on submarines; he had challenged the Army's lunge for preeminence in limited wars by rushing Marines ashore in Lebanon; he had even challenged the CIA's command and control at the Bay of Pigs. Conventional in everything but his drive and his foresight, Burke had nevertheless propelled the Navy into its most unconventional undertaking by drawing from his own inclinations for the offensive, by instinctively seeking to hit the enemy in the flanks, and by his career-long association with men like Mountbatten, Drysdale, Bucklew, and Miles—to whose book, *A Different Kind of War,* he would write the foreword. To navigate the world's mud-colored backwaters, Burke had driven his staff to funnel the Navy's parallel and tributary legacies of beach-marking Scouts and Raiders, guerrilla-running Rogers, and bridge-busting UDTs into a single permanent unit. Though the task of final approval ultimately would fall to Burke's successor, Admiral "Gorgeous George" Anderson, the latter's impression on the SEAL teams would sink not much deeper than his rubber stamp.

Less concerned with the pursuit of new weapons and tactics than his predecessor, Anderson would instead show more interest in his fleet-wide "sermons" on foul language, drunkenness, and church attendance, and for dispatching the fleet's corpsmen ahead of his ships to "feed" portside prostitutes with penicillin. Worried about the SEALs' potential to drain his sailors from his ships, yet "besieged" by President Kennedy's "inquiries" on the Navy's progress in the realm of counterinsurgency, Anderson would actually attempt a half measure to solve both problems—essentially a recycling of the UDT/Marine Recon partnership that would have short-circuited Burke's concept with a unit whose area of expertise would have ended where the surf did. It would also have been an idea that assumed that the Marine Corps would have gladly taken up again the cross of commando raiding, a cause it might have championed had it not come from the organization that was its parent. In the end, despite Anderson's misgivings, Burke's plans would prove too tight to untangle.

When his retirement ceremony ended, Burke excused himself and returned to the reception wearing a civilian's suit and tie. Asked by a reporter what he considered his most important achievement—his six years as CNO? his role in the Revolt of the Admirals? his emphasis on strategic planning?—Burke considered the question not at all. "None of those," he snapped. "It was the battles." Though he could not see his own legacy—none of us can—we might add this to his epitaph: Just like his work on Mitscher's staff, Burke's greatest achievement was preparing the Navy for the battles it had not yet fought.

A decade later, an interviewer for the Navy's Oral History program would sit down with Burke and ask a question: "These days guerrilla warfare is a fairly new and accepted technique, isn't it?"

"Yes," replied Burke. "Guerrilla warfare is fairly new. It's about 5,000 years old. Exactly the same thing . . . We used it even in the Civil War and we've used it in most wars, but we've got in the habit of using tanks and frontal attack and big armies. Both World War I and II, we forgot the use of guerrilla warfare, because we didn't contribute much to [it]. The other nations, European nations, did but we did not."

"It's reborn—for us?" questioned the interviewer further.

"Reborn," Burke snapped. "Every new group that comes into office has got to re-invent the wheel and find all the wonderful things they can do."

Under Burke, the Navy reinvented this wheel for the last time.

Part 4

EXIGENCY

Chapter 10

Kennedy's Army of Gladiators and the Counterinsurgency That Blunted Their Swords, Then Cleared the Way for Another Contender

THE ELECTION OF 1960 initiated for President-elect John F. Kennedy a seventy-two-day-long transition to power. In that time, he would fly some 15,000 airline miles between Boston, Central Texas, Palm Beach, New York City, and Washington, D.C.; at every stop he would submit himself to a whirlwind of meetings with suit-wearing applicants for every executive department—with Eisenhower, on his way out; with Nixon, just defeated; with directors Allen Dulles and J. Edgar Hoover; with labor leaders and civil rights leaders; with Billy Graham; with all the generals and admirals of the Joint Chiefs of Staff. These last were a blur of starred shoulder boards and a fruit salad's worth of chest ribbons, their briefings a horror show of maps dotted with bombers and secret silos.

Given that Kennedy was not a soldier in World War II but a sailor, one could have reasonably guessed that his preferences for containing Communism would have rested on all the modern tools of his former service—the aircraft carriers, fighter jets, Polaris submarines—except that he hadn't been that kind of sailor. As the skipper of a thirteen-man patrol torpedo boat, his mission had been to ply the South Pacific's waters in search of big-deck Japanese cruisers and destroyers, then hit them at night and disappear into the black. Since then, a standoff between the nuclear powers had prevented a World War III but had done nothing to prevent the thousands of miniature wars launched by just the sort of midnight bushwhackers Kennedy himself had been. In China, Cuba, Greece, Malaya, Hungary, Angola, the Congo, Laos, especially in South Vietnam, guerrillas—those "scavengers of revolution," one of Kennedy's advisors would call them—had not only bitten at the heels of the world's shakiest regimes but in some cases had completely knocked out their knees.

Propelled by Maxwell Taylor's theory of flexible response, Kennedy knew that to prevent such collapses he needed a military that could descend beneath the canopy of nuclear deterrence and suck into the mud. To the string of advisors who breached his sanctum, he unleashed a string of questions: "What would you do about Berlin?" he would ask; "What does a division look like?" During the transition, Eisenhower's staffers passed along a potential plan of action for Vietnam prepared by Colonel Edward Lansdale, the architect of victory over the Huk insurgency in the Philippines—a victory won by the double envelopment of guerrilla hunting and nation building. Able to consume some twelve hundred words a minute, and demolish five or six newspapers before 8 A.M., Kennedy devoured the report, then invited Lansdale for a private presentation. A hawkish Democrat who believed in government's power to win wars against both Communists and poverty, Kennedy was transfixed by Lansdale's mobilization of both the scowl and the smile. In short order, Kennedy was tearing through all the "classic texts" on guerrilla warfare, Mao Tse-tung and Che Guevara. He even quizzed the Army's generals on them. Their responses were "skeptical," even "sullen"; "too grand for these mean little messes," an aide recalled. In short order, Kennedy himself would be quoting Mao's most famous maxim from memory—Guerrillas are like fish, and the people are the water in which the fish swim—and "personally [supervising] the selection" of new guerrilla warfare equipment: steel-soled sneakers to withstand a sharpened bamboo puncture; field radios light enough for a malnourished guerrilla to carry; and a new, lightweight jungle rifle called the M16. "Far more than any of his generals or even [his secretary of defense]," remembered an advisor, the president would personally provide the leadership necessary to push the military into—Kennedy's phrase—"this new and ancient kind of warfare."

Carrying gasoline to the flame would be Kennedy's brother and attorney general, Robert, who would enthusiastically recommend to the president the recently released movie *Spartacus,* which told the almost-victorious tale of an escaped gladiator who raised a slave army and took on Rome. Arriving at the theater at 8:24 P.M.—notably with the under secretary of the Navy, who had an extra ticket—Kennedy paused briefly for a cup of coffee with the theater manager, who stopped the movie during the opening credits to restart it for the president. Almost three and a half hours later, Kennedy—along with the rest of the audience—

would marvel as Kirk Douglas cradled the body of his friend and declared, "He'll come back. He'll come back and he'll be millions."

But where to find more gladiators who could turn the third world's slaves into an army? As Kennedy would quickly learn, only one unit in Eisenhower's inventory had even considered such a mission—the US Army's Special Forces, guerrilla warfare experts who just so happened to be the closest thing left to American gladiators. What Kennedy did not consider—no one did—is how the mission of training peasants would blunt them and leave vacant their arena for another contender to fill the lists.

2

ESTABLISHED IN 1952, the Special Forces had been intended to replicate the experiences of its founder and first commander, former OSS operative Colonel Aaron Bank. In 1944, as a forty-one-year-old Jedburgh, he had dropped into France and led resistance fighters, then in 1945—as improbable as it sounds—had almost led an Operational Group of German POWs into the Alps on a mission to capture Hitler. Guided by these examples, Bank and his successors had erected an organization to match their mission: 2,000 airborne-qualified soldiers spread across three forward-staged battalion-sized groups—one in Okinawa, one in Germany, and one at Fort Bragg in North Carolina—all ready at a moment's notice to drop into an enemy country and lead a ready band of resistance fighters. To physically create these groups, a Special Warfare Center had been hacked out of a remote corner of Fort Bragg in the mid-1950s, and volunteers had been recruited—plenty of former Rangers, "old jockstrap commando-types"; no first enlistments or second lieutenants permitted to apply—and ushered through a three-month course in guerrilla warfare with a staggering 90 percent dropout rate. This was followed by language instruction and individual courses in one of four specialties—weapons, demolition, radio communication, and longest of all, medicine. The pipeline culminated with a multiweek exercise in which candidates infiltrated a notional enemy country, linked up with a band of dissidents (other candidates), set up a hinterland base camp, imparted their individual specialties, then led their guerrillas on a series of raids and ambushes, all while avoiding an aggressor force of local deputies, National Guardsmen, and state police. Upon graduation, Special Forces soldiers were split into twelve-man A-Detachments, or A-Teams, which mostly cross-trained with the world's elite units or played the part they had prepared for: leading bands of fifty or so foreign-tongued soldiers in midnight maneuvers against the US Army's conventional divisions, notionally blowing bridges, wrecking rail lines, raiding command posts.

Inspired by their exotic assignments and convinced of their own uniqueness, the men of Special Forces had adopted an unapproved uniform appendage as distinct as they believed themselves to be: a lopsided green beret. In 1956, angry after his headquarters had been raided and three of the four tires stolen from his personal jeep, Fort Bragg commandant General Paul Adams, former executive officer of the Devil's Brigade, went on to forbid the wearing of the beret as an offense of court-martial proportions. When a beret with a general's stars had been good-humoredly placed on his head during a briefing, he had "snatched it off," thrown it across the room, and stomped out. The men of Special Forces had responded predictably—wearing them anyway, especially overseas. Green berets not being a readily available item, the men had shelled out their personal dollars to local tailors, resulting in a variety of "shades and textures." The German version laid as flat as a pancake; rain often shrank them to a wearer's scalp or dripped dye onto a wearer's face. The most reliable berets were shipped in from Dorothea Knitting Mills in Canada; the color—Dorothea's Rifle Green—reportedly being the same shade worn by Rogers' Rangers, the prototype of all American raiders. And these the Special Forces most assuredly were.

Never intended to replace the Rangers, the Special Forces, with their early commitment to the guerrilla warfare legacies of various OSS units—the Jedburghs, the Operational Groups, and the Kachin Rangers in Burma—had nevertheless provided Army planners with a theoretical substitute: a promise of indigenous fighters for behind-the-lines reconnaissance, sabotage, raids, and ambushes. This promise was premised on one obvious-yet-essential ingredient: the availability of guerrillas. The problem: There were none. Since World War II, spy hunters in every Communist country on the globe had hounded down and choked off just about every throat with the courage to volunteer for such an enterprise—a fact made plain by the three failed attempts of UN Partisan Command to drop teams into North Korea to raise guerrillas, attempts that had resulted in the disappearance of all 175 UN operatives.

Faced with a shifting battlefield, the Special Forces had shifted too and adopted a peacetime role, that of Army Jesuits—missionary instructors to host-nation regulars and border police. Their scriptures: a menu of courses, everything from close-order drill to close-quarters killing. This mission had yielded a variety of assignments running the entire length of importance. On the low end, there had been basic training for Ethiopian recruits; airborne training for a crack squad of Jordanian soldiers that turned out to be the Jordanian national soccer team; even jump training for an 800-man Saudi Arabian airborne battalion whose questionable cotton parachutes succeeded in saving the lives of 797 jumpers. On the more important end, there had been Ranger training for Royal Thai soldiers (ironic since the down payment for the creation of the Army's Special Forces had been paid with the proceeds of the Army Rangers' disbandment); a yearlong course of instruction for the first fifty-eight members of the Luc Luong Dac Biet, or LLDB, South Vietnam's Special Forces; and the establishment of three separate training centers for the creation of sixty South Vietnamese Ranger companies, forty-five more than the US Army had disbanded during the Korean War.

The most ambitious effort had been in Laos. Code-named White Star and commanded by a former World War II–era Ranger, Colonel Arthur "Bull" Simons, the first A-Teams to deploy there had been smuggled into the country wearing slacks and golf shirts on a nondescript CIA plane. After changing into their jungle greens and the jaunty wide-brimmed hats of Australian bushmen, the A-Teams had then provided to their Laotian paratroopers the usual months-long menu of training, but once finished they had this time led their students on a series of actions against the Laotian Communists: first, to capture a critical road junction, then a river assault—battlefield miracles if one considers the Laotian officers' oft-reported tendency for drunkenness at the time, and the cascading effect this had on what was described as the Laotian soldiers' "low fighting spirit." Frustrated by this partnership, Colonel Simons had proposed a new recruiting pool: the hardy mountain tribesmen, a people indifferent to the Laotian government, but whose isolation made them vulnerable to Communist petitions. To win the tribesmen's favor, Simons had presented his soldiers like suitors, ready to attend to any tribal need: providing basic medical care; setting up cooperative trading markets; even dismantling an Army truck, helicoptering it over the mountain jungles, and reassembling it as a rice mill. Before long, sixty Special Forces advisors had smiled, courted, and bribed 600 illiterate tribesmen into their own guerrilla army, and moreover had denied them to the enemy. There was a name for this kind of war: counterinsurgency.

For President-elect Kennedy, here was exactly the sort of mission that matched the strategy he'd been looking for, and equally important, here was the unit that could carry it out. After a month and a half of meetings and questions in the days leading up to his inauguration, he was sure that the grounds around the Special Warfare Center at Fort Bragg possessed a potential for growing something far richer than its current crop. All he needed was someone with the foresight to grow this nursery of guerrilla advisors into something the US military had never had: a graduate school of counterinsurgency. For a recommendation on who this man should be, Kennedy turned to his military aide, Major General Ted Clifton, who in turn suggested a personal friend, a classmate since West Point and an "oddball" by Army standards: Colonel Bill Yarborough. His appointment was set for January 23, 1961, just three days after Kennedy's scheduled inauguration. No appointment would so shape the future character of Special Forces as this.

3

WHISKING OVER SANDHILLS, through sheets of longleaf pine, Yarborough arrived at Fort Bragg in Fayetteville, North Carolina, by a path that wound him to a remote pocket of the base at the intersection of two lonely roads—Reilly and Ardennes—and stopped at a low rise known as Smoke Bomb Hill. At the change of command ceremony, his soldiers observed him as he was: average size, chest out, shoulders back; a rooster of a man, his narrowed eyes and pursed lips locked into a stoic's gaze as revealing as a Roman bust. Son of an Army colonel, married to an Army brat, with a son on his way to an Army commission and two daughters on their way to Army husbands, Yarborough was the very picture of Army tradition. Forty-eight years old now, in pressed slacks and bloused boots, with no prior experience in Special Forces, nothing on the surface seemed to indicate anything besides a conventional background and a preference for more of the same. But that was just the surface. Beneath his obvious soldierly bearing was hidden an ambition for a military organization as unconventional as had ever existed.

Born into a military family and predictably funneled into a West Point education, where his only step out of formation seems to have been as a cartoonist on the school newspaper, Yarborough's early Army career was, in fact, a litany of nonconformities. Four years with the Philippine Scouts, one of the most unconventional assignments in the US Army. Two years as a Parachute Test Officer, during which his creativity had burst open as wide as the thing he was testing. This had manifested

Brigadier General William P. Yarborough briefing
the new organization at the Army's Special Warfare Center.

in everything from redesigning the paratroopers' pants and boots to promoting his untested unit by acting as a stunt double for a Hollywood movie—for which he was afterward nicknamed "Showbiz"—and in creating a silver badge that looked like an ice cream cone–shaped parachute flexed with angel wings that was ultimately adopted as the symbol for the entire Airborne. In World War II, Yarborough survived an incomparable five combat jumps, five campaigns, two combat commands (one of which had fought alongside Darby's Rangers at Cisterna and later earned a Presidential Unit Citation), and one crash landing. And except for a brief sidelining resulting from an outburst against his division commander Matthew Ridgway, it was an almost unblemished record of direct action, a record with honors so compelling that any normal soldier would have coveted its repetition. Yarborough wasn't normal.

The next fifteen years for Yarborough was a period of learning and, inevitably, of adaptation. Forced to shed his paratrooper past for a constabulary role as the provost marshal of Vienna, he learned by trial and error how to command a multinational force of Americans, Brits, French, and Russians; how to cut down on occupational abuses—graft, theft, arson, rape, and murder; how to short-circuit interservice arguments by insisting that his military police jeeps carry representatives from every nation. He called them "4-power jeeps." As a postwar student at both the US and British war colleges, then as a faculty member at the US Army's, Yarborough studied and thought deeply about the US military's coming role in what he would call "the warm edges of the Cold War." While preparing a paper on guerrilla warfare, he visited Fort Bragg for a briefing on the Special Forces but was not convinced. Any attempt to mobilize partisans, he concluded, would be as impactful as those of the Korean War partisans. In 1956, Yarborough accepted a yearlong posting as the deputy chief of the US military's advisory mission in Cambodia. To learn the territory and its challenges, he braved monsoon rains and jungle trails to trek his way between remote frontier outposts. In the course of inspecting fortifications—hardly more than Stone Age fences of sharpened stakes—he discovered something he did not expect to: the individual hardiness of the Cambodian, just the right material to "make superb irregular warfare soldiers." In 1958, Yarborough took command of a counterintelligence group in Stuttgart, Germany, the operational front rank of the Cold War, and for two years ran a network of counterintelligence teams throughout Europe—identifying Communist cells and chasing spies, a pale reflection of Soviet measures—measures, he knew, that had long since made it impossible to launch an OSS-type resistance mission in Eastern Europe that resulted in anything but suicide.

When unexpectedly ordered to return to the United States to take command of the Army's Special Warfare Center, essentially a training billet, Yarborough was, as he would confess, "far from pleased." It was, according to many of his Army peers, a "dead-end unit," an adolescent organization whose size had outpaced its maturity; a teenager, in conflict with itself. Striding over a carpet of North Carolina pine needles to inspect his new dominion, however, it did not take long for Yarborough to discover the potential value of the ground that was passing beneath his feet. Long gone were the old ghost town "firetraps" and in their place a headquarters, a library, several barracks, a mess hall, language classrooms, and beyond all these, numerous drop zones, rappel towers, rifle ranges, and gear lockers with everything from skis to scuba tanks. With a little imagination, here was both the well and the potential refinery for turning the world's raw, untapped masses into the armies of anti-Communists for which every soldier in the US Army knew the president was now clamoring. Whatever were Yarborough's initial misgivings, it was an invigorating demand. And Yarborough had more than a little imagination.

4

Yarborough's first action as commander of the Special Warfare Center and head trainer of Special Forces was to initiate a top-to-bottom review of training and curriculum—an effort to match his men with their mission. From his experience in counterintelligence, he knew that guerrilla bodies were not simply milling around behind the Iron Curtain waiting for American heads to lead them. If the United States wanted to mobilize the kinds of indigenous populations he had met in Cambodia, then the Special Forces would need to earn their loyalties. Before Yarborough had been at Fort Bragg a month, Special Forces candidates were learning Mao's rules of conduct, reading Edgar Snow's book *Red Star Over China*—a favorite of Marine Raider Evans Carlson—and receiving classes in everything from well digging to field irrigation, all the comprehensive keys to victory learned by the British in Malaya and ignored by the French in Vietnam and Algeria. Those examples were studied too. Under Yarborough, the archetype for Special Forces soldiers grew from that of Rogers' Rangers and OSS-led guerrillas to a laundry list of examples: Francis Marion and John Hunt Morgan; Sitting Bull and Geronimo; T. E. Lawrence and Orde Wingate; even Fidel Castro and Ho Chi Minh.

To educate his soldiers in what seemed like the graduate level of warfare, Yarborough began hosting renowned authorities in psychology, history, and anthropology, along with guerrilla warfare experts like Roger Hilsman, a White House advisor and veteran of Merrill's Marauders and OSS Detachment 101, and even Air Force General Edward Lansdale, the victor over the Huks in the Philippines who was the American oracle on counterinsurgency. Despite spasms of annoyance on the part of his superiors, he repeatedly hosted Bernard Fall, the left-leaning author of *Street Without Joy,* a firsthand account of the French collapse in Vietnam. In his presentation—"Guerrilla Warfare and Subversion"—Dr. J. K. Zawodny, the behavioral scientist and veteran of the Polish underground, ponderously explained the various motivations of partisans as everything from their political beliefs to their community status, the only bright spot in his lecture being one guerrilla fighter's reason: "When I mention my name, girls' pants drop off by themselves." Before long, the Special Warfare Center began to feel less like a commando course and more like a college campus, complete with courses in bridge building, sanitation, animal husbandry, blacksmithing, crop raising, pigpen construction, swine inoculation, leaflet creation, field irrigation, seed planting, and rice cultivation.

Not all of Yarborough's staff approved of the changes, particularly, said Yarborough, the "old jockstrap commandos, the Ranger types"—"gallant bloodletters" and "fighting machines" to be sure, but men who were "anything but diplomats, and rejected any suggestion that they ought to be." They were, he continued, men devoid of the "more humane qualities . . . compassion, pity, and mercy," men who bristled at the idea of lying on their bellies to teach an illiterate tribesman how to aim a rifle. In the nine years since the establishment of the Special Forces, these Martin Watson–sized personalities had cultivated a culture of "macho fun"—parties, booze, women, even "other guys' wives"; common adjuncts to the confidence required for a mission as daring as the behind-the-lines raid. The problem, a sympathetic Special Forces officer would later write, is that "being 'macho' is the opposite of having concern for other people and realizing the need for their support." Yarborough, in spite of his career of airborne assault, likewise did not envision the Special Forces soldier as "a direct combat instrument," but as a "catalyst who could gather around him those whom he could then train and lend help to lead." To convert his men to this new philosophy of warfare—"my religion," he would one day call it—in which the battle's objective was not the destruction of an enemy's army but the winning of indigenous "minds and sympathies," Yarborough enjoined every one of his officers above the rank of captain to accompany him into the pine barrens for what he called his "talk in the woods."

"As long as I'm in charge of Special Forces," he would say, "there will be no womanizing, no drunkenness, no wild parties, no adultery. There'll be no troublemakers. No wild men . . . that stuff is out. There will be moral standards . . . disciplinary standards . . . appearance standards." "The rules are going to change," he would promise portentously. "There will be a new start."

5

On April 22, on the other side of the world, the Pathet Lao shelled and overran a Special Forces–led Laotian battalion. In the battle, they captured thirty-eight-year-old advisor Captain Walter H. Moon and scattered his three American enlisted men—one into an attempted river escape (he was caught later); and two into an armored car flight, both ambushed and killed, one in a downpour of stick grenades and the other shot through the neck while manning a machine gun. After being wounded in the head and chest during his second escape attempt, Moon was judged by his captors mentally "unbalanced," and executed. It was the kind of catastrophe that would have focused the nation's attention on US guerrilla warfare efforts, except that it was already focused on those efforts, but in Cuba.

While Moon and his men were fighting for their lives, former Special Forces officer Grayston Lynch and his UDT-trained frogmen were still fishing the watery margins of the Bay of Pigs in search of any brigade survivors. Days later, the Taylor Commission convened and went on to topple two long-held American Cold War fantasies: first, that the CIA had sufficient capacity to run its own guerrilla war, and second, that an overt external invasion was a starting pistol for a popular uprising. The corollaries were obvious: If the Kennedy administration wanted an uprising of freedom-seeking indigenous peoples, it would have to earn them the hard way—just like Colonel Simon and his men were doing with the mountain tribes in Laos. And there was only one entity that could do that.

In the summer of 1961, Yarborough was besieged by two events: The first was the president's impending visit to Fort Bragg, a chance that planners had not had for eight years to showcase the Army's limited-war flexibility, everything from an airborne corps to an A-Team. In anticipation, Yarborough and his men had taken great effort to prepare a dress rehearsal—essentially a walking tour of the center's grounds with stations to highlight both the Special Forces soldiers' commando capabilities and their new skills in counterinsurgency. The second event was neither planned nor comparable to anything Yarborough had ever experienced.

On the rain-pelted morning of June 28, while approaching a traffic circle near Fort Bragg's post exchange, Yarborough's twenty-one-year-old daughter, Norma, accidentally drove her car into the path of an Army wrecker, killing her just three days before her scheduled wedding to a young lieutenant at the Fort Bragg chapel. Yarborough's initial reaction to the tragedy was to remove every trace of memory from his sight—the wedding dress, the pile of unopened presents. Within twenty-four hours, all traces of his daughter had been removed from the house, and every future mention of her would be met with stony silence.

Weeks after the tragedy, Yarborough—per the demands of his position—was forced to cinch down his grief in order to preview his walking tour demonstration to General Earle G. Wheeler, the Army's chief of staff, who noted one problem: Kennedy's back was in no shape for a walking tour, the lingering result of a collision with a Japanese destroyer in 1943 that had killed two of his men and sliced his PT boat in half. Over the next several months, Yarborough would grieve for his daughter and overhaul his demonstration—a distraction as welcome as any he had known. At one point, he was contacted by his friend Major General Ted Clifton, the White House military advisor, who suggested an addition to Yarborough's demonstration that was a blatant violation of a standing Army injunction: "I think the President would like to see your guys in their green berets."

6

LANDING AT POPE AIR FORCE BASE on the bright blue day of October 12, Kennedy descended the steps of a four-engine Air Force turboprop and took the rear seat of a white Lincoln convertible. Impeccable in his dark blue suit and sunglasses, he was slow-rolled across the airfield until every horizon was filled with concrete tarmac and the North Carolina pine of the Army's adjacent property of Fort Bragg. There, arrayed before him, stood the entire 82nd Airborne Division—10,268 men, all grouped into companies: the paratroopers' bayoneted rifles slung over their shoulders, some of their helmets twined with leaves; one whole company set off in arctic white parkas, their skis in hand, snowshoes tied to their packs. At the drop-zone demonstration, Kennedy and his entourage—bemedaled Joint Chiefs, cabinet secretaries, and the entire White House press corps—sat cross-legged in bleachers, some craning through binoculars and marveling at a 500-pound napalm blast followed by a C-130 cargo plane that dropped a series of howitzers and equipment, and then the most improbable: an 18,000-pound bulldozer whose six separate 100-foot-wide parachutes "blossomed like giant flowers." A newscaster distinguished the Airborne Division by describing its unique ability to deploy at a moment's notice, to land in an enemy's backyard—the perfect instrument to "snuff out a brush-fire war"; the perfect nickname for which "might very well be 'the Fire Brigade.'" Even for the military chiefs, it was an impressive demonstration, and yet not what the president had come for. Fort Bragg's star attraction still remained to be seen.

Relocated to Fort Bragg's Rod and Gun Club, the president and his entourage occupied another bank of shaded bleachers, this time overlooking a dirt beach and a lagoon reservoir—dredged deep enough for amphibious vehicles and scuba divers for just this occasion. Once seated, the audience was treated to a slow-rolling, Rose Bowl–style parade of floats, Yarborough's solution to the president's back problems—a series of twelve-ton flatbed trailers. Backdropped with hand-painted billboards and palm trees, and staged with awkwardly frozen, living role players, each diorama highlighted another aspect of the Special Warfare Center's range: things like providing security to indigenous peoples, isolating guerrilla bands, destroying them, and training local security forces. One trailer presented a scene in which several soldiers worked a printing press, then stuffed the resulting propaganda leaflets into artillery shells for dynamic distribution. The last flatbed was a veritable forest of multicolored flags and a simulated classroom of seated students from Africa, Latin America, Southeast Asia, and Europe. Written on every billboard but the last was the word of the hour: counterinsurgency.

When the final truck had passed, the audience was treated to a series of demonstrations: a rubber boat insertion of wetsuited divers; a daisy chain of tree-line explosions; a soldier with a .45-caliber pistol against a string of red, head-sized water balloons; even the catching and skinning of a live snake. Then came a series of paired judo encounters in which every assailant was flipped into the dirt, kicked, and pounded with fists. On the 100-foot Ranger-emblazoned rappel tower came a litany of ascents and descents, the most complicated being the last, in which two rappellers slowly lowered a simulated casualty strapped to a stretcher. Next all eyes snapped back to the lagoon, where a soldier strapped to a harness of over-the-shoulder silver tubes and aluminum tanks filled with hydrogen peroxide rocketed free of his boat platform, improbably hovered fifteen feet above the water, and in a fogbank of mist and mystery zoomed seventy-five yards to shore, flared into a dust cloud, and touched down as lightly as he had lifted. After a short walk to demonstrate the jet pack's manageable 125-pound weight, the rocketeer turned to the president and crisply saluted. It had been a demonstration with no rival, much like the men who had presented it—many of whom now wore a type of headgear heretofore unseen by most in the US military.

As soon as the demonstration ended, the president took off his sunglasses and moved to the edge of the bleachers. Striding toward him was Yarborough, who snapped his right hand to the edge of his green beret, then extended it to the president. After shaking hands, Yarborough introduced Kennedy to a twelve-man A-Team, their packs camouflaged with leaves, their heads topped with a "grand variety" of berets of various shades, textures, and shapes.

"Those are nice," the president said casually, still smiling, pointing the sunglasses in his hand to Yarborough's cover. "How do you like the green beret?"

"They're fine, sir," Yarborough replied, straight-faced, almost stern, ignoring the shutter clicks of the nearby photographer. "We've wanted them a long time." He then added that, per Army regulations, the beret was "not authorized."

"It is now," Kennedy replied casually.

Later that day, the president scratched down a note to Yarborough. "My congratulations to you personally for your part in the presentation today," he began. "The challenge of this old but new form of operations is a real one. I know that you and the members of your command will carry on for us and the free world in a manner which is both worthy and inspiring. I am sure that the green beret will be a mark of distinction in the trying times ahead."

The impact of the president's note was immediate: The Army's uniform barons lifted their ban and shortly afterward published guidance on the newly approved beret's exact shape, shade, and "angle of droop," making it so identifiable with the institution that the Special Forces were ever after also known as the Green Berets. More important, they were now simply known.

Yarborough talks with President John F. Kennedy following the special warfare demonstration at Fort Bragg on October 12, 1961.

"In those palmy days," a *Time* magazine reporter would write, "the Green Berets were the darlings of the New Frontier." No other entity would so remind the Kennedy administration's members of themselves—themselves being "the damndest bunch of boy commandos," Adlai Stevenson would call them. In the coming year, many more of Kennedy's aides would make the pilgrimage to Fort Bragg to watch Yarborough's exhibition, a performance so fantastic that they would come to call it "Disneyland." Demand would force Yarborough to dedicate an entire detachment to its production and increase its showings to five times a month. Before long, Robert Kennedy—the most swaggering boy commando of them all, a man who kept a green beret on his desk—would even be "importing" a scaled-down version of this demonstration to the family's weekend retreat in Hyannis Port. There, guests would be entertained by a tree-swinging, barricade-jumping spectacle so intense that Sargent Shriver, Kennedy's brother-in-law and the founder of the Peace Corps, would protest its potentially damaging influence on the children. Conventional soldiers, whose luster was dimmed by this comparison, groused about Camelot's preferences, slurring the Green Berets as "Jacqueline Kennedy's Own Rifles." But this was more than just preference; this was patronage.

Even after the Cuban Missile Crisis, a victory won by the deterrent power of nuclear stockpiles, Kennedy's interest in the Special Forces—his "pride," an aide would describe them—would never waver. In a meeting with Maxwell Taylor to discuss the nuances of limited war, Robert Kennedy would act as the megaphone to his brother's interest: "Why can't we just make the entire Army into Special Forces?" This attitude had benefits too: Over the next two years, Yarborough would have direct telephone access to White House staffers—"my great advantage," he would call it, and leverage he would never hesitate to apply when stymied by conventional Army resistance. In return, Yarborough provided the president with what one reporter called a "new American breed" of soldier; "uncommon men . . . physical specimens . . . intellectual Ph.D.s swinging from trees, speaking Russian and Chinese, eating snake meat"; elite specialists "trained to train local partisans in guerrilla warfare, prepared to perform a wide range of civilian" projects. In short, here finally were the men who could—like Spartacus's gladiators—transform slaves into soldiers for freedom.

What Kennedy did not consider—what no one did—was how the mission of counterinsurgency in Vietnam would transform the gladiators themselves.

7

IN FEBRUARY 1962, Kennedy authorized a series of actions that catapulted the Special Forces to the forefront of US strategy. Among these were the establishment of Military Assistance Command Vietnam, or MACV, and the increasing of American troops in that country from roughly 700 to almost 5,000, with a mandate to act as advisors to the 170,000-man Army of the Republic of Vietnam, or ARVN. So close was this mission to what Yarborough's men were already doing that when a *Time* reporter wrote his story on MACV, he opened with a description of the Special Forces and titled the article "To Liberate from Oppression," the English translation of the Latin motto *De Oppresso Liber* placed beneath the badge of blade and crossed arrows sewn onto every green beret. Having positioned the Special Forces as the keystone to the entire gray endeavor, it was only a matter of time before that keystone took a hit.

Within weeks of Kennedy's actions, an encampment of thirty-one blue-uniformed Catholic youth volunteers and four Green Beret advisors near Danang were roused by a nighttime "rustling in the saw grass," followed by the back-and-forth sounds of a dog's bark, a cock's crow, then the "tap of a bamboo tocsin." They were surrounded. Out of the dark rushed five guerrillas who were immediately shot down, then five from another direction, a terrible routine that persisted until dawn, when Sergeant James "Kimo" Gabriel, a twenty-four-year-old native Hawaiian—the oldest of nine children and about to be a father himself, already shot in the arm and stomach—gripped his radio handset and transmitted a final message: "Under heavy attack from all sides. Completely encircled by enemy. Ammunition expended. We are being overrun." By the time a rescue force arrived from Danang, all four Americans had been marched off into captivity. When Gabriel and another badly wounded Green Beret comrade had fallen behind, both were shot in the head by one of their own indigenous fighters, a defector, their bodies found stacked one atop the other.

Kennedy's next insinuation of the Special Forces was even more explicit. Less than a week after Air Force Globemasters started delivering the first crop of fresh troops to Saigon's sweltering airfield, a Special Forces A-Team, detachment A-113, arrived at the 400-person village of Buon Enao to break ground on the flagship camp of an experimental program called the Civilian Irregular Defense Group, or CIDG. Controlled and funded by the CIA—"you report to no other military or civilian officials unless it suits your purposes," a CIA briefer had told the men at a luxurious villa near Saigon—the Buon Enao experiment was intended to determine the likelihood of mobilizing not South Vietnam's 170,000 regular soldiers, who were the responsibility of conventional MACV troops, but instead the roughly 700,000 backcountry tribesmen known as Montagnards, French for "mountain people." "Old in the days of Julius Caesar," said an Army education video of Montagnard villages, the thirty or so barefoot tribes that still lived in stilt-and-thatch longhouses in hills and mountains so misty, so remote, that they were virtually inaccessible except by helicopter. There, temperatures could brush the thirties; there, chanting village sorcerers still conjured spirit guidance through elaborate sacrificial offerings of rice wine beer. Called Moi by their lowland countrymen, a word variously translated as "savage" or "worthless savage," and despised for their backwardness and past friendship with the hated French, it was hoped that an alliance with the Montagnards—"Yards" to the Green Berets—could solve two strategic problems. Given their position athwart the literal spine of the Central Highlands, it was hoped that an inkblot trail of fortified Montagnard camps and fighters might act as something of a breakwater against overland infiltration from Cambodia and Laos. Second, if such camps could be built, then the Montagnards would cease to be an all-too-ready resource pool for Communist supplies and recruits.

Disappointed that their year of team training would be wasted on a six-month deployment to Vietnam and not the real war zone in Laos, when the Green Berets arrived at Buon Enao they nevertheless unpacked the first plank of counterinsurgency strategy: securing the population. To do this, they constructed a rectangular stockade, underground shelters for mortar attacks, identification checkpoints, and finally a series of bamboo fences whose gaps were studded with sharpened pungi stakes to pierce the tire-soled sandals of any potential invader. To man these defenses, plus those of the forty or so villages within a fifteen-kilometer radius, the detachment swapped out the villagers' crossbows and poisoned arrows—outlawed by the Communist insurgents—for M1 rifles, then offered a two-week curriculum of militia training that progressed from marching to sentry duty, even to improvising rifle tripods out of bamboo stakes. To help count passing enemy guerrillas, the Green Berets taught their illiterate tribesmen to use their toes as units of ten: "two toes and three fingers equaled 23 Reds."

To earn the loyalty of the locals, Special Forces soldiers were shameless. Medics treated tuberculosis, delivered babies, doled out antibiotics and sometimes dapsone pills to lepers, stitched wounds, even amputated limbs. To reward Montagnard children for bathing, twenty-seven-year-old camp commander Captain Terry Cordell—a burly Citadel graduate and father of a newborn baby girl—kept his pockets filled with sourball candies, an incentive that prompted many youngsters to bathe three times a day and, more important, engendered warm feelings in their parents. Cordell's additional blandishments included the replacement of pigs and cattle killed by Communist insurgents and the personal accompaniment of wounded Montagnards to the hospital. In due course, Cordell's efforts were rewarded with a blood-swapping ceremony with the village chief in which he was initiated into the tribe. (In the coming years it would not be at all uncommon for a Green Beret to strip down to a tasseled loincloth and eagerly submit himself to an elaborate two-hour ceremony with the chanting local sorcerer, who would pledge the village's loyalty by wrapping the soldier's wrist with a thin metal band. To goose this loyalty, Special Forces commanders would rush in crates of World War II–era bore-cleaning rods to hammer into additional bracelets.)

8

To extend the influence of the CIDG camp at Buon Enao as a base for counterinfiltration, the A-Team advisors trained the most able villagers in more than defense. Leaning on their experience in training Vietnamese Rangers, the Green Berets began offering a six-week curriculum in patrolling, ambushing, and raiding. Graduates were formed into mobile strike forces later known as "Mike Forces," quasi-Ranger companies complete with mortar teams, recoilless rifles, occasionally flamethrowers. Employed directly by the US government and thereby eligible for $10 more per month than regular ARVN soldiers as well as treatment in US hospitals, Mike Force guerrillas could claim one more advantage over their Vietnamese Ranger peers: They were not burdened by ARVN officers, ARVN regulations, ARVN anything. Before long, Mike Force guerrillas would start attending airborne training, making them the closest thing the US Army had to its own airborne Rangers—a generous comparison, as Mike Force guerrillas could grasp about as much English as the difference between "bang bang" and "no bang bang," and whose bodies were so light that thermal updrafts could almost suspend their parachutes indefinitely.

In two months, the Green Berets at Buon Enao trained about 975 village defenders and 300 Mike Force guerrillas. The follow-on A-Team expanded this protective umbrella from 40 villages to a staggering 200, completed training for some 10,600 village defenders, and grew the province's Mobile Strike Force from 300 fighters to 1,500—enough for eight companies, about half the number of Ranger companies created for the Korean War. Before long, the gateway to Buon Enao was arched by a white, hand-scrawled sign warning Communists to "not apply . . . [because] we're not afraid . . . we have taught our friends small unit tactics." By the fall of 1962, planners considered the Buon Enao experiment so successful that Terry Cordell, the man a reporter would soon call "the Sourball Captain," was complaining that he was spending more time in "squiring dignitaries" on camp tours than he was in fighting the enemy. That ratio didn't last long.

In October, guerrillas hit Buon Enao with a multipronged attack. Just recovered from a bedridden bout of food poisoning, Cordell wasted no time and took to a single-prop spotter plane to call airstrikes against the Communist wave assaults. As the Montagnards watched, Cordell's plane was circling above the besieged camp—low and slow, said a witness—when it banked straight up, its nose aflame, then twisted into an uncontrolled spiral all the way to the jungle floor. As Cordell was the first Special Forces officer killed in the war, his death might have prompted planners to question the cost of the Buon Enao experiment, had it not been quickly followed by two bright spots that proved the value of Yarborough's counterinsurgency curriculum. First, the Montagnards succeeded in repelling the invaders, a testament to the Green Berets' ability to turn aborigines into competent soldiers; second, the Montagnards insisted on accompanying Cordell's body from the Highlands to Saigon—a testament to the Special Forces' ability to create not just allies, but brothers-in-arms. It was an accomplishment of which the Special Forces were jealously proud.

Ever sensitive to the aspirations of other unconventional units that might have tried to horn in on their success, specifically those of the Marine Corps and the US Air Force, Special Forces planners had not bothered to wait for the results of the Buon Enao experiment before breaking ground on additional camps. By the time of Cordell's death, they had already built twenty-three more. (It's worth noting that these planners had not been at all worried about the unconventional ambitions of the Navy.) As these other camps were being built, the Army had also established a fifty-seven-man Special Forces headquarters unit in Saigon, a much-needed entity for managing the sprawl, much of which was the result of the gradual takeover of many CIA programs, including CIDG. Set up in an old four-story colonial-style apartment building, the headquarters office was marked by a large sign bearing a cartoonish green beret. Head-scratching visitors often disappointedly mistook it for a French restaurant. Like a commander of World War II infantry, of which he was himself a veteran, Special Forces commander Colonel George Morton used a jeep and an airplane—both kept at constant idle—to direct a countrywide order of battle that by year's end consisted of 194 trainers for Vietnamese Rangers and LLDBs, plus 336 men spread out in twenty-eight A-Teams, advising twenty-eight CIDG camps.

In total, Special Forces in Vietnam numbered 587 men—around 10 percent of the entire 5,000-man American effort—and were well on the way to creating some 30,000 indigenous fighters. What other unit could promise so steep a return on investment? More important: how to franchise this success?

9

THE ARMY'S INCREASE of Green Berets in this period was nothing less than explosive. Prior to Kennedy, the three Special Forces Groups—the 1st in Okinawa, the 7th at Fort Bragg, the 10th in Germany—had each numbered around 750 men. Now, each was double that size, which had brought the total complement of Green Berets to about 4,500, a number that Army planners had already agreed to more than double in a single year. With a total of 10,000 Green Berets, the Army would have enough to not only build more CIDG camps in Vietnam, but also to add three new groups, each one to cover a different section of the globe: the Middle East, Africa, and Latin America. This demand would require from Yarborough and the Special Warfare Center a staggering increase in output, from around 400 graduates a year to around 3,200.

Over the course of 1963, the Special Forces in Vietnam did not just increase in size—the entire American force expanded to just under 17,000 men—but also assumed the very front rank of risk in MACV's advisory mission. One by one, freshly cut CIDG camps were awakened to the predawn thunder of bamboo drums, followed by the splash of mortar rounds, the cracking hailstorm of machine gun fire, then the inevitable waves of black-pajama-clad guerrillas funneling through the gaps in exploded barbed-wire fences, not stopping until they crested the ramparts with hoarse screams of *"Tien-len! Tien-len!"*—Forward!

At the CIDG camp in Plei Mrong, four Green Berets fought for five straight hours from a single sandbagged mortar pit. By the time the sun rose, every one of them was wounded. From January to July, CIDG detachments conducted some 400 patrols and incurred some 100 camp attacks—the cost to Special Forces being six dead: five in various firefights; one to a sniper. At a solemn medal presentation at a field hospital, Colonel Morton was unable to find enough Purple Hearts to present to the fourteen Green Berets wounded in a mortar barrage at Can Tho, which meant that each presentation was immediately followed by a less solemn medal removal so the award could be recycled to the next soldier's bedside. In spite of such risks, by the end of summer Special Forces in Vietnam had trained between 40,000 and 50,000 tribal militiamen, almost 11,000 Mike Force guerrillas, and had expanded their highland umbrella from 200 villages to over 800. Already Special Forces planners were imagining a future of at least 49 camps and commanding as many as 125,000 militia and Mike Force irregulars—hardly a fifth column, more like a parallel army.

The publicity concerning this growth period, a Special Forces commander wrote, would "[flow] like wine" and produce for the Green Berets a reputation not simply as American heroes but as "Middle America's answer to *The Graduate* . . . a final flowering of glory . . . the last Lone Rangers . . . Apaches with diplomas from Fort Bragg." Much of this reputation would be due to Yarborough, who would never miss an opportunity to promote his troops within the Army as the extreme tip of the president's counterinsurgency spear. That catalogue of promotions would include the enlisting of West Point's bandmaster to produce a Green Beret march; the authoring of several articles for scholarly journals on the necessity of counterinsurgency specialists; and the showcasing of these by having them rappel from the top of the six-story Sheraton-Park Hotel in Washington, D.C., for the 1962 Army Association's annual meeting. His showcase to the public would be even more explicit: the authorizing of a thirty-minute documentary narrated by no less a figure than Henry Fonda, and the official sanctioning of the first book on the Green Berets, provided that its author—a Sheraton Hotel executive—complete the three-month guerrilla warfare course, then deploy with an A-Team to Vietnam. It was a campaign whose objective was to convince its audience that the Special Warfare Center had pushed past its origins of OSS raiders, past the tactical preferences of its many former Rangers, and emerged as a strategic-level laboratory for the alchemy of illiterate tribes into the gold of indigenous legions. It was also a campaign so effective that Kennedy was said to be considering the catapulting of Yarborough to the top billet at MACV—a catapulting that would have carried with it to Vietnam an unshakable belief in the strategy of counterinsurgency, plus a belief in the men most prepared to perform it. Presented by Yarborough as the guiding example for victory in Vietnam, the Special Forces were—though no one yet realized it at that moment—shining like a star whose brilliance had peaked and whose fade was about to begin.

10

THE SITUATION IN SOUTH VIETNAM went from match to conflagration when six months of Buddhist protests—of orange-robed monks immolating themselves for world cameras—gave way to brutal crackdowns by President Ngo Dinh Diem in the form of midnight abductions, assassinations, and temple raids. Many of these had been performed by disguised soldiers of the LLDB, the Green Beret–trained Vietnamese Special Forces. Under the direct control of Diem's brother, Ngo Dinh Nhu, the LLDB had devolved into a throne-preserving praetorian guard, overwhelmingly Catholic and anti-Buddhist, "arrogant and privileged," at home in South Vietnam's backwaters of "kickbacks, payroll juggling, and misappropriation." So far, the LLDB's anti-Communist efforts had been confined to limp participation in the CIDG program and, said one contemporary, the "[occasional poke] along the Laotian border."

On November 1, 1963, antiregime ARVN elements staged a coup d'état in which they laid siege to the French-built presidential palace in Saigon. At a separate location, antiregime officers forced LLDB commander Colonel Le Quang Tung to issue orders to his Vietnamese Special Forces soldiers to surrender. Once Colonel Le complied, once his lone purpose was accomplished, the rebels shot and toppled him into a pre-dug grave. The murder effectively stripped President Diem of his most loyal defenders. Having escaped in Catholic frocks from the palace through secret tunnels yet finding no sanctuary, the next day Diem and his brother Nhu surrendered to ARVN troops, who tied their arms behind their backs, crammed them into an armored troop carrier, then shot and bayoneted them to death. The shockwaves of this assassination expanded to encircle every aspect of US involvement in Vietnam.

For his connection to Diem's brother Nhu and the regime-supporting LLDB, and for his support of various programs of the coup-complicit

CIA, Special Forces commander Colonel George Morton was immediately whisked out of the country. Before such tremors had subsided, a far larger earthquake split the ground beneath everyone's feet.

Three weeks after Diem's assassination, President Kennedy was shot and killed in the back of a limousine bound for a meeting with the Dallas Citizens Council. Over a steak lunch, he would have delivered a speech that, among other things, would have enumerated his administration's first thousand days' worth of increases to various defense programs, a speech compressed and collated into thirty-seven typed notecards. The list included a 30 percent increase in tactical air squadrons; 30 percent more broadcasting hours for Voice of America; a 45 percent increase in combat divisions; a 50 percent increase in Polaris submarines and in strategic bombers on fifteen-minute alert; a 100 percent increase in available nuclear weapons; 100 percent more dollars for ship construction, conversion, and modernization; and an annual commitment of space-launched vehicles that surpassed all those deployed in the 1950s combined. Last to be listed in the speech would have been the president's favorite entity of all: the Special Forces. Per the speech, he would have announced its increase by an incomparable 600 percent—500 percent more than the next closest entity. The president's speech would have gone on to define the Special Forces' role—notably the only entity he would have taken the trouble to define—as those "prepared to work with our allies and friends against the guerrillas, saboteurs, insurgents and assassins," a list of sinister irony, considering the reason the speech was never delivered. "Reducing our efforts to train, equip and assist [these] armies can only encourage communist penetration" and increase the demands of American troops. "We in this country, in this generation," the president's speech would have continued, "are—by destiny rather than choice—the watchmen on the walls of world freedom . . . We dare not weary of the task."

That very same day in Vietnam, a battle demonstrated just the sort of risks that Kennedy had warned about, and the Special Forces reaffirmed their standing as the front rank of the world's watchmen. A little after midnight, a vanguard of Communist guerrillas silently threaded the floodlit sugarcane fields surrounding the CIDG camp at Hiep Hoa—under the watchtowers, over a three-foot-deep moat, through three lines of snipped barbed-wire fences. This accomplished, they silently knifed the camp's guards, then, after a bugle blast, scaled the stockade's fence, then rushed the longhouses to gun down the sleeping defenders, resulting in forty-one killed—many still in their beds—plus a beheaded Vietnamese cook and 120 wounded. Of the camp's Green Berets, four were captured, bound and blindfolded, then slogged off to captivity. Over the next few days as they were dragged through various hamlets, Communist sympathizers "turned out" to mock them with the same chorus, *"Kennedy di-et, Kennedy di-et."* Kennedy is dead.

In response to Jacqueline Kennedy's request for Special Forces soldiers to serve in her husband's funeral guard, Yarborough hand-selected twenty-one men who upon arrival at the Capitol returned their dead president's patronage by taking thirty-minute turns in the rotunda, standing silent guard over his coffin. On November 25, as the black horse-drawn caisson was clopped through the city's streets, the flag-draped casket was accompanied on each side by pairs of white-gloved servicemen from each of the military's branches, all in dress blues, all except for four men, distinct in every way—from their bloused jump boots to their forest-green berets. To the wail of bagpipes and the roar of jets overhead, past black-veiled mourners, past priests and nuns, past uniforms of every sort, past de Gaulle towering in his kepi, the pallbearers carried Kennedy's coffin up Arlington's slopes through a final gauntlet of saluting Green Berets, their polished bayonets glinting in the setting sun. Long after the crowds departed and the November air turned from crisp to cold, these troops remained at the gravesite to stand watch. At some time in the night, Sergeant Major Francis Ruddy removed his beret and solemnly laid it atop the wreaths surrounding the eternal flame.

Not simply a salute nor an epitaph to a kind of patronage that the Special Forces would never enjoy again, it was a moment that marked an end to the US military's wholesale commitment to counterinsurgency, the only kind of warfare that the Green Berets were—at that moment—prepared to wage.

11

With the ascension of Lyndon Johnson to the presidency, all MACV's plans for victory turned from counterinsurgency—the winning of hearts and minds—to fulfilling a single imperative: preventing supplies and insurgents from crossing South Vietnam's borders. Almost immediately, this imperative shifted the focus of the CIDG program from the well digging of counterinsurgency to the headhunting of anti-infiltration. Never enthusiastic about the former strategy, MACV planners viewed the latter as simpler to accomplish, as it was essentially a problem of blocking the geography over which supplies were being carried. Yet geography is never simple.

Curved like a ragged cocktail shrimp, the belly of South Vietnam was bordered on its western side by Laos in the north and Cambodia in the south. Skirting the edge of this "trackless" border stretched the entire length of Highway 559, so named for the fifth month of the fifty-ninth year in which North Vietnam's leaders had decided to support the southern insurgents. Already, the highway was more infamously known as the Ho Chi Minh Trail. "More a maze than a road," wrote an American pilot who would soon be charged with splashing its traffic with bombs, the trail zigzagged beneath a blanket of trees, many of their top branches lashed together for concealment, and beneath which it "contracted, expanded, split, reunited, vanished." In Laos alone, the trail would eventually occupy a "piece . . . of real estate the size of Massachusetts . . . hundreds of miles of road, communication centers, ammo dumps, stockpiles of food and fuel, truck parks, troop bivouacs." From this main arterial line, thousands of off-ramps split into South Vietnam to stock the insurgency with everything from machine guns and mortar rounds to penicillin and mosquito netting.

To create a Maginot Line of anti-infiltration, many of the original Montagnard-manned Special Forces camps were abandoned and their

Map of Special Forces camps, South Vietnam, summer 1964.

A-Teams and Mike Forces airlifted to the empty edges of Vietnam's inaccessible border. In short order, airdropped bulldozers were carving airstrips out of jungle, creating a series of watchtower camps from which the Green Berets could lead border patrols and ambushes. Instead of leading only Montagnard tribesmen, all recruited from nearby villages and thus invested in their own security, the A-Teams assumed control of what one witness described as a volatile "hodge-podge" of privileged LLDB advisors, disinterested Mike Force irregulars, and, invariably, criminals, prostitutes, pimps, press-ganged teenage hoodlums, even "car sharks" (presumably used-car salesmen), and another feature of the war, anti-Communist Chinese mercenaries called Nungs. In every camp, there were never fewer than "five languages spoken and sometimes as many as eight." Combat patrols with such an assortment of misfits, said one veteran, were "something else"—a train of men "smoking, chattering, holding hands, playing transistor radios, shooting monkeys, sucking on sugarcane." Originally intended to "put roots in the population," to deny the tribes to the enemy, "without people" to protect, said a senior Special Forces officer of CIDG, "the effort became a conventional military operation with no real stake in the area, no human intelligence nets, no source of recruits, no hearts and minds to win." Internal divisions were commonplace; infiltration was always a risk. Always. Isolated Green Berets, said a veteran, "slept nights on end with one eye open, wondering which of his troops would cut the wire, open the gate, turn a machine gun into the camp, or roll a grenade under his bunk."

At the camp at Plei Do Lim, the Montagnard garrison simply left; later, a defector tossed a grenade at a group of Green Berets who were combating a generator fire, wounding three. After the collapse of the camp at Polei Krong, a defeat as devastating as the one at Hiep Hoa, several Vietnamese were found in their beds, necks broken, a sure sign of infiltration. As it was quickly being learned by the men in these new camps, the strategy of anti-infiltration was producing a situation in which the only heads being hunted were their own. And there was only one way to win a war like that: pull in and prepare to fight to the death.

On July 6, 1964, after a day of fistfights between the Chinese Nungs and the Montagnard tribesmen over a prostitute, the 400-man camp at Nam Dong learned exactly this lesson when the darkness exploded in a midnight mortar barrage, quickly followed by a ground assault by more than double the entire garrison. Communications severed, command post aflame, the ground splashing with white explosions, thirty-year-old Green Beret Captain Roger Donlon led a five-hour defense—dashing waist-bent between foxholes, dousing flames, pinpointing fire, shuttling ammunition, lobbing grenades, gunning down infiltrators, propping up wounded, tearing his shredded clothing into bandages, at one point manning an almost vertical white-hot mortar tube to lob rounds at a nearly throwable distance. Much of his time was spent cajoling his indigenous troops to fight. With defenders dying around him, including two Green Beret comrades, Donlon was repeatedly tossed and folded by successive explosions, each one puncturing another part, his stomach, his arm, his leg, stripping him of all of his equipment, including his boots—a loss that forced him to run several yards dragging a piece of plywood, the board's nail sticking out of the top of his foot.

After several more months of similar scrapes, some 3,000 Montagnards across the highlands launched a revolt—a "war within a war," wrote a newsman—capturing five CIDG camps, tying up their Special Forces advisors, raising the Montagnard flag, and demanding a 50,000-man Green Beret–led Tribal Army untethered to South Vietnam's corrupt government. Before the Green Berets quelled the rebellion, an effort that tested their commitment to moderate force with diplomacy, the revolutionaries killed eleven LLDB soldiers and another thirty-nine ARVN troops.

None of these were victories, just survivals of the narrowest sort, survivals that should have warned American leaders of the risks in expecting such heights of bravery from so precarious a platform.

12

Originally created as a compact corps of elite commandos for leading partisans on behind-the-lines raids, the Army's Special Forces had long since been overhauled by Yarborough to match Kennedy's priority of transforming illiterate tribesmen into third world freedom fighters. Naturally, the success of this overhaul had led to an unprecedented expansion, which had prompted the Army's "numbers merchants" at the Pentagon to press Yarborough to soften Special Forces training—essentially to trade quality for quantity—backing him into an accession that soon reduced his pipeline's notorious attrition rate from 90 percent to 70 percent and producing graduates less like the program's original elite commandos. This was a disparity that would only increase as the pipeline's attrition rate declined even more—eventually bottoming out at an abysmal 30 percent. The only thing that had thus far preserved the reputation of the Green Berets as the Army's premier commandos was the A-Team itself, two officers and ten enlisted specialists whose capabilities in small-unit tactics—the bedrock of commando raiding—were the direct result of each team's cohesiveness. This in turn was the direct result of each A-Team's operational cycle: an arduous period of predeployment training, followed by six-month temporary duty orders to Vietnam, followed by a return home the same way they had left, together. Besides promoting unit cohesion and thereby improving small-unit tactics, it was an operational cycle that just so happened to pad each Green Beret's pockets with per diem while deployed—a perk so detrimental to the Army's overall budget that it would force planners to settle on a solution that would inadvertently do more damage to the Green Berets' prospects as commando raiders than Yarborough's shift to counterinsurgency had done.

On October 1, 1964, the 5th Special Forces Group was established in Nha Trang, a founding that once again raised the status of the Green Berets in Vietnam, this time by doubling their numbers to 1,297—numbers needed as soon as possible to shore up the western border camps. Because of the cost in per diem payments, however, this increase would have also hollowed out the force if not for the fix that came with 5th Group's founding. That fix was the establishment of 5th Group itself—as permanent a posting as the 10th Group in Germany—that enabled the Army to double the length of all Green Beret deployments to Vietnam from six-month temporary duty assignments to twelve-month permanent change-of-station orders.

It was a solution that cured the problem of per diem, but at a cost as taxing as chemotherapy. In no time, graduates of the rapidly relaxing Special Warfare Center—graduates still perfecting the droop to their green berets—were reporting to their first A-Teams without having received any predeployment platoon training and without ever having met the other members of their platoons. The results were predictable. From the fall of 1964 to the end of the war, A-Teams in Vietnam were a revolving door of arrivals and departures, and on-the-job training—many of the new advisors possessing less combat knowledge than the guerrillas they were meant to advise.

No one noticed the Green Berets' decline from guerrilla raiders to well-digging border guards more acutely than Captain Charlie Beckwith, whose year away from the Special Forces had been spent in Malaya with the British Special Air Service, or SAS, the world's best commandos, who cared not at all about well digging or border guarding. Sensing a need in the US Army for a similar unit—a Special Operations

Force, he called it—Beckwith had wasted no time in drafting the concept: a subunit less "hung up" on advising guerrillas and more focused on the "blocking and tackling" of commando operations—essentially, an American version of the SAS. Considering that Beckwith's proposal flew in the face of nearly every one of the Special Warfare Center's recent initiatives, Yarborough's response was predictable: "Captain, you don't understand, I have a full plate here handling what I got." Not that it mattered at that point anyway; Yarborough's shift to counterinsurgency was not the only gap left by the Special Forces' rise that needed filling.

By the end of 1964, the Special Forces were manning a total of forty-four CIDG camps. From Hue in the north to Saigon in the south, thirty-five of these were evenly distributed from the western border to the Central Highlands; a handful of others were situated along the eastern coast. Below Saigon, however, this evenness stopped. There, in the south, the Special Forces were manning a total of nine camps, seven of these crammed up against the 100-mile-long border with Cambodia. It was a distribution as regular as a row of fence posts, and one that left just two A-Teams and their imported guerrillas to cover the more than 40,000 square miles of rivers, marshes, and tidewater known as the Mekong Delta.

More than ever before, here was neglect and opportunity all in one.

Chapter 11

The First SEALs, Their Search for a Mission, and the Report That Found It for Them

At one o'clock on January 1, 1962, a Monday, SEAL Team ONE was—without fanfare of any kind—unceremoniously commissioned on Naval Amphibious Base, Coronado, right where the neck of San Diego's palm-treed resort island met the flat, seven-mile-long sandy isthmus called the Silver Strand. Located on this base—a peninsula of military-grade right angles that jutted into the sparkling waters of San Diego Bay—the team's physical footprint was little more than a single World War II–era Quonset hut. The team's authorized strength was for ten officers and fifty enlisted men, most of whom had not yet been pulled from their West Coast underwater demolition teams. The man most responsible for recruiting, equipping, and training these men was their twenty-nine-year-old commanding officer, Lieutenant David Del Giudice (pronounced Judas). Raised just outside of Newark, New Jersey, by Italian-speaking, working-class parents, Del Giudice was of average height and athletic build, and like nearly every other frogman, well tanned. As an officer at UDT 12, he had been selected to lead a ten-man detachment to Vietnam on a two-week trip up the Mekong River to deliver landing craft to Laotian troops—troops that the Army's Special Forces were already training for combat. Briefed on the insurgents and the menu of reptiles that he and his men were sure to encounter, they had seen neither, just 100 miles of mud-brown river. Now, Del Giudice was in charge of a unit that had been created in no small part to return to that river, but to what end, no one quite yet knew.

The same could be said of his counterpart on the east coast.

A week after SEAL Team ONE was commissioned, on January 6, twenty-seven-year-old Lieutenant John Callahan, Jr., reported for duty as the new commanding officer of SEAL Team TWO, a command that had not existed until the moment he arrived. Located north of Virginia Beach at the lower lip of the mouth to the Chesapeake Bay, the Navy's amphibious base at Little Creek was a sandy, pine-barren backwater as unlike the postcard setting of SEAL Team ONE as was Callahan to his counterpart. Full-faced for a frogman, when Callahan had reported to Class 19, an instructor had taken one look at him and pronounced, "Forget it, you're too heavy. You'll never make it." To prove that instructor wrong, Callahan had shed fifty pounds and then after graduation had gained every pound back—so much insulation that, in Norway, he had skinned an ocean swim for which others had opted to wear two wetsuits. In spite of his hulking appearance, as an officer at UDT 11 he had been around the world, from Japan to Samoa, measuring beach gradients, laying sonar cables, and proving himself a problem solver on every odd job the Navy had assigned him. Now, like Del Giudice on the other side of the country, Callahan's problem was to transform his fifty-nine fellow frogmen into something they had never been—all while possessing not much more than some vague guidance from the CNO about naval guerrilla/counterguerrilla operations and coastal raiding.

As Callahan and Del Giudice would soon learn, the SEALs' future would be determined not simply by the direction toward which they bent their rudders, but also by the current that would emanate from Navy planners. These currents would be influenced—in no small part—by a report written by one of the most inland-leaning sailors in the unconventional Navy's entire past.

2

THE FIRST FACTOR that explains the distance the SEALs ultimately traveled in their evolution to what they are today can be found in the genes of the group from which they were drawn: the UDTs, an organization whose reputation was already percolating with potential.

At the time of the SEAL teams' creation, the UDT Replacement course, or UDTR, was sixteen weeks long—twice the length of Kauffman's NCDU course—and at that point was held only twice a year, once on each coast. It had become, wrote a *Collier's* reporter, "a course so tough that only about a quarter of the original 'tadpoles' ever [got] to be real frogmen." According to a contemporary, because of the course's difficulty, UDT instructors would actually "apologize to trainees for what they are about to do to them." What they did to them was apply grating sand, very little sleep, uncountable hours of push-ups, uncountable soft-sand runs, an obstacle course with a twenty-foot-high balance beam, a fifty-foot-long track of monkey bars, and a pile of logs called the nutcracker. All of these were attended by the instructor's unscheduled harassments, even of student officers. "Move faster. What's the matter, mister, can't you take it? How in blazes did you ever make it into this outfit?" (Said a witness of the officer's abuse: It was "an enlisted man's dream come true.") To all this was added the neck-breaking enterprise of interminably carrying a 300-pound rubber boat on their heads; hours of calisthenics with telephone poles; and soul-crushing round-the-clock boat races through the surf. For West Coast classes, there were bone-slamming rock portages at a breakwater of sharp boulders beneath the lights and red-pinnacled rooftops of the architectural fairy tale that was the Hotel del Coronado. Throughout the entire course, the trainees' teeth chattered with cold, hip flexors swelled from shivering, and when not in the water, arms and legs instinctively contorted to pull wet fatigues away from icy ribs. In winter classes in Virginia Beach, students braved water temperatures as frigid as thirty-eight degrees. During Hell Week, the ground shook from explosives that choked each student's mouth with sand, and at the tail end of the course, swim pairs finned from Vieques to Roosevelt Roads, a distance of seven miles that made each man's tongue swell from salt water.

When the Navy's academics had arrived in 1955 to observe UDT training, their purpose had been to validate the course's individual "selection tests"—the soft-sand runs, the ocean swims, the harassments of Hell Week—and short of invalidating any of those, to develop what they called "realistic" selection standards that would reduce what the Navy admitted was the course's "excessive attrition." Subjecting students to a battery of personality tests and classifying their individual traits (age, education, intelligence, and so on), the academics hoped to predict not only a candidate's likelihood of success in training, but also his success in an actual underwater demolition team. In the course of these assessments, they learned that students below the age of twenty-one were 8 percent more likely to fail (roughly the same rate as high school dropouts), while students from broken homes were just as likely to graduate as anyone else. Based on the number of times a student had voluntarily visited the dispensary, assessors determined that a candidate in moderate health "who [minimized] the psychological importance of pain, fatigue, and intense discomfort" stood a much higher chance of success than "the most physically fit . . . [who] were overly concerned" about their injuries. The least common traits among successful frogmen seemed to be restraint, thoughtfulness, sociability, and cautiousness; the most common were responsibility, emotional stability, original thinking, objectivity, and, most of all, "masculinity." Later studies had gone on to test a variety of variables, including the benefits of wheat germ in a student's diet, which proved predictably negligible, and a series of Rorschach tests and psychiatric interviews to determine the effect of sexuality on a candidate's success or failure. "Successful frogmen," said the sex report's author, "appear to require this specific rather masculine and adventurous occupation with all its self-destructive and masochistic implications" because—and this was just the author's "speculation"—of their "magical attraction" to the "depth of the sea, and the security of the womb," and an "unconscious motivation . . . to prove their masculinity coupled with a fear of involvement with women." Setting aside the psychoanalysts' tendency to project their own insecurities onto their subjects, the Navy had not been able to argue with the UDTs' results.

"I have never met a group of more self-reliant, hell-for-leather characters," wrote reporter Bill Stapleton after accompanying a UDT to St. Thomas in the Virgin Islands in 1955. Besides their typical reconnaissance exercises, submarine lockouts, and tests with miniature submersibles, the frogmen had also salvaged a fifty-foot yacht from a reef, twisted the tails of passing sharks, and, when an American sailor had disappeared into a harbor on a moonless night, had commandeered a truck, roared to the wharf's edge, and as if they'd been scouting the contours of an enemy beach, dove on-line until they found the drowned man. In their free time, they spearfished, drank untold amounts of beer, erected beachside bonfires, and in overflowing pots of seawater and vinegar boiled lobsters and astonished the superstitious natives by broiling barracuda steaks. "You eat barracuda, barracuda eat you," they had said.

"Promises," replied a frogman. "Nothing but promises."

"So exclusive" were the UDTs, said one observer, "that even rank [meant] nothing to them." When seen in their standard swim trunks and knife belts, surrounded by charts and diving equipment, and asked by passersby if they were indeed in the Navy, the frogmen would invariably reply, regardless of the asker's rank, "Nope. We're all in UDT." Such impertinence had become the price of their utility to the Navy.

Originally conceived as "subsurface detectives," they were now the "Navy's Neptunes," the Navy's toughest, the Navy's impromptu ship salvagers and cable layers, the Navy's best "combination of sailor and Marine," who could blow up a bridge, a ship, or a floating mine, or "knife an enemy sentry." Wherever they had gone, they had proved themselves adaptable, aggressive, full of initiative, and inversely free of military bearing and courtesy. "The men were self-motivated, hard chargers," said Del Giudice. "Everybody was an innovator." By the time SEAL Teams ONE and TWO were established, no group of men in the US military had been so primed for adaptation.

3

POSSESSING NOTHING MORE than a vague idea of the missions they would soon be expected to perform, both Del Giudice and Callahan did what they could and gathered supplies, managed budgets, purchased equipment—automatic weapons, parachutes, scuba tanks—and bartered their UDT expertise in explosives and diving to enroll their men in a series of non-Navy courses. Among these were the Army's Airborne School at Fort Benning; the Marine Corps' Escape and Evasion Course at Pickle Meadows; the Royal Canadian Air Force's Survival Training School in British Columbia; the US Army's Jungle Warfare School in Panama; and Yarborough's Special Warfare Course at Fort Bragg, plus a rap sheet of lesser classes: kitchen table demolition, Soviet weapons, judo, sailboat handling, lockpicking, safecracking, even hot-wiring tutorials at various prisons.

Most important of all, many of the first SEALs attended Ranger School. There, they learned Robert Rogers' Rules of Ranging—just as Darby's men had—as well as map reading, land navigation, hand-and-arm signals; they learned how to set an L-ambush and how to defeat one; they learned the five-paragraph order, a concise primer for planning any operation, but ideal for raiding and still in use today. Once they'd completed the course, the SEALs returned to their teams, where their knowledge was linked to that of other Ranger School graduates, a quirk that turned two Navy units into the tightest concentration of Ranger Tabs since the Korean War—hardly the people the Army could have intended to be the beneficiaries of the Rangers' history, but a fact that seemed to settle any question as to the SEALs' most likely future mission.

This likelihood of a future as Navy Rangers seemed further confirmed by the cameo of several past characters whose brief appearance on the SEALs' stage now all but nudged them in this same direction. Following their postinvasion rescue of Bay of Pigs Brigaders, the unrepentant Cuban frogmen had gone on to volunteer for a second CIA program known as Operation Mongoose, in which they had been folded into a larger commando group, then dispatched on a hundred or so boat-launched raids on the Cuban mainland—missions on which they had improvised lessons as invaluable as avoiding the buoyancy and heat of their black wetsuits in warm water by swapping them out for the same black tights worn by ballerinas. Since then, four of the frogmen had accepted Kennedy's offer of a presidential commission in the US Navy and now found themselves on temporary duty orders to SEAL Team TWO—as best these frogmen could tell, a unit that seemed poised to mimic the example set by the Operation Mongoose commandos. Or at least would have if only the job options available to the SEAL teams hadn't seemed to be pulling them in the opposite direction.

Just ten days after taking command, Del Giudice flew from San Diego to Saigon to meet with MACV and CIA planners. His goal: to discuss the best possible use for the SEAL teams in Vietnam. With the SEALs barely two weeks old, no one yet knew what the unit was, or how to employ them. The latter problem was solved by simply looking around.

For the past six months, UDT advisors had been turning Vietnamese sailors into Vietnamese frogmen, the graduates of which had formed the LDNN, Lien Doc Nguoi Nhia, "soldiers who fight from the sea." With this example, and with a country already awash with green-beret-wearing trainers teaching everyone from Catholic teenagers to Vietnamese Rangers, planners naturally imagined a mission to turn Vietnamese frogmen into coastal raiders. Eager to assist, Navy planners approved the idea, and within two months of inception, the SEAL teams had their first mission: a Mobile Training Team of ten advisors to train several batches of thirty Vietnamese sailors from the coastal blockade's Junk Force, soon to be called the Biet Hai or Sea Commandos.

In time, many of the native volunteers to this unit would be recognizable for the words *sat cong* ("kill Communists") tattooed to their chests, but in the beginning were so slight, so malnourished, so racked by tuberculosis and plague that they did not have the strength to fin through a long-distance ocean swim. Set up in a beachside, French-built house in the village of My Khe, near Danang, the SEALs organized for their diminutive students a three-month curriculum of swimming, small-boat handling, patrolling, and marksmanship; the last lesson possible only after each student learned to close only one eye: "Vietnamese no wink," explained a Nung instructor. To increase the endurance of their rice-accustomed students, at one point the SEALs would chip in to buy a cow and slaughter it, an act that sent most of their Biet Hai running for the latrine.

Had the United States maintained this advisory character in the war, it's unclear how such employment would have influenced the SEALs' ultimate development, but one can venture a guess: When the second batch of Biet Hai advisors from SEAL Team TWO arrived in Vietnam, they marched off the plane in "full regalia"—meaning pressed Marine Corps fatigues, bloused boots, patches from all their various schools, even the braided shoulder-loop aiguillettes worn by boot camp instructors. Whatever their expectations, the most telling accoutrement would be this: On every SEAL's head would be a lopsided black beret.

4

In April 1962, just as he had done with the Army at Fort Bragg, President Kennedy embarked on a trip to the area around Norfolk, Virginia, to inspect the Atlantic Fleet. From four-acre flight decks to windblown conning towers, the president and his retinue rode at flank speed on cruisers and craned over rails to watch deafening new jets fire deafening new missiles, then counted the exploding geysers of each impact. Tucked into the trip was a late-afternoon pierside review of the SEALs, all ranked at attention in swim trunks, each man strapped with a different type of underwater breathing device, one man with a face mask casually perched on his forehead. With hands stuffed in his suitcoat pockets and his shoulders hunched in the cold ocean wind, the smiling president examined each man, asked questions as he went, and laughed at various answers, his face as winsome as Churchill's at the sight of the shirtless frogmen. It was a memory that would soon inspire a letter from Kennedy to the CNO, saying, "When I was in Norfolk, I noted particularly the members of the SEAL Teams. I was impressed by them as individuals and with the capability they possess as a group. As missiles assume more and more of the nuclear deterrent role and as your limited war mission grows, the need for Special Forces in the Navy and the Marine Corps will increase." The president's comparison to the Army's guerrilla warfare experts would be hard to miss, and even harder to ignore.

Born in the full current of Kennedy's captivation with counterinsurgency, the planned-for commando character of the Navy SEALs could easily have melted into that of a watery version of the Army's Special

President Kennedy (center) speaks with US Navy SEAL team members on the pier at Naval Air Station, Norfolk, Virginia, before boarding the USS *Northampton* (CC-1), April 13, 1962.

Forces—those snake-eating trainers and guerrilla advisors who were, at that moment, being overhauled into third world diplomats and well diggers. With the exception of several reconnaissance probes and a planned-for but canceled raid during the Cuban Missile Crisis, nothing demonstrated this possible melting better than the litany of SEAL operations from 1962 to 1963, which was almost a mirror image of the Special Forces before their overhaul: practice submarine exfiltrations of partisans in Turkey; nighttime harbor raids with guerrillas in Greece; fiord-hopping escape missions from Home Guardsmen in Norway; a submarine-launched assault on a radar station with French commandos in Corsica. In the midst of these, the SEALs were sent on a second Mobile Training Team (MTT) mission—this time to Turkey, where they learned—like the Green Berets already had—the hidden costs that so often accompanied military diplomacy. With Turkish students assembled before him, Lieutenant Junior Grade William Painter submerged beneath the Bosporus, performed a buoyant ascent, then on his second demonstration disappeared into the racing current between the continents. His body was never found.

When not engaged in MTTs abroad or in exercises with host-nation partners, the SEALs participated in cross-training with soldiers from Canada, Italy, and France, and even with their increasingly jealous cousins from Marine Force Recon. The SEALs trained especially with the Army's Special Forces—not just the US military's Jesuits to the third world, but also so favored by the president for the promise of counterinsurgency that no special unit was safe from being converted to that mission.

Originally conceived as commando-raiders, by the end of 1963 it seemed the SEALs were already drifting into a sea awash with competing opportunities. That is, until a former Scout and Raider turned SACO sailor pushed them back on course.

5

In early January 1964, mere weeks after Kennedy's death, the Commander in Chief of the US Pacific Fleet (CINCPAC), Admiral Donald Felt, directed his staff to organize a survey team with orders to deploy to South Vietnam to study Communist infiltration of the Mekong Delta. Short, spare, and "mean as hell," Admiral Felt was well known in the Navy as the former hero of the Battle of the Eastern Solomons, who as a forty-year-old commander had led his squadron from 14,000 feet on a "screaming dive through flak and fighters" to drill a 1,000-pound bomb into the flight deck of a Japanese aircraft carrier. Now, in the words of one peer, Felt was known for routinely grabbing "3-star officers by the lapels, [and] literally [shaking] them."

When the Delta Survey Team leaders presented themselves at the mustard-colored former morgue that now housed CINCPAC headquarters in Honolulu, Admiral Felt greeted them in his customary flight jacket, then propped his moccasin-clad feet on his desk. "A bear for facts and figures" and a vocal skeptic on the expanding US efforts in Vietnam, Felt's instructions to the survey team reflected the military's growing demand for data and the uncertainty of what to do with it.

"I don't know exactly what I want you to do," Felt began, before ordering them to cover the area, study the problem of infiltration, and recommend solutions for curbing it. "I want to know why all I get from Vietnam are glowing reports of accomplishments and meanwhile we are getting the hell kicked out of us. That's your job."

In fact, the survey would fill a more fundamental, and fateful, purpose. It would determine the Navy's future role in what might be its next theater of operations—a delta peninsula whose interior sank beneath the weight of its rivers, swamps, canals, and marshes; what one reporter called "the least attractive theater for [Admiral Felt] to apply his talents." Not since the American Civil War had US Navy planners actively committed their ships to such a theater, and even then they had initially balked, considering "inland operations" to be the responsibility of the US Army, which had made up for the Navy's negligence by purchasing steamboat rams and commissioning several intrepid soldier-skippers to command them. Now, the Navy was facing the exact same dilemma in Vietnam—naturally, a puzzle best solved by sailors who had already served there.

Though no one explicitly said it, there was another puzzle the survey would need to solve: the future role of the Navy's unconventionals in Vietnam.

Commanded by Rear Admiral Paul Savidge, the head of Amphibious Training Command in Coronado and a lifelong veteran of the blue-water surface Navy, the rest of the survey team consisted of eight naval officers, all but two with past service in Vietnam. Along with prior experience in Vietnam, three of the eight members of Savidge's team possessed service records that spanned the entire history of the US Navy's modern experiments in unconventional warfare. The first of these was a former MACV staff officer, Lieutenant Commander Phil Koehler, who had spent the past sixteen months in Vietnam, and who had earned a Silver Star as a UDT officer at Okinawa in World War II. Next was Savidge's aide-de-camp for the trip, Lieutenant David Del Giudice, who had already ridden up the Mekong River as a UDT officer and was now the skipper of SEAL Team ONE.

Last and highest ranking was the World War II Scout and Raider turned SACO sailor, Captain Phil Bucklew, who had just been appointed to command of Naval Operations Support Group, the parent authority of all UDT and SEAL operations in the Pacific. Who better than he to scout out the future landing beaches of the infant SEAL teams?

Checked in to the seven-story pink hotel in downtown Saigon known as the Brink's BOQ, or bachelor officer quarters, the survey team found themselves in a city pulsing with heat, traffic, and temptation. After securing an office space with typewriters and a conference table, the team members set about gathering maps—mostly those from the French colonial era—and switchbacked the city, presenting themselves to various Vietnamese and air-conditioned American compounds, arranging for the boats, planes, and junks they knew they would need to accomplish their mission. In the evenings, the survey team dined at any one of Saigon's hotels, where waiters brought libations and a sampling of French and Vietnamese cuisine. Except for what one team member called the "bulging" presence of green-fatigued American servicemen and the bars, theaters, pools, and bowling alleys that now catered exclusively to them, it was almost impossible to tell that there was a war going on—at least during the day. At night, the survey team would stand atop their hotel, drinks in hand, and in the distance all around them marvel at the arcing streaks of green and red tracer fire followed by the disjointed clatter of their reports. Despite the sunny statistics being collated by MACV for Washington's planners—numbers of ARVN soldiers trained and graduated; numbers of strategic hamlets created; numbers of insurgents killed—the survey team already knew firsthand and from newspapers that the real story was far cloudier. Just two months earlier President Diem had been murdered, along with the principal partner of the US Navy's advisory effort, the CNO of the Vietnamese Navy, stabbed in the chest while driving, which prompted his crash into a water-filled culvert, where he was ultimately shot three times in the head and dumped in a rubber plantation. Since then, the Navy's future in Vietnam had only become more and more choked with obstacles, things that surface sailors like Admiral Savidge had spent their lifetimes avoiding, and what might have foreshadowed the team's recommendations for the Navy's ultimate involvement in Vietnam if not for what happened next.

Within days of the survey team's arrival in Saigon, its leader, Admiral Savidge, suffered a trip-ending health emergency, alternately described by various team members as "heart trouble" or "closet" alcoholism. Whatever the truth, command of the survey immediately fell to the team member of the next highest rank, a disappointing start for the survey had it not led to the promotion of Savidge's highest-ranking subordinate—none other than Captain Phil Bucklew, an officer who had long ago learned to deal with obstacles by just driving through them.

6

WHEN HE HAD LEFT his house on December 7, 1941, Phil Hinkle Bucklew was a six-foot-two-inch, 235-pound former fullback for the Cleveland Rams whose major concern that morning had been to choose one of the four football contracts burning a hole in his pocket. With thinning hair and a heavy jaw, a curled lip and downturned eyes, not to mention a torso as thick as a tree trunk, Bucklew at twenty-six looked ten years older than he was, and ten times as mean. While intimidating from a distance, Bucklew up close actually possessed a personality that accomplished the opposite. He had even attracted to his orbit enough players to found and coach his own football team, the Columbus Bullies—a team on its way to another league championship had the Japanese not exploded the afternoon as they did.

Turned away by the Army because a recruiter had told him he was too big for the paratroopers, Bucklew had settled for the Navy, where instead of landing a warship he had been railroaded into instructor duty for Gene Tunney. Eventually escaping into what he thought was the Army-Navy Scouts and Raiders, he had instead been pigeonholed into the role of Scout Boat Officer, as which he had ferried his Army raiders from ship to surf on invasions from North Africa to Malta—and on the last of these, had even watched a soldier swim ashore and, with directional flashlight, valiantly signal the landing fleet from under the lip of a machine-gun-barking enemy pillbox. Eager to emulate such bravery, Bucklew—as soon as the Army had pulled out of the Scout and Raider program—had not simply filled the gap, he had set an example for others to follow.

In the Sicily campaign, he had checked the beach himself, then signaled the fleet from the bobbing shell of a blackened kayak while screaming "balls of fire" skipped off the water around him. In the weeks before the Normandy invasion, he skimmed to the coast and collected density-testing bottom samples up to twenty yards from the shore, then evaded a flotilla of six enemy trawlers and a crash of bullet snaps from an MG42 machine gun by escaping into the night and fog. On the smoke-gray dawn of D-Day, Bucklew and his LCT Scout Boat Crew led the first wave of floating tanks to Omaha Beach, fired earsplitting rockets and twin .50-caliber machine guns to silence an enemy pillbox, then spent the day throttling through red-clouded water and mine-topped obstacles to pluck drowning soldiers from burning landing craft. Stashed at Fort Pierce to pass on his experience to the Scouts and Raiders School, Bucklew had pulled every string within reach to get back to the war. The effort had landed him in front-line duty with Mary Miles's guerrillas in China, where, disguised in black peasant clothes, straw hat, and sandals—an impossible disguise for a man of his size, which he made barely believable only by contorting himself into a stoop—he had led an overland reconnaissance of possible landing beaches that had ultimately turned into a foot-wrecking flight to escape the Japanese, who had apparently heard the rumors about "Big Stoop." For this and every other one of his inland excursions, Bucklew—in the final days of the war—had been entrusted to lead an assault force of Scout and Raider veterans on an amphibious raid of the well-defended airfield at Amoy to capture a secret Japanese codebook; this might have been a redemption of Unit Six's attempt at an all-Navy raid had the war not abruptly ended.

Undated photo of Phil Bucklew (left)
and John Tripson conducting recon of the Amoy coast, 1945.

For his service in World War II, Bucklew had received an unheard-of number of commendations—a Bronze Star for North Africa, a Silver for Salerno, then a brace of Navy Crosses, one for Sicily, another for Omaha Beach. Not even his friend and fellow footballer Buck Halperin had been awarded as many. Naturally, such a record had opened doors to more unconventional opportunities, including two and a half years in Korea—more than twice the length of a standard war tour—where Bucklew had doubled as the Navy's representative to the CIA and led the Beachjumpers, a Navy unit created to collect and jam the enemy's electronic communications or periodically mimic them to sow chaos in their transmissions.

By 1963, Bucklew's Navy career had been remarkable for two reasons. First, only a handful of sailors had carried into the postwar fleet such a wide range of operational experiences—multiple shipwrecks, multiple amphibious landings, multiple reconnaissance missions, multiple chances at leading and organizing guerrillas—all of which had given weight to his opinion with the Navy's top leaders, even with Arleigh Burke. The second reason: Unlike Draper Kauffman's, Bucklew's Navy career had only rarely had anything to do with the regular, blue-water Navy—a factor of supreme importance now that he had been promoted to lead the Navy's survey in Vietnam.

In other words, if Admiral Felt—the hero of carrier fliers—had hoped that Savidge's team would validate the Navy's general inclination for blue-water support missions in Vietnam (blockading, bombing, and transporting), he could hardly have done worse than to choose a deputy who had not only shown an ambivalence about blue water, but more important had already carried naval special warfare past the beach and into the mountains of China.

7

When Bucklew assumed command of the team, he knew his first job was to understand the field of play. To do this, he and his men embarked upon what he later described as an "extensive physical survey." Seen through the sun-drenched plexiglass of a prop plane or from the open fuselage of a helicopter, the Mekong Delta stretched out beneath them like an upside-down green spade. The wedges of this spade sliced between the sparkling blue waters of the Gulf of Thailand in the west and the South China Sea in the east. Twice the size of New Jersey but as flat as Florida, the delta's interior revealed innumerable glinting gash lines, the traces of "more than 5,000 miles of navigable waters." Beginning on the northwest border, two major parallel rivers draped southeast across the delta like twin caramel-colored sashes—the Bassac River in the south, the Mekong, or Nine Dragons, River in the north. Both rivers fed a femoral's worth of tributaries striped with thin-waked sampans, plus a "gridiron" of "arrow-straight" French-built canals. Along these byways lay hamlets so connected to the water that they rarely extended farther than two thatch-roofed hootches from the riverbank, but whose length could stretch for ten kilometers.

Gliding over these prop-fouling waterways on the decks of diesel-thumping gunboats, Bucklew and his men watched riverbanks spill into flooded rice fields or rise into walls of sixty-foot-tall green palms, then collapse into plantation-sized tracts of six-foot-tall reeds. Though they never saw insurgents, their presence was evident everywhere: in increased numbers of recoilless rifle attacks; more discoveries of saltpeter caches for making gunpowder; no more enemy conservation of ammunition in mortar barrages; even signs of enemy artillery being carried upon the backs of elephants. At night, the air rattled with the echoes of inshore gunfire. "Don't we do something about it? Don't we assist?" asked Bucklew of his gunboat's skipper. The only thing they could do was impotently monitor the desperate voices of ARVN soldiers crackling over the radio.

In Saigon, Bucklew and his team boarded a creaky junk and set off down the twisting, mud-brown Long Tau River until they emerged onto the vastness of the South China Sea. With a coastline cluttered with innumerable coves and besieged by the fluttering sails of uncountable fishing junks, at first glance there seemed no question that the insurgency was exploiting both to lash together an aquatic equivalent of the Ho Chi Minh Trail. Supplies "couldn't be coming from elsewhere," MACV's operations officer Joe Stilwell, Jr., had concluded to Bucklew

Map of the Mekong Delta.

(this coming from a man whose father had nineteen years earlier built a 700-mile-long inland mountain road into China's back door intended to supply men like Bucklew and his SACO guerrillas).

To choke off these coastal entry points, MACV's Naval Advisory Detachment had already twisted together a blockade of American-advised Vietnamese Navy patrol craft and a junk fleet crewed by some 4,000 civilian fishermen, and even enlisted a handful of SEALs and Junk Force commandos as a coastal quick-reaction force that mirrored the anti-infiltration mission of the highland Green Berets. But had this all worked?

Beset by complications, including many of the blockade's broken junks left to rot on the beaches, these coastal measures suffered from a more fundamental problem: In spite of the reports of paid agents, evidence of large-scale seaborne smuggling simply did not exist—no captured boats buckling with supplies; no "direct observation" of blockade runners; no conspiracy of ocean convoys.

So, where were the endless supplies coming from? The answer was exactly the one that Navy planners had least wanted to hear.

8

All except for an abrupt ridge of low-rise mountains near the coast, the Cambodian border of the Mekong Delta was a 100-mile-long tract of flattened farmland, now a free-fire zone for a string of seven Special Forces camps—an impregnable rampart blocking the final stretch of the Ho Chi Minh Trail—except that it wasn't. The Communists had found a weakness common to every impregnable castle in history: a forgotten, unguarded aqueduct beneath the walls. Standing on the banks of the Mekong River at the Cambodian border checkpoint, Bucklew and his men watched South Vietnamese customs officials "lackadaisically" inspect only those craft whose crews volunteered to be inspected—none at night; none that crossed on the far, Communist-held side of the river. As best as Bucklew and his men could guess, every back-strapped grenade and bullet hauled in from North Vietnam was being unburdened upriver into a sampan, and from there directly injected into the delta's bloodstream. And what was to stop them?

To curb infiltration, MACV had already divided the entire country of South Vietnam into four separate tactical zones, each one the responsibility of a US Army commander; each commander responsible for his section of the Army's traditional terrain: "from high water mark inland."

This arrangement had worked relatively well in the top three-fourths of the country, where dry land and sparsely populated provinces had permitted use of the Army's best assets: infantry boots and artillery barrages. In the Mekong Delta—the area designated by MACV as the IV Corps Tactical Zone (referred to simply as "Fourth Corps")—these conditions existed only as exceptions. There, 65 percent of the country's entire population was squeezed onto just 23 percent of the country's landmass—a by-product of fertile fields that were themselves a by-product of the water. Because a decisive battle was achievable only in those areas where the water was shallow enough for the Army's "moderately amphibious" M113 personnel carriers, commanders in IV Corps had mostly left the delta's marshes, rivers, and canals to the least capable force in the entire country—the Vietnamese Navy.

Since 1961, the US Naval Advisory Detachment had grown the Vietnamese Navy to just over 8,000 sailors—an achievement until compared to the US Army's training of the ARVN's 196,000 soldiers. Of these 8,000 sailors, only about 1,200—a scant 15 percent of the total—were now assigned to the River Assault Group, or RAG. The gross imbalance had enabled Army and ARVN commanders to completely exclude the RAG from operational planning in the delta—even operations that required the RAG's boats; even the counterinfiltration plan that governed IV Corps' entire strategy. This exclusion had turned the RAG's 200 or so assault vessels—mostly a mixture of hardened, World War II–era landing craft—into what one historian called the ARVN's "taxi service," essentially ferries for administrative movements over river sections so secure that many soldiers dangled their legs over the gunwales. The entire RAG, said one advisor, had turned into the Army's "lackey boy."

In the Army's defense, the RAG to date had been capable of little else. After three years of US Navy sponsorship, RAG radiomen could hardly operate their own radios or fix their own antennas; RAG boat chiefs could barely prevent a swamped boat from sinking, even pierside; and despite the threat of sappers and floating mines in the rivers, RAG boats could often be found anchored under a bridge with every crewman asleep, even the boat's American advisor. Dressed in rakish mixtures of bush hats and khaki uniforms that actually seemed to attract enemy fire, most of these advisors, wrote Bucklew's former frogman Phil Koehler, were "disgruntled and discouraged," some doing "more harm than good," many of them sore about not listening to their Stateside detailers, who had warned them that their service in Vietnam would be less beneficial to their careers than a year at the Naval War College. "They were the most frustrated men I have ever encountered in the military," Bucklew would say. And why wouldn't they have been? Unable to command their own crews without a translator, unable to break free of Army transport duty, unable—except by great effort—to get soldiers or Marines assigned to their boats to pursue ambushers beyond the riverbanks, RAG advisors in January 1964 were in the front rank of the most reactive mission in Navy history. Only one thing suggested otherwise: Aside from the RAG's backwater fleet of landing craft, the Navy had also fielded a strange vessel—as low-riding as an alligator with a turret on its nose, and a name that reminded every professional sailor who saw it of the most aggressive, most unconventional episode in US Navy history. The class of craft was called a Monitor.

9

ONCE BUCKLEW AND HIS TEAM had uncovered the methods of infiltration, the next step was to chart a course for curbing it. At every outpost and headquarters, Bucklew and his men received a briefing in which they learned what was working and what was not. At the Special Forces camps, the team observed the "slow and time consuming effort" of winning the assistance of the local population, an effort that the Navy's Seabees were already lending a shoulder to. The notable downside of this assistance, wrote former frogman Phil Koehler, was that the sailors seemed to be "rapidly losing their naval identity." More important, Bucklew and his team discovered that none of the A-Teams had yet discovered an effective way to pursue the enemy into the delta. One tactic that had worked and was "worthy of further stress in the future" was "the deployment of river craft with combat troops embarked." But there was an obvious problem in replicating such a tactic—the Green Berets had no high-speed boats; the ARVN troops were never available; and the SEALs—whom the survey team also visited—were stashed away in Danang, about as far from the delta as one could get and still be in South Vietnam.

Back in Saigon, Bucklew seemed to meet with everyone. He dined with Ambassador Henry Cabot Lodge; he had coffee with MACV commander Paul Harkins; he lunched with Harkins's deputy commander William Westmoreland, who pestered him without success for the yet-unpublished survey's contents. In the evenings, while the team scrambled to find answers to the report's final questions, Bucklew and

Del Giudice usually retired to one of several hotel restaurants, where the senior of the two reflected on the report's implications for the Navy, and the junior one dug for stories about North Africa and Omaha Beach. Bucklew graciously entertained all questions. When the report's various sections were completed, the team met in their conference room and went around the table. When they had a question, they summoned advisors from the field for answers. To double-check the survey's most controversial conclusion, Bucklew met with MACV intelligence colonel Dutch Kramer, the same Marine who had enlisted Atcheson and the UDTs as advisors for coastal raids in Korea. Like Bucklew, Kramer had served in SACO and knew full well the Asian guerrilla's ability to walk long distances overland. Whether this informed his understanding of the problem is not known, but this is: Kramer also recognized the Navy's preferred threat of seaborne smuggling for what it largely was: a myth.

After each team member submitted his handwritten section, Bucklew typed the final report himself. In it, he generously gave credit to Admiral Savidge, his long-since-departed predecessor—he even kept the admiral's name in the first sentence of the first paragraph and only mentioned himself among the team's "working members." It was almost the report's only generosity. Forty-six pages long, each one vertically stamped Secret, the report's language was diplomatic, almost sterile, but its contents were anything but, each enumerated bullet another carefully worded indictment of the Navy's Vietnam planners, all guilty of the peacetime military's most predictable blunder: They had brought the fleet they wanted to the battlefield instead of the fleet the battlefield needed.

And what kind of fleet did the battle need? According to Bucklew, the battle required something not unlike the riverine force used in the American Civil War, in which, said Abraham Lincoln, "Uncle Sam's web feet" had fought "not only in the deep sea and the broad bay . . . but also up the narrow muddy bayou and wherever the ground was a little damp." For an unconventional example in a "modified amphibious" environment, Bucklew could have drawn attention to his own legacy. He didn't; he never did. Lincoln's fleet was example enough.

In practical terms, his solution for the Navy's heretofore failure was a comprehensive overhaul of the entire counterinfiltration effort: more Navy boats, more Navy boarding teams; more river checkpoints, submarine nets, navigation lights; a system for checking cargo manifests and enforcing curfews; and in exchange for all this, more Navy representation in IV Corps planning. On the question of whether the Navy was "missing the boat" on counterinsurgency—the winning of locals' loyalty through civic action and the leading of indigenous troops—Bucklew's report was comparatively silent, especially given the date: just eighty-six days since Kennedy's assassination. Though he recommended increased boat support to the Special Forces camps, he had already judged the Green Berets' efforts as slow and time consuming, and therefore ineffective. Only two of the report's pages dealt with the Navy's limited efforts in civic action (coastal medical assistance and so on), and cautioned that additional expenditures in this area could actually "cause the effort to lose its sincerity."

10

DESPITE DEL GIUDICE's presence on the survey team, the final report mentioned the word "SEAL" only once, and then just to advocate for a single entity in Vietnam to command all the Navy's special units. Attached to this was no recommendation for the SEALs' future employment, but based on what the report did not recommend, there was really only one option left. Had the evidence of coastal smuggling existed, Bucklew and his team would have likely recommended a redoubling of the Navy's blockade, limiting SEAL operations to that sliver of dry land within reach of the blue-water fleet. Had MACV's civic action efforts and the Special Forces' camps proved more effective, Bucklew and his team would have probably recommended for the Navy its first comprehensive counterinsurgency mission: more advisory billets, more medical missions, more support to the civilian junk fleet, the creation of a civilian river variant; and for the SEALs, a redoubling of their advisory missions to groups like the Biet Hai commandos. Instead, in its forty-six pages the report used the term "counter-insurgency" only three times—a "somewhat nebulous field," Bucklew would one day call it—four fewer mentions than the term "counter-infiltration," the report's preferred mission. Appearing a total of ten times was a variant of the term "raiding," a tactic that could, said the report, "engender more fight back spirit" among the RAG's sailors, but would require companies of "pursuit raiders," preferably Marines or Rangers. And who would command such raids? On this question, the former Scout and Raider turned SACO guerrilla did not blink: "the over-water transport of raiding and landing forces . . . should be a Navy responsibility."

With no intention of letting Harkins or Westmoreland see the report first, as soon as it was completed Admiral Felt recalled Bucklew on the first available all-night flight to Honolulu. The next morning, a Sunday, Bucklew joined Felt and a handful of his staffers on the CINCPAC patio, where they "cross-examined" him over the team's conclusions.

"Do you feel it is right to subject American personnel to things you are recommending?" Felt asked skeptically, controlling his temper—easier to do, perhaps, when confronting a man twice his size.

"That's why we recommend them," Bucklew answered, then elaborated on his own advisory experience in World War II and his successes in his past service with the troops. Our sailors are "just as capable today," he added.

"I hope so," Felt replied.

Nine days later, on February 25, 1964, the Bucklew Report—the name by which even McNamara would refer to it—was officially distributed to leaders across the Navy, MACV, and the Joint Chiefs of Staff, eventually even rising to the office of the secretary of defense. It was handled, said Bucklew, like a "hot potato." Actually, it was more like a gauntlet—a challenge to the Navy's leaders to not only directly fight an inland river war, but to fight it in a way that mostly deviated from the consensus strategy of counterinsurgency. Over the next two years, this challenge would propel the Navy toward the development of new vessels, new organizations, and, most important, new missions, including the report's most recommended: raiding beyond the riverbanks.

For the SEALs, Bucklew's recommendations—once adopted by the Navy's senior leaders—were exactly the sort to solidify their future as inland commandos, except for one problem: The report had failed to explicitly nominate the SEALs as the river fleet's exclusive raiders. It was an oversight that had the potential to widen into a gap—a gap that could have quickly been crowded with other candidates.

Chapter 12

The Dam Break of Conventional War in Vietnam, and the Following Flood of Raiders That Failed to Beat the Navy to the Mekong Delta; All but One

Established in January 1964 with a nonspecific mandate to retaliate against North Vietnam for its support of the southern insurgency, MACV's Studies and Observations Group, or SOG, was an organization—part military, part CIA—whose blade was forged of indigenous guerrillas but whose hilt shrouded the controlling hand of American advisors—mostly Green Berets. To avoid any overt provocation of American involvement in North Vietnam, SOG's advisors not only ceased to influence their guerrillas the moment they crossed the border, but for airborne operations they also employed aircraft so sanitized of US-made equipment that they could only fly in perfect weather and only on the four full-moon nights per month. In the short term, such restrictions on American participation were resulting in airdropped guerrillas who were simply trying to survive without resupply, never mind any scouting or raiding. In the long term, this imperative to conceal American fingerprints would so drastically backfire that soon American arms would be dragged into an all-out war.

SOG's only operational bright spot of this period was its Maritime Study Group, a section staffed by some 150 LDNN guerrillas—many stripped from duty in the Mekong Delta, and all advised by a handful of enlisted SEALs and Force Recon Marines—whose relative success was owed to a getaway flotilla of six Norwegian-built torpedo boats called Nasties—all equally hamstrung by their lack of US-made equipment, a disadvantage relatively mitigated by the fact that their weapons were usually only a surf zone away from the guerrillas they were meant to support. As such, the Maritime Study Group's successes included a raid on a coastal warehouse, the demolition of a bridge, and destruction of a reservoir pumping station that prompted a North Vietnamese counterattack and a running gunfight that forced the SEAL-skippered Nasties to crowd the coast and thump the enemy with 81-millimeter mortars. Subsequent Nasty-born operations followed a similar rhythm of raid, run, and shell—a rhythm that almost perfectly synchronized with the echoes of SOG's namesake in Korea, but this time produced an outcome that reverberated much farther than any beachside counterattack.

On the last day of July in 1964, North Vietnam retaliated against SOG's coastal cuts by launching an unsuccessful torpedo boat attack against the USS *Maddox,* a destroyer on patrol that was believed to be the source of SOG's coastal raids. On the night of August 4—a night so fraught with bad weather that visibility was limited to adjacent whitecaps—sensors on board the *Maddox* and the USS *Turner Joy* detected another suspected attack by North Vietnamese torpedo boats. Three days later, after much exaggeration of the incident and pressure by the Johnson administration to act, Congress passed the Gulf of Tonkin Resolution—the authorization to use conventional US forces in South Vietnam. The decision was ironic, considering that SOG's operations had been intended to avoid such an escalation, but more important, one that demonstrated again the potential of raiders to act as a lever for strategic consequence. Now that consequence was taking the form of conventional American troops who would no longer need to disguise themselves as advisors.

Only if these troops had appeared on the horizon in square-sailed Viking longboats could the coming of American raiders have seemed more imminent. It especially seemed so for that corner of the country to which Bucklew had already drawn the US military's attention, and whose lack of LDNNs meant it was now completely open for a non-Navy competitor, however, only one of which would beat the SEALs to their battlefield; not so much as a competitor but as a pathfinder.

2

AT THE TIME of the Gulf of Tonkin Resolution, the only all-American special operations unit in the Vietnam battlespace was Sub Unit 1, a squad of Force Recon Marines assigned to a Navy minesweeping flotilla for the limited purpose of surveying potential landing sites for invasion. But what was a Force Recon Marine? Originally drawn from the Marine Corps' divisional reconnaissance units, Marine Force Recon had been established in 1957 for the purpose of strategic-level reconnaissance missions, and as such was capable of "deep surveillance up to 100 miles inland"—a sort of bird dog for finding the enemy for the rest of the Fleet Marine Force. Since then, Force Recon Marines had stretched the length of their legs to 300 miles, and in the process had mastered everything from parachuting and pathfinding to scuba diving and submarine lockouts. For these reasons, they had come be to be viewed, said journalist Martin Russ, as the "Commandos of the Corps," the unit that other Marines "surreptitiously" stared at "with awe." While this status did not necessarily qualify Force Recon Marines as raiders, their adaptability did indicate that they could have availed themselves to just such a mission shift. Other indicative traits included the following: Reconnaissance Marines had been raiding since Captain James Jones had led the VAC Recon Marines against Apamama in 1943; Force Recon had plenty of Ranger School graduates—by their accounts, even more than the SEALs; and except for their four billets to SOG—one officer, three enlisted men—Force Recon had no advisory commitments. Even Victor "Brute" Krulak, the legendary commanding general of all Marines in the Pacific, was in favor of adding the raiding mission to their portfolio. So, what stopped them from seizing the raiding mission recommended by the Bucklew Report?

On March 8, 1965, a battalion of the 3rd Marine Division landed in Vietnam—not another group of beret-wearing advisors, but the war's first combat troops, sloughing from the surf in the same blotch-camouflaged helmets worn in the campaigns of the Central Pacific. Greeted by a line of lei-bearing Vietnamese girls and a welcome sign stretched between two downturned paddles courtesy of UDT 12, the Marines landed not in the murky Mekong Delta—the most logical theater of operations for the US military's most amphibious branch of service—but on the white sands of Danang, the beachhead to the I Corps Tactical Zone, or "Eye Corps," the northernmost quadrant of the country. From the eastern coast, the landscape darkened into a veil of triple-canopy jungle, then rose gradually into the western highlands—not exactly *The Sands of Iwo Jima,* but a beachhead to a kind of war the Marines had always wanted, one in which they would be untethered to their traditional Navy anchor and could finally be the masters of their own battlespace.

In less than three months' time, the I Corps battlespace would contain some 18,000 Leathernecks—all of them ready for a war, if only they could find one. In May, the Force Recon Marines of Sub Unit 1 were reassigned to various Special Forces camps in I Corps. Their mission: to scout the surrounding mountains and report their findings, preferably the locations of the enemy's redoubts, to slake the battle hunger of their fellow Marines. Based on his résumé, none seemed hungrier than the Marine who now assumed command over all the others—a raider whose bona fides were challenged only by his preference for a different style of warfare.

On June 4, 1965, General Lew Walt assumed command of all Marines in Vietnam. Square-headed and burly, and a veteran of Red Mike Edson's 1st Raider Battalion as well as yard-by-yard Pacific fighting that had earned him two Navy Crosses, Walt would soon be known throughout the Marine Corps as the "squad leader in the sky"—10,000 miles a month of "flying so low," a witness would say, that the pilot would have to "yo-yo over every bump in the ground." By all external indications a high priest of direct action and the Marine Corps' prerogatives, Walt had actually acquired the same respect for counterinsurgency as had Bill Yarborough, and in the near future, when not bird-dogging for his infantrymen, would often be found in the evenings watching an outdoor movie with some "250 cross-legged Vietnamese kids." Within two months of his arrival, he would approve the establishment of the Combined Action Program, essentially a Marine version of the Special Forces' early CIDG initiative—the harnessing of villagers through civic action and guerrilla training.

Just as it had originally appeared, Walt's inherent affinity for counterinsurgency would consign the majority of Force Recon Marines to an advisory role in I Corps' Army Special Forces camps, but with one distinction: unlike the Green Berets that had metastasized into a parallel army with parallel operations, Force Recon was still seen by Marine planners as a support unit for the rest of the Fleet Marine Force, their mission of reconnaissance, as one historian would describe it, as "a means to an end, not an end in itself." Put simply—the preferred complexity of every Marine—Walt foresaw for Force Recon an operational future that could be summed up in two punchy sentences: "You find. We'll bail you out." It was a phrasing that suggested Force Recon's value to the Marines in Vietnam would not be as raiders, but as bait.

In six months, this concept of operations would contribute to the cornering of a unit of Force Recon Marines, Green Berets, and CIDG troops on a hilltop surrounded by as many as 200 North Vietnamese soldiers. Before the cavalry could "bail them out," the enemy overran the hilltop and killed fourteen defenders, three of them Marines. This disaster would ultimately convince General Walt to pull Force Recon out of the Special Forces camps altogether and place them under the command of the 3rd Reconnaissance Battalion. Tantamount to placing the SEALs under the UDTs, this action effectively subordinated Force Recon's future to a unit of lesser capability—effectively disbanding them—and in a section of the country that disqualified them from raiding the Mekong Delta's riverbanks. So, who would?

3

A TOTAL OF FIFTEEN ARMY DIVISIONS and brigades would ultimately serve in the Vietnam War, divisions including the Big Red One of Omaha Beach, the 101st Airborne of Bastogne, and the Iron Horses of the Hurtgen Forest. All would arrive wanting to hoist the pennant of another victorious battle of annihilation. But how to annihilate what could not be found? In the summer of 1965, two Army initiatives emerged to help solve this problem, both with missions similar to that of the Marine Corps' Force Recon and both with the potential to be something more.

The first of these initiatives was an outgrowth of the Special Forces' Leaping Lena operation, based in the centrally located coastal city of Nha Trang. Leaping Lena was run by the thirty Green Berets of a detachment called Project Delta, whose four- to eight-man teams of irregulars had been trained to parachute into the western jungles to locate enemy units, but, more important, were teams that had the potential to take on a countrywide commando role. Or might have, if not for their posting to Nha Trang, a city of French restaurants, inviting beaches, and abundant brothels. Exposed to such temptations, Project Delta's Green Beret advisors had quickly settled into a comfortable routine of booze, prostitutes, and weeklong jungle patrols, this last chore converted into profit by using their absences to rent out their beachside hotel rooms. As with SOG, early results had been atrocious. Of the first forty newly trained Lenas who had airdropped into the Laotian jungle's 120-foot-tall, parachute-tangling trees, only five had made it back to Vietnam; one had died trying to rappel himself out of a treetop.

Because of such results, Project Delta's role—in the year since its inception—had shifted from reconnaissance missions for the 5th Special Forces Group on the Laotian border to reconnaissance missions for the conventional Army's rapidly arriving divisions in their respective areas of operations—all in the II and III Corps Tactical Zones in the center of the country. In this new capacity, most of Project Delta's after-action recommendations had centered on the improvement of tactical air support—all recommendations in keeping with their outlined mission of finding the enemy so Air Force bombs and Army boots could crush him. None of these recommendations reflected any interest in transforming Project Delta into a Special Forces–led raiding unit; at least, not until June 1965, when Project Delta was taken over by its new commander.

Army Major Charles Beckwith,
commander of Project Delta, conducting defense of Plei Me.

As prepossessing as a comic-book Superman—albeit one with a high-and-tight haircut—when Major Charlie Beckwith assumed command he immediately took stock of Project Delta's accumulation of women, nonchalance, and graft, and dismissed the twenty-three Green Berets most responsible for it. This completed, he distributed a Wanted flyer across all Special Forces' posts in Vietnam with the following announcement: "Will guarantee you a medal, a body bag, or both." Eager to replicate the commando example of the British SAS with whom he had recently completed a tour, Beckwith ferried his stalwart volunteers to one of Nha Trang's coastal islands and subjected them to a three-week selection course. Within a month, he had forty Green Berets trained in long-range navigation and Special Air Service–type tactics plus four companies' worth of Vietnamese Rangers. In August, he led four recon teams into Pleiku Province for a three-day mission to detect enemy movement. The results were mixed: One team grew so spooked about being ambushed that they ditched four rucksacks and the radio they would have needed to call for help if they had been. In another team, the point man accidentally circled back to the tail of his own patrol, where the rear security man shot him dead. After spying two companies of brown-shirted insurgents snaking through the jungle carrying the litters of thirty-three dead or wounded comrades (a perfect target), one team managed to call in an airstrike but in their excitement forgot to confirm that they hit anything. Quick to record the "deficiencies" of his own men in his after-action report, Beckwith nevertheless could not help but simultaneously promote Project Delta's suitability for the operations he really wanted: what he called Hunter-Killer-type missions, "in areas where other units [found] it difficult to operate." Similar to the legendary Bill Darby in his bravery, aggressiveness, ambition, concern for his men, and even in the impenetrability of his southern accent, Beckwith also shared Darby's most consequential deficiency: that thing Shakespeare had called the "better part of valor," and the underwriter of every disaster from Cisterna to Hwaachon Dam, discretion. Or if not discretion, at least a rank not superior enough to say no to misuse.

In October, multiple regiments of North Vietnamese troops crossed the Laotian border and besieged the Special Forces camp at Plei Me—an isolated, triangular stockade of red dirt, sandbags, and tin-roofed shelters surrounded on all sides by a green sea of treeless free-fire slopes. Beyond these, in every direction, a curtain of flashing hilltops loomed like the memory of Dien Bien Phu—the final defeat that had collapsed the last of French resolve in Indochina. Inside the camp, huddled against the splashing mortars and "ropes of green and orange tracers," were some 400 mud-caked Montagnard fighters and their families, plus a platoon of LLDBs and one American A-Team. Already, enemy attacks had filled a pyramid of some sixty stacked body bags and left the successive lines of perimeter barbed wire interrupted with grotesquely swollen dead now strung up like sagging scarecrows.

Faced with the annihilation of one of his border camps, the commander of the 5th Special Forces Group, Colonel William "Bulldog" McKean, a man with no experience in the Special Forces he commanded, ordered Beckwith and his men to reinforce Plei Me—not even close to the kind of mission for which Project Delta had been intended. More concerned with saving lives than adhering to principle, Beckwith gathered a force of some fourteen specially trained Project Delta Green Berets and two companies of his Vietnamese Rangers, then landed them well outside the camp for a mad morning dash through a break in the enemy's lines that left two rescuers dead—one of them a long-haired American photographer shot in the side of the face. Upon relieving the A-Team commander, Beckwith immediately set to inspecting his new post and securing his lines; he even press-ganged two reporters into crewing a machine gun. He also saw what no one else did: not a besieged camp, but a base of operations. Within four hours of his arrival, Beckwith was forming ad hoc raiding parties, everything from multiple companies of Rangers to clear out the enemy-held hilltops to what he called "commando type" squads with flamethrowers to knock out the enemy's individual machine gun bunkers.

During the day, his radiomen directed a constant wheel of Air Force and Navy fighter-bombers, each attack blowing the surrounding green into hell-black balloons of jellied napalm while tendrils of gray smoke streaked the skyline, the residue of what were ultimately 672 sorties. When the siege was finally broken, Beckwith estimated the camp's surroundings to be littered with the khaki-clad bodies of 800 to 900 enemy troops—not quite the number of Confederates killed in Pickett's Charge. In his conclusions about the battle, the stone-faced Beckwith marveled at the enemy's combat skill—"the best troops I have ever seen," he told a reporter—and officially reprimanded Plei Me's A-Team for failing "to patrol the close in area around their camp." To him, the lesson validated everything he had done in Nha Trang and emboldened him to officially reiterate that his Rangers and Project Delta operators should be trained "in straight-forward offensive tactics."

Having not only survived misuse but thrived in it, Beckwith—in the aftermath of Plei Me—was finally allowed to form four "all-American" Recon Teams, another step closer to the SAS commandos for which he had long advocated. There was only one problem: In 1965, the Army didn't really want SAS commandos, let alone Rangers. Instead, the Army's division commanders still wanted the same kind of unit as the Marine Corps' Force Recon, pathfinders to guide as many troops to the battlefield as possible. Soon to be known as the hero of Ia Drang, Lieutenant Colonel Harold G. Moore—commander of the 1st Battalion, 7th Cavalry—conveyed his desires to Beckwith in much the same words as General Walt had to Force Recon: "you go find them, I'll come kill them." After all, what good was a hit-and-run raid by commandos compared to a full-scale beating by a battalion of helicopter-borne infantrymen? The only problem: After the enemy's thrashing at Ia Drang, insurgents would rarely linger anywhere long enough for such troops to pounce on them, a heresy to Army planners still cleaving to the lessons of the last war.

The Army's most fervent apostle for the new faith of raids and raiders left Vietnam in January 1966 when Beckwith, while scouting a landing zone from a helicopter, was shot through the gut by a .51-caliber machine gun, ending his command of Project Delta and consigning him—after four months of hospitalization and the removal of his gallbladder and twenty-one inches of small intestine—to instructor duty at the one place his ideas could flourish: the Army's Ranger School at Fort Benning. In Vietnam, he left behind a stack of after-action reports of Project Delta's operations, each including a variation of the same complaints made by every other commander in the history of the US Army's unconventional efforts: subordination of the unit to less-than-divisional control; failure by Army leaders to understand the unit's proper employment; misuse of the unit as conventional infantry. To free Project Delta from these and presumably to allow them to transform into the SAS commandos he had always wanted, Beckwith—in one of his final reports—had even recommended that "all Infantry Units of Brigade size develope [*sic*] [their own] Long Range Patrol capability." As it happened, the brigades were already on their way to creating these: quasi-commando raiders with the potential to reach every corner of the country, including the one that needed them the most.

4

At about the same time that Beckwith had begun his initial overhauls of Project Delta, the 1st Brigade of the 101st Airborne Division had arrived in II Corps with an unexceptional-looking operations officer in its ranks whose serial adventures in past conflicts seemed better suited to a square-jawed superhero. Briefly a member of the Eighth Army Ranger Company in the Korean War, then a company commander of the 27th Infantry Regiment's Wolfhound Raiders—a unit that had been created to fill the gap left by the Ranger companies' disbandment—Major David Hackworth, at thirty-four years old, had already earned a battlefield commission, three battlefield wounds, three Silver Stars, and as much combat experience as any other American soldier at that time. Eager to re-create his Wolfhound Raiders—as is anyone who has had to let go of an elite unit—Hackworth, upon arrival in Vietnam, had assessed the jungle and the enemy's tactics and immediately advocated for the recruitment of what he called the 1st Brigade's biggest "studs" for service in a fifty-man unit called Tiger Force that could "out-G the G": outguerrilla the guerrillas.

The result had been the Army's first all-American, long-range reconnaissance patrol unit, or LRRP (pronounced lurp), a unit not unlike the one Beckwith had been in the process of trying to create with Project Delta. Unlike the Green Berets of Project Delta, however, the soldiers of Tiger Force had been subjected to no real training program beyond their various occupational specialties, nor had those in the variously named copycats of the 101st's other subordinate commands—the 2nd Battalion's Hawks; the 502nd's tomahawk-wielding Hatchet Team. The first real training program did not come until September, when just ten soldiers from the 101st had been permitted to attend Beckwith's three-week course in Nha Trang. It was an invaluable education for the student-soldiers, but only moderately successful, since the graduates' commanders had not yet discovered the optimal employment for their LRRP units. The arrival of more divisions would not improve the problem, as none would arrive in Vietnam with an already established capability. Compounding this problem was the Army's increasingly diluted pool of motivated soldiers, as the rolls were increasingly flooded by draftees. Before long, replacements for the various LRRP units would gain acceptance by simply volunteering, then completing three patrols. This lack of training and selection would naturally have consequences.

In February 1966, Hackworth's Tiger Force was ordered to join in the daytime attack of the enemy-held village of My Canh as though it were any other infantry company. For the assault, Tiger Force's twenty-three-year-old commanding officer, 1st Lieutenant James Gardner, a redheaded West Point washout, spread his men along a skirmish line, bayonets affixed, and literally charged them across an open field of waist-high grass. Predictably, they were cut down by machine gun fire. The results: eleven wounded, three killed, one of these being a newly arrived Black soldier shot beneath the jaw and practically decapitated. This was not merely a deficit of advanced tactics, but a bankruptcy of basic infantry principles—a debt that Gardner was honor-bound to settle by single-handedly crawling to four of the enemy's machine gun bunkers to destroy each with grenades. At the last one he was shot four times in the chest and killed. Gardner would not be the last LRRP who would have to compensate for his lack of training with bravery.

More than a year after Hackworth's creation of Tiger Force, MACV commander William Westmoreland would order the 5th Special Forces Group to correct the training deficiencies of the Army's various LRRP teams by reproducing the three-week course Beckwith had created for Project Delta. Established as the Recondo School—Westmoreland's mash-up of three words: reconnaissance, commando, and doughboy—the course would do more than just correct deficiencies. It would quickly boast a nearly 40 percent attrition rate and essentially function as a forward-deployed Ranger School, rappel towers and all. Training blocks would cover a swath of long-range reconnaissance subjects, but also many prerequisites for amphibious raiding, including 180 minutes of swimming, small-boat handling, over-the-beach landings, even a sixty-minute section on the searching and transporting of captives and the writing of property receipts for the equipment taken from them. Standing at attention in front of desks cleared of everything but ashtrays, Recondo graduates would receive a downturned, arrowhead patch signifying their "Indian skills of field craft" and would be welcomed, said one speaker, into the ranks of the Army's elite—the paratroopers, the pathfinders, and yes, the Rangers. "No matter how toughened up [the Army's other troops] became in the war," correspondent Michael Herr would soon write, "they still looked innocent compared to the Lurps." Bedecked in boondock hats and tiger-striped fatigues, with faces smeared green and armed with an experimental arsenal of suppressed M16s and sawed-off M79 grenade launchers—the latter often carried like Old West revolvers in modified canteen pouches—no other Army troops in the entire war could have so readily filled the raider gap in Vietnam. And yet they did not, for reasons that should be less than surprising.

Addressing the Recondo School graduates at their commencement ceremony, one speaker would essentially reiterate the same injunctions General Walt had given to Force Recon and Colonel Moore had given to Project Delta: "Do not lose sight of your basic mission . . . which is to return to your respective units . . . [as] the 'eyes and ears' of your brigade, division and corps commanders who must be able to find the enemy to destroy him." Valued primarily for their eyes and ears, it would take some time before the LRRP teams would be able to exert the potential of their teeth and claws, an evolution that would be as erratic as the staggered arrival dates of each division. It was an evolution that would be especially protracted for the LRRPs of the Army's 9th Infantry Division—a late arrival to the war, but more important, a late arrival to that tactical zone for which Bucklew's report had been written.

5

At the time of the Bucklew Report's publication, the war's prohibition on American regulars meant that the only raiders who could have rolled back the enemy's grip on the Mekong Delta's riverbanks were those various collections of American-advised indigenous guerrillas. One of the first such groups had been led by Lieutenant Roy Boehm, the black-beret-wearing former UDT swimmer who had risen to become the first executive officer of SEAL Team TWO before becoming an advisor to the LDNN in the coastal Mekong Delta. Preferring not to waste his war in measuring beach gradients but rather in performing the one mission for which he had spent his last two years preparing, Boehm had, upon taking command, hustled his watered-down, indigenous UDT swimmers—forty-two giggling, hand-holding, mostly barefoot Vietnamese sailors—through a two-month combat course that had ended their use of explosive primer cord as rope and succeeded in overhauling them into the Mekong Delta's first coastal raiding force. Widemouthed as a duck and so bowlegged that one observer declared that he wore his "balls in parentheses," Boehm quickly taught his frogmen to stop treating patrols like shopping trips—kidnapping chickens, haggling with villagers over corn, and so on—and had begun conducting a series of successful raids, the most celebrated being an on-line, daylight assault through knee-sucking mud and rifle fire to capture six beached enemy junks. Some of their operations, Boehm later claimed, had ventured so far from the riverbanks that they had even jostled up against Vietnamese Rangers and prompted complaints that the LDNN were "poaching" ARVN territory and exceeding the boundaries of their "maritime environment." Boehm's defense: "our canteens were full of water." It was a justification that might have led to more inland encroachments had Boehm's guerrillas not also been poached—stripped from him and shipped north to support MACV's Studies and Observations Group.

With these units rendered ineffective, the only raiders still led by Americans in the IV Corps Tactical Zone—at least until the Delta's LDNN had been replenished and the prohibition on American regulars relaxed—were also the least like any in American history. But their examples would soon help steer the future of the SEALs that helped create them.

Unlike the war's other indigenous advisory efforts—the SOG guerrillas, the Green Berets' Mike Forces, the SEALs' LDNNs—which had all been created to confront the enemy in head-to-head combat, the CIA's Counter-Terror Teams, or CTTs, had instead been created to cut out the enemy's kneecaps, to harass those human beings that made up the VCI, or Viet Cong Infrastructure. These were the tax collectors who shook down peasants for rice and piasters; the well-heeled buying agents who shopped Saigon's streets for penicillin, cement, and spare parts; the tireless women in makeshift jungle factories who primed Chinese grenades and Frankensteined new rifles out of dead ones. Most of all, these were the province chieftains and village commissars who indoctrinated new fighters, and whose rosters, vouchers, and receipts papered the trails to the hideouts of all the rest. As the CIA's planners had seen it, each one of these was a separate cog in a deceptively hierarchical bureaucracy, so Byzantine that it was only possible to dismantle it by enlisting those who had been in it—that being CTTs' ideal recruit, a Viet Cong deserter or turncoat. Called Hoi Chanhs in Vietnamese, at best these were disillusioned Communists—hungry, tired, or just plain homesick; at worst, they were scorned guerrillas who carried out vendettas against their former comrades, the cruelest rumored to have been a traitor turned avenger who had waged a "one-man, two-year war" against the Viet Cong; "God knows how many VC he killed," said the reporter who broke his story. After the Hoi Chanhs, the best recruits to rob the Viet Cong of their support were common criminals—thieves, toughs, ARVN deserters; all paroled from various jails and who were, said an adviser, like the cast from *The Dirty Dozen*. As that movie would show and as the CIA had already discovered, there were challenges in attempting to break a herd of wild mustangs into wearing a war chariot's yoke.

The CIA's initial solution to this mustang breaking was—as usual—to outsource the job to the US military's trainers and advisors. In this case, however, the CIA's planners did not offer the job to their standby pool of Special Forces A-Teams, but instead took a long-shot chance on a three-man element from SEAL Team ONE—a gamble due to the element's leader, a man who had convinced the CIA planners that he was the equivalent of an entire Special Forces A-Team. He almost was. With a boxer's jab that could "part the Red Sea," said one who saw it, and a six-foot-three-inch frame that could have waded through it anyway, it had been natural to assume that Storekeeper 1st Class Robert Wagner's most likely contribution to the SEAL teams would have been in pure pugilistic combat. His instincts for it were undeniable. Driving a jeep through a MACV compound and passing so close to an Army sergeant that the offended man had taken a swing at Wagner's lieutenant in the passenger seat, Wagner had responded by slamming on the brakes, then beating the sergeant so savagely that the lieutenant had feared for the man's life. "I never saw anything like that," the lieutenant said later. Not an uncommon expression whenever Wagner was around.

As one of the only enlisted UDTR graduates of that period to be selected to skip the mandatory stint at a UDT for direct assignment to a SEAL team, Bob Wagner—despite a wife and four young children—had predictably risen to become one of his team's most eager volunteers for repeat deployments to train the Biet Hai and LDNN: three six-month tours in three years. In this role he had earned a reputation among superiors that had swung between the superlatives of "perfectionist advisor" and "perfect SEAL," reputations he had cultivated while simultaneously building a name as a wheeler-dealer for his part ownership of a beachside bar in Danang called the Blue Moon. Clean-cut for a SEAL, even by 1960s standards—his face a graph of hard angles and straight lines below a flattop deliberately ranked to attention—his only physical feature that suggested he was anything more than a lockstep conventional were his eyes: hard, focused, a bit like a predator's in pursuit of its prey and implying a similar pace.

From July 1966 to May 1967, Wagner was a blur in green fatigues or slacks and golf shirt, either directing construction for a miniature UDTR training camp at Vung Tau or sloughing from the beach to the rifle range to the classroom to the various CIA offsites, everywhere

Wagner training PRU candidates on the rifle range.

coaching students, meeting case officers, recruiting his first batch of volunteers, almost all of which were Hoi Chanhs and looked like a gang of adolescent pickpockets armed with switchblades. As soon as these were sufficiently trained, Wagner personally led them to Vinh Binh Province, on the coastal edge of the northern Mekong Delta, the same area from whence they had been recruited. There, they patrolled the jungle trails and village pathways—Wagner's black beret towering above his turncoats—and ferreted out from the locals the information that only they, as former neighbors and Viet Cong, could. Relying on this information, Wagner led his men on thirteen operations, all but one a success. On the greatest of these, Wagner and his indigenous troops conducted a raid on an enemy-held village, a stunning exposition of artillery and aircraft that culminated with a well-coordinated ground assault. The village had been, in Wagner's words, "entirely obliterated"—the natural outcome of finding a target that matched the SEALs' original purpose, but not what had made the raid remarkable. That had been Wagner's capture of what he described as "3 high ranking VC political types"—not just a gold mine of Viet Cong locations and supply routes, but a treasure map to an entirely new kind of raiding target.

Rarely the goal of military operations but often a by-product, the capturing of prisoners for follow-on interrogation was, as any big-city policeman would have said, not only the best way to dismantle a criminal enterprise but also the best way to generate new targets—essentially, the best way to stay employed. Here had been the operational cornerstone of the CIA's entire Counter-Terror Program, and, as Wagner had recognized, a gateway to new SEAL opportunities. This is "really down our alley," this is "our foot in the door," Wagner had exclaimed to his own chain of command. "If we could show these people that the SEALs not only can train people, and train them well—better than anybody else . . . [and] can also effectively operate these teams, work with them and guide their operations, [then we can] create a demand so to speak for our services in this field." As Wagner had predicted, demand had been high indeed.

To make his case for a full partnership with the CIA, Wagner sat down and drafted a concept paper that formally detailed all of his proposals. The first of these was a name change from Counter-Terror Teams to Delta Reconnaissance Units, a less forward-leaning title but one that also attempted to drive the program toward that region where, more than any other, the Viet Cong's infrastructure spread out like spiderwebs. It also happened to be the area of Vietnam best suited for the

SEALs' expertise. That region was, of course, the Mekong Delta. The next proposals were equally self-serving. At the end of each eight-week training course, Wagner proposed to assign two SEAL advisors to each Reconnaissance Unit, which would in turn be assigned to a different delta province—sixteen provinces in total, thus creating a demand for thirty-two SEALs. Once there, these teams would "outguerrilla the guerrilla" by targeting the "political and economic structure in the VC controlled area." But what did this mouthful mean? Wagner's answer was a lot of the usual—harassment (better known as ambushing) and patrolling (better known as intel collection)—but also some of the unusual, including a mission not ever mentioned in Arleigh Burke's list of original SEAL operations. That mission—in Wagner's words—was abduction.

In the fall of 1966, the CIA half approved Wagner's recommended name change and recast the Counter-Terror Teams as the Provincial Reconnaissance Units, or PRUs (pronounced prews), a name that indicated a broader ambition than just the Mekong Delta—ironically, an ambition made possible only by Wagner's pace. His reward was a succession of hassles: a recall to SEAL Team ONE to justify his back-alley negotiations; an attempted power play by the Australian SAS to horn in on all his efforts; even the CIA's hiring of a Special Forces master sergeant who was meant to serve as the camp's intelligence officer, but who used his higher rank to try to wrest control of the entire program. When physical intimidation didn't clear such obstacles (it worked with the Special Forces master sergeant), Wagner always resorted to the same two levers. First, to his superiors in the Navy and the CIA he reiterated the SEALs' comparative edge over their competitors: in his words, "more flexible, more adaptable than the Special Forces or Marine Recon." Second, like all deal makers, he threatened to pack up and go home—a ploy that never failed to inflame the ambitions of his higher-ups in the US Navy.

By year's end, such maneuvers had convinced his superiors to enter into a miniature SACO-like arrangement in which the Navy agreed to provide a steady supply of SEALs to the CIA for advisory duty with the PRUs; an agreement that the chief of the CIA's counterterror group followed up by explicitly advocating for a PRU in every one of South Vietnam's forty-four provinces. Forget the Bucklew Report, forget the Mekong Delta, here was an opportunity for the SEALs to start raiding targets up and down the entire length of South Vietnam; and yet, it was an opportunity so overwhelming that—if accepted—would require more men than existed in all of SEAL Team ONE. Moreover, it would require them not as twelve-man platoons of direct-action commandos, but as two-man pairs of advisors.

In short, it was a chance to finally push the SEALs past their narrow expectations of raiding the delta's riverbanks and into a horizon as broad as that of the Army's Green Berets; or it might have been, if not for the competing crosswind that had already set the SEALs on a course that foreclosed this option.

Part 5

CULMINATION

Chapter 13

The Derailing of the First Direct-Action SEALs in the Rung Sat, and the Detachment That Restored Their Prospects

In December 1965, right about the same time that General Walt began pulling Marine Force Recon from the Special Forces camps in I Corps and the Army's division commanders began casting the LRRPs and Project Delta into the outlands of II and III Corps, Navy planners finally decided to dip a toe into that area for which Bucklew's two-year-old report had been written: the IV Corps Tactical Zone, the Mekong Delta. The physical manifestation of this toe would be Operation Game Warden, a traditional naval blockade intended to stop the flow of enemy contraband—meaning river patrols and cargo checks—but enforced by a fleet that would be tradition's opposite. Soon to be known as Combined Task Force 116, or CTF-116, this unconventional fleet would mostly be made up of 120 river patrol boats, or PBRs—green-painted civilian pleasure craft with a water-jet propulsion system and a draft of eighteen inches; perfect for skimming over waterways cluttered with logs, reeds, fish, snakes, and sandbars—but a fleet unlike any that Navy planners had ever conceived; moreover, one that the blue-water traditionalists were, even now, reluctant to launch. For signs of this reluctance, one needed to look no further than the Navy's early plan to dock its PBRs not at a series of riverbank outposts, but rather at one of four immobilized barges, their insides racked with bunks and outfitted with polished galleys, their bottoms anchored to the mouths of various rivers near the coast, and, more important, within reach of the blue-water ships that could support them.

At any other time, the Navy's self-imposed containment would have been commendable, a rare example of a government institution staying in its lane. But Westmoreland, the commander of MACV, needed troops, not temperance. He especially needed them for an increasingly hostile area near Saigon on the very northeastern edge of the coastal Mekong Delta known as the Rung Sat Special Zone, but for which he reportedly had "no troops to spare." Considering the locations and orientations of every other American special operations unit in Vietnam, Westmoreland could just as accurately have said that he had no troops available—not Force Recon, not Project Delta, not even a divisional LRRP team. So, who would cover it?

Already in the process of positioning the vanguard of a brown-water navy in the extremities of the Mekong Delta, it was no great leap for the commander in chief of the Pacific Fleet to attach to CTF-116 a detachment from SEAL Team ONE for onshore, direct-action operations. This was especially no great leap since those operations wouldn't be located anywhere near the heart of the Mekong Delta, but would be confined to the Rung Sat, a barely dry corner of coastal tidewater well within arm's reach of the Navy's blue-water comfort zone. Or at least that's how Westmoreland's invitation seemed at the outset. In hindsight, not since Tai Li had made his midnight proposal to Mary Miles to lead a guerrilla army in China had the US Navy been faced with such an opportunity for a landgrab.

Once the decision was made to attach the first batch of SEALs to CTF-116, it took Rear Admiral Norvell G. Ward, the commander of US Naval Forces in Vietnam, about two months of planning to prepare the infrastructure needed to support them: everything from boats to bedrolls. Unlike the barge-based PBR crews who would often have to motor for as many as four hours from the coast just to reach their upriver patrol areas, Ward decided to base the SEALs at the inland naval facility at Nha Be, a sweltering riverbank compound of green tents, saltwater showers, and barrel latrines whose disadvantages of stench and mosquitos were offset by convenient placement at the edge of the SEALs' intended area of operations. But as yet operations for which the Navy had not developed any standardized procedures. Who would the SEALs report to? How would their targets be selected? Probably most important: How best to interpret the meaning of direct action? This last was a question that would so stump the first direct-action SEALs in Vietnam that the Navy would nearly abandon the entire idea—that is, until the SEALs discovered a definition that would in turn define them.

2

GENERALLY UNDERSTOOD BY THE SEALs themselves as the behind-the-lines raiding of radar installations, railways, bridges, fuel depots, and command posts, the term "direct action" was mostly ambiguous to Navy ears. Wasn't all military action *direct*? The term only really made sense when compared to the *indirect* operations of other special units—those performed by all the various reconnaissance scouts and the Army's Special Forces advisors. It just so happened that the latter of these was, at that very moment, skyrocketing in public esteem as the sappy "Ballad of the Green Berets" neared number 1 in *Billboard.* To a susceptible listener, this ballad might have served as a subliminal nudge to interpret the SEALs' upcoming purpose as more like the civic action and advisory role performed by the song's wholesome singer. Fortunately for the SEALs, there was nothing susceptible about Admiral Ward.

Bald-headed and so plain-faced that his only outstanding features were a pair of horn-rimmed glasses and a set of horn-tipped caterpillars for eyebrows, Ward had defied expectations by succeeding in life with a personality that was just as captivating. Described by a reporter as "utterly unflamboyant," a comparison as descriptive as "ostentatiously bland," Ward—on the surface—telegraphed no obvious signs of innovation, nor did he appear a man queued to stretch the boundaries of naval warfare. It was a first impression that would prove the limitations of first impressions.

Having barely survived the attack on Manila Bay in December 1941—where Japanese bombers and an exploding pier fire had nearly sunk his submarine—Ward had gone on to serve on three different vessels on which he had thrived in countless more emergencies: instantaneous crash dives to the ocean floor to avoid enemy aircraft; prayer-lipped escapes through shuddering depth charges; even the emergency appendectomy of a nineteen-year-old shipmate in which Ward had had to white-knuckle two bent tablespoons to stretch open the man's stomach while an improvising pharmacist's mate had cut out the infection. In every one of Ward's wartime patrols, the operational orders had been the same: patrol a grid square, stalk the enemy's ships, launch a sneak attack, then escape into the depths to do it all again. Not since the age of sail had there been a military assignment as cut off from support or, more important, from supervision. As such, no other assignment had required as much personal initiative from a commander, or trust by those in authority. Taking command of his first submarine at just thirty years old, Ward had not been paralyzed by this freedom but propelled. Straining his eyes into a periscope lens, in just seven weeks he had orchestrated six separate torpedo attacks whose impacts had multiplied to sink an astonishing eight vessels. The feat had earned him a Navy Cross and a promotion to an operations billet at headquarters. Ultimately, this had placed him in the chain of command of all US submarines in the Pacific, including the USS *Barb,* whose skipper, in 1945, had enlisted eight unmarried crewmen to paddle a rubber boat to Sakhalin Island, where the sailors had trudged inland and blown up a sixteen-car Japanese train.

Twenty-one years since this historic raid, Ward was now in command of a fleet for which there was no true historical example, and from this position was responsible for setting the operational brackets that would likely channelize the SEALs into one of several possible futures—Force Recon–type reconnaissance, PBR indentured ship boarding, maybe even Green Beret–style civic action, a mission for which there still existed ample enthusiasm at Fort Bragg. In a war controlled by the US Army—a branch of service for which the chain of command had never been delinked, but only progressively thickened—it would prove no small advantage for the first direct-action SEALs in Vietnam to serve under a commander whose career in submarines had taught him the value of the hit-and-run raid and, just as important, the potential windfall that could be achieved in a policy of "latitude." This was Ward's term for entrusting his sailors with operational freedom. It was, however, a policy with one vulnerability: Latitude only really succeeded when handed to someone who wanted to push its limits.

3

When the SEALs of Detachment Delta—or Det. Delta, as it was called—arrived in February 1966, they numbered just three officers and fifteen enlisted men, not much more than a single enhanced platoon, but a platoon so important to SEAL aspirations that it was led by Lieutenant James Barnes, SEAL Team ONE's commanding officer. Known as a friendly and capable administrator, the ideal sort for forging partnerships and acquiring in-country assets, Barnes was also a firm believer in the SEALs' traditional interpretation of direct action and upon arrival set to gathering intelligence on all the enemy's command posts, radar dishes, and bridges. Barnes's problem: These simply did not exist.

On a map, the 400 or so square miles' worth of rivers and canals of the Rung Sat Special Zone looked like the splitting, curving bronchioles seen in a cross-section of a human lung. On the ground, this lung was a putrid tidewater swamp that when flushed left behind a "morass" of boot-sucking mudflats and root-twisted peninsulas, the high ground of which could mostly be measured above the waterline with a yardstick. Called the "evil place" by the locals or the "forest of assassins" by the Americans, and known as a past hideout for pirates, the Rung Sat was, by the time of the SEALs' arrival at Nha Be, reinforcing all of these reputations, since it was the source of an increasing number of rocket attacks on Saigon plus riverbank ambushes along Saigon's main shipping channel.

At the end of April, MACV planners tried to curb these attacks with Operation Jackstay, a battalion-sized, amphibious landing of Marines on a coastal peninsula that was said to be the Rung Sat's most likely enemy base and the hub for all the hardened targets that Barnes and his SEALs were anxious to discover. It wasn't. At a cost of five Americans killed, plus another fifty-five collapsed from heat exhaustion, the twelve-

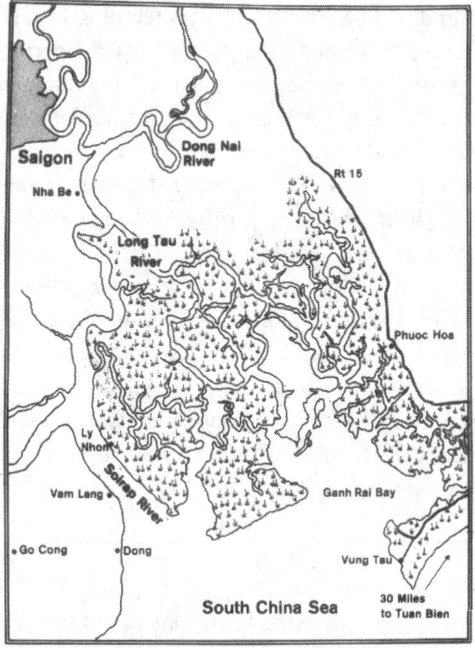

Map of the Rung Sat Special Zone (RSSZ).

day operation yielded little more than a handful of freshwater wells and rice caches; some rudimentary weapons factories and black-powder depots; and—the closest thing to a commando target—a hidden jungle hospital whose outbuildings were connected by an elevated log walkway.

The most obvious alternative to the enemy's nonexistent bridges and command posts was the enemy himself—South Vietnam's actual Communist insurgent, the slipperiest soldier in history. Known to all as the Viet Cong, or VC—a shorthand that had been stretched by the US military's phonetic alphabet into Victor Charlie, then shortened again by the American soldier to just Charlie—by any name this enemy combatant possessed a list of attributes that made him notoriously hard to pin down. Generally weighing in at around 100 pounds and reaching not much higher than the average GI's armpit, the Viet Cong guerrilla was further concealed by his uniform: nothing more than the same tire-soled sandals and black pajamas worn by all Vietnamese peasants. It was a costume born out of economy, but one with a handsome payoff: To the American serviceman the Viet Cong was both everywhere and nowhere, almost unidentifiable until he sprung his attack—everything from the traditional guerrilla's assault of a Special Forces camp to the terrorist's infiltration of a city. In the year preceding Det. Delta's arrival, the Viet Cong had detonated an explosive-packed sedan at the US embassy (killing twenty), blown up a popular floating restaurant in Saigon (killing forty-three), and inspired a new generation of anarchists to eye every street crowd as the prospective recipient of a tossed grenade. Outfitted with little more than a waterproof nylon sheet, a mosquito net, a hammock, and about two cents' worth of salted rice per day, the Viet Cong guerrilla could disappear into the jungle for weeks at a time without resupply. As if that alone had not made him impossible to find, just after Det. Delta's arrival in Vietnam, American soldiers had discovered below the Saigon suburb of Cu Chi a sprawling, multistory, subterranean city of tunnels whose breathing tubes had been burrowed out by an ingenious application of open-topped cages and gophers. It was a head-scratching discovery: How on earth did you find an enemy who wasn't even on top of it?

4

To FIND THE VIET CONG in the Rung Sat, Barnes tentatively accepted the only operations left to a unit of his size and disposition: 1) search-and-destroy patrols, and 2) canal-side ambushes. The patrols amounted to aimless walks through the Rung Sat's notoriously dense mangroves—called "the forest of iron-trees" by the locals—where the best possible outcome was to stumble upon an enemy camp. The ambushes were worse: Hours of prone silence in the mud, eyes straining through coal-mine darkness to glimpse the shadow of a sampan violating the government's nighttime travel ban, a marathon of endurance while the misery of biting insects was replaced by the misery of fetid tidewater rising from one's ankles to one's ears. "Our legs would go to sleep, our faces would be swollen by mosquito bites, we'd be wet and cold and miserable," said one SEAL to a RAND researcher.

Disenchanted with a war that did not conform to the one he wanted, Barnes did not respond by adjusting his operational expectations but by ending them. After reducing his detachment's operations to underwater inspections of the Navy's moored ship hulls, Barnes made use of his free time with daily trips to Saigon to shack up with an American nurse. In this vacuum of leadership, Barnes's men naturally set out to find their own nurses, and in the process discovered Saigon's bars, plus all the trouble that attended them. The most memorable example of this occurred when one enlisted SEAL attempted to avoid a reprimand for some incidental infraction with an egregious cover-up, allegedly using his own gun on his jeep's windshield to fake survival of an enemy ambush. Barnes's reaction to this incident and others was to "quarantine" his men to base, where they would wait out the remainder of their deployment in the usual SEAL fashion: working out and sunbathing. "Don't unpack, this isn't for us," Barnes would soon tell an arriving SEAL officer, whose response would be utter puzzlement that his fellow SEALs were so ready to abandon the war. Perhaps only if they had been massacred in Operation Jackstay could the first direct-action SEALs in Vietnam have managed such a disappointing first impression.

Though Admiral Ward could never have predicted what his policy of latitude for the SEALs might have achieved, he definitely had not expected an outcome so underwhelming, let alone one of near criminality. In response to this scandal, Ward's operations officer, Captain John Shepherd, arranged a conference call with the Coronado-based commander of Naval Operations Support Group, the administrative head of all UDTs and SEALs in the Pacific. Once the call commenced, Shepherd ran through the rap sheet of Det. Delta's failures: the lack of aggressiveness, the lack of operations, the booze, the girls—all problems that Shepherd proposed to solve by kicking the SEALs out of the country. Had this proposal been met by a man whose opinions resembled those of Commandant Thomas Holcomb, who had disbanded the Marine Corps' Raiders, or of General Mark Clark, who had twice lent a hand in the disbandment of the Army's Rangers, it might very well have been interpreted as proof that the SEALs were not cut out for Vietnam or that the mission for which they had been created no longer existed. Either verdict could have snowballed the SEALs into the same trash heap as every other disbanded unit in the US military's commando past. At the very least, such verdicts could have proved that the SEALs were best used as they had been, as advisors. But that is not what happened.

Though most historians have treated the Bucklew Report as the most important factor in establishing the basis for the SEALs' direct-action role in Vietnam, there was another that was equally important: the ongoing influence of Bucklew himself. Now, as he listened to Shepherd's accusations on the phone, his response would be the hinge upon which turned the SEALs' raiding ambitions.

Upon hearing Shepherd's proposal to kick the SEALs out of Vietnam, the unflappable scout turned raider offered another solution. The problem, Bucklew contended, was leadership: Fix that, and everything else would sort itself out—an unassailable argument to Shepherd, an officer in a service so transfixed by leadership that it regularly fired its skippers for hull scrapes that happened while they slept. In the end, Shepherd agreed to give the SEALs another chance at Rung Sat raiding.

The only problem that remained: Better leadership or not, the Rung Sat was still a battlefield with almost nothing worth raiding.

5

In early July, two handpicked platoons from SEAL Team ONE—a total of four officers and twenty enlisted men—touched down on the sunbaked tarmac of Ton Son Nhut airfield and stepped into the brick-wall heat of Vietnam. There to greet them was Lieutenant Maynard Weyers (pronounced "wires"), the recently appointed twenty-eight-year-old commander of what was now called Detachment Golf, or Det. Golf, an intentional rebranding meant to erase the memory of Detachment Delta's embarrassments.

Suntanned, well built, and sandy-haired, Weyers looked more like the top bill in a 1960s-era surf movie than the top option to resurrect the SEALs' reputation, but here he was—rushed over to Nha Be so fast from an exercise in Taiwan that he had not even been permitted the time to collect his own rifle. He was fully aware of the reasons for his abrupt installation, so it was now his job to explain to his new arrivals what he had already been told: Forget what you think is a traditional SEAL mission. This is the only war in town, and we are not about to let it go to waste. It was a mandate that fell just short of one of Patton's most famous, to "attack everywhere with everything"—an order meant to expose the enemy and his weaknesses. To achieve a similar end, Weyers's first move was to lead each of his platoons on a handful of terrain-learning familiarization patrols. Once Weyers felt he had developed as complete an intelligence picture as he could, he did something his predecessor had never dreamed of: He turned his men loose to plan their own missions—proposals that Weyers himself typed into official orders, then hand-carried to his Navy superiors at CTF-116. As Admiral Ward the submariner had intended, for CTF-116, "oversight" was an overstatement. Not since the wolfpacks had been unleashed to sink without warning had a military unit been entrusted with so much leeway. Like teenagers, it would take the SEALs some time to grow into it.

When the men of Det. Golf turned out for their first missions, there was a quaintness to their appearance that would not be seen in future SEAL detachments—clean shaves, bloused boots, nearly high-and-tight haircuts, and either the classic, blotch-patterned olive-and-brown fatigues similar to those worn by the Raiders in the South Pacific or the tiger stripes designed by Yarborough for the Special Forces. Their headgear was one of three options: eight-point Marine Corps covers, wide-brimmed Australian bush hats, or the majority's choice, the convention of all snake-eating American commandos: a foppish French beret. Even their support was quaint: for transportation a single LCM-8 (Landing Craft Mechanized, Mark 8), or Mike Boat, a World War II–era landing craft of ponderous speed and paltry defenses, and for fire support, no battery of artillerymen, no hovering gunships, nothing but their own weapons.

Det. Golf's initial operations were also less than sophisticated. With mission areas chosen nearly at random, these mostly consisted of endless nights spent shivering in waist-deep water just watching for sampan traffic or crouched against the edge of a trail listening for voices or footfalls. As it had been with Det. Delta, such efforts were attended by swarms of mosquitos and "an especially irritating species of large, biting ant," plus an orchestra of "scuttling" crabs and the odd, periodic slap of a crocodile pushing off from the shore, immediately followed by total silence as every man held his breath and watched the water around himself to be sure that a black tail glided past. Chief Petty Officer Joe Churchill was prostrate on one of these nightlong marathons, his endurance further depleted by the sudden appearance of a black python that descended from a branch to coil itself on the jungle floor, then lock eyes with him until it slithered off some four hours later. These efforts resulted in predictable enemy contact: a glimpse of a "startled face," a "quick ducking behind trees," maybe a "clamber" into a sampan. If synced with low tide, an extraction swim to the Mike Boat could devolve into an hours-long, hip-deep slog through sewer-stinking mud, a marathon for Petty Officer 1st Class Roger Moscone, a 260-pound mountain who would collapse so deep into the muck that one day he would return to his tent to find his boots nailed to a pair of two-by-fours, the improvised water skis stamped "Moscone's Jungle Boots."

"We didn't know what the hell we were doing," remembered platoon commander Tom Truxell of those early days. It was essentially the refrain of every green soldier from every war in history, but compounded by the SEALs' nonexistent support, nonexistent playbook, nonexistent dry ground. Sharing the same mud, the same frustrations as his men, Weyers responded to this refrain with sympathy but, unlike Barnes, with

Undated photo of Det. Golf with the *Mighty Mo* in the background. Maynard Weyers is kneeling at the far left; Billy Machen is kneeling, third from left; Roger Moscone is standing, third from left.

no curbing of Det. Golf's operational tempo. It was a posture that inevitably pushed the frogmen turned SEALs to do what they already had: adapt.

6

WITHIN WEEKS OF THEIR ARRIVAL, the SEALs of Det. Golf were shaking off their initial jitters and even displaying some measure of proficiency. Signs of this were apparent in every aspect of their operations. On ambush, no one cleared his throat, coughed, spit, sneezed, or even sniffled; on insert and extract, the men stepped heel to toe to reduce the "sucking explosion of mudwalking" and above all avoided the footprints of the man in front to keep from sinking even deeper.

To improve their in-field support, the SEALs befriended the pilots and crews of the Navy's helicopter squadron at Nha Be and overhauled their denuded landing craft into an up-armored ironclad: six heavy machine guns mounted to the gunwales, a 60-millimeter mortar bolted to the rusted deck plate, and a bunker-busting recoilless rifle pinioned to the top of the sandbagged pilothouse. It was so much armament that the men quickly recommissioned the LCM the *Mighty Mo*. To it they added a canopy to block the sun and rain, a two-burner stove for meals, then draped hammocks between everything that didn't pivot or fire—essentially turned it into a houseboat littered with empty hot sauce bottles, coffee cups, clotheslines, all aids to reduce the number of trips back to Nha Be and increase the amount of time they could spend in a mission area.

To improve the quality of their encounters with the enemy, they experimented with a variety of tactics: false insertions that made the Viet Cong think the SEALs had landed where they hadn't; false extractions that made the Viet Cong think the SEALs had left; and probably most important, squad-sized missions that halved the SEALs' punch but correspondingly increased their stealth and the amount of swampland they could cover, thus doubling their chances of Viet Cong contact—no small challenge in an area as empty of enemy as was the Rung Sat.

And what results did these innovations yield? A handful of captured documents and North Vietnamese currency, some freshwater wells, some rice caches—one so monstrous that it merited an airstrike. Then, finally, after more than a month of frustrations, Det. Golf landed a jackpot ambush of two sampans that killed seven suspected Viet Cong guerrillas. The SEALs' reaction was the same as that of anyone who has just caught a hot streak.

Undated photo of Maynard Weyers on board the *Mighty Mo* after an op.

A little more than a week after their first coup, one squad pursued a tip from the crew of a hovering Navy gunship that had spotted several camouflaged sampans not far from the *Mighty Mo*'s anchorage. Despite having already blown their cover in that area from several days' worth of patrolling, the squad landed in full daylight and fell in behind point man Billy Machen, a keen-eyed twenty-eight-year-old Texan, the father of a daughter and a five-week-old boy he had never seen. Stepping alone into the middle of a sun-drenched clearing and spotting a Viet Cong bunker, Machen managed a single burst from his M16 before he was cut down by an eruption of machine gun fire that left him stranded. Hugging the ground to get under the rush of snapping bullets and splintering branches, the SEALs fell back on their training and clawed themselves into a rough firing line, but one that was not nearly stiff enough to break the wall of lead that blocked the way to their fallen comrade. To Tom Truxell, engaged in the untested platoon commander's perennial two-front war—the enemy and his own doubts—it seemed that the only recourse might be to pull back to the river and the *Mighty Mo*'s guns—that is, until one of his men fired a 40-millimeter grenade into the bunker's mouth. The shock forced a momentary flinch in the enemy's ambush, just long enough for the heavyweight Moscone to bull a mad dash for Machen, who was carried to safety just in time to whisper a final message to his wife while the corpsman ransacked his tiger stripes to find his wounds.

7

Considering that Machen's death in combat was not simply the first for the SEAL teams but that it was also nearly a 2 percent manpower loss for SEAL Team ONE, no one would have faulted Weyers if he had forced a pause to assess the operation that had led to the tragedy. He didn't. The reason was no more complicated than the same one taught to anyone who has ever looked up to see the belly of the horse that just bucked them off. Weyers ordered his men back into their saddles and back into the Rung Sat. This perseverance would have payoffs.

Within a month, the SEALs of Det. Golf were expanding their operational repertoire from planned patrol and ambush to unplanned quick-reaction counterattacks along the Rung Sat's choke points. In theory, it was an operational expansion that finally fulfilled the Bucklew Report's recommendation for riverbank raiders; in practice, it was a resurrection of the Navy's grapnel-swinging boarding parties. Encounters now included the inland pursuit and cornering of black-pajama-wearing attackers, firefights that varied from a few sharp rifle exchanges to fifteen-minute skirmishes, one of these against an enemy-packed haystack that did not stop firing until the SEALs launched forty-eight grenades into it.

Before long, the operational impact of Det. Golf's aggressiveness was considered so substantial that Admiral Ward approved its increase from two platoons to three, all but a guarantee of a corresponding increase in impact. While this blossomed, so too did the SEALs' confidence, best evidenced by their swagger around Nha Be, but also by a wooden sign above the entrance to their tent scrawled "Yea, though I walk through the valley of the shadow of death, I will fear no evil: because I'm the meanest bastard in the valley." Though the helmets and flak jackets of uncountable GIs would soon boast the same thing, by mid-autumn of 1966 the SEALs' claim to "meanest in the valley" was undisputed; in the Rung Sat, no other unit was as lethal.

On October 7, while two of Det. Golf's squads motored downriver from Nha Be they were hit in the sides by a massive, "viselike" ambush from opposing shorelines—sheets of machine gun bullets snapping overhead, pinging armor, geysering water all around them, followed by plunging mortar rounds, one squarely to the belly of the *Mighty Mo* that splashed flaming metal into sixteen of the nineteen men aboard. With several men blown clear of their weapons and "sewed head to foot with shrapnel," the Det. Golf SEALs nevertheless ignored their wounds and manned the gunwales to fire everything they had with a trigger—including Petty Officers John Henry Penn and James Campbell, who had been so shredded by the mortar blast that they had only gotten to their guns by crawling to them. Once there, the men unleashed an ear-deadening counterattack so savage—"Campbell's machine gun grew so white-hot that they could see the stream of bullets feeding out through it," said one account—that US intelligence later reported a kill count of forty Viet Cong. Accurate or not, it was a number just below that claimed by an entire battalion of US Marines in two weeks during Operation Jackstay.

Almost uninvited to the war and within just four months of their arrival, Weyers and Det. Golf had not only resurrected the reputation of the SEAL teams but were now on the cusp of earning the greatest of all honors for the SEALs' first direct-action detachment: a request for another direct-action detachment.

8

Nine months after the establishment of Det. Golf, Rear Admiral Norvell Ward, the hit-and-run submariner, escorted the commander in chief of the Pacific Fleet, Admiral U. S. Grant Sharp, and MACV commander William Westmoreland to the PBR base at Nha Be. The purpose of their jaunt: to express their personal admiration for Det. Golf's performance in the Rung Sat, a performance that had all but eliminated the rocket attacks on Saigon. Touring the base, the visitors were able to inspect Det. Golf's new accommodations, no longer a stifling tent but a two-story, air-conditioned barge. One of the men present—Lieutenant Franklin Anderson, SEAL Team ONE's compact commanding officer—had met Westmoreland two years before when the general had pinned a Bronze Star to his uniform for recapturing the port of Vung Ro Bay. Now, after spotting Anderson in the group, Westmoreland immediately picked up their two-year-old conversation right where they had left off—an indication either of Westmoreland's incomparable memory or the SEALs' incomparable ability to make an impression. "I would like to have a thousand like them," Westmoreland was reported to have declared. At the time of his comment, the US Navy—"the biggest navy on the planet," a reporter was quick to note—had only created 200 total, not even 15 percent of the number of Green Berets in Vietnam. But the SEALs were about to receive a Green Beret–sized portion of attention.

From their inception in 1962 to the end of 1966, the SEALs were, said a reporter, "one of the most publicity-shy outfits of the decade." Up to that point, their only significant exposure—"to every SEAL's horror"—came from the *Buz Sawyer* comic strip, a syndicated serial in which the cartoon hero usually saved the world or a female, but in this case, wetsuited ashore in North Vietnam to steal a Soviet missile. Shortly thereafter, Navy planners decided for some unknown reason to increase the SEALs' exposure by cracking open a window to their training and disclosing a handful of what the official report called their "adventures." The result was a mounting roll of publicity: *The San Diego Union* printed an article titled "Navy Unwraps Its SEALS," which was followed by their description in *The Christian Science Monitor* as the "Navy's Black Berets" and by the Long Beach (California) *Independent Press-Telegram* as "Navy James Bond Types." In less than a month, the SEALs made their television debut on a Navy-approved documentary film produced by the KOGO station in San Diego, much of the footage shot in the Chocolate Mountains and nowhere near San Diego. Ultimately, this chorus of publicity reached what must have seemed like a maximum pitch with the publication of a six-page story in the *Reader's Digest*. In that article one enlisted SEAL was quoted saying, "I would never downgrade any other American outfits, but they're not like us . . . Just give us a mission. If it can be done, we'll do it; if it can't be done, we'll try, and nine times out of ten we'll do it anyway." After listening to their assertions, to their stories, to their breadth of knowledge drawn from all the US military's top guerrilla warfare schools—"a variety of skills never before invested in a single unit"—the article's author declared the SEALs the "century's supercommandos" and already "the most deadly combat outfit in American history."

Never mind for a moment that the *Reader's Digest* was not exactly a known authority on American military history, these superlatives were also just the things reporters had said about the Raiders and Rangers right before misuse and misfortune had led to their disbandment.

9

As if sensing that all was not as rosy with the SEALs' first direct-action assignment as the reporters were soon to say, in January 1967 Lieutenant Commander David Del Giudice, now assigned to the Naval Operations Support Group and the officer in charge of all West-PAC SEAL Detachments, convened a conference at Naval Amphibious Base Coronado. In attendance were the commanders of both SEAL teams: Lieutenant Commander Franklin Anderson of SEAL Team ONE and William Early, his counterpart at Team TWO. Their discussions, according to the record, included an overview of Det. Golf's 1966 casualties—sixteen wounded but only one killed, a relatively shallow investment for a high return of eighty-six Viet Cong. This proportion seemed to show that Det. Golf had discovered a predictable method for finding and fighting the enemy, but actually these operations were yielding about as much as they ever had—the most common phrase among the current after-action reports: "negative contact." The number of enemy captured was not listed. Further discussions revealed Det. Golf's efforts to improve this ratio.

Frustrated with the enemy's retreat from the Rung Sat's riverbanks, Det. Golf had already started pushing further inland—so far, in fact, that SEAL Team ONE's replacement platoons were now anticipating almost nothing but helicopter insertions. To better prepare for this inland warfare, SEAL Team ONE's Anderson had ordered Guy Stone—a former Korean War soldier and forward observer who had left the Army to become an enlisted SEAL—to create a six-week-long predeployment course in basic infantry tactics. With a training camp carved into the Chocolate Mountains some 100 miles east of the Pacific Ocean, Stone had trained his Team ONE comrades in every skill of soldiering that he knew, everything from contour navigating to mortars; every skill a step closer to Navy infantrymen.

To the commanders now convened in Coronado, such developments seemed to justify an official revision to the SEALs' Navy-imposed operational boundaries; in other words, what Del Giudice, Anderson, and Early were describing as direct-action missions "outside of a purely naval or maritime environment." As they already knew, there was only one other available area that could present a Navy unit with that kind of opportunity, an area a contemporary described as the war's "true bastion of iron": the Mekong Delta.

Chapter 14

The Direct-Action SEALs Who Dodged Diversion, Then Perfected a Mission That Propelled the Teams Past the Riverbanks, into History

On January 31, 1967, with arms still sore from final immunizations, twenty-five men belonging to SEAL Team TWO's 2nd and 3rd Platoons descended onto Binh Thuy airfield near Can Tho, in the very heart of the Mekong Delta. Their orders: establish Det. Alfa, the first all-American commando unit dedicated for direct action in the IV Corps Tactical Zone—an entire corps, just theirs for the taking. Finally. But not so fast. Exactly one day after Det. Alfa arrived in the Mekong Delta, so too did the first batches of the Army's 9th Infantry Division, a vanguard to a battlespace that its soldiers would dominate the moment they arrived. The result: Before the SEALs had even unpacked their weapons crates, it was already clear, said Det. Alfa's official history, that they had "no jurisdiction to prosecute a land war . . . beyond the [delta's] high water mark," nor had any official agreement yet been reached among all "interested parties" that would allow the SEALs to set one wet foot onto the IV Corps' riverbanks. Reaching such an agreement required three weeks' worth of unemployed saluting, politicking, explaining to soldiers what SEALs were, and most of all, promising that these would not overstep their welcome; a promise that finally granted the SEALs permission to start setting "simple ambushes along the banks of the Bassac [River] and its tributaries." As important a hurdle as any the SEALs had overcome, it was nevertheless a hurdle, and as in any race, there were more right behind it.

Within a week of Det. Alfa's unlocking of the Bassac's riverbanks, the SEALs were melting into the brush and setting their first canal-side ambushes—ambushes in districts more populated than the entire Rung Sat. In no time, they bumped into the enemy and predictably discovered the gulf between their training and actual combat. Early examples of this gulf included a friendly-fire incident that killed a Vietnamese frogman, and a squad-sized ambush of an enemy sampan whose success was besmirched by everything afterward—the Det. Alfa SEALs' inability to control their excitement or their fire; an errant grenade that nearly killed SEAL Bob Gallagher, who had waded into the canal to collect the sampan's remnants; and, worst of all, a next-day rumor that was started by the squad's commander, Lieutenant Junior Grade Dick Marcinko, that accused the SEAL in charge of the team's extraction of the abandonment of the squad in the middle of a running gun battle. The subsequent investigation revealed that not only had the accused officer done none of the things that had been alleged, but neither had there been a running gun battle. It was a controversy ringing the same warnings that had nearly sunk the SEALs in the Rung Sat, an alarm that soon coincided with a chorus of others.

In the last week of June, Rear Admiral Kenneth Veth, Admiral Ward's replacement as the commander of naval forces in Vietnam, convened a symposium "centered around," said the official record, answering "the questions of who could effectively use SEAL personnel." The interpretation of the responses to this question depended much on the man who had asked it. Having made the bones of his naval career almost exclusively in the art of mine laying—floating graveyards of area denial—Admiral Veth brought to this symposium none of his predecessor's instincts for offensive warfare, and would, over the length of his nine-month tenure, preside over an eight-hour-a-day staff described as sleepy and moribund, the result of his preference for the traditional Navy missions of support. At the time of the symposium, Veth's options for less-than-direct-action/support-type missions for the SEALs fell into one of two categories.

The first of these were the SEALs' various advisory efforts—SOG, the LDNNs, but also now the CIA's Provincial Reconnaissance Units, or PRUs. One month before Veth's symposium, the sprawl of the Navy's commitment to the last had been officially recognized with the establishment of Det. Bravo in Saigon, the third SEAL detachment in Vietnam, to manage a 100-man PRU company in fourteen of the Mekong Delta's sixteen provinces, and an effort whose potential for terrorizing the Viet Cong's infrastructure had been limited only by the SEALs' contributions to it.

The SEALs' second support option was with the just-established Mobile Riverine Force, or MRF, whose 2,000 soldiers of the Army's 9th Infantry Division—based out of Dong Tam in the Central Mekong Delta—had not only received their predeployment amphibious training at Fort Riley, in Central Kansas, but had been so rushed through it that one battalion commander had described it as "almost indecent." Now, the MRF's representatives made use of Veth's symposium to attempt to make up for these shortcomings by advocating their use of SEALs "both as a training and operational force." In other words: as a cohort of instructors and a quick-reaction reserve whose inland operations would—per the policy since World War II—fall under Army command, and, whether anyone realized it or not, decrease with the graduation of every soldier that the SEALs trained.

As Veth chewed on the options of shifting more of his direct-action SEALs to serve as indigenous advisors or Army instructors, two platoons from SEAL Team ONE descended from the decks of the USS *Brush,* a destroyer assigned to the US Navy's coastal blockade, then rowed their blacked-out rubber boats to a beach in II Corps. There, they threaded over sand dunes and up hillsides to raid an enemy rest area, during which they killed the leader of a Viet Cong women's organization and captured three others, then—under a protective umbrella of 164 shells from the destroyer's five-inch guns—escaped aboard a flight of Navy helicopters. Not only was it the most perfect naval commando mission in the history of the SEAL teams, it was—for anyone who cared to notice—a showcase for opportunities with the coastal fleet. Just one more potential diversion to draw the SEALs away from a future of inland direct action.

Just as these various alternatives for SEAL employment were appearing down the length of Vietnam, the men of Det. Alfa simultaneously started to notice a change. Gone now were the nights of simply setting up on some random canal and hoping for a passing enemy sampan. Just like they had in the Rung Sat, the Viet Cong in the delta were learning to avoid such confrontations, an evolution that now placed the SEALs of Det. Alfa at a crossroads: either wait for the lack of activity to prompt unenthusiastic planners like Admiral Veth into redistributing them into any one of the aforementioned programs, or start stalking inland.

As if timed to help make this decision, a ghost from the US Navy's past appeared just offstage in the form of Mary Miles and his posthumously published book, *A Different Kind of War*—a 629-page record of the Navy's greatest infringement ashore, and a skeleton key for any naval unit looking to unlock the opportunities that were just beyond their reach. As both the man and book now showed, the secret of the key was competence, and it was a secret the Det. Alfa SEALs would likewise reveal again—this time by developing a cycle of operations that not only stretched their legs beyond the riverbanks, but also stretched their reputation for direct action so far that they would soon set an example for every American commando unit that came after them.

2

As all these options were being considered, SEAL Team TWO was simultaneously preparing for its third platoon rotation to Det. Alfa. On deck for this was the 7th Platoon—twelve SEALs, one hospital corpsman, and one German shepherd named Rinnie. On the surface, this platoon was nothing remarkable. Several men were on their first deployments as SEALs, including the second-in-command, a warrant officer named Charlie Watson whose decision to volunteer had shocked many, since his earlier service in the UDTs had been mostly spent as a yeoman, or staff secretary. Only one platoon member had ever deployed

Undated predeployment photo of SEAL Team TWO, 7th Platoon. Front row, left to right: Chief Robert Gallagher, Petty Officer Richard Tuure, Petty Officer Roy Matthews, Petty Officer Mike Boynton, Lieutenant Robert Peterson. Back row, left to right: Warrant Officer Charles Watson, Chief Erasmo Riojas, Seaman Fred Keener, Seaman Harry Constance, Petty Officer Curtis Ashton, Petty Officer Jack Rowell.

to Vietnam in a direct-action capacity, and only two had ever experienced combat, one of those a SEAL, the other the hospital corpsman—and that was thirteen years earlier, in the Korean War. Only a few members—namely those youngsters on their first deployments—resembled the widely held image of the muscular frogman; several—including Petty Officer 1st Class Mike Boynton—were so insulated that they looked more like Budweiser-swilling dockworkers. Probably most unremarkable—at least at first assessment—was the 7th Platoon's officer-in-charge, Lieutenant Pete Peterson, mild-mannered and lanky, who had only checked in to SEAL Team TWO nine months earlier—and not from a UDT but from a blue-water destroyer, a snapshot that could hardly be considered ideal for leading a platoon into the most inland war the SEALs had ever faced. But it was also just a snapshot.

Tall and lean, dark-haired and thin-faced, sincere in speech and expression, twenty-eight-year-old Robert "Pete" Peterson had taken a twisted path to his command of the 7th Platoon. Raised in Newcastle, Pennsylvania, the red-brown center of the rust belt, and educated at nearby Slippery Rock State Teachers College, Peterson owed his 1961 commission not to any attempt to sidestep the draft but to a lack of local opportunity and a last-minute realization that he had no interest in being a teacher. At OCS he had learned about the Navy's frogmen, and having been a college swimmer had volunteered for the UDT, an almost accidental career path that had immediately led to an accidental opportunity. Graduating with UDTR Class 27 in 1962, the year the Navy's frogmen were first plundered for their experience, Peterson's maturity in underwater demolition training had determined that he would serve not a day in an underwater demolition team, and instead would be directly assigned to SEAL Team TWO. What followed had been some of the usual, and some of the not: Like all SEAL officers on Team TWO, Peterson had been sent to Ranger School, but while there he had stood out from his twenty-four fellow officers for his reluctance to shout at the enlisted men—for the Ranger instructors a trait that had made him seem anything but a Ranger; for another audience, a trait in high demand.

Peterson's first real-world assignment, when he was just twenty-three years old, had been to lead a squad to Miami and the Florida Keys, where under aliases and covers as civilian utility divers they had spent a year on loan to the CIA to pass on their UDT knowledge to Cuban exiles. Like the servant in the book of Matthew, Peterson's stewardship of these talents had unlocked an even greater responsibility. This had been a twelve-month staff posting to the naval advisory group in Saigon, where he had—as the lowest-ranking officer on staff but the only one with the requisite security clearance to do it—been in charge of all operational planning for the Biet Hai's commando raids on North Vietnam's coast. This had included the one that resulted in the Gulf of Tonkin affair, after which he had had to race to Danang to oversee the hasty flight of all Nasty-class patrol boats to a new hideout in Cam Ranh Bay. It was an assignment as strategic as any thus far performed by a SEAL, and yet not exactly one to which any SEAL had aspired. After two tours as a naval commando, both relegated to the caretaking of other naval commandos, Peterson—despite his obvious talents—had decided to resign his commission to seek his fortune elsewhere. As was often the case with such quests, his had led him right back to the Navy, but having quit—the only blasphemous word that existed in the teams—he had been required to atone for his sin in the surface fleet, an atonement he had tried to shorten with persistent phone calls to the detailer as soon as he heard that SEALs were to be used for direct action.

Of the two types of SEALs—the self-sacrificing and the self-promoting, either of which could make a successful frogman—Peterson was completely the former. Agreeable, free of the impulse to showcase

Official Navy photo of Robert "Pete" Peterson, undated.

his virtues, and often wearing a half smile that had more in common with Mayberry than it did with *Gunsmoke,* at first meeting it was easy to superimpose upon him the traits often associated with such clues: credulity, cautiousness, lassitude—misimpressions that would make the truth that much starker. The reality of Peterson was that he possessed all the traits of an outstanding naval officer—he was honest, honorable, diligent; the feeder traits of courage, but without which were useless. He was self-deprecating, generous with praise, and, unlike many in authority, had an interest in details, plus the enthusiasm to pursue them when they were not readily available. Above all he was adaptable and eager to confront the enemy—the relentless challenge of every SEAL platoon commander, but a burden that each would share with one other platoon member.

On paper, the rank structure of every SEAL platoon flowed down from the platoon commander to the assistant platoon commander to the platoon chief to the platoon leading petty officer to the men. Neat, uncomplicated—and inaccurate. Being that each assistant platoon commander was usually on his first deployment, for most practical purposes the role of second-in-command was usually performed by the platoon chief, or chief petty officer, the equivalent of a Marine Corps gunnery sergeant, or an Army sergeant first class. On a ship, chief petty officers were responsible for maintaining the good order and discipline of the crew, and as such were afforded their own mess, khaki uniforms, and, due to the experience evidenced by their permanently black-stained coffee cups and crow's feet, a level of respect that more often than not outranked all but the ship's most senior officers. In the SEAL teams, where no policy yet existed to allow an officer to stay in the community without periodically rotating out of the fleet, the chiefs, for their continuity of experience, commandeered respect like no one else in the Navy.

At the forming of the 7th Platoon, this billet had been occupied by Chuck Newell, a perfectly capable chief whose tenure was cut short the second he was hit in the stomach with a 40-millimeter grenade fragment during a training exercise. Not only did such an accident threaten to upset the 7th Platoon's cohesion and final preparations, but with SEAL Team TWO now in a constant state of rotating deployments, it wasn't immediately clear from where Peterson might pull a replacement. In the end, he needn't have worried. The replacement found him—a chief as eager as any in the SEALs' entire history to pursue the enemy wherever he hid.

3

Almost as soon as it was decided that Newell would not be able to deploy, Chief Petty Officer Robert T. Gallagher volunteered to take his spot. Called "the Eagle" for his early baldness—a scalp as smooth as a bird's pate and rimmed by a horseshoe of black fuzz—and for his unforgivingly hard-eyed stare, if it hadn't been for the latter, Gallagher would have looked as physically unlike a SEAL as any who had ever existed. Pale and often paunchy, with a bulk that always settled in his gut and shoulders, Gallagher's resemblance to a deck-plate chief in the surface fleet was further exaggerated by a well-trimmed mustache and a disposition so severe that he never betrayed a smile within range of a camera. When he volunteered for 7th Platoon, he had already completed a tour with Det. Alfa and at the time of Newell's accident was the senior enlisted advisor at Team TWO's training detachment in Little Creek. In this capacity he had been responsible for a predeployment curriculum whose lessons were the building blocks of patrol and ambush: everything from hand-and-arm signals to overlapping fields of fire; more recently, lessons as granular as substituting swamp mud for insect repellent and marking trip wires by draping them with sheets of toilet paper.

Undated photo of Chief Bob Gallagher (seated at left, in shorts and no shirt).

Such latter lessons were now returning home with every veteran of Det. Alfa. Unlike them, however, and despite a wife and six-month-old twin sons at home, Gallagher had never really returned.

Struck by tragedy at just three years old when his mother had died from tuberculosis—a tragedy that had simultaneously incapacitated his father for fathering—Gallagher's early life had nevertheless been salvaged by a well-to-do but childless aunt and uncle in Naugatuck, Connecticut. With them, he and his sister had been raised and loved, and educated at the local Catholic school. Unlike Peterson, who had never seen the ocean until he joined the Navy, Gallagher had grown up barely thirty minutes from it. Intelligent and athletic, had it not been for this proximity—and the Richard Widmark movie *The Frogmen*—Gallagher would have been a natural fit at any New England college. Instead, he had enlisted in the Navy at his earliest opportunity.

In the winter of 1956, Gallagher joined UDTR Class 17 at Little Creek, a class made up of ninety-seven personnel, including five Navy officers, five US Army soldier-graduates from Ranger School, and one Black sailor from Ohio who, remarkably, had taught himself to swim in a creek after a town order to integrate the local pool had prompted the owner to fill it with rocks. At one point in the first few weeks, the temperature had dropped so low that Gallagher and his classmates had been forced to break the ice that had crusted the edge of the Chesapeake Bay so their instructors could torture them in it, a ritual not unheard-of in the UDT's East Coast winter classes. After four weeks of this—four weeks of heaving logs over windswept sand dunes; four weeks of wet fatigues freezing to their skin; four weeks of elephant marches with boats on their heads, a misery that had rubbed Gallagher's already thinning widow's peak raw—more than 50 percent of the class had quit, including one of the Navy officers and all five of the Ranger School graduates. "It was just too psychological for them," one man remembered. And there had been so much farther to go. After a total of sixteen weeks, Class 17 had shrunk to a mere shadow of itself. Of the ninety-seven who had started, only fourteen graduated. One of those, incidentally, was the undaunted Black sailor from Ohio; another, of course, was Gallagher.

Gallagher's subsequent career in the UDTs was more than commendable; wherever he went he excelled, and more. This reputation, plus his standing as a sturdy drinker, had made him a natural choice for the first batch of frogmen to join SEAL Team TWO. There, he had excelled again, undertaking the most difficult assignments, including a course to qualify as an explosive ordnance disposal technician, or EOD Tech, one of the military's more cerebral ratings, and an eight-month overseas advisory billet to Istanbul, where he had helped train the first all-Turkish Navy UDT class.

From these assignments it was possible for Gallagher's peers to assemble a portrait of his personality: hard-charging and intense, yet entirely devoid of pretense. When deployed, it was only on the rare occasion he was seen in anything but a rumpled pair of UDT shorts. He was above all known for his quiet confidence—the oxygen of his leadership—but with an emphasis on quiet. He had all the "sensitivity of a rock," remembered one teammate. Unless at a bar—the only place he seemed to allow his sense of humor to walk around off-leash—he was just more "pulled into himself [than others]," remembered a teammate; "just tough to get to know." It was even tougher when he returned from his first tour with Det. Alfa carrying a reputation as one of SEAL Team TWO's top hunters, but a reputation that had come at a cost.

Welcomed home after his last tour by his wife and twin sons—born just weeks before his arrival, and two and a half months premature—Gallagher should have reacted with relief and contentment. Instead, to his wife he was unrecognizable, a brooding presence whose entire focus had split between the training of Team TWO's outgoing platoons and his own return to Vietnam as soon as possible, a wish come true as a result of 7th Platoon's unexpected vacancy.

For the force of his personality, for his combat experience, Gallagher was—from the moment he joined—the 7th Platoon's unofficial leader. "No one argued with him," said Roy Matthews, about to depart on his first deployment. "You might win the fight, but you'd never want to go to sleep again." The reality was actually slightly less severe. Certainly, Gallagher was all of the aforementioned; was remote, intense, almost humorless; but there was another quality that would soon help him become one of the best combat leaders in the history of the Navy. Essentially an orphan, from the day Gallagher had joined the SEALs, they had been—whether they knew it or not—his family. Nothing mattered as much to him; nothing except maybe the mission. A mission whose evolution would have no greater contributor than Gallagher.

4

On October 24, 1967, six deuce-and-a-half cargo trucks rumbled into the city of My Tho carrying Peterson, Gallagher, and the eleven other members of the 7th Platoon. All around them stretched a war-battered Mekong Delta city of cement, alleyways, waterfronts, fishmongers, street vendors, and the casual reminders of 100 years of French dominion, everything from Versailles architecture and brothels to open-air cafés and checkered tablecloths. Threading through it all was a pulsing traffic of pedaled gondolas and motorbikes, bouncing conical hats and parasols. In the heart of this bustle stood the 7th Platoon's accommodations: the entire third floor of the Carter Billet, a four-story French-style hotel leased by the Navy, three men to a room, the only air-conditioning in each supplied by one lazy overhead fan and whatever breeze blew through the screened-in exterior patio. The hotel's security measures were about as sophisticated as the air-conditioning: a sandbagged guard shack and some wire mesh around the lower two floors to prevent a passing guerrilla from lobbing a grenade inside.

The 7th Platoon's operational home was located three-quarters of a mile south of the hotel inside the castellated perimeter of the US Navy's smallest PBR base in Vietnam. There, beyond the chain-link gate and sandbags, the cyclones of concertina wire, the base was little more than a hasty construct of dirt-packed gravel, plywood, and tin roofing. Within this maze of prefabs and Quonset huts, the men of the 7th Platoon found a small campus of structures earmarked for their command post and spent the first hours of the war hand-wrenching crate after crate of weapons and gear into a small, wood-floored hangar adjacent to the PBR docks. Those crates included some 900 pounds of dog food and everything from sawed-off, duck-billed shotguns that could blast an oval-shaped spread of nine-ball buck to 150-round, drum-fed Stoner machine guns that were as lightweight as rifles but could dump 500 rounds in the time it took to read the title page in the weapon's manual.

From this pier-side hangar and just beyond the rows of PBRs moored gunwale to gunwale, each man got a glimpse of the My Tho River, a half-mile-wide, rust-colored highway with uncountable tributaries into the inland Mekong Delta—every off-ramp another inland operational opportunity. What they couldn't see, however, was the amount of traffic competing for such off-ramps. Located just east of a regular ARVN outpost, just south of an ARVN Ranger compound, and just a fifteen-minute boat ride downriver from the bulk of the Army's 9th Infantry Division at Dong Tam, the 7th Platoon's SEALs had just moved into a neighborhood with rivals whose claims to these hinterlands were all more legitimate than theirs. A funny thing about legitimacy: It's usually bestowed upon the person or entity that proves most capable.

Having some sense of this, Peterson—though jet-lagged by the four-prop flight from Norfolk and far from acclimated to the delta heat—wasted not a moment and, though he lacked a jeep, set off to flat-foot the city and introduce himself to any entity that might connect his platoon to the Viet Cong. Among the first of these meetings were with CTF-116's local commander, a fleet officer who knew nothing of land warfare, and the commander's naval intelligence liaison officer, or NILO, who knew almost as much about the locations of the Viet Cong. More productive meetings included those with the skippers of the base Mike Boat and the various PBRs, plus the nearby squadron of Seawolves at Dong Tam, Army-owned gunships manned by all-Navy helicopter crews. Beyond these, Peterson also met with the SEALs assigned to the local PRUs and the LDNNs, plus the American advisors to the ARVN regulars and the ARVN Rangers, the latter of these actually being one of Peterson's former classmates at Ranger School. From these latter groups—the PRUs, the LDNNS, and the ARVN—Peterson also enlisted commitments for additional operators to act as scouts and interpreters.

On October 28, Peterson produced a burst of activity and nerves by issuing his first warning order to his men, followed immediately by an op plan to the Det. Alfa commander, Lieutenant Henry "Jake" Rhinebolt, for concurrence by CTF-116 in Can Tho. Once the mission was approved, the men of the 7th Platoon straggled into one of the Carter Billet's third-floor hotel rooms, where Peterson and Gallagher took turns disseminating a detailed briefing, everything from the order of march to the number of rounds to be carried in each man's loadout. When the briefing concluded, the men filed down to the PBR base and their dockside hangar, where they swapped T-shirts and cutoffs for tiger-striped fatigues and load-bearing harnesses. For headgear, most of the men donned camouflaged boonie hats; Peterson and a handful of others opted for their camouflaged berets while Gallagher wore nothing more exotic than a faded eight-point Marine Corps cover. Everyone smeared their faces and necks with a combination of green and black paint. About half of them draped themselves with crossed belts of machine gun ammunition. Erasmo "Doc" Riojas, the platoon's Korean War vet corpsman, carried a medical loadout that consisted, said one man, "of 50,000 rounds and one bandaid." In appearance, the 7th Platoon looked sinister and resolved, equal parts Comanche and gangster, but also no different from any of the other recent SEAL platoons that had served in Vietnam.

The 7th Platoon's looks weren't the only similarity to those that had come before them. Their first mission was similarly unremarkable: a PBR insert, a short patrol, a nightlong laydown in jungle muck for an ambush that never happened; a routine that had mostly become the rule for SEAL operations in the delta. The only atypical aspect of the mission was Peterson's employment of nine indigenous troops on loan from the LDNNs, the PRUs, and the ARVN, which had enabled him to multiply his chances for enemy contact with three separate patrols—7A led by himself, 7B led by Gallagher, and 7C led by Warrant Officer Charlie Watson—but more important, had supplied his men with information gleaned from five detained Vietnamese peasants; or would have, if any of the indigenous scouts had spoken English. If there was another remarkable aspect to this shake-out patrol it was this: It had been launched just four days after the 7th Platoon's arrival in My Tho, barely enough time for the men to have learned the route from their hotel to their PBR docks.

After the 7th Platoon reboarded the Mike Boat for the three-hour transit back to My Tho, the men laid out their wet clothes in the sun, held Zippos to the leeches stuck to their bodies, and took turns being dragged in the washing machine that was the landing craft's heavy chop. Lounging on the available deck plate, with cigarettes and Ba Muoi Ba beers in hand, the men recounted the individual details of their first mission until their laughs and the boat's steady thrum uncoiled the night's tension and lulled many of them to sleep. When the Mike Boat re-docked at My Tho, Gallagher oversaw the offloading of gear and the cleaning of everything fouled by mud—weapons, magazines, ammunition belts—then held an all-hands debrief to discuss what had worked, what hadn't, and what could be done better. This completed, Peterson hand-wrote an after-action report for Doc Riojas—the platoon's only competent typist—to peck onto a postcard-size document called a Barndance Card, then forwarded it up to Lieutenant Rhinebolt at Det. Alfa. Most important, he immediately started planning another mission.

Mimicking nearly every operational aspect of their first mission, the 7th Platoon's second differed mainly in location—this one a six-hour boat trip away on the coast of the South China Sea, where, said one participant, they "hit the beach like a John Wayne movie." Within two hours of establishing three separate ambush sites between the beach and a nearby canal, Peterson's 7A ambushed its first sampan, killing two Viet Cong, then patrolled south to a complex of bunkers. From these, the squad itself was ambushed with rifle fire and grenades, initiating the 7th's first immediate action—a belly-crawling, machine-gunning counterattack that Peterson concluded with a radio-directed sortie from the Navy's Seawolf gunships. While this was happening, Gallagher's 7B and Watson's 7C swept north through a Viet Cong village of bunkers and structures, destroying them as they went. Their first kill was an old man with a Sears, Roebuck rifle. "I think we killed that guy twenty-five times," one platoon member said. The result of this sweep was a series of sharp skirmishes, the most dramatic being the pursuit of five insurgents fleeing south through the sand dunes, followed by a hasty extraction to the Boston Whalers that was covered by a line of thumping explosions from the Mike Boat's 81-millimeter mortar. Returning to My Tho with a body count of four Viet Cong, a small stash of documents, and a tally of thirty-four structures destroyed, the 7th Platoon had just accomplished about as much as any other SEAL mission to date.

And they had only been in-country for a week.

5

On November 6, while the entire platoon swept through a "heavily booby trapped bunker complex," Gallagher found himself on a path lined with trip wires connected to a string of seven grenades, their pins already removed. Trained as an EOD technician, he inspected the devices and then—one by one—began securing their spoons with safety pins he carried for just such a purpose. For the first three, this method worked. For the fourth, it didn't. Blown into the air, Gallagher landed hard, his face burnt black, his stomach punctured with tiny holes, his left-hand fingers shredded at the tips. For almost anyone else, such teeth-clenching injuries would have prompted all the normal questions: Am I going to live? Are my genitals intact? With tears in his eyes, Gallagher asked only one: "Is this going to survey me out?" It did. After a brief medevac flight to the field hospital at Dong Tam, he was flown to Japan.

The departure of Gallagher meant that the 7th Platoon had lost not only one of its squad leaders but also its most important engine of activity and anchor of stability. In the wake of this, Peterson reduced his patrols from three squads to two—with one exception—then initiated a series of squad-sized operations: 7A led by himself, and 7B led by Warrant Officer Charlie Watson, a man whose war so far had been overshadowed by a second front with dysentery. The results were predictably mixed. In the third week of November, Peterson's squad conducted four missions that resulted in a total of three Viet Cong killed, another one listed as "probable," plus two more captured. By comparison, Watson's squad conducted three missions that resulted in none killed and only one detained. It was a tally that did nothing to reverse his growing reputation for caution among the platoon's enlisted men—a reputation that was quickly becoming not unlike Jonah's before his shipmates threw him overboard.

A yeoman for almost his entire career in the UDTs, a rating of secretary-sailors responsible for paperwork and not exactly known for exceeding the margins of their assignments, Warrant Officer Charlie Watson was in possession of the kind of personality that irritated every man who was not his superior. When accompanied by the presence of a strong chief petty officer, this kind of personality was mostly neutralized, but without that, it was toxic. Even the affable Peterson—Watson's hotel roommate—was not immune, one time taking vengeance on Watson's quirks by eating an entire box of cookies that had been shipped in by his wife. In response, Watson moved out, then just as thoroughly irritated his new roommate, Jack Rowell, a former Golden Gloves boxer who—in spite of his lesser rank—never failed to remind Watson of this fact. In response to all similar affronts, Watson had dangled the peril of court-martial, the kind of nuclear threat that made fast friends of the threatened, who—before long—began using Watson's physical ailment as an excuse to say "he was scared shitless." True or not, it was a rumor that Watson exacerbated by being the only man on patrol who often wore a helmet.

Just before the enlisted men of the 7th Platoon erupted into outright mutiny, a disheveled man wearing a Navy doctor's uniform and his arm in a sling appeared on the streets of My Tho. It was Gallagher. How he had escaped the bureaucracy of the Navy medics no one knew, but it did nothing to decrease the size of his legend. And he had done it just in time.

For the entire 7th Platoon (not just Peterson's 7A), the return of Gallagher produced an effect not unlike that of a nitrous injection on an engine. Just after dawn on November 24, squad 7B, with a contingent of ARVN scouts, bushwhacked and captured two Viet Cong, then called fire support on an out-of-rifle-range contingent of some twenty armed guerrillas. Three days later, 7B swept a Viet Cong–controlled village and killed two more. In no time after Gallagher's return, Harry Constance and Roy Matthews—the most junior SEALs on 7A and 7B, respectively—were locked in a neck-and-neck competition for most kills.

Undated post-mission photo of SEAL Team TWO, 7th Platoon.

By mid-December, the men of the 7th Platoon were already exhibiting the swagger and nonchalance of experienced commandos. In part, the effect was due to mission attire that for several had evolved from tiger stripes and berets into blue jeans and bandanas. Mostly, though, this was the result of the 7th Platoon's growing ability to find and fight the Viet Cong, an ability that was starting to attract a reputation. Not even two months into the 7th Platoon's six-month deployment, a pair of LRRPs from the Army's 9th Infantry Division braved the precarious road from Dong Tam to find the SEAL compound in My Tho. Young, eager—"all e-nothings and lower," remembered one man—the LRRPs confessed to the SEALs that they had had some trouble in tracking down the Viet Cong mortar teams that were constantly harassing Dong Tam. Though they were tentative swimmers at best and a little clumsy in the dark, Peterson nevertheless agreed to help the LRRPs gain some experience in night patrolling in exchange for the added firepower that such "daredevils" brought to his platoon. He might also have had another reason.

6

UPON ARRIVAL IN the Mekong Delta, the 7th Platoon was informally relegated to an area of operations that was—for the most part—situated to the east of My Tho all the way to the coast of the South China Sea. Therefore, Peterson's agreement to help the LRRPs may have been an unconscious attempt to parlay that relationship into a westward invitation into the 9th Division's greener pastures. In any event, on December 19, just after a week of joint operations with the 9th Division LRRPs, the 7th Platoon did just that.

By the second week of January 1968, the SEALs' reputation as a competent land warfare unit was further acknowledged by two starkly different entities. The first of these were the planners of the Mobile Riverine Force—that two-headed hydra of the Army's 2nd Brigade of the 9th Infantry Division and the Navy's CTF-117—who decided to employ the 7th Platoon in Operation Preakness III—an Old Testament annihilation of a Viet Cong–controlled village near the coast—first as an ambush/blocking force, then as house-to-house search teams, and finally as bunker-busting demolitioneers. The second was none other than *Time* magazine, which printed a two-page article declaring that the Navy SEALs—the Navy's elite, the Navy's unconventionals, the Navy's "animals"—had transformed the Viet Cong from the hunters into the hunted.

For all of these outside acknowledgments of the SEALs' increasing prowess, Peterson nevertheless knew that the 7th Platoon's operations were still not as successful as they could be. So far, its missions had been planned with whatever information Peterson had been able to stitch together from his various meetings around My Tho, meetings with everyone from his friend at the ARVN Ranger compound to various Army sources at Dong Tam, and units that—another SEAL officer in Peterson's position would soon say—possessed "a natural feeling to withhold the most lucrative operations for units in [one's] own branch of service." As a result, the 7th Platoon's encounters with the enemy had been unpredictable, more a result of persistence than intelligence. Even the captives and documents that the 7th Platoon had turned over for analysis and interrogation by the Navy's intelligence liaison officer had so far proved dead ends, in part due to this particular NILO's collateral commitment to guarding a bottle at the local officers' club.

Attempts to improve the 7th Platoon's knowledge of enemy whereabouts had included near-daily overflights of suspected enemy locations, attempts to lure the Viet Cong into the open by running PBRs past known ambush sites, even experimental manhunts behind Rinnie, the 7th Platoon's scout dog, who proved a failure at everything but terrifying captured suspects into soiling themselves. To ease the burden of Peterson's intelligence collection across the breadth of My Tho and thereby increase the 7th Platoon's success rate, Gallagher borrowed a pair of bolt cutters from nearby EOD techs, then ordered Petty Officer 2nd Class Eugene Fraley to use them in stealing a jeep from the Army exchange in Saigon. An amateur magician known to pocket a white bra into a bar to make the girls momentarily think he could remove them from their bodies without first removing their shirts, Fraley accomplished Gallagher's task and negotiated the various checkpoints back to My Tho by wearing a set of lieutenant's bars and the gold-cross insignia of a Navy chaplain.

The most promising gold mine of Viet Cong routes and locations was the local Chieu Hoi Center, essentially a rehabilitation prison for Hoi Chanhs, or turncoat Viet Cong guerrillas, the same recruiting pool for the CIA's Provincial Reconnaissance Units. Peterson's ability to tap into this pool, however, had so far suffered from the same problem that the 7th Platoon had faced with every other Vietnamese from civilian to suspect: naturally, they only spoke Vietnamese. To overcome this language barrier, the 7th Platoon had thus far relied on the interpretive abilities of a string of LDNN frogmen and ARVN scouts, troops who had often been recruited from the far ends of Vietnam and whose accents had been met with mistrust by the locals, and whose English had proved only passable. Peterson's other option would have been to formally hire an interpreter, the only eligible candidates being those who had already received a draft deferment by the ARVN and who could, by law, refuse to go on missions without loss of pay unless their contract specifically classified them as a "combat terp." In any event, Peterson had no official monies to pay for an interpreter, combat or not.

In the second week of January, an American PBR sailor approached Gallagher and introduced him to a Vietnamese interpreter named Minh. Similar to his countrymen in frame and height, Minh at first glance seemed no different from any of the 7th Platoon's previous interpreters, but different he most certainly was. A former sailor in the Vietnamese Navy who had been jailed for insubordination, Minh had been paroled a year earlier by some PBR sailors who had heard rumors about his language abilities. Since then, he had served on a PBR, where he had not only sharpened his English and adjusted his accent to that of the local area, but had become so adept with American weapons and in small-boat handling that his American shipmates had come to rely on him as another crew member—a steady gun in a fight, even a cheerful drinking companion at the Victory Hotel. Recognizing the value in such bona fides, Gallagher wasted no time in asking Minh to accompany him on the 7th Platoon's next mission.

At 4:30 A.M. on January 16, squad 7B landed on the north shore of the northern branch of the Mekong River some fifteen miles east of My Tho. Nominally led by Warrant Officer Charlie Watson, in reality the squad looked to Gallagher for all decisions regarding mission objectives. In this instance, those consisted of a routine ambush of a Viet Cong tax collector, with a footnote to audition the new interpreter. By 8:00 A.M., after three and a half hours of no contact and neither objective accomplished, Watson ordered the squad to break their position and patrol north through the stubby palms of a banana grove. Beyond this strip of trees, sprawling in every direction, was a sea of green rice paddies—flat as pancakes and just as dry—the only noticeable interruptions being the brown gash lines of irrigation dikes and a tree line several hundred yards to the north. Happening upon three peasant farmers, Gallagher ordered his men to halt and surrounded the suspects with a protective perimeter. Once they were in custody, Gallagher turned to Minh.

"Ask [them] where the japs are," he said.

What followed was a rapid patter of Vietnamese. When it stopped, Minh motioned north and told Gallagher that there were 300 Viet Cong encamped in the far tree line.

"There isn't 300 VC in this whole damn IV Corps," Gallagher responded, so far unimpressed with Minh's abilities. "Ask [them] again."

Minh's answer was the same.

Carrying the squad's only radio, Watson requested an overflight by a Swamp Fox reconnaissance plane, whose pilot reported no visual confirmation of anything.

Bent on discovering the truth, Gallagher stashed the squad and Minh in a firing line at the peasants' farm, then enlisted Mike Boynton—his most senior petty officer and the one who looked most like a dockworker—in following him the 200 yards to the tree line by skirting the rice paddy's only concealment, a fence-topped irrigation dike thinly shaded by a row of measly palms.

They made it only halfway.

At approximately 9:15, under a hot sun, the cracks of a half-dozen rifle shots forced Gallagher and Boynton to their bellies and snapped into focus every eye that had remained at the farm. Half a breath later, ten to twelve machine guns erupted from the entire length of the northern tree line, a barrage so intense that for a moment the squad's firing-line defenders became little more than a base of huddling ineffectives. Initially concealed by a forest of shivering rice stalks, Gallagher and Boynton managed to roll themselves into a dike's shallows, but not before Boynton's sling was shot through by a bullet. There, outgunned and exposed, willing the mud to swallow them whole, the two men played dead until fire from 7B's own arsenal and a forty-round mortar barrage fired from the nearby Mike Boat that had been directed from the circling Swamp Fox opened a window for them to escape. As soon as they did, the entire area exploded with twenty-seven rockets launched from a flight of Seawolf gunships, 550 pounds of napalm dropped by two thundering A-1 Skyraiders, and a teeth-rattling bombardment by a 105-millimeter artillery battery out of My Tho.

Throughout this symphony of explosions, Boynton's ears nevertheless managed to register one other sound, that of Minh's voice—at every lull in the fire, taunting, cursing, berating the enemy, each shouted slur from the farmhouse another distraction that pulled the enemy's attention from the two men still stranded in the open. Just as the PBR sailors had said, Minh had shown himself capable in a fight and, what was more important, had proved the value of an interpreter who could be trusted by the locals and communicate their real-time intelligence to the Americans. It would take a little time before Peterson and the 7th Platoon fully appreciated how to make use of this advantage.

7

Over the next three weeks, this process of appreciation was hindered by three obstacles.

The first came on the heels of 7B's last mission, which had produced a rumor that Warrant Officer Charlie Watson's immediate reaction to the tree-line ambush had been to bolt to the river, taking with him the squad's only radio. True or not (and there are facts that support each side of the story), the rumor was a cancer on the platoon's cohesiveness, and one that spread all the way to the ears of Lieutenant Rhinebolt in Can Tho.

The second obstacle to this process occurred on January 21, while

Petty Officer 2nd Class Eugene Fraley—the amateur magician who had stolen the Army jeep—was down at the SEALs' armory near the PBR docks indulging his other hobby: improvised explosives. So far, Fraley's most sinister inventions had been booby-trapped ammunition cartridges designed to be left behind at a mission site where they might eventually be fired by the enemy's rifles and exploded into the enemy's faces. Looking to create an even bigger blast, Fraley, on this day, was finishing up a C-4–packed flashlight when the fuse malfunctioned and blew him onto the top of the Quonset hut, from where he slid down the side until his body was lodged between the corrugated wall and the abutment of protective sandbags. Nearby sailors tore down this abutment as fast as they could, but they reached him too late.

Both of these incidents—the spreading of Watson's rumor and the tragedy of Fraley's death—were obstacles enough to squander the entire head of steam the 7th Platoon had thus far accumulated. Neither, however, could compare to what happened next.

In most sections of the country, the Vietnamese New Year, or Tet, was accompanied by a thirty-six-hour truce. In My Tho, this truce brought with it a waterfront carnival with all the trimmings: puppet shows, jugglers, fire-eaters, even a .22-caliber shooting gallery. Throughout the city and late into the night, the air popped with firecrackers. For most American servicemen stationed in the area, the festivities were an opportunity to relax, to visit the bars, to momentarily forget the war. But not for the SEALs.

On the night of January 30, while the carnival was in full swing, the 7th Platoon was nowhere near it. Probably sensing the need to keep his men from thinking about Fraley and plotting against Watson, Peterson had lobbied for special permission to set up several ambush sites—called "observation posts" because of the truce—and now they were set up in an area not far from where Gallagher and Boynton had almost been killed, an area whose lack of activity stood as a stark monument to their lost momentum.

Well. At 3:07 A.M., after several hours of zero enemy contact, Peterson received a crackling radio transmission that the New Year's truce had just been canceled; return to base. Additional information was scant, but it wouldn't have mattered. No one could have told them the most important truth: From here on, the war was forever changed.

8

THOUGH NO ONE had yet quite grasped what was happening, at the moment of Peterson's radio transmission some 80,000 North Vietnamese troops and Viet Cong irregulars were initiating near-simultaneous attacks throughout many of the cities and towns across the entire length of South Vietnam, including in thirteen of the IV Corps' sixteen provincial capitals. These attacks were the result of several weeks of prodigious infiltration and weapons smuggling, the most effective method being in coffins whose contents were dug up on the night of the attack, then test-fired amid the fireworks and such noises as those being created at the carnival's shooting gallery.

At My Tho, the first IV Corps city to be hit, the attack started right around 3:30 A.M. Numbering around 1,200 fighters, the attackers' first objectives were the destruction of every airfield that might resupply the local defenders and the blocking of every road upon which reinforcements might travel. Next came assaults on all of the ARVN outposts that ringed the city, followed by a house-to-house cleansing of all local politicians, teachers, civil servants, plus a list of unfortunates fingered by Communist agents as "insufficiently friendly to the cause."

When the PBRs carrying the 7th Platoon neared My Tho, much of the city was already silhouetted in flame and reverberating with the staccato clatter of competing machine guns. With the skies noticeably free from the thunder of American jets and the whomp of American rotor blades, every crunch from a mortar round and its booming answer by artillery confirmed that the Viet Cong were in control. Overhead, the intermittent flash and drift of parachute illumination flares across the sky chased horrific, elongating shadows across the landscape. Into this mayhem the SEALs arrived.

Landing at the PBR docks in full battle attire, the hollows of their faces still dark with the traces of green paint, the 7th Platoon's first job was to figure out where they were needed. Without an abundance of information on the enemy's locations or the status of pro-government forces, Peterson ordered the platoon to split into squads and figure it out. Leaving the sandbagged protection of the PBR base, he and 7A bounded over the rubbled sidewalks to their hotel, where they distributed weapons and ammunition and organized the PBR sailors into a defense force.

While 7A was doing this, Gallagher and 7B cut north through the center of My Tho along the Bao Dinh Canal until they found the 32nd

ARVN Rangers under Viet Cong attack, their backs already pushed up against the river. With the ARVN Rangers separated from their American advisor and thus the radio that could connect them to the safety of American aircraft and artillery, the SEALs of 7B volunteered to step in and act as substitutes. Though they couldn't have predicted how long their support would be needed, Gallagher and the rest spent the next twenty-seven hours—all day and all night—fighting a land battle and employing their PRC-25 radio in, as one contemporary called it, "dropping rings of ruination around" their positions; and—in one of history's twists—repaying the Army Rangers' contributions to the development of the Navy SEAL teams by stiffening the backs of Darby's only direct descendants.

When the 32nd Rangers' American advisor finally returned, Gallagher and 7B hustled back to the Carter Billet, where Peterson and 7A were still busy turning it into an Alamo. From the second floor to the fourth, the hotel's patios now bristled with shooting pairs of enlisted sailors behind sandbagged emplacements. On the roof, several of the SEALs were staking out sniper nests and machine gun positions, and linking their 200-round belts of ammunition into belts of a thousand. Not sure how long the siege would last, Peterson and Gallagher wasted no time in organizing raiding parties, first for the pantries of the Navy's nearby facilities—bottles of water, soup cans, bologna logs, bread loaves, cheese and crackers—and second for the armories at the PBR base—everything from grenades to LAW rockets.

Before long, the 7th Platoon's preparations were inevitably tested by the Viet Cong's scout-snipers, each of which was quickly answered by one of the rooftop SEALs, who so thoroughly proved the hotel's transformation into a citadel that a large-scale attack never followed. Realizing the strength of his position, Peterson took to dispatching his SEALs throughout the city to scout the enemy's positions. One of these patrols resulted in Gallagher's decision to unburden the local CIA station of what one of the patrol members called a "twenty-nine-million-cubic-foot" Frigidaire, which the SEALs trucked back to the hotel and lugged up three flights to Gallagher's room.

On the second full day of fighting, three companies of the Mobile Riverine Force landed to the city's west, then fought north and east until their advance eventually enveloped the Carter Billet. When it finally did, the soldiers were treated to the sight of SEAL snipers in swim trunks and sunscreen, and outside the hotel's adjacent hospital, a pile of stacked corpses already as swollen as hot dogs.

Largely relieved of the responsibility for the Carter Billet's safety, Peterson—for the remainder of the week—folded the 7th Platoon into the general campaign to retake the Dong Tam/My Tho battlespace. During this period, his SEALs detonated unexploded ordnance, captured enemy caches, and rescued civilian holdouts. The only difference between the SEALs and the 9th Division's soldiers was that the former weren't soldiers.

In My Tho, as it did in most other places in the IV Corps Tactical Zone, the Tet Offensive died a relatively quick death, much of this due to the Mobile Riverine Force's ability to shuttle troops to trouble spots without having to rely on the Army's already overburdened helicopter squadrons. In this battle, the 7th Platoon's contributions—though lauded in reports—were mostly incidental, and in the end did not permanently contribute to the SEALs' general development. But that is not to say that they didn't matter. As with the 8th Platoon in Chau Doc, on the Cambodian border, which had joined up with a local PRU advisor to rescue a nurse and retake the city, the 7th Platoon's contributions to the My Tho battle were important for similar reasons: First, they helped put the past problems of Fraley's death and Watson's leadership out of their minds, and second, they demonstrated for all to see that the Navy's SEALs were just as competent at ground combat as were the Army's infantrymen. And they still had three more months left on their deployment.

9

In the immediate aftermath of Tet, Lieutenant Jake Rhinebolt, the coon-hunting commander of Det. Alfa, paid a visit to the 7th Platoon in My Tho—a city still smoldering and choking beneath the competing aromas of burning cordite and the sweetness of decomposing bodies. The purpose of his visit was to once and for all deal with the issue of Warrant Officer Charlie Watson's leadership and a reputation that had not improved with the Tet Offensive's many opportunities for bravery. To get to the bottom of these accusations, Rhinebolt conducted interviews with several of the platoon members, then met with Peterson and Gallagher. In the end, whatever the truth, Rhinebolt decided that Watson had lost the confidence of the squad, and ordered Doc Riojas to find an Army doctor who could evaluate Watson for hepatitis and—whether he found it or not—send him home. The corollary to this decision meant that squad 7B would not—for the time being—have the benefit of an officer, meaning that Gallagher would have to fill in. In the history of the SEAL teams, there have been few leadership adjustments that produced better results.

On the day of Gallagher's promotion to assistant platoon commander, squad 7B underwent a change—not overt, but significant. The first indication of what was to come occurred that night, when Gallagher led his squad some 1,500 meters north of their riverbank insertion point—about as far as one could get from the water in that part of the delta and a distance from the boat's protective fan that Watson had never been inclined to exceed—then had his men steal into the empty house of a suspected Viet Cong guerrilla, where they waited for the occupant to return. At the arrival of an eleven-man patrol, Gallagher again distinguished himself from Watson by ordering the group to halt, and opened fire only when the panicked men attempted to flee, a decision that yielded numerous killed and five captives.

Three nights later, the entire 7th Platoon went ashore some ten kilometers southeast of My Tho, then split into squads 7A and 7B to patrol to separate ambush sites—or that was the plan, anyway. Encountering a village with signs of Viet Cong influence, Gallagher decided to improvise. It being 7B's turn to patrol with the interpreter, Gallagher and Minh snuck into one of the houses, woke the occupants, and then, illuminated by a red-lens flashlight, introduced themselves as casually as they could under the circumstances and questioned the startled peasants about enemy locations. Familiar with the local Viet Cong agents, who were the taxers of their monies and their sons, the information the peasants provided—the hideout of a Viet Cong village chieftain and a Viet Cong tax collector—represented enough of a score that they could have returned to My Tho to plan a follow-on mission. Or, rather, that would have been enough for someone else.

As soon as he and Minh emerged from the peasant's hooch, Gallagher circled his men, whispered the bones of a new plan, and immediately pointed the patrol in the direction of the new suspect's hideout. What had been a typical patrol-and-ambush had just turned into something new: a mission to capture or kill two Viet Cong leaders. The results were equally original.

By the time of their rendezvous with Peterson and 7A—who hadn't had the benefit of a competent interpreter, and thus spent another uneventful night in an ambush site—Gallagher and 7B had successfully killed a Viet Cong chieftain and captured a Viet Cong tax collector and a packet of documents, along with an American rifle, a .30-caliber machine gun, and eight American fragmentation grenades. But those weren't the only results. More important than what was found was what was discovered, and for the 7th Platoon, it was something of a revelation. Normally as dry as toast and completely free of conjecture, Peterson's after-action report on this occasion carried a number of comments and superlatives, including the shining of a spotlight on "having a competent aggressive operational interpreter," but what was more important, on being able to turn that interpreter into a real-time producer of intelligence for the killing or capturing of Viet Cong leaders—preferably the latter, as those captives could then be squeezed to provide additional Viet Cong leaders.

From February 12 to March 12, just twenty-nine days, the 7th Platoon planned and conducted thirteen direct-action operations, averaging about one mission every two days, the same tempo they had kept before Tet. The character of these missions, however, differed in several respects. First of all, Minh's knack for talking the truth out of peasants in the middle of the night proved just as valuable when talking to actual intelligence sources: Hoi Chanhs at the Chieu Hoi Center, ARVN soldiers and Rangers, even the National Police, which Minh's wife just happened to work for. This ability, plus the knowledge gained by Minh's previous work with the PBR fleet, added to the 7th Platoon's roster a presence not unlike that of a beat cop. Armed with such an asset, Peterson and Gallagher ceased to satisfy themselves with simple canal-side ambushes and instead focused their energies not merely on capturing or killing Viet Cong, but on capturing or killing individual Viet Cong, Viet Cong with names. It was a mission change with others right behind it.

Prior to Tet, deference to the Army's elbows at Dong Tam had mostly consigned the 7th Platoon to an operational area that stretched southeast from My Tho to the coast. After Tet, Peterson and Gallagher dropped this pretense, and, like hunters, followed the game wherever it led them. Of their thirteen missions during this period, seven were conducted either near Dong Tam or even farther west of it. Of these, only three failed to make successful contact with the enemy. Of the ten that did, seven missions succeeded in killing at least one or more insurgents, and eight resulted in the successful capture of the same. All of this had been due to Peterson's and Gallagher's adoption of a self-sustaining operational cycle: first, the ransacking of local intelligence for enemy locations; then the raiding of Viet Cong hideouts to capture the cadre and kill those they couldn't; and finally, the interrogating of captives for even more Viet Cong hideouts. It was a cycle that couldn't help but add to the SEALs' reputation, a reputation that others were already trying to mimic.

Starting in the last week of February, the Army's 9th Infantry Division once again began permitting its LRRPs—two at a time—to accompany 7th Platoon SEALs on their operations. It was a courtesy that Peterson also extended to a single Force Recon Marine—a stray cat in a part of the country with no other Force Recon Marines, and just one more awkward example of a soldier or Marine coming cap in hand to the Navy for a bit of direct-action charity. About the only local unit that didn't look to learn from the SEALs' example was the one whose operational cycle most closely matched the 7th Platoon's: the local PRU.

In the first week of March, Peterson approved Gallagher's request to take a small element of 7th Platoon SEALs on a short sabbatical from My Tho in order to support a need by the PRU in Vinh Binh Province some forty kilometers to the south, a sabbatical that culminated in a several-hours-long daytime land battle—a battle supported by Navy Seawolf gunships—that killed as many as twenty Viet Cong fighters, including their company commander, and wounded as many more; results that Gallagher ascribed to the "maximum use of a Navy Team." What he didn't call it was a "maximum use of a Navy team in performing an Army mission." But he could have.

It was something that could also be said of the 7th Platoon's next mission, the most impactful capture/kill raid of its deployment, or that of any other SEAL platoon to date. A thirty-year culmination of sorts that would not only prove the potential impact of inland commando raids, but also demonstrate that a Navy unit could perform them as well as any of the units that had come before.

10

In the second week of March 1968, an Army troop helicopter, or slick, assigned to the 9th Infantry Division was shot down in the Mekong Delta. Later, upon the discovery of the crash site, it was learned that the body of one crew member was missing, forcing the chain of command to concede the possibility that the missing man was now a prisoner of war. Perceived as the closest thing that the Army still had to the Rangers, the 9th Infantry Division's LRRPs were the most obvious candidates to mount a rescue; to the LRRPs themselves, the most obvious unit for the operation was the one that had spent the past four months in the delta perfecting the art of finding and capturing people that did not want to be found and captured. They turned to the 7th Platoon.

Having bootstrapped his various sources into one of the most sophisticated intelligence networks in the region, Peterson, at the time of the LRRPs' request, had also already made several single-engine overflights of a Viet Cong–controlled area said to be a way station for POWs on the ratline to Hanoi. Some twenty kilometers east of My Tho and some three kilometers north of the northern branch of the Mekong River, the physical location of this way station lay at the end of a "tortured," twisting snake of a canal too narrow for the SEALs' support boats and farther from the water than even Gallagher had ever ventured. It was also rumored to be an area bristling with enemy bunkers. No matter. Flying over the canopy of a monstrous coconut grove, Peterson could only imagine that somewhere, hidden beneath him, was an American in a cage. And if he was there, the 7th Platoon was going to find him.

Throughout the morning of March 13, the members of the 7th planned and prepared. For Peterson and Gallagher, this meant booking all the units that would support them: the sailor crews of the Mike Boat, PBRs, and the newly arrived SEAL Team Assault Boat, or STAB, a twenty-six-foot, blunt-nosed bathtub that could crowd so close to a riverbank that its occupants need never get their feet wet; plus, alerting the Airedales who would pilot the Navy Seawolves and Army slicks. It also meant dispatching a concept of operations to Lieutenant Rhinebolt, who deconflicted the operation with CTF-116. For Jack Rowell and Richard "Hook" Tuure, the radio operators for 7A and 7B, respectively, these preparations meant programming frequencies into their PRC-25s, then confirming that someone on the other end could hear them. For everyone else—including Minh, two LDNN frogmen, and two LRRPs—it meant loading their gear with extra magazines and grenades, based on the knowledge of where they were going, more than they had ever taken, so much that most men decided to forgo the extra weight of water.

Watching these preparations and pitching in wherever he could was Lieutenant Junior Grade Ronald Yeaw, a blond, square-jawed college swimmer born and raised just outside of Philadelphia. Yeaw's first Vietnam assignment as a SEAL had started a couple months earlier as a replacement for a 6th Platoon officer who had gotten shot, then in subsequent assignments with the 8th and 9th Platoons, participating in each one's operations—standard platoon missions of patrol and ambush. Having arrived in My Tho just a few days earlier to fill the vacancy left by Charlie Watson, Yeaw was now about to embark on his first mission with the 7th, a mission that was unlike anything he had experienced before, and as the second-in-command of a unit in which he knew nobody but radio operator Hook Tuure, who had been one of Yeaw's UDTR instructors.

As soon as preparations were complete, the men of the 7th Platoon did as they always had and gathered in one of the third-floor hotel rooms for their mission briefing. Though these briefs had long since stopped specifying the content of each man's individual loadout, Peterson and Gallagher nevertheless took their time, alternately detailing the locations of insertion and extraction, and the complicated target area—well outside of the Army's artillery fan. Most of all, they focused on the mission itself—essentially the same sort of thing they had been perfecting: an intelligence-driven capture/kill. It is worth noting that if they couldn't accomplish the former, certain personalities would ensure that the 7th Platoon at least accomplished the latter.

11

THAT NIGHT, RIGHT AROUND 10:00 P.M. local time, with the glare from a nearly full moon magnifying itself in the mirror of the black river, the 7th Platoon's STAB slowly turned toward a steep riverbank and dropped into a drifting idle. Crowding the bow in a pirate trunk's worth of tiger stripes, blue jeans, bandanas, and boondock hats, the men crouched like sprinters, waiting for the shore's abrupt bump and the light wash of exhaust fumes to release them into the wildlands. Ashore, the men did as they always had and fanned into a hushed semicircle and sank into the grass, where their eyes widened to separate the blackness into identifiable shapes and their ears bent to parse the croaks of bullfrogs and the buzz of insects from anything that wasn't. The sudden absence of boat breeze and the onset of the night's oppressive heat told each man's sweat glands to start soaking his clothes and melting his face paint into a smudge. In a few minutes, the low growl of the STAB's twin outboards returned with the second squad, which likewise fanned ashore and threaded into the perimeter. Only after several minutes of silent waiting with no order to start patrolling did anyone realize that something was amiss.

"What the hell are we waiting for?" Mike Boynton hissed to the black shape next to him.

"Gallagher's not here," came the muffled response.

In a few moments, this mystery was solved by the STAB's return and the silhouette of a single shape storming ashore.

"You guys didn't wake me up," Gallagher growled, furious at having nearly slept through the mission for which he, as much as anyone else, had proved the Navy capable of performing. But never mind.

The events that immediately followed were typical of most of the 7th Platoon's previous missions, save for some minor distinctions. For a unit accustomed now to squad-sized operations, the sudden doubling to fifteen men meant a patrol file of about half the length of a football field, which meant that the normal accordion effect of stretching and bunching was exacerbated, especially by terrain. In this instance, that terrain initially consisted of a dense forest, meaning obsidian darkness and trip-hazards, the latter made worse by the extra weight of ammunition belts crossed around almost everyone's shoulders. Setting the pace through this jungle was the patrol's point man, a position normally entrusted to those raised in the rurals and steeped in the art of deer stalking, but on this occasion falling to the man who had personally overflown the area, Peterson himself.

After about an hour and roughly one kilometer of this, the jungle's darkness gave way to a dry rice paddy flooded with moonlight. Interrupting the clearing was a checkered pattern of dikes and thin tree lines, plus small clusters of thatched houses. Avoiding the last of these, Peterson led the patrol north, hugging what shadows he could. At one point, remembered Harry Constance, the whole patrol froze at the distant sight of two men standing outside a hooch, their bodies oriented toward the SEALs, who were now just blackened statues. As the platoon wondered if they'd been seen, that question was answered when one of the distant men raised his hand in a friendly wave, to which Constance responded the only way he knew how; he waved back.

At the far end of the rice paddy, right around 1:00 A.M. on March 14, the patrol finally ducked under the edge of the coconut grove Peterson had seen from the air. They were relieved to find themselves back beneath a blanket of darkness, but this feeling didn't last long, as every step took them deeper into the mystery that the palm fronds had been hiding all along: a landscape cluttered with mud-and-log bunkers, structures that were obviously guarding something. But what, and where?

At the end of his intelligence rope and with no locals left to question, here Peterson did as he had planned and split the platoon into squads to start sweeping the area for signs of POW imprisonment—7A to the east with Peterson and two LDNNs; 7B to the west with Yeaw, Gallagher, and Minh; one LRRP accompanying each squad.

From here, events began to quicken.

Patrolling to the east, Peterson—still on point—led 7A some 500 meters farther into the patchwork of bunkers until they were funneled onto a path that seemed to be leading toward a hub of structures. While picking his way along this path, keeping careful watch for trip wires that might be protecting an enemy outpost, Peterson looked up to see not far ahead the black shapes of two men carrying rifles and heading directly toward him—so far oblivious to his presence. As he shrank to the trail's edge and drew his knife, Peterson simultaneously turned to the man behind him—one of the LRRPs—and tried to pantomime a hasty plan to capture the oncomers, not kill them, the only way the SEALs might still discover the POW's whereabouts. Anyway, it was too much to communicate and too late. As soon as the first guerrilla was within arm's length, Peterson violently shunted him toward the LRRP, then tackled the second. Within a breath, however, the startled LRRP stepped out of the path of the stumbling guerrilla and shot him dead, each muzzle flash illuminating another snapshot of the man's crumpling body and each report shattering the night's calm for miles around. In the wake of this mistake, Peterson was forced to immediately "engage" the second guerrilla with the weapon in his hand—or so read the official report. Except for the fading pulses of the two unfortunates, the whole episode was over in seconds, and so was any chance that the 7th Platoon had to find the captured American.

So, what now?

Even before Peterson had unwrapped himself from the dead man's body, the sounds of startled Vietnamese voices could be heard to the east, not far from where the two guerrillas had come. In fact, there were lots of voices. Not overly eager to fight his way through them or pick his way back over the coconut grove's bunkers, Peterson quickly gathered his men, told radioman Jack Rowell to pass a message to 7B to head to the landing zone, then faced north and started moving, fast. As he knew from his overflights, there was a large clearing about a kilometer ahead, large enough for several Army slicks to land, but first they had to get there. In that moment, this prospect was a doubtful one. All around them Vietnamese voices were growing louder—angrier too—forcing Peterson to make abrupt changes in the patrol's direction. Before long, the voices were joined by the crack of rifle shots, probing fire meant to elicit a response but from which Peterson's men judiciously held their fire. This was easier when the LDNNs began whispering translations of what the voices said they would do to those they captured. Spurred on by the prospect of being skinned alive (among other things), the squad finally made it to the edge of the clearing Peterson had seen from the air.

At the edge of this sea of grass surrounded by unbroken tree lines, Peterson and his men crouched, then dashed beneath the moonlight to the clearing's center and a square berm containing what looked like rows of cement structures. When they got there, they quickly spread out in a perimeter along the berm, from where they watched the edges of the darkened forest undulate with movement, like water spreading around a rock. While they watched, Jack Rowell plotted the location of the clearing, then keyed his handset to pass the squad's coordinates to the Army slicks. The reply was only static. While Rowell was problem-shooting his settings and cleaning his connectors, the rest of the squad focused their attention on what they feared was coming. And if it wasn't already hard enough to put the worst out of their minds, they only had to glance over their shoulders. They had taken cover in a cemetery.

12

BY THE TIME they had heard the shots to their east, squad 7B had already patrolled for four straight hours. With more weight than they had ever carried, many without water, their concentration had already reached its ebb. Since splitting with 7A, their last leg had taken them some 500 meters to the west along the edge of a tree line, then north—slowly, almost deliberately—into a forest as dark as they had ever seen. Along the way, there had been plenty more bunkers, but nothing to indicate a campsite or a way station for POWs.

At the transmission to abort the operation, Yeaw and Gallagher quickly conferred, then pointed the squad east to make for the landing zone—a direction that would, despite the men's exhaustion, take them there by another route than the one they had come by, thus increasing their chances of enemy contact. This route took them to the edge of a deeply cut canal, forcing each footsore man, once again, to delicately sidestep his way down the near face into a shallow rivulet of water, then heave his weight up the far side. There, after a few more steps into the brush, the point man halted the patrol. Just ahead was a clearing awash in moonlight, with something that none of them had ever seen in the Mekong Delta.

Staying in the darkness of the brush line, Yeaw and Gallagher stepped out of their patrol positions and crept forward to join the point man at the edge of the clearing. In front of them was a campsite dominated by two structures: the first, a normal-sized, almost circular hooch that was hovering just along the lip of the stream they had just crossed; the second, a thatched longhouse some forty-five feet in length, roughly the size of an American barracks—a "huge sucker by Vietnamese standards," remembered one man. Around these structures lay numerous trails and signs of normal camp life, including several Vietnamese picnic tables, rice bowls tied to their tops. If there existed a POW way station in the My Tho area, this was it. So, what now?

Faced with too big a target for one squad to handle but unable to call for support from Peterson and 7A, who were already running for their landing zone, the question was ultimately Yeaw's and Gallagher's to decide, but what choice did they really have? An American soldier was still missing and possibly inside one of these two structures. Once that realization dawned, Yeaw and Gallagher wasted no time establishing a firing line on the edge of the clearing, and then sent to the longhouse a pair of scouts—Hook Tuure, the radioman, and Roy Matthews, the twenty-five-year-old Floridian on his first deployment with SEAL Team TWO, but already one of its top-ranked killers. When the pair reached it, they took a few careful steps into what Matthews described as pitch black, then with a brief scan by red-lens flashlight confirmed the structure as a barracks—row upon row of bunks, the walls lined with rifles—not exactly the kind of environment in which to keep an American soldier.

To search for a more likely location for a POW cage, Gallagher, Yeaw, and Minh left the firing line and stalked to the threshold of the hooch, where one by one they disappeared inside. There, under the shaded loom of Yeaw's red-lens flashlight, they found themselves between a pair of bunks, four cots total—each covered in mosquito netting, not bamboo bars, and each containing two sleepers, none of whom were the missing American. At the base of each bunk stood a rank of AK-47 assault rifles. In the amount of time it took Yeaw to fully absorb these surroundings, Gallagher was already leveling his CAR-15 at the sleepers on his side and about to turn this rescue into the kind of mission the 7th Platoon had long been perfecting. Unable to wield flashlight and rifle simultaneously, Yeaw hustled to set his M16 next to the stack of AK-47s, then slipped his .38-caliber revolver from his shoulder holster, lifted the mosquito screen with his light, and, like Gallagher, aimed his muzzle at the first of two black-haired heads. Minh did the same.

From the outside, what followed looked and sounded like an explosion of fireworks erupting inside a box—the shredding rattle, the screams, the pops from Yeaw's .38. From the inside, it was unimaginable—three different muzzles blasting split-second freeze-frames of thrashing bodies and tortured faces. In the chaos, one of the victims burst from his cot toward Yeaw, who turned his .38 into a club and pistol-whipped the fighter to the ground, then shot him in the head. At the rear of the hooch, a back door—not noticed until now—flew open, and another fighter rushed outside.

Watching from the brush line for just that sort of flight from either of the structures, Mike Boynton and the LRRP immediately spotted the outline of a runner and released a spasm of red tracer fire that illuminated the silhouette enough to see that it was a woman sprinting behind the back of the smaller hooch.

"Get the son of a bitch! Get her," someone yelled just as she doubled back across the clearing. This time she crumpled beneath a red streak of bullets from the skirmish line, but it was too late; she had already accomplished what she had set out to do.

Still exhaling clouds of gun smoke from above the slaughterhouse floor in the hooch, Yeaw pushed past Minh and Gallagher—the latter in a hand-to-hand fight of his own—to reach the back door's open threshold and the fighter he had seen escaping from it.

Then, as he stepped outside, a flash of light completely engulfed him.

13

When Yeaw regained consciousness, he was on the ground just outside the hooch, an unidentifiable pain stabbing him in the back. The first sound he heard was Gallagher's voice yelling that he had been hit—strangely audible because of a lull in fire from the skirmish line, a lull that at that moment Yeaw could not possibly understand or explain.

The reason was actually simple: a pair of grenades—apparently tossed by the female runner when she had neared the hooch's back door—had thrown Yeaw into the clearing and blown Gallagher and Minh beneath the bunks and the bodies they had just killed, and sprayed fragmentation so far that even the men in the skirmish line were now stitched with bits of metal beneath their skin. Trying to make sense of his injuries, Yeaw clambered to his knees, attempted to stand, and immediately passed out again, this time toppling into the adjacent stream and disappearing from sight.

Ignoring his own injuries, Mike Boynton—the thick-necked, broad-faced survivor of 7B's last tree-line ambush—ordered the skirmishers into the clearing, where they swept forward until they reached the hooch. Surrounded by the dead and dying, those unfortunates whose last living act had been to escape from their beds, Boynton and his skirmishers swept over them, shooting bodies as they passed. In between shots, they looked and listened for any signs of their own men.

First to be found was Yeaw, still lying where he had rolled, writhing in pain, his entire left side frayed with holes from the top of his back to the heel of his foot.

"If you don't shut up, I'll kill you," Boynton matter-of-factly told him from the lip of the canal, still fearful that the enemy was—even now—trying to mount a counterattack.

At the sound of these voices, Gallagher began calling for Boynton, who stepped inside the hooch to a scene he simply described as "bodies all over the place." Clearly in pain, his right side and legs "peppered" with holes, Gallagher ignored this and simply ordered Boynton to "Get Minh." After moving a bed and finding the interpreter, Boynton tried to comply with Gallagher's order but found Minh so shredded up the middle of his body that not only was he unable to walk, he could only be lifted by Boynton as if cradling a baby.

Outside, Hook Tuure was alternately attempting to radio the squad's need for support and shouldering Yeaw's weight by draping the wounded man's arm around his neck. He succeeded in neither—and worse, exacerbated Yeaw's problems by lifting his arm and spreading several of the holes in his side farther apart. But what other option was there? Because he could not be airlifted on a medevac flight and because he was so big that he would have required at least two men to carry him out—probably three, the squad's current number of nonwounded operators—Yeaw, without saying a word, now presented his teammates with a deadly problem. Or would have if they had been inflicted on any normal person. Having already earned a reputation in UDTR training for one-armed pull-ups and for an occasional bar trick of chewing glass (there wasn't much trick to it), Yeaw solved his own problem by asking for two things: a shot of morphine and his rifle, which he turned into a crutch and in this way was just able to manage a tortured shuffle. Because he knew the task of staying upright would now require every shred of his concentration, Yeaw found Gallagher's eyes and managed to mouth two words: "It's yours," he said, a handoff of command that for the second time in one deployment placed the fate of 7B in the hands of the man who cared the most for it.

Cut off from air support and with more wounded than not, Gallagher's only option was to make for the river, a distance of just over three kilometers, or two miles, but at a pace and in a state that practically begged the Viet Cong to attack them. Between Yeaw and Gallagher, only the latter was still in any condition to fight, but his ripped and bloodied pants shivered at every step. Worse still was Minh, who screamed if carried in any position besides a cradle, a transport method that required both of Boynton's arms, which meant one less gun available while the squad was moving. And this was clearly going to be a problem.

As with 7A's dash north, 7B's dash south was likewise attracting a following—before long, more recon by fire, more Vietnamese voices. At the same dry rice paddy whose thin tree lines the platoon had previously attempted to skirt during their infiltration, Gallagher plunged the squad directly across—too late now for any caution; their only concealment was an occasional log-rolled rice bale. Had every man in the squad still been healthy, the sprint likely would have worked, and at the end of it 7B could have inflated their life vests and swum into the river's center, where loitering PBRs would have surely picked them up. But they were far from healthy, and the river was still two kilometers away.

Realizing the enemy was already moving to cut them off, Gallagher decided the only thing left to do was fight. This decision made, he directed his men to make for the rice paddy's lone position of cover, an isolated peasant's house—but situated just twenty uncomfortable yards away from the nearest tree line. When they reached it, their first job was to calm the family inside; not an easy task for any home invader, and one in which the squad was only partially successful as two children quickly escaped, sure to eventually tell the Viet Cong their position. Next most important was to check the wounded—Yeaw's entire left side was starting to freeze up—and fix whatever was wrong with the radio, the same troubleshooting checklist of cleaning connectors, swapping out handsets, changing batteries, plus a healthy amount of cursing and praying. This troubleshooting, however, was only partially successful. When Tuure finally got the radio back on-line, the only other person who could hear him was Jack Rowell, the radioman for 7A, and they had problems of their own.

14

AT A LITTLE before 3:00 A.M., Peterson and squad 7A considered themselves in a very difficult position. Everywhere they looked in the surrounding tree lines there was movement; at one point, Peterson had even seen torches, what seemed like hundreds of them moving to their south. But as they were now finding out over the radio, it could have been worse. Once Gallagher's and 7B's situation was learned, Peterson was quick to count his blessings. First, he had none of Gallagher's casualties, and except for the LRRP who had shot the man Peterson had meant to interrogate, every one of his men still had a full loadout of ammunition. Next was his position, clear fields of fire in every direction and the cemetery's berm for cover, even concrete vaults if the enemy brought in his mortars. Most important of all: Rowell's radio was now working as it should, putting the squad in reach of the Army slicks and the Navy Seawolves, who were, at that moment, on their way to 7A's rescue. Or at least they had been.

Recognizing 7B's overwhelming need, Peterson quickly made two decisions: First, he ordered Rowell to relay 7B's position to the helicopters, effectively putting his own squad at the back of the line; second, and this decision was made by the default of the first, 7A would now fight the encircling enemy alone.

Just as Peterson's decision was made and the helicopters began diverting south, a group of some thirty Viet Cong fighters—as if sensing 7A's sudden vulnerability—stepped clear of their eastern wood line, spread themselves into a screen of skirmishers, and started forward. The first wave was coming, and no one knew what was coming behind it.

15

HAVING BEEN FORCED to spend the first few minutes at the farmhouse calming peasants, dressing wounds, and fixing the radio, Gallagher—despite the shards of metal in his legs—was now checking each man's field of fire and telling him to hold that fire until he gave the order. As men organized their positions with easily accessible stacks of ammunition and grenades, they scanned their sectors for any sign of movement. They didn't have to scan long. Soon, between the rice bales, there was movement everywhere.

"Look at them all," said Boynton. "It looks like hundreds of them"—

but, as best he could tell, hundreds who by their milling around still had no idea where the Americans were.

Right about the time that Boynton was making this assessment, Hook Tuure received what they had all been quietly desperate for: the check-in procedures from Lieutenant Commander Myers of the Navy Seawolves, who rattled off the loadout for his flight of two helicopters—wings racked with 2.75-inch rockets and machine guns—then gave his altitude and vicinity, a racetrack in the sky far enough away so as to not reveal 7B's position. In response, Tuure gave a physical description of the rice paddy and 7B's location in it, along with the rapidly deteriorating situation—multiple wounded, and enemy everywhere. The next call was with the lead pilot of the Army's flight of slicks, who, upon hearing of 7B's situation, replied that he would not be able to help as it was "a violation of squadron policy to land in a hot LZ."

What happened next is a matter of some dispute. One account suggests that the Seawolf pilots may have shamed their Army peers by offering to pick up the SEALs themselves—or at least the wounded; the Navy fuselages could only hold one or two men. Another explicitly claims that the Seawolf commander told the Army pilot that "you're gonna go down or I'm gonna shoot you down." Whatever the truth, within a few minutes the matter was resolved, and Gallagher told Tuure to tell the helicopters what he wanted.

At a little before 3:15 A.M., the moon behind them, two Seawolves started their attack run across the rice paddy. As they closed with the tree line, someone in the squad—there is some dispute as to who—stepped out of the farmhouse, ripped the pull ring on a Mark 13 signal flare, and tossed it in the grass. Within a second, the flare ignited a bonfire-size glow that told the pilots exactly where the SEALs were, but also drew the bullet snaps of every muzzle now blazing from the tree line. As the SEALs flinched beneath the fire and responded with their own, the world above them exploded with the whomp and whoosh of two gunships strafing the enemy's muzzle flashes with their rockets and four machine guns. With landing skids directly above them, the combination of rotor blades and rocket exhaust nearly ripped the roof off the farmhouse. As the Seawolves unleashed this chaos, several SEALs got on-line and followed suit, launching grenades and shredding through the belts of Stoner rounds they had so assiduously linked. "The noise was unbelievable," wrote one man afterward, "and it looked like something not of this world."

Behind this cover, the Army pilot reluctantly landed his slick, and

Gallagher directed the firing line of SEALs to begin bounding back toward it. While the firing line covered, Mike Boynton transformed himself into an ambulance, cradling Minh from the hooch to the helicopter, then helping to shoulder Yeaw to a seat crammed between the pilot and the co-pilot. Finding Gallagher limping away from the firing line—his rifle still in hand, and compressing a fresh gunshot wound—and leaning into the rotor wash like it was a driving rain, Boynton picked him up and heaved him so hard into the helicopter's open door that he flew right out the other side. The accident forced Boynton to run all the way around and repeat the effort, finally stashing Gallagher all the way in the back. Once everyone was finally loaded, the pilot eagerly applied his collective pitch control lever—until several knocks on the helmet forced him to look back.

"Hey, we've still got men on the ground!" Boynton yelled above the din. At this, the pilot depressed his collective, just in time for Roy Matthews, the barrel of his Stoner still glowing red, to dash from the hooch and clamber aboard, rounds now clanking against the fuselage.

This time the pilot's liftoff sent a shudder throughout the entire helicopter, prompting Yeaw to crane his head toward the instrument control panel, where he saw an RPM indicator flashing red. While gaining the next 100 feet of elevation, the helicopter shook like it would suddenly drop out of the sky, a feeling that only intensified when every gun still connected to a living Communist finger started firing and surrounding the slick with green tracers. It was a barrage that had resulted from the near-simultaneous liftoff of the Seawolves, because they had somewhere else to be.

16

By the time the Seawolves reached Peterson and 7A, they had been in direct combat for some thirty minutes. Lacking the support of the Seawolves, Peterson had let that first group of skirmishers get close—closer than most of his teammates probably would have liked—then had unleashed upon them a barrage not unlike those that had turned the Western Front into a no-man's-land. Since this episode, the enemy had learned its lesson in frontal assault but had kept up a consistent fire, making Peterson think they were most likely trying to buy some time while they mobilized their crew-served weapons—mortars, recoilless rifles, anything that might keep the Americans' heads down while a second assault force drove across the clearing.

Anyway, if those were their plans, they crumbled the moment the Seawolves arrived to eviscerate the tree line and once again pave the way for the landing of an Army slick. Last to board, Peterson stayed at the edge of the helicopter door and watched the cemetery shrink beneath his feet, then saw every inch of tree line that had surrounded it erupt with machine gun fire. Once safely out of range, Peterson turned his attention to learning the mission's impact on his teammates, and in that moment not at all realizing that those impacts would extend far beyond his teammates in 7B.

17

When the slick carrying 7B landed in the bright lights of the H-marked landing zone of the US Army's field hospital at Dong Tam, a thin stream of blood was draining from the rear fuselage. Before the rotor blades even stopped spinning, a squadron of medics was already at the helicopter's door to load the wounded aboard stretchers, their eyes scanning for bleeders no less intently than the SEALs had just been scanning the tree line for Viet Cong. The other members of 7B were left with nothing to do but get out of the way and marvel at the evidence of their own survival—empty magazine pouches, mud-caked fatigues still damp with sweat and blood. Being the most senior man on-scene now, Mike Boynton felt obliged to thank the Army pilot, whom he melodramatically kissed, then added something about how he would have shot him if he hadn't landed the helicopter for Matthews.

When the slick carrying 7A arrived at the field hospital, Peterson met quickly with the men of 7B, just long enough to find out where all the wounded had been taken. Inside, Army nurses were busy stabilizing the SEALs (apparently Minh had already been rushed into surgery) and jotting clipboards with answers to the typical questions asked of dying men: name and religion. Taking hold of Gallagher's hand—already cold—Peterson said not a word, just watched while a nurse probed Gallagher's body for a vein with enough pressure to provide a blood type. In the end, they were forced to start an IV near his collarbone.

Yeaw's condition was just as serious. As the medics cut the clothes from his body, they counted no fewer than eight holes up the length of his left side, and all so packed with fragmentation that they would require the special assistance of an ice cream scooper. Removing Yeaw's left boot, the orderlies were met by the sight of a GI-issued green sock, now red, from which fell a chunk of heel half the size of a baseball.

Eventually, several members of the 7th Platoon got up the nerve to come inside.

"Where's the Eagle?" Boynton bellowed while storming through the crowded operating room, his startling appearance prompting one orderly to drop an IV bottle. When he found him, Boynton kissed Gallagher's bald forehead, then looked him in the eyes and matter-of-factly said, "I'll see you later"—at least that's how the story goes; just about every other platoon member would claim something similar.

After hitching a ride on a PBR on its way downriver—a ride that had taken him into the relief of a rising sun—Peterson finally arrived back in My Tho, where his men were already reliving the night's events with beers in hand, and would relive them for several hours more. Peterson was not so lucky. After making an oral accounting to Det. Alfa commander Rhinebolt of the operation's results, his responsibilities also required a formal after-action report, but that was not all. Over the next several days, Peterson convened a general debriefing to gain an overview of 7B's actions, then interviewed each member separately. When this was done, he submitted awards citations up through CTF-116's chain of command: Bronze Stars for just about every member of 7B, a Silver Star for Boynton, and for Gallagher, a Navy Cross—an award that he had to justify to an awards officer with multiple statements, but who responded by saying that the evidence could actually support a Medal of Honor. For himself—despite his quick-thinking command at the cemetery and his decision to push the helicopters to 7B's location—Peterson drafted nothing. Having set out to rescue an American POW, Peterson felt he had instead presided over an operation in which his two squads had barely escaped annihilation, and needed rescue themselves. Besides this, five of his fifteen men had been wounded—three severely—for a total casualty figure of 33 percent. By all these measures, it was hard for him to consider the mission anything but a failure—a good reminder that none of us really know our own impact.

On March 26 at 7:30 A.M.—twelve days after the attempted POW rescue; twelve more days of Peterson's unrelenting operational tempo—Peterson and the men of the 7th Platoon initiated a second mission in the same area, but this time in the form of a nine-and-a-half-hour sweep at the head of two companies from the Army's 9th Infantry Division. By the end, much had been learned. First, said Peterson's official report, was that the placing of SEALs on a "company level to advise and guide" was not an effective use of their time—something they had already known; second, and more important, was that the 7th Platoon's failed rescue had taken them through an area dominated by some 200 bunkers and two battalions of North Vietnamese Army regulars, as many as 600 well-trained troops. In his first after-action report, Peterson had made a conservative estimate of twenty-six Viet Cong killed, but by local accounts the total had been that plus more than a hundred. So, while the SEALs of the 7th Platoon had not succeeded in rescuing the POW, they had in fact succeeded in pivoting to execute a capture/kill mission whose enemy body count had exceeded all of SEAL Team TWO's from the previous year. Not necessarily the best measurement of a mission's impact, it nevertheless proved the value of—and shined a spotlight on—the 7th Platoon's entire deployment and its incomparable achievement in the exploitation of intelligence.

It was also a method that no other all-American commando-type unit in the IV Corps Tactical Zone could come close to mimicking, a fact due to the Army's neglect to attempt such a venture or even to assert their own copycat version. Now, with the 9th Division's authority established over all the land within reach of its infantrymen's boots, a reversal of the 9th Division's neglect in commando-type operations could have easily meant an end to Det. Alfa's opportunity for direct-action missions in the delta—an outcome, the SEALs knew, that was best averted by doubling down.

18

As if to reassert the importance of the intelligence exploitation that had made the 7th Platoon's deployment remarkable, just two days after this last mission Peterson's routine check-in at the Chieu Hoi Center produced a Hoi Chanh with information on what sounded like a too-big-to-be-true weapons cache. Enlisting this Hoi Chanh as a guide, Peterson then led a combined force of the 7th Platoon and an entire squad from SEAL Team ONE's Delta Platoon to the edge of a four-hooch village. There, while preparing an assault, two Viet Cong guerrillas stumbled into the SEALs' perimeter and were silently killed before they could alert their comrades. The subsequent clearance resulted in two more Viet Cong killed and, more important, in the capture of a villager who volunteered to lead them the final stretch to two 360-cubic-foot underground concrete bunkers, practically warehouses of Viet Cong weapons and ammunition—water mines, rockets, German machine guns, even a crate of the same Chicom grenades that had shredded Minh, Yeaw, and Gallagher. After its contents had been totaled, the cache was found to be one of the largest in IV Corps history. This earned a personal "well done" from Westmoreland himself and initiated two more weeks of joint operations with the squad from SEAL Team ONE, nearly all just as dramatic.

At the tail end of this period, and for the second time in one deployment, a bandaged and bald-headed chief petty officer reappeared on the streets of My Tho. Released on his own recognizance and the doctor's expectation that he would take it easy, Gallagher had managed his escape from the hospital at Vung Tau in order to participate in the 7th Platoon's final missions, feats he accomplished by having Doc Riojas wrap his stitches with duct tape.

On April 22, 1968, SEAL Team TWO's 10th Platoon arrived in My Tho to relieve the 7th. The latter had been in-country for 181 days, and in that time had completed eighty operations, a little less than one mission every two days. Peterson, by his own admission, was exhausted. With gear packed and ready for home, the men of the 7th Platoon had only one last thing to do: provide a turnover with the incomers. This consisted of an overview of the past six months, including the best target areas and the most supportive helicopter squadrons. And most of all, a description of the missions that had best generated new ones: hands down, the intelligence-driven capture/kill raid. To help the 10th accomplish this, the 7th provided a pass-down of all the relationships that they had cultivated with intelligence sources: the Navy's local NILOs, the interrogators at the Chieu Hoi Center, the advisors to the ARVN Rangers and the PRUs, their contacts with the local "white mice" of the national police, even a handful of Hoi Chanhs who had proved trustworthy or at least amenable to payments—every one of those pulled from the 7th Platoon's own personal pockets.

To make sure that this pass-down was both received and understood, the 7th Platoon left behind two of its best: Mike Boynton, who overstayed his deployment by two weeks to help with mission planning and tactical know-how, and Minh, back from the dead and the MACV hospital at Vung Tau, an all-American facility to which Gallagher—out of loyalty—had ensured Minh's admittance, thus ensuring Minh's loyalty to all future SEAL platoons in My Tho and, more important, ensuring the SEALs' access to the intelligence networks that they and Minh had built.

While many of the other direct-action SEAL platoons in Vietnam had been similarly and simultaneously learning the value of local intelligence sources and the turning of captives into guides for their next operations, none had, as yet, quite matched the 7th Platoon's results. No other outfit had so dramatically shown what the SEALs were capable of—not simply the coastal raids on easily located bridges and command posts that the SEAL units had been designed to execute, nor the simple ambushes that the lack of these had forced the SEALs to undertake, but an entirely new kind of direct action that was targeted and self-perpetuating, and completely transferable to a follow-on platoon. This transferability took almost no time to revalidate.

Within days of their arrival in My Tho, the 10th Platoon harnessed the intelligence network and operational example that had been passed down to them by the 7th and enlisted a Hoi Chanh to lead them to a secret Viet Cong Infrastructure meeting. The result: the capture of six Viet Cong cadre. After interrogation, these six provided the locations of more than 100 Communist agents who had already infiltrated "every US and Allied agency and military unit in My Tho," every one another gold mine of Viet Cong locations. In very short order, Rudy Boesch, the former seventeen-year-old volunteer for the Scouts and Raiders in World War II and now the chief petty officer for the 10th Platoon, was crediting the exploitation of this intelligence, and its "timely [use]," to his platoon's ability to hit as many as three targets per night, most of these ripped right out of their hammocks.

Almost relegated to the delta's riverbanks or farmed out to a variety of less-than-direct-action-type assignments, Det. Alfa had instead gone on to set an example for every SEAL who came after.

19

On November 5, 1968, a Tuesday, in the open-air Rockwell Hall gymnasium at Little Creek Amphibious Base in Virginia, twenty-four men from SEAL Team TWO stood in dress blue uniforms to receive a total of forty-two awards from the commander in chief of the Atlantic Fleet. Approaching its second year of direct-action operations in Vietnam, SEAL Team TWO had at this point already earned a total of 252 combat decorations—a "division-size" success, said a reporter—and could account for the bodies of some 1,000 Viet Cong fighters, at a loss of only five of their own. Among these had been Petty Officer Joseph Albrecht—killed in the Seven Mountains on the Cambodian border and nowhere near any water—whose young wife, with short hair, horn-rimmed glasses, and an expression of anxious sadness, now presented herself to receive her husband's awards. In the end, said the official account, the "[highlight] of the ceremony" was the presentation of the Navy Cross—the highest award ever bestowed on a SEAL—to Chief Petty Officer Bob Gallagher, who, despite having been told that he would never walk again, now stood to receive the honor. With his mustache gone and his bald head covered by his garrison cap, Gallagher somehow looked smaller than he had, not as fierce as the Eagle they all knew. For the evidence of that, however, one needed only glance at SEAL Team TWO's command history for 1968.

Just five days after the presentation of Gallagher's Navy Cross, the 10th Platoon completed their six-month deployment and returned to Little Creek. Having inherited Minh, and the intelligence network that Peterson and Gallagher and the men of the 7th Platoon had worked so hard to establish, the 10th had also linked arms with the local PRU and—in the words of SEAL Team TWO's command history—"succeeded in shifting [their operational] emphasis" from "obtaining a body count, to being more capture-oriented." This shift, along with the efforts of every other SEAL platoon that had served in the Mekong Delta, had "extended the arm of Task Force 116 into . . . uncontested territory wholly under VC control," and "for the first time" even beyond this territory. In short: Not since SACO had any naval unit pulled the Navy so far from its origins.

And what of the men who had done so much of the pulling?

Nearly every member of the 7th Platoon would return to Vietnam for another SEAL deployment, some for several. Almost the only one who didn't would be Pete Peterson. His return to Little Creek had not only reunited him with his wife and the three-month-old son he had never met—born during the Tet Offensive—but had also handed him a set of orders to UDT 13 as its executive officer. For one of the most successful platoon commanders in the history of the SEAL teams, it was a ludicrous downgrading, but one whose side effect would be the nudging of UDT 13's operations toward those of the SEALs. In other words, Peterson's was a legacy that would live on through subordinates. Especially one.

Though physically wrecked by the wounds he had incurred with the 7th Platoon, Gallagher would convince the Navy's doctors that he was fit for duty and return to Vietnam almost immediately, this time as a PRU advisor in Ba Xuyen Province. The assignment would earn him a Silver Star and, more important, another direct-action platoon. On this final combat deployment he would employ all the lessons that his previous three had taught him—interpreters, intelligence exploitation, Hoi Chanhs, helicopter fire missions within ten meters of his position—and despite the rapidly increasing rules of engagement would nevertheless contribute to the killing, capturing, or arresting of 187 Viet Cong guerrillas and North Vietnamese Army soldiers. This was "an impressive and remarkable record" that outshined even that of the 7th Platoon, but without whose example (plus those of every other SEAL platoon that had stretched itself beyond the comfort of the coast) would have been impossible.

All of this would also come at a cost.

Following his retirement from the Navy, Gallagher was so unable to stomach the loss of his SEAL Team TWO family that he quickly migrated from Virginia Beach to Fort Pierce, Florida, the Navy's long-since-abandoned World War II training site and the location of the UDT-SEAL Museum. There, some fifty years after the end of the Vietnam War, he would receive two reminders of his service with the 7th Platoon. First, he would learn the whereabouts of Minh, who had gone missing after the war—jailed for years by the Communists—and who had since fallen on hard times. Having arranged for Minh's medical care at the US hospital in Vung Tau, Gallagher could easily have considered his debt fulfilled. He didn't, and instead cut a check for $200, and did so every month thereafter. Next, in 2017, a Navy official would present himself at Gallagher's door and inform him that a review of the 7th Platoon's attempted POW rescue had determined that his actions might merit the Medal of Honor. Gallagher—his health failing, barely able to walk—showed the man out. If he hadn't merited it back then, he didn't want it now.

About the only thing he did want was to spend the rest of his life near the beach that had given birth to the Scouts and Raiders, the NCDUs, the UDTs, all the various units whose legacies had created the institution to which he had devoted his life—an institution that by all logic should have never been, and whose mission he had, as much as anyone else, been responsible for creating.

Chapter 15

The Navy's Skeleton Key to Inland Combat, and the Final Against-the-Current Achievements in the War's Ebb Tide That Exposed the SEALs' Preeminence as the US Military's Go-Anywhere Commandos

In the sixteen months that followed the 7th Platoon's deployment—roughly the final period of untapered American involvement in Vietnam—every direct-action SEAL platoon engaged in one of three activities: the pursuit of intelligence that could be translated into targets; the pursuit of wider operational boundaries that could be translated into the same; or some combination of both. As most platoons found, the readiest gateway to either path was usually right under their noses.

In the not quite two years since Bob Wagner had created the first PRU training camp at Vung Tau, the SEALs' commitment to the PRU program had led not only to the creation of Det. Bravo and to the sponsorship of a 100-man PRU in just about every one of the IV Corps' sixteen provinces, but also to the establishment of Camp Machen—a Stateside training site for SEAL/PRU advisors that was situated on some 1,000 backcountry acres near Lake Cuyamaca that Wagner had sweet-talked out of a California real estate mogul. There, he had cleared mountain scrub, salvaged more than a dozen old tents, improvised a stream-filled oil drum into a shower, recruited veteran Mekong Delta SEALs as instructors, and, most important, had combined the curriculum of several disparate training schools into—said a local reporter—"one compact punch." As the delta platoons were revalidating by the day, the target of Camp Machen's punch was to educate its students on the importance of, and the methods to accomplish, the taking of captives for follow-on exploitation. Though descriptions of the worst of these exploitations would ultimately include interrogations involving electric wires in the ears, water suffocation, even the removal of a captive's liver to wipe it in the faces of the other captives, the more commonly used methods were little more than the "smothering" of prisoners with kindness, food, and cigarettes, and ultimately offering them a generous bounty for information, all the way up to 1,250 piasters for leading the PRUs to a regional VCI chieftain. Now, by combining these exploitation techniques with the tactics taught at Camp Machen, Wagner's graduates were leading missions every other day and "neutralizing" an extravagant "average of 800 VC or VCI personnel" per month, many of them described in the official record as "former associates," and many more that were a gold mine whose output would benefit more than just the PRUs.

"So far I have got 10 village level cadre," wrote Petty Officer Gary Gallagher—no relation to Bob Gallagher—after only a month of PRU advisory duty. His only complaints: the excessive CIA paperwork, the excessive CIA handlers—"two big pricks," he called them; and a threat from the local Viet Cong leader to blow up his house and "cut [him] up into 10 parts." With more enemy locations than he knew what to do with, toward the end of June 1968 Gallagher started handing off intelligence to Robert Gormly's 9th Platoon. In turn, Gormly's platoon discovered a massive Viet Cong concentration in the U Minh Forest that they survived only by expending nearly every bullet, rocket, grenade, and claymore mine they carried, and by employing successive gun-runs from a flight of Navy Seawolf helicopters piloted by MACV commander Creighton Abrams's nephew and a Cuban-born veteran of the Bay of Pigs invasion whose heavily accented voice was heard to threaten the Army's slick pilots to either recover the stranded frogmen from their hot LZ or be shot from the sky. In the aftermath, Gallagher's generosity in intel sharing—like most generosities—boomeranged.

Though the senior Army officers who dominated the PRU program were generally "enraged" to discover that they had been hoodwinked into entrusting an entire 100-man company to an enlisted SEAL, Gallagher—a yeoman third class, ostensibly a secretary-corporal—nevertheless justified his appointment by parlaying the SEAL platoon's discovery of the enemy concentration in the U Minh Forest into the capture of another Viet Cong leader, whom he drove like a shield across a contested canal in order to rescue half of his PRU from a counterattack, then led them on a five-mile running escape while never dropping one of his wounded comrades. Eventually awarded the Navy Cross for his heroism—the second in the SEALs' entire history—Gallagher's action was noteworthy for one other reason. Encouraged by his fighters to speed their escape by executing their Viet Cong captive, Gallagher had refused, a testament to his humanity and to even a low-ranking SEAL's understanding of the indispensability of captives to a PRU's cycle of operations and, what was more important, a cycle that presented his fellow SEALs with a nearly endless series of opportunities for wider operational boundaries.

Such was exactly the case in late July of 1968, when Sergeant Drew Dix—the same Green Beret/PRU advisor who had fought alongside SEAL Team TWO's 8th Platoon in Chau Doc during the Tet Offensive and was now about to be awarded the Medal of Honor for his actions—offered another opportunity to the SEALs, once again to Gormly's 9th Platoon to help his PRU search for a weapons cache at the base of Nui Coto, in the heart of the Seven Mountains near the Cambodian border. Because it was nowhere near the water, Gormly had to first get approval from Captain Art Price, the commander of CTF-116. Later, when the mission met with near disaster—one SEAL was killed by a foot mine, and the Cambodian troops had to be forcibly disarmed before they mutinied and sold their American advisors into captivity—the Army's IV Corps commander convened an inquiry to determine, among other things, "what the hell [the] SEALs [were] doing on Nui Coto." Hearing Captain Price's answer, that "he'd personally endorsed the operation because [the SEALs] were going after the weapons the VC were using to shoot up his PBRs," the general said not a word, but just laughed. He wasn't the first US Army officer in history to snort at a Navy unit's pluck, but he was among the last to find it funny, for the following reason.

Just as the SEALs had harnessed the PRUs to pull themselves inland, so were the Navy's leaders about to harness the SEALs to do the same—an intentional incursion by the Navy that would soon be made more conspicuous by the ebb of American involvement in Vietnam, an ebb that would so widely expose the SEALs' aptitudes for inland combat that this legacy would forever cut the legs out of any argument that said they didn't belong there.

2

In September of 1968, Admiral Veth—the lackluster minelayer turned commander of US Naval Forces in Vietnam—was replaced by the incomparably aggressive and incomparably sideburned Admiral Elmo Zumwalt. Upon arrival, he adopted a relentless eighteen-hour-a-day schedule that, unlike Veth's, included daily helicopter flights to

Navy outposts to talk with his sailors, an imposition he always atoned for with a generous distribution of beer, charcoal, and medals. Having piloted a commandeered Japanese minesweeper into Shanghai Harbor in 1945 to take custody of twenty Japanese prisoners from one Phil Bucklew—and thus been one of only a handful of fleet sailors to witness the Navy's landgrab in China—Zumwalt needed only a few weeks of outpost-hopping to realize his most important problem: The Navy was not doing everything it could to pursue the enemy. Only one of his units was: the one that seemed least like it belonged to the US Navy, but a unit whose example now rose like a lighthouse to guide the rest of his fleet.

Before a month of his tour was complete, Zumwalt commissioned the Southeast Asia Lake, Ocean, River, and Delta Strategy, as clunky a title as any ever given to a military plan, but as magnificent as Lincoln's Anaconda once it was compressed to SEALORDS, a title whose front half contained a wink to the unit whose example had most led to its adoption. In no time, Zumwalt was saturating the IV Corps' waterways by shifting every craft in his fleet as far up the delta as their drafts would allow and, following the SEALs' example, pushing them right up to the Cambodian border—lifting them over the shallows by helicopters if he had to. Within two months of his arrival, Zumwalt's strategy had pulled Swift Boats from the coastal blockade to take over the PBR patrols in the lower delta and had reclaimed some 90 percent of the vessels assigned to the Mobile Riverine Force to push into the "Blood Alley" of the Parrot's Beak, the portion of Cambodia that stabbed the insurgency's supply lines like a knife into the delta's heart. Before long, Zumwalt was, unlike Veth, briefing the commander of MACV every week on the Navy's initiatives, and so shifting the Navy's role in Vietnam that he was turning the IV Corps into his own. It was a shift that hit the SEALs like a wind at their backs.

With Zumwalt's arrival, the SEALs went from being the fleet's prodigal stepchild raiders to the fleet's skeleton key to inland opportunities—opportunities for Navy boats, Navy ships, Navy fighters, Navy helicopters, Navy gunships, Navy intelligence officers, even Navy Seabees. To goose the Navy's involvement in SEAL operations, Zumwalt—always wearing forest-green fatigues, and occasionally accompanied by a camera crew and reporters—routinely dropped in on his platoons and always posed a variant of the same question: How can I help? In short order that help was showing up in piasters for Hoi Chanhs and interpreters, Navy jeeps to meet with sources, daily grocery drops by the Navy's transport helicopters. After the friendly-fire death of Lieutenant Junior Grade David Nicholas, Zumwalt took less than three days to invest one SEAL compound with an actual Navy physician. All told, it was the kind of self-serving help that infused the SEALs with an even greater operational capacity, so much so that within six months of Zumwalt's arrival the headquarters of the SEALs' task group commander in Vietnam was finally upgraded from a cluttered desk at CTF-116, to an entire Quonset hut.

"I need fifteen more, twenty more, one hundred more SEALs," remembered three-war veteran frogman Frank Kaine of Zumwalt's repeated calls to increase his complement. When such requests collided with the reality of the SEALs' actual manning levels (nowhere close to the Green Berets'), Zumwalt even enlisted the efforts and advice of the commander of US naval forces in the Philippines, none other than the bullfrog himself, Admiral Draper Kauffman.

The SEALs were of "immense value to me," Zumwalt would say years later in an oral history interview, and "better Indian fighters than the VC were." With them, he could almost instantly "cool off an area" where the aggressiveness of his SEALORDS campaign was producing casualties amongst his riverine sailors, one of whom was his own son and who regularly supported SEAL operations from his Swift Boat. In those areas—areas where his "boats were the hunted," Zumwalt said—his SEALs "were the hunters." Because of Zumwalt's ambition to push his fleet into the hinterlands, they were hunters about to range so far beyond their hunting grounds that one might be forgiven for confusing them with poachers.

3

Inside the first few months of Operation SEALORDS, Zumwalt's infusion of support to Det. Alfa, Det. Bravo, and Det. Golf—more money, more jeeps, more helicopters, more gunboats, more intel officers—enabled the SEALs to press deeper into enemy territory than they ever had. In turn, this pressing yielded a series of operations whose results were just as extravagant, just as hair-raising, and just as far from the water as the 7th Platoon's. Several of these bumped right up against the Cambodian border; several were deep inside the U Minh forest, an interior jungle so dark with mangrove trees that local legend claimed it was inhabited by werewolves; two were undertaken on Da Dung Mountain, and both of these were survived only by calling for gunship support and helicopter extract. Crashed in a rice paddy and thrown from his helicopter on a third such mission to the area, Petty Officer R. J. Thomas—with bullet wounds in his chest and abdomen, and his nose barely hanging from his face—tried to stand, collapsed, then staggered back to the burning wreck to drag survivors away from its exploding ordnance. This accomplished, he proceeded to protect the dazed pilot by lying atop him, and then for forty minutes shielded the rest of the wounded from the encircling enemy with the only weapon he could find, a .45-caliber pistol. It was the kind of heroism that not only ripped success from the jaws of failure, but also prevented MACV's planners from saying a word about the SEALs' suitability for inland combat—demonstrations that were deepening by the day and broadening too.

In January 1969, a single platoon from SEAL Team ONE was assigned to CTF-115 to serve as the inland arm of the Coastal Surveillance Group in the II Corps Tactical Zone—ostensibly, an assignment tucked well inside the Navy's traditional tidewater, but in reality as brazen as any along the Cambodian border for trespassing into unchallenged Army territory. Worst of all—worst of all for the Army, anyway—it was also an incursion made more noticeable by one of the most daring missions in the history of the SEAL teams. In the second week of March, a squad from SEAL Team ONE's Delta Platoon—the same platoon that had supported the 7th Platoon on its previous cycle—was tasked with the capture/kill of a Viet Cong sapper team that was supposed to be hiding atop one of the mountainous islands in Nha Trang Bay; not just in II Corps' bailiwick, but in the same general area where Beckwith had trained his first batch of Green Berets for Project Delta. More complex than anything SEAL Team ONE had undertaken in its entire first year of operations in the Rung Sat, the mission of capture/kill was now such a focus of predeployment training that it had become the SEALs' standard fare and an operational expectation of every SEAL who deployed. In command of this particular mission was twenty-five-year-old Lieutenant Junior Grade Joseph "Bob" Kerrey of Nebraska—just three months into his first deployment—who led his men on a multihour climb up a 350-foot cliff in pitch-black darkness to sneak into the enemy camp from behind. So successful was the infiltration that one of Kerrey's men actually stumbled into a fighter asleep in his hammock, prompting a barrage of enemy fire and a grenade that exploded Kerrey into the rocks, practically severing his right leg. Nearly blinded with pain and gushing blood, Kerrey nevertheless used the Viet Cong's green tracers as an anchor to coordinate a two-element counterattack that trapped the enemy in a crossfire and wiped them out. For this, he would be awarded the SEALs' first Medal of Honor, just one more marker of the SEALs' rise to inland relevance—even in the Green Berets' backyard.

At the same time that the SEALs were being welcomed north, Zumwalt was preparing another invitation for them, this one at the opposite end of the country, in the southern Ca Mau Peninsula. The invitation was to come in the form of the most slapdash base in the Navy's entire history: fourteen ammo barges topped with tin roofing, then moored side by side and anchored in the middle of the three-mile-wide mouth of the Cua Lon River. Situated so close to the coast that it floated on a sea of mud-brown salt water, the base was not only given the name of Seafloat, but also at first glance seemed to indicate a general retreat by Zumwalt toward the Navy's traditional comfort zone, except for this: Damp, rat-infested, reeking of diesel fuel, and "severely cramped" by the crew of some 600 other sailors, Seafloat could nevertheless support three entire SEAL platoons, an entire UDT detachment, an entire fleet of river assault craft, and, most important of all, an entire detachment of Seawolf helicopters. For a corner of the country whose isolation had turned it into a haven for Viet Cong fighters but whose majority of "hard targets" were "located away from navigable waterways," this last feature—plus Seafloat's barge-top helipad—now made it possible to connect the SEALs to some 900,000 square meters of untouched hinterland, and for the first time could turn them into commandos whose raids need not have any connection to the water.

The result was a series of fish-in-a-barrel-type raids from above: nearly all in pocket with the target-rich PRUs, nearly all made possible by sliding from the skids of American helicopters, and even more than before, nearly all surrounded. The most dramatic of these occurred when a platoon from SEAL Team ONE attempted to capture a Viet Cong finance chief by dropping directly atop the hooch he was hiding in, a gamble that literally busted when the helicopter crashed through the hooch's roof, exploding the platoon and crew members into a limping and chaotic retreat through hostile terrain that had to be reversed the moment the men realized they were missing Hospital Corpsman 1st Class Richard "Red" Wolfe, found dead amid the wreckage and the bodies of two Viet Cong fighters. Such daring was the inevitable culmination of Zumwalt's inland push, but a push that prompted an equally predictable reaction by the rightful administrator of the now-contested territory, albeit a response that had been delayed by about eighteen years—the elapsed time since the Army's disbandment of its last legitimate raiders.

In January 1969, three months since Zumwalt's SEALORDS campaign had started pushing the SEALs across the lower half of South Vietnam, General Creighton Abrams—the commander of MACV and an enthusiastic devourer of SEAL after-action reports—authorized the consolidation of all LRRP units into companies for reassignment to the 75th Infantry Regiment. This consolidation was followed by renaming these units Long Range Reconnaissance Rangers—a revision in more than name, but in mission too. In March—after two years of being upstaged in the commando game—the Army's 9th Infantry Division authorized its rebranded LRRP Rangers to launch a series of helicopter and waterborne raids throughout the Mekong Delta. Not long after these Army raids were initiated, several SEAL platoons submitted area clearance requests that the 9th Division's planners denied, only to find out later that the 9th Division's soldiers had swept the area simply "because of SEAL interest." Though the Army units had had "no idea as to [the SEALs'] target," such moves by the 9th Division finally seemed to portend an end to the SEALs' poaching and, who knows, maybe a decline in the need for SEALs in general. That is, until everything changed.

In July 1969—in response to President Nixon's pledge to "Vietnamize" the war and end American involvement—the last brigade of the Army's 9th Infantry Division was pulled from the IV Corps Tactical Zone, leaving the SEALs as the "only US commanded ground unit" in the Mekong Delta and its only all-American commando force. This vacuum of competition would continue until December 7, 1971, when the last direct-action SEAL platoon would be pulled out of the Mekong Delta—another two years, four months, and twelve days for the SEAL platoons to fight a war in which their largest operational obstacle would no longer be competition from other all-American ground units but from distance and red tape. This vacuum would also produce one final consequence.

4

From the summer of 1969 to the end of the US military's involvement in Vietnam, the American public was treated to a deteriorating diet of news: the steady withdrawal of American troops; the inevitable advance of Communist forces; and a near-endless litany of American atrocities. These last included the casual massacre of as many as 500 villagers at My Lai and a rising whisper of American officers being fragged by their own soldiers—both brutalities the partial result of padding the US military with disgruntled draftees during an unpopular war, and a condition that especially plagued the recipient of 95 percent of all draftees, the US Army. It was a descent that would only emphasize the heights of the SEALs' final achievements, each one another example establishing their legitimacy for all the sorts of inland missions that had made them famous.

On January 14, 1969, President Lyndon Johnson strode into the White House Cabinet Room wearing a gray suit and his typical Texas-sized smile to greet an assembly of twenty blue-uniformed members of SEAL Team ONE. Exactly one week before his last day in office and the end of all the worries that went with it, the president was almost ebullient as he waded into the group, shaking hands, asking questions of the men, his height towering above them. To Johnson's question if he had ventured too far to sea—"kind of a long way from Montana," the president joked, himself a Navy veteran—Hospital Corpsman 1st Class Wayne Jones responded with puckish confusion; as a four-tour SEAL, he had seen far more of mud and mountain than he had of sand and blue water. There to help explain this unlikely evolution was Lieutenant Commander Franklin Anderson, SEAL Team ONE's former commanding officer, who took advantage of the president's interest in people to describe Team ONE's growth from 60 SEALs in 1962 to an as-yet-unfulfilled allotment of 400 in 1969; then, due to demand, promoted the "crazy" idea that manning levels should be increased again to more than 500. Ultimately, all of these conversations were cut short by the purpose of the visit: the awarding of the Presidential Unit Citation, or PUC, the US military's highest unit-level commendation. Though just the first of five such awards to be presented to the SEAL teams for their service in Vietnam, this inaugural ceremony was the only one to be conducted under the watchful gaze of a bronze bust of Johnson's predecessor, the youthful president who had done so much to elevate the standing of the Army's Special Forces, and who—despite their overwhelmingly larger contribution to the war—would receive only one such award. Not necessarily the surest measure of comparative contribution, each subsequent PUC would nevertheless serve to show the heights to which the SEAL teams would rise in perception; a perception due to the operational reach of the SEALs themselves.

On February 17, 1969—six months and two days after her husband was killed by an improvised explosive device while leading his PRUs on a raid of a VCI encampment in Vinh Binh Province—Bob Wagner's widow received a letter from the Navy's personnel office with an offer to convene a formal presentation of her husband's posthumous awards. Though his rank at the time had been that of a mere storekeeper 1st class, this offer would include the presentation of a Legion of Merit with combat "V," not only a commendation that was rarely awarded with valor distinction but, more important, one that required the personal approval of the secretary of the Navy and was almost never awarded to anyone below the rank of captain or admiral. Less concerned with the unprecedented nature of the award than she was with reopening the wound that had orphaned her five children, Wagner's widow left the decision up to her oldest son, just sixteen, who opted to receive his father's honor in the mail—an understandable decision that didn't change the reasons for its uniqueness. Though no single SEAL had been fully responsible for pushing the teams beyond the riverbanks, Wagner's "inimitable foresight," said the citation, had nevertheless created one of the most "fruitful" programs "ever devised in unconventional warfare," a well of intelligence whose overflow had never failed to fuel the cycle of capture/kill operations that had pulled the direct-action platoons inland. Most important, the awarding of the Legion of Merit to a 1st class petty officer also demonstrated the strategic value that the Navy's leadership had come to place on the SEALs' sacrifices in Vietnam, sacrifices that the drawdown of regular American forces would only magnify.

Coincidentally occurring at the same moment their legs were venturing deeper into enemy territory than ever before, the drawdown of American soldiers and PBR sailors also meant that the SEALs' operations would now be aimed at a higher proportion of enemy fighters, missions that tipped the scales of chance toward the enemy. Among the most heartbreaking casualties of this scale tipping occurred on Thanksgiving Day in 1969, when a platoon from SEAL Team ONE was ambushed from a bunker in the Rung Sat, wounding several and prompting a counterbarrage from Petty Officer Robert Christopher, who didn't stop firing his machine gun until he was shot through the femoral artery, both hands (severing numerous fingers), and his head, the bullet exiting from his jaw. Shot in the arm and back, and stranded in knee-deep water, Lieutenant Junior Grade John "Bubba" Brewton—a handsome twenty-six-year-old from Alabama who was known to don dress blues and fly to random cities just to meet flight attendants—nevertheless managed to radio for gunship support, then coordinate a helo extract. With Brewton's kidneys too severely infected to allow his transfer back to the States, Zumwalt—a dutiful letter writer to the parents of all his casualty sailors—not only visited Brewton as many as ten times over the following weeks, but had a trailer set up so the young man's father and fiancée could be with him when he finally slipped away. Of the hundreds of faces of the wounded he saw during the course of that war, Zumwalt "carried" only Brewton's for the rest of his life, a testament not just to Brewton's courage but to the outsized impact that the SEALs' contributions had on the man whose promotion in a few short months would turn him into the chief of naval operations.

Beginning in March 1970, the drawdown of Vietnamization finally began to dismantle those pillars that had long supported the capture/kill operations of the direct-action SEAL platoons. The first blow to these pillars occurred with the disbandment of Det. Bravo, ending the Navy's contribution to the PRU program and, more important, curtailing the SEALs' access to one of their deepest wells of intelligence. It was a blow that coincided with a sudden shortage of Navy support sailors that forced base skippers to assign noncombat chores to their SEAL platoons: watch standing, garbage collection, prisoner transportation; the last of these an annoyance that quickly tapered off, since the SEALs' base duties usually prevented them from capturing any more prisoners. Behind these time constraints trailed a series of physical limitations, including the mundane interruption of mail, C-rations, and replacement parts for trucks and jeeps, the vehicles that made cultivating new intelligence sources possible, and the critical shortfalls of colored smoke grenades for signaling aircraft, and even ammunition for M60 machine guns and M16 rifles—the latter commodity completely out of stock on one base for three weeks.

In little more than a year, these logistical burdens would be exacerbated by the deliberately imposed roadblocks of MACV planners, whose increasingly restrictive rules of engagement would eventually require an operational stand-down of all SEAL platoons until "a special team from Navy headquarters" could administer a written test to each operator "on their understanding of when they could attack or return fire and when they could not." All told, it would seem a series of setbacks with the potential to pull the rug out from under the SEALs' standing as land-focused commandos—or might have, if not for the strides the SEALs made in the war's final lap.

Beset by enough operational obstacles to have rested on their laurels for the remainder of the war (a posture adopted by many American units) or by enough over-the-shoulder scrutiny to at least have resigned themselves to strictly reconnaissance and advisory missions (a posture that Admiral Robert Salzer, Zumwalt's replacement, would have preferred), the SEALs' aggressiveness instead turned the downhill years of 1970 and onward into a launch ramp that threw a spotlight on their preeminence as the war's go-anywhere commandos.

Compensating for their lack of PRU-produced intelligence by sponsoring their own squads of Kit Carson Scouts—essentially PRU and Viet Cong alumni—the SEALs quickly resumed their up-tempo rhythm of capture/kill. "They hate to sit still and do nothing," said Salzer, who couldn't help but let the animal have his head once in a while. "What they really want to do is find out what the enemy is doing by kidnapping some guy and getting it out of him." Considering the progressively lopsided odds, it was a commitment to the mission of capture/kill that yielded a predictable outcome: a helicopter crash that killed five SEALs, the largest single-incident loss of life for the teams until June 28, 2005; a deployment by SEAL Team ONE's X-Ray Platoon, whose four killed and twelve wounded prompted a month-early return to the States and a nickname as the "hard luck platoon"—losses that had little to do with luck and everything to do with their pursuit of river-removed captives; a long-shot capture/kill raid that was survived only by the efforts of SEAL Team ONE's chief petty officer Barry Enoch, a cheerful Kentuckian who—with a bullet-riddled radio and an appropriate call sign of Threadbare—directed a last-ditch rocket attack by a treetop flight of OV-10 Broncos that exploded a brief escape path in the enemy's tightening encirclement. Supplied with yarns like these—plus one in which a SEAL sprained his wrist while swinging a pair of brass knuckles against a hoochful of VCI officials who apparently didn't want to be kidnapped—Salzer never failed to cheer up MACV commander Creighton Abrams. "That tickled old Abe," Salzer said of the SEAL who sprained his wrist. "It made his whole morning." In fact, such stories made the SEAL teams' future.

In July, an entire SEAL platoon was requested for assignment to Operation Bright Light, MACV's countrywide POW recovery initiative, an effort that collected the whispers of POW whereabouts—the jungle sighting of a western-size silhouette or footprint—then farmed them out for action. As the SEALs were fanning out to accomplish this, planners in I Corps—the northernmost tactical zone in Vietnam, and a zone dominated by the US Army and US Marine Corps—likewise requested a SEAL platoon to put a stop to the sappers who had been mining the Cua Viet River. Both offers were a chance for the SEALs to expand beyond the Navy-dominated IV Corps Tactical Zone; both were a recognition by non-Navy planners that the SEALs were capable of commando-type missions in zones whose commanders shouldn't have needed to ask for commandos in the first place. Not that it mattered anymore. The SEALs in Vietnam had long since left their beachheads behind.

5

In March of 1969, the RAND Corporation, a semiprivate think tank that specialized in research and analysis for the Department of Defense, published a report titled "The Navy SEAL Commandos: A Case Study of Military Decision Making and Organizational Change"—as best I am able to determine, the first academic-level study of the SEAL teams. The report's author was Francis J. "Bing" West, a former Force Recon Marine and Vietnam War veteran whose investigation had begun a year earlier, and whose research had produced a raft of documents, "dozens" of interviews, and the firsthand observation of several SEAL missions into the Rung Sat and the Mekong Delta. From this research, West had produced an eighteen-page report whose introduction provided a brief description of SEAL training—training he estimated at a cost of around $14,000 per man—plus an overview of the SEALs' commitment to Vietnam, at its height a commitment that never exceeded 150 SEALs, or roughly 1,150 fewer than the in-country height of the Green Berets' total complement. It was a commitment that stood out in even starker relief when placed next to the author's obvious admiration for the SEALs' progression from lackluster coastal raiders to the war's most aggressive direct-action commandos—admittedly, commandos who had had no business becoming such, and thus had drawn the interest of the same preeminent think tank that had created the US military's nuclear defense strategy.

Intended as a study on organizational change, the report's true purpose had been to discover how the Navy could have possibly succeeded in creating a land-focused commando force—a force that even the Viet Cong had reportedly dubbed "the men with green faces," a color not normally associated with the Navy's traditional medium. It was a puzzle of personal importance to the author, as the Marine Corps—the far more likely branch of service—had never succeeded in creating anything similar. "How the concept was sheperded [*sic*] through the Joint Chiefs of Staff and the Congress I am still trying to determine," the author wrote, "for the mission of the SEALs . . . exceeded the charter of the US Navy." As best as he could tell, the "legality" of this initial "infringement" had been tolerated because of its negligible size, but later had been allowed to widen because of a series of factors—none of which, at this point, should come as a surprise.

The first of these—at least in the Mekong Delta, submitted the author—had been the neglect of the US Army, in general, and the 9th Infantry Division, in particular, to push their commando-type units to "develop the same aggressive attitude towards ambushing that the SEALs had." It might further be added that neither entity had adequately prepared those commando-type units to make such a transition in the delta environment, a claim best evidenced by one attempt to conceal the river insertion of five LRRP soldiers by having them copy the SEAL method of jumping from the back of a moving boat but that ultimately resulted in the drowning of all five men.

The second factor that accounted for this infringement, the report continued, had been the Navy's senior officers, whose tours, by comparison, were mostly "dreary" affairs—a condition made more noticeable when "in the presence of generals." To compensate for this, the Navy's leaders had allowed the SEALs more latitude than they had their other units, a black-market trade-off that had produced a steady supply of anecdotes for the Navy and thereby "saved the pride of the admirals."

Ultimately, the author decided, the most important factor in the SEALs' "infringement" was owing to the SEALs themselves and the culture that weighed upon them. Drawn from a notoriously selective training program that produced few qualified candidates, the SEALs naturally had had to find a mission that kept casualties low, a circumstance that might have pushed them—like the LRRPs or the Force Recon Marines—into a reconnaissance role had they had anyone to pass the intelligence on to. They hadn't. Nor had there been any great pressure from the Riverine Force to engage in any sort of Green Beret–style advisory duty or civic action. "Organizational orphans" with no larger force to support or control them and possessing "no love or admiration for the Vietnamese," the SEALs had set out into the swamps "not to prove themselves"—their training had already done that, said the author—but "because not to go would have been inexcusable to the others. They had [developed] a collective value system which emphasized physical hardiness and courage . . . [and] they liked to fight." So, when the tactics of patrol and ambush had proved unproductive, "nobody not a SEAL," meaning no blue-water superior officer, had ordered them to try something else—they had just done it. It was an exceptional adaptation, the veteran Marine author made a special note to point out, that his fellow Marines had failed to mimic and, by following the previous logic, for reasons that blamed them for this—a sequence of attribution and blame that, if the preceding pages have proved anything, was not a sufficient explanation.

"What strikes me as most remarkable about the SEAL story," the author concluded, "is their performance and their ability to learn and adapt in a decentralized, suboptimizing environment." Though all true, all commendable, it was also an explanation that had considered only the record that came after 1966. Missing was any analysis that probed deeper than that top layer of history whose soil had fertilized this inland evolution: the Army's and Marine Corps' preceding thirty years of whipsawing interest in raids and raiders, and the Navy's perennial preoccupation with justifying its worth in offensive combat—a preoccupation that had combined with the Navy's traditional latitude and the UDTs' traditional adaptability to create what several unidentified SEALs soon described to a documentary filmmaker as the war's "unsung soldier" and "what we consider without question the best troops that the country has" —both descriptions notable because they didn't use the word "sailors," and just short of the *Reader's Digest* appraisal that had dubbed them the war's "supercommandos." By the end, these would be assessments that were next to impossible to dispute.

6

On March 4, 1976—a year after the last American troops were lifted off the roof of the US embassy in Saigon—the height of the SEALs' rise from coastal raiders to go-anywhere commandos was put on full display in the East Room of the White House. Prior to entering that room, President Gerald Ford met with Lieutenant Thomas R. Norris, a bantamweight thirty-two-year-old SEAL in dress blue uniform whose features included a sunny disposition, a set of nonregulation ear-length sideburns, and, most notably, a prosthetic eye and extensive surgical scarring around his left orbital bone—the residue of a 1972 deployment to the northernmost section of South Vietnam, a deployment that had produced the two longest-shot commando operations of the war's last chapter. On the first of these, Norris and one LDNN frogman—after surviving a week of previous attempts and a rocket attack that had killed twelve of their ARVN Ranger comrades—had disguised themselves in rice hats and long peasant shirts, then paddled a stolen sampan with Army-issued oars up the Mieu Giang River through an estimated concentration of 30,000 NVA soldiers to rescue one downed US Air Force navigator whom eleven other Americans had died attempting to save. On the second of these impossible missions, Norris—while covering the hasty escape of one enlisted SEAL and three LDNN frogmen from a failed attempt to capture an NVA soldier in the sand dunes below the DMZ—had been shot behind the left ear, the bullet blowing away the left front section of his skull, and abandoned for dead until Petty Officer Michael Thornton, a hulking twenty-three-year-old SEAL from South Carolina, had ignored his own numerous fragmentation wounds and fought 400 yards back through enemy troops to shoulder Norris to the ocean, then swim him out to sea and eventual rescue by a Navy cruiser.

Aware of the operations that led to this moment, and having already presented the Presidential Unit Citation to SEAL Team ONE the previous year, Ford now took one look at Norris's near-skeletal frame, the product of four years of surgeries, and with a grin said, "You're too small for this work."

"I've been trying to grow for years, but it hasn't worked out yet," Norris replied. Norris's diminutive size was made even starker by the over-the-shoulder presence of Thornton, whose 220 pounds of muscle was—to all who knew—made even larger by the five-starred 1⅜-inch-long light blue ribbon on his chest.

What followed was a friendly conversation that briefly touched on Ford's Navy service in World War II, service that included carrier duty in the Marshalls and Marianas, campaigns that had coincidentally created the unit from which the SEALs had ultimately sprung. After several minutes of this, Norris's parents and guests were led into the gold-draped East Room—the white-molded walls now lined with state flags and the parquet floors ranked with row upon row of seated spectators encircling the dais—where they were shown to their chairs, two of which had initially been promised to congressmen, but which Norris had claimed by personally calling the CNO and asking him to explain to the president why one of his award winners had refused to show up.

Now, Norris and two other award recipients—Admiral James Stockdale and Colonel Bud Day, two of the war's greatest heroes—stood at attention facing the hushed crowd, their faces guarded against the well-deserved emotion surrounding the ceremony's missing recipient, Captain Lance P. Sijan, US Air Force, whose torture and death had been exactly the sort of fate that had motivated Norris's superhuman rescue mission. Before long, the summary of that mission was read aloud by the secretary of the Navy, whose words—"unprecedented ground rescue . . . through 2,000 meters of heavily controlled enemy territory . . . the finest traditions of the US Naval Service"—were only punctuated by the shutter clicks of the White House photographer, who captured Norris's lowered-eyed solemnity just moments after the president draped his neck with the Medal of Honor, which was, after Thornton's, the third in the history of the SEAL teams and a validation of all the infringements that had elevated them to it.

Watching this validation from the audience was the current CNO, Admiral James Holloway, whose position gave him a better vantage point than anyone else in the US military for the SEALs' rise to prominence, a rise best demonstrated at the moment by the SEALs' disproportionate acclaim. Having accrued a total loss of forty-four men killed in the war, or just 2 percent of the Navy's 2,559 deaths, the SEALs were now the recipients of 20 percent of the Navy's Medals of Honor—a higher percentage even than the Navy's aviators, the branch from which Holloway himself had hailed. Though difficult to discern by the US military's notoriously inflated enemy casualty figures, this lopsided contribution could likewise be seen from the SEALs' battlefield record, namely in their incomparable ability to find and capture enemy combatants, a skill that—as Holloway had just witnessed—they had slightly repurposed in the war's final days to find and rescue friendly forces. Reduced in the end to a skeleton force of only thirty disaggregated operators—a number that was comically below that of the Green Berets assigned to the 5th Special Forces Group, whose declining totals still exceeded that of most regular American divisions—the SEALs in this final period had nevertheless accounted for the rescue of 152 Vietnamese POWs, or 48 percent of the total rescued during the entire Vietnam War. "To this writer," said one of the final commanders of Det. Alfa who was a firsthand witness to this disproportionate effort, "it is obvious . . . that the only units in the Delta which will react to Brightlight intelligence are the US Navy SEALs."

Just one seat removed from a living example of this history, Admiral Holloway now took advantage of the occasional breaks in the ceremony to talk with Petty Officer Thornton—a SEAL whose size and legend were surpassed only by a personality that rarely resisted the urge to compare his battle-punctured body to an 18-hole golf course. It was also a personality as out of place at a formal event—Holloway the aviator believed—as was a land-focused commando unit in a fleet whose future lay primarily in the Navy's traditional blue-water missions. Never mind that the SEALs had unlocked the hinterland of Vietnam for the rest of the fleet, never mind even that the setting of this conversation proved exactly the opposite, Holloway nevertheless took the opportunity to confide to Thornton—a man not normally known for being lost for words—the Navy's long-term intention to "dissolve the teams." Having proved themselves as the US military's preeminent go-anywhere commandos—commandos with a mission as indispensable as the UDTs' had ever been—it seemed the SEALs had come as far as they ever would. And like the Raiders and Rangers before them, would be disbanded at the apex of their achievements.

Conclusion

Nature Abhors a Vacuum

Like all successful entrepreneurs, the SEALs deserved a monopoly on the market they had built. Like all successful entrepreneurs, they didn't get one.

In the same period when the SEALs had been earning a name as an indispensable component of the IV Corps' order of battle, the Army's special operations units had been earning some acclaim in the opposite direction. From May to November 1967, the LRRPs of Tiger Force embarked on a campaign in the Song Ve Valley that prompted an Army investigation that ultimately uncovered a list of atrocities that ranged from the taking of scalps and ears as trophies to the rape and murder of civilians, including the beheading of an infant. At about the same time these rumors began circulating, the Green Berets of Project Gamma—essentially a CIA-controlled variant of Beckwith's Project Delta—executed a double-crossing Vietnamese agent, weighted his body with chains and tire rims, and dropped him in Nha Trang Bay, then concocted a story that the traitor had been sent on a mission into enemy territory. After uncovering the truth, General Abrams flew into a rage and ordered the guilty parties arrested and charged with first-degree murder, including 5th Special Forces Commander Colonel Bob Rheault, the top Green Beret in all of Vietnam. Considering the Army's usual knee-jerk reaction to the mistakes of its special units, both the LRRPs and the Green Berets seemed well on the path to abrupt disbandment. As it happened, an opportunity intervened that once and for all shook the Army awake to the potential of direct-action commandos.

On the night of November 21, 1970, a single American helicopter deliberately crash-landed into a whirlwind of snapping tree trunks inside a walled compound in North Vietnam, some twenty-three airline miles west of Hanoi. Once settled in a cloud of dust and chaos, a fourteen-man assault force armed with chain saws, lock-cutting torches, a fireman's ladder, red-dot rifle sights, and state-of-the-art night-vision scopes, seized the guard towers and exploded the walls with satchel charges, then—to the accompaniment of bullhorn-broadcast instructions—stormed the outbuildings, gunned down the North Vietnamese garrison, and scoured every corner of the camp in search of the American prisoners of war that were their objectives, tragically all of them having been moved just one week earlier. Despite the mission's failure to locate any POWs, it was a twenty-seven-minute-long, behind-the-lines commando raid of historic precision, a testament to the Green Beret volunteers of the 6th and 7th Special Forces Groups who had conducted it, and whose performances had been, in no small part, enabled by the experience of two principal participants: the assault force commander, Captain Dick Meadows, a mustang Green Beret and SAS alumni who had been plucked for the mission from his post at the Ranger School at Fort Benning, and the task force's overall commander, Colonel Arthur "Bull" Simons, a veteran of the 6th Ranger Battalion's raid on Cabanatuan in World War II. The lineage of both men was impossible to ignore.

In the decade that followed the Son Tay Raid, the ember of the Army's interest in direct-action commandos was blown into a flame by the winds of world events. Namely, these included the failure of West German police to rescue Israeli athletes from the clutches of Palestinian terrorists at the 1972 Olympics in Munich, and the successes of Israeli commandos in the Yom Kippur War, then again in the rescue of 102 hostages from their hijackers at Entebbe. As these winds were blowing, the US Army responded by establishing units whose capabilities bracketed those of its Special Forces. First to be formed was the 75th Ranger Regiment, a pet project of Army Chief of Staff General Creighton Abrams—a giddy devourer of SEAL after-action reports while commander of MACV—whose exasperation with what he believed to be the sneaks and "hoodlums" in the Vietnam-era LRRPs and Green Berets had prompted him to champion not another round of scouts and guerrilla advisors, but an entire regiment of soldiers so well trained—with tactics and weapons, even with their bare hands—that they would be recognized as the world's best light infantrymen. Such a unit could also act as a bridge of sorts "between the Army's conventional and special operations forces"—in other words, Darby's spearheaders, just 30 years late.

Next to be established was the 1st Special Forces Operational Detachment Delta, or Delta Force, a culmination of Colonel Charlie Beckwith's ten-year push to create a batch of SAS-modeled Green Berets whose intended purpose as a capture/kill commando unit was almost immediately validated with the need for a rescue of American hostages in Iran.

Considering that the Navy's commando investment had been meant to fill an obvious gap left by both Army and Marine Corps neglect, the SEALs—at that moment—seemed poised to retract toward the sea, their primary role in the history of inland special operations simply having been that of a placeholder for units more suited to the terrain. And why not? If the preceding pages show anything, it is this: From World War II to the war in Vietnam, the greatest threat to an American special operations unit had always been from above, from the US military's planners who had—time and time again—decided such units were no longer needed.

After four years of SEALs pulling the fleet inland, however, of SEALs bird-dogging the relevance of boats and helicopters and Seabees, of SEALs broadcasting sacrifices for spies and POWs and soldiers and downed airmen, the majority of the Navy's top planners—Admiral Holloway notwithstanding—had long since abandoned any such folly. In fact—gap or not—the Navy's planners were already preparing to compound their interest. Damn the torpedoes, you know the rest.

In the wake of Delta Force's failed rescue of American hostages in Iran, the Navy's planners—as if sensing another gap into which they could squeeze—authorized two actions that solidified the Navy's future commitment to land-focused capture/kill commandos.

First, the Navy established SEAL Team SIX, ostensibly a maritime-focused version of the Army's Delta Force, but in reality a unit whose commitment to counterterrorism would soon override its maritime focus. The reason for this override should be no surprise: Unlike Delta Force, whose ranks consisted of former Green Berets whose Vietnam experiences had been a mixed bag of direct-action and advisory duties, SEAL Team SIX was made up exclusively of veteran SEALs whose only wartime experiences had been in direct-action raiding—toward the end of the war, against targets so landlocked that some platoons had simply driven to them. Boasting only the best operators that the teams had produced, and with a training ammunition budget for ninety men (claimed Team SIX's first commander) that was greater than that afforded to the entire US Marine Corps, this unit—in time—would account for some of the most daring commando missions in American military history—but missions whose character would be a perfect echo of the capture/kill raids that the SEALs had mastered in the Mekong Delta.

The next action that solidified the Navy's commitment to such operations occurred when its planners officially acknowledged that the operations of the UDTs and the SEAL teams were less *concurrent* than they were *sequential,* meaning that—in any war—the amphibious operations of the UDT would naturally precede the inland operations of the SEAL teams, and thus both could be performed by one entity—but only the more mature of the two. The Navy's immediate response to this acknowledgment was to turn UDTs 12 and 22 into a pair of SEAL Delivery Vehicle Teams, or SDVs, entities intended not merely to retain all the traditional capabilities of the UDTs—hydrographic reconnaissance, underwater demolition, and the piloting of covert submersibles—but whose very name implied the transport of raiders from the sea to the shore. At the same time, the Navy upgraded UDTs 11 and 21 into SEAL Teams FIVE and FOUR, then laid the groundwork for SEAL Team THREE, additions that brought the total number of SEAL teams to eight—two of these tied to the Navy's traditional medium, and six oriented away from it. It was a ratio lopsided toward inland raiding, but also one that year after year the Navy would continue to lopside even more.

In the coming years, the SEAL teams would be dispatched to conduct direct-action commando raids in Grenada, Panama, the Persian Gulf, and Somalia; raids that would seemingly be justified by each conflict's proximity to a coast, and which—to any bystander in the US Army or Marine Corps—would all reinforce the notion that the SEALs had been corralled into a future as maritime raiders. If not already refuted by the thirty years of history in which the Navy's sailors had progressively crept beyond their stations, it was a notion that would finally be put to rest by two decades of direct-action raids into the deserts, towns, and mountains of Iraq and Afghanistan, where the SEALs would prove—once and for all—the preeminence of salt-crusted boots for this work.

Anyway, enough. Now that you and I—both reader and writer—have come to the end, please allow me this final word.

Though it has been my objective from the beginning of this project to illuminate how the Army's and Marine Corps' shortcomings contributed to the Navy's establishment of the SEALs as land-focused capture/kill commandos, I feel it appropriate to end by drawing attention to a discovery that I had not expected at the outset. That discovery is the depth of the debt that the SEAL teams accrued against the two decades of gap-filling examples that preceded their creation—by Raiders, Rangers, Partisans, and Green Berets; by dozens more unnamed units whose examples had simply been abandoned to history—and were picked up by men whose circumstances had placed them in a branch of service with a waning connection to combat but whose inclinations for it had been sharpened by all the commandos that had come before them. Perhaps never to be fully satisfied, it is a debt that the SEAL teams will continue to pay as they always have: by fighting alongside, and for, all the resurrected units to which they owe their creation.

A Note on Sources

In an effort to spare you—the reader—the extra pages and weight that would have come with a bibliography, I have followed my editor's advice and confined my citations to the following endnotes. This decision followed the letter of the law, so to speak, but not the spirit, as the unattributed sources that supported this narrative are indeed like the unseen nine-tenths of the iceberg. What now follows is my attempt to make amends for this abridgment.

The most important sources of information for this book—the memoranda, operational plans, and after-action reports that were the necessary bricks of the timeline I had to build before writing—were nearly always found in the records of this country's invaluable archives, all of which are made so because of their tireless and enthusiastic cadre of archivists. Among these were John Hodges, Dale Gordon, and Vietnam War naval historian Dr. John Sherwood at the Naval History and Heritage Command on the campus of the Washington Navy Yard; Richard L. Baker at the US Army Heritage and Education Center in Carlisle, Pennsylvania; and Martin Gedra, Laurel Macondray, and Nathaniel Patch at the National Archives and Records Administration in College Park, Maryland, the last of whom is a talented historian in his own right and never failed to respond to my box requests with his own book-enhancing suggestions. Equally crucial to my research was Ruth McSween at the National Navy UDT-SEAL Museum in Fort Pierce, Florida, who—in spite of what seemed like perennial closings for expansions at the museum—never once failed to take pity on my need for documents and always generously granted me access to them. Later, in the spring of 2017, when one of the aforementioned institutions introduced a ludicrously restrictive interpretation of the Department of Defense's guidance for granting research access to previously classified materials, the final chapters of my book were quite literally rescued by the massive infusion of articles, photographs, and documents provided by the historians at US Army Special Operations Command and by Dr. Pedro Loureiro, the command historian at Navy Special Warfare Command—whose public affairs officer, Lieutenant Matthew Stroup, additionally lent vital help in the navigation of DOD's prepublication review process. The last of the principal archives that made this work possible were actually not archives at all but rather the personal collections of two individuals that were so large they might as well have been. Those two collections were in the care of James Barnes, a veteran of the World War II–era Scouts and Raiders and an unofficial historian of Naval Special Warfare; and Kelsey Kauffman, daughter of Draper Kauffman, who has since donated her father's extensive collection of papers to the UDT-SEAL Museum. A similar note of thanks is due to all those individuals whose names are scattered throughout the following endnotes—many of whom are now close friends—and who rummaged through their "attic archives" and shared their finds with me along with their remembrances, and without which this book would have been impossible.

A similarly important thanks is owed to the various libraries (and librarians) that, at different phases of my writing, have not simply afforded me access to the books on their shelves and a quiet nook to escape the chaos of my three young boys, but also—through their interlibrary loan programs—have connected me to a world of hard-to-find publications that, if added together, my budget would never have been able to afford. These libraries include the following: the Cherry Hill Public Library in Cherry Hill, New Jersey; the Nimitz Library at the US Naval Academy in Annapolis, Maryland; the Alfred M. Gray Marine Corps Research Center at Quantico, Virginia; and the College of DuPage Library in Glen Ellyn, Illinois.

Some of the secondary sources obtained by these institutions became so necessary to my efforts that their use extended well beyond the maximum number of allowable renewals, and—because I routinely discovered the accounts that each of these was based on tucked away in the folds of various archive boxes—almost took on the weight and credibility of primary sources. Notable selections in this category include the following in order of their use: *Herringbone Cloak—GI Dagger: Marines of the OSS* by Major Robert E. Mattingly (USMC); *Commandos from the Sea: The History of Amphibious Special Warfare in World War II and the*

Korean War and *Scouts and Raiders: The Navy's First Special Warfare Commandos* by John B. Dwyer; *Raiders or Elite Infantry? The Changing Role of the U.S. Army Rangers from Dieppe to Grenada* by David W. Hogan, Jr.; *The Naked Warriors* by Cdr. Francis Douglas Fane, USNR (Ret.), and Don Moore; *More Than Scuttlebutt: The U.S. Navy Demolition Men in WWII* by Sue Ann Dunford and James Douglas O'Dell; *Darkmoon: Eighth Army Special Operations in the Korean War* by Ed Evanhoe; *Green Berets at War: US Army Special Forces in Southeast Asia, 1956–1975* by Shelby L. Stanton; *War in the Shallows: U.S. Navy Coastal and Riverine Warfare in Vietnam 1965–1968* by John Darrell Sherwood; and *SEALs: UDT/SEAL Operations in Vietnam* by T. L. Bosiljevac. The assiduous efforts of several of these authors—including those of Tom Hawkins, an oracle of NSW history who generously added his edits to the book's first half—in collecting documents and preserving the memories of their many subjects in typed interviews and letters before those experiences were lost forever to history not only demonstrate their craft but, more important, provide those of us who came after with the corroborative details of all those operations for which many of the official supporting documents seem to have vanished, operations like Clark's reconnaissance of Inchon and the Virginia I raid.

To all these sources of information I am grateful, but sources—no matter how detailed—can bring a book only so far along. For me, the support to carry on in a project that took six years longer than the two-year allotted deadline came first from a publisher whose patience for my slog was only outmatched by its enthusiasm for the final product. Throughout this process, that patience and enthusiasm were exhibited by Tracy Devine, Ian Jackman, Jennifer Hershey, Caroline Weishuhn, Steve Messina, and finally my editor, Julian Pavia, whose thoughtful attention to the book's structure rescued its proportions and spared you the pain of additional pages. Deserving of an even higher share of credit for this book is my agent, Jim Hornfischer (whom I met at the 2011 funeral of my friend and former teammate Jon Tumilson), whose endless advocacy made this book a reality, and whose example as a researcher and historian—an example I witnessed firsthand at the Navy Yard while sharing a conference table and going through the papers of Admiral R. Kelly Turner—made this the book that it became.

Finally, I owe the largest of all debts to those who endured this burden with me. Naturally, this includes my immediate family—my ever-encouraging mom, my always interested dad, especially my incomparably patient sons, and yes, my former wife and co-parent, Roni. Much is also owed to my older brother, Jamie Milligan, who read and reread chapters and whose edits never once telegraphed a flagging interest. Over the years, other readers have—whether they knew it or not—also added their shoulders to propping up these pages, including Jon Cleck, Jack Nash, Sophie Hill, Mike Reed, Jim May, Zib Goodman, Drew Ohlson, and Alison Foy. Last to be acknowledged—yet also the men to whom this book is dedicated—are my teammates, living and dead, frogmen and commandos, many of whose stories you now know. Among this last group are three old comrades who deserve special recognition: Mark Robbins, whose weekly encouragements were only outdone by the fact that his sacrifice in Iraq likely saved my life; Tadd Morrison, whose routine checkups on my progress even while he was overseas always acted as a reminder of the SEAL chief's commitment to his men even after the gunfights have stopped, and during which I never saw anyone smile so much; and most of all Jason Hickman, who could easily have written a better book in half the time but who never once failed to drop everything to thoughtfully edit a chapter of mine.

Though numerous hands helped make this book a possibility, only the two that are typing this now deserve fault for any errors contained within, or, for that matter, the structure that I ultimately decided upon. Just as Barbara Tuchman—whose repeated handlings of simultaneous story lines never failed to offer practical tips for this project—wrote in one of her many introductions, I am "conscious" that I could write this book "all over again under the same title . . . and then a third time, still without repeating" the subjects contained in each chapter. Having never set out with the particular objective to write a book with a thesis but rather to simply chart the influence of other special units on the origins of the SEAL teams, I nevertheless found that my arrived-upon argument could be proved by any number of paths that hopscotched their way along the disconnected islands of American special operations history. This path could have easily detoured from the one I chose and progressed from the 1st Rangers at Dieppe to the 2nd Marine Raiders on Guadalcanal to the 2nd Rangers at Pointe du Hoc to the VAC Recon Marines at Apamama to the OSS Maritime Swimmers at Yap to Merrill's Marauders at Myitkyina to the 41 Commandos at Chosin to SEAL Team ONE in the Ca Mau Peninsula. In the end, I settled on the subjects that I did because each was able to simultaneously pull numerous threads forward—the UDTs and VAC Recon Marines at Tinian; the Scouts and Raiders, Marines, and Amphibious Rogers at Camp 6; the Rangers, Partisans, and Navy planners in the Virginia I raid; the LRRPs,

PRUs, and SEALs of the 7th Platoon. Best of all, these were all subjects about which I knew almost nothing at the outset but whose characters are now—after so much time with them—almost as real to me as any that I ever personally served alongside.

Well, now, I suppose that's enough. Having never written a book before, I likewise don't exactly know how to end it except to say that the experience is not unlike collapsing after a long journey, albeit one whose challenges—almost like clues in a treasure hunt—afforded me a constant well of purpose and a steady diet of mysteries to unravel.

What more can any of us ask for?

Ben Milligan, 235
November 3, 2020

Notes

Part 1: Neglect

Chapter 1: The Reluctant Creation and Violent Demise of the Navy's First Commandos, the Marine Corps Raiders

12 OIL, TIN, AND RUBBER: Donald L. Miller, *D-Days in the Pacific* (New York: Simon & Schuster, 2005), 1.

12 "HOLDING OR RETREATING": David J. Ulbrich, *Preparing for Victory: Thomas Holcomb and the Making of the Modern Marine Corps, 1936–1943* (Annapolis: Naval Institute Press, 2011), 20.

13 ACCESS TO THE WHITE HOUSE POOL: Ibid., 50.

13 "5,000 WHITES OR 250,000 NEGROES": Morris J. MacGregor, Jr., "Integration of the Armed Forces, 1940–1965," Defense Studies Series, 1980, 100.

13 WATCHFUL PORTRAITS and SEEK VENGEANCE: "Professional Fighters," *Time,* November 11, 1940.

14 "USE OF 'COMMANDOS'": January 8, 1942, memorandum from King to Holcomb, Major Robert E. Mattingly (USMC), *Herringbone Cloak—GI Dagger: Marines of the OSS,* History and Museum Division Headquarters, USMC, Washington, D.C., 1989, 237.

14 "DONOVAN SERVED WITH DISTINCTION": January 14, 1942, letter from Holcomb to MGen. H. M. Smith, in ibid., 245.

14 "IT DOESN'T BELONG TO ME": Douglass Waller, *Wild Bill Donovan: The Spymaster Who Created the OSS and Modern Espionage* (New York: Free Press, 2012), 30–35.

15 "RACKETEERING ATTEMPT": Ibid., 55.

15 "ALL AMPHIBIOUS FORCE MARINES": January 16, 1942, letter from H. M. Smith to Holcomb, in Mattingly, *Herringbone Cloak—GI Dagger,* 252–253.

15 "I AM TERRIFIED": January 19, 1942, letter from Holcomb to Samuel Meek, in ibid., 254.

15 "UNITS OF 'COMMANDO' TYPE": January 24, 1942, letter from Nimitz to CG, Second Joint Training Force, in ibid., 255.

15 STEEL MILL ON HOKKAIDO: MGen. Omar T. Pfeiffer (USMC), Marine Research Center, Quantico, Virginia, Marine Corps Oral History Collection, 1968, 274.

15 "AS A MEANS OF FORESTALLING": February 10, 1942, letter from Holcomb to MG Clayton B. Vogel (USMC), in Mattingly, *Herringbone Cloak—GI Dagger,* 265–268.

16 "POLISHED GRAPEFRUIT": George W. Smith, *Carlson's Raid: The Daring Assault on Makin* (New York: Berkley, 2003), 134.

17 "SWIFTLY MOVING BLOWS": January 13, 1942, letter from J. Roosevelt to Holcomb, in Mattingly, *Herringbone Cloak—GI Dagger,* 238.

17 2,500 RAILROAD CARS' WORTH: Iris Chang, *The Rape of Nanking: The Forgotten Holocaust of World War II* (New York: Penguin, 1997), 5.

18 UNFORTUNATE ZEALOT JOHN BROWN: See Evans Fordyce Carlson, *The Autobiography of Evans Carlson*, unpublished, undated; John Wukovits, *American Commando: Evans Carlson, His WWII Marine Raiders and America's First Special Forces Mission* (New York: Penguin, 2009), 14.

18 "LONELY GENIUS": Evans Fordyce Carlson, *Twin Stars of China: A Behind-the-Scenes Story of China's Valiant Struggle for Existence by a US Marine Who Lived and Moved with the People* (New York: Dodd, Mead & Company, 1940), 171.

19 LIST OF TEN BOOKS: MGen. Oscar F. Peatross (USMC), *Bless 'Em All: The Raider Marines of World War II* (Tampa: Raider Publishing, 1995), 6.

19 "WHATEVER CARLSON'S SO-CALLED STANDARDS": Wukovits, *American Commando,* 45.

19 "SUBORDINATE SELF": Enclosure A of January 13, 1942, J. Roosevelt letter, "Proposed Organization of Mobile Columns (Commandos), in Mattingly, *Herringbone Cloak—GI Dagger,* 242.

20 "WE MUST STRIKE THE ENEMY": COMINCH press release, in Walter R. Borneman, *The Admirals: Nimitz, Halsey, Leahy, and King—The Five-Star Admirals Who Won the War at Sea* (New York: Little, Brown, 2012), 286.

20 "HELL-FOR-LEATHER": "Battle of the Pacific: In the Coral Sea," *Time,* May 18, 1942.

20 ORDERED TO SEIZE TULAGI: See Jon T. Hoffman, *From Makin to Bougainville: Marine Raiders in the Pacific War*, Marines in World War II Commemorative Series, 10.

21 TO REDUCE THIS PRESSURE: See Peatross, *Bless 'Em All,* 48.

22 THE *ARGONAUT* APPEARED: Cdr. John M. Haines (USN), "Report of Marine-Submarine Raider Expedition," August 24, 1942, 2, fold3.com; Peatross, *Bless 'Em All,* 54.

22 CARLSON COULD HAVE RESOLVED: See Carlson, *Autobiography of Evans Carlson.*

23 HEAP OF MEDICAL SUPPLIES: Smith, *Carlson's Raid,* 111.

23 "BOUNCED AROUND LIKE TOYS": Lt. W. S. Le Francois (USMC), "We Mopped Up Makin Island," *Saturday Evening Post,* December 4, 1943, vol. 1, 21.

23 AS MUCH AS SIXTY POUNDS: Peatross, *Bless 'Em All,* 55.

23 HIS RIGHT CHEEK: Wukovits, *American Commando,* 102.

23 "IT WAS ORGANIZED GRABASS": Wukovits, *American Commando,* 105; Smith, *Carlson's Raid,* 114–115.

24 BOLT SLAMMED SHUT: See Col. Evans F. Carlson (USMC), "Operations on Makin After-Action Report—August 17–18, 1942," August 21, 1942, 2, fold3.com; Peatross, *Bless 'Em All,* 56.

24 TORE IT IN HALF: Le Francois, "We Mopped Up Makin Island," 109.

25 "EVERYTHING LOUSY": Wukovits, *American Commando,* 109.

25 "SITUATION EXPECTED": Peatross, *Bless 'Em All,* 70.

25 AS A COMPANY BEGAN: See Le Francois, "We Mopped Up Makin Island," 109; Peatross, *Bless 'Em All,* 71.

26 "LET 'EM HAVE IT" and "WE HAD JAPS IN FRONT OF US": Le Francois, "We Mopped Up Makin Island," 109–110.

26 "ANYTHING OUT IN THE OPEN": Ibid., 109.

26 ENEMY ORDER OF BATTLE: Carlson, "Operations on Makin After-Action Report—August 17–18, 1942."

26 "PLEADED WITH [THOMASON] TO STAY DOWN": Peatross, *Bless 'Em All,* 73.

26 "WE HAD JAPS IN FRONT OF US": Ibid., 72.

26 "I LAY AS FLAT AS I COULD" and ALSO KILLED: Ibid., 72.

27 USING THE ONE RADIO: Haines, "Report of Marine-Submarine Raider Expedition."

27 SHOUTS OF "BANZAI": See Michael Blankfort, *The Big Yankee: The Life of Carlson of the Raiders* (Boston: Little, Brown, 1947), 49.

27 EIGHTY-TWO JAPANESE BODIES: Le Francois, "We Mopped Up Makin Island," 110.

27 SMOKING HIS PIPE: Blankfort, *Big Yankee,* 42.

28 CARLSON'S CASUALTIES: Peatross, *Bless 'Em All,* 78.

28 "IT DID NOT LOOK TOUGH": Carlson, "Operations on Makin After-Action Report—August 17–18, 1942."

28 BOBBED AWAY: Peatross, *Bless 'Em All,* 61.

28 "PALE SHADOWS": Ibid., 61.

29 UNHINGED HIM: Ibid., 65.

29 FIND THE JAPANESE COMMANDER: Ibid., 80.

29 CARLSON ORDERED ROOSEVELT: Carlson, "Operations on Makin After-Action Report—August 17–18, 1942."

29 FIVE STOUTHEARTED RAIDER VOLUNTEERS: Tripp Wiles, *Forgotten Raiders of '42: The Fate of the Marines Left Behind on Makin* (Washington, D.C.: Potomac Books, 2007), 30.

30 RANSACKED THE ISLAND'S STORES: Carlson, "Operations on Makin After-Action Report—August 17–18, 1942"; Le Francois, "We Mopped Up Makin Island," 43.

30 "A CHILD'S-PICTURE-BOOK VERSION": Le Francois, "We Mopped Up Makin Island," 45.

30 PLACID LAGOON ENTRANCE: Carlson, "Operations on Makin After-Action Report—August 17–18, 1942."

30 ALL SURVIVORS HAD BEEN EVACUATED: Haines, "Report of Marine-Submarine Raider Expedition."

30 "MORE BRASS THAN IN A FOUNDRY": Blankfort, *Big Yankee,* 71.

31 "ADMIRAL NIMITZ": Ibid.

31 "I HOPE THE ADMIRAL IS PLEASED": Le Francois, "We Mopped Up Makin Island," 48.

32 "FOR FOLKS WITH STRONG STOMACHS": Bosley Crowther, "The Screen: 'Gung Ho!' a Lurid Action Film About the Makin Island Raid, with Randolph Scott, Opens at the Criterion Theatre," *The New York Times,* January 26, 1944.

32 "A RAIDER GROUP": "The Roughest and the Toughest," *The New York Times,* November 8, 1942.

32 "LOSSES WERE SOMEWHAT LARGER": Admiral Chester W. Nimitz (USN), "Solomon Island Campaign—Makin Island Diversion," October 20, 1942, fold3.com.

32 AN APACHE WHO HAD BEEN LEFT: Wiles, *Forgotten Raiders of '42,* 57.

32 "PFEIFFER, HAVE YOU READ THIS?": Pfeiffer, Marine Corps Oral History Collection, 278.

33 "THE BASIC TRAINING": Col. Joseph H. Alexander, *Edson's Raiders: 1st Marine Raider Battalion in World War II* (Annapolis: Naval Institute Press, 1995), 236; Ulbrich, *Preparing for Victory,* 143–144.

34 VERGED ON NAUSEA and "MISSED HIS CALLING": Pfeiffer, Marine Corps Oral History Collection, 279.

34 "ORTHODOX MARINES" AND "PLAIN FOOLS": Ibid., 277.

34 CARLSON SUCCUMBED: See "Win the Peace for Whom," *Time,* September 16, 1946.

34 "CARLSON'S RAID ON MAKIN": Holland M. Smith and Percy Finch, *Coral and Brass* (New York: Bantam Books, 1948), 111.

34 NEVER TALKED ABOUT THE MAKIN RAID: Author interview with James Roosevelt III, 2014.

35 "THIS IS GOING TO BE A MARINE REGIMENT": Alexander, *Edson's Raiders,* 310.

Chapter 2: The Sidelining of the Army's Amphibious Soldier-Scouts and the Call-up of the Navy's Second-String Sailors

37 JOINT UNIT CALLED THE OBSERVER GROUP: John B. Dwyer, *Commandos from the Sea: The History of Amphibious Special Warfare in World War II and the Korean War* (Boulder: Paladin Press, 1998), 9–10.

37 "THAT DID NOT WORK AT ALL": Capt. Lloyd Peddicord, Jr. (USA), interview of Lloyd Peddicord, undated, audio recording provided courtesy of James Barnes.

38 "AMPHIBIOUS COMMANDOS": Capt. Phil Bucklew (USN), *Reminiscences of Captain Phil Bucklew, US Navy (Retired),* US Naval Institute Oral History Program, Annapolis, Maryland, 1980, no. 1, 34.

38 "EDUCATED MUSCLEMEN": "Navy: Potbellyacher," *Time,* September 22, 1941.

38 "A HAIRCUT AND A SHAVE" and *RICHARD III:* "Strong Boy," *Time,* January 10, 1927.

38 "DO SOMETHING BIG IN OTHER FIELDS": "Tunney Out," *Time,* August 13, 1928.

38 "THE GENE TUNNEY EXERCISER" and "MORAL COLLAPSE": "Navy: Potbellyacher," *Time.*

39 "I COULD TAKE TWO INSTEAD OF YOU": *Reminiscences of Captain Phil Bucklew,* no. 1, 31.

39 CONSIDERING THAT THE SMALLEST SOLDIER: Leonard D. Heaton (editor), Robert S. Anderson (editor), and Charles M. Wiltse, *Physical Standards in World War II,* Department of the Army, 1967, 278.

39 NUMBER OF ORIGINALS: George Connery, "The Unsung 200 Whose H-Hour Was Minus 4," *The Washington Post,* March 24, 1946; *Reminiscences of Captain Phil Bucklew,* no. 1, 34.

40 ACCOUNT OF ACCIDENT: Rusty W. Brown, *The US Navy's Scout and Raider Teams of World War II, 1942–1944,* unpublished account, 19–20, courtesy of James Barnes.

40 "WELL, CHIEF": *Reminiscences of Captain Phil Bucklew,* no. 1, 36.

41 UNLIKE MANY SONS: Author interviews with Dan Halperin; Connery, "Unsung 200."

42 LOCAL UNION BOSS: Author interviews with Dan Halperin.

43 HE NOW WELCOMED: Brown, *US Navy's Scout and Raider Teams,* 23.

43 HAD CREATED A CURRICULUM: Colonel Louis B. Ely, *Report of Instruction in Landings by Rubber Boat,* To CO, Atlantic Amphibious Training Center, October 10, 1942, courtesy of James Barnes.

44 9TH INFANTRY DIVISION: Ibid.

45 ACCOUNT OF PATTON VISIT BY JOHN BELL: Brown, Aftermath—The Scout and Raider Story Continued.

45 DOZEN SIGNAL FLASHES: Connery, "Unsung 200."

45 THE RIGHT BEACHES: Ibid.

46 "CONSIDERED LANDING-CRAFT PROPELLERS": Lt. Gen. Lucian K. Truscott, Jr., *Command Missions: A Personal Story,* Kindle edition (Auckland, New Zealand: Pickle Partners Publishing, 2013), loc. 1634.

46 "LIKE A FILE OF INDIAN SQUAWS": Ibid., loc. 1692.

46 HAD NOT BEEN EXPECTED: John B. Dwyer, *Scouts and Raiders: The Navy's First Special Warfare Commandos* (Westport: Praeger Publishers, 1993), 14.

46 NO ENLISTED WERE ALLOWED INSIDE: *Reminiscences of Captain Phil Bucklew,* no. 1, 39.

47 "FROM DAKAR CLEAR TO ICELAND": John Bell, *War Diary of John Bell,* courtesy of James Barnes.

47 OPERATION TORCH PREPARATIONS: Capt. Lloyd Peddicord, Jr. (USA), *Report of Scout Boat Operations and General Observation: Mehdia, French Morrocco, Landing Operation (Draft),* undated, courtesy of James Barnes.

47 ACCOUNT OF HALPERIN'S SELECTION OF ARMY SCOUTS: Dwyer, *Scouts and Raiders,* 15.

48 "BATTLE STATIONS": Ibid., 19.

50 IN THE ARMY THEY FOUND: Dwyer, *Commandos from the Sea,* 143–145.

51 "SHOT US FORWARD LIKE AN EXPRESS TRAIN": Chet Cunningham, *The Frogmen of World War II: An Oral History of the US Navy's Underwater Demolition Units* (New York: Pocket Books, 2005), 30; Cdr. Francis Douglas Fane (USNR) and Don Moore, *The Naked Warriors* (New York: Appleton-Century Crofts, 1956), 11.

51 "MAKE IT BACK ON YOUR OWN": Author interview with Dexter Freeman, April 6, 2014.

51 AS HENNEY: See Cunningham, *Frogmen of World War II,* 30–32.

51 "LET'S GET THE HELL OUT OF HERE!": Ibid., 31; Fane and Moore, *Naked Warriors,* 11.

52 JUST THEN, FIVE OR SIX: Truscott, *Command Missions,* loc. 2103.

53 "I HAD NO TROUBLE TAKING THEM PRISONER": Dwyer, *Scouts and Raiders,* 21.

53 "AS FAR AS I COULD SEE": Truscott, *Command Missions,* loc. 2179.

53 "YOU BRAVE CRAZY": Peddicord, *Report of Scout Boat Operations and General Observation.*

54 "ALL SPIRITS ROSE" and AFTER THE FAILED ATTEMPT: Dwyer, *Commandos from the Sea,* 143–145.

54 THE USS *DALLAS* POSSESSED A DRAFT: *Ships of the US Navy, 1940–1945,* available at http://www.ibiblio.org/hyperwar/USN/ships/DD/DD-199_AlexanderDallas.html.

56 "I DON'T KNOW HOW THE HELL WE DID IT": Author interview with Dexter Freeman.

56 WHO BROKE HIS ANKLE: James Douglas O'Dell, *The Water Is Never Cold: The Origins of the US Navy's Combat Demolition Units, UDTs, and SEALs* (Washington, D.C.: Brassey's, 2000), 116.

57 "PARTED IT WITHOUT A TREMOR": Cdr. Robert Brodie, Jr. (USN), "Report of Action Against Enemy Between November 7 and 11, 1942," *USS DALLAS War Diary,* November 19, 1942.

57 JUST OVER AN HOUR: Ibid.; Peddicord, *Report of Scout Boat Operations and General Observation.*

58 "I THINK IT VERY IMPORTANT": Adm. Kent Hewitt (USN), "Post-Operation Torch Letter from Adm. Kent Hewitt to Rear Adm. James L. Hall," undated, papers of H. Kent Hewitt, Archives Branch, courtesy of Naval Heritage and History Command, Washington, D.C.

58 “BUNDLED”: Undated book review by Jim O’Dell of John B. Dwyer, *Scouts and Raiders: The Navy’s First Special Warfare Commandos,* courtesy of James Barnes.

58 “WHEN OUR ARMY”: Capt. Lloyd Peddicord, Jr. (USA), “Orientation Talk—Scout and Raider Training Course,” July 1943, courtesy of James Barnes.

59 FIVE OF THE ORIGINAL TEN: Dwyer, *Scouts and Raiders,* 34.

59 ONE HIGHER THAN THE SILVER STAR: Ibid.; Robert W. Black, *The Battalion: The Dramatic Story of the 2nd Ranger Battalion in WWII* (Mechanicsburg: Stackpole Books, 2013), 28.

59 NAVY PLANNERS WOULD DISPATCH: Dwyer, *Scouts and Raiders,* 34.

60 THE LAST ONE TRAPPING HIM: *Reminiscences of Captain Phil Bucklew,* no. 1, 41–47.

60 “SURVIVOR’S LEAVE”: Ibid., 46.

60 MORE THAN JUST COCKLESHELLS: Dwyer, *Scouts and Raiders,* 39.

60 “HAVE SIXTEEN NAVY VOLUNTEER SWIMMERS”: Ensign Phil Bucklew (USN), letter to John Bell and Lloyd Peddicord, undated, courtesy of James Barnes.

61 ODDLY ENOUGH: Capt. George H. Bright, Jr. (USA), “Certificate of Receipt for Material of Scouts and Raiders Field Manuals,” February 2, 1944, courtesy of James Barnes.

Chapter 3: The US Army’s First Commandos and the Raid That Wasn’t

62 “DEVELOP A REIGN OF TERROR”: Russell Miller, *The Commandos* (Chicago: Time-Life Books, 1981), 21.

62 ON THEIR FIRST CROSS-CHANNEL NIGHT RAID and ANOTHER GROUP HAD BOTCHED: Ibid., 23–24.

63 HAVE HIS EAR STITCHED: James Ladd, *Commandos and Rangers of World War II* (New York: David & Charles, 1989), 18.

63 ONLY SUCCESSFUL RAID: Miller, *Commandos,* 21.

63 “BUTCHER AND BOLT”: “Battle of Europe: Why Are We Waiting,” *Time,* June 8, 1942.

63 “IF THEY COULD” and “THE FAT MAN WASN’T THERE”: “Goring’s Narrow Escape,” *Time,* November 10, 1941.

63 “A STEEL HAND FROM THE SEA”: Ladd, *Commandos and Rangers of World War II,* preface.

63 HIS SILVER CIGARETTE LIGHTER: “Battle of Europe,” *Time.*

64 ARRIVED IN BRITAIN: “World Battlefronts: Joint Responsibility,” *Time,* April 20, 1942.

64 BRUSSELS SPROUTS: “Foreign News: Union Now,” *Time,* May 18, 1942.

64 HE HAD OVERHAULED: Barbara W. Tuchman, *Stilwell and the American Experience in China, 1911–45* (New York: Grove Press, 1970), 123.

64 HIS OVERHAULS HAD TAKEN: “New Army,” *Time,* April 8, 1940.

65 A SPECIALLY TRAINED FORCE: Robert H. Adelman and George H.

Walton, *The Devil's Brigade* (Annapolis: Naval Institute Press, 2013), 19–22.

65 "BATTLE EXPERIENCE AS SOON AS POSSIBLE": W. G. Stirling, Offices of the War Cabinet, Great George Street, letter to General Chaney, April 10, 1942, courtesy of George C. Marshall Research Library, papers of Lucian K. Truscott.

65 "INEVITABLY": "Marshall Pledges Action in Europe," *The New York Times,* April 19, 1942.

65 "SHORT PUGNACIOUS NOSE": "Military Brains," *Time,* July 29, 1940.

66 "MARSHALL PLEDGES ACTION IN EUROPE": "Marshall Pledges Action in Europe," *The New York Times,* April 19, 1942.

66 SKULKING RAIDS: "Skulking" used from Plymouth to the Plains of Abraham to describe guerrilla tactics.

66 "HELL, WE REHEARSED": David W. Hogan, Jr., *Raiders or Elite Infantry: The Changing Role of the US Army Rangers from Dieppe to Grenada* (Westport: Greenwood Press, 1992), 37.

67 "YOU ARE AN OLDER MAN": Truscott, *Command Missions,* loc. 268.

67 "YOU WILL KEEP IN MIND": Ibid., loc. 317.

68 "EVERY WAR IN WHICH THE NATION": Ibid., loc. 646.

68 MARSHALL TELEGRAMMED: Gen. George C. Marshall, "Message: AGWAR to USAFBI, Subject: Commando Unit," May 27, 1942, GCM Library, papers of LKT.

68 575 VOLUNTEERS: Henry Paul Jeffers, *Command of Honor: General Lucian Truscott's Path to Victory in World War II* (New York: Penguin, 2008), 34.

68 REQUIREMENTS FOR RACE and "EACH APPLICANT": Lt. Col. Theodore G. Holcombe (Adjutant General First Armored Corps), "Subject: Volunteers for Ranger Battalions, by order of Commanding General Wilson," May 17, 1943, NARA, RG 407, entry 427.

68 TYPICAL SPREAD OF CITIZEN-SOLDIERS: "Ranger Reconversion," *Yank: The Army Weekly,* November 16, 1945, vol. 4, no. 22, courtesy of UDT-SEAL Museum.

68 ONE LION TAMER, A BULLFIGHTER: Rick Atkinson, *An Army at Dawn: The War in North Africa, 1942–1943* (New York: Owl, 2002), 79.

68 FOUND THEMSELVES AT ACHNACARRY CASTLE: William O. Darby and William H. Baumer, *We Led the Way* (Novato: Presidio Press, 1993).

68 "EVERYTHING HERE": James Altieri, *The Spearheaders: A Vivid Personal History of Darby's Rangers, America's First Commando Unit* (Indianapolis: Bobbs-Merrill, 1960), 38.

68 104 MEN WERE RETURNED: Jeffers, *Command of Honor,* 34.

68 ONE MAN DROWNED and FIRED LIVE ROUNDS: Ibid., 58.

68 "ME-AND-MY-PAL" COURSE: Ibid., 50.

69 SOAP BULLETS: Darby and Baumer, *We Led the Way,* 38.

69 "DEATH SLIDE": Ibid., 32.

69 "SLAB OF FISH": Altieri, *Spearheaders,* 51.

69 "MARTIN, A LADY KILLER": Darby and Baumer, *We Led the Way,* 31–38.

69 TROOPS CAPABLE OF MARCHING: Ibid., 31.

70 "BRILLIANT RED SCAR": Altieri, *Spearheaders,* 31.

70 SON OF A PRINTER and A BORN SALESMAN: Darby and Baumer, *We Led the Way,* 1.

70 "HE IS THE IDEAL COMMANDO LEADER": Lt. Col. L. E. Vaughan (HMA), "Report on 1st Bn. US Rangers," August 2, 1942, appendix A, GCM Library, papers of LKT.

71 "PENCIL-PUSHING AIDE-DE-CAMP": Altieri, *Spearheaders,* 56.

71 "THIS INFORMATION YOU HAVE JUST HEARD": Ibid., 94.

71 "EL DARBO": Jeffers, *Command of Honor,* 52.

71 "YOU'LL NEVER FIND HIM THIS FAR BACK": Darby and Baumer, *We Led the Way,* 180.

72 "MY GOD, THOSE COMMANDOS CAN FIGHT!": Ibid., 45.

72 "YOU'VE GOT TO FIGHT": Ibid., 45.

72 "MY GOD, COLONEL": Ibid., 13.

72 "NOISILY" and *"QUI VA LÀ?":* Capt. M. Jacob, "Report: Subject: Attack on Fort de la Pointe," November 16, 1942, NARA, RG 407, entry 427.

73 MEDIEVAL RAMPARTS AND MOAT and BALANCING LAUNDRY: Atkinson, *Army at Dawn,* 79.

73 WAIL OF SIRENS and T-5 MURRAY KATZEN: Jacob, "Report: Subject: Attack on Fort de la Pointe."

73 THE SECOND RAID: Altieri, *Spearheaders,* 121.

73 "ROY, PULL YOUR COMPANY": Darby and Baumer, *We Led the Way,* 19.

73 "HIHO, SILVER! AWAY!": Jacob, "Report: Subject: Attack on Fort de la Pointe."

73 PEACOAT, PAJAMAS, AND SLIPPERS: Darby and Baumer, *We Led the Way,* 20.

74 "FIRST ONE BACK": "Sport: Little War," *Time,* December 14, 1942; see also "Ranger Commandos," BoardGameGeek, available at http://boardgamegeek.com/image/29256/ranger-commandos.

74 EASY COMPANY ATTACKED AT LA MACTA: Altieri, *Spearheaders,* 141.

74 "THAT DOES IT": Ibid., 149–150.

75 SHINE COLORED-PINHOLE FLASHLIGHTS: Ibid., 187; and Col. William O. Darby, letter to BGen. George H. Weens, Asst. Commandant, the Infantry School, undated, in response to Weens's letter of May 27, 1944, NARA, RG 407, entry 427.

75 TAPE GIANT WHITE LETTERS: Ibid.

75 "FROM HERE ON IN": Altieri, *Spearheaders,* 182.

75 "I'M SORRY, DAMNED SORRY": Ibid., 184.

75 "THE TERRIBLE LETDOWN": Ibid., 186.

75 "I KNEW IT!": Ibid., 184.

75 "IF THIS KEEPS UP": Ibid., 187.

76 "HOW CLOSE DID HE GET?": Ibid., 202.

76 "STYGIAN BLACKNESS" and ALTIERI STABBED A MAN: Ibid., 211.
76 "EXCELLENT LEADER": Vaughn Report, Appendix A.
76 "I THINK I HAVE TWO": Altieri, *Spearheaders,* 225.
76 IN TOTAL, DARBY LOST: Ibid., 213.
76 IN EXCHANGE FOR THOSE LOSSES: Lt. Col. William O. Darby, "Report of Action at Sened Station," March 5, 1943, to the Adjutant General, Washington, D.C. (via II Army Corps), 1st Ranger Bn., Commanding, NARA, RG 407, entry 427.
77 "REGULAR INFANTRY BATTALION": Darby, letter to Weens, undated.
77 "CAN YOU SEND ME": Atkinson, *Army at Dawn,* 380.
78 DARBY TURNED DOWN BOTH OFFERS: Jeffers, *Command of Honor,* 123.
78 "NO BONUS": Altieri, *Spearheaders,* 246.
78 "TAKE THE REGIMENT": Ibid., 293.
79 200 PACK MULES: Ibid., 290.
79 FIGHTING ALONG THE WINTER LINE: Jeffers, *Command of Honor,* 171.
80 FORTY-FIVE DAYS: Altieri, *Spearheaders,* 305.
80 "FLAT AS A TABLE TOP": Sgt. Milton Lehman, "The Rangers Bled Fighting at Dawn," *Stars and Stripes,* March 11, 1944, NARA, RG 407, entry 427.
80 LARYNGITIS AND A LIMP: Truscott, *Command Missions,* loc. 6356.
81 SEVERAL MEN OVERHEARD: Jeffers, *Command of Honor,* 198–199.
82 A THIRTY-YEAR-OLD VIRGINIAN: Carlo D'Este, *Fatal Decision: Anzio and the Battle for Rome* (New York: HarperCollins, 1991), 493.
82 "VERY SMALL": Vaughn Report.
82 AMATEUR POET: Rick Atkinson, *The Day of Battle: The War in Sicily and Italy, 1943–1944* (New York: Henry Holt, 2007), 389.
82 ONE OF THE FASTEST THINKERS: Vaughn Report.
82 TYPED OUT A LETTER and "PROPER": Hogan, *Raiders or Elite Infantry,* 42.
82 PINE NEEDLES and BARBERS: Lehman, "The Rangers Bled Fighting at Dawn."
83 "TRIED TO TELL THE TROOPS": Darby and Baumer, *We Led the Way,* 169; Joseph M. Kolish, "Special Report," March 9, 1944.
83 "THE CITY MAY HAVE CONSIDERABLE OPPOSITION": Atkinson, *Day of Battle,* 389.
83 "WE'VE BEEN ORDERED": D'Este, *Fatal Decision,* 161.
83 BANDOLIERS OF AMMUNITION and STICKY GRENADES: Lehman, "The Rangers Bled Fighting at Dawn."
83 LEAVE THE BAGS UNOPENED: Clarence R. Meltesen, *After the Battle: Ranger Evasion and Escape,* San Francisco, OPFLAG 64 Press, US Army Military History Institute, January 1997, 18.
83 "PISTOL PACKIN' MAMA": Atkinson, *Day of Battle,* 389.
83 "CLOUD-CHOKED SKIES": Lehman, "The Rangers Bled Fighting at Dawn."
83 "OMINOUS SILENCE" and "IRON MIKE": D'Este, *Fatal Decision,* 162.
84 HERE THEY SPLIT: Darby and Baumer, *We Led the Way,* 149–150.

84 antennas: Lehman, "The Rangers Bled Fighting at Dawn."

84 "That's the god-damndest thing": Robert W. Black, *The Ranger Force: Darby's Rangers in World War II,* Kindle edition (Mechanicsburg: Stackpole Books, 2009), loc. 2974.

84 *"Alles geht gut"*: D'Este, *Fatal Decision,* 493.

84 Gliding his knife: Ibid., 163.

84 "We passed two batteries": Lehman, "The Rangers Bled Fighting at Dawn."

85 Eventually, Dobson and his men: D'Este, *Fatal Decision,* 163.

86 "Kill them!" and "Go for Cisterna!": Black, *Ranger Force,* loc. 3030.

86 gliding through the night's last shadows: Ibid., loc. 3041.

87 "Hit the dirt!": Meltesen, *After the Battle,* 27.

87 the tank's first round: Black, *Ranger Force,* loc. 3073.

87 *"Kamarad!"* and wooden stocks: Lehman, "The Rangers Bled Fighting at Dawn."

87 Hiding in a shed: Meltesen, *After the Battle,* 23.

88 "landed running": D'Este, *Fatal Decision,* 165.

88 Two other squads: Ibid., 165.

88 fifteen armored vehicles: Meltesen, *After the Battle,* 22.

88 At Darby's command post: Altieri, *Spearheaders,* 310.

88 None had: Black, *Ranger Force,* loc. 3061.

89 "hit through the head": Darby and Baumer, *We Led the Way,* 167.

89 By civil twilight: Ibid., 159.

89 Having reached the ditch: D'Este, *Fatal Decision,* 165.

89 blasting a chunk: Meltesen, *After the Battle,* 22.

89 Iron Cross emblem: Atkinson, *Day of Battle,* 391.

89 "Then": Lehman, "The Rangers Bled Fighting at Dawn"; Darby and Baumer, *We Led the Way,* 161.

89 "What happened next": Lehman, "The Rangers Bled Fighting at Dawn."

89 Iron Cross–marked tanks: Darby and Baumer, *We Led the Way,* 161.

89 "holed up": Ibid., 163.

89 "Can't adjust fire": D'Este, *Fatal Decision,* 164.

90 "Is 1st Battalion lost?": Meltesen, *After the Battle,* 24.

90 When the tanks lurched: Darby and Baumer, *We Led the Way,* 162.

90 few knew who was in charge: Meltesen, *After the Battle,* 36.

90 "he wasn't so crazy": Lehman, "The Rangers Bled Fighting at Dawn"; Darby and Baumer, *We Led the Way,* 166.

90 Dobson had somehow made it back: Black, *Ranger Force,* locs. 3116–3124.

90 solid communications were finally established: Ibid.

91 At the Calacaprini House: Ibid., loc. 3107.

91 "overwrought and weeping": Ibid., loc. 3107.

91 "Some of the fellows": Altieri, *Spearheaders,* 312.

91 "So long, Colonel": Darby and Baumer, *We Led the Way,* 164.

91 "It apparently was too much": Atkinson, *Day of Battle,* 395.

91 "As enemy shells beat": Altieri, *Spearheaders,* 312.

91 "straight and his chin": Ibid., 313.

92 destroyed their radio: Darby and Baumer, *We Led the Way,* 165–166.

92 "little fellow" and "machine gun nest": D'Este, *Fatal Decision,* 166–167.

92 With hands raised: Capt. Charles M. Shunstrom, "Report of Action: Capture of the First and Third Ranger Battalions (Cisterna, Di Litorria, Italy on the Day of 30 January 1944)," July 10, 1944, NARA, RG 407, entry 427.

92 *For every Churman killed:* Meltesen, *After the Battle,* 34–35.

92 "spray": Shunstrom, "Report of Action."

92 "got hysterical": Ibid.; see also Black, *Ranger Force,* loc. 3155; D'Este, *Fatal Decision,* 166.

92 Even Shunstrom's attempts: Shunstrom, "Report of Action."

92 Ranger Larry Kushner: Black, *Ranger Force,* loc. 3155.

92 Staff Sergeant Wayne Ruona: Meltesen, *After the Battle,* 38.

92 Master Sergeant Ehalt: Black, *Ranger Force,* loc. 3170.

93 a helmetless Ranger and "little jig": Meltesen, *After the Battle,* 36.

93 Darby stood silently: D'Este, *Fatal Decision,* 169.

93 Beyond the reach of the Army: Ibid., 416.

93 only 87 remained: Darby and Baumer, *We Led the Way,* 172.

93 In a few days the remnants: Ibid., 173.

93 Darby just went away: D'Este, *Fatal Decision,* 169.

93 "[Clark] says they were used": Ibid., 171.

94 In the meeting, Clark bemoaned and There was no need, Truscott said: Truscott, *Command Missions,* loc. 6387; Wilson A. Heefner, *Dogface Soldier: The Life of General Lucian J. Truscott, Jr.* (Columbia: University of Missouri Press, 2010), 157.

94 "black uniformed Fascisti": Meltesen, *After the Battle,* 77.

94 open truck: Black, *Ranger Force,* loc. 3222.

94 Churchill Vs and muttered obscenities: Meltesen, *After the Battle,* 46.

94 "Not until I was marching": Ibid., 48.

94 "hunk": D'Este, *Fatal Decision,* 165.

94 interrogators gushed: Ibid., 425.

95 "The Rangers have at last": Ibid., 169.

95 "This is Cisterna": Black, *Ranger Force,* loc. 3253.

96 Frederick ordered them to remove: Hogan, *Raiders or Elite Infantry,* 61.

96 "clumsy": Cdr. John S. Mosher (USNR—Intel Staff, 7th Phib. Force), "Amphibious Scouts and Raiders," lecture delivered at the Army and

Navy Staff College, Washington, D.C., March 2, 1945, UDT-SEAL Museum.

96 "He actually seemed to enjoy fighting": D'Este, *Fatal Decision,* 244.

97 "promiscuous use of artillery": Michael J. King, *William Orlando Darby: A Military Biography* (Hamdon: Archon Books, 1981), 160.

97 "Cheer up, son": D'Este, *Fatal Decision,* 244.

97 "certain exemplary soldiers": Darby and Baumer, *We Led the Way,* 174.

97 "[his] most blood lost since the war began": King, *William Orlando Darby,* 169.

97 "they become egotistical": Mosher, "Amphibious Scouts and Raiders."

98 "half the size of a dime": Darby and Baumer, *We Led the Way,* 219.

98 recruited in-theater: Hogan, *Raiders or Elite Infantry,* 84.

98 had not even heard of other Rangers: Hogan, *Raiders or Elite Infantry,* 85.

98 "postwar doctrinal documents": Hogan, *Raiders or Elite Infantry,* 93.

Part 2: Opportunity

Chapter 4: Draper Kauffman and the Course That Cracked the Atlantic Wall, Then Laid the First Bricks of the Legend of Naval Special Warfare

103 Army's combat engineers: James Douglas O'Dell, "Joint-Service Beach Obstacle Demolition in World War II," *Engineer,* April–June 2005, 38.

103 "communicate what they required": Sue Ann Dunford, *More Than Scuttlebutt: The US Navy Demolition Men in WWII* (privately published, 2009), 13.

103 "Have you seen the pictures": R. Adm. Draper L. Kauffman (USN), *Reminiscences of R. Adm. Draper L. Kauffman* (Annapolis: US Naval Institute Press, 1982), no. 2, 158–159.

104 Tall and thin, lanky even: *Reminiscences of R. Adm. Draper L. Kauffman,* nos. 1 and 2; Elizabeth Kauffman Bush, *America's First Frogman: The Draper Kauffman Story* (Annapolis: Naval Institute Press, 2004); author interviews with Draper Kauffman, Jr., 2016; author interviews with Kelsey Kauffman, 2016.

105 could have palmed a pistol: Kauffman, letter to mother, December 8, 1940, courtesy of Kauffman family.

105 cost of one ambulance and renounced the dry Episcopal faith: *Reminiscences of R. Adm. Draper L. Kauffman,* no. 1, 54–58.

106 weighed 165 pounds: Bush, *America's First Frogman,* 25.

106 "I can't tell you": *Reminiscences of R. Adm. Draper L. Kauffman,* no. 1, 61.

106 NEVER WITH HIS BOOTS OFF: Kauffman, letter to Mr. Johnson, undated, courtesy of Kauffman family.

106 BOCHE BARBARIANS: Kauffman, letter to parents, August 8, 1940, courtesy of Kauffman family.

106 DRAPING DARK BLANKETS: *Reminiscences of R. Adm. Draper L. Kauffman,* no. 1, 61.

106 LOST TEN POUNDS: Kauffman, letter to Mr. Johnson, undated, courtesy of Kauffman family.

107 OUTFIT KNOWN AS THE CORPS FRANC and "THEY WERE FOOLHARDY": *Reminiscences of R. Adm. Draper L. Kauffman,* no. 1, 63.

107 FORMER MANAGER FOR COCA-COLA IN GERMANY: Ibid., no. 1, 71.

107 SURRENDERED HIS PASSPORT: Ibid., no. 1, 81.

107 WHEN FREED: Bush, *America's First Frogman,* 25.

107 "ONE STEP AHEAD OF A FIT": J. L. Kauffman, letter to Kauffman, July 26, 1940, courtesy of Kauffman family.

107 "NOT VALID FOR TRAVEL TO ENGLAND": *Reminiscences of R. Adm. Draper L. Kauffman,* no. 1, 81.

107 POTATO PEELING: Ibid., no. 1, 85.

107 "I AM GOING TO ENGLAND": Kauffman, letter to parents, August 8, 1940.

108 "AS FAR AS I KNOW": Bush, *America's First Frogman,* 29.

108 A GERMAN BOMB LANDED: *Reminiscences of R. Adm. Draper L. Kauffman,* no. 1, 93.

108 "UNEXPLODED BOMB COMING THROUGH!": Cdr. Harold B. Say (USNR), "17 Seconds to Live," *True Magazine,* December 1945.

109 "YOU HAVE NOT THE RIGHT": Ibid.

110 300-POUND PARACHUTE MINE: Ibid.; *Reminiscences of R. Adm. Draper L. Kauffman,* no. 1, 107–108.

110 "HOW DID YOU HAPPEN TO JOIN": Ibid., no. 1, 119.

110 "THE PLACE WAS MINE": Ibid., no. 1, 113.

110 "LITTLE CEREMONY": Kauffman, letter to family, May 16, 1941, courtesy of Kauffman family.

110 "BELIEVE IT OR NOT": BBC broadcast, July 4, 1941, courtesy of Kauffman family.

110 "NURSING THESE GODDAM LAND MINES": "Battle of the Pacific: Aloha," *Time,* July 6, 1942.

111 "I WANT YOU TO COME": Say, "17 Seconds to Live."

111 "IF YOU THINK THE UNITED STATES NAVY": *Reminiscences of R. Adm. Draper L. Kauffman,* no. 2, 125–126.

111 "GET OUT TO PEARL HARBOR": Say, "17 Seconds to Live," 12.

111 "I COULDN'T HAVE SET THAT BOMB OFF": *Reminiscences of R. Adm. Draper L. Kauffman,* no. 2, 132.

111 "D.C. MAN TAKES LIVE JAP BOMB APART": "D.C. Man Takes Live Jap Bomb Apart, Gets Navy Cross," *The Washington Post,* June 27, 1942.

111 "All Florida will rejoice": WQAM radio transcript, Miami Broadcasting Company, June 30, 1942, courtesy of Kauffman family.

112 ample space in Fort Pierce and "sewerage": Adm. Kent Hewitt (USN), "Establishment of Temporary Amphibious Training Base at Fort Pierce, Florida Instead of at St. Augustine, Florida," January 19, 1943, NHHC, H. Kent Hewitt Papers, Coll/138.

112 Shaped like a sausage: Edward T. Higgins, *Webfooted Warriors: A Story of a Frogman in the Navy During World War II* (New York: Exposition Press, 1955), 30.

113 drawing a variety of skill sets: "Scout and Raider Training Manifest," January 1943–January 1944, UDT-SEAL Museum, and NHHC, papers of Adm. Alan G. Kirk, Box 31–32.

113 classes on kicking, choking, escaping: Capt. Clarence Gulbranson (USN), "Hand to Hand Combat for Amphibious Scouts," undated, UDT-SEAL Museum.

113 "temperamental stability": R. Adm. F. W. Rockwell (USN), "Handbook of Naval Combat Underwater Demolition Team Training," Bureau of Naval Personnel Training Standards and Curriculum Division, October 23, 1944, courtesy of UDT/SEAL Museum.

113 "individual initiative": *Reminiscences of R. Adm. Draper L. Kauffman,* no. 2, 163.

113 "very heavy": Ibid., no. 2, 163.

114 "I was standing at a bench": James M. Warnock, "Some Memories and Thoughts About Draper L. Kauffman," unpublished, March 1986, 17–19, courtesy of Kauffman family.

114 Every day at Fort Pierce and adopt names: see Dunford, *More Than Scuttlebutt,* photo array; NCDU Handbook.

115 "You were wet": Capt. Francis R. Kaine (USNR), "Draper Kauffman and the UDTs," *Naval History,* Winter 1990.

115 If an instructor detected: Cunningham, *Frogmen of World War II,* 41.

115 flour bombs: Dunford, *More Than Scuttlebutt,* 53.

115 Jetty landings: Ibid., 53.

115 "So Solly Day": Fane and Moore, *Naked Warriors,* 19.

116 esprit de corps and "If you haven't been": *Reminiscences of R. Adm. Draper L. Kauffman,* no. 2, 172.

116 "I think I have never seen": Warnock, "Some Memories," 28.

116 he passed out: Ibid., 28.

116 "We all knew": Kaine, "Draper Kauffman and the UDTs," 2.

116 "bloody battle cry": Excerpt from "The Ribbon for the First Battle of the Indian River," undated, courtesy of Kauffman family.

116 "The water": O'Dell, *The Water Is Never Cold,* 1.

116 "What is this I hear": *Reminiscences of R. Adm. Draper L. Kauffman,* no. 2, 169.

117 "It became a contest": Warnock, "Some Memories," 24.

117 "A ticket to sure fire danger and excitement": "Demolition Work Ticket to Danger," *Beelines,* October 18, 1943, courtesy of Kauffman family.

118 "It seems the men who have gone": Dunford, *More Than Scuttlebutt,* 46.

118 "This outfit doesn't know much": Warnock, "Some Memories," 29.

118 "big, blonde, good natured Virginian": Craig L. Symonds, *Operation Neptune: The Allied Invasion of Europe and the D-Day Landings* (New York: Oxford University Press, 2014), 202.

118 Already, in the invasions: "American Admirals for the Sea Tasks of Invasion," *The New York Sun,* June 6, 1944.

119 "I'll be with my men": Susan H. Godson, *Viking of Assault: Admiral John Leslie Hall, Jr., and Amphibious Warfare* (Lanham: Rowman & Littlefield, 1982), 118.

119 Viking of Assault: Ibid., 121.

119 "Any tiny island invasion": Symonds, *Operation Neptune,* 193.

119 "It is always necessary": Godson, *Viking of Assault,* 122.

119 "Naval task force commander": Ibid., 122–123.

120 "until such time" and guard duty: "Demolition Units of the Atlantic Theatre of Operations," World War II Histories and Historical Reports in the US Naval History Division, Operational Archives Naval History Division, UDT-SEAL Museum.

120 local brew: Freeman, letter to father, January 7, 1944, courtesy of Dexter Freeman.

120 since his arrival: Ibid.

120 mechanical skills and leadership: "William Freeman, US Navy Fitness Evaluations," courtesy of Dexter Freeman.

120 Hall's increased authority: CO, US Naval Forces in Europe, to CO, Eleventh Amphibious Force, "Subject: Special British Course for Naval Combat Demolition Officers," January 24, 1944, Papers of Adm. Alan G. Kirk, NARA, RG 38, entry UD-09D 30, box 14.

121 in the shape of a bratwurst: Fane and Moore, *Naked Warriors,* 43.

121 "'sailmakers' in lofts throughout England": Ibid., 48.

121 Hall demanded: LTJG H. L. Blackwell, Jr. (USN), "Report of Naval Combat Demolition Units," July 15, 1944, NHHC, D-Day, the Normandy Invasion: Combat Demolition Units, history.navy.mil /content/history/nhhc/research/library/online-reading-room/title-list -alphabetically/d/d-day-the-normandy-invasion-combat-demolition -units.html.

121 In a 1944 training film: "Hand Placed Charges Against Beach and Underwater Obstacles," War Department Film Bulletin, Army Pictorial Service, F.B. 133, *Critical Past,* available at http://www .criticalpast.com/video/65675075894_demolition-charges_landing -craft-underway_barbed-wire-obstacles_Bangalore-torpedoes.

122 "the effectiveness of demolition parties": Joseph Balkoski,

Omaha Beach: D-Day, June 6, 1944 (Mechanicsburg: Stackpole Books, 2004), 144.

122 "I AM RATHER DISTURBED" (TO BRIGADIER GENERAL WILLIAM KEAN): Ibid., 142.

122 "WE ARE AS DISTURBED AS YOU ARE": Ibid., 142.

122 "ADVICE ON OBSTACLE CLEARANCE": Blackwell, "Report of Naval Combat Demolition Units," 3.

122 "DEFENSIVE TACTICS OF THE RIFLE SQUAD": "Division of Responsibility Between Beach Party and Shore Party," Commander US Naval Forces Northwest African Waters, ANPM No. 5, February, 21, 1944, 6, NARA papers of Adm. Alan G. Kirk, RG 38, entry UD-09D 30, box 13.

124 INGENIOUSLY CORKING: Erwin Rommel, translation of "Enclosure 1: Annex to Order of Commander Army Group B," May 7, 1944, 4, papers of Adm. Alan G. Kirk, NARA, RG 38, entry UD-09D 30, 12.

124 STILL THERE WAS MORE: Rommel, "Enclosure 1," 6.

125 CAPTAIN TIMOTHY F. WELLINGS: "The Wellings Family: United States Navy," *Arlington National Cemetery,* available at http://www.arlingtoncemetery.net/wellings-family.htm.

126 "HIS DEMOS" and "HALL PLEADED": Godson, *Viking of Assault,* 124.

126 "POWERFULLY BUILT": David Howarth, *D Day: The Sixth of June 1944* (New York: Pyramid Books, 1960), 155.

126 "PUG-NOSED FIGHTING BANTAM": Fane and Moore, *Naked Warriors,* 47.

126 "STERN, DIRECT, AND OUTSPOKEN": Howarth, *D Day,* 155.

126 THOUGH HE HAD GRADUATED: Ibid., 47.

126 "A NUMBER OF THESE MEN": Capt. T. F. Wellings (USN), "Report of Training Progress of Naval Combat Demolition Units," May 6, 1944, NARA, papers of Adm. Alan G. Kirk, RG 38, entry UD-09D-30, box 14.

126 HAVERSACKS AS BIG AS SADDLEBAGS: Jonathan Gawne, *Spearheading D-Day: American Special Units of the Normandy Invasion* (Havertown: Casemate, 1999), 148.

127 BRACKISH WATER MADE POTABLE: Lawrence Karnowski, "Account of Naval Combat Demolition Unit no. 45," undated, courtesy of UDT/SEAL Museum 16.

127 "AS FLAT AS A TABLE TOP": GM3 Gale Fant (NCDU no. 45), "Memories of WWII Service," undated, courtesy of UDT/SEAL Museum.

128 "I KNEW THAT THEY HAD A VERY TOUGH JOB": Adm. John L. Hall, Jr. (USN), "Oral History of Adm. John Leslie Hall, Jr.," interview by John T. Mason, 1963, Columbia University Oral History Research Office, New York, New York, 205.

128 "NOT A LIVING SOUL": Karnowski, "Account of Naval Combat Demolition Unit no. 45," 15.

128 "I'D LIKE TO GO ASHORE WITH YOU": "Oral History of Adm. John Leslie Hall, Jr.," 205.

128 "If you courageously" and "How do we get": Godson, *Viking of Assault,* 131.

129 "God bless you": "Oral History of Adm. John Leslie Hall, Jr.," 205–208.

129 chewing gum, twelve seasickness pills: "The Invasion: June Night," *Time,* June 12, 1944.

129 three blankets: Karnowski, "Account of Naval Combat Demolition Unit no. 45," 16.

129 "I saw an opening": Cunningham, *Frogmen of World War II,* 95–96.

129 A few miles away: Ibid., 65.

129 After reporting the vessel's condition: Blackwell, "Report of Naval Combat Demolition Units."

130 Despite the problems and "seven-bag case": 2nd Lt. Wesley C. Ross, "Account of Wesley Ross," 5, courtesy of James Barnes and John B. Dwyer.

130 lucky two-dollar bill: James Burke, 299th Combat Engineer Battalion, available at HistoryD-Day2dollarbill.htm.

130 white curls: Balkoski, *Omaha Beach,* 146.

130 "would have blown the helmet off my head": Ross, "Account of Wesley Ross," 5.

131 "waving and yelling frantically": Michael Accordino, 299th Combat Engineer Battalion, available at HistoryD-Day2dollarbill .htm.

131 grass fires: Balkoski, *Omaha Beach,* 148.

131 palmed throttle knobs: Antony Beevor, *D-Day: The Battle for Normandy* (New York: Viking Press, 2009), 94.

131 "Take us on in": Russell Miller, *Nothing Less than Victory: The Oral History of D-Day* (New York: Harper Perennial, 1998), 291.

131 now in command of NCDU #11: NCDU, no. 11 After-Action Report, courtesy of Dexter Freeman.

132 Bible-thumping chaplains: Freeman, letter to Annie, July 16, 1944, courtesy of Dexter Freeman.

133 their bullets stitching across the sand: NCDU, no. 11 After-Action Report.

133 Gripping the condom-protected fuse lighter: Fane and Moore, *Naked Warriors,* 54; NCDU, no. 11 After-Action Report.

134 "shinnied up the stakes": Joseph H. Gibbons, "Oral History—Invasion of Normandy, 6–25 June, 1944," NHHC, World War II interviews, box 11.

134 "drowned out the battle's din": Fane and Moore, *Naked Warriors,* 56.

134 Seaman Farrell alone, still writhing and Bass bent down: NCDU, no. 11 After-Action Report.

135 Team 2, having been forced: Blackwell, "Report of Naval Combat Demolition Units."

135 WOULD NOT ARRIVE FOR ANOTHER HOUR: Fane and Moore, *Naked Warriors,* 57.
135 WHEN THE SOLDIERS AND SAILORS: Ibid., 58–61.
135 PARALYZED BY THE SAME PROBLEM: Ibid., 58–59.
136 A TALL, HANDSOME, COOL-HEADED: Karnowski, "Account of Naval Combat Demolition Unit no. 45," 13.
136 LOST HIS HELMET: Ibid., 17.
136 "IT LOOKED IMPOSSIBLE": Fant, "Memories of WWII Service."
137 "PACK OF EXPLOSIVES": Karnowski, "Account of Naval Combat Demolition Unit no. 45."
137 "I THOUGHT I'D NEVER GET": Ibid., 18.
137 AS OBSTACLES BLEW APART: Karnowski, "Account of Naval Combat Demolition Unit no. 45," 19.
137 CARRYING THE ARMY AND NAVY DEMOLITION COMMANDERS: Fane and Moore, *Naked Warriors,* 64.
137 "GET THE HELL OUT OF MY FOXHOLE!": Ibid., 64.
138 "FAULTY" and "COMPLETELY OFF HIS BODY": Cunningham, *Frogmen of World War II,* 66.
138 OUT TO SEA, HUDDLED: Godson, *Viking of Assault,* 137.
139 "A DESTROYER LOOMED OUT OF THE SEA": Stephen E. Ambrose, *D-Day: June 6, 1944: The Climactic Battle of World War II* (New York: Simon and Schuster, 2013), 389.
139 "DESTROY IT": Ibid., 137.
139 "THERE WAS ONE ELEMENT": Ibid., *D-Day,* 444.
139 HALL WAS MADE: Godson, *Viking of Assault,* 140.
140 "RUN OFF TO FIGHT": Dunford, *More Than Scuttlebutt,* 242.
140 "OLD MAN" and "THE BASTARDS AND SCREWBALLS": Freeman, letter to Annie, July 16, 1944.
140 CAPPED OFF HIS ALMOST TWELVE HOURS: NCDU, no. 11 After-Action Report; Fane and Moore, *Naked Warriors,* 74.
140 STANCH THE SOLDIER'S WOUNDS: Karnowski, "Account of Naval Combat Demolition Unit no. 45," 20.
141 "I AM VERY GLAD TO HAVE THE OPPORTUNITY": Sec. James Forrestal, "Minutes of Press Conference: Excerpts Covering Naval Combat Demolition Unit Presidential Citation Award," Washington, D.C., September 27, 1944, UDT-SEAL Museum.
141 "THEY SAY HERE CASUALTIES": Ibid.
141 "SEVERE INTERNAL BLEEDING": Cunningham, *Frogmen of World War II,* 69.
141 DEMOLITIONEERS WOUNDED AT OMAHA: Dunford, *More Than Scuttlebutt,* 242 (not including Navy or Army Augmentees).
141 DIFFICULTY IN PLANTING EXPLOSIVES: Forrestal, "Minutes of Press Conference."
142 "I KICKED MYSELF EVER SINCE": "Oral History of Adm. John Leslie Hall, Jr.," 210.

142 "ONLY OUR VIGOROUS TRAINING": Cunningham, *Frogmen of World War II,* 65.

Chapter 5: The Evolving Contest That Created the Mermen of War—World War II's Only Indispensable Special Operations Unit

144 "BRIDGE TO THE BEACH": Michael S. Rosenwald, "D-Day's Hero: Andrew Higgins Loved Bourbon, Cursed a Lot and Built the Boats That Won WWII," *The Washington Post,* June 6, 2017.

144 FIFTEEN-BOAT TRIAL: Anne Cipriano Venzon, *From Whaleboats to Amphibious Warfare: Lt. Gen. "Howling Mad" Smith and the US Marine Corps* (Westport: Praeger, 2003), 65.

144 "RECESSED TUNNEL": Rosenwald, "D-Day's Hero."

144 JAPANESE INVASION OF SHANGHAI: Venzon, *From Whaleboats to Amphibious Warfare,* 65.

144 "THAT'S IT! THAT'S IT!": Robert Coram, "The Bridge to the Beach," HistoryNet.com, November–December 2010, *World War II Magazine,* available at https://www.historynet.com/the-bridge-to-the-beach.htm.

144 "YOU WON'T HAVE THREE FEET!": Ronald H. Spector, *Eagle Against the Sun: The American War with Japan* (New York: Random House, 1985), 260.

145 AN AMPHIBIOUS TRACTOR, AN ALLIGATOR, AN AMTRAC: VAdm. George C. Dyer (USN), *The Amphibians Came to Conquer: The Story of Admiral Richmond Kelly Turner* (Washington, D.C.: US Government Printing Office, 1972), 703.

145 CONCEIVED BY DONALD ROEBLING: Venzon, *From Whaleboats to Amphibious Warfare,* 66.

145 AN ABILITY TO CRAWL: Smith and Finch, *Coral and Brass,* 112.

145 "NO LVTS, NO OPERATION!": Col. Joseph H. Alexander (USMC), *Utmost Savagery: The Three Days of Tarawa* (Annapolis: Naval Institute Press, 1995), 64.

145 1,464 MARINES: Martin Russ, *Line of Departure: Tarawa* (Garden City: Doubleday, 1975), 53.

145 FIVE-HOUR TRANSIT: Alexander, *Utmost Savagery,* 126.

146 STEAK AND EGGS: Russ, *Line of Departure,* 53.

146 PINGED LIKE BELLS: Alexander, *Utmost Savagery,* 92.

146 "THE BROKEN TEETH OF A COMB": Alexander, *Utmost Savagery,* 112.

146 "MY DELORIS": Col. Joseph H. Alexander (USMC), "Across the Reef: The Marine Assault of Tarawa," Marines in World War II Commemorative Series, available at https://www.nps.gov/parkhistory/online_books/npswapa/extcontent/usmc/pcn-190-003120-00/sec1.htm.

146 "SOPRANO WHINE": "Battle of the Pacific: Old Man of the Atolls," *Time,* February 21, 1944.

146 RED-BLACK SHELL: Miller, *D-Days in the Pacific,* loc. 1921.

146 "The water never seemed clear": Alexander, *Utmost Savagery,* 7.
146 1,009 Marines killed: Fane and Moore, *Naked Warriors,* 7.
147 half were identifiable: Miller, *D-Days in the Pacific,* loc. 2115.
147 washed away men's hair: Miller, *D-Days in the Pacific,* loc. 2115.
147 tougher, faster, and more: MGen. M. P. Caulfield (USMC), "Second Marine Division Report on Gilbert Islands Tarawa Operation," December 23, 1943, 74, ibiblio.org/hyperwar/USMC/rep/Tarawa/2dMarDiv-AR.html.
148 "solemn owlish expression": Dyer, *Amphibians Came to Conquer,* 593; Joseph Driscoll, *Pacific Victory* (Philadelphia: Lippincott, 1944), 58–59.
148 country parson: Dyer, *Amphibians Came to Conquer,* 66.
148 schoolmaster: Smith and Finch, *Coral and Brass,* 102.
148 "Courtly in courtesy": Ibid., 102.
148 "As abrasive as a file": Dyer, *Amphibians Came to Conquer,* 66.
148 "loose-jointed": Howard M. Norton, "Admiral Turner's Job Is Putting Them Ashore," *Sunpaper,* February 4, 1942.
148 "down to [its] last soggy half-inch": Dyer, *Amphibians Came to Conquer,* 593; Driscoll, *Pacific Victory,* 58–59.
148 "Damn the torpedoes": Norton, "Admiral Turner's Job."
148 "He is known as the 'Alligator'": Translated Japanese Broadcast, NHHC, papers of Adm. Richmond Kelly Turner, Coll 575, Series IX.
148 A subordinate of Admiral Ghormley: Ulbrich, *Preparing for Victory,* 82.
149 "You son of a bitch": James D. Hornfischer, *Neptune's Inferno: The US Navy at Guadalcanal* (New York: Bantam, 2011), 36.
149 "I had never heard anything like it": Spector, *Eagle Against the Sun,* 191.
149 "It stinks": "Admiral Turner Rated Tops," *S.R. Examiner,* January 23, 1944, NHHC, papers of Adm. Richmond Kelly Turner, Coll 575, Series IX.
149 "without lecturing the coxswain": Spector, *Eagle Against the Sun,* 238.
150 "Without authority": BGen. Samuel B. Griffith II (USMC), *The Battle for Guadalcanal* (Philadelphia: Lippincott, 1963), 141.
150 Fleet Tactical Publication 167: Dyer, *Amphibians Came to Conquer,* 226–227.
150 "By and large naval officers": Spector, *Eagle Against the Sun,* 238.
151 "underwater demolition teams": W. B. Phillips, "Subject: Combat Naval and Troop Demolition Units, COMFIFTHPHIBFORCE" communiqué, December 17, 1943, NHHC, papers of Adm. Richmond Kelly Turner, Coll 575, Series V, Subseries G.
151 Commander John T. Koehler: Author interview with Mathilde Rothwell, August 31, 2014; US Navy Biography of John Theodore Koehler, Assistant Secretary of the Navy.

152 "OUR YEAR OF ATTACK" and COMPOSED OF MORE THAN THIRTY ATOLLS: "Year of Attack," *Time,* February 7, 1944.

152 LIKE THE TWELVE SPIES: Bruce F. Meyers, *Swift, Silent, and Deadly: Marine Amphibious Reconnaissance in the Pacific, 1942–1945* (Annapolis: Naval Institute Press, 2004), 45–61.

152 PROVISIONAL UDTS DID NOT IMPRESS: Cdr. E. D. Brewster (USN), "Report on Underwater Demolition—Southern Flintlock Operation," February 8, 1944, NARA, RG 38, entry WWII Action and Operational Reports, box 787.

152 FIFTY MILES NORTH: Fane and Moore, *Naked Warriors,* 35.

152 THE NEXT DAY: O'Dell, *The Water Is Never Cold,* 137.

153 "THE ENTIRE ISLAND LOOKED": Dyer, *Amphibians Came to Conquer,* 798.

154 "THE JAPANESE SEEMED UNAWARE": Dyer, *Amphibians Came to Conquer,* 792.

154 "WE HAVE CERTAIN THEORIES": "The Way to Tokyo," *Time,* January 31, 1944.

154 BABY SATAN: "World: Mop-Up on Kwajalein," *Time,* February 21, 1944.

154 "BLASTING ENEMY STRONG POINTS": Brewster, "Report on Underwater Demolition."

154 "ONE VESSEL TO BE USED": Brewster, "Report on Underwater Demolition."

155 "SHOULD NOT BE ATTACHED": Memorandum for Admiral Turner, RAdm. R. L. Conolly (note sent prior to December 23, 1943), NHHC, papers of Adm. Richmond Kelly Turner, Coll 575, Series V.

155 "WHEN I CAME BACK": Spector, *Eagle Against the Sun,* 302; Dyer, *Amphibians Came to Conquer,* 853.

155 "LISTENED WITH UTMOST ENTHUSIASM": J. H. Doyle, letter to Turner, February 24, 1944, NHHC, papers of Adm. Richmond Kelly Turner, Coll 575, Series V.

155 "HIS BABY": Lt. D. J. Wrysinski (USNR), letter to Turner, June 30, 1953, NHHC, papers of Adm. Richmond Kelly Turner, Coll 575, Series VII.

155 "SOMETHING ENTIRELY NEW": Turner, letter to Kauffman, March 17, 1960, courtesy of Kauffman family.

155 TO CREATE EXACTLY THE KIND: "Command History of Naval Combat Demolition Training and Experimental Base," undated, courtesy of UDT-SEAL Museum and NHHC, RG 38, entry UD-09D-19.

156 "COOKS WHO NEVER COOKED": Higgins, *Webfooted Warriors,* 11; "Command History of Naval Combat Demolition Training and Experimental Base."

156 HE HAD NEVER EVEN LIKED SWIMMING: Patrick K. O'Donnell, *First SEALs: The Untold Story of the Forging of America's Most Elite Unit,* Kindle edition (Boston: Da Capo Press, 2014), loc. 42.

156 "WEE HOURS OF THE MORNING": Dunford, *More Than Scuttlebutt,* 57.

156 "THE BRAIN": Elizabeth Bush, interview with Dan Dillon, August 22, 1985.

156 "COMBINATION OF DON QUIXOTE AND RICHARD THE LIONHEARTED": R. C. Packard Speech, undated, courtesy of Kauffman family.

157 "ASHORE AGAINST HEAVY OPPOSITION": Turner, letter to Kauffman, March 17, 1960, courtesy of Kauffman family.

157 "THE FIRST AND MOST IMPORTANT THING": *Reminiscences of R. Adm. Draper L. Kauffman,* no. 2, 187.

157 ROUGH RUBBER EDGES SANDED DOWN: Dunford, *More Than Scuttlebutt,* 87.

157 WHAT FOLLOWED: "Command History of Naval Combat Demolition Training and Experimental Base."

157 "ROCKS, CORAL": Higgins, *Webfooted Warriors,* 47.

157 SIX HOURS A DAY: O'Dell, *The Water Is Never Cold,* 145.

157 "WHEN POSSIBLE": O'Dell, *The Water Is Never Cold,* 145; Higgins, *Webfooted Warriors,* 48.

157 "FINGERS BLOWN CLEAR OFF": Higgins, *Webfooted Warriors,* 53.

157 "WITH 100 POUNDS": Bush, *America's First Frogman,* 121.

157 FLAT-TRAJECTORY FIRE: Ibid., 123.

158 SOME RECENTLY ENLISTED SEABEES: Higgins, *Webfooted Warriors,* 10.

158 "GO BACK IN THERE": Dyer, *Amphibians Came to Conquer,* 894.

158 "MISERABLE": Cunningham, *Frogmen of World War II,* 260.

158 NEVER UTTERED A WORD OF PROTEST: Kauffman Recollections, undated, courtesy of Kauffman Family.

158 "LOTS OF LOVE": Bush, *America's First Frogman,* 128.

158 "SAIPAN LOOKED LIKE": Sherrod, "Beachhead in the Marianas," July 3, 1944.

159 "HONOLULU SEEN THROUGH": "Saipan New Phase in War in Pacific," *Time,* June 16, 1944.

159 STRADDLED BY PLUMES: UDT 5 Official History, UDT-SEAL Museum and NARA, RG 38, WWII Action and Operational Reports, box 788.

159 "CAFÉ ROYALE": Ens. Robert P. Marshall (CEC USNR), "Notes Prepared at the Time of Action," UDT 5, courtesy of UDT/SEAL Museum.

160 "FROM TOE TO CHIN": Fane and Moore, *Naked Warriors,* 95.

160 TWO LEAD PENCILS: Marshall, "Notes Prepared at the Time of Action."

160 SANDBLASTED PLEXIGLASS SLATE: Higgins, *Webfooted Warriors,* 49.

160 THE DUAL WAKES: UDT 5 Unit History.

160 TURNED SHARPLY: Marshall, "Notes Prepared at the Time of Action."

160 TWENTY-SIX CONSECUTIVE PLUMES: Fane and Moore, *Naked Warriors,* 95.

160 REEL OF FISHING LINE: O'Dell, *The Water Is Never Cold,* 141.

161 "I WAS THE CENTER OF ATTENTION": Marshall, "Notes Prepared at the Time of Action."

161 "HIS SEEING EYE": *Reminiscences of R. Adm. Draper L. Kauffman,* no. 2, 196.
161 630 BINOCULARS: UDT 5 History.
161 BLOWGUN 5: Marshall, "Notes Prepared at the Time of Action."
161 "FOR GOD'S SAKE": *Reminiscences of R. Adm. Draper L. Kauffman,* no. 2, 207–208.
161 USS *CALIFORNIA* WAS HIT: UDT 5 Unit History.
161 DITCHING THEIR LIFE BELTS, THEN "DOLPHINING": Marshall, "Notes Prepared at the Time of Action."
161 SOUVENIRS: Sgt. Harry J. Tomlinson (USA), "Paddlefoot Commandos," *Yank: The Army Weekly,* November 16, 1945, vol. 4, no. 22, 10–11.
161 TREE-LIMB-FASHIONED TRIPODS: Marshall, "Notes Prepared at the Time of Action."
162 BLOWN COMPLETELY OUT OF THE WATER: UDT 5 History.
162 "POINT-BLANK": Fane and Moore, *Naked Warriors,* 97; UDT 5 History.
162 PULLING THEMSELVES ALONG: Marshall, "Notes Prepared at the Time of Action"; UDT 5 Unit History.
162 "GET THAT DAMNED THING": Fane and Moore, *Naked Warriors,* 98.
163 "VOCIFEROUS": Marshall, "Notes Prepared at the Time of Action"; UDT 5 Unit History.
163 WHEN A CRUISER REPORTED: *Reminiscences of R. Adm. Draper L. Kauffman,* no. 2, 197–199.
164 DECIPHERED THE PENCIL SCRATCHES and NO FEWER THAN EIGHT HOLES: UDT 5 History.
164 INSTANTLY HUSTLED BEFORE TURNER: *Reminiscences of R. Adm. Draper L. Kauffman,* no. 2, 199–200.
164 "WHOSE TANKS DO YOU": Ibid., 199–201; Fane and Moore, *Naked Warriors,* 102.
164 AN HOUR AFTER THAT: Alexander, *Storm Landings,* 84.
164 CLOSE BEHIND: Fane and Moore, *Naked Warriors,* 103.
165 DRESSED AS CONSPICUOUSLY AS TOURISTS: Ibid., 104.
165 IT WOULD BE SEVERAL DAYS: Marshall, "Notes Prepared at the Time of Action."
165 "I DON'T THINK THERE ARE THREE MEN": *Reminiscences of R. Adm. Draper L. Kauffman,* no. 3, 210–214.
165 "HIS OWN ALL-AMERICAN FOOTBALL TEAM": UDT 5 History.
165 NOR DID HE HAVE: Fane and Moore, *Naked Warriors,* 107–108.
166 KAUFFMAN HAD ONLY MADE THEM: Bush, *America's First Frogman,* 148.
166 CAPTAIN JACK TAYLOR APPEARED: *Reminiscences of R. Adm. Draper L. Kauffman,* no. 3, 210–213.
166 "NOW, JUST CALM DOWN" and *JACKS OF ALL TRADES:* Ibid., 212–213.
166 "HEDGEHOPPING": Fane and Moore, *Naked Warriors,* 123.
167 "INFINITESIMAL": Smith and Finch, *Coral and Brass,* 192.
167 "YOU CAN'T POSSIBLY LAND": Ibid., 193.

167 "You are not going to land": Richard Harwood, *A Close Encounter: The Marine Landing on Tinian* (Washington, D.C.: US Government Printing Office, 1994), 6.

167 "We'll send Draper": *Reminiscences of R. Adm. Draper L. Kauffman*, no. 3, 215–217.

168 Magicienne Bay: Harwood, *Close Encounter*.

168 dummy mines: UDT 5 History.

168 condom-encased penlights and dye packets: Fane and Moore, *Naked Warriors,* 124.

168 Aboard the *Stringham:* Harwood, *Close Encounter.*

168 admittedly swam badly: Bush, *America's First Frogman,* 140.

168 In charge of the reconnaissance: "World Battlefronts: 379-Mile Hop," *Time,* February 28, 1944.

168 "Pin-up": *Reminiscences of R. Adm. Draper L. Kauffman,* no. 3, 221.

168 recovered as blondes: Fane and Moore, *Naked Warriors,* 127.

168 coughs had been silenced: Ibid., 125.

169 designated as Yellow Beach: Harwood, *Close Encounter;* Fane and Moore, *Naked Warriors,* 125.

169 White 1: Fane and Moore, *Naked Warriors,* 126.

170 wrapping a garrote: Ibid., 127.

170 silently circle until confirming: Ibid., 127.

170 "How many blondes?": Ibid., 127.

170 At around 0430: *Reminiscences of R. Adm. Draper L. Kauffman,* no. 3, 221–222.

170 reflect off his dive mask: Fane and Moore, *Naked Warriors,* 127.

171 a ratio reversed: Ibid., 128.

171 reflectors made of wire and SCR-200 radios: Mosher, "Amphibious Scouts and Raiders."

171 Pressing his hands: *Reminiscences of R. Adm. Draper L. Kauffman,* no. 3, 232.

171 "as big as houses": Fane and Moore, *Naked Warriors,* 128.

171 "so mean and cantankerous": Dyer, *Amphibians Came to Conquer,* 957.

171 held his breath: Ibid., 956.

171 it was clear that Smith: *Reminiscences of R. Adm. Draper L. Kauffman,* no. 3, 223.

172 The ploy worked: Bush, *America's First Frogman,* 145.

172 At 0717: Harwood, *Close Encounter,* 7.

173 So fast and unexpected: Dyer, *Amphibians Came to Conquer,* 949–969; *Reminiscences of R. Adm. Draper L. Kauffman,* no. 3, 236; Fane and Moore, *Naked Warriors,* 131.

173 1,500 yards inland: Mosher, "Amphibious Scouts and Raiders."

173 "fatal to the Jap mentality": Smith and Finch, *Coral and Brass,* 191.

173 eleven tons of special equipment: Cdr. R. Davis Halliwell,

USNR, letter to Charles S. Cheston, OSS Assistant Director, June 7, 1945, courtesy of NARA.

174 "[The UDTs] are an essential": Turner, letter to W. B. Philips, August 1, 1944, NHHC, papers of Adm. Richmond Kelly Turner, Coll 575, Series VII.

174 640 obstacles: Meyers, *Swift, Silent, and Deadly,* 87.

174 3,000 yards of beaches: Tomlinson, "Paddlefoot Commandos."

174 "landings could not have been made": Fane and Moore, *Naked Warriors,* 122.

174 "U.S. MARINES, WELCOME TO USO": Tomlinson, "Paddlefoot Commandos."

174 "Wait till I tell Turner": Bush, *America's First Frogman,* 148.

174 "the largest mass recommendation": Ibid., 150.

174 "importance of the job": Fane and Moore, *Naked Warriors,* 122.

174 presented by none other: Bush, *America's First Frogman,* 147.

174 rumors circulated: Author interview with Draper Kauffman, Jr.

174 awards board: Bush, *America's First Frogman,* 157.

174 "Thank the Lord": Ibid., 157.

175 Owen Churchill–patented swim fins: Higgins, *Webfooted Warriors,* 47.

175 "flight-speed tempo": Dunford, *More Than Scuttlebutt,* 56.

175 "could lick any man": Fane and Moore, *Naked Warriors,* 159.

175 "the only guy who didn't": *Reminiscences of R. Adm. Draper L. Kauffman,* no. 3, 263.

175 "Have patience with screwball ideas": Fane and Moore, *Naked Warriors,* 159.

176 "into a big business": Turner, letter to Ping Wilkinson, December 5, 1944, NHHC, papers of Adm. Richmond Kelly Turner, Coll 575, Series VII.

176 "The results achieved": Fane and Moore, *Naked Warriors,* 169; Bush, *America's First Frogman,* 156.

176 With no pressing need: Lt. L. J. Gibboney (USNR), "Maritime Unit, Group A, OSS; Combat Operations with UDT 10 from August 10, 1944, to April 16, 1945," May 23, 1945 (OSS Maritime Unit, Group A Command History), NARA, RG 226, entry A1 139, miscellaneous files, file 1.

176 including the white-knuckling: Gibboney, "Maritime Unit, Group A, OSS."

177 "Golden Horseshoe": Fane and Moore, *Naked Warriors,* 154.

177 cocoa butter: Dick Camp, *Iwo Jima Recon: The US Navy at War, February 17, 1945* (St. Paul: Zenith Press, 2007), 99–100.

177 Making up this army: Fane and Moore, *Naked Warriors,* 174.

177 "falling leaves": Ibid., 177.

177 timing his breaths: Camp, *Iwo Jima Recon,* 112.

177 smoked ashore and "shake his fist": Tomlinson, "Paddlefoot Commandos."

178 "ZIGZAG ORANGE": Fane and Moore, *Naked Warriors,* 174.
178 SHREDDING THE BULKHEADS: Camp, *Iwo Jima Recon,* 79.
179 FLIMSY RINGS: Ibid., 77.
179 HANDS STITCHED WITH SHRAPNEL: Ibid., 79, 86.
179 "CLIMBED TO THE CONNING TOWER": LTJG Charles Crandall, LCIG 471, quoted in Camp, *Iwo Jima Recon,* 96.
179 "[LIKE] A GENERAL WHO HAD HIS HORSE": Fane and Moore, *Naked Warriors,* 176.
179 "RETURN TO THE FIRING LINE": Camp, *Iwo Jima Recon,* 80.
179 JUST TWO UDT SWIMMERS: The MIA swimmer was A. E. Anderson, and Boatman Frank W. Sumpter was shot through the head by a sniper while extracting. Fane and Moore, *Naked Warriors,* 179.
179 LOSSES HAD TOTALED: Ibid., 176.
180 HIS BORROWED SHOES: Ibid., 176.
180 THREE MEN ABOARD: Camp, *Iwo Jima Recon,* 87.
180 THREE HUNDRED COPIES: Ibid., 116.
181 NIGHTTIME KAMIKAZES: Kauffman, 266.
181 ONE BLOND UDT PETTY OFFICER: Fane and Moore, *Naked Warriors,* 203.
181 "FREEZING BY INCHES": Higgins, *Webfooted Warriors,* 63.
181 "THE INCESSANT MACHINE GUN FIRE": Ibid., 61.
181 "SMALL HEAVEN": Ibid., 63.
181 JUST HAPPENED TO COINCIDE: Ibid., 55.
182 SHOULDER-WORN: Ibid., 60.
182 ENSIGN ROBERT KILLOUGH: Fane and Moore, *Naked Warriors,* 193.
182 "I WAS PERFECTLY SAFE": Ibid., 207.
182 AT MAUI IN JUNE: Dunford, *More Than Scuttlebutt,* 95.
182 MARINE CORPS VOLUNTEERS: Fresh from combat in a mountain artillery unit, my grandfather—PFC Harry Hirschman, USMC—was one of these volunteers.
182 SPLICING MAUI'S TRAINING: Edwin P. Hoyt, *SEALs at War: The Story of US Naval Special Warfare from the Frogmen to the SEALs,* Kindle edition (New York: Dell Books, 1993), loc. 1691.
183 "I AM THE COMMANDING OFFICER" and "I KNEW IT WAS": Comments by RAdm. Draper L. Kauffman, October, 1975, courtesy of Kauffman family.
183 EVEN THE IRREPRESSIBLE ERNIE PYLE: Bush, *America's First Frogman,* 183.
184 "THE FIRST LINE!" and "SHIPS, PLANES AND SUBMARINES": Arthur Meyerhoff & Company, Chicago, Radio Script, WBBM–CBS, October 25, 1945, courtesy of Kauffman family.
184 A SCANT 126 POUNDS: Bush, *America's First Frogman,* 187; *Reminiscences of R. Adm. Draper L. Kauffman,* no. 3, 273.
185 THIRTEEN-DAY, TWELVE-NIGHT BRANDY-FUELED BASH: *Reminiscences of R. Adm. Draper L. Kauffman,* no. 3, 282–285.
185 ALL THE WAY TO A FUTURE: Bush, *America's First Frogman,* 187.

185 "I WOULD LIKE VERY MUCH TO WORK": Kauffman, letter to VAdm. Blandy, January 29, 1946, courtesy of Kauffman family.

185 PROOFREADING MANUSCRIPTS: Don Moore, letter to Kauffman, March 2, 1966, courtesy of Kauffman family.

185 "LOSS OF STATURE": Henry E. Coe, letter to Kauffman, Farrar, Straus, & Young, Inc., Publishers, December 16, 1952, courtesy of Kauffman family.

185 "ITS MARINE CORPS": Fane and Moore, *Naked Warriors,* iii–v.

185 "SENTIMENTAL AS AN OLD WOMAN": Untitled/undated newspaper article, by AP reporter Leif Erickson, January 14, NHHC, papers of Adm. Richmond Kelly Turner, Coll 575, Series IX.

186 "OR EVEN APPROACHED": Kauffman, letter to Turner, March 12, 1960, courtesy of Kauffman family.

186 "THE UDTS TURNED OUT": Turner, letter to Kauffman, March 17, 1960, courtesy of Kauffman family.

186 "GRANDPAPPY BULLFROG": *Reminiscences of R. Adm. Draper L. Kauffman,* no. 3, 280.

186 GENEROUS MENTORSHIP: Rick Woolard, email to author, December 15, 2017.

186 SERVICE INSIGNIA and "WITH PLEASURE": Kauffman, letter to Chief of Naval Personnel, "Subject: Request Authority to Wear UDT and EOD Insignia," May 14, 1970; Sheldon H. Kinney (Asst. Chief for Education and Training), letter to Kauffman, "Subject: Authorization for Wearing of UDT and EOD Officer Breast Insignia," June 12, 1970, courtesy of Kauffman family.

186 BUDAPEST and NAVAL ACADEMY CHAPEL: Bush, *America's First Frogman,* 201–202.

Chapter 6: The Contest for the Guerrilla War in China and the Organization That Had "No Damn Business" Fighting in It: The US Navy's Army of Sailors

187 "BESTIAL": Gunther E. Rothenberg, *The Napoleonic Wars* (New York: HarperCollins, 1999), 157.

187 "NO IRREGULARS": Adm. Milton E. Miles (USN), *A Different Kind of War: The Little Known Story of the Combined Guerrilla Forces Created in China by the US Navy and the Chinese During World War II* (New York: Doubleday, 1967), 86.

188 "EAST COAST FAGGOTS": Waller, *Wild Bill Donovan,* loc. 93.

188 "A CLOAK AND DAGGER STORY": Cdr. Roy Olin Stratton (USN), *Saco—The Rice Paddy Navy* (Pleasantville: C. S. Palmer Publishing, 1950).

189 "WE ARE GOING TO HAVE TOUGH" to "HECKLE": Miles, *Different Kind of War,* 18.

189 BORN MILTON E. ROBBINS: Cdr. Roy Olin Stratton (USN), *The Army-Navy Games* (Falmouth: Volta, 1977), 14.

189 "THE WICKEDEST TOWN": Michael Price, "Jerome: A Ghost Town That

Never Gave Up the Ghost," *Travels in Geology*, January 2007, available at http://www.geotimes.org/jan07/Travels0107.html.

190 GRADUATED FORTY-FOURTH: Stratton, *Army-Navy Games,* 15.

190 NEARLY ORANGE WATERS: Ibid., 61.

191 "OUT OF A HOLD UP": Miles, *Different Kind of War,* 247.

191 PACKED FIVE SUITCASES: Stratton, *Army-Navy Games,* 15.

191 HITCHING, DRIVING, SAILING and "DADDY, THERE AREN'T VERY MANY": Stratton, *Saco,* 28–30.

191 DURING THE FLIGHT: Capt. Milton E. Miles (USN), "US Naval Group, China," *Proceedings Magazine,* vol. 72/7/521, July 1946, 125–128.

191 THERE, MILES STARED UP: Stratton, *Army-Navy Games,* 61; Stratton, *Saco,* 65.

192 "SELDOM PHOTOGRAPHED, NEVER INTERVIEWED": LCdr. Charles G. Dobbins (USN), "China's Mystery Man," *Collier's,* February 16, 1946; Stratton, *Saco,* 8; Gen. Joseph W. Stilwell, *The Stilwell Papers,* ed. Theodore H. White (New York: Da Capo Press, 1948), 220.

192 "THOUGHT POLICE" and "HIMMLER OF CHINA" and MURDER OF HIS MOTHER: Dobbins, "China's Mystery Man."

192 THAT HE NOW INSISTED: *Reminiscences of Captain Phil Bucklew,* no. 3, 166; no. 4, 175.

192 "HE'S A SKUNK": Stratton, *Army-Navy Games,* 23.

192 "COMMANDER MILES HAS GOTTEN OFF": Maochun Yu, *The Dragon's War: Allied Operations and the Fate of China, 1937–1947,* Kindle edition (Annapolis: Naval Institute Press, 2006), loc. 1654.

192 TAI LI ALTERNATELY INTRODUCED: Miles, "US Naval Group, China."

193 ONE PREDAWN MORNING: Dobbins, "China's Mystery Man"; Miles, "US Naval Group, China."

193 "OK": Miles, *Different Kind of War,* 51–53.

193 "THE MOST IMPORTANT GUN BATTLE": Linda Kush, *The Rice Paddy Navy: US Sailors Undercover in China* (New York: Osprey Publishing, 2012), 55.

193 "YOU SHOULD STICK TO THE SEA": Miles, *Different Kind of War,* 73–74.

194 WHAT FOLLOWED WAS: Yu, *Dragon's War,* loc. 1893; Stratton, *Army-Navy Games,* 49.

194 "ILLEGAL ACTION" and "RUNNING LOOSE IN HIS THEATER": Miles, *Different Kind of War,* 76.

194 "THE MOST FOR THE LEAST": Ibid., 76.

194 "I'LL TELL THE BOYS": Ibid., 77.

195 HE FOUND 200 ACRES: Stratton, *Saco,* 13.

195 IN SEPTEMBER 1942: S. Shepherd Tate, "The Rice Paddy Navy: SACO and the China I Knew," *Experience,* Spring 2003; Clayton Mishler, *Sampan Sailor: A Navy Man's Adventures in WWII China* (Washington, D.C.: Brassey's, 1994), 50–51.

195 COTS OF INTERLACED ROPES: Mishler, *Sampan Sailor,* 50–51.

195 A CRISSCROSSING SYSTEM: Stratton, *Saco,* 224.

195 To prevent dysentery: Miles, *Different Kind of War,* 139.
195 Maybe the worst feature: Mishler, *Sampan Sailor,* 53.
195 triangular white pennant and "What the hell?": Miles, *Different Kind of War,* 137.
196 list of don'ts and "Treat the Chinese": Yu, *Dragon's War,* locs. 1780–1781.
196 "No high hat": Yu, *Dragon's War,* locs. 1742–1744.
196 "foreigners' contempt": Miles request for recruits, SACO Papers, undated, NARA, Records of US Naval Group China and VAdm Milton E. Miles, 1942–1957, RG 38, entry NHC-75.
196 "The less our recruits know": Miles request for recruits.
196 "fight the Nips": Ibid.
196 "[Volunteers] must be slightly crazy": Ibid.
197 but always "Mary": Stratton, *Army-Navy Games,* 100–101.
197 "You are expected to learn Chinese": Stratton, *Army-Navy Games,* 100–101.
197 crippling pace: *Reminiscences of Captain Phil Bucklew,* no. 3, 145.
197 To officers returning: Stratton, *Army-Navy Games,* 100–101.
197 "goddamn": Miles, *Different Kind of War,* 203.
197 "But he had the personality": Stratton, *Army-Navy Games,* 155; taken from RAdm. Walter G. Ebert (then a LCdr.), a submariner liaison to SACO.
197 "shoes filled with blood": US Information Service, "Chinese and American SACO Directors Had Highest Priced Heads in Orient," September 14, 1945, NARA, RG 38, entry NHC-75.
198 "left a blur of color": Miles, *Different Kind of War,* 89.
198 a plan to parachute: Stratton, *Army-Navy Games,* 56.
198 Miles offered Hayden: Miles, *Different Kind of War,* 87–90.
198 "Mary has a lot of nerve": Stratton, *Army-Navy Games,* 69.
198 "a renegade white man": Yu, *Dragon's War,* locs. 1795–1796; Adm. Milton E. Miles (USN), *The Navy Launched a Dragon,* unpublished manuscript, undated, US Naval War College, Naval Historical Collection MSC26, Miles Papers: box 11, 62.
198 "A big-hearted gent, that Marshall": Miles, *Different Kind of War,* 113.
198 "After investigation": Yu, *Dragon's War,* locs. 1965–1969.
199 When Miles and Metzel: Miles, *Different Kind of War,* 114–115.
200 "We're no longer bastard": Ibid., 116.
200 "socko": Sino-American Special Technical Cooperation Agreement, NARA, RG 38, entry NHC-75, box 3.
200 "Every time we meet": Yu, *Dragon's War,* loc. 1697.
200 "Brigadier General of the Sea": Miles, *Different Kind of War,* 250.
200 "belly laugh": Ibid., 218.
201 beat-up trucks: Mishler, *Sampan Sailor,* 54.
201 "about tigers": Miles, *Different Kind of War,* 148.
201 barely visible roads: Stratton, *Saco,* 79.

201 "300 PER CENT": Miles, *Different Kind of War,* 153.
201 "THE WALKING DOOMED": Robert J. Hoe, letter to John B. Dwyer, May 6, 1994, in Papers of John B. Dwyer, courtesy of James Barnes.
201 TYPICAL MAILBAG: Miles, "US Naval Group, China."
202 MILES SECURED FOUR DC-4: The Navy variant of the DC-4 was an R5D. Miles, *Different Kind of War,* 128.
202 "WITH SUPPLIES ROLLING": Metzel, letter to Miles, August 24, 1943, NARA, RG 38, entry NHC-75, box 1; Stratton, *Army-Navy Games,* 108.
202 FORCED TO NEGOTIATE: Maj. C. M. Parkin, Jr. (USMC), message from Commander Pao of the 7th Commando Group, October 25, 1943, NARA, RG 38, entry NHC-75, box 15.
202 "I SHOT THE CHINESE GENERAL RESPONSIBLE": Stratton, *Army-Navy Game*, 137.
203 WHERE HE HAD HUMBLY AFFIXED: Waller, *Wild Bill Donovan,* loc. 152.
203 ACCOMPANIED BY AN ENTOURAGE: Miles, letter to Metzel, December 10, 1943, NARA, RG 38, entry NHC-75, box 1; Waller, *Wild Bill Donovan,* loc. 214.
204 "FAR TOO HEAVY": Waller, *Wild Bill Donovan,* loc. 212.
204 "HARANGUED ON THREE SIDES": Miles, letter to Metzel, December 10, 1943.
204 A NIGHT OF WINE, FOOD, AND SINGING: Ibid.
204 TAI LI OFFERED DONOVAN: Waller, *Wild Bill Donovan,* locs. 212–213.
204 "YELLED AND BECAME UNGENTLEMANLIKE": Miles, letter to Metzel, December 10, 1943.
204 "IF OSS TRIES TO OPERATE": Waller, *Wild Bill Donovan,* loc. 212–213.
204 SHOUT WITH A LOWERED VOICE: Miles, letter to Metzel, December 10, 1943.
205 "HUMPTY DUMPTY [HE] HAD BROKEN": Miles, *Different Kind of War,* 172.
205 TEN BATTALIONS OF GUERRILLAS: Miles, letter to Metzel, December 20, 1943, NARA, RG 38, entry NHC-75, box 1.
205 "THE NAVY WAS [NOW] PERFORMING": Adm. Frederick J. Horne (USN), "Aide Memoire of SACO Meeting with Admiral Horne, VCNO," February 23, 1944, NARA, RG 38, entry NHC-75, box 1.
205 "I SHOULD BE RELIEVED IN CHINA": Miles, *Different Kind of War,* 207.
205 "WE KNOW YOU WANT TO GO TO SEA": Ibid., 206.
205 "HAPPY BIRTHDAY, MARY!": Ibid., 207.
206 INCREASING HIS ROLLS TO 600 OFFICERS: Adm. Frederick J. Horne (USN), "Operating Force Plan 1945–46—Personnel Requirements for NAVGROUP, China, Memorandum for CNO," August 3, 1944, RG 38, entry NHC-75, box 17.
206 GAS ALONE FOR THESE PLANES: Miles, *Different Kind of War,* 273; Stratton, *Army-Navy Games,* 148.

206 a small, blue-eyed thirty-one-year-old: Stratton, *Army-Navy Games,* 66.

206 "He don't look so tough": "Enumerated Manifest with Personality Profiles of Personnel Assigned to SACO," undated, NARA, RG 38, entry NHC-75, box 1.

207 "standing-room-only": Miles, *Different Kind of War,* 216.

207 "consorting with the wrong type": Stratton, *Army-Navy Games,* 151.

208 hero's gauntlet: Dobbins, "China's Mystery Man."

208 "He looks like a Chinese": Miles, *Different Kind of War,* 215.

208 "explosive argument": Dobbins, "China's Mystery Man."

208 "This is the green light": Miles, *Different Kind of War,* 292.

208 the typical preparation: Mishler, *Sampan Sailor.*

208 specially designed psychological evaluation: Charles Miles, email to author, November 9, 2020.

208 held together by a spine of Marines: SACO Friendship Action Report, April 30, 1945, NARA, RG 38, entry NHC-75.

208 "We have a clique": Miles, letter to Metzel, December 29, 1943, NARA, RG 38, entry NHC-75, box 1.

209 "divided equally between": COMINCH order to COMPHIBTRALANT, "Subject: Fort Pierce," August 4, 1944, NARA, RG 38, entry NHC-75, box 17.

209 good digestive system and "Officers must combine": COMINCH US Fleet and CNO Letter to Commander in Chief, US Atlantic Fleet, "Subject: Amphibious Training for Special Project," undated, NARA, RG 38, entry NHC-75, box 17.

209 finished off by a raid: Dwyer, *Scouts and Raiders,* 147.

209 "substitute": Adm. W. R. Purnell (USN), letter to Chief of the Bureau of Naval Personnel, "Subject: Orders for Enlisted Men in Training at Amphibious Training Base, Fort Pierce, Fla.—Request For," December 21, 1944, NARA, RG 38, entry NHC-75, box 17.

209 "dissolved": Capt. Clarence Gulbranson (USN) to Cdr. of Amphib Training Command, Atlantic Fleet, February 8, 1945, NARA, RG 38, entry NHC-75, box 17.

210 "the most outstanding": RAdm. Milton E. Miles (USN), Memo to Capt. Clarence Gulbranson (USN), "Subject: Amphibious Roger Training," March 27, 1945, NARA, RG 38, entry NHC-75, box 17.

211 "swallowed a lump": Miles, *Different Kind of War,* 335.

211 "I just stumbled": Ibid., 344–345.

211 "Big Brain": "Big Brain," *Time,* June 25, 1951.

211 "coordination" and "Nimitz does not have": Miles, *Different Kind of War,* 437–441.

212 Friends since their days: Ibid., 475.

212 "What is the Navy doing": Ibid., 437.

212 "a seagoing sailor": Ibid., 447.

212 "slopes": Ibid., 452.

212 "a rather embarrassing problem" and "Commodore Miles": Gen. Albert C. Wedemeyer, *Wedemeyer Reports* (Auckland, New Zealand: Pickle Partners Publishing, 1958), loc. 6330.

212 "I am in favor": Miles, *Different Kind of War,* 456.

213 "well hemmed": Stratton, *Saco,* 221.

213 bean curd sampans and "a strange feeling of relief": Ibid.

213 Marco Polo: Frank Ruggieri, letter to Barry Dwyer, August 23, 1984, Dwyer Papers, courtesy of James Barnes.

213 an abandoned American mission: Mishler, *Sampan Sailor,* 111, 121.

213 shared their space with the snorts: Stratton, *Saco,* 222.

213 Chinese temple large enough: LCdr. William J. Birthright, letter to Miles, undated, response to Miles, letter to Birthright, August 22, 1944, NARA, RG 38, entry NHC-75, box 17.

214 "Since you are to be tangled": RAdm. Milton E. Miles (USN), letter to LCdr. Birthright, August 22, 1944, NARA, RG 38, entry NHC-75, box 1.

214 "issued orders right and left" and pistol shooting contest: Mishler, *Sampan Sailor,* 164.

214 a patch of high ground and "luxury": Stratton, *Saco,* 224.

214 classes on ship and plane identification: Ibid., 223.

215 collecting the hot brass: Mishler, *Sampan Sailor,* 56.

215 skies unleashed forty-seven days and "unpleasant bathtub" and "cultivated" and "off and on key": Stratton, *Saco,* 225.

215 images of salacious women: Ibid., 224.

215 "Get the Americans Drunk": Mishler, *Sampan Sailor,* 124.

215 "backing a tortoise": Miles, *Different Kind of War,* 499.

215 Dead End Kids: Ibid., 492.

215 "ideal" and "sorely needed combat experience": Unit Six War Diary, January 1 to 15, 1945, signed Lt. Robert J. Jantzen, NARA, RG 38, entry NHC-75, box 17.

215 "as they are the only men qualified": Ibid.

216 Wearing a peaked cap: Stratton, *Saco,* 227.

216 invasions that had claimed: Connery, "Unsung 200."

216 "top secret within a top secret": Ibid.

216 "[A job] which not one man": *Canadian Jewish Chronicle,* June 16, 1944.

217 Navy's Interior Control Board and "gave him the business": Connery, "Unsung 200."

217 "participate directly in combat action": Hoe, August 30, 1993.

217 Every Man a Tiger: Miles, *Different Kind of War,* 499.

218 "Bam Bam Boo": Stratton, *Saco,* 227.

218 many of his guerrilla trainees racked: Unit Six War Diary, January 16 to 31, 1945, NARA, RG 38, NHC-75, box 17.

218 change of clothing: Unit Six War Diary, February 1 to 15, 1945, NARA, RG 38, NHC-75, box 17.

218 AN INEXPLICABLE HABIT: Unit Six War Diary, January 16 to 31, 1945, NARA, RG 38, NHC-75, box 17.

218 "RESTLESS": Miles, *Different Kind of War,* 431.

218 LOST A MUSETTE BAG: Unit Six War Diary, February 1 to 15, 1945, NARA, RG 38, NHC-75, box 17.

218 FIRST ORDER OF BUSINESS: Ibid.

219 "GREATLY ELONGATED PREPUCE" and GOLD EQUIVALENT and SANDALS: Unit Six War Diary, February 15 to 28, 1945, NARA, RG 38, NHC-75, box 17.

219 TWO-DAY MOCK BATTLE: Ibid.

219 UMPIRED ON HORSEBACK: Stratton, *Saco,* 228.

219 "THE ELEMENT OF SURPRISE": Unit Six War Diary, February 1 to 15, 1945, NARA, RG 38, NHC-75, box 17.

219 ONE OF HIS OWN RADIOMEN: Unit Six War Diary, February 16 to 28, 1945, NARA, RG 38, NHC-75, box 17.

219 FIRST NIGHTTIME RAID: Unit Six War Diary, March 16 to 31, 1945, NARA, RG 38, NHC-75, box 17.

219 AS IT HAPPENED: Ibid.; Stratton, *Saco,* 228.

220 "THOSE DIRECTLY ESSENTIAL": Miles, *Different Kind of War,* 458.

220 "ROADBLOCKS" and MORE HOURS THAN HE HAD EVER and "ACCEPTABLE": Ibid., 461.

220 "LITTLE PENTAGON" and NAVY SHOULD HAVE A SEAT: Ibid., 462.

220 "PROSECUTE THE WAR": Miles, RAdm. Milton E. Miles (USN), letter of instruction to staff of Naval Group China, March 20, 1945, NARA, RG 38, entry NHC-75, box 17.

221 "GO OUT OF EXISTENCE": Adm. Jeffrey Metzel (USN), "Naval Message: COMINCH to COMNAVGRCHINA," May 25, 1945, NARA, RG 38, entry NHC-75, box 17.

221 "MALICIOUS GADGETS" and "UNDESIRABLE PERSONS": Stratton, *Saco,* 227.

221 AGGRESSIVE AND CAN-DO: Miles, *Different Kind of War,* 430.

222 RECENTLY ARRIVED FORMER SWIMMER: Mishler, *Sampan Sailor,* 153; USMC casualty list for Iwo Jima.

222 "RPT FIFTY": Unit Six War Diary, April 1 to 15, 1945, NARA, RG 38, entry NHC-75, box 17.

222 ONE OF HIS SWIMMERS: Stratton, *Saco,* 229.

222 MAGNETIZED LIMPET MINES: Unit Six War Diary, May 1 to 15, 1945, NARA, RG 38, entry NHC-75, box 17.

222 CADAVER-COLD HULL: US Information Service, "Navy Lifts Secrecy Curtain on Chinese-American Guerilla Cooperation," September 13, 1945.

222 NEWLY FILLED LAND DOCK: Capt. I. F. Beyerly (USN), message to Metzel, May 7, 1945, NARA, RG 38, entry NHC-75, box 17.

222 TWO SWIMMERS WERE FORCED: Unit Six War Diary, May 1 to 15, NARA, RG 38, entry NHC-75, box 17.

222 ONCE ALL MINES WERE AFFIXED: Connery, "Unsung 200"; Mishler,

Sampan Sailor, 169; Unit Six War Diary, May 1 to 15, 1945, NARA, RG 38, entry NHC-75, box 17.

223 QUIETLY LED THE SHORE PARTY: Connery, "Unsung 200."

223 "DAMN PENCILS MUST NOT": Mishler, *Sampan Sailor,* 169.

223 "A GREAT RUMBLING NOISE": Ibid., 169.

223 "GEYSER OF FIRE": Ibid., 170.

223 WITHIN THIRTY MINUTES: Connery, "Unsung 200"; John B. Dwyer, "US Scouts and Raiders Harassed the Japanese in China at Every Opportunity," *Undercover,* undated, Dwyer Papers, courtesy of James Barnes.

223 "AMOY AREA": Beyerly, message to Metzel, May 7, 1945.

223 LARGER IN SQUARE FOOTAGE: Connery, "Unsung 200."

223 "CLEANING UP": Unit Six War Diary, June 16 to 30, 1945, NARA, RG 38, entry NHC-75, box 17.

223 ANXIOUSLY AWAITING THEIR ORDERS: Stratton, *Saco,* 232.

224 "THE STEEPEST, ROCKIEST, MOST SLIPPERY": Ibid., 233.

224 FEWER THAN A HUNDRED DEFENDERS: Hoe, letter, August 30, 1993.

224 HALPERIN WASTED NO TIME: Unit Six War Diary, June 15–30, NARA, RG 38, entry NHC-75, box 17.

224 SEVERAL SIGNAL LIGHTS: Hoe, letter, August 30, 1993.

225 PLANK AND HIS MACHINE GUN CREW: Dwyer, *Commandos from the Sea,* 209–212.

225 FIRST OF SEVERAL JAPANESE GUNBOATS: Hoe, letter, August 30, 1993.

225 "SPLATTERED" and "LITERALLY PLASTERED": Stratton, *Saco,* 235.

226 "THIS WAS BELOW THEIR POSITION": Hoe, letter, August 30, 1993.

226 WHEN ALL THE CREWS: Dwyer, *Commandos from the Sea,* 209–212.

227 BLACK BUSINESS SUITS: Connery, "Unsung 200."

227 FOR TWENTY DAYS AND NIGHTS: Ens. Richard T. Davis (USNR/Roger 1), "Report on Unit Six Group Attached to the 2nd Battalion, to LCdr. Halperin," Dwyer Papers, courtesy of James Barnes.

227 "WITH OR WITHOUT" and "TURNED THEIR SWORDS OVER": Connery, "Unsung 200."

228 "WHAT THE HELL?" PENNANT: Connery, "Unsung 200."

228 UNDERCUTTING A CNO-DIRECTED RAID: Stratton, *Saco,* 238–239.

228 SPECIALLY TRAINED FORCE: Ibid., 238.

228 "SOMETHING ABOUT A 'BIG BOMB'": Miles, *Different Kind of War,* 519.

228 "THE END OF THE WAR SHOULD": Ibid., 522.

228 INTELLIGENCE INFRASTRUCTURE: Navy Department, "NOW IT CAN BE TOLD!," press and radio release, September 13, 1945, NHHC, history.navy.mil/content/history/nhhc/research/library/online-reading-room/title-list-alphabetically/s/saco.html.

228 ASSISTED BY MARINES: Kush, *Rice Paddy Navy,* 269; taken from Charles Miles estimates, number of Japanese killed includes Puppet troops.

228 BEST ESTIMATES OF THE TIME: In the years that followed Miles's death, his son Charles Miles assembled what many consider a more

accurate scorecard of SACO's achievements. Those tallies include the following: Japanese killed—31,345; Japanese wounded—12,969; Japanese captured—349; Japanese ships sunk—141; locomotives destroyed—84; bridges destroyed—209. A 1964 estimate places the number of Japanese dead at 71,000, or "two and a half Japanese killed for every US weapon placed in a Navy-trained guerrilla's hands." Charles Miles, email to author, November 9, 2020.

229 "THE MONTH THAT FOLLOWED": Miles, *Different Kind of War,* 522.

229 "ALMOST ABSOLUTE CONTROL": Ibid., 521.

229 "ROILED AS A SHIP'S WAKE": Ibid., 558.

229 "A METHOD OF WARFARE": Ibid., 557.

229 "MILES, I DON'T HAVE": Ibid., 558.

229 "THE GREATEST JOINT OPERATION": US Information Service, "Chinese and American SACO Directors Had Highest Priced Heads in Orient," September 14, 1945, NARA, RG 38, entry NHC-75.

230 "TO GET MILES THROWN OUT": Miles, *Different Kind of War,* 602.

230 "CRACK THE WHOLE THEATER": Ibid., 559.

230 "NOW GENERAL WEDEMEYER" and "ARREST THAT MAN": *Reminiscences of Captain Phil Bucklew,* no. 3, 160.

230 TWO NIGHTS LATER: Miles, *Different Kind of War,* 559.

230 AFTER THE CAMP DOCTOR CONFINED: Stratton, *Army-Navy Games,* 241–242.

230 AND HIS RAZOR WAS CONFISCATED: Kush, *Rice Paddy Navy,* 261; Miles, *Different Kind of War,* 560.

231 "COMPLETE MENTAL BREAKDOWN" and "HE HAD NOT SUFFERED PERMANENT": Stratton, *Army-Navy Games,* 242–243.

231 "OPPOSITION TO THE SACO EFFORT": Miles, *Different Kind of War,* 602.

231 TWO CHINESE GENERALS and "PLATE-SIZED MEDALS": *Stratton, Army-Navy Games,* 244; SACO website. The medals were presented by Chinese generals Mao Jen-feng and Pan Chi-wu.

231 WAS DISSOLVED AND MILES'S RANK: Kush, *Rice Paddy Navy,* 266 (taken from Stratton, *Army-Navy Games,* xii). The SACO agreement itself was dissolved on March 1, 1946 (ibid.).

231 "STOP WHAT YOU'RE DOING": Rudy Boesch account in Bill Fawcett, ed., *Hunters and Shooters: An Oral History of the US Navy SEALs in Vietnam* (New York: HarperCollins, 1995), 1–2.

232 DEMOLISHING EVERYTHING: Charles Brown, letter to John B. Dwyer, August 14, 1994, Dwyer Papers, courtesy of James Barnes.

232 CONFUSE WITH THOSE OF THE ARMY'S RANGERS: Connery, "Unsung 200."

232 COURT-MARTIAL: Brown, letter, August 14, 1994.

232 JUMPED FROM THE TRAIN: Fawcett, ed., *Hunters and Shooters,* 2.

232 "THE GODDAMNDEST ROAD": *India-Burma Theater Roundup,* vol. 4, no. 1, Delhi, September 13, 1945.

232 "DESTROYER MIGHT HAVE NAVIGATED": Stratton, *Saco,* 50–51.

232 The Rogers completed: Dwyer, *Commandos from the Sea,* 222.
232 losing four trucks: Stratton, *Saco,* 50.
232 football game: Dwyer, *Scouts and Raiders*, 170; and Shanghai Rice Bowl Program, Dwyer Papers, courtesy of James Barnes.
233 Tai Li's plane crashed: Stratton, *Saco,* 23.
233 serial number: Stratton, *Army-Navy Games*, 256.
233 four large pictures: Miles, *Different Kind of War,* 583.
233 At his retirement ceremony: Ibid., xiii (Wilma Miles).
233 "an awful lot of pages": Ibid., xiv (Wilma Miles).
234 "[stumble] upon the guerrillas" and "At least a dozen": Ibid., 507.
234 former Chinese cook: Kush, *Rice Paddy Navy,* 271, and Charles Miles, email to author, November 9, 2020.
234 prepared a eulogy: Program from St. Angela's Rectory, 917 Morris Avenue, New York 51, New York, Dwyer Papers, courtesy of James Barnes.

Part 3: Relevance

Chapter 7: The US Navy's Postwar Plight, and the Sailor-Raiders Who Led Her Back to Significance in Korea

237 "Well, I do have a rowboat": "Off to Ireland," *Time,* July 9, 1951.
237 "Admiral, the Navy": E. B. Potter, *Admiral Arleigh Burke* (Annapolis: Naval Institute Press, 1990), 323.
238 "stunned silence": "The Incorrigible and Indomitable," *Time,* October 31, 1949.
239 Between July 1 and 12: "Battle of Korea: The Retreat from Taejon," *Time,* July 31, 1950.
240 "unto the enemy": "US Rangers Answer to Prayers for Troops to Slip Behind Red Lines in Korean Conflict, *Seattle Post Intelligencer,* March 10, 1951.
240 Korea's geography pushed: Capt. Walter Karig (USNR), Cdr. Malcolm W. Cagle (USN), and LCdr. Frank A. Manson (USN), *Battle Report: The War in Korea* (New York: Rinehart, 1952), 152.
240 the peninsula exposed: Malcolm W. Cagle and Frank A. Manson, *The Sea War in Korea* (Annapolis: Naval Institute Press, 1957), 231.
241 "The Navy could not have": Adm. Charles Turner Joy (USN), "Testimony of Adm. Charles Turner Joy," Subcommittee to Investigate the Administration of the Internal Security Act and Other Internal Security Laws of the Committee on the Judiciary, United States Senate, 83rd Congress, December 29, 1954.
241 "We are losing men": John Toland, *In Mortal Combat: Korea, 1950–1953* (New York: William Morrow, 1991), 519.
241 "Stonewall Joy": "Cease-Fire: The Round Table," *Time,* August 27, 1951; "Joy's Patience," *The Washington Post,* August 14, 1951.
241 "like hungry dogs": Cagle and Manson, *Sea War in Korea,* 287.

241 “THE LITTLE SLOT”: “Last Train from Vladivostok,” *Time,* July 24, 1950.

242 BURKE WOULD BET: Potter, *Admiral Arleigh Burke,* 353–354.

242 “DISRUPT THE EAST COAST”: Cagle and Manson, *Sea War in Korea,* 290.

242 “A SMALL COMMANDO OUTFIT”: Ibid., 290.

242 “YOU ARE ALL VOLUNTEERS”: “Last Train from Vladivostok,” *Time.*

243 PORTER SLIPPED OUT OF THE BOAT: Cagle and Manson, *Sea War in Korea,* 291.

243 WILSON FIELDER: “The Press: Missing in Action,” *Time,* July 31, 1950.

243 “IT WASN’T BAD”: “Last Train from Vladivostok,” *Time,* July 24, 1950.

243 “STICKING OUT”: Cagle and Manson, *Sea War in Korea,* 290–292.

244 “SPECIAL RAIDING FORCES”: F. F. Draper (MTT Chief), “Report to Commander Amphibious Forces, Pacific Fleet, Report of Team Operations for the Period of 24 July 1950 to 7 November 1950,” November 7, 1950, NARA, RG 313, entry P66, box 4.

244 “EARLIEST POSSIBLE”: VAdm. Charles Turner Joy (COMNAVFE), COMNAVFE Operation Order No. 11-50 to CTF-90, “To Conduct Harassing and Demolition Raids Against North Korean Military Objectives,” July 28, 1950, NHHC, Post-1946 Operation’s Plans Forces, Far East, January 1946–January 1950, box 230.

244 ALLOCATED TO ITS TRAINING: John J. Hourihan, Memo from CO Naval Amphibious Test & Evaluating Unit to Chief of the Bureau of Ships, “LCVP Type Craft for Troop Carrier Submarines,” August 10, 1949; Jerauld Wright, Memo from Cdr. Amphibious Force, US Atlantic Fleet to Chief of the Bureau of Ships, “LCVP Type Craft for Troop Carrier Submarines,” August 30, 1949, NARA, RG 313, entry P66, box 3.

244 SONOBUOY-FLOATED ANTENNA: John J. Hourihan, Memo from CO Naval Amphibious Test & Evaluating Unit to Chief of Naval Operations, “Request for Equipment for Communication Between Submerged Troop Carrier Submarine and Debarked Landing Force,” October 12, 1949, NARA, RG 313, entry P66, box 3.

244 “HAIRTRIGGERED”: Dyer, *Amphibians Came to Conquer,* 604.

245 DOYLE IMMEDIATELY SUMMONED: Karig, Cagle, and Manson, *Battle Report,* 152.

245 “RAW”: Author interview with Chuck Thiess, March 29, 2015.

246 SO QUALIFIED: Dwyer, *Commandos from the Sea,* 119–120; Grouper’s AAR; and Fane and Moore, *Naked Warriors,* 289.

246 “RESPONSIBILITY WAS STRICTLY UNDERWATER” and “RAIDING BEHIND THE BEACH”: Fane and Moore, *Naked Warriors,* 194.

246 “CONFUSION AND UNCERTAINTY”: Atcheson account in Dwyer, *Commandos from the Sea,* 237.

246 “SUICIDE MISSIONS”: Ibid., 237.

247 “I’M SORRY IT HAD TO END”: “Foreign Relations: It Can’t Be Helped,” *Time,* August 25, 1947.

247 "GAUDY SOUVENIR KIMONOS": Ibid.

247 IT WAS A TOPIC ABOUT WHICH: Author interview with Mack Boynton, December 6, 2015.

247 "CATCHING A TRAIN" and THEN PASSED OUT: Dwyer, *Commandos from the Sea,* 112.

247 "WAVING ARMS": Karig, Cagle, and Manson, *Battle Report,* 91–93.

248 DESPITE HIS EXPERIENCE: George Atcheson account, *US Naval Special Warfare Archives: 1942 to Present Day,* available at http://www.navyfrogmen.com/Atcheson.html.

248 "WAR-BAGS": Phil Carrico, "The First Inland Demolition Raid in Korea," *Stories of Naval Frogmen in Korea: Pioneers in Naval Special Warfare,* navyfrogmen.com/carricobook.html.

248 PACKED INTO A SEAPLANE: Dwyer, "UDTs in Korea," *Soldier of Fortune,* 71.

248 FLANK SPEED: Carrico, "First Inland Demolition Raid in Korea."

248 "THE BIG TEN" and "THOUSANDS OF ROUNDS": Ibid.

249 "BREAK A LEG": Ibid.

249 ATCHESON RELAXED: George Atcheson account, navyfrogmen.com/Atcheson.html.

250 "HANG IN THERE, LT": Carrico, "First Inland Demolition Raid in Korea."

250 "YOU IDIOTS": Ibid.

250 "GRITTING HIS TEETH": Ibid.

250 AFTER DOCTORS DETERMINED: Ibid.

251 "JOHN WAYNE": Carrico, "First Inland Demolition Raid in Korea."

251 "CARRY OUT HER ASSIGNED MISSION": VAdm. Charles Turner Joy (USN), COMNAVFE Memo to Commander in Chief, Far East (MacArthur), Subject: "Assignment of Undersea Raiding Force for USS Perch (ASSP313)," September 14, 1950, NARA, RG 313, entry P66, box 3.

251 THE NEXT DAY: Draper MTT Report, November 7, 1950.

251 AFTER SOME OPENING REMARKS: Ibid., Enclosure A.

252 RIGHT ABOUT THE SAME TIME: S. C. Small, Transport Division 111, Commander (CTD), War Diary for August, September 1, 1950, NARA, RG 38, entry UD-09D 28, box 39.

252 AS A JUNIOR OFFICER: Robert Peters and Roger Staley, "Pineapple Marines: The Journey from Citizen to Marine Combat Veteran," 2017, 22, available at http://kbaymarine.com/images/Pineapple_Marines.pdf.

252 AFTER MENTALLY ADAPTING: Miles, *Different Kind of War,* 360.

253 TARGET KING: CTD 111 War Diary for August.

253 MARINES BEDECKED THEMSELVES: Dwyer, "Special Operations Group Korea, 1950," *Leatherneck,* July 1994.

253 WAISTS: Jerry Ravino, *Elite: USMC First Reconnaissance Company of the Korean War, 1950–1953* (Memory Works, 2009), 19.

253 "TORTURE CREW": Karig, Cagle, and Manson, *Battle Report,* 154.

253 ACCLIMATE THEIR EYES: Ibid.

253 WHO STARTED THE ENGINE: Ibid., 155.

254 "CONSIDERABLE ENEMY ACTIVITY" and GUNNERS UNLEASHED: CTD 111 War Diary for August.

254 WOODEN RIFLE: Fane and Moore, *Naked Warriors,* 241.

255 "CHARGES EXPLODED": CTD 111 War Diary for August.

255 REQUEST FOR A SMALL SQUAD: VAdm. Charles Turner Joy (USN), "Submission of War Diary, Commander Naval Forces, Far East, August 1 to 31, 1950," December 2, 1950, Plans Section, August 14, 1950, NARA, RG 38, entry UD-09D, box 3.

255 OFFER WAS QUICKLY ACCEPTED: Ibid., August 15, 1950.

255 FOUR SLEEPING PEASANTS: Karig, Cagle, and Manson, *Battle Report,* 155. Note that the account has the incorrect date; see CTD 111 War Diary for August.

255 "CHATTERING LIKE A BUNCH OF MAGPIES": Dwyer, "Special Operations Group Korea, 1950."

255 *"QUIET!":* Fane and Moore, *Naked Warriors,* 240.

255 IF DUPRAS HAD HOPED: Karig, Cagle, and Manson, *Battle Report,* 153; Dupras: "The hardest part of my job was continually to impress the boys that our job was demolition, not fighting."

256 BLUE FLAMES: Karig, Cagle, and Manson, *Battle Report,* 156.

256 IMMEDIATELY PREPARE: CTD 111 War Diary for August.

256 DUPRAS AND A RADIOMAN: Ravino, *Elite,* 34.

256 "STANDING PATIENTLY": Fane and Moore, *Naked Warriors,* 243; Dwyer, "Special Operations Group Korea, 1950."

256 "THE BEACH IS HYDROGRAPHICALLY UNSUITABLE": CTD 111 War Diary for August.

257 ALL SENIOR THEATER COMMANDERS and "THE MOST POWERFUL TOOL WE HAVE": William Manchester, *American Caesar: Douglas MacArthur, 1880–1964* (New York: Little, Brown, 1978), 575.

258 "I MIGHT HAVE MORE [FAITH]": David Halberstam, *The Coldest Winter: America and the Korean War* (New York: Hyperion, 2007), 300.

258 "GENERAL, THE NAVY WILL": Halberstam, *Coldest Winter,* 300.

258 COLONEL WILLIAM HOWE: Eliot A. Cohen, *Conquered into Liberty: Two Centuries of Battles Along the Great Warpath That Made the American Way of War* (New York: Simon & Schuster, 2012), 88; Francis Parkman, *Montcalm and Wolfe: The French and Indian War* (New York: Barnes & Noble Books, 2005), 436.

258 ON AUGUST 26: Eugene Franklin Clark, *The Secrets of Inchon: The Untold Story of the Most Daring Covert Mission of the Korean War* (New York: G. P. Putnam's Sons, 2002), 3.

259 "GRAVE DISSATISFACTION": Ibid., 5.

259 "HOW WOULD YOU LIKE TO GET" and "I'D CERTAINLY LIKE": Ibid., 4.

260 AN EARLY CHILDHOOD AS BLEAK: Author interview with Genine Franklin Clark, March 30, 2015.

260 INTENDED TO PROTECT CIVILIAN POPULATIONS: Clark, *Secrets of Inchon,* 7.

260 "FORCED-DRAFT EDUCATION IN SOLDIERING": Karig, Cagle, and Manson, *Battle Report,* 177.

260 HE WITNESSED: Clark, *Secrets of Inchon,* 5.

261 MATURE, DELIBERATE, AND CALCULATING: Karig, Cagle, and Manson, *Battle Report,* 177.

261 IN MANNER HE WAS AGREEABLE: Author interview with Genine Franklin Clark.

261 SELECTED TWO MEN: Clark, *Secrets of Inchon,* 7.

261 FIRED FROM HIS COUNTERINTELLIGENCE POST: Ibid., 21.

262 TRANSFORMED THE TEAM'S WISH LIST: Ibid., 11.

262 "ETCHED IN DEEP BLUE VELVET": Ibid., 17.

262 SLEEP-DEPRIVED DAYS: Karig, Cagle, and Manson, *Battle Report,* 177.

263 ONLY THE SKIPPER WORE: Ibid., 177.

263 GREEN MARINE CORPS FATIGUES: Clark, *Secrets of Inchon,* 35.

264 THREE MILES FROM THE TARGET: Ed Evanhoe, *Dark Moon: Eighth Army Special Operations in the Korean War* (Annapolis: Naval Institute Press, 1995), 20–26.

264 "FRANTIC": Clark, *Secrets of Inchon,* 41.

264 SET UP A COMMAND POST and RECRUITED SEVEN BOYS: Ibid., 31.

264 "WATCH AND RUN": Karig, Cagle, and Manson, *Battle Report,* 181.

264 LIKE A DRAIN BEING PULLED: Clark, *Secrets of Inchon,* 73.

265 "EARLIEST POSSIBLE": VAdm. Charles Turner Joy (USN), COMNAVFE Message to HMS Whitesand Bay, DTG:080346Z, NHHC, Post-1946 Operation's Plans Forces, Far East, January 1946–January 1950, box 230.

265 A MISHMASH OF TIES: Fred Hayhurst, *Green Berets in Korea: The Story of 41 Independent Commando* (Cambridge: Vanguard Press, 2001), 25–27.

266 "I DON'T KNOW HOW THE HELL": Adm. Arleigh A. Burke (USN), *Oral History of Adm. Arleigh Burke* (Annapolis: Naval Institute Press, 2003), no. 10, 319–321.

266 "UNDERSEA RAIDING FORCE" and "OPERATIONAL CONTROL": COMNAVFE, memo to CICFE, September 14, 1950, NHHC, Post-1946 Operation's Plans Forces, Far East, January 1946–January 1950, box 230.

266 SET SAIL FOR TAEMUUI-DO: Clark, *Secrets of Inchon,* 167.

267 DESCENDING INTO A RICE PADDY: Ibid., 170.

268 WHILE BEING PURSUED: Ibid., 170–175.

268 PERCHED LIKE AHAB and "RAKED A GASH": Ibid., 218.

269 "MISERABLE LOOKING": Ibid., 222.

269 "MELTED": Ibid., 220.

269 BENZEDRINE TABLETS: Ibid., 225.

269 "WHOLE KEY TO SUCCESS OR FAILURE": Ibid., 209.

269 COATING THEMSELVES: Ibid., 225; Karig, Cagle, and Manson, *Battle Report,* 198.

269 SPARKS: Clark, *Secrets of Inchon,* 317.

270 TOOTHY and MONSTROSITY: Ibid., 243.

270 BEGAN PLOTTING THE MISSIONS: Karig, Cagle, and Manson, *Battle Report,* 198.

270 CROSS-TAPED: Clark, *Secrets of Inchon,* 249.

270 "SEEMED TO BE SUSPENDED": Ibid., 225.

270 MUDFLAT AS FIRM: Ibid., 251.

270 SENTRY'S BOOTS: Clark, *Secrets of Inchon,* 254.

270 PRACTICALLY BEHEADED: Ibid., 261.

270 UNREMARKABLE RAID: Hayhurst, *Green Berets in Korea,* 44; Andrew Salmon, *Scorched Earth, Black Snow: The First Year of the Korean War,* Kindle edition (Aurum Press, 2011), 142.

271 ONE CAMPFIRE: Clark, *Secrets of Inchon,* 280.

272 "MADE IN FRANCE": Karig, Cagle, and Manson, *Battle Report,* 189; see also Clark, *Secrets of Inchon,* 318.

272 "BEATING LIKE A TRIP-HAMMER": Clark, *Secrets of Inchon,* 318.

273 "DARK AS THE INSIDE OF A COW'S BELLY": Karig, Cagle, and Manson, *Battle Report,* 214.

273 "SLAMMED DOOR": "War, the Proposition Was Simple," *Time,* September 25, 1950.

273 "QUIVERING": Joseph C. Goulden, *Korea: The Untold Story of the War* (New York: Times Books, 1982), 211; Karig, Cagle, and Manson, *Battle Report,* 225.

273 "I THOUGHT IT WOULD ROLL": Goulden, *Korea,* 211.

273 THE FIRING STOPPED: Ibid., 212.

273 CAPTURE COST THE MARINE BATTALION: Karig, Cagle, and Manson, *Battle Report,* 222.

273 "THE NAVY AND MARINES": Goulden, *Korea,* 213; "War: Operation Chromite," *Time,* September 25, 1950.

274 "WHO THE HELL ARE YOU?": Karig, Cagle, and Manson, *Battle Report,* 190–191.

274 "CHOKED WITH FUMES" and "PALL OF PURPLE SMOKE": "For God, for Country, but Not . . . ," *Time,* September 25, 1950.

274 "TRUMAN POLICE FORCE": Karig, Cagle, and Manson, *Battle Report,* 225.

274 ALLUSION TO TRUMAN'S LETTER TO CONGRESSMAN GORDON L. MCDONOUGH SUGGESTING THAT THE USMC HAVE THEIR OWN GENERAL ON THE JCS: "For your information, the Marine Corps is the Navy's police force and as long as I am president that is what it will remain. They have a propaganda machine that is almost equal to Stalin's . . ." "The President: When I Make a Mistake," *Time,* September 18, 1950.

274 ANTENNAED BEETLES: "For God, for Country, but Not . . . ," *Time.*

274 FIFTEEN SECONDS: Karig, Cagle, and Manson, *Battle Report,* 225.

274 ROCK-SLAB SEAWALL: "For God, for Country, but Not . . . ," *Time.*

274 MEN SIMPLY CATAPULTED: Karig, Cagle, and Manson, *Battle Report,* 225.

275 BEHIND THE LANDING CRAFT: Cagle and Manson, *Sea War in Korea,* 99.

275 REASONS BOTH MATERIAL AND POLITICAL: "The Presidency: The Face in the Lamplight," *Time,* September 25, 1950.

275 "WHY IS THE NAVY": Michael E. Haas, *In the Devil's Shadow: UN Special Operations During the Korean War* (Annapolis: Naval Institute Press, 2000), 150.

275 "THE URGENT NEED": US Pacific Fleet Operations, Korean War, "Commander in Chief US Pacific Fleet Interim Evaluation Report No. 1: Period 25 June 1950 to 15 November 1950, Combat Operations Sections: Amphibious and Ground," NHHC, Special Collections, 732.

276 "THE 41 ROYAL MARINE COMMANDO": Haas, *In the Devil's Shadow,* 50.

276 "GO DOWN IN HISTORY'S BRIGHTEST PAGES": Hayhurst, *Green Berets in Korea,* 425–426.

276 DRYSDALE AND FIVE OTHERS: Ibid., 446–447.

277 "DECAPITATING": Christopher Pontrelli, "The 'Butchers of Kapsan,'" *Naval History Magazine,* October 2007, vol. 21, no. 5.

277 WOULD LEAD A DEMOLITION RAID: "George Atcheson," *The Hall of Valor Project,* available at http://valor.militarytimes.com/recipient.php?recipientid=55200.

277 HE RECALLED THAT HE LOST: Karig, Cagle, and Manson, *Battle Report,* 189.

278 "MASS OF GORE": Ibid., 350–351.

278 "NO MORE WIND, WAVES, AND ROCKS": Ibid.

278 CLARK AND YOUN WERE AGAIN TAPPED: Dwight Jon Zimmerman, "Operation Sams: A Mission to Confirm Plague or Propaganda," *Defense Media Network,* October 9, 2014.

279 WOULD PECK AWAY and "HERE YOU GO, SUSIE": Author interview with Genine Franklin Clark.

279 "SHUNT OFF A LARGE BODY": Clark, *Secrets of Inchon,* 283–284.

279 CAST HIS CLOUD OF ASHES: Author interview with Genine Franklin Clark.

Chapter 8: The Resurrection of the Army's Rangers, and the Guerrilla Raid That Failed to Forestall Their Second Death

280 IN EARLY JULY 1950: Author interview with Kathy McGee Rose, April 25, 2016.

280 SOMETHING LIKE AN AMPHIBIOUS: John B. Dwyer, untitled draft article on US Army special units in the Korean War, unpublished, undated, courtesy of James Barnes.

281 "SUGAR-COATING": "Command: Old Pro," *Time,* July 31, 1950.

281 AN APPROPRIATE SELECTION: Dwyer, untitled draft article.

281 GRID-SQUARED QUONSET HUTS: Ellery Anderson (MBE, MC), *Banner Over Pusan* (London: Evans Brothers Limited, 1960), 56.

281 COMMAND OPERATIONS OFFICER: BGen. John Hugh McGee (USA, Retired), letter to Colonel Rod Paschall, Director, US Army Military History Institute, March 24, 1986, USAHEC, John Hugh McGee Papers, box 38, folder 7.

281 SUPPLIES INCLUDED NOT EVEN: Ibid.

281 "STAFF STUDY": Ibid.

282 McGEE PACKED HIS PREGNANT WIFE: BGen. John Hugh McGee (USA, Retired), *Rice and Salt: Resistance, Capture, and Escape on Mindanao,* Kindle edition (Uncommon Valor Press, 2014), loc. 296.

283 A HUMILIATING, BLINDFOLDED SALUTE: McGee, *Rice and Salt,* loc. 1170.

283 McGEE'S DARK BROWN HAIR: Author interview with Kathy McGee Rose.

283 IRON GRAY: Anderson, *Banner Over Pusan,* 56.

283 ALLOTMENT OF FORTY PESOS: Capt. W. J. Lincoln, Brief Interview with Colonel John H. McGee following escape from Philippine Military Prison Camp No. 2, NARA, RG 389, entry 460 A, box 2177.

283 LITTER OF PUPPIES: McGee, *Rice and Salt,* loc. 2321.

284 "HEELLESS SLIPPERS": Ibid., loc. 2827.

284 "AS BRIGHT AS A CIGAR TIP": Ibid., loc. 2852.

284 STUMP OF THE ANIMAL'S TAIL: Ibid., loc. 2866.

284 "ANY DAMN THING BUT SURRENDER": John Keats, *They Fought Alone: A True Story of an American Hero* (Philadelphia: Lippincott, 1963), 10.

284 McGEE'S REQUEST: McGee, *Rice and Salt,* loc. 3285.

285 "EASY TIME": Ibid., loc. 3297.

285 "INVARIABLY COURTEOUS AND KIND": Anderson, *Banner Over Pusan,* 61.

285 COMPOSED A MANIFEST: McGee, *Rice and Salt,* locs. 10–39, foreword by RAdm. Dan Gallery, September 19, 1962.

286 "A FINAL LIBERATING ADVANCE": McGee, *Salt and Rice;* McGee, letter to Col. Rod Paschall, March 24, 1986.

286 MORO TRIBESMEN: Ibid.

287 "CHOKED" and "APPARENT COWED PEOPLE": Ibid.

287 "DIRECTED TO ORGANIZE A UNIT": McGee, letter to Col. Rod Paschall, March 24, 1986.

287 SUCH A TO&E: Ibid.

287 McGEE'S MANPOWER POOL: Hogan, *Raiders or Elite Infantry,* 106.

287 WEST POINT CLASS OF 1949: Black, *Rangers in Korea,* loc. 172.

287 "I'LL DO ANYTHING": Neil Sheehan, *A Bright Shining Lie: John Paul Vann and America in Vietnam* (New York: Random House, 2009), 454.

287 IMMEDIATELY LIKED THE YOUNG: McGee, letter to Col. Rod Paschall, March 24, 1986.

287 "IF YOU ARE NOT WILLING": Black, *Rangers in Korea,* loc. 179.

288 CURRICULUM WOULD BE COBBLED: Col. John H. McGee (USA), memo to CG, Eighth Army, "Training Report of Eighth Army

Ranger Company," October 1, 1950, USAHEC, Robert W. Black Collection, box 10, folder 1.

288 ISSUED A DIRECTIVE: Hogan, *Raiders or Elite Infantry*, 106–108; Black, *Rangers in Korea*, locs. 216–241. Black says that the directive was sent to Army G-3, not AFF.

288 A COPY OF THE NAZI BRANDENBURGERS: Hogan, *Raiders or Elite Infantry,* 108.

289 COLONEL JOHN VAN HOUTEN REPORTED: Col. John G. Van Houten, memo, CG Infantry Center Fort Benning, "Diary of the Ranger Training Center," March 19, 1951, USAHEC, Robert W. Black Collection, box 10.

289 TALL, QUIET, AND HANDSOME: Martin S. Hayden, "History Rolls Back for Army Rangers," *The Detroit News,* March 6, 1951.

289 "COME ON, SON": MGen. John K. Singlaub (USA) and Malcolm McConnell, *Hazardous Duty: An American Soldier in the Twentieth Century* (New York: Summit Books, 1991), 172.

290 "COMMAND POSTS": Hogan, *Raiders or Elite Infantry*, 111.

290 "SUSTAINED COMBAT": Ibid., 111.

290 DRAWLY, MEANDERING JOURNEY: Ranger Newsletter, "Commandant Welcomes 4th Cycle Rangers to Command," undated, USAHEC, Robert W. Black Collection, box 10.

291 "YOU SEE, SIR": Hayden, *The Detroit News,* March 6, 1951.

291 "POUND AWAY": Ibid.

291 "COMBAT VALUE": McGee, memo, October 1, 1950.

291 FOOT SPEED and "DETAILED": Ibid.

291 2,500-YARD-WIDE RIVER: "Air War: Some Crazy War," *Time,* November 27, 1950.

292 ON NOVEMBER 21: Black, *Rangers in Korea,* locs. 464–488.

292 TO DESERT THE COMPANY: Sheehan, *Bright Shining Lie,* 458.

292 A CASCADE OF SPARKS: Ibid., 462.

292 TAN, WINTER-PADDED UNIFORMS: Singlaub and McConnell, *Hazardous Duty,* 175.

293 WHEN HE WOKE UP: Sheehan, *Bright Shining Lie,* 464.

293 "HOLY MARY": Black, *Rangers in Korea,* loc. 518.

293 "I'M A RANGER": Sheehan, *Bright Shining Lie,* 465.

293 "THIS PERSONAL SATISFACTION": Col. John H. McGee, letter to Capt. Ralph Puckett, March 7, 1951, USAHEC, John Hugh McGee Papers, box 38, folder 7.

293 OF PUCKETT'S FIFTY-SEVEN MEN: Black, *Rangers in Korea,* loc. 539.

294 "I FELT A LITTLE USELESS": Singlaub and McConnell, *Hazardous Duty,* 177.

294 DISPATCHING HIS UDTS WITH and LARGEST NONATOMIC: Haas, *In the Devil's Shadow,* 165.

294 "WE DON'T WANT": "The Enemy: Poor Showing," *Time,* January 8, 1951.

294 THE EVACUATION RESCUED SOME: Cagle and Manson, *Sea War in Korea,* 191.
295 ON JANUARY 8, 1951: 8086 Army Unit—AFFE Military History Detachment, "UN Partisan Forces in the Korean Conflict, 1951–1952: A Study of Their Characteristics and Operations," US Army Military History Institute, May 5, 1954, USAHEC.
295 THE NEXT DAY: Ibid.
296 MCGEE REITERATED HIS IDEA: Ibid.; Enclosure: Col. John H. McGee (USA), Memo to G-3 Section EUSAK APO 301, "Employment of a Ranger Company in a Penetration Operation," January 13, 1951; reiterated in McGee, letter to Col. Rod Paschall, March 24, 1986.
296 "EMPLOYMENT OF A RANGER COMPANY": McGee, "Employment of a Ranger Company in a Penetration Operation," January 13, 1951.
297 PARTISAN COMMAND HEADQUARTERS: Anderson, *Banner Over Pusan,* 56.
297 "THIN HAZE OF CIGAR SMOKE" and "CHARMING" and "INVARIABLY COURTEOUS": Ibid.
297 "SCHOOL BOY": McGee, letter to Col. Rod Paschall, March 24, 1986.
297 "A LARGE DISORGANIZED FAMILY": Anderson, *Banner Over Pusan,* 61.
297 THE FIRST OF THESE: Frederick W. Cleaver, George Fitzpatrick, John Ponturo, William Rossiter, and C. Darwin Stolzenbach, "UN Partisan Warfare in Korea," Chevy Chase, Johns Hopkins University, Operations Research Office, 1956. Numbers include those assigned to McGee's HQ (3 Officers/2 Enlisted).
298 TO FIND VOLUNTEERS: McGee, letter to Col. Rod Paschall, March 24, 1986.
298 MCGEE HUSTLED: Ibid.
298 "THE COMING ADVANCE": Ibid.
299 "THIS RANGER COMPANY": Ranger Newsletter, "Commandant Welcomes 4th Cycle Rangers to Command," undated, USAHEC, Robert W. Black Collection, box 10.
299 "I CANNOT REMEMBER": Black, *Rangers in Korea,* loc. 635.
300 "NEGROID": Ibid., loc. 708.
300 "THEIR IMPATIENCE IS BEGINNING": Ibid., loc. 644.
300 RIDING TOBOGGANS: Ibid., loc. 1037.
300 "LIKE BEES OUT OF A HIVE": Ibid., loc. 1047.
300 "RANGERS ANSWER TO PRAYERS": "US Rangers Answer to Prayers for Troops to Slip Behind Red Lines in Korean Conflicts," Associated Press, March 10, 1951; "New US Rangers Make Life Tough for Reds," *Seattle Post-Intelligencer,* March 11, 1951.
300 "LIKE HELL FOR HOME": "New US Rangers Make Life Tough for Reds."
301 "BECAUSE THEY DEPEND PRIMARILY": Lloyd Norman, "Tough Rangers Now Harassing the Enemy," *Chicago Tribune*, February 19, 1951.
301 "CHRIST, JOHN": Russell A. Gugeler, *Combat Actions in Korea,* Office

of the Chief of Military History, US Army (Washington, D.C.: Government Publications, 1970), 118.

301 Ultimately, the Rangers' daylight assault: Black, *Rangers in Korea,* loc. 1280.

302 still just a skeleton: McGee, letter to Col. Rod Paschall, March 24, 1986.

302 airborne jump towers: Evanhoe, *Dark Moon,* 47.

302 a tunnel near the mountain river town: Ibid., 49–52.

302 "an OSS type mission": Ranger Newsletter, "Reports from Ranger Companies Overseas," undated, USAHEC, Robert W. Black Collection, box 10.

303 McGee strode onto: Anderson, *Banner Over Pusan,* 68–69.

303 Unfortunately, the airborne instructors: Evanhoe, *Dark Moon,* 52.

304 "secured": 8086 Army Unit, "UN Partisan Forces in the Korean Conflict, 1951–1952," May 5, 1954, USAHEC, Enclosure: McGee, Col. John H. (Chief of Miscellaneous Division), Memo to Eighth Army HQ, "Conference Aboard HMS Belfast," March 15, 1951.

305 As before every other longshot: "Final POW Name Rewards a Father," *The New York Times,* September 7, 1953.

305 accidentally: Evanhoe, *Dark Moon,* 54.

305 Keep Perry on the plane: Ibid., 54.

305 Raised in Hartford: Author interview with Kate Smith, July 29, 2016.

305 learning the languages of each group: John T. Flynn, "Post Captivity Interview of John T. Flynn Account, Subject: Martin R. Watson," September 1953, Corporal Martin R. Watson, POW file, NARA, RG 319, entry A1-134E.

306 German shepherd: Author interview with Martin R. Watson, Jr., July 26, 2016.

306 "rabbit": Flynn, "Post Captivity Interview."

306 jailed for thirty days: "FBI Record, Rap Sheet of Martin R. Watson," October 9, 1953, Watson POW file.

307 essentially a corporal: Confirmed in McGee, letter to Col. Rod Paschall, March 24, 1986; numerous documents in Watson POW file, and letter from Capt. Dorsey B. Anderson, 4th Ranger Company, to Col. Van Houten, April 23, 1951, USAHEC, Robert W. Black Collection, box 8, folder 7.

307 "wished them Godspeed": McGee, letter to Col. Rod Paschall, March 24, 1986.

307 brought his M1 rifle: Black, *Rangers in Korea,* loc. 1405.

308 peasant's hut: Ibid., 1405.

308 rolled up and slung: Evanhoe, *Dark Moon,* 55.

309 on the other side of the world: Col. John G. Van Houten, memo to CG Infantry Center Fort Benning, "Diary of the Ranger Training

Center," March 19, 1951, USAHEC, Robert W. Black Collection, box 10.

309 "SIPHONED OFF": Gen. Mark W. Clark (USA), "Courage Test," *The Des Moines Register,* April 13, 1952.

309 "PREPARE AND SUBMIT IDEAS": Hogan, *Raiders or Elite Infantry,* 125.

310 "I LOOK FOR NO TROUBLE": 8086 Army Unit, "UN Partisan Forces in the Korean Conflict, 1951–1952," May 5, 1954, Enclosure: McGee, Col. John H. (Chief of Miscellaneous Division), Memo to Eighth Army HQ, "Policies for Eagle," March 16, 1951, USAHEC.

311 THEY REPORTED THAT THE TUNNEL: Evanhoe, *Dark Moon,* 57.

311 BUSY AS AN ANTHILL: Described by Pucel in Black, *Rangers in Korea,* loc. 1405.

311 BURNING SMALL CHUNKS OF EXPLOSIVES: Ibid., loc. 1419.

311 SOME SIXTY MILES: Evanhoe, *Dark Moon,* 58.

312 "VIRGINIA ONE": Ibid., 58.

312 "RUBBERNECKED" and "STONY SILENCE": Capt. John W. Thornton (USN), *Believed to Be Alive* (Middlebury: P. S. Ericksson, 1981), 65.

313 SMALL AS FLIES: Jim G. Lucas, "Helicopter Lands with Dangling GI," *The Pittsburgh Gazette,* June 25, 1951.

313 THORNTON NOW RESEMBLED: Thornton, *Believed to Be Alive,* 64.

313 "A LONG NIGHT": Ibid., 81.

313 BELOW AND AROUND HIM: Ibid., 68.

314 "CARVED A TRENCH": Ibid., 75.

314 "ESCALATOR RIDE": Ibid., 68.

314 "BUG OUT OF HIS HEAD": Ibid., 68.

314 "HAILSTORM": Ibid., 69.

314 "DROPPED LIKE A STONE": Ibid.

315 STILL PUMPING GAS: Ibid., 70.

315 A BULLET SLICED: Ibid., 71. Thornton claims Miles was hit on second lift, not third.

316 "WRENCHED": Lucas, "Helicopter Lands with Dangling GI."

317 "CARTWHEELING": Thornton, *Believed to Be Alive,* 75.

317 "THIS IS GONNA BE IT!": Ibid., 76.

317 "SHOWERS OF GLOWING WHITE STREAMERS" and "KEEP YOUR HEAD DOWN!": Ibid., 77.

318 "TAKE THIS": Ibid., 78–79.

318 "STUMBLING, RISING, RUNNING" and "NOOSE": Ibid., 80.

319 "EXCEPT FOR THE BLOWING WIND": Ibid., 80.

319 "THEY'LL NEVER GET ME": Ibid., 101.

320 "PROCESSION OF THE DEAD": Ibid., 87.

320 "LIKE A DEMON POPPING": Ibid., 90.

320 LOST HIS BOOTS and "DIED A LITTLE": Ibid., 92.

320 CORNERED IN A CAVE: Sgt. Martin R. Watson, "Security Information Form," September 19, 1953, NARA, Watson POW file.

320 TWICE THEIR NORMAL SIZE: Sgt. Martin R. Watson Interview, Army

Security Center, 8589th AAU, Fort George Meade, Maryland, June 7, 1954, NARA, Watson POW file.

321 ON THE PREDAWN MORNING: Martin Blumenson, "Hwachon Dam—Korea, 1951: The 4th Ranger Company and the 7th Cavalry in Action," *Infantry,* May–June 1996; Blumenson, 1st Lt. Martin (3d Historical Detachment), "Various After Action Interviews for Hwachon Dam Raid," April 1951, USAHEC, Robert W. Black Collection, box 8, folder 7.

321 "THERE WAS AN INADEQUACY": Blumenson, "After Action Interview with Lt. Col. John Carlson, G-3, 1st Cav Div.," April 11, 1951, USAHEC, Robert W. Black Collection.

321 ASKING FOR AN IMMEDIATE INACTIVATION: Hogan, *Raiders or Elite Infantry,* 128 (taken from Ridgway, letter to Maxwell Taylor, Assistant Chief of Staff for Operations, May 19, 1951).

321 "IMPRACTICAL": Hogan, *Rangers or Elite Infantry,* 128.

322 BLAMED THE FAILURE ON: McGee, letter to Col. Rod Paschall, March 24, 1986.

322 PERMANENT ANNEXATION: Evanhoe, *Dark Moon,* 96.

323 "RANGER ACTIVITIES" and "WOULD BE": Col. Aaron Bank (USA), *From OSS to Green Berets: The Birth of Special Forces* (New York: Pocket Books, 1986), 173.

323 OF THE ROUGHLY 748: See Black, *Rangers in Korea,* appendices.

323 WHO TRAINED HIS PARTISANS: Evanhoe, *Dark Moon,* 153–155; Haas, *In the Devil's Shadow,* 67.

323 "SPUR OF THE MOMENT": 8086 Army Unit, "UN Partisan Forces in the Korean Conflict, 1951–1952," May 5, 1954; Enclosure: Purcell, Lt. Col. Francis R. (USA), "Interview of Lt. Col. Francis R. Purcell, G-2 Section, Eighth Army," May 13, 1953.

323 OXEN, FILM PROJECTORS: Cleaver et al., "UN Partisan Forces in the Korean Conflict," May 13, 1953.

324 OF THE 19: Cleaver et al., "UN Partisan Warfare in Korea," 1956, 91–93.

324 THEY WERE EXECUTED: Evanhoe, *Dark Moon,* 61.

324 BY THE END OF THE WAR: Cleaver et al., "UN Partisan Warfare in Korea," 1956, 142.

324 BIRD-DOGGING TARGETS: UN Partisan Forces in the Korean Conflict, May 13, 1953, 36.

324 FOR A PRINTING PRESS OPERATOR: "Final POW Name Rewards a Father," *The New York Times,* September 7, 1953.

324 A SOLDIER NO GUARD OR PRISONER: Post-captivity interview of William R. Runyan, Subject: Martin R. Watson, July 26, 1954, NARA, Watson POW file.

325 THIRTY DAYS AFTER: Post-captivity interview of Cpl. Thomas A. Lyke, Subject: Martin R. Watson, September 1, 1953, NARA, Watson POW file; Watson interview, Army Security Center, 8589th AAU,

Fort George Meade, Maryland, June 7, 1954, NARA, Watson POW file.

325 NEVERTHELESS ESCAPED AGAIN: Ibid.

325 SHREDS OF BROWN PAPER: Sgt. Martin R. Watson (USA), Written Statement of Sgt. Martin R. Watson, 5-page statement and 3-page statement, September 22, 1953, NARA, Watson POW file.

325 PLUS AN ATTEMPTED SUICIDE: Ibid.

325 "SPARSE": Col. W. A. Perry (Chief, Security Division) to CG, First Army, New York, New York (ATTN: Asst. Chief of Staff, G-2), "Recommendation for Recognition of Meritorious Action," January 6, 1954, NARA.

325 OSS SPY: Jeffords, A/2C Jacque (USAF), Post-captivity interview of A/2C Jacque M. Jeffords (USAF), Subject: Martin R. Watson, undated, NARA, Watson POW file.

325 "PARATROOP": "Phase 1 Questionnaire for Recovered UN POW," USNS *Howze,* September 20, 1953, NARA, Watson POW file.

325 WATSON'S RESPONSE TO THESE: Watson interview, Army Security Center, June 7, 1954, Watson POW file.

325 "DIDN'T KNOW WHAT COMMUNISM WAS": Ibid.

325 SENTENCED TO DEATH: Perry, "Recommendation for Recognition of Meritorious Action," January 6, 1954.

325 SECOND-TO-LAST: The last man to be repatriated was Lt. Harris (USAF), who was only reluctantly repatriated. Watson's description of this event is detailed in "Written Statement of Sgt. Martin R. Watson," September 22, 1953, NARA, Watson POW file.

326 HAVING BEEN STARVED: "POW Cited for Valor: Connecticut Man Tortured by Reds Refused to Break," *The New York Times,* February 19, 1954.

326 NEVER AGAIN: McGee, letter to Col. Rod Paschall, March 24, 1986.

326 "BRANDED" THE "SCAPEGOAT": Ibid.

326 "NEW WAR IS MARKED": McGee, letter to Col. Rod Paschall, March 24, 1986.

Chapter 9: Arleigh Burke, the Bay of Pigs, and the Launching of the Navy's Limited-War SEALs

327 SECLUDED ON A REMOTE BEACH: Eduardo Zayas-Bazán, unpublished autobiography of Eduardo Zayas-Bazán, undated, courtesy of Eduardo Zayas-Bazán.

328 TRADITIONAL UDT SACRAMENTS: Author interview with Andres Pruna, September 28, 2020.

328 MORE ACCESSIBLE "OLD-TIMER" and "MORE EMPHASIS ON THE LAND": Ibid.

328 "KITCHEN EXPLOSIVES": Peter Wyden, *Bay of Pigs: The Untold Story* (New York: Simon and Schuster, 1979), 132.

328 "BEAT THE SHIT OUT OF HIM": Author interview with Andres Pruna.

328 DEMOLITION RAIDS ON INLAND INSTALLATIONS: Ibid.
328 DAILY INTERRUPTION FOR MASS: Unpublished autobiography of Eduardo Zayas-Bazán.
328 12 APOSTLES: Wyden, *Bay of Pigs*, 132.
328 "SEA ROLL TO HIS STRIDE" and BASS VIOLIN: Potter, *Admiral Arleigh Burke*, 401.
328 FREIGHTER: "The Admiral and the Atom," *Time*, May 21, 1956.
328 "SUNNY": Ken Jones and Hubert Kelley, Jr., *Admiral Arleigh (31-Knot) Burke: The Story of a Fighting Sailor* (Annapolis: Naval Institute Press, 2001), 188.
329 "SLEPT IN A STABLE": David Alan Rosenburg, "Arleigh Burke: The Last CNO," Naval History and Heritage Command, December 18, 2016.
329 "FLUKE": Ibid.
330 "ARLEIGH BURKE WILL BE DEAD": Potter, *Admiral Arleigh Burke*, inset picture.
330 A COURSE SO INTENSE and "ONE DAY, MY FRIEND": Jones and Kelley, *Admiral Arleigh (31-Knot) Burke*, 79.
330 "NIGHT OF THE LONG LANCES" and "THE DOCTRINE OF FAITH": Ibid., 93.
330 "IF IT WILL HELP KILL JAPS": Ibid., 94.
331 A LITTLE AFTER MIDNIGHT and "HOLD YOUR HATS, BOYS": "The Admiral and the Atom," *Time*.
331 "SHEER EXHAUSTION": "90 Miles Below Rabaul," *Time*, December 6, 1943.
331 "EVERY SHIP IN THE ROADSTEAD": "The Admiral and the Atom," *Time*.
331 "THE CLASSIC SEA ACTION": Ibid.
331 "PROCEEDING AT 31 KNOTS": Ibid.
331 "BOILER-BUSTING": Jim Rasenburger, *The Brilliant Disaster: JFK, Castro, and America's Doomed Invasion of Cuba's Bay of Pigs* (New York: Scribner, 2011), 76.
331 CHIEF OF STAFF TO MARC MITSCHER: Jones and Kelley, *Admiral Arleigh (31-Knot) Burke*, 139–140.
331 "AGAINST THE SPOT": "The Admiral and the Atom," *Time*.
332 ALWAYS UP AT 0330: Jones and Kelley, *Admiral Arleigh (31-Knot) Burke*, 142.
332 "FOR YEARS TO COME": Ibid., 143.
332 "I WILL FIGHT THIS SHIP": Ibid.
332 THE NEXT FIVE YEARS: Burke, *Oral History of Adm. Arleigh Burke*, no. 4, 306.
332 BURKE PUSHED THE GROUP: Jones and Kelley, *Admiral Arleigh (31-Knot) Burke*, 149.
332 "COMBAT": Ibid., 25.
332 "ANOTHER TYPE OF WAR": Arleigh Burke, "Burke Speaks Out on Korea," *Proceedings*, May 2000.

332 "He was his own Chief of Staff": "An Admiral's 31-Knot Career," *Time,* June 6, 1955.

332 rotated them to the front: Potter, *Admiral Arleigh Burke,* 354–355.

332 "artillery commander": Jones and Kelley, *Admiral Arleigh (31-Knot) Burke,* 152.

333 watch alarm sounded: Potter, *Admiral Arleigh Burke,* 354–355.

333 he was forever pleased: Burke, *Oral History of Adm. Arleigh Burke,* no. 10, 320.

333 "general": Jones and Kelley, *Admiral Arleigh (31-Knot) Burke,* 163.

333 "five years ahead, ten years ahead": Ibid., 167.

333 MacArthur-style corncob pipe: Potter, *Admiral Arleigh Burke,* 401.

333 "battleship smokestack": Wyden, *Bay of Pigs,* 79.

333 "man-killing personal example": "The Admiral and the Atom," *Time.*

333 "You could hear the sighs": Jones and Kelley, *Admiral Arleigh (31-Knot) Burke,* 181.

333 Burke usually retired: Ibid., 166.

334 "direct foreign commitment": Edward Marolda, "The Influence of Burke's Boys on Limited War," *US Naval Institute Proceedings,* August 1981, 37.

334 "champion of limited war": Cdr. Malcolm W. Cagle (USN), "Sea Power and Limited War," *US Naval Institute Proceedings,* July 1958, 25.

334 "I have never heard": Rasenberger, *Brilliant Disaster,* 116.

334 Just before midnight: Unpublished autobiography of Eduardo Zayas-Bazán.

335 high-and-tight Pacific War Marine: Author interview with Andres Pruna.

335 No longer naked warriors: Unpublished autobiography of Eduardo Zayas-Bazán.

336 Once reoriented: Grayston L. Lynch, *Decision for Disaster: Betrayal at the Bay of Pigs* (Washington, D.C.: Potomac Books, 2009), 85.

336 Erupting with a deafening clatter: Unpublished autobiography of Eduardo Zayas-Bazán.

336 Never mind for a moment: Gen. Maxwell Taylor, Taylor Commission Report, ed. Kornbluh, Peter, assisted by Rafael Cohen, Michael Evans, and Catherine Nielsen, "The ULTRASENSITIVE Bay of Pigs," National Security Archive, George Washington University, May 3, 2000, available at https://nsarchive2.gwu.edu/NSAEBB/NSAEBB29/index.html: Gen. Maxwell Taylor, "Paramilitary Study Group Meeting at the Pentagon, Ninth Meeting," May 3, 1961, Document 4: After Action Report on Operation Pluto, May 4, 1961.

336 Burke's alarm clock: Wyden, *Bay of Pigs,* 206.

337 "wiping out": Rasenberger, *Brilliant Disaster,* 283.

337 "STRICKEN": Wyden, *Bay of Pigs,* 267.
337 "LET ME TAKE TWO JETS": Rasenberger, *Brilliant Disaster,* 282.
337 "BURKE, I DON'T WANT": Wyden, *Bay of Pigs,* 270.
337 IN THE THREE DAYS SINCE THEY HAD SEIZED: Author interview with Andres Pruna.
338 AS FOR THE FROGMEN LEFT BEHIND: Unpublished autobiography of Eduardo Zayas-Bazan; author interview with Eduardo Zayas-Bazán, September 26, 2020.
339 BELT BUCKLES: Wyden, *Bay of Pigs,* 303.
339 SEATED IN THE BACK OF A BUICK: Unpublished autobiography of Eduardo Zayas-Bazán; author interview with Eduardo Zayas-Bazán.
339 GET THEIR GEAR: Author interview with Andres Pruna.
339 FROM THIS PLATFORM OF DETERRENCE: Author interview with Andres Pruna; author interview with Amado Cantillo, September 28, 2020.
339 "HAD TWO SETS OF KHAKIS": Wyden, *Bay of Pigs,* 297.
339 OF THE 1,500 MEN: Taylor Commission Report, Ninth Meeting, May 3, 1961, recorded in After Action Report on Operation Pluto, May 4, 1961.
339 "DID WE WIN?": Author interview with Andres Pruna.
339 FOR THE DEAD BRIGADERS: Author interview with Andres Pruna.
340 "I'D NEVER SEEN": Author interview with Andres Pruna; author interview with Amado Cantillo.
340 "INCREDIBLE": Author interview with Amado Cantillo; author interview with Andres Pruna.
340 "SLOUCHING": Lynch, *Decision for Disaster,* 149.
340 NO RECORDING EQUIPMENT: Ibid., 148.
340 SKIN SUNBURNED BLACK: Wyden, *Bay of Pigs,* 301.
341 "AND WHAT THE ARMY": Adm. Arleigh Burke (CNO), Memorandum for OP-01, subject "Guerrilla Warfare," May 3, 1961, CNO papers, Immediate Office Files 1960–1969, NHHC, AR/134, box 17, folder 3300/2.
341 PROJECTED NUMBERS: W. R. Smedberg III, memo, "Record of Naval Personnel Trained in Guerrilla Warfare," June 2, 1961, CNO papers, Immediate Office Files 1960–1969, NHHC, AR/134, box 17, folder 3300/2.
341 "RECOMMENDED": Burke, "Guerrilla Warfare" memo, May 3, 1961.
341 "HOW CAN THE NAVY IMPROVE": William E. Gentner, Jr. (Director Strategic Plans Division), memo to CNO (OP-00), March 10, 1961, CNO papers, Immediate Office Files 1960–1969, NHHC, AR/134, box 17, folder 3300/2; Tom Hawkins, *The History and Heritage of US Navy SEALs* (Chicago: Pritzker Military, 2014), 30.
342 "I'M FIRST TO RECOGNIZE": Taylor Commission Report, Fourteenth Meeting, May 11, 1961.
343 "SMALL AMPHIBIOUS RAIDING PARTIES": Wallace M. Beakley, memo to CNO, "Program for the Development of an Improved Naval

Guerrilla/Counterguerrilla Capability," May 13, 1961, CNO papers, Immediate Office Files 1960–1969, NHHC, AR/134, box 17, folder 3300/2.

343 "The risks he ran": "Chief of Staff," *Time,* July 28, 1961.

343 caretaker's schedule: Potter, *Admiral Arleigh Burke,* 401.

344 "I think Napoleon himself": "Chief of Staff," *Time.*

344 *The Unclean Strumpet:* Ibid.

344 "strategy of Flexible Response": Maxwell D. Taylor (USA ret.), *The Uncertain Trumpet* (New York: Harper and Brothers, 1959), foreword.

344 "unmistakable honesty": "Chief of Staff," *Time.*

344 "entire southern half of the globe": Pres. John F. Kennedy, "Urgent National Needs" May 25, 1961, available at https://catalog.archives.gov/id/193915.

345 "attacks on enemy shipping": Wallace M. Beakley, CNO Memo to CIC US Atlantic and Pacific Fleets and Naval Forces Europe, "Planning for Development of an Improved Naval Guerrilla/Counterguerrilla Warfare Capability," June 5, 1961, CNO papers, Immediate Office Files 1960–1969, NHHC, AR/134, box 17, folder 3300/2.

345 "Sea Warriors": Roy Boehm and Charles W. Sasser, *First SEAL* (New York: Pocket Books, 1997), 127, 153.

345 "for all seasons": Ibid., 154.

345 holy man: Ibid., 93.

345 Che Guevara, and Mary Miles: Ibid., 153.

346 "seriously attacked": Mott, "Jungle River Operations" (Mott's "jungle river operations" in memo from Paul Stroop to CNO Anderson: 11/21/1961, attached to a memo in CNO papers, AR/134, box 17, folder 3300/2.

346 left breast of his white uniform: Burke's retirement photo.

346 "Will you please": Jones and Kelley, *Admiral Arleigh (31-Knot) Burke,* picture inset.

347 Anderson would instead show: "Nation: The CNO: The Unfaltering Competence and an Uncommon Flair," *Time,* November 2, 1962.

347 "besieged": Edward J. Marolda and Oscar P. Fitzgerald, *The United States and the Vietnam Conflict, Volume II, from Military Assistance to Combat, 1959–1965* (Washington, D.C.: Naval Historical Center, Department of the Navy, 1986).

347 Burke excused himself: Potter, *Admiral Arleigh Burke,* 438.

347 "None of those": Jones and Kelley, *Admiral Arleigh (31-Knot) Burke,* 193.

347 "These days guerrilla warfare": Burke, *Oral History of Adm. Arleigh Burke,* no. 3, 180.

Part 4: Exigency

Chapter 10: Kennedy's Army of Gladiators and the Counterinsurgency That Blunted Their Swords, Then Cleared the Way for Another Contender

351 15,000 AIRLINE MILES: Theodore C. Sorenson, *Kennedy* (New York: Bantam, 1966), 233.

351 "SCAVENGERS OF REVOLUTION": David Halberstam, *The Best and the Brightest* (New York: Random House, 1972), 123.

352 "WHAT WOULD YOU DO ABOUT BERLIN?": Cecil Stoughton, MGen. Chester V. Clifton, and Hugh Sidey, *The Memories: 1961–1963* (New York: W. W. Norton, 1980), 3–7.

352 ABLE TO CONSUME: Ibid., 3.

352 "CLASSIC TEXTS": Sorensen, *Kennedy,* 632.

352 "PERSONALLY [SUPERVISING] THE SELECTION": Ibid., 633.

352 "FAR MORE THAN ANY": Ibid., 632.

352 WHICH TOLD THE ALMOST-VICTORIOUS TALE: "Kennedy Attends Movie in Capital," *The New York Times,* February 4, 1961.

353 "OLD JOCKSTRAP COMMANDO-TYPES": Tom Clancy, Gen. Carl Stiner, and Tony Koltz, *Shadow Warriors: Inside the Special Forces* (New York: Berkley Books, 2002), 86–87.

353 MULTIWEEK EXERCISE: Bank, *From OSS to Green Berets,* 195–196.

354 FORT BRAGG COMMANDANT: "Embattled Badge of Courage," *Time,* August 22, 1969.

354 COURT-MARTIAL PROPORTIONS: Charles M. Simpson, III, *Inside the Green Berets: The First Thirty Years* (Novato: Presidio, 1983), 36.

354 "SNATCHED IT OFF": Ibid., 46.

354 "SHADES AND TEXTURES": Clancy, Stiner, and Koltz, *Shadow Warriors,* 69.

354 FLAT AS A PANCAKE and DOROTHEA KNITTING MILLS: Simpson, *Inside the Green Berets,* 31.

354 THE SAME SHADE: Barbara Gamarekian, "Washington Talk: John F. Kennedy, 1917–1963; Hundreds Are in Capital for 25th Remembrance," *The New York Times,* November 22, 1988; "The Real Berets," *Time,* July 19, 1968.

354 NEVER INTENDED TO REPLACE: Cleaver et al., "UN Partisan Warfare in Korea," 1956, 93.

355 JORDANIAN NATIONAL SOCCER TEAM and SAUDI ARABIAN AIRBORNE BATTALION: Simpson, *Inside the Green Berets,* 70–71.

355 SLACKS AND GOLF SHIRTS: Ibid., 86.

355 DRUNKENNESS and "LOW FIGHTING SPIRIT": Ibid., 87; Shelby L. Stanton, *The Green Berets at War: US Army Special Forces in Asia: 1956–1975* (Novato: Presidio, 1986), 31.

355 HARDY MOUNTAIN TRIBESMEN: Yarborough foreword in Simpson, *Inside the Green Berets,* xvii.

355 600 ILLITERATE TRIBESMEN: Simpson, *Inside the Green Berets,* 89.

356 "ODDBALL": Clancy, Stiner, and Koltz, *Shadow Warriors,* 67.

356 LITANY OF NONCONFORMITIES and "SHOWBIZ": Ibid., 72–74.

357 Yarborough survived an incomparable: Ibid.; Lt. Gen. William Pelham Yarborough, *Bail Out of North Africa: America's First Combat Parachute Missions 1942* (Williamstown: Philips Publications, 1979).

357 "4-power jeeps": Clancy, Stiner, and Koltz, *Shadow Warriors*, 78.

358 "the warm edges": Col. William Pelham Yarborough, "Unconventional Warfare: One Military View," *The Annals of the American Academy of Political and Social Science*, May 1962, vol. 341, 1–7.

358 "make superb irregular warfare soldiers": Ibid., 81.

358 "far from pleased": Ibid., 72.

358 "dead-end unit": Ibid., 70.

358 "firetraps": Simpson, *Inside the Green Berets*, 211.

359 Mao's Rules of Conduct: Yarborough foreword in Simpson, *Inside the Green Berets*, xi.

359 receiving classes in everything: Clancy, Stiner, and Koltz, *Shadow Warriors*, 71, 93.

359 laundry list of examples: "The Big Picture: This Is Our Strength," US Army Audiovisual Center, October 12, 1961, available at archive.org/details/gov.archives.arc.2569780.

359 hosting renowned authorities and Dr. J. K. Zawodny: Clancy, Stiner, and Koltz, *Shadow Warriors*, 89.

359 "When I mention my name": J. K. Zawodny, "Guerrilla Warfare and Subversion as a Means of Political Change," lecture prepared for delivery at the 1961 Annual Meeting of the American Political Science Association, Sheraton-Jefferson Hotel, St. Louis, Missouri, September 6–9, 1961, in CNO: Immediate Office Files 1960–1969, NHHC, AR/134, box 17, folder 3300/2, 10.

359 complete with courses: Simpson, *Inside the Green Berets*, 68.

360 "old jockstrap commandos": Clancy, Stiner, and Koltz, *Shadow Warriors*, 86–87.

360 "macho fun": Ibid., 88.

360 "being 'macho' is the opposite": Simpson, *Inside the Green Berets*, 212.

360 "a direct combat instrument": Clancy, Stiner, and Koltz, *Shadow Warriors*, 95.

360 "my religion": Lt. Gen. William Pelham Yarborough, "Tribute to LT General William Yarborough," December 26, 2016, available at https://www.youtube.com/watch?v=rHQYtcl1wiI.

360 "minds and sympathies": Yarborough, "Unconventional Warfare."

360 "talk in the woods": Clancy, Stiner, and Koltz, *Shadow Warriors*, 88.

360 "The rules are going to change": Ibid., 88.

361 "unbalanced": Stanton, *Green Berets at War*, 22.

361 On the rain-pelted morning: Author interview with Col. John F. Reed, November 10, 2017.

361 Kennedy's back was in no shape: Charles H. Briscoe, PhD, "JFK

Visits Fort Bragg," *Veritas,* vol. 14, no. 2, 2018, available at https://arsof-history.org/articles/v14n2_jfk_fort_bragg_visit_page_1.html.

362 "I THINK THE PRESIDENT": Clancy, Stiner, and Koltz, *Shadow Warriors,* 69.

362 LANDING AT POPE: Briscoe, "JFK Visits Fort Bragg."

362 "BLOSSOMED LIKE GIANT FLOWERS": "The Big Picture."

362 "SNUFF OUT A BRUSH-FIRE WAR": Ibid.

362 DREDGED DEEP ENOUGH: Briscoe, "JFK Visits Fort Bragg."

363 ROSE BOWL–STYLE: Ibid.

363 WORKED A PRINTING PRESS: Ibid.

363 DESCRIPTION OF EVENTS: "Tribute to LT General William Yarborough."

363 SKINNING OF A LIVE SNAKE: Simpson, *Inside the Green Berets,* 67.

363 TWO RAPPELLERS SLOWLY LOWERED: "The Big Picture."

363 125-POUND WEIGHT: Briscoe, "JFK Visits Fort Bragg."

363 "GRAND VARIETY": Clancy, Stiner, and Koltz, *Shadow Warriors,* 69.

363 DESCRIPTION OF DIALOGUE: Obituary of William Pelham Yarborough, Arlington National Cemetery.

364 SCRATCHED DOWN A NOTE: President John F. Kennedy, letter to Col. William Yarborough, JFK Library, October 12, 1961.

364 "ANGLE OF DROOP": Simpson, *Inside the Green Berets,* 33.

365 "IN THOSE PALMY DAYS": "Embattled Badge of Courage," *Time,* August 22, 1969.

365 "THE DAMNDEST BUNCH": Lawrence Freedman, *Kennedy's Wars: Berlin, Cuba, Laos, and Vietnam* (New York: Oxford University Press, 2000), 7.

365 "DISNEYLAND": Simpson, *Inside the Green Berets,* 67; "Embattled Badge of Courage," *Time.*

365 FIVE TIMES A MONTH: Ibid.

365 KEPT A GREEN BERET: Judie Mills, *John F. Kennedy* (New York: Franklin Watts, 1988), 204.

365 "IMPORTING" and PROTEST ITS POTENTIALLY DAMAGING: Harris Wofford, *Of Kennedys and Kings: Making Sense of the Sixties* (New York: Farrar, Straus & Giroux, 1980), 386.

365 "JACQUELINE KENNEDY'S OWN RIFLES": Simpson, *Inside the Green Berets,* 63.

365 "PRIDE": Sorensen, *Kennedy,* 632.

365 "WHY CAN'T WE JUST MAKE": Andrew F. Krepinevich, Jr., *The Army and Vietnam* (Baltimore: Johns Hopkins University Press, 1988), 35.

365 DIRECT TELEPHONE ACCESS: Author interview with Col. John F. Reed.

365 "MY GREAT ADVANTAGE": Yarborough foreword in Simpson, *Inside the Green Berets,* x.

365 "NEW AMERICAN BREED" and "UNCOMMON MEN": Halberstam, *Best and the Brightest,* 124.

365 "TRAINED TO TRAIN LOCAL PARTISANS": Sorensen, *Kennedy,* 632–633.

366 "TO LIBERATE FROM OPPRESSION": "To Liberate from Oppression," *Time,* May 11, 1962.

366 Within weeks of Kennedy's actions: "South Viet Nam: We Are Being Overrun," *Time,* April 20, 1962.

366 a twenty-four-year-old native Hawaiian: Leslie Wilcox, "Interview with Billie Gabriel," *Long Story Short with Leslie Wilcox*, PBS Hawaii, January 24, 2018, available at https://www.pbshawaii.org/long-story-short-with-leslie-wilcox-billie-gabriel/.

366 By the time a rescue force: Stanton, *Green Berets at War,* 44–45.

366 "you report to no other military": Simpson, *Inside the Green Berets,* 100–101.

367 roughly 700,000 backcountry tribesmen: Eugene G. Piasecki, "Civilian Irregular Defense Group: The First Years: 1961–1967," *Veritas,* vol. 5, no. 4, 2009.

367 "Old in the days of Julius Caesar": "The Big Picture."

367 "Yards": Howard Sochurek, "American Special Forces in Action in Vietnam," *National Geographic,* January 1965.

367 To do this, they constructed: Piasecki, "Civilian Irregular Defense Group."

367 crossbows: Col. Francis J. Kelly (USA), *The Green Berets in Vietnam, 1961–1971* (New York: Brassey's, 1991), 25.

367 poisoned arrows: "The Sourball Captain," *Time,* October 26, 1962.

367 two-week curriculum: Kelly, *Green Berets in Vietnam, 1961–1971,* 37.

367 tripods: "The Big Picture."

367 "two toes and three fingers": "The Sourball Captain," *Time.*

368 dapsone pills: Kelly, *Green Berets in Vietnam, 1961–1971,* 61.

368 engendered warm feelings: Ibid.

368 it would not be at all uncommon: Sochurek, "American Special Forces in Action in Vietnam."

368 rush in crates: Stanton, *Green Berets at War,* 42.

368 "Mike Forces" and $10 more per month: Lt. Col. L. H. "Bucky" Burruss, *Mike Force,* iUniverse, 2001, 56.

368 "bang bang" and thermal updrafts: Ibid., 59.

369 expanded this protective umbrella: Piasecki, "Civilian Irregular Defense Group."

369 "not apply": "The Big Picture."

369 Terry Cordell: "The Sourball Captain," *Time.*

369 twisted into an uncontrolled spiral: Ibid.; https://army.togetherweserved.com/army/servlet/tws.webapp.WebApp?cmd=ShadowBoxProfile&type=Person&ID=44513.

369 Montagnards insisted on accompanying: "The Sourball Captain," *Time.*

369 Ever sensitive to the aspirations: Stanton, *Green Berets at War,* 42.

369 By the time of Cordell's death: Piasecki, "Civilian Irregular Defense Group."

370 Head-scratching visitors: Stanton, *Green Berets at War,* 53.

370 Colonel George Morton: Ibid., 54.

370 a countrywide order of battle: Piasecki, "Civilian Irregular Defense Group."

370 bamboo drums and *"Tien-len!"*: "To Liberate from Oppression," *Time.*

371 At the CIDG camp: Stanton, *Green Berets at War,* 56–57. SF casualties by July 1963 include SSFG Robert J. Hain, Capt. James H. Brodt, Pfc. Neil K. MacIver, Capt. Laurence E. Hackley, MSgt. Jack L. Goodman, and Capt. Robert K. Mosier; see Stanton, *Green Berets at War,* 58–59.

371 At a solemn medal presentation: Ibid., 59.

371 In spite of such risks: Kelly, *Green Berets in Vietnam, 1961–1971,* 37.

371 "[flow] like wine": Simpson, *Inside the Green Berets,* 66.

371 "Middle America's answer to *The Graduate*": "Goodbye to All That," *Time,* February 8, 1971.

371 West Point's bandmaster: Clancy, Stiner, and Koltz, *Shadow Warriors,* 76.

371 articles for scholarly journals: Yarborough, "Unconventional Warfare."

371 Sheraton-Park Hotel: Simpson, *Inside the Green Berets,* 67.

371 no less a figure than Henry Fonda: "The Big Picture."

372 "arrogant and privileged" and "[occasional poke]": Stanton, *Green Berets at War,* 36.

373 immediately whisked: Stanton, *Green Berets at War,* 64.

373 would have delivered a speech: President John F. Kennedy, "Undelivered Remarks for Dallas Citizens Council," Papers of John F. Kennedy, Presidential Papers, President's Office Files, November 22, 1963.

373 A little after midnight: "The War Heats Up," *Time,* December 6, 1963.

373 through three lines: Anna Kavic, "Oral History of Isaac Camacho," Voces Oral History Project, Moody College of Communication, University of Texas at Austin, April 24, 2010.

374 "turned out" and *"Kennedy di-et"*: Eddie Morin, "Isaac 'Ike' Camacho: Escaped from Captivity During the Vietnam War," *Vietnam Magazine,* June 2000.

374 funeral guard: David Martin, "Green Berets Share Special Bond with JFK," CBS News, November 25, 2013.

374 JFK Funeral: "John F. Kennedy Funeral November 25, 1963," YouTube, available at https://www.youtube.com/watch?v=3KJQkn6zUvM.

375 "trackless": "To Liberate from Oppression," *Time.*

375 Highway 559: Merrill A. McPeak, "Bombing the Ho Chi Minh Trail," *The New York Times,* December 26, 2017.

375 "More a maze than a road": Ibid.

375 branches lashed together: Alan Hoe, *The Quiet Professional:*

Major Richard J. Meadows of the US Army Special Forces (Lexington: University Press of Kentucky, 2013).

375 "PIECE . . . OF REAL ESTATE": McPeak, "Bombing the Ho Chi Minh Trail."

376 "HODGE-PODGE": Stanton, *Green Berets at War*, 68.

376 "SOMETHING ELSE": Ibid., 108.

376 "PUT ROOTS IN THE POPULATION": Ibid., 106.

376 "SLEPT NIGHTS ON END": Ibid., 104.

376 OVER A PROSTITUTE: Stanton, *Green Berets at War*, 75.

376 WHEN THE DARKNESS EXPLODED: Edward F. Murphy, *Vietnam Medal of Honor Heroes* (New York: Ballantine Books, 1987), 9.

377 "WAR WITHIN A WAR": Sochurek, "American Special Forces in Action in Vietnam."

377 FIVE CIDG CAMPS: "Rights for the Mountain Men," *Time*, October 28, 1966.

377 MONTAGNARD FLAG: Sochurek, "American Special Forces in Action in Vietnam."

377 "NUMBERS MERCHANTS" and REDUCED HIS PIPELINE'S NOTORIOUS ATTRITION RATE: Simpson, *Inside the Green Berets*, 66.

378 TEMPORARY DUTY ORDERS and PER DIEM: Simpson, *Inside the Green Berets*, 168.

378 REVOLVING DOOR: Stanton, *Green Berets at War*, 89.

379 "HUNG UP" and "BLOCKING AND TACKLING": Col. Charlie A. Beckwith (USA) and Donald Knox, *Delta Force: A Memoir by the Founder of the Military's Most Secretive Special Operations Unit* (New York: William Morrow, 1984), 58.

379 "CAPTAIN, YOU DON'T UNDERSTAND": Ibid., 45.

Chapter 11: The First SEALs, Their Search for a Mission, and the Report That Found It for Them

380 AT ONE O'CLOCK: Thomas H. Keith and J. Terry Riebling, *SEAL Warrior: Death in the Dark: Vietnam 1968–1972* (New York: Thomas Dunne Books, 2009), 135.

380 THE TEAM'S AUTHORIZED STRENGTH: SEAL Team ONE Command History, 1966, NHHC, Post-1946 Command File, see microfiche #138 for CH and reports (1963–1973), (17 fiche), says initial complement was five officers, fifty enlisted.

380 RAISED JUST OUTSIDE OF NEWARK: Author interview with David Del Giudice, January 5, 2018.

381 "FORGET IT": Tad Devine and Ron Smith, "John Callaghan, Jr.: A Biography," *The Blast: Journal of Naval Special Warfare*, vol. 41, no. 4, 2009.

381 TWICE THE LENGTH: James Wood Tuma, "UDT Candidate Attrition, US Navy: The Influence of Exercise and Diet Supplement (Wheat

Germ Oil) on Fitness Changes During Training," Thesis for the Degree of Doctor of Philosophy in Physical Education, University of Illinois, July 1959.

381 "A COURSE SO TOUGH": Bill Stapleton, "Navy Frogmen—Top Skin-Divers of Them All," *Colliers,* May 27, 1955.

381 "APOLOGIZE TO TRAINEES": Ed Hymoff, "Our Navy's Undersea Commandos," *Real: The Exciting Magazine for Men,* vol. 8, no. 4, August 1956.

382 UNSCHEDULED HARASSMENTS: Edward F. Alf and Leonard V. Gordon, "A Fleet Validation of Selection Tests for Underwater Demolition Team Training," Bureau of Personnel: Technical Bulletin 57-6, July 1957.

382 AS FRIGID AS THIRTY-EIGHT DEGREES and A DISTANCE OF SEVEN MILES: Ibid.

382 "SELECTION TESTS": Alf and Gordon, "A Fleet Validation of Selection Tests for Underwater Demolition Team Training."

382 "REALISTIC" and "EXCESSIVE ATTRITION": Alfred F. Hertzka and Adolph V. Anderson, "Selection Requirements for Underwater Demolition Team Training," Bureau of Personnel: Technical Bulletin 56-4, March 1956.

382 IN THE COURSE OF THESE ASSESSMENTS: Cdr. J. W. Richmond (USN), "Evaluation of UDT Training," memo from Executive Officer of US Naval Amphibious School to Director of Analysis and Evaluation, October 6, 1966.

382 "WHO [MINIMIZED]": Alf and Gordon, "A Fleet Validation of Selection Tests for Underwater Demolition Team Training."

383 BENEFITS OF WHEAT GERM: Tuma, "UDT Candidate Attrition."

383 "SUCCESSFUL FROGMEN": D. W. Heyder (MD) and Helen S. Wambach (MA), "Sexuality and Affect in Frogmen: An Investigation of Personality Factors in Resistance to Prolonged Stress," *Archives of General Psychiatry,* vol. 2, September 1964.

383 "I HAVE NEVER MET": Stapleton, "Navy Frogmen—Top Skin-Divers of Them All," May 27, 1955.

383 "YOU EAT BARRACUDA": Ibid.

383 "SO EXCLUSIVE": Hymoff, "Our Navy's Undersea Commandos."

383 "SUBSURFACE DETECTIVES": Stapleton, "Navy Frogmen."

383 "NAVY'S NEPTUNES": JO3 Jim Deken (USN), "Navy's Neptunes—Grim Reapers, Good Samaritans," press release, Navy Office of Information, August 25, 1971.

383 "COMBINATION OF SAILOR AND MARINE": Hymoff, "Our Navy's Undersea Commandos."

384 "EVERYBODY WAS AN INNOVATOR": "Coast-to-Coast Celebrations Mark 40th Anniversary of Navy's First Two SEAL Teams," *Coronado Eagle and Journal,* vol. 92, no. 5, January 30, 2002.

384 AMONG THESE: LCdr. Roy Henry Boehm, Officer Biography Sheet; author interview with William Goines, November 26, 2018.

384 Most important of all and five-paragraph order: Author interview with Ronald Yeaw, July 11, 2018.

384 second CIA program: Author interview with Andres Pruna; author interview with Amado Cantillo.

385 flew from San Diego: Author interview with David Del Giudice.

385 "soldiers who fight from the sea": T. L. Bosiljevac, *SEALs: UDT/SEAL Operations in Vietnam* (Boulder: Paladin Press, 1990), 16.

385 within two months of inception: Ibid., 18.

385 *"sat cong"*: LCdr. W. L. Earley (USN), "Command History SEAL Team TWO: 1 January 1962 to 31 December 1966," May 31, 1967, NHHC, Post-1946 Command File, see microfiche #140 for CH and Reports (1962–1973), (13 fiche).

385 racked by tuberculosis and plague: Barry W. Enoch and Gregory A. Walker, *Teammates: SEALs at War* (New York: Pocket Books, 1996), 30.

385 "Vietnamese no wink": Ibid., 30.

386 "full regalia": Lt. JG Al Routh, "Addition for SEAL/Specwar History . . . MTT Section," undated, Office of the Command Historian of Naval Special Warfare Command (NSWC).

386 inspect the Atlantic Fleet: Pres. John F. Kennedy, "Trips: US Atlantic Fleet, April 1962: 13–14," available at https://www.jfklibrary.org/asset-viewer/archives/JFKPOF/107/JFKPOF-107-019.

386 late-afternoon pierside review: Pres. John F. Kennedy, "President Kennedy Greets SEALs; Boards USS Northampton (CC-1), 5:20 PM," available at https://www.jfklibrary.org/asset-viewer/archives/JFKWHP/1962/Month%2004/Day%2013/JFKWHP-1962-04-13-F?image_identifier=JFKWHP-KN-C21119.

386 "When I was in Norfolk": Bosiljevac, *SEALs,* 19.

387 litany of SEAL operations: Earley, "Command History SEAL Team TWO: 1 January 1962 to 31 December 1966."

387 submerged beneath the Bosporus: Ibid.

388 When not engaged: Ibid. Marine Corps animosity exemplified in quote by a Marine Force Recon officer to his superior after bumping up against the Navy's commandos in a fleet-wide exercise in the Philippines: "I personally feel [that] SEAL is infringing on USMC missions by moving inland from the high water mark." Michael Lee Lanning and Ray Stubbe, *Inside Force Recon: Recon Marines in Vietnam* (Lanham: Stackpole Books, 2017), 49–50.

388 "mean as hell": "Mr. Pacific," *Time,* January 6, 1961.

388 "screaming dive through flak": "Big Man, Big Moment," *Time,* June 9, 1958.

388 "3-star officers": Potter, *Admiral Arleigh Burke,* 407.

388 mustard-colored former morgue : "Mr. Pacific," *Time.*

388 moccasin-clad feet: *Reminiscences of Captain Phil Bucklew,* no. 7, 323.

388 "A bear for facts and figures": Ibid.

388 "I DON'T KNOW EXACTLY": *Reminiscences of Captain Phil Bucklew,* no. 7, 323.

389 "THE LEAST ATTRACTIVE THEATER": "Mr. Pacific," *Time.*

389 "INLAND OPERATIONS": James M. McPherson, *War on the Waters: The Union and Confederate Navies, 1861–1865* (Chapel Hill: University of North Carolina Press, 2012), 70.

389 BRINK'S BOQ: Philip W. Koehler, letter to John B. Dwyer, March 4, 1993, NSWC.

390 IN THE EVENINGS: Author interview with David Del Giudice.

390 "BULGING": *Reminiscences of Captain Phil Bucklew,* no. 7, 332.

390 BARS, THEATERS, POOLS, AND BOWLING ALLEYS: LCdr. Philip W. Koehler (USN), "Counter-insurgency Efforts in Vietnam, Personal Comments Concerning," unaddressed memorandum, January 2, 1964, NSWC.

390 ATOP THEIR HOTEL: *Reminiscences of Captain Phil Bucklew,* no. 7, 334.

390 STABBED IN THE CHEST: John Darrell Sherwood, *War in the Shallows: US Navy Coastal and Riverine Warfare in Vietnam 1965–1968* (Washington, D.C.: Department of the Navy, 2015), 21–22.

390 "HEART TROUBLE": *Reminiscences of Captain Phil Bucklew,* no. 7, 325–326.

390 "CLOSET": Koehler, letter to John B. Dwyer, March 4, 1993, NSWC.

390 FOUR FOOTBALL CONTRACTS: *Reminiscences of Captain Phil Bucklew,* no. 1, 20.

391 COLUMBUS BULLIES: Ibid., 19.

391 LEAGUE CHAMPIONSHIP: "Columbus Bullies," *Ohio History Central,* available at https://www.ohiohistorycentral.org/w/Columbus_Bullies?rec=2961.

391 "BALLS OF FIRE": *Reminiscences of Captain Phil Bucklew,* no. 2, 65.

391 HE SKIMMED TO THE COAST: "Phil Hinkle Bucklew, Navy Cross Citation," *The Hall of Valor Project,* https://valor.militarytimes.com/hero/19876.

392 "BIG STOOP": Stratton, *Saco,* 226.

393 "EXTENSIVE PHYSICAL SURVEY": Capt. P. H. Bucklew (USN), "Report of Recommendations Pertaining to Infiltration into South Vietnam of Viet Cong Personnel, Supporting Materials, Weapons and Ammunition," February 15, 1964, 1, NSWC.

393 "MORE THAN 5,000 MILES": Navy News Release, no. 287-69, "Mekong Delta," March 29, 1969, UDT-SEAL Museum.

393 "GRIDIRON": Georgie Anne Geyer, "The CIA's Hired Killers," *True Magazine,* February 1970.

394 NEVER SAW INSURGENTS: Author interview with David Del Giudice.

394 RECOILLESS RIFLE ATTACKS: Bucklew Report.

394 "DON'T WE DO SOMETHING": *Reminiscences of Captain Phil Bucklew,* no. 7, 334.

394 CREAKY JUNK: Bucklew Report.

394 “COULDN’T BE COMING”: *Reminiscences of Captain Phil Bucklew,* no. 7, 345–346.
395 To CHOKE OFF: Sherwood, *War in the Shallows,* 12.
395 “DIRECT OBSERVATION”: Bucklew Report, Appendix 1, 1, NSWC.
395 “LACKADAISICALLY”: Bucklew Report, Appendix 2, 1, NSWC.
395 “FROM HIGH WATER MARK INLAND”: Bucklew Report, Conclusions.
396 65 PERCENT: Bucklew Report.
396 “MODERATELY AMPHIBIOUS”: “M113 Armored Personnel Carrier,” Wikipedia, available at https://en.wikipedia.org/wiki/M113_armored_personnel_carrier.
396 HAD GROWN THE VIETNAMESE NAVY: Sherwood, *War in the Shallows,* 12–17.
396 COMPLETELY EXCLUDE THE RAG: Bucklew Report, Conclusions.
396 ASSAULT VESSELS: Sherwood, *War in the Shallows,* 17.
396 “TAXI SERVICE”: Ibid., 10.
396 “LACKEY BOY”: Ibid.
396 COULD HARDLY OPERATE: Ibid.
396 BARELY PREVENT A SWAMPED BOAT and EVERY CREWMAN ASLEEP: Ibid., 18.
396 BUSH HATS AND KHAKI UNIFORMS: Ibid., 16.
396 “DISGRUNTLED AND DISCOURAGED” and LESS BENEFICIAL TO THEIR CAREERS: Koehler, “Counter-insurgency Efforts in Vietnam,” January 2, 1964, NSWC.
397 “THEY WERE THE MOST”: Sherwood, *War in the Shallows,* 12.
397 “SLOW AND TIME CONSUMING EFFORT”: Bucklew Report.
397 SEABEES and “RAPIDLY LOSING THEIR NAVAL IDENTITY”: Koehler, “Counter-insurgency Efforts in Vietnam,” January 2, 1964.
397 “WORTHY OF FURTHER STRESS”: Ibid.
397 STASHED AWAY IN DANANG: *Reminiscences of Captain Phil Bucklew,* no. 7, 335.
397 DINED WITH AMBASSADOR HENRY CABOT LODGE: *Reminiscences of Captain Phil Bucklew,* no. 7, 325–327.
397 HE HAD COFFEE: Ibid.
397 DEPUTY COMMANDER WILLIAM WESTMORELAND: Ibid., no. 7, 331.
398 GRACIOUSLY ENTERTAINED ALL QUESTIONS: Author interview with David Del Giudice.
398 MACV INTELLIGENCE COLONEL DUTCH KRAMER: *Reminiscences of Captain Phil Bucklew,* no. 7, 345.
398 HANDWRITTEN SECTION: *Reminiscences of Captain Phil Bucklew,* no. 7, 352.
398 BUCKLEW TYPED: Author interview with David Del Giudice.
398 “WORKING MEMBERS”: Bucklew Report.
398 “UNCLE SAM’S WEB FEET”: McPherson, *War on the Waters,* 1.
398 “MODIFIED AMPHIBIOUS”: Bucklew Report.
398 COULD HAVE DRAWN ATTENTION: Author interview with David Del Giudice.

399 “MISSING THE BOAT”: LCdr. Philip W. Koehler (USN), “Missing the Boat . . . ,” undated, NSWC.

399 SLOW AND TIME CONSUMING: Bucklew Report.

399 “CAUSE THE EFFORT”: Bucklew Report, Appendix V, 3, NSWC.

399 MENTIONED THE WORD: Bucklew Report, 11.

399 “SOMEWHAT NEBULOUS FIELD”: *Reminiscences of Captain Phil Bucklew,* no. 9, 432–433.

399 FOUR FEWER MENTIONS: Bucklew Report, 11.

399 “ENGENDER MORE FIGHT BACK SPIRIT” and “PURSUIT RAIDERS”: Ibid., 13.

399 “THE OVER-WATER TRANSPORT”: Bucklew Report, Conclusions.

400 “CROSS-EXAMINED” and “DO YOU FEEL IT IS RIGHT”: *Reminiscences of Captain Phil Bucklew,* no. 7, 347.

400 OFFICIALLY DISTRIBUTED: Bucklew Report, cover sheet; *Reminiscences of Captain Phil Bucklew,* no. 7, 352–354.

400 “HOT POTATO”: *Reminiscences of Captain Phil Bucklew,* no. 7, 354.

Chapter 12: The Dam Break of Conventional War in Vietnam, and the Following Flood of Raiders That Failed to Beat the Navy to the Mekong Delta; All but One

401 AIRBORNE OPERATIONS: MACVSOG Command History, Annex N to Appendix B, July 10, 1970, Tab A, NSWC.

401 SUCCESSES INCLUDED: Bosiljevac, *SEALs,* 24–27.

402 “DEEP SURVEILLANCE”: Lanning and Stubbe, *Inside Force Recon,* 37.

403 “COMMANDOS OF THE CORPS”: Ibid., 2.

403 WHILE THIS STATUS DID NOT: Ibid., 49.

403 ONE OFFICER, THREE ENLISTED MEN: Bosiljevac, *SEALs,* 25.

403 IN FAVOR OF ADDING: Lanning and Stubbe, *Inside Force Recon,* 62.

403 LEI-BEARING VIETNAMESE GIRLS: Colin Leinster, “The Two Wars of General Lew Walt,” *Life,* May 26, 1967.

403 TWO DOWNTURNED PADDLES: Bosiljevac, *SEALs,* 36.

403 REASSIGNED TO VARIOUS SPECIAL FORCES CAMPS: Lanning and Stubbe, *Inside Force Recon,* 63.

404 “SQUAD LEADER IN THE SKY”: Leinster, “The Two Wars of General Lew Walt,” May 26, 1967.

404 “A MEANS TO AN END”: Lanning and Stubbe, *Inside Force Recon,* 4.

404 “YOU FIND”: Ibid., 62.

404 BEFORE THE CAVALRY COULD: Ibid., 69–72.

404 PLACE THEM UNDER THE COMMAND: Ibid., 72–73.

405 FRENCH RESTAURANTS: Burruss, *Mike Force,* 88.

405 USING THEIR ABSENCES: Beckwith and Knox, *Delta Force,* 58.

405 OF THE FIRST FORTY: R. C. Morris, *The Ether Zone: US Army Special Forces Detachment B-52, Project Delta* (Ashland: Hellgate Press, 2009), 15.

405 IMPROVEMENT OF TACTICAL AIR SUPPORT: Project Delta AARs prior

to August 20, 1965, NARA, RG 472, entry 5th Special Forces Group Det. B-52, box 2.

406 This completed, he distributed and "Will guarantee": Beckwith and Knox, *Delta Force,* 58.

406 three-week selection course: Ibid., 58–60.

407 The results were mixed and "deficiencies": Maj. Charles A. Beckwith (USA), After Action Report to OPORD 16-65 (Dan Thong 7 II Corps), August 20, 1965, NARA, RG 472, entry 5th Special Forces Group Det. B-52, box 2.

407 "ropes of green and orange tracers": Beckwith and Knox, *Delta Force,* 74.

407 sixty stacked body bags: Ibid., 72.

407 a man with no experience: Ibid., 56.

407 Beckwith gathered a force: Ibid., 71–72.

408 "commando type": Maj. Charles A. Beckwith (USA), Sequence of Events for Plei Me Operation for Period 21–28 October, 1965, November 15, 1965, NARA, RG 472, entry 5th Special Forces Group Det. B-52, box 2.

408 672 sorties: Stanton, *Green Berets at War,* 112–116.

408 khaki-clad bodies: Beckwith and Knox, *Delta Force,* 77.

408 "the best troops": Ken Burns and Lynn Novick, "Plei Me and the Ia Drang Valley," *The Vietnam War: A Film by Ken Burns and Lynn Novick,* PBS, 2017.

408 "to patrol the close in area": Beckwith, Sequence of Events for Plei Me Operation for Period 21–28 October, 1965.

408 "in straight-forward offensive tactics": Ibid.

408 "All-American": Beckwith and Knox, *Delta Force,* 78–79.

408 "you go find them": Ibid., 86.

409 while scouting a landing zone: Ibid., 89.

409 "all Infantry Units of Brigade size": Maj. Charles A. Beckwith (USA), After Action Report to OPORD 23-65 (III Corps, 1st US InfDiv), December 23, 1965, NARA, RG 472, entry 5th Special Forces Group Det. B-52, box 2.

410 "out-G the G": Michael Sallah and Mitch Weiss, *Tiger Force: A True Story of Men and War* (New York: Little, Brown and Company, 2006), 13.

410 The first real training program: MACV Recondo School Unit History, 5th Special Forces Group, Annex A to Section III, undated, NARA, RG 472, entry P1108, box 1.

410 none would arrive in Vietnam: Michael Lee Lanning, *Inside the LRRPs: Rangers in Vietnam* (New York: Presidio Press, 1988), 52.

410 increasingly diluted pool: F. J. West, Jr., "The Navy SEAL Commandos: A Case of Military Decision Making and Organizational Change," RAND Study, March 1969, UDT-SEAL Museum and NHHC, Vietnam Command File Collection (Coll 372), box 264.

410 SIMPLY VOLUNTEERING: Lanning, *Inside the LRRPs,* 101.

410 REDHEADED WEST POINT WASHOUT: Col. David H. Hackworth, *About Face: The Odyssey of an American Warrior* (New York: Touchstone, 1990), 485.

410 SPREAD HIS MEN ALONG A SKIRMISH LINE: Phil Neel, "Vietnam Memories My Canh II," *327th Infantry Veterans,* available at www.327infantry.org/homescreamingeagles/inside-the-wire/discussions/vietnam-memories-my-canh-ii/.

410 ELEVEN WOUNDED, THREE KILLED: Ibid.

411 ESTABLISHED AS THE RECONDO SCHOOL: MACV Recondo School Unit History, Annex A to Section III.

411 MANY PREREQUISITES: Maj. James H. Morris (USA), MACV Recondo School Program of Instruction, 5th Special Forces Group, December 14, 1968, NARA, RG 472, entry P1108, box 1.

411 EVERYTHING BUT ASHTRAYS: Class Opening Ceremony and Rehearsal, MACV Recondo School, 5th Special Forces Group, undated, NARA, RG 472, entry P1108, box 1.

411 "NO MATTER HOW TOUGHENED UP": Michael Herr, *Dispatches* (New York: Vintage Books, 1991), 7.

411 BEDECKED IN BOONDOCK HATS: Hackworth, *About Face,* 485.

411 SUPPRESSED M16S AND SAWED-OFF: Lanning, *Inside the LRRPs,* 125.

411 "DO NOT LOSE SIGHT": COC Class Opening Remarks, Recondo and Airborne Class Graduation Speech, 5th Special Forces Group, undated, NARA, RG 0472, Entry P1108, box 1.

412 PREFERRING NOT TO WASTE: Boehm and Sasser, *First SEAL,* 235.

412 HAND-HOLDING: Ibid., *First SEAL,* 232–236.

412 TWO-MONTH COMBAT COURSE: Boehm's Bronze Star citation, July 13, 1964.

412 PRIMER CORD: Boehm and Sasser, *First SEAL,* 232–236.

412 "BALLS IN PARENTHESES": Ibid., 265.

412 TREATING PATROLS: Ibid., 244–245.

412 VENTURED SO FAR: Boehm's Bronze Star citation, July 13, 1964.

412 "POACHING" and "OUR CANTEENS": Boehm and Sasser, *First SEAL,* 258.

413 THESE WERE THE TAX COLLECTORS: "Organization Man," *Time,* August 25, 1967.

413 SEPARATE COG: Ibid.

413 "ONE-MAN, TWO-YEAR WAR": Geyer, "The CIA's Hired Killers," *True Magazine,* February 1970.

413 *THE DIRTY DOZEN:* Randall B. Woods, *Shadow Warrior: William Egan Colby and the CIA* (New York: Basic Books, 2013), 288.

413 "PART THE RED SEA": Author interview with Michael Wagner, July 8, 2018.

414 "I NEVER SAW ANYTHING LIKE THAT": Author interview with Maynard Weyers, June 10, 2018.

414 "PERFECTIONIST ADVISOR": Author interview with Franklin Anderson, July 8, 2018

415 "ENTIRELY OBLITERATED": SKC Robert K. Wagner, *Profile and Interview of Bob Wagner*, Recorded on June 20, 1967, available at http://www.navyfrogmen.com/BobWagner.html.

415 "REALLY DOWN OUR ALLEY": Ibid.

416 "OUTGUERRILLA THE GUERRILLA": Ibid.

416 IN THE FALL OF 1966: Ibid.

416 "MORE FLEXIBLE": Ibid.

Part 5: Culmination

Chapter 13: The Derailing of the First Direct-Action SEALs in the Rung Sat, and the Detachment That Restored Their Prospects

422 "NO TROOPS TO SPARE": RAdm. Norvell G. Ward (USN), letter to John B. Dwyer, April 26, 1984, NSWC. A "special zone" was classified as such because it was believed to conceal a vast and hidden network of enemy supply dumps. Josiah Bunting, *The Lionheads* (New York: George Braziller, 1972), 86.

422 TWO MONTHS OF PLANNING: Ward, letter to John B. Dwyer, April 26, 1984.

422 SALTWATER SHOWERS: Woolard account in Fawcett, ed., *Hunters and Shooters,* 244.

422 BARREL LATRINES: Author interview with Maynard Weyers.

422 HOW BEST TO INTERPRET: Ibid.

423 "UTTERLY UNFLAMBOYANT": Adam Bernstein, "Navy Rear Admiral Norvell G. Ward Dies," *The Washington Post,* August 2, 2005.

423 EMERGENCY APPENDECTOMY: George Weller, "'Doc' Lipes Commandeers a Submarine Officers' Wardroom," *Chicago Daily News,* December 14, 1942.

424 UNMARRIED CREWMEN: John Farrier, "The Submarine That Sank a Train: The Extraordinary Raid of the USS *Barb,*" *Neatorama,* November 12, 2014, available at https://www.neatorama.com/2014/11/12/The-Submarine-That-Sank-a-Train-The-Extraordinary-Raid-of-the-USS-Barb/.

424 "LATITUDE": Ward, letter to John B. Dwyer, April 26, 1984.

424 TRADITIONAL INTERPRETATION OF DIRECT ACTION: Author interview of Franklin Anderson, June 16, 2018; author interview with Maynard Weyers.

425 "MORASS" and "EVIL PLACE": "South Asia Briefing Report No. 1—Vietnam, Jackstay 24890 HD," Periscope Film LLC 2009, available at https://youtu.be/byKDu4zHgMY.

425 "FOREST OF ASSASSINS": "Three Years with the River Patrol Force," Navy News Release: River Patrol Force, Public Affairs Office, FPO San Francisco 96627, Release Number: 287-69, March 29, 1969, NHHC, Post-1946 Command Files.

425 HIDEOUT FOR PIRATES: P. E. Kane, River Squadron FIVE Command History, from Cdr. River Squadron FIVE to CNO, January 19, 1968, NHHC, Post-1946 Command Files; also known as "the killer jungle."
425 OPERATION JACKSTAY: Sherwood, *War in the Shallows,* 100–103.
426 NOT MUCH HIGHER THAN THE AVERAGE GI'S ARMPIT: "To Liberate from Oppression," *Time.*
426 EVERYWHERE AND NOWHERE: Ibid.
427 "THE FOREST OF IRON-TREES": West, "Navy SEAL Commandos," 5.
427 "QUARANTINE" and "DON'T UNPACK": Author interview with Maynard Weyers.
427 RAP SHEET and ONGOING INFLUENCE: Author interview of Franklin Anderson, June 16, 2018.
428 INTENTIONAL REBRANDING: Ibid.
429 NOT EVEN BEEN PERMITTED: Author interview with Maynard Weyers.
429 FORGET WHAT YOU THINK: Ibid.; confirmed in author interview of Franklin Anderson, June 16, 2018.
429 WEYERS HIMSELF TYPED: Author interview with Maynard Weyers.
429 EVEN THEIR SUPPORT: Ibid.; author interview with Tom Truxell, June 16, 2018.
429 "AN ESPECIALLY IRRITATING SPECIES" and CHURCHILL ACCOUNT: John G. Hubbell, "Supercommandos of the Wetlands," *Reader's Digest,* June 1967.
430 "STARTLED FACE": West, "Navy SEAL Commandos," 5.
430 "MOSCONE'S JUNGLE BOOTS": Deployment photographs of Tom Truxell; author interview with Tom Truxell.
430 "WE DIDN'T KNOW": Ibid.
431 "SUCKING EXPLOSION OF MUDWALKING" and AVOIDED THE FOOTPRINTS: Hubbell, "Supercommandos of the Wetlands."
431 TO IT THEY ADDED: Author interview with Tom Truxell.
431 JACKPOT AMBUSH: Ibid.; author interview with Maynard Weyers.
432 PURSUED A TIP: Ibid.
432 KEEN-EYED TWENTY-EIGHT-YEAR-OLD: Ibid.; "Remembering Radarman Second Class Billy W. Machen, USN," Naval History Blog, NHHC, August 19, 2010, available at https://www.navalhistory.org/2010/08/19/remembering-radarman-second-class-billy-w-machen-usn.
432 CUT DOWN BY AN ERUPTION: Author interview with Tom Truxell.
433 ENEMY-PACKED HAYSTACK: Hubbell, "Supercommandos of the Wetlands."
433 "YEA, THOUGH I WALK": Email from Truxell to author, July 9, 2018.
434 "VISELIKE": Hubbell, "Supercommandos of the Wetlands."
434 ACCURATE OR NOT: LCdr. F. W. Anderson (USN), Command History SEAL Team ONE, 1966, NHHC, Post-1946 Command File, see microfiche #138 for CH and Reports (1963–1973), (17 fiche).
434 ALL BUT ELIMINATED THE ROCKET ATTACKS: Ibid.; Bosiljevac, *SEALs,* 74.

434 HAD MET WESTMORELAND: Author interview of Franklin Anderson, June 16, 2018.

435 "I WOULD LIKE TO HAVE": LCdr. F. W. Anderson (USN), Command History SEAL Team ONE, 1967, March 29, 1968, NHHC, Post-1946 Command File, see microfiche #138 for CH and Reports (1963–1973), (17 fiche).

435 "THE BIGGEST NAVY ON THE PLANET": Hubbell, "Supercommandos of the Wetlands." At that moment there were eighty-two 12-man A-Teams in Vietnam, or 984 Green Berets assigned to A-Teams. This did not include B-Teams, or C-Teams, and did not include those Green Berets in Fort Bragg or around the world. By comparison, Det. Golf had three 12-man platoons; and Det. Alfa had two 12-man platoons, or 60 men—6 percent of the Green Berets' A-Team allotment.

435 "ONE OF THE MOST PUBLICITY-SHY": Ibid.

435 "TO EVERY SEAL'S HORROR": Ibid.; "Unconventional Commandos," *Time,* January 12, 1968.

435 "ADVENTURES": Anderson, Command History SEAL Team ONE, 1967.

435 "NAVY UNWRAPS ITS SEALS": Ibid.

435 "I WOULD NEVER DOWNGRADE": Hubbell, "Supercommandos of the Wetlands."

436 CONVENED A CONFERENCE: Anderson, Command History SEAL Team ONE, 1967.

436 "NEGATIVE CONTACT": Det. Golf Operational Summaries, 1967, NHHC, Post-1946 Command File, see microfiche #138 for CH and Reports (1963–1973), (17 fiche).

436 WAS NOT LISTED: Anderson, Command History SEAL Team ONE, 1966.

436 ANDERSON HAD ORDERED: Anderson, Command History SEAL Team ONE, 1967.

436 SIX-WEEK-LONG PREDEPLOYMENT COURSE: Author interview with Guy Stone, October 20, 2018.

436 "OUTSIDE OF A PURELY NAVAL": LCdr. W. L. Earley (USN), Command History SEAL Team TWO: 1 January 1967 to 31 December 1967, February 8, 1968, NHHC, Post-1946 Command File, see microfiche #138 for CH and Reports (1963–1973), (17 fiche).

436 "TRUE BASTION OF IRON": "Organization Man," *Time.*

Chapter 14: The Direct-Action SEALs Who Dodged Diversion, Then Perfected a Mission That Propelled the Teams Past the Riverbanks, into History

437 "NO JURISDICTION TO PROSECUTE": LCdr. W. L. Earley (USN), Command History SEAL Team TWO: 1 January 1967 to 31 December 1967.

437 THREE WEEKS' WORTH: Larry Bailey account in Fawcett, ed., *Hunters and Shooters,* 133.

437 "SIMPLE AMBUSHES": Earley, Command History SEAL Team TWO: 1 January 1967 to 31 December 1967.

438 THE SUBSEQUENT INVESTIGATION: Fawcett, ed., *Hunters and Shooters,* 135; Dale Andrade, "*Rogue Warrior:* Is Truth the First Casualty in War Books?," *Soldier of Fortune,* March 1994.

438 "CENTERED AROUND": Anderson, Command History SEAL Team ONE, 1967, March 29, 1968.

438 SLEEPY AND MORIBUND: Adm. Elmo Russell Zumwalt, Jr., USN (Ret.)—Staff Officers Oral History (Capt. Howard J. Kerr, Jr., USN (Ret.), Capt. W. Lewis Glenn, Jr., USN, and Adm. Worth H. Bagley, USN (Ret.)), US Naval Institute, 1989, 29–30.

439 "ALMOST INDECENT": Sherwood, *War in the Shallows,* 168.

439 "BOTH AS A TRAINING AND OPERATIONAL FORCE": Anderson, Command History SEAL Team ONE, 1967.

439 AS VETH CHEWED ON THE OPTIONS: Hoyt, *SEALs at War,* loc. 2473.

441 HAD TAKEN A TWISTED PATH: Author interview with Robert Peterson, October 22, 2018.

441 PETERSON'S FIRST REAL-WORLD ASSIGNMENT: Ibid.

443 THIS BILLET HAD BEEN OCCUPIED: Ibid.; author interview with Robert Peterson; Fawcett, ed., *Hunters and Shooters,* 71.

444 SUBSTITUTING SWAMP MUD: Harry Constance and Randall Fuerst, *Good to Go: The Life and Times of a Decorated Member of the U.S. Navy's Elite SEAL Team Two* (New York: Avon, 2014), 62.

444 DRAPING THEM WITH SHEETS: Ibid., 76.

445 GALLAGHER'S EARLY LIFE: Author interview with Neena Gallagher, November 25, 2018.

445 GALLAGHER JOINED: Author interview with William Goines.

446 FIRST ALL-TURKISH NAVY UDT CLASS: Earley, Command History SEAL Team TWO: 1 January 1962 to 31 December 1966.

446 RARE OCCASION HE WAS SEEN: Author interview with Erasmo Riojas, January 25, 2018.

446 "SENSITIVITY OF A ROCK": Constance and Fuerst, *Good to Go,* 11.

446 "PULLED INTO HIMSELF": Author interview with William Goines.

446 CARRYING A REPUTATION: Rudy Boesch account in Fawcett, ed., *Hunters and Shooters,* 22.

446 A BROODING PRESENCE: Author interview with Neena Gallagher.

446 "NO ONE ARGUED": Author interview with Roy Matthews, May 6, 2017.

446 ESSENTIALLY AN ORPHAN: Author interview with Neena Gallagher.

446 SIX DEUCE-AND-A-HALF CARGO TRUCKS: Constance and Fuerst, *Good to Go,* 5.

447 900 POUNDS OF DOG FOOD: Boynton account in Fawcett, ed., *Hunters and Shooters,* 71.

448 ONE OF PETERSON'S FORMER CLASSMATES: Author interview with Robert Peterson.

448 DISSEMINATING A DETAILED BRIEFING: Author interview with Roy Matthews.

448 "OF 50,000 ROUNDS AND ONE BANDAID": Ibid.

449 THEIR FIRST MISSION: SEAL Team TWO, 7th Platoon Barn Dance Card 7-1, 29OCT67, UDT-SEAL Museum.

449 AFTER THE 7TH PLATOON REBOARDED: Author interview with Robert Peterson.

449 "HIT THE BEACH": Author interview with Erasmo Riojas.

449 WITHIN TWO HOURS: SEAL Team TWO, 7th Platoon Barn Dance Card 7-2, 31OCT67, UDT-SEAL Museum.

450 "I THINK WE KILLED THAT GUY": Author interview with Roy Matthews.

450 THE RESULT OF THIS SWEEP: SEAL Team TWO, 7th Platoon Barn Dance Card 7-2, 31OCT67, UDT-SEAL Museum.

450 "HEAVILY BOOBY TRAPPED BUNKER COMPLEX": SEAL Team TWO, 7th Platoon Barn Dance Card 7-4, 06NOV67, UDT-SEAL Museum.

450 SECURING THEIR SPOONS WITH SAFETY PINS: Author interview with Erasmo Riojas.

450 GALLAGHER LANDED HARD: Author interview with Robert Peterson.

450 "IS THIS GOING TO SURVEY ME OUT?": Boynton account in Fawcett, ed., *Hunters and Shooters,* 88.

450 7TH PLATOON HAD LOST NOT ONLY: SEAL Team TWO, 7th Platoon Barn Dance Cards: 7-5, 08NOV67 / 7-6, 11NOV67 / 7-7, 14NOV67 / 7-10, 14NOV67, UDT-SEAL Museum.

451 SECOND FRONT WITH DYSENTERY: Author interview with Erasmo Riojas.

451 IN THE THIRD WEEK OF NOVEMBER: SEAL Team TWO, 7th Platoon Barn Dance Cards: 7-10, 14NOV67 / 7-10, 15NOV67 / 7-11, 16NOV67 / 7-13, 19NOV67, UDT-SEAL Museum.

451 WATSON'S SQUAD CONDUCTED THREE MISSIONS: SEAL Team TWO, 7th Platoon Barn Dance Cards: 7-7, 14NOV67 / 7-8, 17NOV67 / 7-9, 20NOV67, UDT-SEAL Museum.

451 IRRITATED EVERY MAN: Author interview with Erasmo Riojas.

451 "HE WAS SCARED SHITLESS": Henry Rhinebolt, *Deposition of Henry Rhinebolt*, Watson v. Constance, et al., Federal Civil Lawsuit, Virginia Eastern District Court, Case No. 2:98-cv-00072-JBF, filed February 8, 1999.

451 A RUMOR THAT WATSON EXACERBATED: Author interview with Ronald Yeaw.

451 BUSHWHACKED AND CAPTURED: SEAL Team TWO, 7th Platoon Barn Dance Card 7-16, 24NOV67, UDT-SEAL Museum.

451 THREE DAYS LATER: SEAL Team TWO, 7th Platoon Barn Dance Card 7-18, 27NOV67, UDT-SEAL Museum.

452 NECK-AND-NECK COMPETITION: Author interview with Roy Matthews.

452 "ALL E-NOTHINGS AND LOWER": Ibid.
452 VIET CONG MORTAR TEAMS: Author interview with Robert Peterson.
452 TENTATIVE SWIMMERS: Ibid.
453 "DAREDEVILS": Author interview with Roy Matthews.
453 PARLAY THAT RELATIONSHIP: SEAL Team TWO, 7th Platoon Barn Dance Card 7-27, 19DEC67, UDT-SEAL Museum.
453 OPERATION PREAKNESS III: SEAL Team TWO, 7th Platoon Barn Dance Card 7-37, 11JAN68, UDT-SEAL Museum.
453 "ANIMALS": "Unconventional Commandos," *Time.*
453 "A NATURAL FEELING": "End of Tour Report," SEAL Team TWO, 5th Platoon, April 1969, UDT-SEAL Museum.
453 COLLATERAL COMMITMENT TO GUARDING A BOTTLE: Boynton account in Fawcett, ed., *Hunters and Shooters,* 89.
454 EXPERIMENTAL MANHUNTS BEHIND RINNIE: Ibid., 84.
454 STEALING A JEEP: Author interview with Erasmo Riojas.
454 AN AMATEUR MAGICIAN: Boynton account in Fawcett, ed., *Hunters and Shooters,* 99.
454 LIEUTENANT'S BARS AND THE GOLD-CROSS INSIGNIA: Author interview with Erasmo Riojas.
454 THE ONLY ELIGIBLE CANDIDATES: "End of Tour Report," SEAL Team ONE, Zulu Platoon, June 1971, UDT-SEAL Museum.
454 "COMBAT TERP": "End of Tour Report," SEAL Team TWO, 8th Platoon, February 1971, UDT-SEAL Museum.
454 NO OFFICIAL MONIES: Author interview with Robert Peterson.
454 A FORMER SAILOR: Mary Ann Koenig, "A Bond Unbroken: The Why of Minh," ABU Productions, 2015.
455 LANDED ON THE NORTH SHORE: SEAL Team TWO, 7th Platoon Barn Dance Card 7-39, 16JAN68, UDT-SEAL Museum.
455 "ASK [THEM]": Boynton account in Fawcett, ed., *Hunters and Shooters,* 93–97.
455 WATSON REQUESTED AN OVERFLIGHT: SEAL Team TWO, 7th Platoon Barn Dance Card 7-39, 16JAN68, UDT-SEAL Museum.
456 TEN TO TWELVE MACHINE GUNS: Ibid.
456 BOYNTON'S SLING WAS SHOT: Boynton account in Fawcett, ed., *Hunters and Shooters,* 93–97.
456 ENTIRE AREA EXPLODED: SEAL Team TWO, 7th Platoon Barn Dance Card 7-39, 16JAN68, UDT-SEAL Museum.
456 MINH'S VOICE: Boynton account in Fawcett, ed., *Hunters and Shooters,* 93–97.
456 PRODUCED A RUMOR: *Deposition of Henry Rhinebolt,* Watson v. Constance et al., February 8, 1999.
457 REACHED HIM TOO LATE: Constance and Fuerst, *Good to Go,* 102.
457 IN MOST SECTIONS: Tobias Wolff, *In Pharaoh's Army: Memories of the Lost War* (New York: Alfred A. Knopf, 1994), 131.
457 LOBBIED FOR SPECIAL PERMISSION: Author interview with Robert Peterson.

457 "OBSERVATION POSTS": SEAL Team TWO, 7th Platoon Barn Dance Card 7-47, misdated 30JAN68, UDT-SEAL Museum.
457 TRUCE HAD JUST BEEN CANCELED: Ibid.; Barn Dance 7-48, 01FEB68, UDT-SEAL Museum; author interview with Robert Peterson.
458 NEAR-SIMULTANEOUS ATTACKS: James H. Willibanks, *The Tet Offensive: A Concise History* (New York: Columbia University Press, 2008), 41.
458 THE MOST EFFECTIVE METHOD: "The General's Gamble," *Time*, February 9, 1968.
458 FIRST IV CORPS CITY TO BE HIT: Willibanks, *Tet Offensive,* 41.
458 ATTACK STARTED RIGHT AROUND: Wolff, *In Pharaoh's Army,* 132.
458 NUMBERING AROUND 1,200 FIGHTERS: Sherwood, *War in the Shallows,* 285.
458 "INSUFFICIENTLY FRIENDLY": Wolff, *In Pharaoh's Army,* 132.
459 "DROPPING RINGS OF RUINATION AROUND": Ibid., 138.
459 STIFFENING THE BACKS: SEAL Team TWO, 7th Platoon Barn Dance Card 7-50, 07FEB68, UDT-SEAL Museum.
459 CARTER BILLET: Ibid.; author interview with Robert Peterson; Constance and Fuerst, *Good to Go,* 191–202.
459 HOTEL'S TRANSFORMATION INTO A CITADEL: SEAL Team TWO, 7th Platoon Barn Dance Card 7-50, 07FEB68, UDT-SEAL Museum.
459 "TWENTY-NINE-MILLION-CUBIT FOOT": Constance and Fuerst, *Good to Go,* 199; author interview with Roy Matthews.
459 UNTIL THEIR ADVANCE EVENTUALLY: Sherwood, *War in the Shallows,* 290; Hunt, 123.
459 SWIM TRUNKS AND SUNSCREEN: Constance and Fuerst, *Good to Go,* 206.
459 SWOLLEN AS HOT DOGS: Ibid., 209.
460 THE ONLY DIFFERENCE: SEAL Team TWO, 7th Platoon Barn Dance Card 7-50, 07FEB68, UDT-SEAL Museum; author interview with Robert Peterson.
460 SWEETNESS OF DECOMPOSING BODIES: Wolff, *In Pharaoh's Army,* 139.
460 WATSON HAD LOST THE CONFIDENCE: *Deposition of Henry Rhinebolt,* Watson v. Constance et al., February 8, 1999; author interview with Erasmo Riojas.
461 WHEN GALLAGHER LED HIS SQUAD: SEAL Team TWO, 7th Platoon Barn Dance Card 7-51, 09FEB68, UDT-SEAL Museum.
462 "HAVING A COMPETENT": SEAL Team TWO, 7th Platoon Barn Dance Card 7-52 12FEB68, UDT-SEAL Museum.
462 7TH PLATOON PLANNED AND CONDUCTED: SEAL Team TWO, 7th Platoon Barn Dance Cards 7-52, 12FEB68 to 7-65, 10MAR68, UDT-SEAL Museum.
462 FOLLOWED THE GAME: West, "Navy SEAL Commandos," Rand Study 8.
462 OF THE TEN THAT DID: SEAL Team TWO, 7th Platoon Barn Dance Cards 7-52, 12FEB68 to 7-65, 10MAR68, UDT-SEAL Museum.

463 ITS LRRPs and SINGLE FORCE RECON MARINE: Ibid.
463 SUPPORT A NEED BY THE PRU and "MAXIMUM USE OF A NAVY TEAM": 7th Platoon AAR, March 7, 1968, UDT-SEAL Museum.
463 CONCEDE THE POSSIBILITY: Author interview with Robert Peterson.
464 "TORTURED": Ibid.
464 PLANNED AND PREPARED and EXTRA WEIGHT OF WATER: Boynton account in Fawcett, ed., *Hunters and Shooters,* 101.
464 SQUARE-JAWED COLLEGE SWIMMER: Author interview with Ronald Yeaw; author interview with Erasmo Riojas.
465 MISSION BRIEFING: Constance and Fuerst, *Good to Go,* 105.
465 "WHAT THE HELL": Boynton account in Fawcett, ed., *Hunters and Shooters,* 101.
466 PATROL'S POINT MAN: Author interview with Robert Peterson.
466 DRY RICE PADDY: Author interview with Ronald Yeaw.
466 HE WAVED BACK: Constance and Fuerst, *Good to Go,* 107.
466 MUD-AND-LOG BUNKERS: Yeaw account in Orr Kelly, *Never Fight Fair: Inside the Legendary Navy SEALs—Their Own True Stories* (New York: Open Road, 1995), 1792; author interview with Robert Peterson.
467 WHILE PICKING HIS WAY and "ENGAGE": Ibid.; SEAL Team TWO, 7th Platoon Barn Dance Card 7-66, 14MAR68, UDT-SEAL Museum.
467 LOTS OF VOICES: Author interview with Robert Peterson.
468 SKINNED ALIVE: Ibid.
468 HAD TAKEN COVER IN A CEMETERY: Ibid.
468 7B HAD ALREADY PATROLLED: Author interview with Ronald Yeaw; Boynton account in Fawcett, ed., *Hunters and Shooters,* 101.
469 ALMOST CIRCULAR HOOCH and "A HUGE SUCKER": Ibid.; author interview with Ronald Yeaw.
469 RICE BOWLS TIED: Author interview with Roy Matthews.
469 CONFIRMED THE STRUCTURE AS A BARRACKS: Ibid.
469 FOUND THEMSELVES BETWEEN A PAIR: Author interview with Ronald Yeaw.
470 IN THE CHAOS: Ibid.
470 "GET THE SON OF A BITCH!": Boynton account in Fawcett, ed., *Hunters and Shooters,* 103.
470 THIS TIME SHE CRUMPLED: Author interview with Roy Matthews.
470 WHEN YEAW REGAINED CONSCIOUSNESS: Author interview with Ronald Yeaw.
470 THE REASON WAS ACTUALLY SIMPLE: Ibid.; Boynton account in Fawcett, ed., *Hunters and Shooters,* 103.
471 BOYNTON AND HIS SKIRMISHERS: Ibid.
471 WRITHING IN PAIN: Author interview with Ronald Yeaw, July 11, 2018.
471 "IF YOU DON'T SHUT UP": Boynton account in Fawcett, ed., *Hunters and Shooters,* 103–104.
471 "BODIES ALL OVER THE PLACE": Ibid.

471 Having already earned a reputation: Author interview with Gordon Boyce, November 4, 2018.
472 "It's yours": Author interview with Ronald Yeaw.
472 log-rolled rice bale: Boynton account in Fawcett, ed., *Hunters and Shooters*, 106.
472 lone peasant's house: Ibid., 106; author interview with Roy Matthews.
472 two children quickly escaped: Boynton account in Fawcett, ed., *Hunters and Shooters*, 104.
472 Yeaw's entire left side and fix whatever was wrong: Author interview with Ronald Yeaw.
472 radio back on-line: Author interview with Robert Peterson.
473 Recognizing 7B's overwhelming need: Ibid.
473 The first wave was coming: SEAL Team TWO, 7th Platoon Barn Dance Card 7-66, 14MAR68, UDT-SEAL Museum.
473 "Look at them all": Boynton account in Fawcett, ed., *Hunters and Shooters*, 106.
474 Lieutenant Commander Myers of the Navy Seawolves: SEAL Team TWO, 7th Platoon Barn Dance Card 7-66, 14MAR68.
474 "a violation of squadron policy": Author interview with Ronald Yeaw.
474 may have shamed: Boynton account in Fawcett, ed., *Hunters and Shooters*, 106.
474 "you're gonna go down": Author interview with Ronald Yeaw.
474 ripped the pull ring: SEAL Team TWO, 7th Platoon Barn Dance Card 7-66, 14MAR68.
474 Mark 13 signal flare: Boynton account in Fawcett, ed., *Hunters and Shooters*, 107.
474 As the Seawolves unleashed and "The noise was unbelievable": Ibid.
475 Mike Boynton transformed himself: Author interview with Ronald Yeaw.
475 a fresh gunshot wound: Gallagher's Navy Cross citation.
475 heaved him so hard: Boynton account in Fawcett, ed., *Hunters and Shooters*, 107; author interview with Ronald Yeaw.
475 "Hey, we've still got men": Boynton account in Fawcett, ed., *Hunters and Shooters*, 107.
475 liftoff sent a shudder: Author interview with Ronald Yeaw.
475 surrounding the slick: Boynton account in Fawcett, ed., *Hunters and Shooters*, 107.
475 some thirty minutes: SEAL Team TWO, 7th Platoon Barn Dance Card 7-66, 14MAR68.
475 making Peterson think: Author interview with Robert Peterson.
476 machine gun fire: Ibid.
476 thin stream of blood: Author interview with Ronald Yeaw.

476 WHOM HE MELODRAMATICALLY KISSED: Boynton account in Fawcett, ed., *Hunters and Shooters,* 109.

476 ARMY NURSES WERE BUSY: Author interview with Ronald Yeaw.

476 PROBED GALLAGHER'S BODY FOR A VEIN: Ibid.; author interview with Robert Peterson.

477 GREEN SOCK, NOW RED: Author interview with Ronald Yeaw.

477 "WHERE'S THE EAGLE?": Boynton account in Fawcett, ed., *Hunters and Shooters,* 109.

477 SUPPORT A MEDAL OF HONOR: Author interview with Robert Peterson.

478 "COMPANY LEVEL TO ADVISE AND GUIDE": SEAL Team TWO, 7th Platoon Barn Dance Card 7-73, 26MAR68, UDT-SEAL Museum.

478 THROUGH AN AREA DOMINATED BY: Author interview with Ronald Yeaw; Yeaw account in Kelly, *Never Fight Fair,* 1759.

478 CONSERVATIVE ESTIMATE: SEAL Team TWO, 7th Platoon Barn Dance Card 7-66, 14MAR68, UDT-SEAL Museum.

478 THE SUBSEQUENT CLEARANCE: SEAL Team TWO, 7th Platoon Barn Dance Card 7-75, 29MAR68, UDT-SEAL Museum.

479 "WELL DONE": Bosiljevac, *SEALs,* 107.

479 WRAP HIS STITCHES WITH DUCT TAPE: Author interview with Erasmo Riojas, January 25, 2018.

479 LATTER HAD BEEN IN-COUNTRY: SEAL Team TWO, 7th Platoon Barn Dance Cards.

479 BY HIS OWN ADMISSION: Author interview with Robert Peterson.

479 PROVIDED A PASS-DOWN and AMENABLE TO PAYMENTS: Ibid.

479 OVERSTAYED HIS DEPLOYMENT: Boynton account in Fawcett, ed., *Hunters and Shooters,* 111.

479 HAD ENSURED MINH'S ADMITTANCE: Koenig, "Bond Unbroken."

480 "EVERY US AND ALLIED AGENCY": Bosiljevac, *SEALs,* 107–108.

480 "TIMELY [USE]": Boesch account in Fawcett, ed., *Hunters and Shooters,* 14.

480 ROCKWELL HALL GYMNASIUM: LCdr. E. Lyon III (USN), Command History SEAL Team TWO: 1 January 1968 to 31 December 1968, February 7, 1969, NHHC, Post-1946 Command File, see microfiche #140 for CH and Reports (1962–1973), (13 fiche).

480 252 COMBAT DECORATIONS: *The Gator,* vol. 27, November 8, 1968, UDT-SEAL Museum.

481 "[HIGHLIGHT] OF THE CEREMONY": Lyon, Command History SEAL Team TWO: 1 January 1968 to 31 December 1968.

481 "SUCCEEDED IN SHIFTING": Lyon, Command History SEAL Team TWO: 1 January 1968 to 31 December 1968, Enclosure 1.

481 "EXTENDED THE ARM": Lyon, Command History SEAL Team TWO: 1 January 1968 to 31 December 1968.

481 HIS RETURN TO LITTLE CREEK: Author interview with Robert Peterson.

481 RETURN TO VIETNAM ALMOST IMMEDIATELY and "AN IMPRESSIVE

AND REMARKABLE RECORD": "End of Tour Report," SEAL Team TWO 9th Platoon, 28OCT70 to 01APR71, UDT-SEAL Museum.

482 GALLAGHER COULD EASILY HAVE CONSIDERED: Koenig, "Bond Unbroken"; author interview with Robert Peterson.

482 SHOWED THE MAN OUT: Ibid.

Chapter 15: The Navy's Skeleton Key to Inland Combat, and the Final Against-the-Current Achievements in the War's Ebb Tide That Exposed the SEALs' Preeminence as the US Military's Go-Anywhere Commandos

483 "ONE COMPACT PUNCH": Lee Dye, "Navy Seal Teams Invade Cuyamaca," *Evening Tribune Military Writer,* undated, courtesy of Michael Wagner.

483 WIRES IN THE EARS, WATER SUFFOCATION: Geyer, "The CIA's Hired Killers."

483 REMOVAL OF A CAPTIVE'S LIVER: Zumwalt—Staff Officers Oral History, 108.

484 "SMOTHERING": SEAL Hoi Chanh Exploitation Guide, July 20, 1971, UDT-SEAL Museum.

484 1,250 PIASTERS: Official MACV Pay Scale for Informers, NSWC.

484 "NEUTRALIZING" and "AVERAGE OF 800": LCdr. D. L. Schaible (USN), Command History SEAL Team ONE, 1968, May 13, 1969, NHHC, Post-1946 Command File, see microfiche #138 for CH and Reports (1963–1973), (17 fiche).

484 "FORMER ASSOCIATES": "End of Tour Report," Det. Golf, June 1970, UDT-SEAL Museum.

484 "SO FAR I HAVE GOT": Gary Gallagher, letter, June 2, 1968, NSWC.

484 SEAWOLF HELICOPTERS PILOTED: Capt. Robert A. Gormly, USN (Ret.), *Combat Swimmer: Memoirs of a Navy SEAL* (New York: Penguin, 1999), 139–140.

484 "ENRAGED": Zumwalt—Staff Officers Oral History, 106.

484 JUSTIFIED HIS APPOINTMENT: Gallagher's Navy Cross citation; Gormly, *Combat Swimmer,* 146–147.

485 "WHAT THE HELL": Ibid., 155–162.

485 RELENTLESS EIGHTEEN-HOUR-A-DAY SCHEDULE: Zumwalt—Staff Officers Oral History, 187.

486 BEER, CHARCOAL, AND MEDALS: Ibid., 80.

486 LANDGRAB IN CHINA: Dwyer, *Scouts and Raiders,* 166.

486 A WINK TO THE UNIT: Adm. Elmo R. Zumwalt, Jr., US Navy (Ret.), Oral History of Admiral Elmo R. Zumwalt, Jr. (US Naval Institute, 2003), interview #8, 501.

486 BEFORE LONG: Ibid., 490 and 494.

486 TURNING THE IV CORPS INTO HIS OWN: Ibid., 490–533.

486 ACCOMPANIED BY A CAMERA CREW: McPartlin account in Fawcett, ed., *Hunters and Shooters,* 294.

486 PIASTERS FOR HOI CHANHS: Each platoon issued 100,000 piasters to pay for intel. Hawkins account in ibid., 195.

487 ACTUAL NAVY PHYSICIAN: Ibid., 289–290.

487 FINALLY UPGRADED FROM A CLUTTERED DESK: "End of Tour Report," Det. Alfa, May 1969, UDT-SEAL Museum.

487 "I NEED FIFTEEN MORE": Orr Kelly, *Brave Men, Dark Waters: The Untold Story of the Navy SEALs* (New York: Pocket Books, 1992), 151.

487 EVEN ENLISTED THE EFFORTS: Ibid.; Zumwalt Oral History.

487 "IMMENSE VALUE TO ME": Zumwalt Oral History, 505.

487 INHABITED BY WEREWOLVES: "Organization Man," *Time*.

488 TRIED TO STAND: Thomas's Navy Cross citation, and Bosiljevac, *SEALs*, 153–154; https://www.facebook.com/HombresOfTheDelta/photos/petty-officer-3rd-class-rj-thomas-was-part-of-a-detachment-from-us-navy-seal-tea/160598900785902/.

488 JUST THREE MONTHS INTO HIS FIRST DEPLOYMENT: Kerrey's Medal of Honor citation; Murphy, *Vietnam Medal of Honor Heroes*, 164–166.

489 "SEVERELY CRAMPED": "End of Tour Report," SEAL Team ONE, Foxtrot Platoon, March 1971, UDT-SEAL Museum.

489 "HARD TARGETS": "End of Tour Report," Det. Golf, June 1970, UDT-SEAL Museum.

489 FOUND DEAD AMID THE WRECKAGE: Bosiljevac, *SEALs*, 167; https://www.facebook.com/HombresOfTheDelta/posts/-remembering-hm1-richard-o-wolfe-kia-nov-30th-1969-seal-team-one-republic-of-vie/480768388768950/.

490 FOLLOWED BY RENAMING THESE UNITS: Lanning, *Inside the LRRPs*, 71–73.

490 HELICOPTER AND WATERBORNE RAIDS: Hunt, 76.

490 "BECAUSE OF SEAL INTEREST": "End of Tour Report," Det. Alfa, 10May69 to 17Nov69, UDT-SEAL Museum.

490 "NO IDEA": Ibid.

490 "ONLY US COMMANDED GROUND UNIT": "End of Tour Report," Det. Alfa, 8th Platoon, November 24, 1969, UDT-SEAL Museum.

491 PRESIDENT LYNDON JOHNSON STRODE and "KIND OF A LONG WAY" and "CRAZY": Author interview with Franklin Anderson, June 3, 2020.

492 BOB WAGNER'S WIDOW RECEIVED A LETTER: Capt. S. W. Vejtasa, USN, Chief of Staff to the Commandant to the Eleventh Naval District, letter to Mrs. Robert K. Wagner, Feb. 17, 1969, courtesy of Michael Wagner.

492 WHO OPTED TO RECEIVE: Author interview with Michael Wagner, May 31, 2020.

492 "INIMITABLE FORESIGHT": Wagner's Legion of Merit citation.

492 PROMPTING A COUNTERBARRAGE: Kelly, *Never Fight Fair*, 1581.

492 WHO WAS KNOWN TO DON DRESS BLUES: Woolard account in Fawcett, ed., *Hunters and Shooters*, 246–247.

493 A DUTIFUL LETTER WRITER TO THE PARENTS: Zumwalt Oral History, interview #8, 498–543.
493 OF THE HUNDREDS OF FACES: Ibid., 248–249.
493 "CARRIED": Ibid., 498.
493 FORCED BASE SKIPPERS TO ASSIGN: "End of Tour Report," SEAL Team ONE, Golf Platoon, 17May70 to 1Nov70, UDT-SEAL Museum, and "End of Tour Report," SEAL Team ONE, Zulu Platoon, 30Aug70 to 30Jun71, UDT-SEAL Museum.
493 SERIES OF PHYSICAL LIMITATIONS: "End of Tour Report," SEAL Team ONE, Kilo Platoon, Jul70 to Jan71, UDT-SEAL Museum.
493 CRITICAL SHORTFALLS: "End of Tour Report," SEAL Team ONE, Golf Platoon, November 1970, UDT-SEAL Museum.
493 "A SPECIAL TEAM": Craig R. Whitney, "Navy's 'Seals,' Super-Secret Commandos, Are Quitting Vietnam," *The New York Times,* November 29, 1971.
494 A POSTURE THAT ADMIRAL ROBERT SALZER: Kelly, *Brave Men, Dark Waters,* 146.
494 "THEY HATE TO SIT STILL" and LET THE ANIMAL: Ibid.
494 ENEMY'S TIGHTENING ENCIRCLEMENT: Enoch and Walker, *Teammates,* 278–287.
494 "THAT TICKLED OLD ABE": Kelly, *Brave Men, Dark Waters,* 146–147.
495 AROUND $14,000 PER MAN: West, "Navy SEAL Commandos," 11.
495 "THE MEN WITH GREEN FACES": John Gordon, "Men with Green Faces," US Navy, 1979.
495 THE FAR MORE LIKELY BRANCH: Ibid., 13.
495 "HOW THE CONCEPT": Ibid., 2.
496 "DEVELOP THE SAME AGGRESSIVE ATTITUDE" and DROWNING OF ALL FIVE MEN: Ibid., 12.
496 "DREARY" and "SAVED THE PRIDE": Ibid., 15.
496 "ORGANIZATIONAL ORPHANS": Ibid., 7.
496 "NO LOVE OR ADMIRATION": Ibid., 13–14.
496 "NOBODY NOT A SEAL": Ibid., 4.
497 FAILED TO MIMIC: Ibid., 13.
497 "WHAT STRIKES ME": Ibid., 4.
497 "UNSUNG SOLDIER": Gordon, "Men with Green Faces."
498 ARMY-ISSUED OARS: Stephen Talty, *Saving Bravo: The Greatest Rescue Mission in Navy SEAL History* (New York: Mariner Books, 2018), 201.
498 "YOU'RE TOO SMALL": Author interview with Thomas Norris, June 14, 2020.
498 PERSONALLY CALLING THE CNO: Ibid.
499 "UNPRECEDENTED GROUND RESCUE": Norris's Medal of Honor citation.
499 "TO THIS WRITER": "End of Tour Report," Det. Alfa, 7APR71, UDT-SEAL Museum.
500 "DISSOLVE THE TEAMS": Author interview with Thomas Norris.

Conclusion: Nature Abhors a Vacuum

501 TIGER FORCE EMBARKED: Sallah and Weiss, *Tiger Force.*
501 WEIGHTED HIS BODY WITH CHAINS: Jeff Stein, *A Murder in Wartime: The Untold Spy Story That Changed the Course of the Vietnam War* (New York: St. Martin's Press, 1992), 129–130.
501 GENERAL ABRAMS FLEW INTO A RAGE: L. Fletcher Prouty, "Green Berets and the CIA," *The New Republic,* August 22, 1969.
502 ONCE SETTLED IN A CLOUD: McRaven, *Spec Ops,* 287–331.
502 "HOODLUMS": Kent T. Woods, *Rangers Lead the War: The Vision of General Creighton W. Abrams* (Carlisle Barracks: US Army War College, 2003), 7.
502 "BETWEEN THE ARMY'S CONVENTIONAL": Ibid., 14.
503 TRAINING AMMUNITION BUDGET: Richard Marcinko and John Weisman, *Rogue Warrior* (New York: Pocket Books, 1992), picture inset.
504 THE AMPHIBIOUS OPERATIONS: Kelly, *Brave Men, Dark Waters,* 245.

Illustration Credits

Pages 18, 22, 31, 57, 109, 132, 135, 149, 175, 178, 180, 190, 196, 329, 394, 425: courtesy of Naval History and Heritage Command

Pages 41, 203, 218, 392: courtesy of Dan Halperin

Pages 44, 59, 117, 210, 245, 295, 414, 444, 452: courtesy of Navy SEAL Museum

Pages 70, 79, 248, 254, 277, 299, 317, 357, 364, 375, 406: courtesy of Office of the Command Historian, US Army Special Operations Command

Page 128: courtesy of Dexter Freeman

Pages 194, 207: courtesy of Charles Miles

Page 267: courtesy of Genine Franklin Clark

Page 282: courtesy of Kathy McGee

Page 306: courtesy of Martin R. Watson

Page 335: courtesy of Dr. Eduardo Zayas-Bazán

Page 387: © Robert Knudsen, White House Photographs, John F. Kennedy Presidential Library and Museum, Boston

Pages 430, 432: courtesy of Maynard Weyers

Pages 440, 442: courtesy of Erasmo Riojas

Index

Page numbers of photographs and maps appear in italics.

Key to frequently used abbreviations:
CIA = Central Intelligence Agency
CTTs = Counter Terror Teams
LCVP = Landing Craft Vehicle Personnel (Higgins Boat)
MACV = Military Assistance Command Vietnam
MRF = Mobile Riverine Force
NCDU = Naval Combat Demolition Unit
OSS = Office of Strategic Services
PBRs = Patrol Boats, Riverine
POWs = prisoners of war
recon = reconnaissance
SACO = Sino-American Cooperative Organization
SAG = Special Activities Group
SOG = Special Operations Group
UDTs = Underwater Demolition Teams
WWII = World War II

PHOTO: © BENJAMIN H. MILLIGAN

BENJAMIN H. MILLIGAN became a US Navy SEAL in 2001 and served until 2009. He is a recipient of the Bronze Star and other awards. A native of Indianapolis, he received a BA in history at Purdue University and an MA in international relations at the University of San Diego. Since the publication of *By Water Beneath the Walls*, he has balanced his writing with speaking and lecturing on leadership, organizational change, and American history at various universities, military commands, and veterans events. When not traveling for research or leading a tour of an overseas battlefield, he lives in the Chicago area with his three sons.

benhmilligan.com
Twitter: @benhmilligan
Instagram: @ben.h.milligan